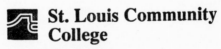

St. Louis Community College

Forest Park
Florissant Valley
Meramec

Instructional Resources
St. Louis, Missouri

GAYLORD

Racial and Ethnic Relations in America

Fourth Edition

Racial and Ethnic Relations in America

S. Dale McLemore
The University of Texas at Austin

Allyn and Bacon
Boston • London • Toronto • Sydney • Tokyo • Singapore

Senior Editor: Karen Hanson
Editor in Chief, Social Sciences: Susan Badger
Editorial Assistant: Sarah Dunbar
Production Administrator: Susan McIntyre
Editorial-Production Service: Ruttle, Shaw & Wetherill, Inc.
Photo Researcher: Kathy Smith
Cover Administrator: Suzanne Harbison
Composition Buyer: Linda Cox
Manufacturing Buyer: Louise Richardson

Copyright © 1994, 1991, 1983, 1980 by Allyn and Bacon
A Division of Simon & Schuster, Inc.
160 Gould Street
Needham Heights, MA 02194

Library of Congress Cataloging-in-Publication Data

McLemore, S. Dale.
    Racial and ethnic relations in America / S. Dale McLemore. — 4th
  ed.
        p.   cm.
    Includes bibliographical references and index.
    ISBN 0-205-14346-6
    1. Minorities—United States. 2. United States—Ethnic relations.
  3. United States—Race relations. I. Title.
  E184.A1M16 1993
  305.8′00973—dc20   93-2934
                                                                         CIP

Printed in the United States of America

10 9 8 7 6 5 4 3 2   98 97 96 95 94

Photo Credits: Chapter 1, AP/Wide World Photos; Chapter 2, North Wind Picture Archives; Chapter 3, The Bettmann Archive; Chapter 4, The Bettmann Archive; Chapter 5, The Bettmann Archive; Chapter 6, Jean-Claude Lejeune, Stock, Boston; Chapter 7, Elizabeth Crews, Stock, Boston; Chapter 8, AP/Wide World Photos; Chapter 9, Jean-Claude Lejeune, Stock, Boston; Chapter 10, AP/Wide World Photos; Chapter 11, Lionel J-M. Delevingne, Stock, Boston; Chapter 12, Paul Sakuma, AP/World Wide Photos; Chapter 13, AP/Wide World Photos; Chapter 14, Fredrick D. Bodin, Stock, Boston.

This book is dedicated to two remarkable women
Opal, my mother, and
Imogene, my mother-in-law

Contents

Preface   xi

1 Natives and Newcomers   1
A Popular View of Americanization   2
Some Non-European Instances   5
Some Factors Affecting Inclusion   6
    Voluntary Entrance and Race   6
    Group Size, Cultural Similarity, and Time of Entry   9
    Race and Ethnicity: A Conceptual Note   10
From Tradition to Modernity   13
Key Ideas   15
Notes   16

2 Together or Apart? Some Competing Views   19
The Cycle of Race Relations   20
The Subprocesses of Assimilation   21
Three Ideologies of Assimilation   25
    The Anglo Conformity Ideology   25
    The Melting Pot Ideology   27
    The Ideology of Cultural Pluralism   30
Key Ideas   37
Notes   38

3 The Rise of Anglo-American Society   41
The English Legacy   42
Native American–English Relations   45
Servants and Slaves   49
The Colonial Irish   53
The Colonial Germans   55
The Revolutionary Period   57
Key Ideas   60
Notes   62

4 The Golden Door   65
The First Great Immigrant Stream   67
    The Nineteenth-Century Irish   68

The Nineteenth-Century Germans   71
Changing Patterns of Immigration   74
The Second Great Immigrant Stream   76
The Italians   77
The Jews   80
The Third Great Immigrant Stream   85
Key Ideas   92
Notes   93

5 Nativism, Racism, and Immigration Restriction   95
Nativism   96
Racism   100
Racial Differences   101
The IQ Controversy: Before 1924   104
Immigration Restriction   105
Initial Steps: The Chinese   105
The Culmination: 1924   108
The IQ Controversy: Since 1924   111
Key Ideas   115
Notes   116

6 Prejudice and Discrimination   119
Theories of Prejudice   123
Cultural Transmission Theories of Prejudice   123
Personality Theories of Prejudice   128
Group Identification Theories of Prejudice   133
Which Theory Is Best?   138
Theories of Discrimination   139
Situational Pressures Theories of Discrimination   140
Group Gains Theories of Discrimination   144
Institutional Structure Theories of Discrimination   149
Key Ideas   152
Notes   153

7 Reducing Prejudice and Discrimination   155
The Educational Approach   157
Factual Information   157
Vicarious Experience   158
Intergroup Contact   159
The Legal Approach   165
The Laws and the Mores   165
School Busing   169
Affirmative Action   172
Organized Social Protest   179

Conclusion   180
Key Ideas   181
Notes   182

8 Japanese Americans   183
Japanese Immigration and Native Reactions   186
    Anti-Asian Sentiment   186
    Anti-Japanese Protest   187
    The School Board Crisis   189
    The "Picture Bride" Invasion   191
The Japanese Family and Community in America   192
    Family and Community Cohesion   192
    Japanese Occupations and the Alien Land Laws   195
    Exclusion   197
    The Second-Generation Period   198
War, Evacuation, and Relocation   200
    The Relocation Program   202
    Life in the Camps   204
    Legal Issues   207
Japanese American Assimilation   210
    Cultural Assimilation   210
    Secondary Structural Assimilation   213
    Primary Structural Assimilation   215
    Marital Assimilation   215
Japanese American "Success"   218
    The Cultural View   218
    The Structural View   221
    A Comparison of Success Theories   224
Key Ideas   226
Notes   227

9 Mexican Americans   231
The Colonial Model   232
    Indian–Spanish Relations   236
    The Texas Frontier   237
    Conflict in the Borderlands   239
The Immigrant Model   243
Mexican Immigration and Native Reaction   247
    The Great Depression   249
    The Bracero Program   250
    The Zoot Suit Riots   252
    The Chicano "Awakening"   255
Generation and Identity   258
    Intergenerational Overlap   258
    Census Identifiers   259

Mexican American Assimilation   261
    Cultural Assimilation   261
    Secondary Structural Assimilation   265
    Primary Structural Assimilation   269
    Marital Assimilation   271
Mexican American "Success"   272
Key Ideas   276
Notes   278

10 African Americans: From Slavery to Segregation   281
The Period of Slavery   282
Immigrant or Colonized Minority?   287
Emancipation and Reconstruction   289
The Restoration of White Supremacy   292
Migration, Urbanization, and Employment   297
The Civil Rights Movement   299
    Tuskegee and Niagara   299
    Separatism   302
    Strategy, Tactics, and Conflict   305
    Victories in the Courts   309
Key Ideas   311
Notes   312

11 African Americans: Protest and Social Change   315
The Rise of Direct Action   316
    Black Power   319
African American Assimilation   325
    Cultural Assimilation   325
    Secondary Structural Assimilation   330
    Primary Structural Assimilation   338
    Marital Assimilation   339
African American "Success"   341
Key Ideas   348
Notes   349

12 Native Americans   353
The English Penetration of the Continent   355
Anglo-American Indian Policies   357
Indian Removal   359
    Legal Issues   359
    The Trail of Tears   360
Plains Wars and Reservations   362
From Separatism to Anglo Conformity   367
    The Bureau of Indian Affairs   368

The End of Treaty Making   368
The Dawes Act   369
Indian Education   370
The Ghost Dance and Wounded Knee   371
Alternations between Anglo Conformity and Cultural Pluralism   373
The Indian Reorganization Act   374
The "Termination" Policy   375
Pan-Indian Responses and Initiatives   377
Protest Organizations   377
The New Tribalism   380
Immigrant or Colonized Minority?   383
Native American Assimilation   386
Cultural Assimilation   386
Secondary Structural Assimilation   390
Primary Structural Assimilation   394
Marital Assimilation   395
Native American "Success"   397
Key Ideas   398
Notes   400

13 A Renewal of Ethnicity and Immigration   405
An Ethnic Revival   406
The New Immigration   412
The Vietnamese   414
An Involuntary Immigrant Minority?   420
Vietnamese American Assimilation   421
Resurgent Nativism?   430
Key Ideas   433
Notes   433

14 The Future of Ethnicity in America   437
When Is Soon?   438
White Ethnic Assimilation   439
Primary and Secondary Ethnic Groups   445
Conclusions   447
Key Ideas   453
Notes   455

References   457

Author Index   491

Subject Index   501

Preface

When the members of different racial and ethnic groups come together, many interesting, intricate, and sometimes volatile patterns of social relations and interactions are created. Examples of these patterns exist throughout the modern world. The United States, of course, contains numerous racial and ethnic groups, each with a different history and set of problem, but the countries of the former Soviet Union, the former Yugoslavia, the Middle East, China, Australia, Africa, India, and many other places also present striking examples of racial and ethnic relations.

The struggles and conflicts that frequently characterize these relations are the subject of political discussion and intense examination. People who are themselves engaged in racial and ethnic relations, understandably, may have deeply held opinions concerning the situation in which they find themselves. In addition, many social commentators and academic specialists wish to understand the complicated problems that arise out of racial and ethnic contacts and differences. The widespread interest in this field has produced a literature that is rich, diverse, and constantly increasing. This increase in our knowledge and understanding is of crucial value in a shrinking and multicultural world, but it does complicate the task of presenting a coherent overview of this intellectually stimulating field.

This volume continues the basic strategy adopted in the previous editions. It focuses on the United States and joins two of the broadest, most illuminating approaches to the study of racial and ethnic relations: the sociological analysis of intergroup processes and the history of racial and ethnic groups in the United States. These two approaches combine nicely because the study of social processes, such as competition, conflict, segregation, stratification, and accommodation, and the various subprocesses of assimilation is inherently temporal. The flow of these processes (and subprocesses) in the interactions of the members of different racial and ethnic groups is most readily grasped through an examination of the history of the relations of these groups.

At the most general level, our "processual-historical" approach proceeds from the beginnings of contact among different groups in North America to the pressing racial and ethnic issues of the contemporary United States, but we deviate from this general thrust to encompass many other topics of interest. We devote some attention to such conventional topics as prejudice and discrimination, race and racial differences, stereotyping, social distance, desegregation, affirmative action, vertical mobility, variations in group goals, variations in types of economic responses to discrimination, and various approaches to social change. These topics are introduced as elements in the general development of the relations among racial and ethnic groups in the United States. Contemporary prejudice, for instance, is seen against the background of the intergroup struggles for control following various racial and ethnic contacts in the United States, and the ideas of "scientific racism" are discussed in relation to the rise of the movement to restrict immigration that came to prominence at the turn of the twentieth century.

New materials were added to every chapter in this fourth edition, and many chapters were extensively revised. The most noticeable changes occur in chapters 1 through 5. The topics of these chapters have been rearranged and substantially rewritten with a view to strengthening the theoretical and conceptual framework of the book. Chapter 1, as before, focuses on certain ideas that have been advanced to answer the question, "How do people acquire and American identity?" but the chapter also now contains a section on the concepts of race and ethnicity. Chapter 2 brings together the discussions of the four main models (or ideologies) of intergroup adjustment, which affords the most general framework within which all of the book's materials are presented. Chapters 3 and 4 focus on the development of racial and ethnic relations in America during the colonial period and the period of the three great immigrant streams, respectively, and on the variations in the hostility of the dominant group to the many subordinate groups. Chapter 5 now focuses exclusively on the rise and interrelationships of nativism, racism, and immigration restriction in American life.

Chapter 6 is devoted to a discussion of the most prominent theories of prejudice and discrimination, and chapter 7 discusses some of the techniques that have been most important in the effort to reduce prejudice and discrimination. Chapter 8 and 9 discuss, respectively, the experiences of the Japanese and Mexican Americans; chapters 10 and 11 discuss the African American experience; and chapter 12 is devoted to an analysis of the experiences of the Native Americans. The discussions of each of these chapters is organized to aid our analysis of the materials in terms of the main models of intergroup adjustment discussed in chapter 2. Chapter 13 considers the reawakening of ethnic consciousness in the United States during the 1960s and 1970s and resumes, within this context, our discussion of the third great immigrant stream to the United States. This discussion amplifies the materials introduced in chapter 4 through an analysis of the experiences of the Vietnamese in the United States. We close, in chapter 14, with a consideration of evidence on the group adjustments of the descendants of the second immigrant stream and with conjectures, suggested by our analysis, concerning the future of ethnicity in the United States.

Although the ideas presented here may be applicable to racial and ethnic relations anywhere in the world, the book is not expressly comparative; however, since the primary aim of this volume is to reveal to the reader a set of key ideas concerning racial and ethnic relations, there is a special sense in which the book definitely is comparative. The key ideas are developed and illustrated mainly through comparisons of the experiences of different racial and ethnic groups in the United States. Fifteen groups in all are discussed, nine of them briefly. The Japanese Americans, Mexican Americans, African Americans, and American Indians are the subjects of complete chapters; most of one chapter is devoted to Vietnamese Americans, and the dominant Anglo-Americans are discussed throughout. The remaining nine groups are the Chinese, English, Dutch, colonial Irish, colonial Germans, nineteenth-century Irish, nineteenth-century Germans, Italians, and Jews.

The choice of groups and of emphasis is not intended to slight the many other groups that might have been included and have contributed in their different ways to the development of the United States. There is no intention, in any case, to present complete profiles of the groups that have been chosen for discussion. The choices were dictated chiefly by an interest in presenting and illustrating the key ideas listed at the end of each chapter. The reader may find, in fact, that it is useful to read the key ideas pertaining to a given chapter both before and after reading the chapter itself. This procedure may help the reader to distinguish more clearly the central points under discussion from the many details that are useful in understanding those points.

My debts to others have continued to grow. As the reader will see, I am deeply indebted to the many scholars whose efforts have produced the rich literature on which this volume is based and whose continued research is rapidly increasing our knowledge of racial and ethnic relations in the United States and throughout the world; and I continue to profit from the inspiration and intellectual guidance of many memorable teachers.

I also wish to thank Karen Hanson, my editor, and the staff at Allyn and Bacon, for their support throughout the writing of this book. I wish to thank Dottie Caddick at Allyn and Bacon and Thomas J. Conville, III at Ruttle, Shaw & Wetherill for coordinating the many tasks connected with the preparation of the manuscript for publication. I am grateful also to the scholars who reviewed the manuscript and offered criticisms and suggestions for its improvement. Chief among these are Allen Martin, The University of Texas at Tyler, and Fernando Parra, California Polytechnic State University. In addition, I wish to thank Frank Bean, John Sibley Butler, Jack P. Gibbs, Gideon Sjoberg, Teresa A. Sullivan, and Norma Williams for their continuous support and valuable suggestions.

Chapter 1

Natives and Newcomers

Send these, the homeless, tempest-tost, to me: I lift my lamp beside the golden door. —*EMMA LAZARUS*

e pluribus unum.
—*MOTTO OF THE UNITED STATES OF AMERICA*

The United States of America frequently is described as a nation of nations, a mixture of immigrants from all over the world. Most Americans cannot trace their stay in this land to more than five or six generations, and only Native Americans can claim to have been here for more than a few centuries. As a result, many Americans still think of themselves as having a "nationality" in addition to their identity as Americans. Despite the somewhat romantic insistence that Americans are the product of an international melting pot, that they are the first "self-created People in the history of the world" (MacLeish 1943:115), newspapers, magazines, and television bring us daily reminders—often through accounts of intergroup disagreements and conflict—that the fabric of modern American society is comprised largely of people who are immigrants from, or are the descendants of immigrants from, Africa, China, Cuba, El Salvador, England, Germany, Ireland, Italy, Mexico, Poland, Puerto Rico, Syria, Turkey, Vietnam, and many other places from around the globe. Our national, racial, and religious diversity has been a source of pride and of problems.

The basic problem has been to answer the question, "Who wishes to be considered, and will be accepted as, full participants in American society?" How can we accomplish what Glazer called "the difficult task of fashioning a single national identity" (1972:175)? If an American citizen's national origin is Irish, Italian, Nigerian, Polish, or Vietnamese, is the person *first* an American and *then* a member of a *racial* or *ethnic group*?[1] Or is the order of priority and loyalty reversed? When people speak of "my people" or "we," what group do they have in mind? Behind questions such as these lie some others of critical importance. If many people in the United States have divided group loyalties, how is the underlying unity of the nation affected? What should be the official policy of the United States toward those citizens who feel primarily or significantly loyal to some subgroup within the American nation rather than to the nation itself? Should the long-standing differences of opinion between blacks and whites, to take one of the most striking examples, or among Protestants, Catholics, and Jews, to take another, be encouraged as sources of variety and strength or be discouraged as sources of disunity and distrust? Whether they are discouraged or not, will these types of groups naturally disappear with the passage of time? Some of these perplexing questions call for factual answers. Others are concerned mainly with the goals, values, and purposes of American society as a whole and of the various groups within it. Together they have been, and continue to be, the subject of an enormous amount of public and scholarly attention and controversy.

We begin our exploration of the ideas that have been prominent in sociological thought on the subject of racial and ethnic groups in America by tracing very briefly a popular view of how a person's identity may be transformed from that of an "alien" or "foreigner" to that of an "American."

A Popular View of Americanization

The principal stages through which a newcomer to the United States generally is presumed to travel have been portrayed in many biographies, novels, plays, movies, and scholarly books and articles. Both in fact and in legend, millions of people have crossed the oceans in search of economic, religious, and other opportunities in the United States. The central image is familiar: A ship enters New York harbor within view of the Statue of Liberty; the weary and awe-struck immigrants are cleared through Ellis Island ("The Gateway to the New World") for entry into the United States; after clearance, they come ashore and, if possible, seek a place to live in an area where some or many others from their home country have settled. Those who arrived earlier already may have established "national churches, immigrant-aid societies, foreign-language newspapers, and other institutions" (Petersen 1980:239) to form an immigrant community within the city.

The life of the "greenhorn," though exciting, is filled with problems to solve and obstacles to overcome. In addition to finding a place to live, he or she must find a job and manage to cope with the countless difficulties that arise daily when a person is trying to learn a new language and adopt a new way of living. The old-country ways and ideas are no longer appropriate. The newcomer must do his or her best to learn rapidly the "American way" to speak, dress, think, and act. Gradually, the greenhorn begins to "learn the ropes," to speak and act less like someone F.O.B. ("fresh off the boat") and more like an "American." But even an immigrant who wishes to do so probably will not be able to make a complete transition to the new way of life. His or her name, speech, dress, manner, religious observances, food preferences, place of residence, or type of occupation may continue to mark him or her as "foreign." In most cases, newcomers do not want to be divorced entirely from the old-country ways. They may wish to be accepted as Americans in all ways that are essential to their livelihood and immediate welfare; they may wish for the members of their families to be able to participate as fully as they like in the mainstream of American life; but they may find life's greatest pleasures and satisfactions in the sights, smells, sounds, and companionship that exist only in the ethnic community—Little Italy, Little Poland, or Little Hungary—that the members of their national group have developed. Nevertheless, these new, *first-generation* Americans who are unable or unwilling to give up certain elements of their foreign culture and society may hope that their children will move further in the direction of losing their identities as foreigners and become completely "American."[2]

The children of the immigrant, the *second generation,* may learn many of the old-country ways from their parents and may also be unable or unwilling to drop all vestiges of their parents' culture and behavior.[3] They will attend public schools and become much more fluent in English than their parents; and they may fail to learn, or may actively reject, certain features of the old-country ways. When these second-generation Americans are grown, they will move up the ladder of economic success and may move out of the old neighborhood or take a job in another city. They may even marry someone of a different ethnicity or change their name to something more "American." Still, many elements of the old culture may remain, either by preference or by necessity, and the individuals may be regarded by themselves or by others as still remaining in some significant ways Italian, Polish,

Hungarian, or Greek. Such people are *marginal,* having one foot in the "host" society and one in the immigrant society.[4]

Finally, according to the familiar view being sketched, the grandchildren of the immigrant, the *third generation,* will move completely into the mainstream of American life. Their parents will not have transmitted to them a noticeable portion of the old culture. This failure of transmission may occur partly because the parents do not wish to have the children maintain an ethnic identity (other than American) and partly because the parents do not themselves know enough of the old culture to transmit it. The children of the third generation, of course, may learn to speak a few words of the old-country language, especially if the grandparents are still alive, and they may learn certain old-country recipes, folk songs, and proverbs; they may feel a strong sense of attachment to the country of their grandparents and to other Americans who share a similar ethnic heritage; but they will speak English without an accent, and questions concerning their nationality will seldom arise. The third-generation Americans will have completed, for all practical purposes, the process of Americanization set into motion by their grandparents. At this point, the individual's ethnicity becomes essentially invisible. The grandchildren of immigrants may think of themselves simply as "Americans" and be so regarded by other "Americans" (who probably are themselves the descendants of immigrants); or they may choose to emphasize one or more aspects of their ancestry to a greater or lesser degree (Waters 1990). The individual has now become a full member of the host society, sharing equally with the "charter" members in the distribution of social rewards. No ethnic restrictions on the individual's participation in the society remain. He or she may "rise" to any position the society has to offer.

A number of different terms used in both popular and scholarly discourse refer to the transformation of a person's identity from foreign to American. Some of the more prominent of these are *acculturation, assimilation,* and *integration.* Frequently it is suggested that the foreigner becomes an American through a process of "melting," "merging," or "fusing." For the moment, though, let us refer to the experience of Americanization simply as one of *inclusion.* When a person first enters a society, he or she may be included only in a physical sense. The person may be "in" the society but, socially speaking, not "of" it. Our primary interest here is how a person does or does not become more nearly "fitted into" the various parts of a society.

The particular process of inclusion outlined previously is usually called the *three-generations process.*[5] It is one description of the sequence of stages through which members of successive generations may pass to become "completely American," and it may be summarized as follows: "Except where color is involved . . . , [t]he specifically *national* aspect of most ethnic groups rarely survives the third generation in any significant terms" (Glazer and Moynihan 1964:313). Even if one accepts this account as a general description of the way some immigrants have been included in American society, however, certain aspects of it must be altered to fit many other cases. For example, many immigrants have gone directly to farms or small towns rather than remaining in a large city. Also, the process of inclusion may have been completed in some cases by the end of the second generation, or it may have continued beyond the third. Another interesting phenomenon is that, in many instances, the grandchildren of immigrants (the third generation) attempt to recover the heritage of the first generation. This phenomenon, in which "what the son wishes to forget the grandson wishes to remember," is referred to as Hansen's thesis or law (Hansen 1938:9). The basic idea is that if the second generation successfully forgets its heritage, the third generation has a feeling of rootlessness and therefore attempts to fill the void through cultural revival.

Some Non-European Instances

All of the examples mentioned refer to people from southern or eastern Europe, and though no time period was specified, the examples actually suggest the experiences of those who came to the United States from Europe during a particular period of high immigration: the years from 1880 to 1924. What assumptions are to be made, however, concerning the process of including immigrants from other parts of the world and other periods of immigration? More specifically, has the same process of inclusion (with the appropriate geographical and temporal modifications) been at work among all of the different peoples who comprise the present population of the United States?

Since the grandparents (or earlier ancestors) of most African Americans, for example, came to the United States from Africa as bonded servants or slaves, they obviously did not emigrate to the United States in the sense being discussed. While much human migration involves, to some degree, both voluntary and involuntary elements, it is clear that the involuntary element was enormously greater in the migration of the ancestors of most African Americans than was true of any other group that has come to the United States.[6] It also is clear that after many more than three generations (in most cases), African Americans, on the average, have not entered fully into the mainstream of American life and become simply "Americans."

In a similar vein, it is plain that Native Americans did not enter American society as immigrants at all. Since they preceded American society, one may say that American society has migrated to them! Moreover, as has been true for African Americans, Native Americans have for the most part been brought into American society involuntarily, in this case through conquest and the occupation of their territory.

Mexican Americans present a somewhat more complicated case. Like Native Americans, the ancestors of some Mexican Americans were brought to the United States involuntarily through conquest. The ancestors of some others, however, joined in and supported the military operations that resulted in the transfer of enormous tracts of land to the United States, while the ancestors of still others—and this is by far the largest category—migrated more or less voluntarily to the United States from Mexico. Many of those in the latter group, however, did not consider the border between the two countries to be very important psychologically and did not think of themselves as immigrants to a foreign country (Alvarez 1985). Like

African Americans and Native Americans, most Mexican Americans have not completed the process of inclusion in three generations.

The experience of the African, Native, and Mexican American groups should leave little doubt that the three-generations process (even with some fairly large modifications) does not describe very well what has happened to some of the groups that have been brought into American society. Some scholars also doubt that the three-generations idea is applicable to the current conditions of newcomers to the United States. Portes and Rumbaut (1990:7–8), for example, argue that the ethnic diversity of newcomers to America is greater now than ever before, and they find the idea that there is a "uniform" generational process leading to economic advancement to be "increasingly implausible." They state that "there are today first-generation millionaires who speak broken English, foreign-born mayors of large cities, and top-flight immigrant engineers and scientists in the nation's research centers: there are also those, at the other extreme, who cannot even take the first step toward assimilation because of the insecurity linked to an uncertain legal status."

Why have some groups in the past not merged uniformly into American society? Is it likely, given still longer periods of time, that even groups that have not gone through the three-generations process gradually will be included fully? And will the newcomers who now are reaching America follow the three-generations patterns or some other pattern? Stated more generally, the primary question to be considered here and throughout this book is this: *What factors affect whether, to what extent, and the rate at which the members of a given group are included in American society?*

Some Factors Affecting Inclusion

Voluntary Entrance and Race

The simplified sketch presented so far indicates that the members of some groups are more likely to approximate the three-generations process of inclusion in American society than others. The discussion also implies that at least two factors may increase or decrease the speed of inclusion. The first of these factors is whether people enter American society mainly voluntarily or involuntarily. Those who choose to come to the United States may exert special efforts to learn English and to alter many other established ways of acting. Their goal may be full inclusion. People who are enslaved or conquered, on the other hand, may be less willing to become members of a society that is responsible for those acts. Their goal may be to escape the new society and return to the homeland.[7] Please note, however, that even though a voluntary entrance into the society may initially lead people to be more favorable toward the adoption of American ways, and an involuntary entrance may favor the rejection of Americanization, the two types of entrance do not necessarily lead to different results.

Americanization may be viewed, even by those who migrated voluntarily, as having both desirable and undesirable aspects. For example, the members of a racial or ethnic group may view full inclusion in American life as a process whereby a cherished way of life is destroyed or gradually eroded rather than as progress; consequently, they may not *wish* to relinquish those traits that make them distinctive and may struggle to maintain an ethnic identity. From this standpoint, a major problem for newcomers is their inability to resist inclusion. Groups of this type usually stir resentment and are described by other Americans as being "clannish." Frequently, too, the members of a group may be uncertain regarding whether, or in what ways, inclusion should be sought. Nearly all Jews, for example, may agree that the members of their group should learn English and be permitted to attend public schools, but they may disagree sharply concerning the extent to which their religious ceremonies should be conducted in English.

A second factor implied as having an effect on inclusion is the racial identification of the individual or group. Although white Americans have generally shown some hostility toward all foreigners, they have been more willing to accept the members of some groups than others. The history of the United States shows, in particular, that white resistance to the inclusion of different groups is greater against those who are defined as "nonwhite" than against those who are considered to be "white." For reasons discussed later, white Americans generally have considered those labeled as nonwhite to be especially inferior and unacceptable as social equals.[8]

The latter point focuses on the preferences of white Americans for a simple, but most important, reason. White Americans have been not only the numerical majority throughout most of the history of the United States, they also have been the most *powerful* group in the society. The racial and ethnic groups to be included, on the other hand, have been minorities in power as well as in number. For our purposes, this point is crucial. Racial and ethnic relations, not only in the United States but throughout the world, may be viewed as one among a family of human relationships in which one group is more powerful and dominates another. In all human societies, some group or groups will have greater social power and, therefore, a greater capacity to *control* than others, and the kinds of relations these more or less powerful groups have with one another represent a vital element in the operation of the society.[9]

The power of many groups is accepted as legitimate by those below them, and their commands are willingly obeyed; however, sometimes subordinate groups do not obey powerful groups, and then concealed or open conflicts may erupt between the dominant (controlling) and subordinate (controlled) groups. *The relative power or degree of dominance of various racial and ethnic groups, rather than their sheer size, is of paramount sociological significance.* When the terms *majority* and *minority* refer to power differences, therefore, rather than merely to differences in size, we are encouraged to pay close attention to *the extent to which the minority group's behavior and life circumstances are related to the superior control exercised by the majority.* We are also alerted to the possibility that conflicts may erupt between the groups.

These ideas suggest that the rate of a group's inclusion in American society may be affected by the extent to which its members seek inclusion, by the extent to which white Americans desire or resist their inclusion, or by the combined effects of these forces. It seems likely that the resistance of the majority will be stronger in the case of a racial minority than in the case of a white minority. Figure 1-1 depicts these possibilities in a highly simplified form.[10]

On the basis of Figure 1-1, one may speculate that if either the majority or the minority rejects the desirability of inclusion (as in cells II and III), then the rate of inclusion will be slower than if both groups accept inclusion as a goal. The rate will be slowest of all in a situation in which both groups reject the desirability of inclusion (as in cell IV). Whether a particular minority's slow rate of inclusion reflects a rejection mainly from the side of the majority, the side of the minority, or both sides can be settled only by specific research. For example, the existence of ethnic enclaves and ghettos does not by itself demonstrate the relative effects of enforced separation (*segregation*) or voluntary separation (*congregation*) as antecedent factors.

Without further investigation, one might well believe that a satisfactory reason has been found for the comparative speed or slowness of the inclusion of various American groups. For instance, since German Americans were not forced to come here, and since they are considered to be white, both the minority and the majority probably have accepted inclusion as a desirable goal; hence, one might argue that German Americans illustrate the situation described in cell I of Figure 1-1. African and Native Americans, by contrast, did not generally enter the society voluntarily, and they generally are considered members of nonwhite races; therefore, on the basis of the discussion thus far, the assumption seems to be supported that these two minorities and the majority have rejected full inclusion as a desirable goal. This is the situation depicted in cell IV of Figure 1-1. To illustrate further, although Japanese Americans are racially nonwhite, they were voluntary immigrants; so we might expect that they would be included more rapidly than the African and Native American groups, as shown in cell II.

This line of explanation seems to describe, in rough outline at least, the actual situation existing in the United States, but the apparent "fit" between the suggested

FIGURE 1-1 Majority and minority reactions to inclusion

		Majority	
		Accepts	Rejects
Minority	Accepts	+ + **I**	+ − **II**
	Rejects	− + **III**	− − **IV**

explanation and the facts may be no more than accidental. Remember that voluntary entrance into a country does not guarantee that the minority will wish to be included, certainly not in every respect. Many German Americans, as we discuss later, originally wished to set up a separate state or nation within the United States. Even though that effort was unsuccessful, many German American communities were established and have continued to maintain a distinctive German "flavor" to this day. For this reason, one may wish to place some German Americans in cell III instead of cell I of Figure 1-1.

Similarly, as mentioned previously, an involuntary entrance into a country does not guarantee that the minority will wish to remain apart. There are many reasons to suppose, for instance, that large numbers of African Americans have worked vigorously to achieve full inclusion despite the involuntary entrance of their ancestors. From this perspective, African Americans illustrate cell II rather than cell IV of Figure 1-1. These shortcomings, and others that may occur to the reader, indicate that we must know a great deal about a particular minority and its relation to the majority before we can answer the questions that have been raised. *It is absolutely essential in this regard that we study the historical sequences that have created the dominant–subordinate group relations of interest.*[11] In this way, we will gain an appreciation of the part played by many other factors affecting inclusion.

Group Size, Cultural Similarity, and Time of Entry

Consider, for example, how the *size* of the minority group affects its relationship to the majority. It is familiar knowledge that majority group members are much more concerned about the presence of minority group members and give much more evidence of rejecting them in those places in which the minority group is relatively large or has grown rapidly in size.[12] If the minority group becomes larger than the dominant group, the concern of the dominant-group members may be greater still. This situation has been common in the experience of African Americans in many towns in the southern United States and of Mexican and Native Americans in many towns of the southwestern and western United States. Outside the United States, the positions of non-whites in the Union of South Africa and of French-speaking Canadians in Quebec afford illustrations. In South Africa, although the white English and Dutch groups jointly dominate the economic and political affairs of the nation, they constitute only about 15 percent of the total population. English-speaking Canadians are politically and economically dominant in the country as a whole but are a numerical minority in the province of Quebec.

Another factor affecting the rate of inclusion of a minority group in the United States is the *similarity* between the culture of the minority and the culture of the majority. People whose native languages are Chinese, Korean, or Japanese, for instance, may experience more difficulty in mastering the speech patterns and inflections of the English language than those whose native languages are Dutch, German, or Spanish. And since Judeo-Christian beliefs are dominant in the United States, those who have been raised in a different religious tradition may find many

"American" ways difficult to accept.[13] Much the same may be said concerning American approaches to politics, education, courtship, marriage, and many other aspects of life.

As another illustration (among several that might be presented), consider the effect the *timing* of a group's entry into the United States may have. Generally speaking, the earlier a group arrived in America, the more likely its descendants are to have adopted the ways of the dominant group. Lieberson and Waters, for instance, found that among those who described their ancestry as "American" in the decennial census of 1980, 98 percent "also have at least three generations' residence . . . " in the United States (1988:43). An additional way the time of a group's entry affects its inclusion is that the possibility of finding work, or certain types of work, varies from time to time. When the country has been in periods of economic expansion and more "hands" have been needed to do the work, immigrants have been encouraged to move to the United States, and during such times they have been accepted more cheerfully than during depressions, when many of those already here have been out of work.

A racial or ethnic group's actual level of inclusion, then, is the result of many different factors acting in combination. Some of these factors pertain to the social and cultural conditions faced by the emigrating group in the home country (e.g., whether the group is being forced to leave); other factors pertain to the way the immigrants are received in the host country (e.g., whether the host group welcomes more laborers or feels threatened by competition for jobs); and other factors concern an immigrant group's level of organization or sophistication (e.g., how fully their skills and talents are applicable in the new setting (Greeley 1971:32; Portes and Rumbaut 1990:156).[14] These sets of factors may guide our effort to explain why some groups experience higher or lower levels of inclusion in American life; however, the variable effects of these factors means that no neat formula can be offered for determining which ones among them have the greatest influence on a specific minority group at a given moment. Although this discussion has been focused on the United States, it is probable that sociocultural conditions in both sending and receiving countries have shaped the outcomes of the inter-group contacts among peoples that have been occurring throughout the world during the past several centuries.

The discussion so far has suggested a way to identify some of the factors that may be important in helping to understand why some groups apparently have been fully included in American life within three generations and others have not, and we have noted in passing the special importance of visible physical and sociocultural differences. These differences are key elements of the central terms of our discussion—*race* and *ethnicity*.

Race and Ethnicity: A Conceptual Note

The terms *race* and *ethnicity* have been assigned a variety of meanings and are the subjects of continuing discussion. Each term refers in part to the fact that people may believe they and certain other people are the descendants of common or related ancestors and, further, that those of common ancestry comprise natural social groups or categories.[15] In current use, racial group or category designations refer mainly to a person's physical heritage (e.g., skin color, hair form, facial shape, and so on), while ethnic group or category designations refer mainly to a person's sociocultural heritage (e.g., country of origin, religion, language, manners, and so on). Since one's line of descent is not a matter of choice, people tend to assume that groups based on physical and social inheritance are of special importance and are more or less immutable (Allport 1958:106; Petersen 1980:239). The plausibility of this viewpoint rests primarily on the centuries-old observation that family members usually resemble one another more in both appearance and behavior than do unrelated individuals.[16]

The practice of distinguishing between people's heritages in primarily physical (racial) or sociocultural (ethnic) terms is widely accepted. Its common acceptance, indeed, and the social groupings that are generally recognized thereby, provide the underpinnings for the analyses of this book, but let us note that the boundaries between and within racial and ethnic groups are not nearly as sharp and fixed as many people assume. They in fact overlap and, in many ways, are blurred.

To illustrate, let us consider briefly some issues that arise in the process of attempting to determine a person's racial group membership. In everyday situations, most people are defined by themselves and others as belonging to a particular racial group even when they are aware that some racial "mixing" has occurred. They are thought to be (and are treated as) members of this race or that race or some other race. Under these circumstances it is easy to assume that the boundaries of this system are "real" and have been imposed upon us by nature. In fact, however, the conclusion that a person is a member of a single race involves a much larger element of choice and social agreement than may be apparent. The most frequently chosen defining trait, skin color, obviously varies by degrees. Some "white" people have skin that is as dark as, or darker than, the skin of some "black," "brown," "red," or "yellow" people; hence, a common defining racial trait (skin color) cannot be used to establish sharp boundaries. Since all of the other commonly employed visible traits (hair form, nose shape, and so on) suffer this same defect, any effort to establish sharp boundaries among the races on the basis of any one of these commonly used physical traits is bound to be imperfect and, to some extent, arbitrary. Blumenbach, an early anthropologist, appreciated this point far better than many later observers. In his words, the "innumerable varieties of mankind run into one another by insensible degrees" (quoted by J. King 1971:113).

The problem of overlapping boundaries cannot be surmounted by combining the various traits, either. It is true that in the United States people who are judged on the basis of skin color to be "white" are more likely to have "narrow" noses than people who are judged to be "black" (i.e., skin color and nose shape are *correlated*), but some people who are considered to be white have broader noses than some people who are considered to be black. As a third trait is added, and then a fourth and a fifth, the probability that all of the traits will lead to the same racial assignments declines.[17] The low levels of correlation among these different socially accepted criteria of racial grouping explain why scholars who have employed the criteria of skin color, head shape, nose shape, geographical location, and so on, either singly or in combination, frequently have arrived at different numbers of human races. Linnaeus distinguished 4 races, Buffon distinguished 6, Deniker concluded there are 29, Coon et al. constructed 30, and Quatrefages listed 150 (Dunn and Dobzhansky 1964:110; Loehlin, Lindzey, and Spuhler 1975:33). These illustrations run directly counter to the prevalent idea that the "races" people usually distinguish on the basis of visible physical traits are quite distinctive, specific, unvarying entities. People may be grouped into the same or different races depending on the criteria used as defining traits.[18]

These considerations support the conclusion that *although people commonly think of races, and sometimes ethnic groups, as sharply distinguishable biological entities, their boundaries, in fact, are set by social agreement.* Whatever sharpness racial boundaries may have springs from the fact that people react to the members of these socially recognized groups in quite different, socially important ways. The logic of this conclusion has led some students of racial and ethnic groups to argue that the concept of race is a sociopolitical rather than a scientific concept and to recommend that it be abandoned completely as a scientific term (Littlefield, Lieberman, and Reynolds 1982:644).[19]

Although the concept of ethnicity now usually emphasizes a person's sociocultural rather than his or her biological heritage, many of the visible elements that are believed to characterize an ethnic group may be thought by those outside the group to have some basis in biology as well as in culture, reflecting the fact that "a biological connotation sometimes adheres still to 'ethnic' . . . " (Petersen 1980:235);[20] but even when a person's appearance or behavior is generally acknowledged to derive exclusively from culture, there is a common tendency to treat the characteristic in an all-or-none fashion and to create derogatory images (*stereotypes*) of various groups' members.[21] Both majority group and minority group members may well believe that "we" who appear to share certain physical, social, and cultural characteristics are more honest, or skillful, or loyal, or humane than "they" who appear to share other physical, social, and cultural traits. Such judgments about *in-groups* and *out-groups* are made routinely and with little reflection in our daily lives, and they may seem to rest on hard experience and firm foundations. We must stress here that even when such views are poorly founded, they nevertheless exist as social realities and have important consequences in people's lives. They also serve as formidable barriers to intergroup understanding and the full inclusion of minority groups in a society.

As we analyze racial and ethnic relations in America, then, we must recognize the social reality of the racial and ethnic categories that exist in our society and simultaneously maintain an awareness that these categories have not been imposed on us by nature. They are socially constructed (even when physical traits have been used as building materials), and they are, in principle, subject to reconstruction.

Some scholars have argued that the alteration of our existing racial and ethnic categories will occur naturally with the passage of time. The argument is that racial and ethnic distinctions are inherently at odds with the requirements of a modern urban-industrial, scientific-rational society and that, consequently, "the forces of history" are against the maintenance of such distinctions. To understand the basis for this argument, let us turn briefly to some ideas pertaining to a related sociological problem.

From Tradition to Modernity

A central concern of sociologists is to describe and understand what happens when a society undergoes the enormous shift from a premodern to a modern form of social organization. In western Europe, for example, the transformation was from the traditional patterns of social life that characterized the feudal system to the radically different patterns of life that characterize modern industrial societies. Feudal societies are regulated mainly by custom and are organized primarily in terms of kinship. The members of families work together and form the basic economic unit of the society. Since neighboring families live in essentially the same way, mutual understanding and cooperative activity are promoted, and a strong sense of community attachment or solidarity develops. In such a setting, religion is a powerful force that tends to permeate all segments of individual and community life. The pervasiveness of religion combines with the force of custom and tradition to maintain a slowly changing, comparatively static social order. The ordinary person in a society of this type lives a hard life in many physical respects and probably is poor and illiterate. This person is compensated for these disadvantages, however, by the continuous social support of family, friends, and religious leaders. These supports create in the individual a strong sense of belonging, community purpose, and reverence, and they foster the impression that the social order in which the individual lives is timeless and unchanging.

The defining properties of modern societies frequently are portrayed as the exact opposites of those contained or implied in the description of traditional societies. If the central tendency of traditional societies is to create and maintain a strong family and community in which people live with a sense of belonging and purpose, the central tendency of modern societies is to weaken the bonds of family and community and to atomize the individual. In modern societies, economic activities shift away from the family to the city and the corporation. Work tasks are more likely to be divided and organized according to rational plans than according to custom. Instead of engaging in the same kinds of work, family members and neighbors usually engage in different kinds of work. As a result, the intimate knowledge and mutual understanding of one another that are cultivated when people work together at the same activities are hindered or do not develop. Even individuals who work together are less likely to develop strong personal ties in the modern setting. People move around so frequently in modern societies that it is difficult to develop enduring personal bonds. Life, in general, becomes more hurried and more bureaucratic. The individual's sense of commitment to his or her family and community declines.

This comparison of the traditional and modern forms of social life suggests mainly the losses that individuals suffer in the shift from the former to the latter. But the picture may be painted in terms of the ways in which individuals gain. The term *modern* usually connotes progress for both the individual and the society. For the individual, modern life represents a release from the bonds of traditional life—a life in which the individual's place is determined largely by *ascribed* characteristics, such as family status, sex, and age. Under modern conditions, the individual's place presumably depends more heavily on *achieved* characteristics, such as educational level and occupational skill.

At the societal level, modernization frequently is advocated as a way to decrease poverty, disease, and death rates. It is a way to increase material abundance and the enjoyment of life. Modern life is seen by many as more enlightened and more efficiently organized than traditional life. Moreover, those who emphasize the advantages of modern life frequently assume that the individual's attachment and loyalty to kinship and community groups will be transferred to other groups in modern societies. This capacity to transfer allegiance frees the individual from the accidental restraints of birth and tradition, enabling him or her to pick and choose personal attachments on the basis of more "rational" considerations. From this standpoint, a loyalty to the family, clan, tribe, or village that interferes with a person's ability to change group memberships is "irrational" and "inefficient." In modern life, rewards are *supposed* to be distributed on the basis of *the principle of achievement* rather than on the basis of *the principle of ascription*. Giving individuals rewards for their achievements is regarded as "fair," while giving rewards to individuals because they have been born into privileged groups is considered "unfair."

With these ideas in mind, one may understand more easily why many sociologists believed that racial and ethnic distinctions would become decreasingly important in the modern world. It was assumed that the historical trend of American society is away from tradition and toward modernity. From this perspective, social distinctions based on racial and ethnic differences are leftovers, so to speak, from the traditional form of social organization. The ties that bind individuals to racial and ethnic groups in American society are expected, from this perspective, to continue to become progressively weaker. Racial and ethnic loyalties and "consciousness" should decline. If they do not, this fact is likely to be seen as a problem that needs to be solved.

Several questions are raised by the ideas just presented. For instance, even though there is much evidence to support our general description of the positive and negative changes that accompany modernization, one still may wonder whether such changes *must* occur.[22] Is it possible that traditional loyalties to family and tribe are compatible with the efficient operation of a modern nation? Or is it true that the retention or.creation of ethnic loyalties may afford a valuable, even necessary, anchorage for people facing the "future shock" of rapid social and cultural change? If racial and ethnic consciousness has been declining throughout the twentieth century, why have civil rights activities become more prominent in the United States since the 1950s? And why is it true, as Spickard (1989:11) noted, that "Everywhere one looks, ethnic division persists"?

These considerations suggest that we may not take for granted the idea that racial and ethnic differences automatically will decline as a society becomes more modern. Numerous conflicts almost certainly will arise between dominant and subordinate groups as a society reorganizes along new lines. Nevertheless, even if the process is not automatic, shouldn't the passage of time generally lead interacting racial and ethnic groups in a modern society gradually to adjust to one another and become more alike? The implications of various answers to these questions must be examined in some detail, and we begin this examination in chapter 2.

Key Ideas

1. Many people assume that the usual and normal course of Americanization requires three generations. In this view, the adult grandchild of the immigrant generally is, and should be, fully Americanized.

2. A basic sociological task is to try to understand the factors affecting whether, to what extent, and the rate at which the members of a particular group have been included in a given society.

3. Many factors may affect the rate at which different groups move toward full inclusion in a society. Some of the most important of these factors are: (a) the extent to which the group's entry into the society was voluntary; (b) the wishes and strength of the minority; (c) the wishes and strength of the majority; (d) the racial and cultural similarity of the minority and majority groups; and (e) the relative population sizes of the minority and majority groups.

4. Numerous problems exist in the effort to classify people as members of specific racial and ethnic groups. A basic problem is that the boundaries between and within racial and ethnic groups overlap and, in many ways, are blurred. Even though people commonly think of races, and sometimes ethnic groups, as sharply distinguishable biological entities, their boundaries are set, rather, by social agreement. Hence, the members of the groups that people recognize socially may not necessarily exhibit any particular trait they are supposed to possess, and people in different socially recognized racial and ethnic groups may possess identical genes for biologically significant traits.

5. Judgments about in-groups and out-groups are made routinely and may rest on poor foundations. Such judgments, nevertheless, exist as social realities and have important consequences in people's lives. They serve as significant barriers to intergroup understanding and the inclusion of minority groups in a society.

6. Many scholars have assumed that as societies move away from traditional forms of social organization, loyalties based on kinship and cultural similarity tend to recede in importance or disappear. These forms of loyalty (based on the principle of ascription) are thought to be incompatible with the requirements of modern social organization (based on the principle of achievement). From this point of view, the kinship and cultural loyalties that remain within a modern nation are problems to be solved.

Notes

1. Generally speaking, the term *racial group* is used here to refer to groups (or categories) of people whose inclusion in the group (or category) is based primarily on certain physical resemblances. The term *ethnic group* refers to groups (or categories) of people whose inclusion in the group (or category) is based primarily on similarities of national or religious origin. These concepts are discussed further later in the chapter.

2. There is no completely satisfactory way to identify different racial and ethnic groups. The practice followed in this book is intended to be both neutral and as close as possible to the contemporary preferences of the groups involved. We usually describe a group by race or ethnicity followed by the word *American*.

3. Immigrants to a new country may bring with them infants and young children. Although these youngsters are technically members of the first generation, their experiences while growing up in the new country usually resemble those of their siblings who are born in the new country. From a social and psychological standpoint, therefore, these individuals are best viewed as members of the second generation.

4. Marginality has been a subject of sustained interest to students of racial and ethnic relations. For the classic work, see Stonequist (1937).

5. We assume here that a generation is approximately twenty-five years.

6. Schermerhorn presented a valuable classification of migrations according to the amount of coercion involved (1970:98). Slave transfers are the most coercive type.

7. The most influential analysis of minority groups in terms of their goals was presented by Wirth (1945:347–372).

8. Distinctions also are made within the white group. Dark-skinned whites are generally less acceptable to the dominant group than are whites with lighter skin. For an excellent discussion of this point, see Warner and Srole (1946:285–286).

9. For a comprehensive treatment of the concept of control and of its importance in sociological analysis, see Gibbs (1989).

10. For a comprehensive depiction of these possibilities, see Schermerhorn (1970:207).

11. Schermerhorn stated in this regard "that historical reality must receive primary attention" (1970:93). Heraclitus, a scholar of ancient Greece, put it this way: "He who watches a thing grow has the best view of it."

12. R. Williams stated that the "migration of a visibly different group into a given area increases the likelihood of conflict; the probability of conflict is greater (a) the larger the ratio of the incoming minority to the resident population, and (b) the more rapid the influx" (1947:6–7). This viewpoint has been referred to as the visibility-discrimination hypothesis, the competition hypothesis, and the minority size hypothesis (Burr, Galle, and Fossett 1991:833).

13. For a careful statement of the way language and religious differences are generally appraised against the accepted American standards, see Warner and Srole (1946:286–288).

14. Additional useful discussions of the factors affecting the rate of inclusion are given by Berry (1965:263–271) and Lieberson (1980:19–47).

15. *Social groups* are small aggregates of people who know one another and interact on a personal level. *Social categories* are large aggregates of people who share one, or several, social characteristics. These terms generally are used interchangeably.

16. The idea that clans, tribes, nations, and races owe their resemblances to shared blood was discredited by the discoveries of Mendel and others. A person's characteristics result not from "mixed" blood but from the operation of separate particles ("genes") from the germ plasm of the parents (Dobzhansky 1962:27). The genetic ele-

ments are either present or absent; they do not "mix." An element may be present within the gene structure of an individual (the genotype) but find no expression whatever in the visible characteristics of the individual (the phenotype). The unexpressed characteristic is nonetheless still there.

17. Swedes typically are thought to be tall, long-headed, blond, and blue-eyed, but a study of Swedish people found only 10.1 percent of those studied to have *all four* of these traits (Loehlin, Lindzey, and Spuhler 1975:22).

18. Genetic approaches to defining races are based on counting the *frequencies* with which genes appear within different "breeding populations." They may also require decisions concerning where to draw boundaries, and the resulting number of races may be very large. Loehlin, Lindzey, and Spuhler concluded there may be as many as one million "local breeding populations" (i.e., races) within the human species! (1975:33)

19. I wish to thank Jack P. Gibbs for calling this study to my attention.

20. Petersen states that *ethnic* comes from the Greek *ethnikos,* meaning a nation or race, and that *nation* comes from the Latin *nasci,* meaning "to be born"; hence, both ethnicity and nationality are derived from terms that originally referred to a group's biological heritage (1980:234).

21. We return to the discussion of stereotypes in chapter 6.

22. Blumer, for example, argued that modern societies are more likely to adapt to the preexisting patterns of interethnic relations than the other way around (1965).

Chapter 2

Together or Apart?

Some Competing Views

They must cast off the European skin, never to resume it. They must look forward to their posterity rather than backward to their ancestors. —JOHN QUINCY ADAMS

America is God's crucible. The great melting pot where all the races of Europe are melting and reforming! —ISRAEL ZANGWILL

Thus "American civilization" may come to mean the perfection of the cooperative harmonies of "European civilization" . . . a multiplicity in a unity, an orchestration of mankind. —HORACE KALLEN

The Indians are not willing to come to live near to the English. . . . A place must be found somewhere remote from the English, where they must have the word constantly taught, and government constantly exercised. —JOHN ELIOT

Chapter 1 introduced the view that we may not merely assume that racial and ethnic differences will decline automatically as a society becomes more modern. Numerous conflicts almost certainly will arise between dominant and subordinate groups as a society reorganizes along new lines. These conflicts may strengthen rather than weaken group divisions, and the level of disagreement between the groups may increase. Even so, shouldn't we expect interacting groups within a given society *usually* to adjust to one another and become more alike with the passage of time? An important answer to this question was provided by the influential theorist Robert E. Park.

The Cycle of Race Relations

Park was deeply interested in the experiences of racial and cultural groups throughout the world. His professional work on this subject covered a span of more than thirty years. The framework of his thought was presented in the form of the now famous *cycle of race relations:* "In the relations of races there is a cycle of events which tends everywhere to repeat itself. . . . The race relations cycle . . . contacts, competition, accommodation and eventual assimilation, is apparently progressive and irreversible. Customs regulations, immigration restrictions and racial barriers may slacken the tempo of the movement; may perhaps halt it altogether for a time; but cannot change its direction; cannot at any rate, reverse it" (Park [1926]1964:150).

The stages of this cycle are "the processes by which the integration of peoples and cultures have always and everywhere taken place" (Park 1964:104). Groups of people first come into *contact* through exploration or migration. Once they are in contact, a *competition* between the groups is set into motion for land, natural resources, and various goods and services, a competition in which violent conflict frequently erupts. After a period of time, overt conflict becomes less frequent as one of the two groups establishes dominance over the other. The groups develop some fairly regular or customary ways of living together; at this point, they are said to have *accommodated* to one another.[1]

Beginning with the first contacts, various individuals within the two groups learn some of the language, customs, sentiments, and attitudes of those in the other group. This process, initiated in the contact phase of the groups' relations with one another, gains momentum after the more or less stable period of accommodation has been reached. As the groups continue to live together, there occurs, according to Park, a "progressive merging" of the smaller group into the larger (1964:205). The members of the smaller group increasingly adopt the language, manners, and public customs of the larger group. Except in the case of physical differences, this process has "erased the external signs which formerly distinguished the members of one [group] from those of another." When the external signs have been "erased," the members of the smaller group are said to be *assimilated*. Although Park lists *eventual* assimilation as the final stage in the cycle, *the assimilation process commences with contact and occurs throughout the cycle,* reaching its completion when all distinguishing external signs of group membership have disappeared.

Compare the cycle described by Park with the popular view of Americanization presented in chapter 1. Park, of course, was attempting to understand the results of racial and ethnic contacts "always and everywhere," while our interest is centered on the United States; however, even though the two accounts differ in a number of ways, they appear to be entirely compatible in their main features. In this sense, the popular view of Americanization may be regarded as a "special case" of Park's general theory.

The term *assimilation* is in some ways unsatisfactory. To begin with, as Park said in his earliest paper on this topic, "It is not always clear . . . what assimilation means" (1964:204). Even though the word has a precise ring to it and is used in technical discussions, people with quite different or incompatible ideas may use it to describe their particular points of view on racial and ethnic problems. Park's work has been criticized particularly for seeming to confuse the idea of assimilation as an historical reality or matter of fact with the idea of assimilation as a desirable condition that groups should work to achieve. Analyses based on the race cycle idea have been criticized, too, for seeming to give insufficient attention to conflict.[2]

In the course of criticism, many valuable contributions have been made to our knowledge of this subject. Although we will discuss several of these at various points, the framework of our discussion is heavily indebted to the outstanding work of Milton M. Gordon (1964). Gordon effectively made the point that it is useful to view assimilation as a *collection of subprocesses* rather than as a single process, and he identified several important subprocesses.[3] He also distinguished three main *ideologies of assimilation* that have been significant in the development of the United States as a nation.

The implications of the major ideas introduced so far must be examined in much greater detail. We begin with a brief discussion of three of the subprocesses of assimilation described by Gordon. To illustrate the ideas being presented, we will refer to certain events drawn from the early colonial period of American history; in so doing, we will make certain statements concerning colonial American society that will be discussed further in chapter 3.

The Subprocesses of Assimilation

The European "discovery" of the western hemisphere near the end of the fifteenth century was followed by a long period of competition among several European nations for control of the land and resources of the new territories. The Spanish and Portuguese had been colonizing the New World for more than a century when the English established their first successful colonies in Jamestown, Virginia (1607) and Plymouth, Massachusetts (1620). All of the territories claimed and occupied by these and other European powers had been held previously by various indigenous, so-called "Indian," peoples. As the Jamestown and Plymouth colonies expanded— by armed conquest and other techniques—the English became the dominant or occupying group in an increasingly large territory. The indigenous people gradually were forced either to retreat to lands that the English did not occupy or, if they wished to be included in English colonial society, to remain where they were on terms set by the English.

This process of expansion and dominance by the English led, in time, to the seizure of New Netherland, which had been established earlier by the Dutch. New Amsterdam (1626) became New York (1664), giving the English tentative control of a strip of coastal territory stretching from Massachusetts to Virginia. During the next three decades, the mainly English population of this still-expanding territory became much larger, gained a stronger grip on the land, and came increasingly to think of itself as comprised of "Americans"; as their sense of "Americanness" developed, they distinguished more sharply between themselves and more recent newcomers, who were likely to be regarded as "foreigners."

These considerations support a very important point: *By the last quarter of the seventeenth century, the Anglo-Americans had become established as the dominant, "host," or "native" group along the Atlantic seaboard from Massachusetts to Virginia.* Obviously, this does not mean that the Anglo-Americans were natives in the same sense that Native Americans were natives. It means that they had displaced the Native Americans as the principal occupants of the land and had established their own ways of living as dominant. In this way, the *standards* of American life were set, at least in a tentative way. The extent to which someone was American or foreign could now be determined in a rough way by a comparison with the accepted Anglo-American pattern. The more nearly a person approximated the Anglo-American ethnic model, the more nearly American he or she was judged to be.[4]

Let us examine more closely the phrase "the Anglo-American ethnic model" and attempt to describe some of its component parts. Consider, for instance, some of the main features of Anglo-American culture. English was the accepted language, and foreigners were expected to learn and use it; Protestant religious ideas were dominant, and non-Protestant practices were discouraged; the system of law and government that was established throughout the territory clearly was imported from England, as was the system of business practices that was established. It is true, of course, that various non-English elements were being added to the culture of the Anglo-Americans. Many foods, planting practices, hunting methods, and other knowledge that were crucial to survival in North America were borrowed from Native Americans, and many other cultural items were contributed by other groups. Dutch place names, for example, already had supplanted Native American names in some parts of New York and continue to be used there even now. Moreover, many aspects of English culture had been affected by the "long intimate and cranky relationship" (Tuchman 1988:57) that had existed between the English and the Dutch prior to 1664. In addition to the Dutch, New Amsterdam contained people of Swedish, French, Portuguese, Jewish, Spanish, Norwegian, Polish, Danish, African, German, and several other ethnicities when the English arrived there.[5] Given this diversity, the culture of the Anglo-*Americans* was no longer identical to that of the English. In its major contours and social structure, nevertheless, it was distinctively English. It was a transplanted "sprig" of English life growing on foreign soil.

Within this context, we may say that as the Native Americans or the Dutch or the members of the many other groups already present in the English colonies abandoned their previous cultural practices and took up those of the colonists, they were undergoing what Gordon called *cultural assimilation*. This term refers to the subprocess whereby the members of a subordinate group relinquish their own language, ideas of law, commercial and religious norms, and customary modes of dress and behavior and, at the same time, acquire those of the dominant group. The complete "merging" and disappearance of one group into another, though, requires more than this. It requires also, for example, that the members of the two groups interact with one another as friends and equals and that they select marriage partners without regard to ethnic or racial identities. Gordon referred to these two additional subprocesses as *structural assimilation* and *marital assimilation,* respectively. Hence, to continue our illustration, the Native Americans, Dutch, and others could be considered assimilated at each of these more intimate levels of association only when friendships and marriages among these groups and the dominant group were taking place without regard to racial or ethnic distinctions.

We may now list three subprocesses of assimilation: (1) cultural assimilation, (2) structural assimilation, and (3) marital assimilation.[6] The meaning and value of these distinctions will become progressively clearer. For the moment, though, let us make four observations. First, each of the subprocesses of assimilation "may take place in varying degrees" (Gordon 1964:71). Second, although the subprocesses are distinctive and relatively independent, Gordon hypothesized that the rate of change in each one will correspond to its position in the list just given. Third, it is possible for a group to assimilate culturally without assimilating in the other respects mentioned. Gordon stated that *"this condition . . . may continue indefinitely"* (emphasis added) (1964:77).

Our fourth observation on Gordon's subprocesses of assimilation concerns the structural type. As previously defined, structural assimilation does not focus on the kinds of human relationships that people experience most frequently at work, in schools, in commercial transactions, at political meetings, and in places of public recreation. In these settings, most of our contacts with others are not of the close, personal type that sociologists call *primary*. They are, rather, of the relatively cold, distant, impersonal type called *secondary*. Our analysis, consequently, will be aided greatly by dividing structural assimilation into two more refined subprocesses, each focusing on one of these two different types of settings. *Secondary structural assimilation* refers to nondiscriminatory sharing (even if it is impersonal) by subordinate-group and dominant-group members of occupational, educational, civic, neighborhood, and public recreational settings (i.e., interactions in the "public" sphere of secondary relations). *Primary structural assimilation* refers to close, personal interactions between dominant-group and subordinate-group members in churches, "social" clubs, neighborhoods, families, and so on.[7] Please observe that, stated in terms of Gordon's theory, the secondary structural assimilation of a subordinate group should occur earlier and proceed more rapidly than its primary structural assimilation. The reasoning is simply that since people typically interact with one another in impersonal settings before they become close friends, we should expect assimilation into jobs, schools, political parties and positions, and so on to precede primary structural assimilation. With this refinement, our list now includes four subprocesses of assimilation: (1) cultural assimilation, (2) secondary structural assimilation, (3) primary structural assimilation, and (4) marital assimilation. For the purposes of discussion, we generally will refer to the second and third subprocesses simply as secondary assimilation and primary assimilation.

Gordon's theory leads us to expect that even though all of the subprocesses we have identified may be underway simultaneously, the rate at which each type of change occurs depends on its place in the preceding list. But, *in sharp contrast to Park's view, a group may assimilate culturally without necessarily proceeding through the remaining stages.* Past a certain point, however (and in this way Gordon's theory resembles Park's), assimilation in all four respects becomes inevitable. The crucial point in the process for Gordon is the formation of primary group relations. Once the minority group enters "into the social cliques, clubs, and institutions of the core society at the primary group level" marital assimilation will follow (Gordon 1964:80).

These ideas permit us to delineate more sharply the degrees and types of assimilation that have occurred (or are occurring) between a given dominant group and a given subordinate group. For example, we may now say that although most of the Anglo-Americans expected the Native Americans, Dutch, and other ethnically distinctive peoples who lived among them to undertake cultural assimilation, this task posed greater problems for some groups than others. For one thing, the "cultural distance" between the ideas, beliefs, and manners of the Native Americans and those of the Anglo-Americans was far greater than that between the latter and the Dutch; so a greater cultural change on the Native Americans' part was involved in their cultural assimilation (if they chose to undertake it). For another thing, and partly as a consequence of cultural differences and similarities, the dominant group was more willing to accept the members of some groups than of others; so the Dutch as a group were more acceptable than the Native Americans. Additionally, various obstacles were erected to slow or prevent the secondary assimilation of these subordinate groups. Even more emphatically, primary and marital assimilation generally were opposed actively (and in the case of Africans, legally). The white, Protestant, European, Dutch, on the other hand, faced no insuperable barriers to a steady movement through the remaining stages of assimilation. Even so, we must not conclude that all of the Dutch moved through all of the subprocesses rapidly (e.g., within three generations), or that they wished to do so. Even though the Anglo-Americans and the Dutch were able to understand one another fairly easily and to establish many forms of cooperation, the Dutch language was maintained in some families far beyond three generations, as was a preference for Dutch friends and marriage partners.

Recall that Gordon presented, in addition to a theory of assimilation, a description of three ideologies of assimilation. An understanding of these ideologies is crucial to our analysis of the processes through which groups come together, partially or completely, or remain apart.

Three Ideologies of Assimilation

The Anglo Conformity Ideology

We have said that from the standpoint of the Anglo-American ethnic group in colonial America, an American was someone who fitted exactly (or closely resembled) the pattern of life, standards of behavior, and racial type they preferred. He or she spoke English, was of a Protestant religious persuasion, was of the so-called white physical type, had an English surname, and practiced the customs, behavior, and manners of the Anglo-Americans.

Viewed in this light, assimilation is a process of inclusion through which a person gradually ceases to conform to any standards of life and behavior that differ from the majority-group standards and, at the same time, adopts all of those standards. The process of inclusion involves the replacement or substitution of one heritage and behavior pattern for another (McFee 1972). Assimilation is complete, in this view, when foreigners merge fully into the dominant group in regard to each of the four subprocesses of assimilation we have described. From this perspective also, the colonial groups that were racially distinct, such as the Native Americans and Africans, could not satisfy all of the requirements of assimilation even if they were disposed to try. The members of these groups who adopted the Anglo-American culture were not permitted, as a rule, to move freely into the economic and political life of the Anglo-Americans, let alone into their social gatherings and families.

The notion that alien groups should assimilate into Anglo-American society by "disappearing" within it has been labeled the *Anglo conformity ideology* of assimilation. This phrase is generally accepted and will be used in this book.[8] But it should be understood that the "Anglo" standards to which minority-group members are expected to conform are Anglo-*American,* not purely English. Note, also, that the process we have described may be applicable to any dominant-subordinate group setting; hence the idea that everyone in Russia or Spain should conform to the dominant group's standards may be called the Russo conformity ideology or the Hispano conformity ideology, respectively.

To summarize these points, we may say that complete Anglo conformity assimilation exists when:

1. A minority group's members exhibit a very high degree of cultural assimilation and, simultaneously, lose all or nearly all of their native culture. Cultural

assimilation has occurred by the *substitution* of the majority-group's culture for the native culture. Some vestiges of the native culture may be acceptable to the majority group and may even be regarded as "colorful" and "quaint." These cultural remnants include such things as special holiday celebrations, ethnic foods and recipes, and folk costumes, dances, and songs.

2. The minority's members exhibit a very high degree of secondary assimilation in education, occupations, places of residence, civic participation, and mass recreation (i.e., the *public sphere* of secondary relations); and they participate little or not at all in such activities organized specifically for members of their ethnic group (i.e., the *private sphere* of secondary relations). They have equal civil standing with the majority. Equality of opportunity is guaranteed. The law is "colorblind." It prohibits both discrimination against them and preferential treatment for them.

3. They exhibit a very high degree of primary assimilation. Friendship choices are made without reference to race or ethnicity.

4. They exhibit a very high degree of marital assimilation. Choices of mates are made without reference to race or ethnicity.

This model of assimilation is depicted in Figure 2-1 and represents what sociologists call an *ideal type*. The model does not necessarily represent the actual level of assimilation of any particular group or groups. It represents, rather, a goal or set of standards toward which a group may elect or be expected to move; it portrays Anglo-American culture and membership in the white race as *the standards against which any group's location and "progress" toward assimilation may be measured.*

The argument presented so far is that the English colonial efforts during the seventeenth century created an Anglicized version of *the very meaning of the word "American"* and that Anglo conformity was established tentatively as the accepted way to achieve full inclusion. Those who championed this idea looked down on the members of any group that departed very much from the Anglo-American ideal or who appeared not to wish to become Americans. If a person believed that Anglo-American standards of behavior were normal and desirable, then he or she probably also would believe that the standards of others were abnormal and undesirable; hence, groups could be graded as more or less desirable according to how closely they resembled the Anglo-American pattern at the outset, how rapidly they departed from their own cultural and social patterns, and how "successful" they were in becoming socially invisible.

This view of Americanization was not accepted by all members of the dominant group, of course, but by the end of the first century of English colonization it had become paramount. Its continued force into the second century of colonization depended on the continuing dominance of the Anglo-American group itself, and that dominance was tested in some ways we will discuss in chapter 3. We turn first to two major competing alternatives to the ideology of Anglo conformity. The first of these is the ideology of the melting pot.

Subprocesses of Assimilation	Level of Minority's Participation in Majority Group		Level of Minority's Participation within Own Group	
	High ——————— Low		High ——————— Low	
1. Cultural assimilation:	**X**_____ (very high acceptance of the majority's culture)	AND	_____**X** (very low acceptance of own-group's culture)	
2. Secondary assimilation:	**X**_____ (very high "integration" in education, occupations, residence, civic matters, and mass recreation with majority)	AND	_____**X** (very low "integration" in religious, health and welfare, and "social" recreational activities within own group)	
3. Primary assimilation:	**X**_____ (very high acceptance of majority-group friends)	AND	_____**X** (very low acceptance of own-group friends)	
4. Marital assimilation:	**X**_____ (very high acceptance of majority-group mates)	AND	_____**X** (very low acceptance of own-group mates)	

FIGURE 2-1   **A model of assimilation: Anglo conformity (X indicates a person's preferences, or goals, concerning the assimilation of minority groups)**

The Melting Pot Ideology

In 1782, J. Hector St. John Crevecoeur ([1782]1976:25–26) asked, "What, then, is the American, this new man?" and then proposed the following answer: "He is neither a European nor the descendant of a European. . . . Here individuals of all nations are melted into a new race of men." The basic idea behind the melting pot ideology is that while racial and ethnic groups should move toward the culture and society of the host, giving up their distinctive heritages along the way, the host culture and society itself should also change. The culture of each ethnic group should be blended with the culture of the host group. In this way, the heritages of both the minority groups and the host group would come together in a unified, but new and different, culture. Similarly, the groups would merge in all social matters. Like Anglo conformity, the melting pot view embraces the goal of the disappearance of minority groups in America. It adds to Anglo conformity, however, the further idea that the host culture and society also will "disappear," reflecting the influence of the groups that have been assimilated into it. The melting pot ideology is thoroughly assimilationist but rejects the idea that the Anglo-American core should remain as it was before assimilation occurred. The goal of the melting pot theory may be depicted as shown in Figure 2-2.

FIGURE 2-2 A model of assimilation: The melting pot (arrows indicate the preferred direction of social and cultural change

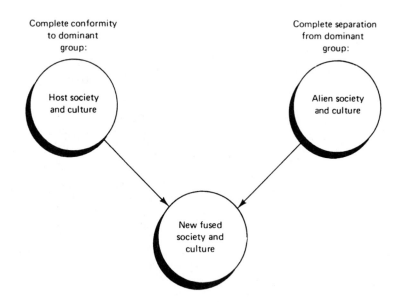

Although a complete merger occurs here, as in the Anglo conformity ideology, the Anglo-American core is also substantially changed. Advocates of this ideology believe the new host society resulting from the blend of the previously separate groups would be stronger and more nearly consistent with the fundamental ideals of the United States. This view began to receive widespread attention near the beginning of the twentieth century.

One of the most influential and persuasive expressions of this viewpoint is the "frontier thesis" of the historian Frederick Jackson Turner (1920). According to Turner, the western American frontier functioned as a great leveler of persons and a blender of cultures. On the frontier, people had to adapt to the harsh conditions confronting them by devising and sharing solutions to the problems presented. People borrowed freely from the various cultures there and, in the process, developed a new blend. The new American culture that arose on the frontier contained significant contributions from the various cultures and societies but was distinctly different from any of them.

When applied to the frontier experience, the melting pot ideology seems plausible. As already noted, the creation of Anglo-American society began on the Atlantic coast during the seventeenth century, and many different peoples contributed various cultural and social elements to it. Also, many non-English people gradually relinquished their previous heritages and social patterns and adopted the new. The main result, however, was that the framework of the new culture and society still was fundamentally English and did not represent a substantial blending of the Native Americans, Dutch, and other sociocultural elements that were present. Although Anglo-American society undoubtedly represented an adaptation to frontier conditions, *the "melting" that took place was overwhelmingly toward Anglo conformity.*

The vast changes that have taken place in America since the seventeenth century have done little to strengthen the melting pot view. Glazer and Moynihan (1964:v) observed in relation to New York, for example, that "The point about the melting pot . . . is that it did not happen." The same comment seems appropriate for most other parts of the country, although some instances of this type of group fusion may be found (Adams 1934). But as we shall see, even when they have adopted high levels of cultural assimilation, some minorities, especially nonwhite minorities, either have not wished to disappear or have not been able to disappear into the "mainstream" of the society. Moreover, the Anglo-American core, while changing in certain ways through time, even yet has not been altered in its essential characteristics.

At least two distinctions are crucial in relation to this judgment. First, even though we argue that the changes in the essential framework of Anglo-American society (e.g., in language, law, commercial organization, basic values) have been relatively small, the framework certainly has not been static. Second, if the rate of change of the past two hundred years continues, the framework of Anglo-American society, in time (i.e., "eventually"), *will* be altered fundamentally.

Consider further the "American" culture that we have taken as our primary point of reference. This culture consists not only of indigenous, English, Dutch, African, and many other elements that were brought to North America but, also, of the fused elements of thousands of other cultures that existed on the earth during a period of several millenia. In the long view of history, even a society that is changing at a comparatively rapid rate will not easily be divorced from this vast accumulation. As is illustrated in a well-known commentary by Linton (1936:326–327), the "solid American citizen" may thank "a Hebrew deity in an Indo-European language that he is 100 percent American." This observation highlights a point we stress again in chapter 14. It is vital that analyses of intergroup relations include clear statements concerning the lengths of the periods of time that are assumed to be needed for given sociocultural changes to take place.

There is one way in which the melting pot ideology has been noticeably successful. Although the dominant group clearly prefers the Anglo conformity ideology, its advocates frequently employ the melting pot metaphor. For instance, St. Patrick's Day celebrations may be discussed as proof that America is a melting pot. On this day, the president may declare that all Americans are Irish. While such declarations may serve to create the impression that a fusion of the cultures of the natives and the newcomers has occurred and has significantly altered the dominant culture, it seems more convincing to argue that the St. Patrick's Day celebrations are a form of make-believe, illustrating less the fusion of two cultures than the continued dominance of one over the other. The melting pot, in Hirschman's words, is "a political symbol used to strengthen and legitimize the ideology of America as a land of opportunity where race, religion, and national origin should not be barriers to social mobility" (1983:398).

Everything considered, it seems clear that the melting pot ideology represents a possible alternative to Anglo conformity but does not, in fact, describe very well what has taken place in America.[9] As expressed by Herberg (1960:21), "Our cultural assimilation has taken place not in a 'melting pot,' but rather in a *'transmuting pot'* in which all ingredients have been transformed and assimilated to an idealized 'Anglo-Saxon' model" (emphasis added); consequently, the melting pot ideology has served, to date, primarily as a literary and metaphorical challenge to Anglo conformity as the leading ideology of intergroup relations in America.

The Ideology of Cultural Pluralism

While the idea of cultural pluralism is quite old in American thought, its formulation as an explicit ideology is usually traced to the writings of the Jewish philosopher Horace Kallen (Gordon 1964:141; Meister 1974:53–61; Newman 1973:67). Beginning in 1915, Kallen attacked the idea that it was necessary for ethnic groups to give up their distinctive cultures in order to be *completely* American. Kallen argued that all Americans should master Anglo-American culture and participate on an equal footing in such things as occupation, education, and politics, but he believed also that the members of each ethnic group should be free to decide for themselves how much of their ethnic heritage to retain. In his view, neither the Anglo conformity nor the melting pot ideologies are acceptable goals for America. True Americanism, he thought, requires us to protect the various distinctive cultures that exist within the United States. Unlike the other two assimilationist ideologies, which assume (or hope) that intergroup relations will end in a merger in which the distinctive groups will disappear, cultural pluralism is based on the idea that the members of minority groups should be accepted as completely Americanized and assimilated without being required to disappear as distinctive groups. Proponents of Anglo conformity, who use the words *completely assimilated* to mean that group distinctions have disappeared, consider this idea to be, at the very least, a contradiction in terms.

How can the processes of assimilation and Americanization be completed even though ethnic diversity continues? The logic of the Anglo conformity view proceeds as follows: (1) complete Americanization can be achieved only through complete assimilation; (2) complete assimilation can be achieved only through Anglo conformity; therefore, (3) complete Americanization can be achieved only through Anglo conformity. Pluralists accept the first premise of this syllogism but reject the second and, consequently, the third. Both Anglo conformists and pluralists accept the idea that for there to be a *United* States of America, ethnic groups should somehow assimilate into American society and become unambiguously American, but pluralists do not believe that Anglo conformity is the only legitimate path to that shared goal.

The problem for pluralists is this: When members of the dominant group say that minority-group members are "unassimilated," are they merely making an observation or are they raising a question about the minority members' loyalty and credentials as Americans? Are the dominant-group members really asking "How can people claim to be 100 percent Americans while at the same time they stand apart from the larger society?" "Isn't such a stand 'divisive' and, perhaps even, evidence of divided loyalties?" "How can we create 'one nation, indivisible' while encouraging group separateness?"

One way to answer these questions is to attempt to uncouple the concepts of assimilation and Americanization, to insist that one may be fully American without being fully assimilated. This approach is logical, but it is not very promising. Advocates of Anglo conformity generally interpret the rejection of assimilation as a rejection of American society, and they are likely to respond to such a stance by saying "If they don't like it here, why don't they go back where they came from!"—or words to that effect. Hence, instead of continuing to maintain that one may be fully American while remaining "unassimilated," many pluralists prefer to discuss a different *model of assimilation*—one that rejects Anglo conformity but emphatically does not reject the desirability of complete Americanization. The aim of the model is to show that individuals and groups may become "100 percent Americans" without following the path of Anglo conformity. For our purposes, pluralism of this type exists when:

1. A minority group's members exhibit a very high degree of cultural assimilation but retain a large proportion of their native heritage for use within the group. They are bilingual and bicultural. Cultural assimilation has occurred through the *addition* of the majority's culture to the minority's culture, rather than by the substitution of the former for the latter. The differences of the majority and the minority are mutually accepted and respected.
2. The minority's members exhibit a very high degree of structural assimilation in education, occupations, places of residence, political participation, and mass recreation (i.e., "integration" in the *public sphere*), but they also remain very highly integrated in the religious, health and welfare, and "social" recreational activities of their ethnic group (i.e., the "ethnic group" or *private sphere* of secondary relations). They have equal civil standing with the majority. Equality of opportunity is guaranteed. The law is "colorblind": it prohibits both discrimination against them and preferential treatment for them.
3. They exhibit a low level of primary assimilation. Friendship choices depend substantially on racial and ethnic identities.
4. They exhibit very low marital assimilation. Out-marriage (exogamy) is strongly discouraged. Mates are chosen almost exclusively from within the racial or ethnic group.

This version of pluralism is depicted in Figure 2-3 on page 32.[10]

The goals of this version of pluralism (like those of Anglo conformity) represent an acceptance of the Anglo-American culture as the "standard" pattern of the country. Advocates of this view have no desire to be separated from the society's educational, occupational, and political mainstream. They wish to be assimilated *by addition* in the cultural realm, to be fully assimilated in the public sphere of the secondary structural realm, but to remain more or less separate in the other aspects of intergroup life. We will refer to this type of pluralism as *cultural pluralism* or

Subprocesses of Assimilation	Level of Minority's Participation in Majority Group		Level of Minority's Participation within Own Group
	High ——————— Low		High ————— Low
1. Cultural assimilation:	**X**_____ (very high acceptance of the majority's culture)	AND	**X**_____ (very high acceptance of own-group's culture)
2. Secondary assimilation:	**X**_____ (very high "integration" in education, occupations, residence, civic matters, and mass recreation with majority)	AND	**X**_____ (very high "integration" in religious, health and welfare, and "social" recreational activities within own group)
3. Primary assimilation:	_____**X**_____ (low acceptance of majority-group friends)	AND	**X**_____ (very high acceptance of own-group friends)
4. Marital assimilation:	_____**X** (very low acceptance of majority-group mates)	AND	**X**_____ (very high acceptance of own-group mates)

FIGURE 2-3   A model of assimilation: Cultural pluralism (X indicates a person's preferences, or goals, concerning the assimilation of minority groups)

simply as pluralism.[11] It is vital to note that if a group were to achieve the goals outlined here it would have completed, from this perspective, the requirements of assimilation. Its members would be viewed as being *as completely American as if they had disappeared in accordance with the goals of Anglo conformity*. Although pluralism and Anglo conformity specify different degrees of intergroup merger, they both envision high levels of similarity and cooperation in regard to the mainstream of the culture and society. This version of pluralism rejects Anglo conformity but, nonetheless, expects high levels of assimilation along the cultural dimension and in the public sphere of secondary assimilation. Although it accepts high levels of separation in the "social" and marital arenas, it nonetheless has an "assimilationist tone."

Pluralists, however, do not agree among themselves concerning the degrees and types of separation and merger that should be sought; hence, unlike Anglo conformity and the melting pot, there exists a range of possible pluralist solutions to the problem of dominant-subordinate group relations, some of which include greater degrees of merger with the dominant group than others; so the model of pluralism depicted in Figure 2-3 is not acceptable to all who consider themselves to be pluralists. Pluralists who are members of the dominant group, in particular, are likely to consider even the cultural pluralism we have described to contain an extreme or radical acceptance of separation. Pluralists of this persuasion might specify, for instance, that cultural assimilation should take place by substitution rather than addition and that white ethnics, at least, should be expected to participate fully in the voluntary associations of the general society rather than attempt to maintain voluntary associations that are comprised primarily of coethnics. They might argue that separate, ethnic churches should be discouraged. Please note that a model of pluralism conforming to these criteria could be depicted as in Figure 2-3, but some of the *X*s would be placed at different points along the four assimilation dimensions.

In opposition to those who believe pluralism should represent a higher degree of merger than is shown in Figure 2-3, some pluralists desire a higher degree of separation. They may suggest establishing separate school systems, separate economies, and even separate states or autonomous regions within the United States. Whenever such separate institutions cannot be organized, the rights of the minority should be legally protected through the establishment of quotas in schools, jobs, and political offices. They may object to the idea that only members of minority groups should be bilingual. Perhaps English should not be the general language in all parts of the country or in every institutional setting; perhaps the members of the majority should also be expected to be bilingual. Equality of results, not of opportunity, is the watchword.

We will simplify the problem of numerous pluralisms by distinguishing a second model of pluralism as a contrast to the one portrayed in Figure 2-3. The second model emphasizes separation and is generally antiassimilationist in "tone." For our purposes, complete pluralism of this second type exists when:

1. A minority group's members exhibit a low degree of cultural assimilation and retain or construct a distinctive heritage for use in most everyday activities. Only some members of the group will master the dominant culture and become bilingual and bicultural. Cultural assimilation takes place *by addition* rather than by *substitution,* but it occurs infrequently. The differences of the majority and the minority are mutually accepted and respected.

2. The minority's members exhibit a low degree of secondary assimilation in both the *public* and *private* social spheres. Their education, occupations, places of residence, political participation, recreation, religious observances, and health and welfare activities are separated from those of the broader society insofar as that is possible within the framework of a single society. The minority's members are legally protected against coercive efforts to force their assimilation in any respect. The law is not "colorblind." Each group's share of public offices and benefits depends on the group's relative size.

3. They exhibit very low primary assimilation. Out-group friendships are strongly discouraged.

4. They exhibit very low marital assimilation. Out-marriage (exogamy) is strongly discouraged. Mates are chosen almost exclusively from within the racial or ethnic group.

Subprocesses of Assimilation	Level of Minority's Participation in Majority Group		Level of Minority's Participation within Own Group
	High ——————— Low		High ——————— Low
1. Cultural assimilation:	_____ **X** _____ (low acceptance of the majority's culture)	AND	**X** _____ (very high acceptance of own-group's culture)
2. Secondary assimilation:	_____ **X** _____ (low "integration" in education, occupations, residence, civic matters, and mass recreation with majority)	AND	**X** _____ (very high "integration" in religious, health and welfare, and "social" recreational activities within own group)
3. Primary assimilation:	_____ **X** (very low acceptance of majority-group friends)	AND	**X** _____ (very high acceptance of own-group friends)
4. Marital assimilation:	_____ **X** (very low acceptance of majority-group mates)	AND	**X** _____ (very high acceptance of own-group mates)

FIGURE 2-4   A model of separatism (X indicates a person's preferences, or goals, concerning the assimilation of minority groups)

This version of pluralism is depicted in Figure 2-4.

This second form of pluralism envisions a high degree of separation in the cultural and social lives of the dominant and subordinate groups; so we will refer to it as *separatism.* Please note, however, that separatism in this sense still does not mean complete separation. The goal of complete separation or withdrawal from the society is *secession.* Secession is well illustrated by the withdrawal of the southern states from the United States in 1861 and by the breakup of the Soviet Union in 1991.

Evidently, pluralism represents a broader range of ideas than either Anglo conformity or the melting pot. What we refer to as cultural pluralism contains a high level of assimilation in the more public and visible aspects of life, but, in the model presented in Figure 2-3, it does not call for the complete disappearance of minority groups as do the Anglo conformity and melting pot ideologies. From the latter perspectives, pluralism's goal is not really "assimilation" at all but, rather, specific mixtures of assimilation and separation; however, *from the perspective of cultural pluralism, groups may retain or create separate identities and have separate religious, social, friendship, and family groups and, nevertheless, be judged to have achieved one version of "complete" Americanization.*

Many critics of cultural pluralism have argued that even if one were to consider such a solution to America's racial and ethnic problems to be desirable, it is highly unlikely that it would be durable. American life and tradition, it is said, keep constant pressures on racial and ethnic groups to Americanize in a way that is acceptable to the dominant group. For white ethnic groups, this means a full merger with the host group; for nonwhite groups, this means full cultural assimilation, with moderate to zero secondary, primary, and marital assimilation. Under these circumstances, groups seeking to escape discrimination and poverty may feel they must choose between cultural survival and upward economic mobility. Given such a choice, most disadvantaged groups have been willing, in Steinberg's (1981:256) words, "to compromise their ethnicity for the sake of economic security, social acceptance" and a sense of full participation. Cultural pluralism, from this vantage point, is hardly more than Anglo conformity in disguise. The requirement that minority groups should master the dominant group's culture to participate in the society's rewards places minorities under continuous pressure to discard their own culture and social organization entirely. Essed (1991:6) argues that the pluralist view "explicitly proclaims the existence of 'multiethnic' equality but implicitly presupposes an ethnic . . . hierarchical order."

Recall that the traditional pressures favoring conformity to the dominant group do not represent the only forces acting to modify cultural pluralism. The forces of separation also must be taken into account. These constantly opposing pressures favoring either conformity to the dominant group, at one extreme, or secession, at the other, suggest that cultural pluralism is inherently unstable. No group, the argument runs, can stop just at the point of assimilation defined by cultural pluralist philosophy. The group must continue through the exact point of merger it prefers toward one or another of the two opposing poles. Either the submersion of the minority within the dominant group or the separation (possibly accompanied by open warfare) of the groups is the inevitable result. Contemporary examples of the latter outcome include the ethnic conflicts between Azerbaijan and Armenia accompanying the dissolution of the Soviet Union and between Serbia, Croatia, and Bosnia-Herzegovina accompanying the dissolution of Yugoslavia.

Our discussion so far has attempted to show that the ideology of pluralism embraces varying degrees of merger and separation. As usually presented, this view proposes one form of pluralism that is decidedly assimilationist in tone and intent. Even though cultural pluralism contains certain separatist elements, these are activated mainly in the sphere of private relations. Advocates of this kind of separateness emphasize that it does not detract from the unity of the nation. They argue, instead, that permitting different racial and ethnic groups to retain their distinctiveness without discrimination creates especially loyal citizens. Diversity, not uniformity, is seen as the key to the maintenance of a vigorous democracy. As stated by Wirth (1945:355), its advocates believe pluralism is "one of the necessary preconditions of a rich and dynamic civilization under conditions of freedom."

Our discussion also has attempted to show that some forms of pluralism may be decidedly antiassimilationist in tone and intent. Separatists do not accept the basic values of the dominant group, and they consider the levels of distinctiveness permitted under cultural pluralism to be unsatisfactory. The presumption is made that the supposedly "democratic" inclusion of the minority is in reality a subtle form of repression. True democracy, from the perspective of separatists, cannot occur when the majority has the power to control the destiny of the minority's members. The minority's ability to protect its rights depends, according to this line of reasoning, on a high degree of independence in the economic, political, and educational areas, as well as in more personal matters.

The antiassimilationist view represented by the second form of pluralism—separatism—shades into the more extreme position of secessionism. In principle, of course, secessionism represents the ultimate challenge to the goals of Anglo conformity. One of the most important contemporary antiassimilationist theories, the *theory of internal colonialism,* is discussed in chapters 9 through 14.

To summarize, two ideologies of assimilation, the melting pot ideology and the ideology of cultural pluralism, emerged in reaction to the increased demands that ethnic groups should rapidly fuse with the dominant society. Both of these alternatives to Anglo conformity emphasize the advantages of accepting diverse elements into the mainstream of American life. In its cultural form, pluralism holds that minority groups may retain their distinctive heritages and, at the same time, live in harmony and equality with the dominant society. In its separatist form, pluralism is less confident about the good will of the majority and focuses on what it believes to be basic flaws in the society. It sees majority and minority groups more as adversaries than as cooperating partners in a joint venture.

As generally expressed, all of the assimilationist views—Anglo conformity, the melting pot, and cultural pluralism—share a very important assumption: under "normal" circumstances, white ethnic groups in the United States should move into the mainstream of American economic life within two or three generations. The ideologies of the melting pot and cultural pluralism contain the same expectation for nonwhites. The Anglo conformity view, however, contains the expectation that nonwhites should undergo cultural assimilation but should pursue socioeconomic "success" largely within a separate ethnic economy (e.g., Korean American professionals should serve Koreans or other minority Americans). Nonwhites also, of course, have been expected to remain separate in primary and marital relations. Each of these ideologies, though in different ways, contains the expectation that racial and ethnic groups in America should make socioeconomic "progress." Groups that are not "succeeding" in socioeconomic terms are considered to be "problem" groups.

Each of the models presented, to repeat, helps us to state clearly and to compare both the *goals* different individuals and groups in American society believe they and others *ought* to pursue and the *actual location* of any given individual or group (on the average) in regard to the four subprocesses of assimilation we have selected for our analysis. Stated differently, the models help us to specify both what the members of any group, individually or collectively, want and where they and others stand with respect to those goals.

The implications of the major ideas introduced so far must be examined in much greater detail and in relation to the actual experiences of different groups within American society. We begin this effort in chapter 3 by expanding our discussion of the way the Anglo-Americans consolidated their power on the Atlantic Coast of North America.

Key Ideas

1. Several scholars have maintained that when racial or ethnic groups come into contact, a specific sequence of events is set into motion. Robert E. Park, for example, believed that racial and ethnic contact led to competition, accommodation, and eventual assimilation, in that order.

2. The subject of assimilation is complex. It is important to think separately about *the facts* of assimilation and *the goals* that should be pursued. In regard to facts, it is helpful to view assimilation as a *collection of subprocesses* rather than as a single process. In regard to goals, it is helpful to identify competing ideologies.

3. Milton M. Gordon has identified seven subprocesses of assimilation. Our analysis relies on three of these. We also focus on one additional subprocess. Altogether, therefore, we distinguish four subprocesses: (1) *cultural assimilation,* (2) *secondary structural assimilation,* (3) *primary structural assimilation,* and (4) *marital assimilation.*

4. According to Gordon's theory of assimilation, each of the subprocesses of assimilation may occur simultaneously in varying degrees, and the rate of change in each will correspond to its position in the list given in point three; but, in contrast to Robert E. Park's view, *a group may assimilate culturally without necessarily proceeding through the remaining stages.* Past a certain point, however, Gordon's and Park's theories agree *that assimilation in all four respects becomes inevitable.*

5. Gordon also specified three main *ideologies of assimilation* that favor particular goals, models, or endpoints of assimilation. These three models of assimilation represent *ideal types.* The models do not necessarily represent the actual levels of assimilation of any particular group or groups; *they represent, rather, goals or targets* toward which a group may elect or be expected to move.

6. By the last quarter of the seventeenth century, the Anglo-Americans had become established as the dominant, "host," or "native" group along the Atlantic seaboard from Massachusetts to Virginia. They had displaced the Native Americans and established their own ways of living as dominant. The more nearly a person approximated the Anglo-American ethnic model, the more nearly American he or she was judged to be. This perspective on assimilation is called *the Anglo conformity ideology.*

7. The most prominent assimilationist views opposing the idea that Anglo conformity as *the* way to become an American and the idea that people of white, Anglo-Saxon ancestry make the most desirable citizens are *the melting pot ideology* and *the ideology of cultural pluralism.*

8. The melting pot ideology, like the ideology of Anglo conformity, favors a complete merger of the majority and the minority. Unlike Anglo conformity, however, the melting pot is expected to alter both the majority and the minority, creating a new and different blend. Although many Americans give lip service to the melting pot ideology, its impact on actual social arrangements in America has been comparatively small. People who adopt the melting pot metaphor usually are referring to Anglo conformity.

9. The ideology of cultural pluralism opposes the complete merger of minorities with the majority. It seeks instead various degrees of recognition for the right of minorities to retain their heritage and separate ways of life. In its main form, pluralism stresses equality of opportunity for minority-group citizens plus the right to retain their cultural and social distinctiveness. In this form, the minority seeks to master the culture of the dominant group without losing its own culture. It also seeks secondary assimilation *in the public sphere.* This approach, therefore, has a decidedly assimilationist "tone" even though separation in the private spheres of life is maintained.

10. A second form of pluralism, which we refer to as *separatism,* seeks not only the preservation of the minority's culture but a high degree of separation in many other ways as well. Advocates of this view may urge quotas in schools, jobs, and political offices, or separate schools, economies, and governments. The resulting social arrangements would be pluralist but would involve a great deal more actual and legal separation than would cultural pluralism. Although the emphasis here is on separation rather than merger, the minority would still be an integral part of the larger society. It would not attempt to secede or overthrow the government by force.

Notes

1. An accommodation exists when the "antagonism of the hostile elements is, for the time being, regulated, and conflict disappears as overt action, although it remains latent as a potential force" Park and Burgess (1921:665). It may last for many generations or for only a short period of time.

2. For an excellent discussion of the theoretical status of Park's thesis, see Hirschman (1983:399–402). See also the criticisms advanced by Stanfield (1988).

3. Gordon is not the first to suggest the usefulness of analyzing assimilation in this way. Galitzi (1929), for instance, analyzed the economic, cultural, and marital assimilation of Roumanians in America.

4. Although it is useful for comparison to think of Anglo-Americans as sharing a single set of standards, there obviously was—and still is—a substantial diversity within this "host," "charter," or "core" group. Gordon employed one term, *core*

subsociety, to refer to middle-class Anglo-American standards and another term, *core group,* to refer to the standards of the entire Anglo-American group (1964:74).

5. Eighteen languages were spoken in New Amsterdam at the time it was annexed by the English (Hansen 1945:39).

6. Gordon also distinguished four other subprocesses of assimilation that will not appear directly in our analysis (1964:71). These are identificational assimilation (a sense of peoplehood based exclusively on the host society), attitude receptional assimilation (the absence of prejudice), behavior receptional assimilation (the absence of discrimination), and civic assimilation (the absence of value and power conflicts).

7. Gordon (1964:31–38) discussed at some length the importance of the difference between secondary and primary relationships, but he did not carry the distinction over into the naming of the subprocesses of assimilation. His analysis

clearly recognizes, however, the importance of this distinction.

8. Gordon (1964:85) attributed the term to Cole and Cole (1954).

9. For an excellent summary of what *has* taken place in America, see Hirschman (1983:402–412).

10. For a related effort to describe an ideal or perfect cultural pluralism, see Murguía (1989:109–111).

11. Horton (1966:708) called this view *consensual pluralism*. Gordon (1964:88) suggested the term *liberal pluralism*.

The Rise of
Anglo-American Society

You will do well to inoculate the Indians by means of blankets, as well as to try every other method that can serve to extirpate this execrable race. —SIR JEFFREY AMHERST

. . . all children born of any negro or other slave, shall be slaves as their fathers were for the term of their lives.
—MARYLAND LAW OF 1664

The process through which many immigrants and their descendants appear to have passed to become full members of American society was described briefly in chapter 1. For those considered to be members of the "white race" this process appears frequently to have required a period of about three generations. In chapter 2 we sketched some of the events that enabled the English, by 1700, to gain control over a strip of land along the Atlantic seacoast of North America and to generate and adopt the Anglo conformity ideology of assimilation. We also reviewed two additional ideologies of assimilation—the melting pot and cultural pluralism—and an antiassimilationist ideology—separatism.

This chapter has two main purposes. First, we discuss further how the Anglo-American group came into existence in the seventeenth century and established its standards as paramount. Second, we describe crucial variations in the operation of the processes of intergroup adjustment during the colonial period. Some groups (e.g., the Dutch, the Scotch-Irish, and the Germans) were propelled more or less strongly toward a merger with the Anglo-American group, but two other prominent groups, the Native Americans and Africans as noted in chapter 2, generally were held at or remained at a distance. The varying degrees and qualities of assimilation and separation experienced by different groups during these formative years left a lasting imprint on the social order of the Anglo-Americans. This imprint continues even now to affect intergroup relations in the United States.

The English Legacy

Hardly more than a century after their successful beginnings at Jamestown, Virginia (1607), and Plymouth, Massachusetts (1620), the thirteen American colonies of the English were well established. By that time, the English language, English customs, and English ideas of commerce, law, government, and religion were predominant throughout the region. The conditions in the New World promoted, and sometimes required, new ways of doing things, of course; so the various elements of English culture and society had been modified in myriad and complex ways to produce the complicated mixture of peoples and cultures of the new "American" society and culture. A consideration of some early developments in this new society—English in broad outline but with many non-English elements—is crucial to an understanding of racial and ethnic relations in America today. To illustrate, let's first review how certain legal and political traditions were transplanted from Europe to America.

Both Jamestown and Plymouth were founded by commercial companies that hoped to establish profitable businesses in America. These companies, operating under a charter granted by King James I, worked with varying degrees of success to colonize the territories granted to them. The London Company landed 104 men and boys in 1607 to construct a trading post that became known as Jamestown. When the second boatload of settlers arrived early in the next year, the original group had been reduced by disease and conflicts with Indians to less than half their original number. The next several years were filled with misery and discouragement for these early settlers, and their suffering was made worse by the seeming pointlessness of their efforts (Burner, Fox-Genovese, and Bernhard 1991:34; Morison 1972:87–90). As company employees, most of these unfortunates had little stake in the enterprise. As would be true later for hundreds of thousands of others, they were expected to work as bonded servants for a specified number of years (usually seven) to pay for their passage and keep. Moreover, little was produced in the colony during the early years that could be sent to England for sale; consequently, the investors in the London Company were not making the profits they had hoped for, and the entire enterprise was in danger of failing. Clearly, something had to be done to save this attempt at colonization.

Three important changes were made in the organization of the Jamestown colony. First, the king for a time discontinued his direct control of the colony. Second, the company (now the Virginia Company) began to grant settlers land and stock in the company so that they, too, would have a stake in its success. Third, in 1619, the company permitted a representative assembly to be established. This assembly, which has been widely hailed as the beginning of representative democracy in America, could enact any law that was not contrary to the laws of England. The king retained veto power, but the Virginia settlers had a great deal of control over their own affairs.

But another event was of special importance in helping to secure England's first toehold in North America. Like most other Europeans, the investors in Jamestown thought it possible that gold and silver would be discovered by the expeditions they financed. They also hoped to establish a profitable trade in furs and other goods with the Indians and to use products from the forests to supply England's navy. No riches in precious metals were to be found in the Chesapeake Bay area, however, and factionalism threatened the very existence of the colony. After several turbulent years, it was discovered that Virginia was an excellent place to grow tobacco. This discovery provided the economic underpinning that was needed for the colony to survive. In Morison's words, "Virginia went tobacco-mad . . ." and by 1618 "exported 50,000 pounds' weight of tobacco to England" (1972:90).

Many investors in the London and Virginia companies suffered financial losses; so, understandably, they may have considered their efforts in America to be a failure. Yet from today's vantage point, the events at Jamestown were of the greatest significance in establishing the social and cultural framework of the English colonies and of their descendant, the United States.

The second early success in the colonization of English America—the founding of Plymouth by the Pilgrims—also occurred under the sponsorship of the Virginia Company. In this case, though, the 102 Pilgrims who agreed to cross the Atlantic on the Mayflower sought to separate themselves from the Church of England in order to practice their own version of the Protestant faith, as well as to find improved economic conditions. It is therefore not surprising that the variation of English life they founded emphasized not only English ideas and ways but also those of their particular Protestant religious group. This fact played an extremely important role in the subsequent English immigration to America and in shaping the value system that became predominant in colonial American society.

Another group of dissenters from the Church of England gained a charter to establish a colony in New England, and in 1630 around eight hundred members of this group, who wished to practice a "purified" version of Protestantism, emigrated to Massachusetts Bay. They established several colonies (including Boston) that were more religious than commercial in nature, and many people were attracted to them for religious reasons. During the first ten years, between fifteen and twenty thousand more Puritans reached the Massachusetts Bay Colony (Burner, Fox-Genovese, and Bernhard 1991:37; Jordan and Litwack 1987:25). Possibly twice that number had arrived in other portions of the lands claimed by England, making this the first period of heavy immigration to America.

The comparatively large size of the English immigration at this time is significant. Consider, by contrast, what happened in New Netherland. The Dutch companies that founded New Netherland were attempting to colonize at roughly the same time as the English, but their efforts to increase the population were not as successful. At one point, the Dutch West India Company offered large grants of land along the Hudson River to members of the company who would finance the passage of fifty families. Some who accepted the offer were given, in addition to the land, extremely strong control over the lives of those who settled there. These inducements did not, however, lead to the volume of immigration that was taking place in the English colonies. When the English occupied this territory (1664), the population of the English colonies may have been six or seven times as large as that of New Netherland. The task of conquest, therefore, was greatly simplified, and New Netherland was captured without a struggle. English control of the coast now stretched without interruption from Massachusetts through Virginia.

These considerations remind us again that as Anglo-American society expanded, the *standards* of the new society were being established. The very meaning of the terms *American* and *foreigner* were coming into being, as was the idea that the metamorphosis of the latter into the former required conformity to the Anglo-American pattern of living. These newly established standards involved more than ethnicity, however. Europeans had been taught throughout the Christian era that all people are brothers, but they nevertheless considered some peoples to be inferior to others (Gossett 1963:8–11). For example, each European national group tended to think its culture was superior to those of the other European groups. In addition to this practically universal kind of group vanity (called *ethnocentrism*), the Europeans distinguished the "civilized" from the "savage" and regarded the latter as inferiors.[1] Although some Europeans considered the tribal ways of life to be pure and noble, the belief grew and spread during the seventeenth century that neither the Native Americans nor the Africans were suitable for complete assimilation into the developing white society.

The ethnocentrism of the English at the beginning of the colonization period apparently was not totally devoid of what we today call racial prejudice; however, as we shall soon see, the relation of the Europeans with the Native and African peoples appear not to have been shaped markedly by the *doctrine of white supremacy*—the belief that the growing dominance of the whites throughout the world was a result of biologically inherited differences among racial groups (Fredrickson 1971:242–252). This doctrine (to which we return in chapter 5) has been elaborated mainly in the last two centuries and, thus, is a product of the modern era.

Native American–English Relations

To understand the past and present experience of the Native Americans,[2] we must begin with two central facts. First, they discovered America. Archeological evidence indicates that there were people in Alaska by 25,000 B.C., and that they had reached South America by 15,000 B.C. (Spencer, Jennings et al. 1977:6–12); thus, when the ancestors of some Anglo-Americans disembarked from the Mayflower the ancestors of some Native Americans soon arrived to greet them. From the time of these early contacts to the present, the American Indians' lands gradually have been occupied by invaders.

The second fact concerns the diversity of societies and cultures among the native tribes. At the outset, at least two hundred different tribes or bands stretched across the continent (Spicer 1980a:58). These societies possessed cultures that varied in many significant ways. Consider, for example, the matter of languages. Approximately two hundred separate languages (not counting dialects) were spoken among the American Indians at the time of first contact.[3] Although the members of these societies could communicate with one another through interpreters and sign language, their languages sometimes differed from one another as much as English and Chinese. Even closely related languages might differ as much as French and Spanish (Spencer 1977:37–39).

Their societies differed also in the way people made their living and the manner in which they were organized. Many of the tribes were hunting and gathering societies; others lived primarily from small-scale gardening; still others had developed more advanced agricultural methods. These societies ranged from very small, simply organized groups to comparatively large, highly organized groups. The diversity of cultures and societies was so great that they were seldom able to lay aside their differences to face the invaders in a unified way; hence, the interactions among the different groups resulted in a bewildering array of specific and changing relationships.

The Iroquois confederacy, for example, consisted of an alliance of five tribes: Cayugas, Mohawks, Oneidas, Onondagas, and Senecas. This political organization probably was formed before the arrival of the Europeans as a defensive measure in a longstanding conflict between the Iroquois and the Algonkians. By the time the Europeans arrived, the Iroquois were among the most politically and militarily active people in the Northeast. They had achieved dominance over a large region and had established an active trading network throughout it (G. Nash 1974:13–25).

A different confederation of Indian tribes was present in the Chesapeake Bay area when the English founded Jamestown. This confederation, named the Powhatans after their leading chief, already had had some unpleasant contacts with Europeans and were therefore somewhat suspicious of these newcomers. The Powhatans did not, however, attempt immediately to expel the English settlers. For one thing, they were as curious about the English as the English were about them. For another, the Powhatans were engaged in warfare with other tribes, and they had hoped to form an alliance with the English. Besides, the English were greatly outnumbered, and the Powhatans had no way of knowing about the dangers of European diseases or the size of the immigration to come.[4] Had the indigenous people wished to end Jamestown, they could have done so easily. In fact, the colony would not have survived its first winter without the Powhatans' help.

During the early years, the Jamestown settlers did not have a fixed policy regarding the American Indians. The king had given the land to the Virginia Company, but he had left the problem of dealing with the tribes to the colonists. The colonists knew that the Indians might well object to their presence and might reject their efforts to make use of the land or take possession of it; consequently, it was not at all clear how these delicate matters were to be handled. The English hoped that the Native Americans would welcome the "benefits" of civilization, cede their lands, convert to Christianity, and serve willingly as a labor force for the colonists; however, the Indians soon made it plain that they were not going to volunteer to perform the hard labor required to make Jamestown a self-sustaining enterprise. When the colonists attempted to force them to work, conflict between the two groups erupted.

Despite a slow start, the population of Jamestown grew rapidly after tobacco production commenced. Beginning with the struggling survivors of the first three years (about sixty people), the population reached twelve hundred in 1624 (Jordan and Litwack 1987:21).[5] This rapid increase in population created a great demand for additional land for tobacco plantations, which in turn led to increased friction with the Native Americans. By 1622, the Powhatans realized they had made a serious mistake; so they launched a full-scale effort to drive the colonists out. They killed almost one-third of the invaders but did not succeed in ending the colony. They did succeed, however, in convincing this particular group of English people that there could be no lasting accommodation between the groups. The hope of Christianizing and "civilizing" the "savages" was abandoned as an official policy.[6] Beyond this point, the English generally sought to seize the indigenous people's lands and to subjugate or eliminate the people themselves.

The Indians responded in kind. In 1644, they tried again—though by now they were much weaker—to drive the English into the sea. Again, they inflicted heavy casualties on the whites but could not end English colonization. At the conclusion of this conflict, the English signed a treaty with the Powhatans that, in effect, initiated the reservation system. The treaty, in Nash's words, "recognized that assimilation of the two peoples was unlikely and guaranteed to the indigenous people a sanctuary from white land hunger and aggression" (1974:65). In this way, the whites set into motion a method of conquest that was used repeatedly for the next two centuries. As a rule, major conflicts were ended through the signing of treaties that assured the Indians certain "reserved" lands, which, after a while, would be infiltrated, seized, and occupied. Each time, new reservations would be created over which the Indians would be guaranteed permanent control, but soon a new round of encroachment would begin.

The relationships between the Puritans and the people of several tribes in the Massachusetts Bay region were similar to those that developed in Virginia. The initial contacts, made with the Wampanoags, generally were friendly and, as in Virginia, the assistance of the Indians proved to be essential to the survival of the colonists.[7] The Indians of Massachusetts also were eager to establish trade relations and military alliances with the colonists; in fact, an alliance between the Puritans and Massasoit, Chief of the Wampanoags, was kept in force for over forty years.

The alliance with Massasoit did not prevent the colonists from occupying Native American lands, however. At first this practice caused little difficulty because the Native American population in eastern Massachusetts already had been greatly reduced by epidemics introduced by European fishermen and explorers (Snipp 1989:20–21). But as the main Puritan immigration commenced in the 1630s the desire for land mounted, and so did friction between the groups.

To an even greater extent than in Virginia, in New England the policy of the English regarding the Native Americans was ambivalent. The English definitely wished to occupy the Native Americans' land, which might have the effect of driving the Native Americans away, but they also were eager to force them to discontinue their "heathenish" beliefs and rituals and adopt the "civilized" religion and culture of the English, which required that they remain close at hand.

The Puritans' ambivalence may be seen in the arguments that arose among them concerning their right to occupy the land. Roger Williams, for example, maintained that the king had no right to give away the tribes' land and that the colonists were occupying it illegally. Although the leaders of the Plymouth colony considered Williams to be a radical, his belief that the Indians' land should be purchased from them already had become the basis for the official policies of Spain and Holland. Most of the English, though, did not accept the idea that the Native Americans were the true owners of the land. Various legal doctrines were advanced to justify taking the land, the most important of which was the doctrine of *vacuum domicilium*.[8] According to this view, the land claimed by the American Indians was in reality "unoccupied." This curious contention rested on the conviction that to be occupied land had to be put to "civilized" uses. Civilized uses, in turn, were the very ones to which the Puritans wished to put the land. One passenger of the Mayflower, who felt no one "can doubt . . . the lawfulness of . . . dwelling there," argued as follows: "Their land is spacious and void, and they are few, and do but run over the grass, as do also the foxes and wild beasts. They are not industrious . . . to use either the land or the commodities of it, but all spoils . . . for want of manuring, gathering, ordering, etc. . . . So it is lawful now to take a land which none useth . . . " (Quint, Cantor, and Albertson 1978:11).[9]

In short, the "failure" of the indigenous population to use the land in ways that the settlers deemed appropriate was interpreted by many Puritans to mean that the land was "unoccupied" and could—indeed, *should*—be used as they saw fit. As the settlers acquired additional land, either by seizure or through some form of purchase, they encountered the people of various tribes and attempted to bring them under English rule. As the frontier moved south and west, various small groups of Indians were left behind in "reserved" areas and "praying" villages. The English expected these people to adopt English culture in every particular as rapidly as possible and, simultaneously, to discontinue all of their own ways of thinking and acting. This did not mean that the English were prepared to permit the Native Americans who succeeded in mastering English culture to occupy positions of leadership and wealth within Puritan society, to enter into their homes as friendly equals, or to marry into their families. It meant that the Native Americans were to be tolerated within the physical limits of New England, provided they appeared to the eye to be "civilized."

The Native Americans, for their part, had shown strong resistance to merging into Anglo-American society. They wished to retain their own tribal identities, traditions, and institutions. From their viewpoint, they were the civilized hosts and the whites were the barbaric invaders. Consequently, some leaders, such as the Wampanoag Chief Metacom (whom the English called King Philip), mounted several unsuccessful attempts to unite the tribes in the region and drive the English out.

By the last quarter of the seventeenth century the Anglo-American colonists of Virginia and New England had devised a two-pronged policy toward the American Indians. The indigenous people were expected either to give up whatever lands the colonists wanted and move peacefully beyond the frontier or to remain within the confines of Anglo-American settlement in a condition of marginality. A refusal by the Indians to accept one of these alternatives could lead to their annihilation or forcible removal from the area. The principal outcome in nearly all cases was the same: the Indians either were excluded physically from participation in Anglo-American society or they were permitted to cling to the lower rungs of the social ladder. Despite the numerous differences that existed among the various tribes, including such things as the extent to which they had allied themselves with the colonists, all of those in America at the time of the "discovery" soon were considered by the majority of the English to be essentially alike. The term *Indian* was applied to all of the indigenous people, and they came to be regarded as unassimilable and ineligible for full membership in the new host society being created. This view was not shared by all of the Anglo-Americans, however. Even though the ideology of separatism was paramount for over two centuries, some members of the dominant group continued to hope to "civilize" and assimilate the Native American, and during the latter third of the nineteenth century, the ideology of Anglo conformity regained supremacy in Native American affairs (see chapter 12).

The situation of Native American-English contact, first in the Northeast and then later in other parts of North America, illustrates clearly the way interracial and interethnic contacts may lead to repeated and persistent conflicts as the participants struggle to gain control of land and other resources and to establish themselves as the dominant group. These contacts also represent our first illustration of a vital point to be developed in chapters 9 through 12: *Minority groups that are highly solidary and socially self-sufficient at the time they become subordinate are likely to resist assimilation strongly for long periods of time.* Minorities of this type are highly unlikely to pass, in only a few generations, through the process of assimilation described by Park's race cycle theory or Gordon's assimilation theory.[10] After three generations, most American Indians exhibited low levels of cultural assimilation into Anglo-American society and very low levels of secondary, primary, and marital assimilation.

Servants and Slaves

African or black people were represented among the first groups to arrive among the Spanish explorers in the New World, but the initial instance of black "immigration" to what is now the United States occurred in Virginia in 1619.[11] It is recorded that the Virginia settlers bought "twenty Negers," who arrived on a Dutch warship (Frazier 1957:3). Although not much is known about the treatment of these twenty people, one thing appears to be established: they "were not slaves in a legal sense" (Franklin and Moss 1988:53). They were purchased as indentured or bonded servants rather than as absolute slaves. As we have noted, many of the white people who were a part of the English colony in Virginia had come there under a similar arrangement.[12]

English people who were impoverished or had been convicted of a crime sometimes were sold into bondage for a specified number of years. Even free people who had not run afoul of the law sometimes were willing to accept a period of servitude in return for their passage to the New World. This system was recognized in England as legal and profitable to all parties, and the servants under this arrangement were sometimes referred to as slaves (Handlin 1957:7–9). Through such contracts, England profited by reducing the number of public charges; the purchaser of the servants profited by having cheap, "slave" labor available for a fixed period; and the servants profited by having the opportunity to escape their unpleasant circumstances at home and, perhaps, to get a new start in life. Even during the period of indenture, the slave had certain rights and was, therefore, legally protected from excessive harshness by the master. Initially, these protections apparently applied to the black bonded servants as well as to the white. English law during this period stated that "a slave who had been baptized became infranchised" (Frazier 1957:23). Those who were so treated might then become free. Although it is probable that black servants were not treated in exactly the same way as white servants, even in the early years, much evidence favors the view that the laws regulating the rights and obligations of servitude applied to the members of both races and all nations.[13]

The main issues that provoked racially discriminatory legislation were the question of the length of the term of service, the problem of the standing of Christianized slaves, and the legal position of the children of slaves. For at least twenty years after black servants were introduced into Virginia, many employers had a definite preference for white laborers and were unwilling to commit themselves for long periods to the support of servants. As time passed, however, the profitability of black labor increased, and so did the masters' desire for it; hence, by the 1660s, both Maryland and Virginia had taken legal steps to make the attainment of freedom more difficult for African slaves. For example, in 1664, Maryland's legislature passed an act that required all non-Christian slaves, especially "Negroes," to serve *durante vita* (for life) (Degler 1972:71). This law was later repealed to prevent unscrupulous masters from marrying their white female servants to black male servants to force the women into longer periods of servitude and to gain possession of their children. In the meantime, however, the noose around the freedom of African people was permanently tightened. Since the law of 1664 had left open the possibility that Christianized Africans might someday become free, a new law was passed stating that baptism did not amount to manumission (i.e., being freed).

A similar process of legalizing lifetime slavery for Africans, even those who were Christians, occurred in Virginia. In 1661, a law imposing penalties on runaway slaves distinguished clearly between black and white runaways and implied that the period of indenture for at least some blacks was forever (Franklin and Moss 1988:54; Handlin 1957:13) Another law passed in the same year made this racial distinction hereditary. The ability of any black person to gain freedom in Virginia seems to have ended by 1682. In that year, a law was passed establishing black slavery for life, whether an individual had been baptized or not. In hardly more than sixty years, then, the Africans who had entered the colonies of Maryland and Virginia were downgraded from a legal position similar to that of indentured servants from other nations to a status of lifelong bondage. But the gap in status was not yet absolute. The terms *servant* and *slave* were still sometimes used interchangeably.

The possibility remained that at least some white people also might be reduced to the type of slavery that had been forced on the blacks, and this possibility had an understandable effect on the choices of whites who might otherwise have chosen to come to Maryland and Virginia. The white servants frequently wrote letters to their relatives and friends back home warning them not to come to these colonies and, in some cases, begging for help. Richard Frethorne ([1623]1988:36), for example, wrote his parents that "there is nothing to be gotten here but sickness and death." He pleaded with them to redeem his debt. Travelers also told of the harshness of white servitude.[14] Such places as Pennsylvania and New York, therefore, frequently were more attractive to free-born immigrants who feared they might be bound over as servants if they went to Maryland or Virginia. In the latter colonies, the masters' desire to encourage the immigration of white settlers and an increasing preference for black labor on the plantations led to a gradual strengthening of the position of the white slaves (Handlin 1957:15). The blacks, who had come to the colonies involuntarily and who did not write horror stories to those back home, were unable to benefit from this small source of protection. Neither were they able, at this point, to become enfranchised through baptism and thus claim the protection of the laws of England. In this way, the condition of white servants gradually improved while that of black slaves became worse.

The spread of the plantation system of agriculture increased the status gap between black and white servants. Black laborers could not desert the plantation and disappear among the citizenry nearly so easily as could white laborers. Therefore, the masters' investment in black laborers was protected. Furthermore, black women and children could be used in the fields along with the men, thus increasing the number of productive hands at the masters' disposal (Frazier 1957:29–30).

As the plantation economy developed throughout the South, it was obvious to the members of the planter class that the fewer rights laborers had and the harder they could be required to work, the lower would be the cost of their labor and the larger would be the planters' profits. Thus, the planters encouraged measures that moved the blacks further from the status of human beings and toward the status of mere property. Under these conditions, the blacks had descended, by the beginning of the eighteenth century, into a state of complete, abject, legally defenseless bondage. The term *slave* became unambiguous: it now meant that a person was of African descent. An African heritage, and particularly black skin, had become its symbols. The equation of blackness and slave status became fixed, making it impossible even for "free" blacks to enjoy their legal rights.

The relegation of African slaves to the status of property also increased the masters' desire to own more of them, and the increasing size of the slave population brought with it new problems for the whites. The importation of slaves increased so rapidly that in some places the planters became alarmed by the possibility that the slaves would become too numerous to control. Georgia, for example, attempted at first to prevent the importation of black slaves entirely so that rebellions would be less likely to occur and the colony would be easier to defend. In South Carolina, the number of black slaves had become so large by 1700 that planters were permitted to have no more than six adult black men for each white servant (Frazier 1957:32). Although the white/black ratio throughout the southern colonies in 1670 was over 14 to 1, by 1730 it had declined to less than 3 to 1, and by 1750 it had reached 1.5 to 1.[15]

The concern of the dominant group was well placed. Despite the fact that the masters took extraordinary precautions to keep the slaves under their dominion, slave resistance was a problem from the first. This fact frequently has been obscured by the claim that black slaves were usually happy, contented people— what we may call the *Gone With the Wind* version of slavery (Jacobs and Landau 1971:100). "If slavery was so intolerable," some have asked, "why didn't the slaves rebel?" Many members of the dominant group believed that black people have a naturally cheerful disposition and, provided they are well fed, are "easily made happy."[16] Aside from the fact that such thinking is stereotyped and superficial, a closer inspection of the historical record does not bear out the nonresistance thesis. At the time of their acquisition—usually by purchase from African slave traders who captured their victims in the valleys of the Gambia, Niger, and Congo rivers—many slaves resisted vigorously. And as they were being transported through the infamous Middle Passage to the New World, many incidents occurred aboard ship. Instances in which the slaves overcame the crews and captured the ships on which they were imprisoned were so common that "they were considered one of the principal hazards of the slave trade" (Frazier 1957:85). Moreover, when escape or attack seemed impossible, many slaves jumped overboard to their deaths.[17]

The resistance to slavery by no means ended after the slaves arrived in America. Throughout the nearly two and one-half centuries of American slavery, most known forms of overt and covert resistance were employed. From the beginning, individual slaves revolted against the system by running away, and considering the difficulties of all other forms of resistance, this may have been the most effective way to strike back. In many cases, fugitive slaves banded together into outlaw groups, establishing "maroon communities" in various inaccessible places. The likelihood of escape by running away was dramatically improved near the beginning of the nineteenth century, when existing arrangements for assisting fugitive slaves, primarily in the northern states, were enlarged and made more efficient as the complicated network of people and facilities known as the Underground Railroad gradually took form. Several "tracks," including one to Florida, developed; during the decades immediately preceding the Civil War the center of the Railroad's activities was Ohio. Hundreds of "stations" and "operators" assisted the fugitives in their long journey to havens in the North and in Canada.

Also during the nineteenth century, individual forms of resistance to slavery were supplemented by organized resistance. As noted previously, the leaders of the Georgia Colony recognized slave insurrections to be a distinct possibility and tried, therefore, to restrict the importation of slaves. The same fear existed in the other colonies, and many precautions were taken to prevent uprisings. Efforts were made to keep the ratio of black slaves to whites below a certain level. Slaves of the same tribe frequently were separated or forbidden to speak to each other. Most slaves were not permitted to speak their native tongues or to retain their African names. They were permitted to travel only for short distances and under careful surveillance. White slave patrols were used extensively to police the activities of blacks and to interfere with any disapproved organizational efforts. In most places, it was illegal for a slave to learn to read or write or for anyone to teach a slave these skills. News of slave unrest was suppressed to diminish the possibility that it might generate or strengthen resistance in other places. In brief, the masters were at great pains to keep the slaves in a state of ignorance and to disrupt communications among them. Under such circumstances, planning and executing a revolt was no easy matter.

We return to the issue of slave resistance in chapter 10. For the moment, though, we emphasize that the relations of blacks and whites during the period discussed illustrates the process whereby the white American majority came into being and placed nonwhite people in a subordinate position. By the beginning of the eighteenth century, the blacks as a group were physically within the developing Anglo-American society and played an absolutely vital economic role there, but they were not candidates for full membership in the society. They were not encouraged, in many cases not permitted, to undergo cultural assimilation, and after three generations they certainly exhibited low levels of secondary, primary, and marital assimilation. Again, as for the Indians, the human interactions and acceptance that are necessary for the "eventual" assimilation of Park's race-cycle theory to take place did not exist. The status of Native American and African groups had been degraded during the seventeenth century, and no one knew where or when the descent would end. To the questions, "What is an American?" and "How does a person become an American?" a majority of the members of the dominant group had adopted one answer—Anglo conformity.

The eighteenth century created challenges to Anglo-American dominance. The first test came from a very heavy immigration to America of the Irish, particularly the so-called Scotch-Irish of Ulster. The second test came from a heavy immigration of Germans, and the Revolutionary War of 1776 represented a third.[18] Let us turn first to the immigration from Ireland.

The Colonial Irish

The Irish began to arrive in the American colonies of the English almost at once. By 1610, according to Adamic (1944:315), hundreds of the Irish had reached Jamestown. Throughout the seventeenth century, many more fled from the troubled Emerald Isle to the Atlantic colonies.

The largest and most discussed prerevolutionary immigration from Ireland to colonial America, however, consisted mainly of people from Northern Ireland (Ulster). Many people living in Ulster at this time were descendants of immigrant Scots who had been brought to Northern Ireland by the English early in the seventeenth century to work the Plantation of Ulster.[19] In contrast to the other citizens of Ireland, who were predominantly Catholic, the Irish of Scots descent were mainly Presbyterians. Although their Presbyterianism was involved in their departure from Ireland, economic reasons were probably much more important. The lands on which they lived and worked were generally leased from absentee English landowners. When the landowners began to raise the rents on these leases, a large number of the Ulster Irish, particularly those of Scots descent, decided to go to America (beginning markedly around 1717) rather than to pay the higher rents.

More important to us than their reasons for leaving, however, is their reception in the colonies. At first, the Scotch-Irish headed mainly for New England, where, in general, they were met with reserve. Although these people were from the British Isles, were mainly Protestants, and were needed to help settle the frontier, they definitely were not accepted wholeheartedly by the now-native Americans. They clearly were regarded as "foreigners" who deviated in undesirable ways from the Anglo-American ideal pattern of behavior. They were said to drink too much, to fight too much, and to be generally ill-tempered, troublesome, and coarse of speech. Ulstermen generally were regarded "as illiterate, slovenly, and filthy" (Burner, Fox-Genovese, and Bernhard 1991:72). These presumed differences cre- ated friction between the Americans and the Scotch-Irish. In one case, for example, a Scotch-Irish Presbyterian meeting house was destroyed (Hansen 1945:49). In another instance, "a mob arose to prevent the landing of the Irish" (Jones 1960:45). In 1718, the Scotch-Irish were blamed for a shortage of food in Boston (Seller 1984:141), and a Boston newspaper stated, in 1725, that the difficulty created by the newcomers "gives us an ill opinion of foreigners, especially those coming from Ireland" (Jones 1960:46).

Pennsylvania soon became the most frequent destination of the Scotch-Irish immigrants. Their treatment in New England had something to do with this, of course, but also William Penn was actively advertising in Europe for settlers, especially for the frontier areas; so the Ulster Irish were greeted in a much friendlier way in Pennsylvania. Even here, though, as the number of Irish immigrants mounted, interethnic problems arose. For example, it was said that unless something was done, the Scotch-Irish would "soon make themselves Proprietors of the Province" (Jones 1960:46).

The newcomers apparently were not great respectors of property; they frequently "squatted" on land without paying for it. There was also a strong mutual antagonism between the German and Scotch-Irish settlers of Pennsylvania that led to numerous disturbances. Before long, the Pennsylvania authorities began to discourage the continuation of the Scotch-Irish immigration; so this particular immigrant stream began to move heavily into the frontier regions of Virginia and the Carolinas (Jones 1980:899–900), where they were in constant conflict with the Indians (Burner, Fox-Genovese, and Bernhard 1991:72).

The case of the Scotch-Irish affords an early example of the mixed reactions exhibited by Americans toward most later arrivals. On the one hand, immigrants frequently have been actively recruited to meet labor shortages and populate frontier areas; on the other hand, Americans have been afraid the newcomers would compete for land and jobs and would not conform to Anglo-American traditions and standards. Perhaps they would instead establish an alternative pattern of life or, worse, establish themselves as a new dominant group. This ambivalence usually has been displayed in acts of violence and other forms of discrimination against members of minority ethnic groups. Some of the difficulties encountered by the colonial Scotch-Irish require us to consider them the first large American immigrant minority group.[20]

Feelings of rejection and acts of hostility were not one-sided, however. The Scotch-Irish came to America mainly in groups, and they tended to stick together after they arrived. They were quite conscious of themselves as a distinctive nationality group and did not mingle easily with the host Anglo-Americans. Indeed, they "nurtured a profound hatred for the English" (Burner, Fox-Genovese, and Bernhard 1991:94) and, as mentioned previously, surely did not get along well with the other noticeable immigrant minority group of the day—the Germans. They were "avid politicians" who "demanded a voice in the lawmaking process" but who "totally disregarded the law if it did not suit them" (Burner, Fox-Genovese, and Bernhard 1991:72).

Given this outline of the entry of the Scotch-Irish into American society, what may be said concerning the course of their inclusion in American life? As Park's formulation of the cycle of race relations would lead us to expect, the contacts between the Scotch-Irish and the other main groups in American society at that time—majority and minorities alike—produced a certain amount of competition and conflict. A gradual accommodation was achieved, however, aided by the migration of the Scotch-Irish to the frontier areas in large numbers. So far, so good. But how rapidly did the Scotch-Irish move toward the fourth stage of Park's race cycle, *eventual* assimilation? To expand our understanding here, we refer to the four subprocesses of assimilation derived from Gordon's theory presented in chapter 2.

By the standards of Anglo conformity, the Scotch-Irish were good candidates for complete assimilation in three generations. They were white Protestants from the British Isles, and, although the research evidence on these matters is far from complete, most writers agree that those elements of culture (e.g., speech, dress, manners) that served readily to distinguish them from the Anglo-Americans were fairly rapidly laid aside. This cultural transformation, however, does not mean that the second-generation (or even third-generation) Scotch-Irish simply disappeared or were "erased" as a group. Many, if not most, were likely to select working partners and friends who were Scotch-Irish, and they were likely to marry someone who was Scotch-Irish; hence, secondary, primary, and marital assimilation were still incomplete when cultural assimilation was well advanced. Though by the time of the Revolutionary War the descendants of the early Scotch-Irish immigrants were for most practical purposes a functioning part of the Anglo-American host group, it still is not correct to state, as many writers have, that the Scotch-Irish were at this point thoroughly assimilated into American society.[21]

We conclude, then, that the Scotch-Irish were not completely assimilated into the Anglo-American majority, even culturally, by the end of the eighteenth century; nevertheless, the various types of assimilation mentioned were all underway.[22] The main results of these different processes was to help solidify the American majority as a white, Protestant group of British origin. Even though the Scotch-Irish had created certain difficulties for the dominant Anglo-Americans, there was never any widespread doubt that the Scotch-Irish could and, given time, would conform to the Anglo-American pattern. The case of the colonial Germans, however, presented a more serious problem to the majority.

The Colonial Germans

At approximately the same time the Scotch-Irish settlers were coming to New England and Pennsylvania, a large number of Germans and German-Swiss were moving to America. As was true for the Scotch-Irish, Pennsylvania proved to be the most popular destination, although some members of the German group went originally to New York, Virginia, the Carolinas, and Georgia. These people, generally referred to as the "Dutch" (from Deutsch) or the "Palatines," were quite noticeable to the Anglo-Americans. Many of them were members of various Protestant religious sects (e.g., the Mennonites), who dressed distinctively, settled together in rural areas, and did their best to maintain the language and customs of the old country.[23] Although the majority of those who came later were less militantly Protestant, they still usually clustered in farming regions and held themselves apart from all other groups.

The primary area of settlement lay to the west of Philadelphia. Here the Germans, or "Pennsylvania Dutch" as they are still frequently called, established prosperous and well-managed farms. They quickly earned a reputation for thrift, diligence, and farming skill that has continued to the present. And their numbers grew rapidly. The German population of Pennsylvania may have reached forty-five thousand by 1745; by 1766, Benjamin Franklin estimated that one-third of the colony's people were German (Wittke 1964:71).[24]

This large immigration of people who spoke German, who differed clearly from the Anglo-Americans in culture, and who tended to settle "clannishly" in isolated areas aroused a strong suspicion among many of the "old" Americans. Some of the complaints against the Germans were identical to those lodged against the Scotch-Irish. They were said to "squat" illegally on other people's land, and their manners and morals were frequently thought to be rude and unseemly. To a much greater extent than the Scotch-Irish, however, the Germans posed an apparent threat of disloyalty. It was feared that they might set up a separate German state or even, as Benjamin Franklin put it, "Germanize us instead of our Anglifying them" (Anderson 1970:86). At one point, a law was passed requiring immigrant Germans to take an oath of allegiance, and during the French and Indian War many among the Anglo-American and Scotch-Irish groups suspected the Germans of sympathizing with the French.

An important result of these differences and suspicions was that they intensified the Germans' determination to survive as a group and, thereby, slowed the rate at which they and their descendants adopted the traditions of the Anglo-Americans. The German language, only slightly modified by contact with English, was transmitted quite faithfully from the first to the second generation and even from the second to the third. The Germans did not wish to attend English-speaking schools or participate in the political affairs of the dominant group. Indeed, they did not even strive especially to be "good citizens." The sect Germans, in particular, refused to bear arms, to hold public office, and, sometimes, to pay taxes.

Since German farmers tended to build stone and heavy wood houses and barns, to buy adjacent lands, and to establish orchards and raise large families, they did not move readily; hence, they were likely to remain in close contact with others of their nationality. They organized publishing houses, German-language newspapers, and fairs and other celebrations to bring their people together on a regular basis. Although the sect Germans (such as the Mennonites) were more cohesive than the church Germans (such as the Lutherans), by the end of the eighteenth century, a German's friends were still likely to be Germans, and marriages outside the group, though increasing, were still in the minority. Consequently, the Germans, especially in Pennsylvania, maintained their sense of ethnic distinctiveness beyond the third generation.

It seems fair to say that in terms of each of the four subprocesses we have identified, the assimilation of the Germans into the majority group was slower than that of the Scotch-Irish and was accompanied by greater friction and hostility. This resistance to assimilation meant that the Germans were viewed with greater suspicion by the Anglo-Americans. Nevertheless—and this is an important qualification—the German presence in large numbers in American society *did* strengthen further the dominant position of the white Protestants. Suppose, for example, that the Germans had succeeded in "Germanizing" the Anglo-Americans and the Scotch-Irish. The dominant group in American society still would have been white and Protestant as well as European in culture, even if not specifically of British origin. This is another way of noting that there were important similarities as well as differences between the Anglo-American and German groups, similarities that, through time, enabled the Anglo-American majority to maintain its basic pattern of life as the preferred and "standard" pattern.

The Revolutionary Period

Some interesting evidence bearing on the solidarity of the colonial Germans and the Anglo-Americans as well as on the solidarity of the Anglo-American group itself is afforded by the alignments during the Revolutionary War. As is well known, those favoring the Revolution probably were in the minority at the beginning of the war and may never have been a substantial majority. Of greater interest to us here is that both revolutionaries and loyalists were to be found within the different ethnic groups then present in America. Though many claims have been made that particular ethnic groups were solidly behind Washington and the Congress, it appears that the lines of cleavage varied from colony to colony.[25]

The Scotch-Irish of Pennsylvania, for instance, evidently were strongly behind the patriot cause, but they were more or less divided among themselves in other parts of the country. In New England, members of the Scotch-Irish group served on both sides. In the back country of the southern colonies, the picture was complicated by religious disagreements among the Scotch-Irish. Some were on the patriot side, some were on the loyalist side, and some fought at one time or another for both sides (Jones 1980:901–902). Despite their more intense ethnic identification, the Germans also present a mixed picture. In Pennsylvania, many of the Germans subordinated their dislike of the Scotch-Irish and joined with them against the local loyalists. In Georgia, on the other hand, most of the Germans supported the British. And while most leaders of the German Reformed Church favored the Revolution, most leaders of the Lutheran church and the sectarian churches supported the British. Perhaps most significant is that in all probability the majority of the ordinary German settlers were largely indifferent to the Revolution. As stated previously, they were not really a part of the Anglo-American core group and had tried, in general, to remain outside the orbit of its affairs.

The cleavages within the Anglo-American group were to some extent regional. For example, there were many more supporters of the Revolution in Massachusetts and Virginia than there were in New York and New Jersey. In addition, there were important social and economic lines of demarcation. The decisive point for the present discussion, however, is this: The majority of those who participated actively in the Revolution, who led the Revolution, and who held the reins of government when the Revolution ended were members of the Anglo-American group. This group had become dominant during the seventeenth century and had successfully met the challenges posed by the Scotch-Irish and the Germans during the colonial period. Now a sizable portion of this group had gained full control of the country's political institutions, strengthening still further its claim to represent the ideal pattern for all Americans to follow. More than ever before, to become fully American one had to conform to the Anglo-American model of behavior and appearance.

The events of the first three decades of the existence of the United States worked generally in the direction of consolidating the acceptance of Anglo-American ethnicity as the "standard" or "semiofficial" ethnicity of America. One important factor in this trend was a greatly decreased flow of immigrants to the United States between 1793 and 1815. The Napoleonic Wars in Europe interfered markedly with the free flow of international traffic and were the primary cause of the decline in immigration. Since the existing ethnic groups were not being reinforced by sizable infusions from their homelands, the pressures on them to conform to the dominant Anglo-American pattern were more effective than might otherwise have been the case.

Another important factor that reinforced the dominance of the Anglo-Americans was that by 1790 four of five Americans were immigrants from the British Isles or their descendants (Easterlin 1980:479). Moreover, and despite the fact that more immigrants had arrived during the eighteenth than in the seventeenth century, most of the American population by this time was native-born (Easterlin 1980:477); hence, "native Americans" were becoming an increasingly large proportion of the population.

A third significant factor aiding the consolidation was the success of the Anglo-American leaders in strengthening the powers of the postrevolutionary central government. Many of the leaders of the Revolution were also property owners who felt a strong central government was needed to protect their interests. In *The Federalist Papers,* Alexander Hamilton ([1787]1961:66) argued that unless the national government was strengthened, the states would soon become separate nations and would begin to make war on each other. Concerns of this sort led Congress to convene a meeting of leaders in 1787 to amend the Articles of Confederation. Early in the convention, however, the delegates decided to draft a new document—the Constitution.

Practically all of the delegates who came to the convention represented the dominant white Protestant Americans, in general, and the wealthier portion of that group, in particular. They were an aristocracy of wealth, education, and social position (Sydnor 1965). The Constitution that was finally approved by the states benefited many groups not specifically represented in the convention. Still, there were economic tensions between those who were property owners or merchants, on the one hand, and those who were poor and in debt, on the other, and these economic differences led to lengthy, occasionally violent, conflicts (Rubenstein 1970).

But this is not the place to engage in the debate over the motives of the members of the Constitutional Convention.[26] The point, rather, is this: During the first five years of the postwar period, many internal divisions threatened the very existence of the United States and, simultaneously, the shaky dominance of the white Protestant Americans over a vast territory. The ratification of a new constitution, written and supported by wealthy representatives of the white Protestant group, was an important step in the direction of consolidating the dominant position of this group.

Let us review the argument that has been presented. The effects of the events commencing with the original settlement of Jamestown and Plymouth by people of English ethnicity combined to establish an American nation that was primarily a "fragment" of English culture and society. Outstanding among these events were the conquest of New Netherland; the exclusion of the Native and African Americans from full participation in the developing society; the assimilation, of various types and degrees, of a large number of Scotch-Irish and German immigrants; the successful Revolutionary War against Britain; the decreased flow of immigrants following the Revolution; and the successful beginning of constitutional government.

We must emphasize again that while the social order that had been established by the end of the eighteenth century was decisively patterned after English society and culture, the pattern itself was not inflexible. The developing Anglo-*American* society and culture not only affected the immigrants, Native Americans, and African Americans who were in contact with it, but, also, the society was, to some degree, affected by them. The crucial argument being presented is that the transformations taking place within this dynamic setting were predominantly toward the relatively fixed Anglo-American pattern.[27]

The identification of the Anglo-American standard as the nationality of Americans accelerated during the War of 1812. Paradoxically, even though both the Revolutionary War and the War of 1812 were fought against the English, the essentially English framework of American society was not directly threatened. The wars seemed to serve, rather, to conceal the underlying similarities between the two peoples and to intensify and exaggerate their more obvious differences.[28] The upshot was that by 1815 the Anglo conformity ideology was more firmly established as the normal and accepted view of assimilation than ever before. At this point, the white Protestant Anglo-Americans were the unquestioned majority in American society, both in numbers and in political and economic power. On the surface, at least, it may have seemed only a matter of time until practically all of the Europeans and their descendants would be completely assimilated culturally and, perhaps, in every other way.[29]

Certain stubborn facts appeared to contradict this view. The African and Native Americans, of course, were still very visible, and there was no prospect that they would soon disappear; however, this failure of assimilation was not viewed as a problem. These groups simply lay beyond the scope and intentions of the Anglo conformity ideology—it did not apply to them. The assumption of the dominant group was that America was to be "a white man's country." Fully assimilated Americans and potential Americans were *by definition* white and Protestant. Much more difficult for the dominant group to explain was the continuing visibility of certain European groups, such as the sect Germans. As mentioned earlier, a number of the Mennonite groups lived largely apart from all others and clung to their own traditions, language, and religious observances. One who believed in the goals of the Anglo conformity ideology could argue, of course, that it was wrong for these groups to resist assimilation. The resistors could argue, in turn, that it would be wrong not to maintain their own group life and culture. Here we see illustrated the effort of some groups to work out an alternative to Anglo conformity as the solution to the problem of intergroup adjustment in America. These groups were dissatisfied with the idea that they should "melt" into the Anglo-American majority, but they were unable to present a different view that would be accepted by the dominant group. Their inability to *state* such a view, however, did not prevent them from attempting to *live* along different lines. Pluralism and separatism, thus, were realities in America long before they were expressed systematically as ideologies.

We have seen that the Anglo conformity ideology encountered, survived, and ultimately was strengthened by the challenges of eighteenth-century immigration and the American Revolution; however, the seeds of three rival ideologies—the melting pot, cultural pluralism, and separatism—already were present in American thought. The first two ideologies reached maturity during the first and second halves of the twentieth century, respectively, while the third has appealed more or less strongly to different groups at different times. In chapter 4 we develop these thoughts further against the background of the additional challenges to Anglo conformity that were presented by the heavy immigrations of the nineteenth and twentieth centuries.

Key Ideas

1. The dominant group in American society was created as people of English ethnicity settled along the Atlantic seacoast and gradually extended their political, economic, and religious control over the territory. This group's structure, values, customs, and beliefs may be traced to (a) the English system of law, (b) the organization of commerce during the sixteenth century, and (c) English Protestant religious ideas and practices, especially Puritanism.

2. By 1700, the Anglo-Americans had replaced the indigenous people as the "native" American group along the Atlantic seacoast. Those who came from the outside were likely to be regarded as "foreigners." The more nearly aliens resembled the Anglo-Americans in appearance and in patterns of behavior, the more nearly "American" they were thought to be. The Native and African Americans had been defined as ineligible to participate fully in the developing society. Although the Native Americans often could choose to remain physically within the boundaries of English colonial society, they usually chose not to. The Africans, on the other hand, were required to remain within those boundaries. In both cases, however, their physical inclusion was combined with social exclusion.

3. The Native American tribes were present for thousands of years before the arrival of the European explorers and colonists. This land belonged to them.

4. There were at least two hundred tribes in what is now the United States. The tribes spoke at least two hundred mutually unintelligible languages and exhibited varying levels of social, economic, and political organization. The tribe was the social unit to which the Native Americans gave their primary allegiance. Larger confederations of tribes were rare, and they usually were loosely organized.

5. Native American-English relations illustrate the point that minority groups that are self-sufficient at the time they are brought into a society are likely to resist assimilation for a long time.

6. Africans in the English colonies did not at first occupy the status of chattel slaves. Their status was similar to that of white bonded servants. In little more than half a century, however, their social position was that of mere property and slaves for life. African ancestry had become synonymous with the status of "slave."

7. The argument that the slaves were generally happy and contented ignores many facts. They used every conceivable form of resistance to oppression. Given the oppressiveness of the slave system, however, most of the resistance was unorganized.

8. The position of the Anglo-American majority and, consequently, the preeminence of its pattern of living were challenged during the eighteenth century by heavy immigrations from Northern Ireland (Ulster) and the German states of central Europe. Though these groups exhibited many of the cultural and social characteristics of the Anglo-American majority, to some extent both became objects of hostility and discrimination. They were the first significant immigrant minorities in American history.

9. The complete assimilation of the Scotch-Irish and German groups did not occur within three generations. Each subprocess of assimilation—cultural, secondary, primary, and marital—probably occurred more rapidly among the Scotch-Irish than among the Germans; however, the Scotch-Irish were still a fairly distinct group late into the nineteenth century, and some would argue that they have not completely disappeared even today.

10. The experience of the Scotch-Irish and Germans illustrates the point that groups may reach a high level of cultural assimilation but remain incompletely assimilated in some other respects.

11. Although the Scotch-Irish and German groups posed challenges to the Anglo-Americans and their version of the "semiofficial" pattern of American life, the outcome served to strengthen the main features of the ideology of Anglo conformity. The experience seemed to prove that white Protestant Europeans could and would conform to the Anglo-American pattern.

12. The results of the Revolutionary War and, later, the Constitutional Convention left the Anglo-American majority in firm control of American society. This position

was strengthened further by a decrease in European migration during the Napoleonic Wars and an increase in American nationalism during the War of 1812.
13. By 1815, the Anglo conformity ideology was practically unchallenged. To become fully American, one had to be white and had to be, or become, Protestant. By this definition, nonwhite peoples such as African and Native Americans were not, and could not become, full-fledged Americans.

Notes

1. *Ethnocentrism,* the tendency to consider one's own society to be superior to all others, is discussed further in chapter 6. This term was coined by Sumner (1906:27).

2. Some of the descendants of the indigenous population of what is now the United States prefer to be identified by specific tribal names or the term *Native American,* though many people prefer the term *American Indian.* We will use *Indian, American Indian,* and *Native American* interchangeably as identifiers.

3. Some writers claim there was an even greater diversity of cultures and languages. Cook (1981:118), for example, stated that there were approximately four hundred different cultures and five hundred languages. Jordan and Litwack (1987:2) stated there were "some twelve hundred different dialects and languages."

4. We cannot be certain how large the indigenous population was at this time in various parts of the New World. Spicer (1980a:68) estimated the population of the Powhatans to have been about nine or ten thousand. During the past fifty years, scholars have presented estimates of the total number of American Indians north of Mexico ranging between 900,000 and 18 million (Snipp 1989:6). After reviewing the available studies and discussing alternative methods of estimation, Snipp concluded that the American Indian population of North America probably was no smaller than 2 million and no larger than 5 million, though he stated it may have been much larger (Snipp 1989:10, 63). The estimates for Mexico and the rest of the Western Hemisphere also vary widely. Embree (1970:18) estimated there were around 10 million in all, while Wagley and Harris (1958:15) stated there may have been as many as 20 million Indians.

5. The latter figure does not reflect the somber fact that over four thousand other immigrants either had died or returned to England.

6. The Spanish, in contrast, maintained a major missionary effort for over three centuries.

7. The American Indians received little credit for their charity. Governor William Bradford described Squanto (Tisquantum) as having been sent by God for the special purpose of helping the settlers (Jordan and Litwack 1987:25). Squanto had been kidnapped and taken to England by Captain George Waymouth in 1605 (Dennis 1977:4) and, thereby, had learned to speak English.

8. Two other popular legal theories were based on the idea that you may take land if your cause is just (*the right of just war*) or if you discovered the land (*the right of discovery*) (Fredrickson 1981:35).

9. I wish to thank W. Allen Martin for calling this quotation to my attention.

10. Francis (1976:167–171) suggested that minorities of this type be called *primary ethnic groups.* We return to this distinction in chapter 14.

11. The term *black* seems currently to be preferred by more Americans of African descent than any other, and we generally will use it here. Many people, however, prefer the term *African,* and we will use it interchangeably with black.

12. For information concerning the development and operation of the indenture system see A. Smith (1947).

13. Winthrop Jordan (1972:86) argued, in contrast, "that there is simply not enough evidence to indicate with any certainty whether Negroes were treated like white servants or not."

14. The great streams of migration were not comprised simply of masses of uprooted people moving aimlessly about. They consisted of people

who sought and shared information with relatives and friends and whose actions depended on the information distributed through such social networks (Bodnar 1985:57–84).

15. Calculated from Burner, Fox-Genovese, and Bernhard (1991:74).

16. Sir Harry Johnston, quoted by Frazier (1957:87).

17. The death rate among slaves aboard ship was very high. Bennett (1966:41) reported that "So many dead people were thrown overboard on slavers that it was said that sharks would pick up a ship off the coast of Africa and follow it to America." Bruner, Fox-Genovese, and Bernhard (1991:78) estimate that between 1660 and 1800 about 10 million slaves embarked on the middle passage and that about 2 million of these "died in transit."

18. Estimates of the size of the early immigrations vary considerably, depending on the methods and sources of the historian. There also is sharp disagreement concerning the religious composition of the Irish immigration. Most students of the subject seem to agree that approximately 250,000 Ulstermen of Scots descent and between 100,000 and 200,000 Germans came to America before the Revolution. See, for example, Conzen (1980:407), Dinnerstein and Reimers (1975:2), Faulkner (1948:49), and Jones (1960:22, 29).

19. Although this group traditionally has been referred to as Scotch-Irish, and although we treat them here as Irish, many, perhaps most, of its members may have been considered more Scottish than Irish. Present-day demographers estimate that by 1790, over 8 percent of the U.S. population was Scottish, while about 6 percent was from Ulster (Lieberson and Waters 1988:39). At the same time, nearly 4 percent of the Irish population of the United States was not from Ulster. This sizable population was predominantly Catholic. Some people resent the historical emphasis that has been given to the Ulster Irish. It is argued that this emphasis creates the impression that the Catholic Irish contributed little to the development of colonial America. No such implication is intended here.

20. In Leyburn's (1970:65–76) opinion, the Scotch-Irish were not a minority group. They were "full Americans almost from the moment they took up their farms in the backcountry."

21. Dinnerstein and Jaher (1970:4–5) stated, for example, "Within three generations . . . [the] Scotch-Irish dropped their 'foreign' characteristics, assimilated to the dominant culture, and disappeared."

22. As we shall discuss further in chapter 14, even when a group seems to have "disappeared," some traces of its existence may still be detectable. For most practical purposes, we may say the Scotch-Irish reached complete Anglo conformity assimilation by the end of the nineteenth century. Yet as recently as 1972 a number of seemingly assimilated groups (including the Irish Protestants) still differed from one another in regard to certain basic values (P.A. Taylor 1981). In terms of very strict criteria of "complete disappearance," therefore, one might argue that the Scotch-Irish have yet to be completely assimilated.

23. The Mayflower of German immigration, the Concord, arrived in Philadelphia in 1683. The small group of immigrant families aboard was led by Franz Daniel Pastorius, an extremely able and well-educated man who was the first to issue a public protest against slavery in America (Adamic 1944:168–169).

24. Franklin's estimate appears to have been accurate. Present-day demographers estimate that in 1790 the English comprised around 35 percent of Pennsylvania's population and that the Germans comprised around 33 percent. At the same time, the English comprised around 61 percent of the population of the United States (Lieberson and Waters 1988:39).

25. Adamic argued that "the Germans just naturally supported the Revolution" (1944:174, 321). He also presented evidence that between 38 and 50 percent of the rebel army was of Irish birth or extraction and suggested that the longstanding Irish hatred of the English aided measurably to foment the Revolution.

26. For discussions see Lutz (1987) and Middlekauff (1987).

27. This also is not a claim that the events affecting the development of Anglo-American ethnicity may be understood entirely by focusing on the events occurring in North America. Hartz (1964) argued that since the colonists were partially insulated from many of the restraints that had been imposed on them in Europe, the nature and

direction of the new society's development may have represented to some extent the elaboration of a specific, now unfettered, European tradition.

28. Some have maintained that the anti-English sentiment strengthened a bid by the Irish to take control of the country away from the Anglo-Americans, but there is little evidence to support this contention (Adamic 1944:328).

29. While it is assumed from this perspective that the majority pattern remained essentially unchanged, it is also assumed that as the minority groups adopted the host culture they made enormous contributions to the development of the society (Gordon 1964:73; Lipset 1979:103).

Chapter 4

The Golden Door

. . . the Great Migration was not only one of people but of talents, skills, and cultural traditions. —MAX LERNER

A nation in a state of peace and safety, ought not to deny a hospitable reception to the fugitive from oppression or misfortune at home. —WILLIAM RAWLE

People do not cross continents and oceans without considerable thought, nor do they uproot themselves from family, friends, and familiar terrain without significant strain. —LEONARD DINNERSTEIN AND DAVID M. REIMERS

The greatest human migration in the history of the world has occurred since 1815. Uncounted millions of people have left their ancestral farms and villages to live in cities and cross the oceans. Although the specific reasons for migration varied substantially according to the time and place, some of the general factors contributing to this great movement of people may easily be identified. They include rapid changes in agriculture, population size, and industrial production. A significant effect of these three major factors has been to reduce large numbers of farmers to a condition of poverty and thus simultaneously to "push" them off the land and "pull" them toward jobs in other places.[1]

Two results of the improvement of agricultural methods are especially important. First, the surplus of food made possible a rapid growth in population. In fact, during the seventeenth and eighteenth centuries, the population of Europe more than doubled. Second, the new methods made possible and profitable the farming of larger areas of land with fewer workers. These facts increased the efforts of the more powerful landowners to enlarge their lands. Consequently, many small private farms and much land held in common were gradually "enclosed" by large landowners. With their farms gone, many people faced the choice of remaining as paupers where they were or moving in the hope of finding work and better living conditions elsewhere.

The choice was by no means easy. In many cases, people did not have the money required to make the journey and stay alive until they found work. Even if there were enough money to send one person ahead (usually a young man), the family members left behind frequently remained in desperate conditions. To be sure, the increasing numbers of factories and the growth of cities created jobs for large numbers of the rural poor. But the growth of the population was so rapid that there were seldom enough jobs for those who wished to work. In addition, just as is true today, the number of jobs available fluctuated with the ups and downs of business activity.

The millions of people who were uprooted by these great changes from a preindustrial to an industrial form of social organization comprised the migrant "streams" or "waves" that flowed out of their native lands and into other countries. The United States has been, overall, the most popular destination. Between 1820, when the U.S. government began keeping official records on immigration, and 1990, around 57 million newcomers to the United States were counted (Table 4-1 on page 67). Many other countries—Russia, Canada, Argentina, Brazil, and Australia, to name only a few—also have received millions of immigrants. The country people chose to go to depended to a large extent on such things as the likelihood that work would be found, the availability of transportation, and the presence of friends and relatives in the country of destination.

The waves of immigrants arriving at America's shores have tended to peak when economic conditions in the United States were good and to recede when there were economic downturns.[2] But as has been suggested already, much more than the "pull" of the American economy was involved in the uprooting and movement of so many people. The convergence of many different forces has led to three fairly distinct and astonishingly large immigrant streams to the United

TABLE 4-1 Immigration to the United States, 1820–1990

Years	Number	Rate*
1820–1830	151,824	1.2
1831–1840	599,125	3.9
1841–1850	1,713,251	8.4
1851–1860	2,598,214	9.3
1861–1870	2,314,824	6.4
1871–1880	2,812,191	6.2
1881–1890	5,246,613	9.2
1891–1900	3,687,564	5.3
1901–1910	8,795,386	10.4
1911–1920	5,735,811	5.7
1921–1930	4,107,209	3.5
1931–1940	528,431	.4
1941–1950	1,035,039	.7
1951–1960	2,515,479	1.5
1961–1970	3,321,677	1.7
1971–1980	4,493,314	2.1
1981–1990	7,338,062	3.1
Total	56,994,014	3.4

*Per 1,000 U.S. population.
Source: U.S. Immigration and Naturalization Service, *1990 Statistical Yearbook* 1991:39,47; U.S. Bureau of the Census, *Statistical Abstract of the United States* 1991:9.

States. For reasons to be discussed later, certain generalizations concerning the peoples represented in the three great immigrant streams are the subject of heated debates. For the moment, let us merely note that people from Ireland, Germany, the United Kingdom, France, and Scandinavia were predominant during the period of the first great stream (1820–1889); people from Italy, Austria-Hungary, Poland, Russia (primarily Jews), and French Canada were the largest groups in the second (1890–1924); and people from Mexico, the Caribbean, South American, Cuba, China, Vietnam, the Philippines, and Korea have predominated during the third (1946 to the present). The decade from 1880 to 1889 combined high immigration from both of the first two great streams and was a period of transition from the first to the second. For reasons to be discussed later, immigration dropped dramatically after 1924, resumed after 1946, and assumed some new and distinctive traits after 1965.

The First Great Immigrant Stream

America was not a very popular destination during the 1820s. The economic panic of 1819 destroyed many of the opportunities immigrants were seeking, and many Americans became less hospitable to newcomers and more concerned about problems associated with immigration. This growing concern was foreshadowed by the enactment, in 1819, of the United States' first federal law to supervise the collection of official statistics relating to immigration. In addition, Russia and Brazil were being heralded in Europe as desirable places to go. Whatever the exact reasons for the comparatively small immigration of the 1820s, though, their effects apparently had diminished by the 1830s. During this decade, the number of immigrants to the United States was over 599,000, almost four times as many as in the previous decade (U.S. Immigration and Naturalization Service 1991:47). The heavy immigration in the 1830s stimulated the dissemination of information concerning hiring and travel arrangements. These changes facilitated the still heavier immigrations of the 1840s and 1850s. The 1840s saw the arrival of around 1.7 million people, while the 1850s produced approximately 2.6 million. Although even larger numbers of people arrived in some later years, this wave of immigrants was the largest ever in comparison to the existing total population of the United States.

The Nineteenth-Century Irish

As was true in colonial times, most of the immigrants during the first half of the nineteenth century came from Ireland and Germany. Also as in the previous century, the large immigration of the Irish preceded that of the Germans. During the 1820s, 1830s, and 1840s the Irish continued to arrive in larger numbers than the Germans, though the totals for both groups rose sharply. As this movement of people reached a peak during the 1850s, however, the German immigration became heavier than the Irish, and it remained so throughout the following decades of the nineteenth century. Table 4-2 shows Irish immigration figures from 1820 to 1990.

To understand these large migrations, it is necessary to consider what was happening to many small farmers in Europe during this time. The basic problem consisted of a combination of a high population density, an unsound system of land tenure, and a high reliance on the potato.

In 1815, Ireland was the most densely populated country in Europe (Jones 1976:69). The end of the Napoleonic Wars brought about a deflation of land values, a decline of foreign markets for wheat, and a decrease in the number of jobs available. Many people believed the potato had insured Ireland forever against the dangers of famine. The potato was fairly easy to cultivate, and it took only an acre or so to support a family. As future events proved, however, this heavy reliance on the potato was ill-advised. The potato could not be preserved, it was hard to transport, and it was hard on the soil.

A foreshadowing of later events occurred in 1821, when the potato crop failed and famine followed. Although this famine was not nearly so severe as the one that led to the heavy Irish immigration of the 1840s and 1850s, many of those who were able left the country. Despite the famine (and a relaxation by England of restrictions on emigration from Ireland), the vast majority of the Irish preferred to remain in their homes. For the moment, there was apparently enough food to go around. But a series of disagreements between landowners and tenants made it more difficult to lease land on which to support a family, leading to an increase in the tempo of

**TABLE 4-2 Irish
Immigration to the United
States, 1820–1990**

Years	Number
1820–1830	54,338
1831–1840	207,381
1841–1850	780,719
1851–1860	914,119
1861–1870	435,778
1871–1880	436,871
1881–1890	655,482
1891–1900	388,416
1901–1910	339,065
1911–1920	146,181
1921–1930	211,234
1931–1940	10,973
1941–1950	19,789
1951–1960	48,362
1961–1970	32,966
1971–1980	11,490
1981–1990	31,969
Total	4,725,133

Source: U.S. Immigration and
Naturalization Service, *1990 Statistical
Yearbook* 1991:48–50.

out-migration around 1830. At this time, as in colonial times, a majority of the immigrants to America came from Ulster. However, during the 1830s, an important change occurred in the character of the movement, and by the latter part of the decade most of the immigrants were Roman Catholics from the south and west of Ireland.

The first of two decisive blows came in the fall of 1845. A particularly virulent form of potato rot struck the Irish crop, destroying not only the potatoes in the ground but also many of those already stored. Apparently, between one-third and one-half of the Irish potato crop was destroyed by the disease. Then, in 1846, potato gardens all over Ireland withered and died in the space of a few days. Never before had the crop failed in two consecutive years. At this point, people finally realized that Ireland simply could not support so large a population, and many people left in what soon became a general "flight from hunger."

The reactions of the people to this disaster were pathetic. Some simply waited patiently in their cottages to die. Others took to the road, wandering from place to place begging for food. Those who could arrange passage to England or America did so. Within a year, at least a half million people had starved to death, while perhaps a million more had died of fever. Those who survived were in desperate condition (Jones 1960:109; 1976:67). During the following several years, the total number of Irish immigrants—the so-called famine Irish—reached unprecedented figures. By 1854, approximately two million people representing all social classes had left Ireland as a result of the famine (Jones 1976:69).

Most of those who arrived in America were poverty-stricken. They had no money to proceed westward on their own, and they usually got out of the coastal cities only when they were needed in inland factories and mines or to help construct canals and railroads. Consequently, the conditions in the "little Dublins" and Irish "shanty towns" that sprang up along the East Coast were very poor (Wittke 1964:134). People were crowded together in tenements, and sometimes twenty or more families lived in a single house. The houses tended to be poorly lighted and ventilated, and diseases such as cholera were rampant. Amidst all this, the "drink menace" increased in severity; the Irish reputation as ruffians and brawlers grew, and family ties were weakened. Although there was little serious crime among the Irish, they nevertheless were frequently arrested for minor offenses. All of these things contributed to the native Americans' image of the Irish as an ignorant, practically barbaric, people, which led to a marked increase in hostility toward them and made their task of getting established in America more difficult. Employers often preferred workers from other groups, resulting in many posted notices saying "No Irish Need Apply" (Jones 1976:78–79).

Aside from their high concentration in the eastern cities and towns and the behavior that the dominant group found to be offensive, two features of the social organization of the Irish worried the native Americans. The first of these was their conspicuous Roman Catholicism. The Irish have always dominated the Catholic hierarchy in America, and the spread of Catholicism in the United States between 1825 and 1855 was due primarily to them. Wittke (1964:152) reported that "in 1836 the diocese of New York and half of New Jersey contained about 200,000 Catholics and of the 38 priests 35 were Irish and 3 were German." By 1852, "there were 6 archbishops, 26 bishops, and 1,385 priests in the United States." As Irish laborers were drawn from the East Coast to work on canals and railroads, new Roman Catholic parishes were created to serve them.

The other characteristic of the Irish that attracted the unfavorable notice of the native Americans was that they were very active in politics. The Irish peasants had a history of conflict with their English overlords, and they were well acquainted with many techniques of organizing and carrying through political campaigns. The Irish, said Adamic (1944:344), "took to politics like ducks to water." In most cities, they were solidly behind the Democratic Party and tended to vote as a block on most issues. In cities like New York and Boston, the "Irish vote" became increasingly important. As their numbers grew, the Irish became especially visible in various public service jobs and political offices. It was frequently claimed by angry natives that the Irish sold their votes to the Democratic city political machines in return for jobs and other favors. As we shall see later, the fears of the natives led to various organized efforts to regulate and curb immigration.

The Irish reacted to the hostility of the Protestant Americans and to the problems of adapting to their new environment in much the same way as most immigrants before and after them. Indeed, Irish ethnic communities were established in part because of rejection in their interactions with members of the host society. Immigrants need, first, to solve the problem of making a living; to do that, they frequently rely on others of their nationality group for help. Moreover, the strange and hostile world of the natives typically stimulates the immigrants' desire to associate in a reassuring and friendly way with others of the same nationality—to eat together and engage in familiar recreational or religious activities. These forces encourage the members of a given nationality group to seek one another out, to form benevolent societies, churches, patriotic organizations, newspapers, and social clubs. The ethnic group that is formed through this process, in the words of Francis (1976:169), is "exclusively the result of processes originating in the host society itself." The group is dependent on the host society for the satisfaction of almost all its basic needs and is under strong pressure—from both within and without—to move toward a mastery of the host group's culture. Although the ethnic society that has been constructed within the host society is intrinsically valuable to its members, and although they make vigorous efforts to retain it, its major purpose is to establish a place for its members *within* the host society.[3]

The Irish who immigrated in the nineteenth century shared many experiences with the Irish of the eighteenth century. For example, both groups responded in large numbers to economic pushes in their homeland and sought a better life in America, and both groups were subjected to hostility and rejection by the natives and joined with others of their nationality to construct ethnic communities. But the Irish who came to America in the nineteenth century illustrate more clearly than their predecessors the effects of the industrialization of Western Europe, the rapid growth of its population, and the operations of capitalist economies across national borders. To a larger extent than previously, the destinations and patterns of settlement of these immigrants were affected by the efforts of growing American industries to meet their needs for labor through direct recruitment. We noted, for instance, that most of these immigrants were manual laborers who were forced to take whatever work was available and were unable to move inland until they were needed for canal and road construction. The effects of these large social forces, only barely noticeable at this point, became increasingly visible following the Civil War.

The Nineteenth-Century Germans

As was true for the Irish, the majority of German immigrants were small farmers who had been driven from their lands by widespread crop failures and financial difficulties. By 1845, the situation of many small farmers in Germany had become desperate. Weather conditions had been poor, and the price of food was rising. Many small farmers were deeply in debt. According to Hansen (1945:225), "overpopulation, hunger and employment were the topics that dominated all discussions of social conditions."

The potato crop failed in Germany in 1846, just as it did in Ireland. Although the crop failure created a social crisis in Germany, the situation was not nearly so bad as in Ireland because the Germans had not relied quite so heavily on a single

TABLE 4-3 German Immigration to the United States, 1820–1990

Years	Number
1820–1830	7,729
1831–1840	152,454
1841–1850	434,626
1851–1860	951,667
1861–1870	787,468
1871–1880	718,182
1881–1890	1,452,970
1891–1900	505,152
1901–1910	341,498
1911–1920	143,945
1921–1930	412,202
1931–1940	114,058
1941–1950	226,578
1951–1960	477,765
1961–1970	190,796
1971–1980	74,414
1981–1990	91,961
Total	7,083,465

Source: U.S. Immigration and Naturalization Service, *1990 Statistical Yearbook* 1991:48–50.

crop. Nevertheless, many people were eager to leave before things became worse. A widely circulated rumor that the United States was on the verge of prohibiting immigration encouraged many people to leave immediately. Hence, even though hunger was involved, the "America fever" that developed in Germany at this time was not so directly a flight from famine as was the case in Ireland. During the 1840s, the number of Germans emigrating to America jumped sharply, and more than twice as many emigrated in the 1850s. Table 4-3 shows German immigration figures from 1820 to 1990.

As large numbers of people in Germany became interested in immigration, several colonization societies were formed on both sides of the Atlantic. One of the most famous of these organizations made an effort to settle German immigrants near St. Louis in the 1830s (Jones 1976:125). In the 1840s, another organization sent thousands of German settlers to Texas with the "avowed object of peopling Texas with Germans" (Hansen 1945:231). And in the 1850s, an effort was made to settle Germans in Wisconsin. Altogether, Germany contributed more immigrants to America during the nineteenth century than any other country. By 1900, Germans were "the single largest ethnic minority in 27 states" (Dinnerstein and Reimers 1975:25).

During this time, travel literature concerning America had become very popular in Europe, especially in Germany. In addition to guidebooks, periodicals, and pamphlets published and disseminated by travel agents, there were books written by those who had traveled in America or had already migrated. Most important were personal letters, which were frequently read to audiences, and their impact on the listeners ordinarily was great. The widespread interest in America within Germany and the increasing availability of travel literature led to the formation of village reading clubs. In this way, many people received information concerning the United States and were stimulated to consider moving there.

As in the eighteenth century, the efforts of the Germans to preserve their ethnic distinctiveness in America were very noticeable. And their reasons were the same. The Irish differed markedly from the Germans because of their prior familiarity with the language and the institutions of the Anglo-Americans and in their knowledge of political organization. Although the Germans were more widely distributed throughout the United States than the Irish, they, too, built up large concentrations in cities like New York. For example, by 1850, most of the large German population of New York lived in an area just north of the Irish district. Nearly all of the businesses in this area were owned and operated by Germans, and German was the principal spoken language. There were in this district German schools, churches, restaurants, saloons, newspapers, and a lending library. And the Germans, no less than the Irish, formed numerous mutual aid societies and benevolent associations to assist immigrants in dealing with the complexities of the strange new environment.

One of the most important differences between the German and Irish immigrations concerned politics. Germany at this time was not a unified nation. The governments of the separate states were controlled by hundreds of princes. As the economic conditions of the country worsened, there was an increasing desire, especially among intellectuals and young people, for large-scale reforms. The demands for solutions to the problems of hunger and unemployment and for a more democratic form of government led to a series of revolutions during the year 1848. These uprisings were crushed, and their leaders, many of whom were distinguished people of property, education, and high social standing, fled from the country and eventually made their way to the United States. Although the so-called "Forty-Eighters" numbered only a few thousand and represented only a small proportion of the German immigration to the United States during this period, they played an important role in determining the reaction of native Americans to the German immigration.

Many of the Forty-Eighters were radical reformers who were disappointed to find that the United States was not a democratic utopia. They were shocked by slavery, by the movement to prohibit alcoholic beverages, and by many defects in the operation of American democracy. They also thought there were too many churches and, in general, regarded American life as "half-barbarian" (Wittke 1964:192). Their program of reform included sweeping changes relating to the church, the presidency, the Constitution, slavery, and prohibition. They also founded organizations (called *Turnvereine*) that became known as centers of radical reform and established newspapers to circulate their views.[4]

The Republican Party (formed in 1854) attracted many of the Forty-Eighters. The Republicans' stand on slavery and the treatment of foreign-born citizens were especially appealing to many German idealists. Germans such as Carl Schurz were so conspicuous during Lincoln's campaign for the presidency in 1860 that many observers have claimed his victory in the midwestern states was due to a block vote by the Germans. Although this claim underestimates the deep divisions among the Germans, it highlights the extent to which they had become identified as active in politics and, perhaps, in the other main spheres of secondary assimilation as well (Jones 1960:162).

The radicals in the German American community were sharply opposed by the large majority of German Americans who reached the United States before the 1840s. Many of the German Lutheran immigrants of the preceding century had moved very noticeably in the direction of Anglo conformity in their church services. The American Lutheran church had substituted English for German as the language of worship, and the traditional Lutheran beliefs and practices also had been modified. These modifications led to violent feuds between colonial and nineteenth-century German Lutherans. The Missouri Synod, formed by the nineteenth-century German Lutherans, emphasized the preservation of the German language and the traditional beliefs and practices.

Changing Patterns of Immigration

The Civil War created a comparative lull in immigration but certainly did not stop it. Over 2.3 million immigrants arrived during the decade in which the war occurred, and still more arrived during the succeeding ten years (see again Table 4-1). More significant than the sheer numbers, however, is that during the period 1870–1879, a noticeable change began to occur in the national origins of the newcomers. Before the war, the largest numbers of immigrants were from Germany, Ireland, and England. During and after the war, these groups continued to grow rapidly and, in time, were augmented by large numbers of northwestern Europeans from Scandinavia. Immigration from Scandinavia during the decade preceding the war was about 21,000; but during 1861–1870, the number of newcomers from Norway and Sweden increased more than fivefold to 109,000, and in the years between 1871 and 1880, the number almost doubled again. However, the comparative increases among those arriving from southern and eastern Europe—particularly from Italy, Austria-Hungary, and Russia—were still more dramatic. Although their total numbers were not large, almost five times as many Italians arrived during 1871–1880 as had arrived in the previous decade. Roughly nine times as many came from Austria-Hungary, and nearly fourteen times as many came from Russia. During this period, it became obvious that the federal government would be required, in time, to assume a major role in the control of immigration. The shift to federal control was launched in 1875 when the

U.S. Supreme Court ruled that only the U.S. Congress is empowered by the Constitution to regulate immigration (Bernard 1980:489). In contrast to an earlier ruling, the Court now said that all of the regulations that had been enacted over the years by the states and cities were unconstitutional and that only the federal government had the authority to supervise immigration. As if to illustrate the point, Congress passed on March 3, 1875 an Immigration Act that sought to bar various types of "undesirable immigrants," such as those who engage in "lewd" or "immoral" conduct (Abrams 1984:108; Cafferty, Chiswick, Greeley, and Sullivan 1983:43).

The following decade, 1881–1890, was very significant both for the absolute volume of immigration and because it represents the high point of the first immigrant stream. More immigrants came from Germany, England, and Scandinavia than ever before or since, and more came from Ireland than at any time since the peak in the 1850s. At the same time, however, the immigrant stream from southern and eastern Europe continued the rapid increase started in the previous decade. The Italian immigration increased almost sixfold, and the Austro-Hungarian and Russian arrivals were about five times as numerous as before.

As the decade progressed, the receiving facilities in New York—located at the southern end of Manhattan Island in a former place of amusement called Castle Garden—became increasingly crowded. New York was by far the most popular landing site for immigrants; during the years Castle Garden served as the city's port of entry (1855–1891), over 7.5 million aliens were received there (Bolino 1985:3). By the end of the 1880s, however, the overcrowded conditions at Castle Garden and the misuse of the depot for political purposes led the federal government to take control of immigration and to open a new receiving station just off shore on Ellis Island.[5] The new facility "was officially dedicated on New Year's Day, 1892" (Bolino 1985:4).

For over forty years, the Island served as the "golden door" for approximately sixteen million immigrants and became, along with the nearby Statue of Liberty, a symbol of hope, freedom, and opportunity. The Island also developed a somewhat sinister reputation. Unlike Castle Garden, "Ellis Island was a gigantic sieve, whose sole function was to keep out undesirables" (Jones 1976:54); consequently, many people who attempted to enter the country there were detained and were subsequently deported. For the many who were denied entrance and were sent back to their homelands, Ellis Island became "The Isle of Tears" (Bolino 1985:44).[6] Kraut (1982:55) states that even those who were admitted after only a few hours on Ellis Island frequently considered the experience "the most traumatic part of their voyage to America." In addition to the fear of detention and of families being separated, the cavernous appearance and iron railings of the Great Hall, and the physical examination, the immigrants also had difficulty communicating with the inspectors. In many cases, when immigrants could not spell their names or when the inspectors could not spell them, the immigrants entered the United States with new, "Ellis Island," names (Kraut 1982:54–57).[7] Nevertheless, it is estimated that around one hundred million Americans today are descended from those whose first taste of their adopted land took place there (Horn 1988:63).

During the 1890s, for the first time, more newcomers arrived from southern and eastern Europe than from northern and western Europe. This preponderance of the second immigrant stream continued and increased during the next two decades. Each of the main countries of the first stream had higher levels of emigration to the United States during the 1880s than in the 1890s or 1900s, while throughout this period emigration from the countries of the second immigrant stream increased steadily. The second stream continued its domination during the first two decades of the twentieth century, but the period from 1901 to 1910 proved to be the high point not only of the second immigrant stream, but also of all immigration to America thus far.

The Second Great Immigrant Stream

Soon after Ellis Island began to serve as the federal government's receiving station, officials began to comment on the change in the "types" of newcomers who were arriving. In addition to the Austrians, Hungarians, Italians, and Russian Jews, the second immigrant stream contained significant numbers of Bohemians, Bulgarians, Croatians, Greeks, Lithuanians, Moravians, Poles, Serbs, Slovaks, and Slovenes. All of these "new" southern and eastern Europeans (and a sizeable number of French Canadians) seemed even more foreign to Americans than the "old" foreigners from northern and western Europe.[8] Many of the "old" foreigners, now in their second or third generation as Americans, had assimilated culturally by substitution, were well-represented in the economic and political mainstream, and appeared to be moving toward complete Anglo conformity assimilation; consequently, there was no longer any real question of their "assimilability." But these "new" immigrants appeared to pose a more difficult problem.

What was so new about the second-stream immigrants? Their languages, of course, were further removed from English than was true of most of the old immigrants. Their religions, too, either were not Christian or were so different from the prevailing Protestant and Anglicized Catholic services as to seem un-Christian. Their dress, manners, and foods also seemed especially alien. But in addition to these cultural differences, many Americans soon came to believe that there was something "unnatural" or "artificial" about this new immigration. Rapid improvements in ocean travel had greatly increased competition for passengers among steamship lines, and their agents were working feverishly throughout the southern and eastern European areas to encourage immigration to America. Hence, many more people could arrange passage than had ever been able to in the past. American employers were eager to tap these large pools of cheap labor, and the great improvements in communication and transportation made such recruitment increasingly easy. The changes in the organization of the economic system that we first noted in our discussion of the nineteenth-century Irish were now well underway. The people who were leaving southern and eastern Europe were, like most of their predecessors, poverty-stricken peasants who were being forced off the land by industrialization, but these people, accustomed to life in small villages and farms, arrived in a "new" America—an America that was now well along the road of change from an agrarian to an industrial and urban nation.[9]

The frontier had been declared officially "closed" after the census of 1890. There was no more free land for immigrants to clear and settle. As the demand for land increased, so did the price, and the immigrants increasingly could not escape the port cities in which they had landed. Given the location of Ellis Island, the city of New York, in particular, was flooded with immigrants. Even when they were able to leave port cities like New York, Boston, Baltimore, Philadelphia, or New Orleans, the immigrants usually wound up in inland cities like Cleveland, Chicago, Pittsburgh, or St. Louis (Novotny 1974:133).[10] The main jobs available were as unskilled laborers on the railroads or in factories, and by 1900, new immigrant groups were the main source of workers for nearly all segments of industrial production (Kraut 1982:86). Since in nearly all cases the immigrants could afford only the least expensive housing, a variety of ethnic slums developed in all of America's major cities. Disease was rampant. Novotny (1974:138) reported that "nearly 40 percent of the slum dwellers suffered from tuberculosis." The promise of a new life in America thus became a bitter joke for large numbers of immigrants. Not surprisingly, many of these disappointed people returned to their homelands at the first opportunity.

We should note, though, that despite the hardships and disappointments, many of those who went back home—especially young, single men—later returned to the United States. The emergence of a pattern of two-way or cyclical migration represents another important distinction between the first and second immigrant streams (Portes and Bach 1985:31).

The Italians

Probably the most prominent group of newcomers and slum dwellers at this time were the Italians. Several factors made this group particularly conspicuous. First, of course, were their sheer numbers and the rate at which they arrived (see Table 4-4 on page 78). Well over three million Italians reached the United States during the thirty-year period beginning in 1890.[11] Second, a large majority of the Italians arriving at this time were from the southern regions. The people from these regions were overwhelmingly *contadini*—ignorant, landless peasants—who were escaping from a harsh physical climate, overpopulation, primitive living conditions, economic dislocations, and an oppressive social class structure (Alba 1985:23–27,38–40; Lopreato 1970:25–33; Schermerhorn 1949:232–237; Wittke 1964:441–442). Third, and somewhat surprising, these agricultural people did not move in large numbers directly into farming occupations when they reached America. To be sure, the changing American economy offered fewer encouragements than previously for those wishing to leave the cities; however, despite their lack of industrial skills, the southern Italians generally preferred to remain in the cities (Alba 1985:47). In this setting, they became concentrated in certain lines of work. For example, they were over nine times as likely as other white workers to be barbers or hairdressers and nearly eight times as likely as other white workers to be "hucksters and peddlers"

TABLE 4-4 Italian Immigration to the United States, 1820–1990

Years	Number
1820–1830	439
1831–1840	2,253
1841–1850	1,870
1851–1860	9,231
1861–1870	11,725
1871–1880	55,759
1881–1890	307,309
1891–1900	651,893
1901–1910	2,045,877
1911–1920	1,109,524
1921–1930	455,315
1931–1940	68,028
1941–1950	57,661
1951–1960	185,491
1961–1970	214,111
1971–1980	129,368
1981–1990	67,254
Total	5,373,108

Source: U.S. Immigration and Naturalization Service, *1990 Statistical Yearbook* 1991:48–50.

(Lieberson and Waters 1988:126). Fourth, the southern Italian immigrants consisted, to an unusual degree, of males who did not intend to remain in America—the so-called "birds of passage" who wished to make their fortunes and return with honor to the homeland (Lopreato 1970:14–15; Piore 1979; Schermerhorn 1949:246). Jones (1976:196) quoted a successful Italian American, Stefano Miele, as follows: "If I am to be frank, then I shall say that I left Italy and came to America for the sole purpose of making money." Lopreato (1970:110) observed that the Italians' "zeal for assimilation in American life left something to be desired." Caroli (1973; cited by Alba 1985:40) reported that, in fact, approximately 1.5 million Italians actually returned to Italy between 1910 and 1914. Finally, since the Italians were "too many and too late" (Schermerhorn 1949:232), they had to accept the pick-and-shovel jobs that no one else wanted and to occupy housing that was in many instances unfit for human habitation. The conditions in the Italian slums were frequently so terrible that they were widely publicized. Since many Americans did not understand the circumstances giving rise to the squalid conditions in the slums, the residents themselves, or their culture, were often blamed. As had been true of the Irish in an earlier period, it was assumed that the Italians were "just naturally" depraved.[12]

Among the American mental images or stereotypes of the Italians, one received special notoriety. The Italians acquired a reputation for criminality. Newspapers throughout the country described in lurid detail extortions and murders attributed to the Black Hand, "Mafia," or "Cosa Nostra." Many Americans feared that a notorious criminal organization had been imported by the southern Italians and now posed a serious foreign threat to democratic methods of assuring law and order. While there is little doubt that Mafia-like organizations did develop among the Italians in America, there is substantial disagreement concerning the reasons for this development and the extent to which there was anything peculiarly Italian about it. Among the first-generation Italians, for example, crime rates were no higher than among other immigrant groups, and they were actually lower than those of the native Americans (Schermerhorn 1949:250). A study in Massachusetts in 1912 showed that the Italian-born were greatly underrepresented in the state's prison population (Jones 1976:213). In Alba's (1985:36) opinion, most accounts of organized crime among Italian Americans mistakenly dwell on events in Sicily and on southern Italian culture and falsely portray "organized crime as an alien and almost accidental growth in American soil . . . rather than as a native product that demanded the energies of numerous ethnic groups." He argued further that the many Black Hand gangs that operated within Italian American communities probably were not organized at a higher level and "had essentially died out by 1920" (Alba 1985:62–63). The higher levels of organization did not occur until the 1930s, with Prohibition, and were not confined to people of Italian ancestry.

Peculiarly Italian or not, the idea that America's Little Italys were "seething hotbeds of crime" (Schermerhorn 1949:250) was commonly believed.[13] This belief helped to fuel a rising level of native hostility during this period. It also had another effect of considerable interest to us: it helped to awaken among the Italians a sense of ethnic identity.

As in the cases of the American Indians and blacks (and later the Asians), Americans tended to lump all people from Italy into the same category. But the immigrants themselves had a very different view of the matter, at least at first. The immigrants who left Italy came not as Italians but as representatives of particular villages, cities, or regions. The cleavages among the "Italians" themselves were very deep. The country had only recently become united, and the cultural and economic differences between the northerners and southerners were wide. The people in the north felt and acted superior to the people in the south. And even among the southerners, the social differences among the peoples from different villages and regions were pronounced. Consequently, as Lopreato (1970:104) stated, "When the Italians came to the United States they imported a pitiful tendency to mistrust and avoid all those who did not share their particular dialect and customs." This identification of the individual with groups smaller than the Italian nation was evident in the residential patterns in New York.

Various Little Italys developed along separate streets or city blocks, each one exhibiting village, provincial, or regional loyalties (Wittke 1964:441). Neapolitans, for instance, gathered around Mulberry Bend; Sicilians clustered on Elizabeth and Prince Streets; and Calabrians lived on a portion of Mott Street (Alba 1985:48–49;

Riis [1890]1957:41–52). As had been true for immigrant groups to America from the earliest days, this method of organizing enabled the immigrants to give and receive help from people like themselves and to bask in the warmth and security of their friendship. Here people could speak their native language, eat food prepared in the "proper" way, and escape the insults and inconveniences encountered in the "outside" world. The ethnic slum, for all its terrible faults, served in certain ways to shield and protect the immigrant.[14] But, to repeat, the Americans did not usually recognize the distinctions that existed among the immigrants from Italy, and hostility and rejection were directed at the "Italians." They were called "wops," "dagos," and "guineas" and were referred to as "the Chinese of Europe" (Dinnerstein and Reimers 1975:40); hence, in Schermerhorn's (1949:250) words, "The Sicilians, the Neapolitans, and Calabrians thus became conscious of their common destiny as Italians in America. . . . " Or, as Lopreato (1970:171) wrote, the hostility of the dominant group "Italianized them."

The process illustrated by the Italians through which people from the same geographical origins join together to form a new ethnic group within a different society is called *ethnogenesis* (Greeley 1971; Singer 1962) or *emergent ethnicity* (Yancey, Ericksen, and Juliani 1976). This process may occur initially because the members of a group share certain historical and cultural characteristics, but from this perspective the importance of these shared characteristics derives from the common experiences of the group's members in the new society, especially the experience of rejection by the dominant group (Portes and Bach 1985:25). This common experience, in turn, provides a basis for a *transformed* ethnicity, one that is not a simple derivative of the society from which the immigrants came (Alba 1985:9; Geschwender, Carroll-Seguin, and Brill 1988:516). As Lurie (1982:143) expressed it, "Immigrant communities usually were not communities when they came; their ethnic identities were, to a surprising extent, constructed in America."

The Jews

If the Italians were the most conspicuous portion of the second immigrant stream, the Russian Jews were only slightly less so. Although Jews had been present in the United States since the colonial period, the largest wave arrived from Russia during the period of the new immigration. The earliest Jews (the Sephardim) had come from Spain, Portugal, and Holland. The Sephardim were few in number, but they had a noticeable impact on the subsequent development of Jewry in America. A second and much larger wave originated in Germany and areas dominated by German culture (Sklare 1975:263). The same forces that led the other large groups of nineteenth-century Germans to come to the United States stimulated the immigration of German Jews as well. Many of the Forty-Eighters mentioned earlier were representatives of this group. The German Jews (the Ashkenazim) so outnumbered the Sephardim that they soon became the primary force in Jewish American life.

The rise of the German Jews was not due entirely to their numbers, however. Of great importance, also, is that the German Jews had undergone a high degree of cultural assimilation in Germany. The identification of the German Jews as

Germans continued in the United States. According to Wittke (1964:329), the Jews participated in the activities of the *Turnvereine* and generally supported German cultural activities, hence, the political and social characteristics of the German Jews were more prominent than their religion. And their religious practices were themselves much less distinctive than those of the Orthodox Jews, who had arrived earlier.

Most of the German Jews were participants in the Reform movement. The Reform synagogue differed from the Orthodox in such things as using little Hebrew in religious services, seating men and women together, celebrating Sunday as the Sabbath, approving intermarriage, and omitting prayers for the restoration of the Jewish state (Schermerhorn 1949:391). When combined, these factors stimulated the rapid cultural and secondary structural assimilation of the German Jews in the United States. The members of this group spread out across the country, and many of them rose rapidly into the middle and upper classes. One of the most celebrated occupations of both first and second stream Jews was that of itinerant peddler. Lieberson and Waters (1988:126) reported that in 1900, Russian men (most of whom presumably were Jewish) were over twenty-three times as likely to be "hucksters and peddlers" as were other white men in the labor force. "The new immigrant who was fired with ambition to succeed but hamstrung by limited capital," Kraut (1982:95) observed, " . . . took up the peddler's . . . pushcart." From such beginnings came the establishment of some of America's great department stores, including Macy's, Gimbel's, Bloomingdale's, Filene's, Goldwater's, and Sears Roebuck (Jones 1976:164–165). By the time the Russian Jews began to arrive in significant numbers, the German Jews already were established as the elite of American Jewry (Sklare 1975:263; Wittke 1964:327)—a status reflected by a strict pattern of within-group and intercity marriage alliances (Baltzell 1964:57). Their rapid movement toward the mainstream of American cultural and secondary structural life suggested that in time—perhaps the fabled three generations—the German Jews would proceed through the remaining phases of assimilation and would disappear as a distinctive group.

That the full Anglo conformity assimilation of the German Jews did not occur may be due to the arrival of the extremely large and culturally distinctive Jews of the new immigration. Between 1.5 and 2 million Russian Jews arrived in the United States as a part of the second immigrant stream.[15] Like the German Jews, the Russian Jews had at one time lived in Germany, and their main language was Yiddish, a mixture of Hebrew and German. Because of this historical unity, these two groups are both referred to as the Ashkenazim, but after centuries of comparative separation the German and Russian groups were markedly different. Unlike the German Jews, the Russian Jews had been forced to live apart from the dominant group in certain parts of the country known as the Pale of Settlement. They had been oppressed by various restrictive laws (such as the military draft) and by organized violence (pogroms). Under these conditions, they had remained strongly united and had maintained their native culture and language to a high degree. Moreover, in contrast to the German Jews, the Russian Jews had every intention of keeping their culture intact in the New World. Most of the men wore beards, they organized Jewish schools to teach the ancient religious ways, they held strictly to the Sabbath and dietary laws, and they dressed in distinctive ways. Even the German Jews considered these newcomers to be social inferiors and did not wish to associate with them (Schermerhorn 1949:393). It was, Glazer wrote, "as if a man who has built himself a pleasant house and is leading a comfortable existence suddenly finds a horde of impecunious relatives descending upon him" (quoted by Baltzell 1964:58).

Like the Italians, the Russian Jews were largely trapped in the port cities of the East, especially the Lower East Side of New York. Despite the efforts of Jewish Americans to assist the newcomers in relocating to other parts of the country, most of them remained in the newly formed urban ghettos. The Russian Jews also resembled the Italians in having had little previous experience in urban living: most of them had come from small villages. Finally, the members of these two new immigrant groups did not come to America with the desire to assimilate.

These similarities between the Italians and the Russian Jews did not, of course, mean that their reactions to the new environment were identical. For example, although neither group wished at first to assimilate in America, their reasons were quite different. The Italians, as we noted previously, typically did not bring their families, planning instead to make a fortune and return with it to the homeland. The Russian Jews, however, while bringing their families and planning to remain permanently in America, did not wish to give up the ancient culture they had so zealously defended in eastern Europe.

Two other differences between the Italians and the Russian Jews are noteworthy. The first of these has to do with the psychological impact of American urban living. It is an understatement to say that thousands of people in all of the new immigrant groups were bitterly disappointed by the conditions they found in the New World. They were exploited at every turn, not only by Americans but by many of their own countrymen who "knew the ropes."[16] They were forced to work at unfamiliar jobs, at low wages, and with no job security. Usually, they had no choice but to move into the tenement slums with their crowding, noise, filth, lack of sanitation, and crime. Understandably, many people felt beaten, homesick, and lonely. Both the Italians and the Jews were subject to these tremendous pressures. The Jews, however, were somewhat more insulated than the Italians. Bad as the conditions were, the Jews found in America a degree of freedom from persecution unimagined under the rulers of eastern Europe. They were extremely eager to make use of their new freedom and, consequently, embraced the opportunities that existed in public education and politics much more rapidly than did the Italians. Moreover, that the Jews had come over in families and had quickly erected a cultural tent, so to speak, gave them added protection against the insults and deprivations that were common in the lives of immigrants.

The second notable difference between the two largest groups of the second immigrant stream concerns the types of skills they possessed and the economic possibilities that were available to them. Although neither group was really familiar with the requirements of urban-industrial living, more Jews than Italians happened to possess occupational skills that could be put to quick use in such a setting.

Ironically, some of the varied restrictions that had been placed on the Jews in eastern Europe had forced them into activities that now were of some value. For example, their concentration in the "needle trades" helped the Jews to develop a distinctive wedge into the economy (Novotny 1974:138; Schermerhorn 1949:410). By 1900, Russian (probably mostly Jewish) men were over thirty times more likely to be tailors than were other white men in the labor force (Lieberson and Waters 1988:126).[17] They began making all types of clothing, and the garment industry in New York was soon run disproportionately on Jewish labor (Kraut 1982:82). But many of the Jews were experienced merchants and were especially resistant, in the words of Portes and Bach (1985:38), "to serving as a mere source of labor power"—the Russian Jews, as had the German Jews, sought to establish themselves as entrepreneurs and owners of property. For instance, to return to the "huckster and peddler" example, although both the Italians and the Russian Jews were attracted disproportionately to these occupations, the latter were much more likely to be found there than the former.

While it was advantageous to the Jews, relative to the other immigrant groups, to have some readily saleable skills, they nonetheless worked under poor and oppressive conditions. The garment industry was so competitive that it was very difficult for its workers, large numbers of whom were women and children, to eke out a living. They worked extremely long hours for very low wages, under unsanitary conditions, and they encountered vigorous, sometimes physical, resistance when they organized labor unions to represent their interests. Moreover, the garment shops frequently were extremely dangerous places to work. In one notorious instance, 146 workers were killed when the Triangle Shirtwaist Company's factory in New York was gutted by fire (Burner, Fox-Genovese, and Bernhard 1991:647–650; Jones 1976:180).[18]

There was another deplorable side to all of this that affected the members of many immigrant groups. Several industries, including the garment industry, subcontracted or "farmed out" sizable shares of their work to people who labored in their homes; so large numbers of Jewish homes became "sweatshops." Jacob Riis ([1890]1957:80) observed in 1890 that "the homes of the Hebrew quarter are its workshops also. . . . " The workers were paid according to the number of items they completed. Not only were the working conditions in these home sweatshops frequently worse than those in the factories, but also the contractors often exploited an especially vicious aspect of the piecework payment arrangement. They gradually reduced the prices paid for each piece of work, thereby forcing the workers to increase their productivity in order to keep their earnings at the same level. A frequent result of this method was to force women and children to work as many as eighteen hours a day (Novotny 1974:141–142). As Riis ([1890]1957:80) noted, all of the members of the family, young or old, helped with the work "from earliest dawn until mind and muscle give out together."

Our comparison of some of the differences between the way the Italians and Jews responded to the American setting illustrates a very important point: although the members of these groups came to America as immigrant laborers and constructed ethnic communities in response to native hostility, their communities nevertheless may have represented significantly different modes of adaptation. The neighborhoods of both groups served residential and economic functions, but the economic function appears to have played a more decisive role in shaping the character of the ethnic neighborhoods established by the Jews. Although these neighborhoods resembled one another in appearance and served to shield their residents from the indignities heaped upon them by the dominant group, the Jewish neighborhoods are frequently cited as examples of an entrepreneurial approach by immigrants to the problems of adapting to a new setting. A number of other American ethnic groups, including the Chinese, Japanese, Greeks, Cubans, Koreans, and Asian Indians, also are named frequently as examples of this mode of adaptation.

We discuss later some competing theories that have been advanced to explain the distinctive roles played by entrepreneurial ethnic groups. One prominent view, *middleman minority theory,* argues that middleman minorities concentrate in commerce and trade and "occupy an intermediate rather than low-status position" (Bonacich 1973:583). Another leading view, *ethnic enclave theory,* states that economic enclaves consist of "immigrant groups containing a substantial proportion of individuals with entrepreneurial backgrounds *in the country of origin*" who establish businesses that provide employment for a still larger proportion of others of their ethnicity (Portes and Bach 1985:46–47).

Whether the immigrants of the second stream worked mainly as common laborers for members of the dominant group or for others of their own ethnicity, the human suffering engendered among all of them by the conditions of slum life in America at that time is truly incalculable. Despite great odds, the various new immigrant groups endured and gradually made niches for themselves in American society, though not necessarily through the three-generations process. But they were neither "a cluster of creative, ambitious, and optimistic individuals . . . on the path from rags to riches" nor "a faceless mass of unskilled labor, sadistically exploited by robber" barons (Kraut 1982:75). In time, as the story of their courage, determination, and success became widely known, they became models of what one may accomplish in America through hard work and perseverance. But when their struggle was most intense, native Americans generally did not see the new immigration as a confirmation of the American dream. They saw instead a massive renewal of the assault by aliens on the standards and ideals of American life. Once again, as in the earlier peak periods of immigration, Americans increasingly feared that their social dominance and well-being were threatened; as a remedy, they increasingly demanded various forms of restrictions on immigration.

We will learn in chapter 5 how the demand for immigration restriction was written into the laws of the United States and will expand our discussion of some underlying issues. We will see how increasing agitation for immigration restriction led Congress to pass a series of laws that by 1924 effectively closed the golden door. The 1924 law introduced the principle of national quotas, which became the cornerstone of national immigration policy and a subject of angry political debate. The effects of this important law were reinforced by the Great Depression during the 1930s and by World War II in the 1940s, producing during those two decades the lowest rate of immigration in American history.

The United States has faced a dilemma throughout the twentieth century in its efforts to regulate the flow of immigration while, at the same time, attempting to honor its historic commitment to accept the "huddled masses" of the world. This dilemma has been intensified as rapid increases in the size of the world's population and dizzying changes in the methods of transportation and communication have, in effect, decreased the size of the world. In the short period between 1924 and the end of World War II, the world "shrank" dramatically. The forces of industrialization and urbanization that were just becoming apparent during the first great immigrant stream have now encircled the globe, and their actions have strongly influenced the character of international migration.

As the world has changed, so has the United States. In contrast to the "open door" of the nineteenth century is the proliferation of laws, regulations, and legal agencies created to deal with the increasing complexities of immigration. This contrast will be apparent as we move now from the issues of the second stream to those of the third. We return in chapter 5 to a deeper consideration of the intergroup conflicts that led initially to immigration restriction.

The Third Great Immigrant Stream

Two notable developments in American immigration occurred after World War II. One of these was a large increase in the number of refugees in the world who sought asylum in the United States.[19] The second was a worldwide increase in labor migrations from the poor to the rich nations (Massey 1981:58). Together, these developments produced an immigration stream to the United States greater in number than any since the early 1920s. The decade 1951–1960 witnessed an increase of more than 240 percent over the preceding decade, and the number of immigrants has continued to rise in every decade since. The 1981–1990 period exceeded in number (though not in rate) all previous decades except 1901–1910 (see again Table 4-1).

Since 1980, these numerical increases also have resulted in a rise in the percentage of the U.S. population that is foreign-born. For sixty years, even after the third stream had begun, the percentage of the population that was foreign-born steadily declined. The U.S. census of 1980, however, showed that the trend had reversed. The foreign-born population in that year (14.1 million) comprised 6.2 percent of the total, in contrast to 4.7 percent in 1970. Even so, the relative size of the foreign-born portion of the population in 1980 was still less than half that of 1920 (6.2 versus 13.2 percent) (U.S. Bureau of the Census 1991b:41).

In addition to increasing both the absolute and the relative size of the foreign-born population, the third immigrant stream also has increased the racial and ethnic diversity of the United States, because the composition of this new stream differs from that of the two previous streams. For instance, Europe's contribution to the total number of documented immigrants fell from about 60 percent during the period 1920–1959 to about 10 percent during 1981–1990. By the latter period, Asia's contribution rose to about 37 percent of the total, while the contribution of the countries of the Western Hemisphere (primarily Mexico) rose to almost 49 percent (U.S. Immigration and Naturalization Service 1991:50). The search for jobs has brought large numbers of immigrants from Mexico, the Caribbean, Central America, South America, the Philippines, Korea, China, and India, while military and political upheavals in Cuba and southeast Asia have brought around 750,000 Cubans and 635,000 Indochinese to the United States (Kitano and Daniels 1988:138; U.S. Immigration and Naturalization Service 1991:50).

The immigrants of the third stream differ from those of the first and second streams not only in their countries of origin, but also in their destinations and the diversity of their social and economic backgrounds. Although some states that traditionally have received large numbers of immigrants, such as New York, are still popular destinations, additional states and regions of the country are receiving a large proportion of the third-stream immigrants. The Vietnamese, for instance, have settled mainly in California, Texas, Pennsylvania, and Louisiana (Montero 1979:8; Wright 1980:511); most of the Cubans live in southern Florida but are represented in sizeable numbers in northern metropolitan areas with large Spanish-speaking populations; and the majority of the Mexicans have settled in the border states of the Southwest (Perez 1980:257; Portes and Rumbaut 1990:46). In regard to social, educational, and occupational backgrounds, these latest newcomers exhibit a much wider variety than those in the previous immigrant streams.

In addition to the manual laborers who were so prominent in the earlier periods of immigration, the third stream has contained a sizable group of professionals. These immigrants "do not come to escape poverty, but to improve their careers. . . . " (Portes and Rumbaut 1990:19). In fiscal year 1990, for instance, among the immigrants admitted who listed a previous occupation, 12.7 percent listed "professional speciality and technical" or "executive, administrative, and managerial." Those comprising these categories came from all over the world but were mainly from Asia (43 percent), Europe (16 percent), and Mexico (13 percent). Other areas contributing at least 5 percent of the professionals were the Caribbean, South America, Africa, and Central America (U.S. Immigration and Naturalization Service 1991:86–87).[20] In the same year, slightly more than 27 percent of those admitted with a stated occupation were listed in the category "operator, fabricator, and laborer." These workers, too, came from all over the world, but their origins were much more concentrated in the Western Hemisphere: about 89 percent of these immigrants came from Mexico (67 percent), Central America (12 percent), and South America and the Caribbean (nearly 10 percent).

Speaking more generally, the Hispanics tend to be of low education and to possess mainly blue-collar work skills (thereby resembling the earlier immigrants), and the Asians tend to be more highly educated and to possess white-collar work skills (Cué and Bach 1980:262, 266; Kitano 1981:129, 132, 134). Some ethnic groups within these two large education-occupation categories are themselves quite mixed. Following Fidel Castro's successful communist revolution in Cuba, for instance, the upper and middle classes were adversely affected; so many industrialists, land-owners, managers, and professionals left for the United States (Portes 1969:506). The entrepreneurial activities of these immigrants have attracted widespread notice. In Miami's "Little Havana," for instance, "Cuban-owned firms went from 919 firms in 1967 to 8,000 in 1976 to 28,000 today. Most average 8.1 employees but include factories employing hundreds of workers" (Portes and Rumbaut 1990:21–22). The most recent surge of immigration from Cuba, in contrast, has consisted mainly of people of lower occupational and educational standing (Bean and Tienda 1987:28–29; Cué and Bach 1980:263–264; Massey 1981:59).[21] Notice, too, the contrast among immigrants from Mexico. In 1990, Mexico was the country of origin of the largest group of immigrant manual laborers, but it was an important source of professional immigrants as well.

We noted earlier that as a consequence of World War II the number of refugees throughout the world increased rapidly. The expulsion of people from their lands of residence is nothing new in history, but the problems associated with refugee movements have increased since the seventeenth century. As the world became organized into nation-states, and as the human population skyrocketed, govern-ments increasingly sought to control the composition of their populations by welcoming some groups and driving out others. This tendency increased until, by the twentieth century, the problem of what to do with the rising number of refugees became an important international question.[22] The "refugee problem" of the latter half of the twentieth century has been created by internal and international conflicts in which millions of people have fled from their homelands fearing for their lives. These people have sought resettlement in the United States or some other country not primarily to improve their economic or religious opportunities but, rather, to avoid execution, imprisonment, or persecution for political reasons.

The increase in the efforts of displaced people to gain admission to the United States generated new tensions between Americans' desire to continue applying national quotas and their view of their country as affording a place of asylum for persecuted people. Many people who were displaced by World War II or were refugees from communist countries were admitted to the United States on special nonquota visas. The Hungarian Revolution of 1956, for instance, led large numbers of the defeated anticommunist "freedom fighters" to seek admission to the United States. President Eisenhower set a precedent by admitting thousands of Hungarians above Hungary's quota through a legal provision that enabled the government to grant asylum to people under the "parole" authority of the U.S. attorney general (Reimers 1985:26). The parole provision also was used by President Kennedy in 1961 to circumvent the annual quota to aid anticommunist refugees who fled Cuba following Castro's revolution (Reimers 1985:27).

The legal changes that laid the groundwork for these basic shifts in the character of American immigration began during World War II. For instance, in 1943, a program to admit *braceros* (temporary farmhands) from Mexico was initiated,[23] and in that same year an important change (to be discussed later) occurred in America's policy toward China. The Displaced Persons Act of 1948 created 220,000 nonquota spaces for European victims of the ravages of World War

II. By the beginning of the 1950s, it was clear that the patchwork of immigration laws that had been adopted during the preceding decades needed to be put in better order; so legislation designed to systematize, and to some extent "liberalize," the existing laws was introduced into Congress. The result of this effort was the Immigration and Nationality Act (INA) of 1952 (McCarran-Walter Act). This law continued the established quota approach for the nations of the Eastern Hemisphere and, consequently, was severely criticized by those who wished to do away with the national origins principle. The act did, however, alter U.S. policy toward immigrants from Japan, introduce special preference designations for people who had talents or skills that were needed in the United States, and increase the number of relatives of citizens and permanent residents who could be brought into the country above the quota restrictions (U.S. Immigration and Naturalization Service 1991:A.1–8). And, as already noted, it granted the president the power to admit other people as "parolees" (Reimers 1985:26). Additional numbers of nonquota immigrants were permitted under the Refugee Relief Act of 1953 (Abrams 1984:109), and following the failed Bay of Pigs invasion of Cuba, the Migration and Refugee Assistance Act of 1962 was passed to grant refugee status to resident Cubans. This act illustrates clearly the conflict between the idea of national quotas, on the one hand, and of the United States as an asylum for oppressed people, on the other (Bernard 1980:495).[24] The periodic admission of refugees outside the normal quota limits has left us uncertain whether such additional newcomers demonstrate, in Glazer's (1985:3) words, "our openness and generosity, or our simple incapacity to forge a national policy on the key question of who shall be allowed to become an American. . . . "

Despite the loosening of restrictions permitted under the McCarran-Walter Act, the various refugee and displaced persons acts, and the president's parole power, criticisms of the national origins principle of admission continued to mount. In the 1965 Amendments to the Immigration and Nationality Act (the Hart-Celler Act), Congress broke sharply with the idea that members of some racial or ethnic groups are superior or preferable to those of other groups. The national origins quota system was abolished, "eliminating national origin, race, or ancestry as a basis for immigration to the United States" (U.S. Immigration and Naturalization Service 1991:A.1–14). The new quotas that replaced them raised the total who might be admitted annually from 150,000 to 290,000, beginning in 1968.[25] A ceiling of 170,000 was set for all countries outside the Western Hemisphere, and no single country was assigned more than 20,000 visas per year (Warren 1980:2). In addition, for the first time, an upper limit of 120,000 people annually was set on the entire Western Hemisphere (Reimers 1981:5), though no limits were set on any given country within it. As the volume of immigration from Mexico, Central America, the Caribbean, and South America rose, however, the pressure to assign limits to specific countries of the Western Hemisphere also rose. In 1976, the Western Hemisphere Act established a limit of 20,000 visas per year for each country in this hemisphere (Bernard 1980:495; Keely 1980:16–17). The Refugee Act of 1980 reduced the worldwide ceiling on immigration to 270,000, not counting refugees. This act aimed to establish a "systematic procedure for the admission and effective resettlement of refugees of special humanitarian concern to the United States" (U.S. Immigration and Naturalization Service 1991:A.1–18). The president and Congress were authorized to establish flexible admission ceilings for refugees from various geographic regions for each year. For example, the overall ceiling for 1990 was 125,000; East Asia initially received 51,500 spaces but later this number was increased to 51,800 (U.S. Immigration and Naturalization Service 1991:96).

The 1965 Amendments of the INA also established a new preference system aimed, first, to reunite family members; second, to permit certain professional and skilled workers to enter the country; and, third, to provide a place of asylum for refugees (Seller 1984:156). For example, among the seven preference categories listed, preferences one, two, four, and five (74 percent of the total) were allocated to family members. Preferences three and six were allocated to professional and skilled workers (20 percent of the total), and preference seven was reserved for refugees (6 percent of the total) (Keely 1980:17; Maldonado and Moore 1985:14). Although the family reunification and refugee provisions of the law were viewed as liberalizing the law, labor certification procedures made the entrance of many types of workers more difficult. For example, many people who wish to enter the United States to work are excluded by the visa limits or are unable to find a job in advance (as required by law); consequently, many of these workers find ways to enter without acquiring the proper papers. Such "undocumented" or "illegal" immigrants have been at the center of much contemporary controversy over immigration. Debates rage over several questions, including "How many 'illegals' are in the country? What are their effects on American society? What policies toward them should be adopted?"

There is controversy, too, over the proper terminology to use in referring to these people. The term *illegal immigrant,* for example, may suggest unfairly that the typical undocumented worker is a person of criminal tendencies who schemes to remain permanently in the country. In fact, the undocumented worker appears in general to be "positively self-selected in terms of ambition and willingness to work" (Portes and Rumbaut 1990:11) and is usually a person who is seeking honest work.[26] The undocumented worker also frequently is a bird of passage who may soon return to his or her home. The multiple entrances and exits of particular workers, indeed, has established a cyclical migration flow that has helped to complicate the problem of estimating how many illegals are actually in the country at a given time. No one can be sure, of course, either how many undocumented immigrants are in the United States or from which countries they have come. News stories frequently have raised the specter of an "invasion" of illegals and have suggested that there could be as many as 15 million such persons in the United States. However, based on several studies employing different research methods, Massey (1981:61) concluded that in 1980 there were probably no more than 4 million undocumented migrants and that around 60 percent of those were from Mexico. More recent efforts to estimate the number of illegals in the United States have led to the conclusion that in 1980 there were almost certainly no more than 4 million and there may well have been no more than 1.5 million (Bean and Tienda 1987:119–120).

In any event, the widespread *perception* has been that undocumented immigration is a very important problem and that something must be done to bring it under control. For example, in 1979 the Federation for American Immigration Reform (FAIR) sued the Bureau of the Census to prevent the count of illegal aliens from affecting congressional reapportionment, and during the early 1980s, Congress repeatedly debated immigration reform proposals brought before it by Senator Alan Simpson and Representative Romano Mazzoli. The main issues were the usual: the immigrants were said to be displacing U.S. workers, lowering wages, undermining working conditions, destroying the rule of law, and receiving social service benefits for which they did not qualify (Papademetriou 1987:325).

After years of controversy, a sweeping new Immigration Reform and Control Act (IRCA), sponsored by Senator Simpson and Representative Rodino, was passed in 1986. The objective of the new law was to reduce the flow of undocumented immigration to the United States, but it also hoped to bring about the legalization of undocumented permanent residents (Bean, Vernez, and Keely 1989:59). It spelled out various ways in which aliens could become legal residents, the types of penalties that could be applied to employers of illegal aliens, and the procedures employers should follow to use foreign agricultural laborers. It also required that all newly hired workers present documents (such as a driver's license or a birth certificate) to prove that they are eligible for employment, and it authorized funds to be used to reimburse states for some of the costs of legalization (Keely 1989:161–170). Although this complicated law's effects are difficult to assess, careful analyses of the number and demographic characteristics of undocumented people crossing the Mexican border following the passage of IRCA show that "To the extent that the pattern of apprehensions reflects the flow of undocumented immigrants . . . the new legislation has slowed the rate of undocumented migration across the southern border of the United States. . . . " (Bean, Espenshade, White, and Dymowski 1990:153).

Another major overhaul in immigration policy was the Immigration Act of 1990. Included in this act was an increase in total immigration to 700,000 per year (675,000 after 1994), changes in the grounds for exclusion and deportation, revisions in the requirements for naturalization, and revisions of enforcement activities (U.S. Immigration and Naturalization Service 1991:A.1–20).

Table 4-5 presents a summary of the major legal changes that have occurred during the period of the third immigrant stream.

Our discussion has shown how the increasing number of refugees seeking asylum in the United States, the increasing number of workers wishing to migrate there, and changes in American immigration laws (especially the 1965 Amendments to the INA) helped to create a dramatic shift in the countries of origin of American immigrants and in their social and economic backgrounds. The sharp increases in the volume of American immigration since the 1960s and the changed racial and ethnic composition of this third immigrant stream (now referred to as the *new immigration*) once again focused national attention on questions concerning the role of immigrants in American life and on the processes and ideologies of group adjustment discussed in chapter 2. Moreover, even though this contemporary

TABLE 4-5   A Chronology of Selected Federal Immigration Laws, 1943–1990

Year	Law	Major Provisions
1943	Repeal of the Chinese Exclusion Act	Gave the Chinese a quota under the "national origins" provision.
	Braceros Act	Permitted Mexican laborers to enter the U.S. on a temporary basis.
1948	Displaced Persons Act	Permitted "nonquota" entrance of refugees from Europe.
1952	Immigration and Nationality Act (INA) (McCarran-Walter Act)	Continued quota principle; gave Japan a quota; introduced special preference categories; created parole power for the president.
1953	Refugee Relief Act	Permitted 189,000 nonquota refugee admissions.
1965	Amendments to the INA (Hart-Cellar Act)	Abolished national origins quota principle; raised annual ceiling to 290,000; set limit of 120,000 on the Western Hemisphere; set limit of 20,000 for each country of the Eastern Hemisphere; created seven-tiered preference system.
1976	Western Hemisphere Act	Set limit of 20,000 for each country of the Western Hemisphere.
1986	Immigration Reform and Control Act (IRCA) (Simpson-Rodino Act)	Provided legalization procedures, employer sanctions, and rules for foreign agricultural workers.
1990	Immigration Act	Raised annual ceiling to 700,000; revised naturalization requirements and enforcement procedures.

immigration so far has been smaller in relative size than the first and second immigrant streams, it still has revived many of the same "immigration fears" and responses that were prominent during the earlier periods (Simon 1985; Waldinger 1984:219). Although there are many reasons to believe that, as in the past, such fears are exaggerated, many of the old concerns about America's ability to absorb the newcomers, and the willingness of the newcomers to be absorbed, have again surfaced.[27] In chapter 13, we examine the adaptation experience of one of the third stream's groups—the Vietnamese—and also reconsider the question of contemporary fears about immigration.

In summary, chapters 3 and 4 noted various objections and arguments that have been advanced against newcomers to America's shores and noted further that these arguments frequently have been presented in support of efforts to curb immigration. We turn in chapter 5 to a further consideration of some of these arguments and their role as shapers of America's immigration policies.

Key Ideas

1. The greatest human migration in history has occurred since 1815. Millions of people have come to the United States as parts of three great overlapping immigrant streams. The first two great streams (the "old" and the "new" immigrations) were completed by 1924. The first ("old") immigrant stream consisted mainly of people from Ireland, Germany, England, and Scandinavia. The second ("new") immigrant stream consisted mainly of people from Italy, Austria-Hungary, and Russia.

2. The immigrants from every country have tended to cluster together with others from their land of origin. In the process, they have formed ethnic communities for mutual aid and the preservation of their ethnic heritages.

3. The waves of immigrants arriving at America's shores tended to peak when economic conditions in the United States were good and to recede when there were economic downturns.

4. Before the Civil War, the Irish and the Germans arrived in the largest numbers. These migrations were precipitated largely by a rapidly growing population and crop failures. Both groups were politically active and appeared to the Anglo-Americans to threaten their dominance; consequently, both groups attracted the hostility of the native Americans and stimulated xenophobic reactions.

5. After the Civil War, the effects of industrialization on both sides of the Atlantic brought great increases in the number of immigrants from southern and eastern Europe. The "new" immigrants, like the "old" before them, seemed to threaten the integrity of the Anglo-American society and culture. As their numbers rose, the demand for immigration restriction also rose.

6. Each of the three great immigrant streams aroused the fears of native Americans concerning such issues as competition for jobs, possible disloyalty, and the effects of foreign "radicalism."

7. The experiences of the largest group to reach America during the "new" immigration, the Italians, illustrate the process of ethnic group formation called *ethnogenesis*. The members of this group became "Italian" in response to the conditions and pressures that existed within the host society.

8. The experiences of the second largest group of the "new" immigration, the Jews, illustrate some of the important factors that affect the adjustment of an immigrant group to a new society. Important among these factors are whether individuals or family groups are most prevalent, the extent to which the group already shares a common identity, and the kinds of occupational skills they possess.

9. The 1965 Amendments to the Immigration and Nationality Act, a liberal policy toward political and military refugees, and the search for jobs among the peoples of the poor countries of the world have led to a third great immigrant stream to the United States.

10. The immigrants of the third stream differ from those of the first and second streams not only in their countries of origin, but also in their destinations and in the diversity of their social and economic backgrounds. They have come mainly from Asia and the Western Hemisphere and represent a broad range of educational and occupational levels.

11. The third immigrant stream has revived many of the questions concerning the role of immigrants that were of interest during the earlier periods of massive immigration. Many people again wonder whether the newcomers will fit into the existing structure of American life or will alter it fundamentally.

Notes

1. We rely on the "push-pull" image to help identify some important factors that encourage migration but do not imply thereby that human beings are automata "drawn from their homes against their wills, as if by a 'distant magnet'" (Kraut 1982:9). The decision to emigrate is based on "a web of factors that in varied measure influenced those who uprooted themselves" (Kraut 1982:4). (See also Portes and Bach 1985:3–7, 336; Portes and Rumbaut 1990:8–14, 223–224.)

2. Some evidence indicates that this historic relationship has reversed since the end of World War II (Portes and Bach 1985:57).

3. Francis (1976:209) called groups formed in this way *secondary ethnic groups*. We return to this point in chapter 14.

4. By 1852, they controlled half of the 133 German-language newspapers in the United States (Wittke 1964:193).

5. The report of a congressional committee (the Ford Committee) contributed to the shift from state control to federal control. The committee's report reflected a change from a concern "with protecting the immigrant" to "protecting America" (Kraut 1982:52).

6. After 1924, Ellis Island was no longer used primarily to receive immigrants. By 1954, the facilities were used mainly as a detention center and point of deportation. President Lyndon B. Johnson, in 1965, declared Ellis Island to be a part of the Statue of Liberty National Monument (Bolino 1985:42,52), and in 1989 the Ellis Island Immigration Museum was opened to the public.

7. Kraut (1982:57) recounts the probably apocryphal tale of a German Jew who said "Schoyn vergessen" (which means "I forget" in Yiddish) when he was asked his name. He left Ellis Island with the name "Sean Ferguson."

8. The practice of calling the first-stream immigrants "old" and the second-stream immigrants "new" may be traced to the report of a congressional commission known as the Dillingham Commission. The report portrayed the immigrants of the second stream as something new in American history who could not be expected to become good Americans, as had the "old" immigrants.

9. Portes and Bach (1985:5) note that deliberate labor recruitment may reveal a shortcoming of orthodox economic ("push-pull") theories of immigration.

10. During the period 1890–1920, the major urban areas of the United States became heavily populated by immigrants. For example, in 1890, 54 percent of the population of New York City consisted of people of German or Irish origin. These same two groups comprised 45 percent of Chicago's population, and 54 percent of St. Louis's (Lieberson and Waters 1988:68–69). Approximately 75 percent of the residents of Boston, Chicago, Cleveland, Detroit, and New York in 1910 were immigrants or the children of immigrants (Kraut 1982:77).

11. The United States was not the only destination of Italian immigrants. Many sought work in other European countries and millions went to Argentina and Brazil (Alba 1985:39; Jones 1976:195–196).

12. These are early illustrations of what is now commonly referred to as "blaming the vic-

tim." For a vigorous critique of this mode of thought see Ryan (1971).

13. A particularly telling illustration was reported by Baltzell (1964:30). When New York's Mayor Fiorello La Guardia criticized his fellow Republican President Herbert Hoover, Hoover wrote to him saying that "You should go back where you belong. . . . The Italians are preponderantly our murderers and boot-leggers. . . . "

14. The practice of identifying various neighborhoods as "Italian," "Bohemian," "Greek," and so on may conceal the fact that these neighborhoods were seldom homogenous. Indeed, in many cases, fewer than half the residents of a given area might belong to the most visible group. The African American ghetto is the major exception to this rule. For a well-documented defense of this assertion, see Philpott (1978).

15. The official statistics concerning the Jews are less reliable than for many other groups because some Jews are listed only as nationals of the particular countries from which they came (Schermerhorn 1949:398).

16. Many immigrants relied on others of their group who could speak English to get jobs for them and to handle all relations with the employer—including receiving their pay. These labor brokers (*padrones*) sometimes took advantage of the situation. As Kraut (1982:91) explained, "While the padrone served a crucial function . . . enough of these ethnic labor bosses made illegal profits at the expense of the workers to give a bad name to the entire group."

17. Despite the high prevalence of "needle" skills among the Jews, Jones (1976:176) estimated that only about 11 percent of the Jewish immigrants previously had been tailors.

18. The "shirtwaist" was a fashionable blouse that had a high collar, full bosom, and narrow, pleated waist. Most of the five hundred employees of the factory were young Jewish and Italian women (Burner, Fox-Genovese, and Bernhard 1991:647–648)

19. Refugees and asylees are people who are outside of their country of nationality and are "unable or unwilling to return to that country because of persecution or a well-founded fear of persecution." Those who apply for asylum while they are outside of the United States are called refugees. Asylees apply from within the United States (U.S. Immigration and Naturalization Service 1991:99, A.2-1, A.2-8).

20. These percentages are calculated from Table 20 (U.S.I.N.S. 1991:86–87). Portes and Rimbaut (1990:19–20) state that the immigration of professionals tends to be inconspicuous because they "seldom form tightly knit ethnic communities. . . . " and "are among the most rapidly assimilated."

21. This group, known as the "Marielitos," consists of approximately 130,000 refugees who were brought from the Cuban port of Mariel in 1980 by a flotilla of boats organized by Cuban Americans.

22. For a general treatment of this question, see the special issue of *International Migration Review* 20 (Summer 1986).

23. This "temporary" program—which continued until 1964—is discussed further in chapter 9.

24. Also illustrative is a pathetic incident, known as "the Voyage of the Damned," that took place in 1939. Over nine hundred Jews attempted to escape from Germany aboard a cruise ship bound for Havana. After the ship was denied permission to dock in Havana, an attempt was made to land in Florida. The United States enforced its quota law, and the ship returned to Germany. Most of the Jews on board lost their lives in Nazi concentration camps.

25. The number 290,000 was based on an agreement that no more than 1 immigrant should be admitted annually for every 600 Americans (Abrams 1984:110).

26. We use the terms *illegal* and *undocumented* interchangeably and with no pejorative intent.

27. Consider, for example, the following remarks contained in a report of the U.S. Senate Judiciary Committee: "If the newcomers to a community do not excessively disrupt or change the attributes of the community . . . then the newcomers may well be welcome. . . . On the other hand . . . if the newcomers remain 'foreign,' they may not be welcome, especially if they seek to carve out separate enclaves to embrace only their own language and culture . . . " (U.S. Senate Committee on the Judiciary 1982:3–4).

Nativism, Racism, and Immigration Restriction

As a nation we began by declaring that "all men are created equal." When the Know-Nothings get control, it will read "all men are created equal except Negroes and foreigners and Catholics." —ABRAHAM LINCOLN

These new immigrants were no longer exclusively members of the Nordic race. . . . Our jails, insane asylums and almshouses are filled with this human flotsam and the whole tone of American life . . . has been . . . vulgarized by them. —MADISON GRANT

In thim days America was th' refuge iv th' oppressed in the wurruld. . . . But as I tell ye, 'tis diff'rent now. 'Tis time we put our back again' th' open dure an' keep out the savage horde. —"MR. DOOLEY"

Nativism

From the time the Anglo-Americans became consolidated as the "native" or host group in America, their reaction to immigrants has been both to welcome and to reject them. On the one hand, immigrants have been welcomed as needed additions to the labor force and as a spur to growth and prosperity; on the other hand, their "foreign" ways and their competition for jobs, political power, and cultural dominance have been resented and feared. The effort to subdue the continent, physically as well as politically, helped create the systems of bonded servitude and slavery, but these sources of labor alone never were sufficient. From the earliest days of colonization, therefore, voluntary immigration was encouraged with greater or lesser degrees of enthusiasm. Clearing the land, tilling the soil, producing raw materials for the mother country, and even the survival of the colonies themselves, all required large numbers of newcomers. The host group's reaction to the immigrants, as we discussed in chapter 1, depended on such things as the size of the incoming group, the rate at which they arrived, their concentration, and the similarity between their culture and the Anglo-American culture. If a group arrived in large numbers and behaved in ways that the members of the host society regarded as "too" different, the Anglo-Americans became alarmed and reacted in "protective" ways. Under such conditions, the usual levels of antiforeign activity were greatly increased.

Despite these fluctuating views, Americans generally came to prefer policies that encouraged a heavy flow of immigrants from Europe. One of the stated causes of the American Revolution, indeed, was the British policy of restricting immigration, and after the United States gained independence, an "open-door" immigration policy was adopted. The basic assumption behind this policy was that immigrants helped the country economically.

The door to America was never entirely open, however. The fear that foreigners would not understand or respect democratic institutions, or would in some way work to undermine them, was voiced during the debates over the Constitution. In the first flush of their new-found freedom, the Americans began to view all foreigners—even those from England—as possible carriers of antirepublican beliefs that might threaten the new nation. They tended to suspect that Catholics might be monarchist subversives and that anyone from France might attempt to foment the kind of unrest that had led to the French Revolution. These fears concerning the safety of the fragile new republic created a widespread fear of foreigners, or *xenophobia*.

A contest over the requirements for naturalization during the 1790s is an early illustration of these antiforeign sentiments. The first federal laws concerning naturalization, passed in 1790, provided that "any free white person" who had resided in the United States for two years could apply for citizenship (Ueda 1980:737). By implication, of course, slaves, Indians, and indentured whites were excluded as potential citizens. These laws also ruled out applicants who were not of "good moral character" (Cafferty, Chiswick, Greeley, and Sullivan 1983:40).

In 1798, the growing resistance to foreigners and foreign influences contributed to the passage by Congress of the Alien and Sedition Acts. These acts raised the residency requirement for voting from five to fourteen years, gave the president the power to expel potentially dangerous aliens from the country, permitted the arrest and deportation of the subjects of countries with whom the United States was at war, and set criminal penalties for those who published attacks against the government. These federal laws were soon revoked, however, and the business of naturalization and immigration was left mainly to state and local governments. These bodies continued, for most of the nineteenth century, to engage in a competition to attract immigrants and to provide for their welfare after they arrived. The federal government's role at this point was so slight that, as we have seen, its officials did not even count those entering the country until 1820.

The onset of the first great immigrant stream was believed by large numbers of Americans to represent an extremely serious threat to their way of life. Their reaction included vitriolic attacks on Catholicism and the Pope, on the pauperism and illiteracy of the immigrants, and on the political rights of naturalized citizens. It also included an increasing number of proposals that laws be passed to restrict immigration, limit the rights of immigrants, and increase the length of time needed to become a naturalized citizen.

As the Irish population in America grew and many of its members moved into various political and municipal jobs, there was an outburst of anti-Catholic propaganda. Many Americans believed the authoritarian organization of the Catholic church was incompatible with the democratic institutions and ideals of American society. An increasing number of newspaper accounts, books, pamphlets, and speeches claimed that the Irish Catholics were emissaries of the Pope who were working to undermine American traditions and overthrow the government of the United States. In 1834, for instance, the famous inventor Samuel F. B. Morse wrote several widely publicized statements claiming that the papal conquest was underway (Jones 1960:150). He believed strongly that the most serious threats to America's free institutions were immigration and Catholicism (Morse [1835]1976:61).[1] In 1836, an infamous tract, *The Awful Disclosures of Maria Monk,* portrayed monasteries and convents as dens of immorality (Monk [1836]1976:77). Anti-Catholic sentiments also were expressed in conflicts over the Catholics' opposition to the use of the King James version of the Bible in public schools and to their demands that state funds be used to support parochial schools.

The opposition to Catholicism was fused with a frequent, and not completely untrue, complaint that Europe was using America as a "dumping ground" for its paupers and criminals. There was widespread fear that the immigrants did not understand the American political system and, therefore, could easily be manipulated by corrupt leaders. The Irish were accused of using rough, unfair, "un-American" methods to rig the outcomes of elections. Instances of block voting, electoral fraud, and voter intimidation were cited to show that the very foundation of American democracy was being undermined. Apparently, in some of the large cities, it was common practice for immigrants to be illegally naturalized the day before an election (Jones 1960:154). Moreover, even though the Irish were rapidly becoming naturalized citizens, they maintained an active vocal and financial interest in political affairs in Ireland. Their interest in foreign politics increased the fear that they were not really loyal to the United States.

Although the Irish were the principal targets of the complaints against Catholics, the Germans shared in the growing antiforeign sentiment of the native Americans. The Germans were feared because they were presumed to be revolutionaries. Even Americans who did not accept many of the generally exaggerated charges against immigrants and naturalized citizens nonetheless did not like the Forty-Eighters. They were considered to be atheists and radicals who were contemptuous of American traditions. The Louisville Platform of 1854 was widely publicized as an example of German radicalism. The platform called for the abolition of slavery, the U.S. Senate, and the presidency. Even so, it was moderate when compared to the demands of the Communist Forty-Eighters, who advocated complete social revolution (Jones 1960:155).

The fear of Irish Catholicism and German radicalism seemed to have other justifications. The members of both groups were (as usual) considered to be clannish and resistant to Americanization. Not only did they form all sorts of associations (including militia units and secret societies), but many of their members worked energetically to support political reforms and revolutions in their native lands. It seemed clear to many Americans that these immigrants had little intention of becoming loyal Americans.

The idea that immigrants were destroying the basic fabric of American society was made to seem even more realistic by the rising controversy between the North and the South over slavery, westward expansion, economic policies, and so on. As the possibility increased that the Union would collapse, various political parties were formed to protect the rights and privileges of natives and to combat immigration and immigrants. For example, in 1845 the Native American Party was formed. This new party's stated purpose was to devise "a plan of concerted political action in defense of American institutions against the encroachments of foreign influence . . . " (Feldstein and Costello 1974:147). The party's Declaration of Principles argued that the natives were rapidly becoming "a minority in their own land" and recited some of the charges mentioned previously: the newcomers were working for foreign governments; they were comprised disproportionately of Europe's unwanted criminals, paupers, and imbeciles; they sought unfair political advantage by organizing along ethnic lines; and they "offered their votes and influence to the highest bidder" (Feldstein and Costello 1974:153). The Native American Party did not succeed on a national scale, but it was soon followed by one that did—the American or "Know-Nothing" party.

The Know-Nothing Party grew out of a secret nativist organization, the Order of the Star-Spangled Banner, founded in 1850, and was named for the fact that its members answered "I know nothing" whenever people sought information concerning its principles (Faulkner 1948:345). The party's slogan was "America for the Americans" (Jones 1960:157), and its platform urged that only native Americans be permitted to hold public office. The Know-Nothings opposed the admission of paupers and criminals into the country, and they believed that the period required for naturalization should be extended to twenty-one years.

By 1854, the party had gained enough strength to elect a number of state governors and U.S. congressmen and to dominate several state legislatures. But as the election of 1856 approached, sectional conflict overshadowed immigration as a threat to national life and the party's support weakened sharply. Since the nativists who supported the Know-Nothing movement lived in both the North and the South, the simple alignment of natives versus foreigners was no longer possible to maintain. The Irish, for example, were in direct competition with blacks in both regions and wished to see slavery maintained; hence, the party's support of abolition drove a deeper wedge between the native whites and Irish in the North but brought the two groups closer together in the South. In 1856, the party's presidential candidate, former President Millard Fillmore, was soundly defeated.

The Civil War gave numerous foreigners a chance to demonstrate their loyalty to the natives. "In both sections of the country," according to Jones (1960:170), "immigrants responded to the call to arms as readily as did the natives." But two incidents during the war showed that the immigrants' loyalty had not removed all antialien sentiments. In the first instance, General Grant ordered all Jews out of his part of Tennessee. It was alleged that they were responsible for illegal cotton trading with the South. Although President Lincoln required Grant to rescind the order, it is clear that the Jews had been suspected as a group.

The second incident consisted of a triangle of ethnic hatred. The Irish in New York, in 1863, staged three days of violence directed against both the white Republican establishment and blacks. These so-called Draft Riots were a protest against the practice of permitting rich draftees to avoid military service, which the largely poor Irish were unable to do. However, most of the rioters' attacks were on blacks. A wave of anti-Irish reaction followed the Draft Riots, suggesting again that the war had not submerged all nativist sentiment.

The conflicts between the native Americans and the peoples of the first great immigrant stream subsided markedly immediately following the Civil War. The Anglo-Americans had met the challenge to their dominance. Most Americans still believed that immigrants should discard their foreign ways and adopt the basic pattern of American life as soon as possible; however, even when the "old" immigrants exceeded their prewar rate of arrival, the hostility of the natives toward the newcomers did not revive proportionately. The people from northern and western Europe had proved they could and would fit into the dominant Anglo-American mold, that they were assimilable. Indeed, many of those whose fathers and mothers had arrived during the 1840s and 1850s now exhibited high levels of cultural and secondary structural assimilation and had, for many practical purposes, joined the ranks of the natives, while those whose grandparents had arrived during the 1820s and 1830s had completed the three-generations process and were undergoing primary structural and marital assimilation. The continuation of the first immigrant stream, therefore, no longer raised in the imaginations of the natives the specter of foreign domination.

The beginning of the second immigrant stream, however, aroused doubts anew. As its volume overtook, and then surpassed, that of immigration from northern and western Europe, many people became alarmed again. As noted previously, the peoples of the new immigration seemed to many Americans to be much more foreign than the usual foreigners. Their manners and customs appeared to many to threaten the very basis of Americanism, and their arrival in large numbers as a part of America's shift from an agrarian to an industrial economy made it seem that the newcomers were directly responsible for the many problems associated with that shift. For example, during this period, workers began to organize labor unions in an attempt to ensure employment and decent working conditions. These organizational efforts were, to put it mildly, not well received by the owners and managers of industry. Workers' strikes and picket lines were met by private armies and strikebreakers. Sabotage, assassinations, and open warfare were increasingly common in coal mines, steel mills, and railroads (Rubenstein 1970:29). Since many of these conflicts involved immigrant workers, xenophobia increased.

The bombing of Haymarket Square in Chicago in 1886 aroused widespread fears that immigrant radicals were plotting a revolution. Following the conviction of some foreign-born anarchists, the idea that all immigrants were wild-eyed radicals was disseminated throughout the country. Less than a month later, the leaders of a new nativist political party argued that immigrants were primarily responsible for the violent strikes and riots that had rocked the country (Jones 1960:253). These events added strength to a movement initiated by conflicts between native workers and Chinese immigrants on the West Coast to end America's historic open-door policy by establishing legal restrictions on immigration into the United States.

The charges against the Chinese emphasized the usual economic and political claims relating to the disadvantages of accepting immigrants, but now prominently added were certain scientific and pseudoscientific beliefs about the nature of racial differences. Immigrants were to be hated and excluded, according to this new wisdom, not only because they were a threat to the American working class and were the carriers of radical political viruses, but also because they were presumed to represent the "defeated" and, therefore, biologically "unfit" portions of their respective races. This new line of thought based on biological, historical, sociological, and psychological elements comprise what subsequently was called *scientific racism*.

Racism

We noted earlier that by the last quarter of the seventeenth century the Indians and Africans were excluded as candidates for full assimilation into Anglo-American society. We noted too that this exclusion did not result directly from a sense of biological superiority; however, the Europeans were keenly aware of the differences in skin color, head shape, hair texture, and so on, and some wondered whether their social dominance over the Indians and Africans might be related to, or in some way spring from, the physical differences.

The main line of division on this issue lay between those who believed the social differences among groups primarily reflect hereditary differences and those who believed social differences arise mainly because of different environmental circumstances. This important—though imprecise—line of division between *hereditarians* and *environmentalists* has appeared repeatedly in human thought as people tried to explain differences in human behavior and patterns of living. The opposing views of hereditarians and environmentalists also have figured prominently in the effort to explain and justify the unequal distribution of desired goods, services, and privileges. Many Greek and Roman aristocrats, for example, were sure they owed their position in society to their "natural" superiority. Many common citizens and slaves, on the other hand, were just as sure that the aristocrats owed their position to differences in social power and opportunity, including the good fortune to have been well born. In a similar fashion, from colonial times to the present, white Americans have been inclined to believe their social dominance is a reflection of natural differences in ability, while nonwhite Americans have been inclined to reject this idea.

In this context, we may say that *racism* refers to *the belief that racial and ethnic groups form a natural hierarchy of superiors and inferiors.* In its "scientific" form, this belief is joined by (1) *the idea that the white race is superior to the nonwhite races* (the doctrine of white supremacy) and (2) by *the further idea that the Anglo-Saxon, "Nordic," or "Teutonic" segment of the white race is superior even to its other segments.*

In contemporary times, the term *racism* has taken on a third general meaning with a different focus and a more flexible range of applications than in the past. *Racism* now usually refers to *prejudice, and perhaps discrimination, toward people who are members of particular racial or ethnic groups; it may or may not imply that a specific type of relationship exists between prejudice and discrimination, and the idea of group ranking may be more or less salient.* As van Oudenhoven and Willemsen (1989:15) put it, "Racism always implies prejudice and may encompass discrimination as well. The relations between these different concepts . . . are generally not straightforward and simple." Hacker (1992:19) states that racism involves "a complex of ideas and attitudes. . . . " which "goes beyond prejudice and discrimination. . . . "

We return in chapter 6 to some of the issues relating to this third, contemporary, view of racism. For now, though, our interest lies in the second, or "scientific," form of racist thought, the contributions of scientific racism to nativist thought, and the contributions of both to immigration restriction.

Racial Differences

We noted in chapter 1 that many people believe racial categories are specific, unvarying entities but that, in fact, the boundaries of races (and, more obviously, ethnic groups) are set by social agreement. The traits ordinarily selected to form the basis of the social definitions of race are, of course, biological: skin color, head shape, eye form, hair texture, and so on are biologically inherited. However, as we emphasized, none of the traits that most people view as "racial" can be used to establish clear-cut lines of division among the races. The apparent sharpness of racial boundaries in the United States springs from the fact that when Americans see another person they generally (and without reflection) "recognize" that person as a member of some racial group. Once that is done, their behavior is guided in certain ways by the assumed similarity or difference in racial status. The members of "our" group ordinarily are treated differently than the members of "their" group. Our group's members frequently are viewed as "standing above" those of other groups and as being entitled to favored treatment.

The idea that all members of the white race are superior to or "better than" all members of the nonwhite races illustrates the point. As usually expressed, however, the argument is more specific than this. Many observers have been willing to grant that some of the "lower" groups are superior to the whites in such things as sensory and motor ability, keenness of the senses, quickness of response, perception of details, and emotional sensitivity (Tyler 1965:300). Indians, for instance, frequently are portrayed as having especially keen senses, while blacks are thought by many to possess superior athletic and musical abilities. But even if these "admissions" were true—a point to which we return later—they they do not really contradict the doctrine of white supremacy. This doctrine holds that the different races are naturally superior or inferior to one another in certain respects but that the different kinds of superiority exhibited by the races are themselves higher or lower on the scale of desirable human qualities. That is to say, racists claim that their group possesses the "higher" superiorities! These "higher" superiorities do not depend on physical prowess or emotional sensitivity; they depend, rather, on intellectual abilities, such as reasoning, attention, foresight, and judgment (Tyler 1965:300).

The "admission" that nonwhite peoples are superior in certain nonintellectual ways actually serves to support the idea that the presumed superiority of white people is the more important, the more human, superiority. For this reason, the question of intellectual differences among the races has always been at the core of the race differences controversy. Buffon (Gossett 1963:36) concluded over two centuries ago that although blacks are "endowed with excellent hearts, and possess the seeds of every human virtue," they possess "little genius." Thomas Jefferson, who was very much influenced by the environmentalist thought of European philosophers, argued that black people are brave, adventuresome, and musical and have good memories but are "much inferior" in the ability to reason (Gossett 1963:42). Despite a later friendship and correspondence with the gifted mathematician Benjamin Banneker, a black man, Jefferson apparently entertained doubts about the mental ability of blacks until his death (Bardolph 1961:31–32).

Throughout the first half of the nineteenth century, the debate over the relative qualities and standing of the races intensified. Slavery in America, and the various justifications of it, moved increasingly toward the center of political, moral, and scientific controversy. Scientists and nonscientists, proslavery advocates and abolitionists, Christians and non-Christians all struggled over whether blacks were really human or were, rather, members of a separate and inferior species. The political and moral battles were decided, in principle at least, by the emancipation of the slaves, the victory of the northern armies in the Civil War, and the extension of full citizenship rights to African Americans. The scientific and scholarly controversy, however, was only beginning.

The fusion of several intellectual trends during the latter half of the nineteenth century fueled the dispute concerning racial differences. Darwin's theory of organic evolution profoundly affected thought in nearly every field of human endeavor. Among social thinkers, the view that individuals, nations, and races were engaged in a struggle to select the "fittest" and that social dominance was a sign of natural superiority gained many adherents. If the white people in America were the most powerful and successful, then this must be a result of an inherited capability resulting from their success in competition with other races.

This "social Darwinism" was given added impetus by Galton's studies of British men of distinction. Galton sought to prove that success in worldly matters was due to inherited abilities (Eckberg 1979:182). Nature, not nurture, was responsible for the rise of people to eminence. No social barriers could suppress the naturally talented person, and no social enrichment could cause an untalented person to become successful. Comparing the races, it was clear to Galton that "the average intellectual standard of the Negro race is some two grades below our own" (Gossett 1963:156). Galton also believed that the rise and fall of nations was strongly influenced by the extent to which they followed breeding practices that led to superior or inferior offspring. He feared that the "Anglo-Saxon race" was sliding in the direction of hereditary degeneration. His teachings supported various "eugenic" measures to "improve" the racial stock, such as the sterilization of criminals.

The arguments of the social Darwinists and Galton were highly compatible with a very influential interpretation of American history that flourished during the period of the second great immigrant stream. The conviction grew that the tall, blond, blue-eyed peoples of northern and western Europe were the modern remnants of an extremely talented race called the "Teutons" or "Nordics," who, in turn, were descended from the ancient Aryans of India (Gossett 1963:84–122). This theory held, more specifically, that of all the Teutonic, Nordic, or Germanic peoples, the Anglo-Saxons had made the most important contributions to English and American life. Although this theory contained numerous—sometimes contradictory—strands of thought, it served to foster the impression that different ethnic groups, as well as different races, exhibited different inherited traits. The Anglo-Saxons, for instance, were believed to love freedom and democracy and to be self-reliant, ethical, and disciplined. The Teutonic or Nordic group, as a whole, had a special talent for political organization that enabled its members to form representative governments and create just laws even when they were a numerical minority (Higham 1963:137). From this perspective, members of certain white "races" are destined to rule not only over the nonwhite races but over the other white races as well. Under this more specific version of the doctrine of white supremacy, the Nordic or Anglo-Saxon element of the white race is held to be superior to the shorter "Alpines" and the darker-skinned "Mediterraneans."

The IQ Controversy: Before 1924

Galton and his followers assumed that each person was endowed at birth with a certain intellectual capacity that could be measured. Bache (1895), for example, compared the auditory, visual, and tactile reaction times of three small samples of whites, blacks, and Indians. He reported that the Indians were the quickest in all three tests, the blacks were second, and the whites were last. Bache's concluded from these findings that the slow reactions of the whites meant that they were more "reflective" (and, hence, more intellectual) than the members of the other two groups! Studies by Woodworth and Bruner (Woodworth 1910:174), however, gave different results, and these authors argued that differences in health and training probably explained the test differences. These early examples illustrate the types of arguments preferred by hereditarians and environmentalists.

The effort to measure intelligence soon began to move away from such things as hearing, sight, and reaction times. The inventors of the most influential type of mental testing procedure, Binet and Simon, combined and organized various ideas to produce the first "scale" of intelligence in 1905 (Klineberg 1937:323). The idea behind the Binet-Simon scale is that a child may be said to have normal intelligence or an appropriate "mental age" (MA) if he or she can answer certain questions that most children of the same age can answer. For example, if most children can give their birthday by the age of five years, children who cannot give their birthday at that age are "behind" their age group in this respect.[2] In 1912, William Stern compared children's performances by dividing each child's mental age (in months) by his or her chronological age (in months) to obtain the child's "intelligence quotient" (IQ) (Klineberg 1937:323).[3]

The Binet-Simon scale was developed at about the time of the peak of the new immigration to the United States, a time when the pressure was mounting to shift away from America's policy of excluding only individuals who were considered undesirable and toward a policy of restricting admissions on the basis of racial or ethnic identity. The restrictionists' efforts were aided greatly by the evidence from a massive mental testing program conducted by the army during World War I. This program tested over 1.7 million men and was the first really large mental testing effort. The data gathered during the program have served ever since as an important reference point concerning many crucial questions: What, exactly, is "intelligence"? Do the tests actually measure it? How independent of prior training and experience are the questions and tasks used in intelligence testing? Is human intelligence a unitary thing, or is it composed of different elements? The primary results of the army's program were based on the findings of the *alpha* test (designed for those who were literate in English) and the *beta* test (designed for those who were illiterate or did not understand English).[4]

The first impression given by the results of the army's studies seemed very clear and had a tremendous impact on scholars, policy makers, and the lay public. In general, black people and immigrants did not score as well on the tests as native whites even when efforts were made to take into consideration group differences in schooling and experience. In terms of the average (median) alpha scores, white recruits of native birth ranked first, foreign-born white recruits ranked second, northern black recruits ranked third, and southern black recruits ranked fourth. The beta score median differences were generally smaller and more favorable for the black recruits, but the rank order of the four groups was unchanged.

In an important contribution to the developing controversy concerning racial and ethnic differences in intelligence, Brigham (1923) analyzed the army data further and presented them as "a companion volume" to *America, A Family Matter* by Gould (1922). Gould's book argued for restrictions on immigration to the United States and against "racial mixing." Brigham's analysis showed that on the combined alpha and beta scores, the foreign-born recruits from four countries—England, Scotland, Holland, and Germany—exceeded the average (mean) for the white native-born recruits; however, even the lowest foreign-born groups—from Greece, Russia, Italy, and Poland—exceeded the average of the native-born blacks (Brigham 1923:124).

Brigham asserted that these differences among the racial and ethnic groups could not be explained by differences in social and economic backgrounds but were due to a superior "hereditary endowment." Although he recognized that schooling does have some effect on intelligence test scores, he concluded that "the results which we obtain by interpreting the data by means of the race hypothesis support . . . the thesis of the superiority of the Nordic type" (Brigham 1923:182). This interpretation seemed to confirm scientifically that the immigrants from northern and western Europe were intellectually superior to (and, therefore, more assimilable than) those from southern and eastern Europe. The result seemed to prove further that white men were superior to black men even when the black men had had the "advantage" of growing up in the United States. All of these results combined seemed to provide impressive support for the position of scientific racism and of those who advocated immigration restriction.

Immigration Restriction

In chapter 4, we stated that the Immigration Act of 1924 led to a great reduction in the number of immigrants who were permitted to enter the United States and also greatly affected the racial and ethnic composition of the groups that were admitted. We noted, too, that the passage of this law took place after decades of agitation in favor of immigration restriction. We now examine briefly the major events that culminated in the 1924 Act.

Initial Steps: The Chinese

California had been a center of anti-Asian sentiment since soon after the discovery of gold there in 1848. Thousands of Chinese came to the United States at this time—as had so many other peoples before them—to assist with the hard manual labor of mining, building railroads, and so on. As was true of most European immigrants, the Chinese laborers who came to the United States were peasants who had been driven from the land by changing patterns of land ownership that increasingly concentrated wealth in the hands of a comparatively small ruling group. The peasants' situation was made even worse by the pressure western governments were placing on the rulers of China to open their country to foreign trade (Lai 1980:218). As a consequence of these changes, approximately 2.5 million people left China for other parts of the world (Jiobu 1988a:32). The Chinese who immigrated to the United States, therefore, were only a small part of this much more extensive emigration.

Before the California gold rush, only a handful of Chinese had come to America. During the three decades following 1848, however, over 228,000 Chinese arrived (see Table 5-1).[5] The majority of these immigrants came to California, and their presence in that state soon became the subject of political debate and public protest. White miners in some of the mining camps passed resolutions excluding the Chinese from the camps and, in some cases, launched physical attacks against them (Boswell 1986:356). In 1852, the governor of California recommended that some action be taken to stem the "tide of Asiatic immigration" (Daniels 1969:16). The action taken by the state legislature was to extend a tax on foreign miners (originally aimed at Mexicans) to include the Chinese (Lai 1980:219), but the action taken by many whites was the slaughter, largely unpunished, of hundreds of Chinese people (tenBroek, Barnhart, and Matson 1954:15). In 1854, a former U.S. Commissioner to China, Humphrey Marshall, expressed the fear that America faced an "inundation of oriental barbarism" in the form of Chinese "coolie" labor (Curran 1975:79).[6] Anticoolie clubs were organized beginning in 1862—the same year Governor Leland Stanford argued that the Chinese immigrants represented "an inferior race" and would "exercise a deleterious influence upon the superior" natives (Curran 1975:81).

Also in 1862, Congress authorized the construction of a transcontinental railroad. The building of the railroad required a large number of laborers, but only a few native workers were available to do this kind of hard and dangerous work; therefore, the Central Pacific Company began to hire large numbers of Chinese workers. Jiobu (1988a:35) quoted the historian Alexander Saxton as saying in this regard that "No man who had any choice would have chosen to be a common laborer on the Central Pacific during the crossing of the High Sierra." Uncounted numbers of Chinese workers lost their lives in the process. When the transcontinental railroad was completed in 1869, thousands of men (most of whom were Chinese) were thrown out of work and into direct competition for other jobs. Native workers and small businessmen considered the Chinese workers to be the "slave laborers" of big business, and they deeply resented what they considered to be the unfair competition of the Chinese (Boswell 1986:357–358; Hirschman and Wong 1986:5). This resentment led to the formation of the Workingmen's Party that campaigned with the slogan "The Chinese Must Go!" (McWilliams 1949:174). A statement by this party in 1877 claimed that "white men, and women, and boys, and girls . . . cannot compete with the single Chinese coolie in the labor market . . ." and that "none but a degraded coward and slave would make the effort"

TABLE 5-1 Chinese Immigration to the United States, 1820–1990

Years	Number
1820–1850	46
1851–1860	41,397
1861–1870	64,301
1871–1880	123,201
1881–1890	61,711
1891–1900	14,799
1901–1910	20,605
1911–1920	21,278
1921–1930	29,907
1931–1940	4,928
1941–1950	16,709
1951–1960	9,657
1961–1970	34,764
1971–1980	124,326
1981–1990	346,747
Total	914,376

Source: U.S. Immigration and Naturalization Service *Statistical Yearbook* 1991:48–50

(Kitano and Daniels 1988:22–23). The clamor for action, especially in California, became so strong that by 1880 both major political parties came out against permitting the Chinese to come to America to work, adding impetus to a trend toward immigration restriction that reached fruition in 1882.

Eighteen eighty-two was a watershed year in American immigration history. The number of immigrants reaching the United States in that year was exceeded only by the peak of the new immigration in 1907 (see again Table 4-1). Also in 1882, Congress enacted the first comprehensive immigration law that prohibited the admission of convicts, lunatics, idiots, and people who were deemed likely to become public charges (Abrams 1984:108). Of special relevance to us here is that Congress voted in the Chinese Exclusion Act of 1882 to suspend for ten years the entrance of workers from this specific nation and, also, to declare them to be ineligible to become citizens of the United States. The previous exclusions of immigrants had been based on the personal characteristics of different individuals, but now a new element had gained official recognition. For the first time, American policy accepted the idea that an entire group of people might be undesirable as immigrants and unfit for citizenship because of their race or nationality! As Reimers (1985:4) expressed it, "With the passage of this act the Chinese became the first and only nationality to be barred by name."

The Chinese Exclusion Act represented a major victory for those who sought the general restriction of immigration, and it sharply reduced the numbers of

Chinese coming into the United States.[7] It did not, however, stop discrimination and violence against those who already in the United States. Throughout the 1880s, the Chinese continued to be the objects of physical assaults, evictions, and other forms of harassment, and the political pressure to impose even greater restrictions on them was maintained. Within the next two decades, the rights of the Chinese in the United States were curtailed, and the laws preventing the entrance of Chinese laborers into the United States and its possessions were extended in 1892 and made permanent in 1902 (Lai 1980:221). Although the Chinese were able to gain some protection in the following years through a number of court cases, they still were subject to various forms of discrimination. In many communities they were segregated in schools, refused service in public places, barred from residence in certain towns, and prohibited from marrying whites in certain states (Lai 1980:223). Not until 1943, when China and the United States were allies in World War II, was the exclusion begun in 1882 ended.

The Culmination: 1924

The second great immigrant stream reached its peak in the decade before World War I, though it continued at a high level during 1911–1920 (see again Table 4-1). Numerous accumulated dissatisfactions among Americans (many of whom were themselves recent arrivals)[8] led to an almost continuous agitation to push Congress into passing laws that would restrict, or halt entirely, the immigration of the members of various national groups. By 1917, pressures from those who feared "racial deterioration" and the inundation of American institutions by "hordes" of European and Asian immigrants had reached a very high level. In that year the federal government passed an Immigration Act that barred alcoholics, stowaways, vagrants, and people who had had an attack of insanity (Cafferty, Chiswick, Greeley, and Sullivan 1983:44). The most controversial portion of the Act of 1917, however, was the requirement that all immigrants pass a literacy test before entering the country. This idea had been championed for twenty years by the Immigration Restriction League, had been endorsed by the Dillingham Commission in 1911, and had been repeatedly debated in Congress. Its enactment into law was seen by many as a repudiation of America's traditional role as a place of asylum. President Woodrow Wilson, in fact, vetoed the bill, stating that it embodied "a radical departure from the tradition and long established policy of this country," but his veto was overturned by Congress (Jones 1976:228).

The Immigration Act of 1917 did little to reduce the flow of immigration; so in 1921 the Emergency Quota Act (the Johnson Act) for the first time placed a general limitation on the number of immigrants who could be admitted in a single year (approximately 350,000) and, consequently, represented an historic departure from the open-door policy (Abrams 1980:27). The basic strategy of the Act of 1921 was to decrease sharply the *total number* of immigrants while at the same time increasing the *proportion* of immigrants from the European countries that contributed most heavily to the colonial and first immigrant streams. This dual result was to be obtained, moreover, without legislating specifically against particular nationalities. To produce this diplomatically tricky outcome, the act restricted immigration from Europe, Africa, the Near East, Australia, and New Zealand to 3 percent of the number of *foreign-born* members of each nationality counted in the U.S. census of 1910. Since a larger number of foreign-born immigrants in 1910 were from the countries of northern and western Europe than from any of the other places of origin, this legislation clearly was intended to favor the countries of the first immigrant stream. By this time the nineteenth century immigrants from Ireland, Germany, the United Kingdom, Canada, Scandinavia, France, and the other "old" immigrant countries were sufficiently assimilated into the dominant group (at least culturally) that additional people of those ethnicities were considered, if not "desirable," then, perhaps, the least undesirable newcomers. At this point, immigration from other countries of the Western Hemisphere was not of great concern; so no quotas were set for these nations. Paradoxically, the new law established a preference system that permitted certain people to enter the United States on a nonquota basis according to their individual characteristics, despite its general focus on groups. For example, a preference was shown toward members of certain occupations, such as "actors, artists, lecturers, singers, nurses, ministers, professors . . . and aliens employed in domestic service" (U.S. Immigration and Naturalization Service 1991:A.1–6). This preference system soon was expanded to include the wives and dependent children of American citizens (Bernard 1980:492).

The application of the quota principle had a dramatic effect on the size and sources of American immigration. Before the 1921 act, annual immigration from all nations averaged over 850,000 people, around 79 percent of whom came from countries of the new immigration; after the 1921 act, annual immigration was reduced to around 355,000, about 44 percent of whom came from countries of the new immigration. Still, these changes did not satisfy the strongest advocates of immigration restriction; consequently, as noted in chapter 4, they continued to press for a stricter law. The Immigration Act of 1924 (the Johnson-Reid Act) was the result. This law continued the basic quota strategy of the Act of 1921 but altered it in four main ways. First, it changed the "base" year from 1910 to 1890; second, the annual quota for all countries was set at 165,000 for the period 1924–1929, while the annual quota for each country was set at 2 percent of the number of foreign-born residents in the United States from each country; third, beginning in 1929 the annual quota for all countries was lowered to 150,000, with the quota for each country set as its proportional share of the total; and fourth, the proportional shares were based on the *"national origins"* of all people in the United States in 1920. For instance, if 20 percent of the Americans in 1920 were of English origin, then the annual quota for English immigrants would have been 30,000 (20 percent of 150,000). Since there were in 1890 and 1920 more Americans who either were from Ireland, Germany, the United Kingdom, France, and Scandinavia or were descended from people from those countries than there were from the countries of the second stream, the 1924 law led to higher quotas for the people of the first-stream countries and clearly showed America's official preference for those people (Cafferty, Chiswick, Greeley, and Sullivan 1983:53; Curran 1975:143). In short, with the quota formulas that were adopted, the limits of overall immigration were lowered while the proportions set for the more "desirable" immigrants were increased, as was intended. The Immigration Act of 1924 was the culmination of the effort to supplant America's historic "open-door" policy with one that would permit close control over immigration.

There was one other especially significant aspect of the Immigration Act of 1924, which we will discuss more fully in chapter 8: the act completely cut off immigration from Japan. Everything considered, the golden door was left only slightly ajar.

Table 5-2 presents a summary of some of the most important immigration legislation passed from the time of the first federal law until the establishment of quotas using the national origins principle.

To recapitulate, the fusion of nativist and racist doctrines and agitation led in the 1920s to laws that sharply reduced the acceptance of immigrants into America. The xenophobia of nativists was strengthened and apparently justified by the doctrines of scientific racism. The rise of IQ testing and the analyses of the army's test data by scholars such as C. C. Brigham joined with the charges of nativists to create the appearance that the immigrants of the colonial and first immigrant streams were naturally superior in intellectual capacities to the immigrants of the second stream and to African Americans and to prepare the way for the restrictive immigration laws of 1921. These laws shifted America's policy away from excluding only individuals who were considered undesirable to a policy of restricting admissions on the basis of racial or ethnic group identity. This new principle of restriction had been applied already in the Chinese Exclusion Act, but until after World War I, the idea of excluding immigrants on the basis of their *group membership* rather than their *individual qualifications* had not been extended to any other groups (Ware 1937:592).

The restrictive legislation of the 1920s, as noted in chapter 4, was followed by global changes that further impeded immigration: the Great Depression of the 1930s and World War II in the 1940s. The combined effects of these events produced the lowest rates of immigration to America on record. Numerous changes in American immigration law since then have been based on assumptions that are more consistent with the ideals and traditions of eighteenth and nineteenth century America and run counter to those embodied in the 1921 and 1924 acts. For example, the various acts to assist refugees reaffirms America's commitment to aid "the wretched refuse" of humankind that is produced through war and oppression; and the 1965 Amendments to the INA of 1952 abandoned the nativist and racist principles embraced by the 1921 and 1924 acts. Individual, rather than group, characteristics once again became paramount.

Nevertheless, the continued rapid rise of the world's population coupled with increasing refugee and labor migrations have made a return to the open-door policy unattractive, to say the least; so numerous laws have been enacted since World War II to continue to regulate and limit immigration and naturalization (see again Table 4-5). And although the influences of nativist and racist ideas on immigration laws have waned, they still exist in America and still affect some of the proposed legislation that is introduced into Congress. The role played by the

TABLE 5-2 A Chronology of Selected Federal Immigration Laws, 1875–1929

Year	Law	Major Provisions
1875	Immigration Act	Barred "undesirables."
1882	Chinese Exclusion Act	Suspended immigration of Chinese workers; declared Chinese ineligible for citizenship. (The suspension of immigration became "permanent" in 1904.)
1917	Immigration Act	Required immigrants to take a literacy test.
1921	Immigration Act (Johnson Act)	Set a quota of 3 percent of the number of foreign-born of each nationality counted in the census of 1910.
1924	Immigration Act (Johnson-Reid Act)	Reduced quota to 2 percent of the number of foreign-born of each nationality counted in 1890 census; set total at 165,000; created "national origins" approach; excluded the Japanese.
1929	Implementation of "national origins" provisions of 1924	Replaced 2 percent quota with the percentage of people of each nationality in 1920; set total at 150,000.

results of IQ tests in the framing of immigration policies after World War I has not, so far, been resumed, but the controversy has not ended.

The IQ Controversy: Since 1924

We saw that by 1924 the results of the army testing program seemed overwhelmingly to support the hereditarian perspective on group differences in intelligence. Most psychologists at this time were, in Thompson's words (1934:494), "pretty much of the opinion that the inherent mental inferiority of [immigrants and nonwhites] had been scientifically demonstrated," and most ordinary citizens were convinced the matter had been settled once and for all. But that was not the case. The number of studies comparing the IQ scores of different racial and ethnic groups mounted rapidly, and as their results became known many scholars began to have second thoughts. Certain contradictions and inconsistencies began to appear. Many thinkers wondered if, after all, such things as a person's social status, language, educational level, and test experience might make a *big* difference in test scores. Even Brigham reconsidered his earlier position. On the basis of a reanalysis of portions of the alpha and beta tests, he concluded that "it is absurd" to combine different intelligence test scores as he had done previously (Brigham 1930:160). In a retraction that has delighted environmentalists ever since, Brigham (1930:165) concluded, "The more recent test findings . . . show that comparative studies of various national and racial groups may not be made with existing tests, and . . . that one of the most pretentious of these comparative racial studies—the writer's own—was without foundation."

Brigham certainly was not alone in his conclusion. Earlier criticisms that the intelligence tests are influenced by factors other than native ability were elaborated. Certain questions of method were explored more fully, and the army data themselves were subjected to further and, in some cases, different types of analyses. In addition, many scientists in the United States (and elsewhere) were shocked by the grossly exaggerated "master race" philosophy that was being espoused in Germany by Adolph Hitler during this time. Hitler justified the Nazis' persecution of "racial inferiors," particularly Jews and Gypsies, as necessary to establish the "New Order" of the "Aryans." In a study at this time of the opinions of people who were specialists in the field of racial differences, Thompson (1934) found that *96 percent of the scientists did not accept* racial superiority or inferiority as an established fact, and only 46 percent of those surveyed believed the hypothesis of race inferiority was even "reasonable."[9]

In the period just preceding World War II, therefore, scholarly opinion (though not that of the general public) had reached a position far removed from that of the early 1920s. Although there were still some scientists who accepted the hereditarian thesis, *most agreed that both heredity and environment affected mental test scores in some complicated, poorly-understood way.* For most researchers, the question was no longer "Is intelligence determined by heredity *or* environment?" It was, rather, "How do heredity and environment combine to produce the results obtained on intelligence tests?" Environmentalists had established that the earlier hereditarian interpretations were uncritical and oversimplified. Factors such as the test taker's social class position, self-esteem, and motivation may influence the test results.[10]

In the ensuing debates among scientists surrounding the proper interpretation of these points, the weight of informed opinion continued to shift toward an emphasis on the role of environmental factors in producing group differences in intelligence test scores. For instance, it was demonstrated that a large number of blacks exceeded the average intelligence test score for whites,[11] and it was found that some blacks scored as high on intelligence tests as any whites.[12] Even reputable scholars who continued to favor an hereditarian interpretation clearly recognized the importance of some environmental factors. The distinguished hereditarian Garrett (1945:495), for example, stated that some test differences, though not all, may "be explained in socio-economic terms."

A further consequence of the years of study and argument was an increasing recognition that hereditary and environmental factors are meshed in intricate ways and that the effort to untangle their relative contributions to intelligence necessarily involves quite technical considerations. Some researchers, for instance, focused more carefully on the possibility that racial differences in intellectual functioning may be specific rather than general. Studies of this type attempt to study intellectual abilities such as verbal comprehension, perceptual speed, figural reasoning, memory span, numerical facility, and so on, in a search for patterns of differences among the intellectual functions of racial and ethnic groups rather than for a way to rank the groups on a single intelligence scale (Loehlin, Lindzey, and Spuhler 1975:177–188).

Another line of research—one that led to an acrimonious public debate—focused on efforts to calculate the heritability of intelligence based on studies of relatives (such as identical twins reared apart) and unrelated individuals. A heritability estimate of 1.00 means that all of the observed differences within a population are due to differences in genotypes. An estimate of zero means that all of the observed differences in a population arise from environmental differences.[13]

This approach to the problem of explaining group differences in average IQ scores came dramatically into public view with a publication by Arthur Jensen (1969:49) that reviewed 141 existing studies of heritability. The heritability estimates ranged from a low of .60 to a high of around .90 (Jensen 1976:103), with most near the higher figure. Jensen (1969:51) concluded that "probably the best single overall estimate of heritability of measured intelligence" is .81. Although Jensen (1969:79) acknowledged that "no one . . . questions the role of environmental factors" on intelligence test scores, he went on to state that the effect of heredity on IQ levels is about twice as great as the effect of the environment, and that the average IQ differences between black and white Americans are best explained mainly in genetic terms.[14]

A storm of protest, public as well as academic, followed the publication of Jensen's review.[15] Some authors challenged Jensen's high estimate of the heritability of measured intelligence. Howard Taylor (1980:10–74), for example, argued that a number of the assumptions underlying the .81 figure are faulty. Ehrlich and Feldman (1977:138) concluded "that there is not a shred of evidence to support Jensen's contention that H = .81." And Eckberg (1979:101) cited evidence showing that some heritability estimates for IQ range between .00 and .45.[16]

A subsequent approach emphasized still another idea. In a comparison of fourteen countries, Flynn (1987) found that since 1950 there had been an average increase in IQ scores of around fifteen points. Does this "massive increase" mean that the average person today is more intelligent than in 1950? If so, Flynn believed, the increase should have been, but has not been, accompanied by a general surge in creativity or invention or some other signs of a higher level of intelligence within these societies. He argued that "the real-world problem-solving ability called intelligence" is no more in evidence today than in the earlier period. In his opinion, IQ tests measure "abstract problem solving ability" and, therefore, "psychologists should stop saying that IQ tests measure intelligence" (Flynn 1987:185–188).

Many members of the general public (particularly members of minority groups) went a step further and concluded that psychologists should stop trying to measure mental abilities at all. Throughout the years following the passage of the civil rights legislation of the 1960s, minority groups increasingly have fought against the use of standardized tests (including IQ tests) on the grounds that the tests are racially and culturally biased and that their results often are used in ways that have deleterious consequences for minority children, such as "tracking" them into special classes and schools. An important part of this struggle has taken place in the courts. For example, a Washington, D.C. court ruled in 1967 that the scores on standardized tests are worthless as measures of ability, and in 1979 a California court ruled that IQ tests could no longer be administered to black children in that state (Thernstrom 1992:134).

Psychologists, nevertheless, have continued to search for more sophisticated and valid ways to appraise individual differences in mental ability. A number of neurophysiological techniques have been developed for this purpose, and some of these, Matarazzo (1992:1011) predicts, will be shown during the next several decades "to be valid measures of what is measured by traditional IQ tests." Matarazzo (1992:1012) does not believe, however, that "the discovery of biological correlates of intelligence test scores supports (either) side in the nature versus nurture controversy."

Many specialists, including many who believe that standardized tests are valid measures of ability, believe that performance differences among people reflect both nature and nurture and that the effective schooling of children need not wait upon solutions of the technical aspects of the debate. The Head Start and Chapter 1 education programs, for instance, have proceeded on the assumption that poor children, many of whom are black, have the talent, but not the background, needed to do well in school, and these programs have shown that compensatory efforts can be effective. Between 1969 and 1984, the gaps between the achievement scores of black and white children (nine through seventeen years old), though still sizable, grew smaller in almost every category of reading, mathematics, and science achievement (Jaynes and Williams 1989:348–349), and the gaps between white and minority children on both the verbal and mathematical portions of the Scholastic Aptitude Test (SAT) declined in 1992 (De Witt 1992). These results show the wisdom of basing educational policies, in the words of Boyer and Walsh (1974:61), "on the most generous and promising assumptions about human nature rather than the most . . . pessimistic. . . . "

Of special significance, though, is that the debate over testing is enmeshed, perhaps now more than ever before, in some of the broader conflicts in American society concerning racism, group dominance, and racial justice. The critics of testing believe the tests and the curriculum they reflect are intrinsically "Eurocentric" and unfair, and it is held that only "Afrocentric" or other culturally specific tests and curricula are appropriate for minority children (Thernstrom 1992:138). These lines of argument do not focus on the technical adequacy of particular types of tests or on the possible bias of test items. They proceed from entirely different assumptions concerning the forms of modern racism and the measures that may be required to achieve racial equality.

At stake here, as we discuss in chapter 7, is the answer to the fundamental question, "What constitutes fair and equal education for children?" This question raises others, including "At what point, if ever, should the scholastic achievements of all American children be judged by the same standards?" (Thernstrom 1992:143).

Chapters 2 through 5 have shown that the members of the dominant Anglo-American group in the United States have exhibited strong views concerning the desirability of various groups of "outsiders" and that these views have been defended in economic, political, cultural, and racial terms. We have seen, too, that these views have been accompanied by different types and degrees of physical, social, and legal reactions. In all of the circumstances we have considered, greater or lesser degrees of conflict have been present. In some cases, though, the conflicts were relatively mild and of relatively short duration, while in other cases they were severe and prolonged. What underlying factors have guided these patterns of intergroup likes and dislikes, acceptances and rejections? This question has intrigued students of racial and ethnic relations since the early years of the twentieth century and, indeed, was the central focus of inquiry among students of racial and ethnic relations in America until the 1960s.

Two main assumptions guided research during this period. The first assumption was that the discriminatory behavior of the dominant group should be the principal object of analysis. The second assumption was that the key to understanding the levels of discrimination among dominant group members was an understanding of their levels of prejudice. Work along these lines became, in Metzger's words (1971:637), "a kind of official orthodoxy" in this field, some of which is summarized and discussed in chapter 6.

Key Ideas

1. The United States began to move away from the open-door policy in 1882. Certain individuals were ruled to be undesirable, and, for the first time, American policy accepted the principle that an entire group of people might be unfit for admission because of their race or ethnicity through the passage of the Chinese Exclusion Act.

2. Each of the three great immigrant streams has aroused the fears of native Americans concerning such issues as competition for jobs, possible disloyalty, and the effects of foreign "radicalism." The shift from the first to the second stream, however, brought with it a new concern for physical differences. This concern was heightened during the latter decades of the nineteenth century by developments in several fields of scientific thought. An emerging view, now called scientific racism, held that human races could be ranked in a hierarchy of superiority and that all nonwhite races were inferior to the white race.

3. In addition to the belief that human races may be ranked, the conviction grew that the characteristic that basically determines the superiority of one race to another is "intelligence."

4. The desire to restrict immigrants, and to do so in a way that would favor the countries of the "old" immigration, led to the Quota Acts of 1921 and 1924. These immigration acts restricted admissions on the basis of the numbers of individuals from different countries who were already in the United States. This application of the quota principle achieved the desired results.

5. One important underpinning of the quota approach to immigration restriction was the development of "intelligence" tests that yielded a single score—the intelligence quotient (IQ). When the average IQ scores of different groups were calculated, it was found that white Americans of colonial or old immigrant stock generally ranked higher than those of the new immigration. It was discovered further that whites generally received higher IQ scores than nonwhites.

6. The efforts to define and measure human intelligence have raised many questions. Many scholars vigorously deny that an IQ score is an adequate measure of general intelligence. Even when IQ scores are accepted as having some well-defined meaning, however, there are many objections to the idea that the scores represent an inborn quality. Environmental as well as biological factors are known to affect people's performances on tests, and there has been no conclusive demonstration that the biological factors play the most important role. After more than seven decades of debate, those who favor a hereditarian interpretation of the existing racial differences in IQ scores have not proven their point.

7. An increasing number of Americans view standardized tests as instruments of oppression rather than as scientific and diagnostic tools. Some critics of the tests have taken their cases to court and have tied testing to broad questions of racism and social justice.

Notes

1. The fear of Catholicism was not new. Adamic reported, for instance, that as early as 1728 a number of Pennsylvanians expressed alarm over the "Irish Papists" (Adamic 1944:36).

2. At first, the Binet-Simon scale was intended only to determine whether a child was feebleminded, but in a revision of the scale in 1908 they also attempted to determine the intelligence of normal children.

3. Thus, if a child of sixty-two months has a mental age of sixty-two months, dividing MA by CA (62 by 62) gives a quotient of 1.00. To remove the decimal, this quotient is multiplied by 100, yielding an IQ score of 100. Children who have scores above 100 are "ahead" of their age group; children who have scores below 100 are "behind" their age group.

4. The alpha test tried to discover such attributes of "general intelligence" as the ability to take oral directions, to solve arithmetical problems, and to unscramble disarranged sentences. It nevertheless included questions that depended on a person's experience and training (e.g., "The author of *The Raven* is: Stevenson, Kipling, Hawthorne, Poe"). The standard procedures for the beta test were intended to present a task that may be understood even by those who have had little formal training in verbal or symbolic matters, such as the ability to trace a path through a maze or visualize accurately the number of cubes in a picture (Yerkes 1921:163, 227).

5. By 1990, the U.S. population of Chinese ancestry was about 1.6 million, which was 0.7 percent of the total population (U.S. Department of Commerce 1991).

6. "Coolies" were workers who were paid only a subsistence wage and who frequently were involuntary or indentured immigrants. Although there is little doubt that the Chinese workers in America generally worked for lower wages than native workers, some writers question whether the Chinese actually occupied the semislave status denoted by the term *coolie*. See Kitano and Daniels (1988:21).

7. Merchants and students still were permitted to enter.

8. Portes and Rumbaut (1990:26) state that the most ardent advocates of restriction "are often children of immigrants who wear their second-generation patriotism outwardly and aggressively."

9. Several scholarly societies published resolutions attacking the misinterpretations and distortions involved in Hitler's ideas. In 1938, the American Anthropological Association issued a statement that "anthropology provides no scientific basis for discrimination against any people on the ground of racial inferiority, religious affiliation, or linguistic heritage." And a division of the American Psychological Association stated that "in the experiments which psychologists have made upon different peoples, no characteristic, inherent psychological differences which fundamentally distinguish so-called 'races' have been disclosed" (Benedict 1961:196).

10. This list has continued to be refined and extended. Blau (1981), for example, systematically traced the combined effects on IQ scores of the occupational status of parents, the mother's education, the father's education, the extent to which parents and their children associate with friends and neighbors who have attended college, the average education of the mother's friends, the family's religious and denominational affiliation, the size of the family, the mother's marital status, the mother's views on ways to control children, the mother's use of physical punishment, the mother's belief in the value of education, and several other factors. Blau found (as have a number of other researchers) that factors reflecting social differences account for a substantial portion (between 40 and 70 percent) of the difference between the IQ averages of black and white children.

11. Shuey (1966:501–502) criticized the frequent claim that there is a large overlap (25 to 30 percent) in the distributions of white and black intelligence test scores. Her comprehensive review showed that the overlap has ranged in various studies from 0 to 44 percent, with an average near 12 percent. Nevertheless, even if one accepts the lower figure, the number of African Americans who exceed the white average would be at least 3.7 million people.

12. An additional finding was that northern blacks from certain states had higher average scores than southern whites from certain states. Environmentalists argued that these results were due to the fact that educational opportunities for both races were greater in the North. Hereditarians said the results could stem from a "selective migration" among blacks in which the more intelligent individuals preferred to move, leaving the less intelligent behind. By studying the IQ scores of black children who had lived in New York and Philadelphia for different lengths of time, Klineberg (1935) and Everett Lee (1951) compiled evidence showing that the longer the children had lived in the North, the better their average scores became, suggesting that an improved environment led to higher IQ scores.

13. The estimates of these quantities may vary according to the method that is used (Jensen 1969:50–56; Loehlin, Lindzey, and Spuhler 1975:286–291).

14. He also acknowledged that "as far as we know the full range of human talents is represented in all the major races of man" and that, therefore, "it is unjust to allow the mere fact of an individual's racial or social background to affect the treatment accorded him" (Jensen 1969:78).

15. Although some of the issues raised in this round of the IQ debate are more technical than in the earlier periods, many of the basic arguments recapitulate the central points raised following the army's World War I tests. See, for example, the exchanges between Walter Lippmann and Lewis M. Terman in Block and Dworkin (1976:4–44).

16. Another type of argument accepts the figure .81 as a starting point but asks, "Does this show that the average difference in IQ *between* two populations is due mainly to inheritance?" The problem is that no matter how heritable a trait may be *within* a given population the difference *between* two populations (e.g., blacks and whites) may be due *totally* to environmental differences. To illustrate, although the heritability of height is high (approximately .90) the average height of both Americans and Japanese is increasing as nutrition improves, but the height of the Japanese appears to be increasing faster without any change whatever in the heritability of height (Institute for Research on Poverty 1976:4). Intelligence may be highly heritable within particular populations while at the same time the *difference* between them may be due entirely to environmental influences. Jensen (1976:103–104) agrees that this argument is logical, but he does not believe this logically possible interpretation is correct.

Chapter 6

Prejudice and Discrimination

*. . . we must sound the inside and see what springs
set us in motion.* —M. E. DE MONTAIGNE

Men begin with acts, not with thoughts.
—WILLIAM GRAHAM SUMNER

Since the formation of the dominant Anglo-American group, its members have to some extent resented, downgraded, and harassed the members of all alien groups. We have seen, however, that aliens from countries of the old immigration generally have been more acceptable to the Anglo-Americans than aliens from countries of the new immigration. And we have seen that regardless of their place of origin, whites have been more acceptable than nonwhites. Our analysis has shown, therefore, that the historical sequence of intergroup contacts in America created a particular pattern of social "layers," or a *stratification system* among America's ethnic groups. Our analysis also implied that the dominant group's efforts to prevent the "rise" of different ethnic groups in the stratification system were a reflection of the various group's "places" in the system. In other words, while the members of the dominant group have rated all other groups as "beneath" them socially and have tried to keep each group "in its place," they have displayed greater hostility and rejection toward some groups than others. Why do people act this way? How are hostility and rejection related to racism?

Please recall that in chapter 5 we presented three definitions of racism and stated that in ordinary use today the term usually refers to *prejudice, and perhaps discrimination, toward people who are members of particular racial or ethnic groups; it may or may not specify the type of relationship that exists between prejudice and discrimination; and the idea of group ranking may be more or less salient.* We did not consider then, however, that two central elements of this definition—*prejudice* and *discrimination*—are themselves key concepts in the study of racial and ethnic relations and also have a variety of meanings and implications. Consider this situation: A white employer has the choice of hiring a white person or a black person for a particular job. Both candidates are well qualified, but the white is chosen. Is this an example of prejudice against blacks, in favor of whites, or both? Is discrimination involved? If so, in what direction? Now suppose, to continue the example, that the employer is overheard to say, "Most black people are lazy, and I don't like that." How does this new information affect our thinking? In addition to knowing about the employer's action in choosing the white candidate for the job, we now know something about what he or she thinks and feels. It now seems plausible to argue that the employer chose the white person because he or she thinks the black person may possess an undesirable quality, laziness. If this reasoning were correct, is the employer prejudiced? Has he or she discriminated? And is the person a racist?

Few people would feel entirely comfortable answering all of these questions on the basis of the information presented. Among the more serious difficulties are that we have not yet agreed how prejudice and discrimination should be distinguished from one another; we have not said how prejudice and discrimination are related; and we lack several important facts about the specific case in question. The illustration nevertheless serves to highlight certain points on which there is widespread agreement. First, the term *prejudice* refers to an attitude or some other similar internal state or disposition, feeling, or opinion. The term *discrimination,* in contrast, refers to an overt action. Second, although racial and ethnic prejudice and discrimination may involve attitudes and actions that are intended to favor a particular group or its members, these terms usually refer to actions directed against certain persons. Third, prejudice frequently is thought to precede, lie behind, or be the cause of discrimination.[1]

Several qualifications of these statements may be suggested. For instance, some observers argue that an unfavorable attitude concerning a person or group should be considered a prejudice only if it is a judgment that is not based on fact or experience. This presumably is what Ambrose Bierce had in mind when he defined prejudice as "a vagrant opinion without visible means of support." Others hold that a prejudice must involve faulty logic or must perform some irrational function for the personality of the prejudiced person, while still others stress that prejudices are attitudes that are especially resistant to change. Discrimination, similarly, is used by some to refer only to certain forms of negative actions. Frequently, for instance, it refers only to negative actions that spring from prejudice. In short, there are no precise or universally accepted definitions of prejudice and discrimination. For our present purposes let us say that a *prejudice is an unfavorable attitude toward people because they are members of a particular racial or ethnic group* and that *discrimination is an unfavorable action toward people because they are members of a particular racial or ethnic group*. Both prejudice and discrimination may vary by degrees, ranging from extremely high to extremely low levels.

With these thoughts in mind, we may expand our definition of the concept of racism as it ordinarily is used today. The term *racism* refers to *an unfavorable attitude, and perhaps an unfavorable action, toward people who are members of particular racial or ethnic groups; it may or may not specify the type of relationship that exists between unfavorable attitudes and actions; and the idea of group ranking may be more or less salient.* Clearly, this meaning of racism is more complicated and flexible than are the meanings we have given prejudice and discrimination and, as Hacker stated, "goes beyond prejudice and discrimination" (1992:19). In many, possibly most, contemporary discussions of racism one must infer from the context whether both prejudice and discrimination are involved, whether they are assumed to be related in a specific way, and whether the idea of group ranking is salient. In this form the concept has the advantage of drawing our attention to the complex web of interconnections between the beliefs, attitudes, and actions of individuals, on the one hand, and the social and historical contexts within which these elements emerged, on the other. It reminds us that the reality of ethnic stratification is located in social *systems,* as well as in the attitudes and actions of individuals.[2] Nevertheless, for many analytical purposes it is useful to focus specifically on prejudice and discrimination, on their relationship to one another, and on their many sources, and that is the chief goal of the present discussion.

Consider again the hypothetical situation of the white and black job applicants. The possibility was raised in this example that the white employer rejected the black applicant because the employer was prejudiced. This idea may be diagrammed as shown in Figure 6-1 on page 122.

This way of viewing the relationship of prejudice to discrimination is, to repeat, very common. And it is easy to see why. Much of our everyday experience seems to confirm the idea that people are motivated to act in different ways and that their

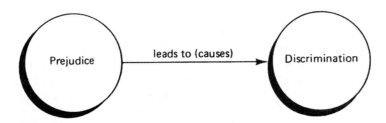

**FIGURE 6-1   A possible relationship between prejudice
and discrimination (arrow indicates
presumed direction of causation)**

actions are an indication of the way they think and feel about things. From this point of view, a person *first* has an attitude or belief about something and *then* acts as a result of that attitude or belief; so if a person harbors a prejudice we may infer (perhaps mistakenly) that the person may engage in discrimination. Conversely, if we are aware that a person has performed an act of discrimination, we may infer (again, perhaps mistakenly) that the person is prejudiced. We may describe either of these situations as examples of racism if, for some reason, the relationship of prejudice to discrimination is not at issue or is of little interest.

Where does the reasoning represented in Figure 6-1 lead? Let us assume that, as a nation, we accept the "American Creed" (Myrdal [1944]1964:209) containing the idea that people should be treated according to their individual merits. This idea (the principle of achievement mentioned in chapter 1) holds that discrimination on the basis of ascribed characteristics (such as race, ethnicity, sex, and color) is both unfair and irrational and that discrimination should be eradicated in the process of building a democratic society.[3] The question now is, "How are we to proceed?" As a first step—in purely logical terms—the answer to this question is, "We must attempt to alter prejudices." If prejudices can be reduced, so the argument runs, discrimination will diminish, and if prejudices can be prevented or removed, discrimination will disappear.

So far so good. But now we must face two hard questions. First, "How are people's prejudices to be altered?" Obviously, the answer to this question depends primarily on what a person believes to be the cause(s) or source(s) of prejudice. Many different sources of prejudice have been proposed, but prominent among these are the process of learning one's culture (at home, at school, and among peers), the process of psychological development (involving frustration, anxiety, personality "needs," and so on), and the human "need" to have a firm anchorage in a well-defined group.[4] This situation may be diagramed as shown in Figure 6-2.

The relative importance of the different sources of prejudice shown in Figure 6-2 has been the subject of a great deal of study, and an enormous literature has been created in the process. Some students emphasize only one of the sources, while others stress the importance of viewing them together. But here we confront

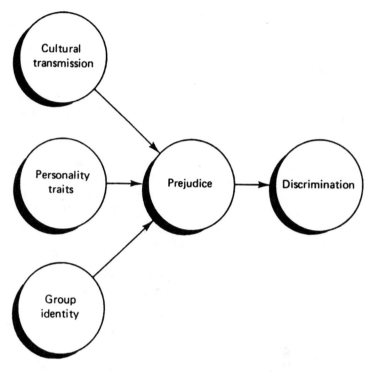

FIGURE 6-2   **Major direct causes of prejudice and indirect causes of discrimination (arrows indicate presumed direction of causation)**

the second (and most surprising) of the two hard questions: "Is discrimination caused entirely, or even mainly, by prejudice?"

Although we cannot hope to examine all of the issues raised by these questions, let us consider some of the more prominent points. We begin at the beginning, with the proposed answers to the first question.

Theories of Prejudice

Cultural Transmission Theories of Prejudice

One important type of theory holds that children learn prejudice in much the same way they learn to speak a particular language, dress in a given manner, or use certain eating utensils. From this viewpoint, the building blocks of prejudice are contained within the society's traditions or culture and are transmitted to children in a natural way as they are exposed to those traditions in the home and community. Two aspects of a culture are particularly closely related to the extent and kind of prejudice found in a given society. The first of these has to do with the shared beliefs that the members of one group have about the members of the other groups in the society. The second has to do with a culture's prescriptions concerning the degrees of intimacy or "nearness" that one group's members should permit or desire from any other group's members.

To illustrate the first point, consider the kind of "information" the children of Anglo-Americans are likely to receive regarding various other ethnic groups in America. Are they not likely to learn—by direct instruction, indirect instruction, and accident—that Germans are hard-working, Mexicans are lazy, Italians are artistic, the Irish are quick-tempered, Jews are mercenary, and the French are amorous? Even the children of quite "liberal" parents are likely to acquire such ideas as they come into contact with a wider circle of people in the neighborhood and school. Moreover, children usually learn that the members of different groups possess not just a single distinctive trait but a cluster of such traits. The extent to which these shared beliefs exist within a society's culture and are transmitted more or less intact from one generation to the next has stimulated many studies of stereotypes. Although theorists disagree concerning whether stereotyping *inevitably* leads to prejudice (Devine 1989), the acceptance of stereotypes frequently is used as one measure of a person's level of prejudice.

Stereotypes

The term *stereotype,* like the term *prejudice,* has been defined in a number of ways. Lippmann defined stereotypes as "pictures in our heads" (Klineberg 1974:631). Howard Ehrlich (1973:20) considered them to be "a set of beliefs and disbeliefs about any group of people" or, as Roger Brown (1986:534) put it, "character profiles attributed to in-groups and out-groups." And Allport (1958:187) stated that "a stereotype is an exaggerated belief associated with a category." As in the case of prejudice, these definitions call attention to certain aspects of the problem and ignore others. For example, these definitions are very broad, having applications beyond the study of racial and ethnic relations. Also, even though none of the definitions specifies the direction of stereotypes, in practice people use the term primarily to call attention to unfavorable beliefs—beliefs that present an out-group in an uncomplimentary way. Furthermore, as is shown by a comparison of either Ehrlich's or Brown's definition with Allport's, the term may or may not presume the accuracy of a given belief. Nevertheless, most people use it to signify, with Allport, an exaggerated or false belief. Indeed, the statement "that is a stereotype" usually means "that is a false generalization." Seldom is it explained, though, just how exaggerated a belief must be before it is to be regarded as a stereotype. Indeed, even a person who rejects a given stereotype may state that "it contains a grain of truth."

Let us explore this problem briefly through a consideration of the major research tradition concerning racial and ethnic stereotypes. This line of work started with a study by Katz and Braly (1933). These researchers compiled a list of eighty-four adjectives that may be used to describe the traits of members of a given racial or ethnic group. Each participant in the study was asked to select five words from the list that he or she thought to be "the most typical of the race in question." By this method, the words that are most frequently selected for a particular group are considered to be the elements of the stereotype for that group. To illustrate, if each participant in a study were to describe Germans as hard-working, intelligent, progressive, practical, and brave, then these five traits would comprise the stereotype of Germans. Such a complete agreement, of course, is extremely unlikely to occur. For instance, in a study on this point by Howard Ehrlich (1973:30) a total of twenty-three traits (including the five listed) were mentioned to describe Germans. We may well ask, therefore, what degree of "shared belief" is required before a trait may be included as an element of a stereotype?

But there is more. What does *typical* mean? Should *each* member of an out-group exhibit a given trait for that trait to be a part of the stereotype? If so, does anyone believe we would ever find such a trait? A more realistic view is that "*typical* means true of a higher percentage of the group in question than of people in general" (R. Brown 1986:592). For example, if a group of people in a study agreed that 50 percent of the world's people are "practical" but that 80 percent of the Germans are practical, then we might say that those in the study believed being practical is more characteristic of Germans than of people in general. This result would acknowledge that many Germans are less practical than are people in general but still would explain why the stereotype of Germans includes being practical. This interpretation is evidently more sensible than one based on the assumption that "typical" refers to every member of a given group, but notice that it still affords no direct evidence that Germans as a group are, in fact, more practical than people in general. Despite this and some other shortcomings, the method of studying stereotypes devised by Katz and Braly (1933) is useful because it does yield information concerning people's beliefs about one another and the extent to which those beliefs are shared.[5] As Roger Brown (1986:590) stated, "a trait can only appear in the stereotype if it is assigned by many people."

For our present purposes *a stereotype is a shared, but not scientifically validated, belief concerning the characteristics of the members of different racial or ethnic groups as compared to some reference group.* This definition recognizes as stereotypes the favorable images that in-groups ordinarily cherish about themselves; however, our main interest centers on the derogatory images that the members of in-groups frequently share about out-groups as compared to themselves or some other group. We assume that the presence of a derogatory stereotype within a culture indicates that those who subscribe to it are prejudiced (i.e., have an unfavorable attitude) toward the members of a given group. And since those who accept negative stereotypes appear to have a tendency to attribute any nonstereotypical behavior of out-groups to luck or favorable circumstances (and thus to "explain away" disconfirming evidence), we assume further that stereotypes assist to sustain prejudice (Hewstone 1989:37).

Returning now to the theory that prejudices are learned as a part of growing up, consider this question: "To what extent do stereotypes exist within American culture?" The evidence on this point appears to be very strong. Katz and Braly (1933), for example, found that more than half of the Princeton College students in their sample agreed that Germans are scientific-minded and industrious, Italians are artistic, the English are sportsmanlike, Jews are shrewd, and blacks are superstitious and lazy. More than a third of the students also believed that Germans are stolid; Italians are passionate and quick-tempered; the English are intelligent and conventional; Jews are mercenary, industrious, and grasping; Americans are industrious, intelligent, materialistic, and ambitious; blacks are happy-go-lucky and ignorant; Irish are pugnacious, quick-tempered, and witty; The Chinese are superstitious; The Japanese are intelligent and industrious; and Turks are cruel. The researchers contended that these high levels of agreement cannot be understood as a reflection of the actual experiences of the study participants and must, therefore, represent the influence of beliefs that exist within the culture and are widely shared.

This conclusion may be qualified by a consideration of the findings of some of the other studies of stereotypes conducted since 1933.[6] Two important qualifications are that the elements of a stereotype are affected to some extent by (1) contemporary events and (2) the kind of research method that is adopted. The effect of contemporary events on the composition of a stereotype was illustrated clearly by studies of Americans' views of their allies and enemies before, during, and after World War II. Public opinion polls in 1942 and 1966 showed that a large proportion of the people who were polled agreed at both times that the Germans, Japanese, and Russians were hard-working (Ehrlich 1973:30); however, the proportion of the respondents who described Germans as warlike fell from 67 percent in 1942 to 16 percent in 1966 and the proportion who described the Japanese as sly fell from 63 percent in 1942 to 19 percent in 1966.

Some illustrations of the way stereotypes changed before and after the war were presented by Gilbert (1951) in a study comparing the stereotypes held by Princeton undergraduates in 1950 with those found by Katz and Braly nearly two decades earlier. For instance, in the 1933 study, 53 percent of the students believed the Italians were artistic, but in the 1951 study, only 28 percent of the students subscribed to this view, and in the 1951 study, the Japanese were no longer intelligent and progressive but were, rather, treacherous and extremely nationalistic. In a 1967 study of Princeton students, Karlins, Coffman, and Walters (1969) found that the Japanese again had become intelligent and progressive. Both the 1950 and 1967 studies found that the students were more resistant than previously carrying out the instructions of the study. By then, criticisms of stereotyping were widely known and the students "sensed that *characterizing* ethnic groups at all would be interpreted as an ignorant and immoral thing to do" (R. Brown 1986:591). In short, the apparent declines in the willingness to stereotype may have represented the student's desire to present themselves in a favorable light to the researchers. People often do that: they give the answers they believe they *ought* to give rather than their true opinions. This distortion is referred to as *social desirability bias* (Lobel 1988:30).

The results of a study of stereotyping also may be affected by the research method that is used. Ehrlich and Rinehart (1965) compared the results of the usual checklist method with those resulting from the use of an open-end method. In the latter case, the participants were not given the eighty-four-item checklist but were asked instead simply to list the traits they thought certain groups possess. It was found that the respondents who used the open-end method listed fewer traits, exhibited greater disagreement with one another, and constructed different stereotypes than those who used the checklist method. In a study using a revised eighty-four-item checklist (Lobel 1988), some of the participants were asked to state which adjectives they personally believed applied to the members of thirteen ethnic groups and the other participants were asked to state which adjectives they believed would be selected by a typical American. The study showed, as have several others, that those who were asked to give their personal ratings presented more favorable stereotypes than those who were asked to give what they considered to be a typical reaction. The study also showed, however, that the divergence of the two types of ratings varied according to the ethnic group being considered. Nevertheless, despite some variability in the results of stereotype research, it is difficult to escape the conclusion that a large number of Americans share discernible clusters of beliefs regarding the traits of different racial and ethnic groups.

This conclusion was supported further by a second line of stereotype research. Although children seem to learn racial and ethnic stereotypes primarily in the home and neighborhood, the mass media of communication tends to reflect and spread the culture's stereotypes (Ehrlich 1973:32). In a well-known study of popular fiction, Berelson and Salter (1946) found that African and Jewish Americans were greatly underrepresented among the characters in the stories and were usually presented in stereotyped ways. Studies of the materials presented in movies, in magazines, on television, and in school textbooks led to similar findings. Elson, for example, showed that elementary school textbooks contain racial and ethnic stereotypes. His findings are consistent with the Anglo conformity view emphasized previously. The ideal American is presented as a member "of the white race, of Northern European background, Protestant, self-made and . . . retaining the virtues of yeoman ancestors" (Elson 1964). On the basis of the many studies that have been conducted, it seems safe to conclude that stereotypes are indeed an integral part of American culture and that people learn the stereotypes as an ordinary consequence of associating with other members of the society.

Social Distance

Is there any other evidence that prejudice is learned in the normal course of acquiring the American culture? The answer is yes. A related, but nonetheless distinct, research tradition offers exceptionally compelling evidence that the very process of learning American culture teaches an individual specific prejudices. The basic idea of the line of research to be described is this: As people grow up in America, they learn more than that various racial and ethnic groups are thought to be intelligent, ambitious, dull, slovenly, and so on. People also learn that some of these traits are preferable to others and that, therefore, it is more desirable to associate with the members of some groups than others. People learn to desire social closeness to some groups and social distance from others. Stated more exactly, *social distance* refers to "the grades and degrees of understanding and intimacy which characterize personal and social relations generally" (Park

1924:339). The idea "includes social nearness or social farness or any degree of distance between the extremes" (Bogardus 1959:7).

The concept of social distance was presented by Simmel ([1908]/1950) and was developed further by Park (1924). But the main research technique for the study of social distance was introduced by Bogardus (1933). Bogardus's method consists of asking people to consider a list of different kinds of social contacts they would be willing to permit with the members of various racial and ethnic groups. The types of social contacts shown in the list are selected to represent fairly evenly spaced points, running from a high willingness to permit social contact (e.g., "would admit to close kinship by marriage") or, at the other extreme, a low willingness to permit social contact (e.g., "would exclude from my country"). The number of the item (usually one through seven) representing the greatest degree of closeness a given person is willing to accept with the members of a particular ethnic group is the one used to calculate the group's average social distance score. Hence, if every person in a study concerning the French selected item three ("would admit to my street as a neighbor"), the social distance score for the French would be three. Using this approach and modifications of it, students of social distance have shown that people who differ widely in such things as occupation, education, and geographical location are nonetheless similar in regard to the pattern of social distance they wish to place between themselves and the members of various racial and ethnic groups.

The pattern Bogardus discovered should not surprise the student of American immigration history. In general, people from the British Isles and from northern and western Europe (the old immigrants) were ranked near the top of the list. People from southern and eastern Europe were next in order, and people of the racial minorities were ranked near the bottom. In short, the general pattern of social distance that is transmitted from generation to generation in the United States coincides with the pattern that was created through the historical sequences of intergroup contact that we already have observed.

As in the case of stereotypes, the conclusion seems warranted that the normal development of people within American society predisposes them to regard some racial and ethnic groups more favorably than others. We cannot know, of course, whether a specific individual's behavior will correspond to the answers given on a paper-and-pencil social distance form, but we can assume, on this basis, that the person at least has learned the answers he or she is expected to give under these circumstances.

Personality Theories of Prejudice

Although cultural transmission theories of prejudice have received a substantial amount of support, few people suppose that, as presented, they are the whole story. Our focus so far has been on the cultural beliefs people learn about racial and ethnic groups as they grow up. Members of out-groups are "dirty," "they" should be kept at a great distance socially. But this is a narrow view of what a person learns during the process of growing up. It is possible that the kind of person an individual learns to be—the kind of personality he or she develops—is of greater importance in understanding prejudice than the kinds of ideas the person "picks up" along the way. Why, for example, do some people accept the racial and ethnic stereotypes that are common in their home community while others reject these stereotypes? How, in particular, is it possible for members of the same family to disagree over these matters? For prejudice to develop, apparently, something more is required than that people learn the content of their groups' stereotypes and social distance norms. It is one thing to learn that the members of a particular group are thought to possess undesirable characteristics and should not be selected as close associates. It is another thing entirely to feel strongly that these are matters of great importance. In the former case, the process of learning prejudice seems to be perfectly normal and understandable. Given the existence of stereotypes and social distance norms within a culture, their acquisition is hardly more surprising than the learning of the group's language or standards of dress. In the latter case, however, something more seems to be involved. It is as if the personalities of some people "need" or depend on prejudice.

Many everyday comments concerning prejudice reflect this idea that some kind of conscious or unconscious personality need or problem lies behind racial and ethnic prejudice. We may hear, for example, that George is "insecure," that Maria has "an inferiority complex," or that Tanya is "afraid of her shadow." Such observations rest on the idea that prejudice is more than a matter of incorrect beliefs or ignorance. They suggest, instead, that prejudice performs some important functions for the personality of the prejudiced person; it serves in some way to help the person cope with his or her inner conflicts and tensions. Although this type of theorizing about the inner causes of prejudice is now commonplace, the basic ideas were developed primarily in the personality theories of various scholars.[7]

One of the most popular of these theories is related to the widespread observation that a person who is frustrated in some way is likely to vent his or her anger in an aggressive action even if the action is only verbal (e.g., shouting, name calling, or cursing). As Baron (1977:22) noted, it is quite likely that most people consider frustration to be the main cause of human aggression. The scholarly version of this idea, called the *frustration-aggression hypothesis,* is generally traced to the important work of Dollard and others (1939). These researchers argued that (1) frustration always leads to aggression, and (2) aggression is always the result of frustration. Stated in this way, however, a number of difficulties arise. For example, common observation reveals that many people who seem to be frustrated do not, in fact, engage in aggressive behavior. Many frustrations (such as rejection by a sweetheart) may result in despair rather than anger. This common-sense conclusion has been supported by numerous laboratory studies showing that while frustration is sometimes followed by aggression and aggression is sometimes preceded by frustration, the two things are not always connected. As Berkowitz (1969:2) and Baron (1977:22) observed, the original formulation of the hypothesis was too simple and sweeping. For these reasons, Miller (1941:30), one of the authors of the original statement, revised the hypothesis and conceded that aggression could be caused by things other than frustration.

Since then, many refinements of the hypothesis (and various definitions of frustration) have been proposed and tested, and many different issues have arisen in the process. Buss (1966), for instance, argued that attack is a much more potent cause of aggression than frustration, while Berkowitz (1969) maintained that frustration creates an emotional readiness to be aggressive that will not be translated into action unless certain other factors (called *aggressive cues*) are present.

A number of studies have been designed to test this controversial revision of the frustration-aggression hypothesis (Krebs and Miller 1985:39–42). To illustrate, Geen and Berkowitz (1967) studied the reactions of college students, some of whom (the experimental subjects) were given insoluble (hence, frustrating) puzzles to solve. Some other students (confederates of the experimenters) were given puzzles that looked the same but were not. Each experimental subject was paired with a confederate, and both students were asked to solve the puzzle in one another's presence. In half the cases the confederate was introduced as "Kirk Anderson" and in the other half he was "Bob Anderson." Sometimes "Mr. Anderson" (who, of course, solved his puzzle) paid no attention to the unsuccessful experimental subject; however, in other cases "Mr. Anderson" openly criticized the subject and boasted of his own cleverness.

When the puzzle task ended, half of each group of students was shown a violent prizefight film starring the actor Kirk Douglas, and the other half was shown a film about a footrace. Still later in the experiment, the subjects were told they had been selected to teach the other member of their pair (the "Mr. Anderson") a certain task. They were told, too, that they could administer electric shocks (in a special apparatus) whenever "Mr. Anderson" made mistakes. One of the several predictions of this study was that the confederates who had been introduced as "Kirk" would be given higher levels of shock from the frustrated subjects than those introduced as "Bob." The association of the name Kirk with the prizefighter in the film was expected to serve as an aggressive cue. This prediction was shown to be correct, thus lending support to the idea that frustration is more likely to lead to aggression if it occurs in the presence of an aggressive cue.

Evidently, the frustration-aggression hypothesis has changed since 1939; however, the core idea—that frustration is related to aggression—has been amply supported. But what has all this to do with prejudice? Dollard and others (1939) recognized that people frequently do not behave aggressively immediately after being frustrated. Many things may prevent a person from doing so. To use a familiar example, a person who causes frustration may be too powerful (e.g., one's boss) to attack directly or openly. In such cases, the frustration and hostility experienced by the individual may have no feasible outlet. It may, instead, be awaiting a safe or convenient substitute target. This situation leads to the frequent admonition to an angry person that he or she should not "take it out on me" (or the dog or your brother). Such a safe, convenient substitute target is called a scapegoat (Allport 1958:236). Since the hostility that lies behind scapegoating may be released against a wide variety of targets, it is described as "free-floating" (Allport 1958:337).

Let us accept the general argument that all people experience various frustrations in their daily lives, that these frustrations give rise to hostile feelings, that the hostile feelings may lead to aggressive behavior, and that the aggression may be aimed at a substitute target. Now, with only one addition to this general line of reasoning, we may apply it to the problem of understanding prejudice. Ethnic groups in America, especially the newest arrivals and those in the racial minorities, frequently afford a weak and convenient target—a scapegoat—for the free-floating aggressions of the majority. In this way, prejudice serves to assist the majority-group members to displace (and possibly to "drain off") their accumulated feelings without exposing themselves to a high risk of retaliation.[8]

As stated so far, the frustration-aggression hypothesis seems to fit well with much everyday experience, as well as with the more formal evidence of many studies. Still, a number of questions remain unanswered. For instance, isn't it the case that when we displace our frustrations through aggression against an innocent person or animal, we usually recognize, if only dimly, that we have not really attacked the true target of our anger? Scapegoating may serve briefly to relieve a sense of frustration, and we may feel better for a moment after such an outburst. But may we not later feel foolish or guilty? If so, would we not soon abandon such an ineffective method of coping?

The frustration-aggression theory points in a different direction. It assumes that the guilt produced by scapegoating—the sense that one may have committed an injustice—may be accompanied by a fear that the injured person will retaliate. The combination of guilt and fear now becomes a new source of frustration, and this new source of frustration, like the original source, arouses aggressive feelings.[9] Once again, the fuel has been provided for a certain amount of free-floating hostility and a new round of scapegoating. In this way, a *vicious circle* is created. Displaced aggression appears to feed upon itself and grow, rather than diminish, in strength. The need of prejudiced people to cope with the frustrations in their daily lives is met by directing the resulting hostility toward the members of minority groups.

Once the members of a minority group are chosen as targets, the displacement of aggression may also lead to an increase in stereotyping, as well as frustration. The possible reasons for this go well beyond our present argument; however, we may note in passing an intriguing explanation that has attracted much interest since it was first proposed by Festinger (1957).

Festinger is one of many so-called balance theorists who maintain that human beings are more comfortable psychologically when their attitudes, beliefs, or ideas ("cognitive elements") are consistent ("consonant") than when they are inconsistent ("dissonant"). The presence of dissonance, therefore, creates psychological pressure within people to change their attitudes, beliefs, or ideas. According to Festinger (1957:30), "the existence of dissonance, being psychologically uncomfortable, will motivate the person to try to reduce the dissonance and achieve consonance." For instance, if a person's behavior (e.g., smoking) is inconsistent with his or her beliefs (e.g., smoking is a health hazard), the person might reduce dissonance either by changing his or her behavior (i.e., giving up smoking) or by changing his or her beliefs (i.e., accepting the belief that smoking is not really dangerous). Either way, the dissonant cognitive elements will become consistent, and the psychological pressure to do something will be diminished. Since for many people it is more difficult to give up smoking than to reject the arguments against it, the latter is a frequent outcome.

Similarly, if a frustrated person displaces hostility onto minority group members whom he or she knows had nothing to do with the frustration, dissonance is created. Two cognitive elements—the knowledge that an aggressive action has occurred and an awareness that the target was innocent—are not in harmony. Consequently, psychological discomfort results. Since the behavior already has occurred and thus cannot be changed, the aggressor may reduce his or her *cognitive dissonance* by accepting stereotyped beliefs about the victim. The more frequently the individual displaces hostility in this way, the more occasions he or she will have for dissonance reduction, and the greater will be the psychological pressure to accept the prevailing stereotypes about the victim. Whether an individual actually does accept the stereotypes, however, or discontinues his or her aggression instead is a very complex matter, depending on much more than we can discuss here. Later in this chapter, we refer again to the theory of cognitive dissonance.

Everything considered, the theory that frustration may lead to aggressive actions against out-groups makes a good deal of sense, but it does not explain why some frustrated people displace aggression onto members of minority groups while some other, perhaps even more frustrated, people do not do so (Allport 1958:210, 332), and it does not explain why some frustrated people vent their anger on members of a particular ethnic minority while others select a completely different group as a target. Furthermore, some proponents of the theory believe that when an ethnic target is chosen, the group in question will be relatively defenseless—that the scapegoat will be, in Allport's (1958:332) phrase, a "safe goat." But the members of ethnic minorities also experience frustration and become filled with aggressive impulses. Does this mean that they do not harbor prejudices against the majority or that they never strike out in anger against the majority? There is every reason to believe, on the contrary, that some African Americans, Native Americans, Jewish Americans, and so on hate Anglo-Americans just as vigorously as the other way around. The hostility that is felt against the members of the dominant group may be expressed in acts ranging from subtle sabotage to ghetto riots (Simpson and Yinger 1972:218–219).

One final limitation of the frustration-aggression theory (and other personality theories) of prejudice is that its emphasis on individual hostility neglects the fact that racial and ethnic groups actually do compete with one another and do frustrate one another's ambitions to a greater or lesser extent. Each group in the competition, of course, will claim that their antagonism toward the other group is well-founded and that the other group richly deserves to be hated. Under these circumstances, it is much more difficult to assert that the negative attitudes are the result of free-floating anxiety. We will return shortly to the issue of the consequences of realistic group conflicts.

Our conclusion concerning personality theories of prejudice resembles the previous one regarding cultural transmission theories: It seems reasonable to suppose that some majority group members react to life's innumerable problems by displacing their hostile feelings onto the members of certain minority groups and that certain minority group members respond in kind. But not all ethnic prejudices are readily explained in this way. Personality structure, like beliefs transmitted through cultures, is one among many things that may lead to ethnic prejudice.

Group Identification Theories of Prejudice

Ethnocentrism

Let us now turn to the last of the three main types of causes of prejudice shown in Figure 6-2: group identification. The importance of a person's group memberships as a molding force has nowhere been stated more powerfully than by Sumner in his famous book *Folkways* (1906). In Sumner's view, a fundamental fact concerning human groups is that as their members are drawn together by a common interest, they simultaneously become distinguished from other groups (1906:12). In this process, those in the newly formed group come to see themselves as the in-group or we-group and to categorize everyone else as members of an out-group or they-group. As our brief review of nativism in the United States showed, the members of an in-group ordinarily have feelings of loyalty and pride toward their own group and feelings of superiority and contempt toward members of out-groups. The in-group is seen as possessing the right, the natural, the human ways of living and thinking. "We" are believed to be virtuous and civilized; "they" are believed to be vicious and barbaric. Outsiders are likely to be described in terms that are scornful and derogatory and that reflect negative stereotypes. In the United States, for example, such terms as *dago, nigger, kike, honkey, spick, mick, limey, chink, gringo,* and so on have been applied frequently to out-groups as terms of extreme disrespect. As noted in chapter 3, this tendency to rate all out-groups as lower than the in-group is called *ethnocentrism* (Sumner 1906:13).

Ethnocentrism is a pervasive sentiment. Children normally learn very early to distinguish the groups to which they belong from all other groups, and they usually have a strong attachment to and preference for their own group and its ways. Since children develop in a specific set of groups, beginning with their families, and since they usually learn only one way to behave, it seems quite understandable that people should regard their groups' ways of thinking and acting as natural and good. From this beginning, it is but an easy step to the rejection of the ways of all out-groups and a general conviction that those ways are unnatural and bad. Thus, children's awareness of themselves as distinct individuals (their personal identities) and their evaluations of themselves (their self-esteem) are inextricably connected to the standards and traditions of specific groups (their social identities). According to this view, the child wishes to evaluate himself or herself positively, and a positive self-evaluation rests on the personal and social identities that develop within the matrix of in-group life (R. Brown 1986:556; Tajfel and Turner 1979). In this way, the group's preferences become their preferences—its standards, their standards;

its beliefs, their beliefs; its enemies, their enemies. To grow up as a member of a given group, this view of social identity states, is automatically to place the group at the center of things and to adopt its evaluations as the best. Prejudice and hostility toward members of out-groups and favoritism toward members of the in-group are seen as predictable consequences of this natural ethnocentrism.[10]

Contemporary sociologists generally are content to accept ethnocentrism as a natural consequence of group living and have not concerned themselves much with the prior question, "Why is ethnocentrism natural?" Is it primarily a highly probable consequence of being socialized by particular others in any human group, or is there also something in the genetic structure of human beings that predisposes them toward this kind of sentiment? Many sociologists believe either that efforts to answer these questions move beyond the boundaries of sociology's scholarly domain or that such answers, if given, would have little bearing on the issues that are of immediate importance. See and Wilson (1988:225), for example, cautioned that the value of such analyses may be only to remind "scholars that . . . there is an ever-present potential for ethnic or racial conflict. . . . " rather than to help explain variations "in ethnic intragroup and intergroup behavior. . . . " Another objection to pursuing these questions is that such research might serve to divert attention from the sociocultural sources of racial and ethnic differences and conflicts and, inadvertently, to undermine the victories against racist doctrines that were won during the half-century following the Immigration Act of 1924.

In recent years, nevertheless, some scholars have maintained that students of race and ethnicity may attempt to describe their assumptions about human nature without fear of encouraging the belief that group inequalities are genetically based. Gordon (1978:23) stated, for instance, that "a view of human behavior which leans in the direction of biological determinism for individual behavior is also not in the least incompatible with the idea of racial equality," while van den Berghe (1978:15) commented that although "our behavior is . . . highly modifiable through learning. . . ," sociologists ". . . must know the biological limits and predispositions of that behavior."

An evolutionary theory that offers stimulating hypotheses concerning both the biological and cultural roots of ethnocentrism, prejudice, and discrimination was presented by Lopreato (1984:304–314). This theory assumed there are some universal predispositions among human beings that have evolved through biocultural selection because they help to maximize the chances of survival. One such predisposition, *homologous affiliation,* may help to produce the familiar fact that people tend to marry others who are phenotypically and culturally similar to themselves (i.e., *homogamy*). It is true, of course, that sometimes "opposites attract." As a rule, though, similarity wins out (Kephart and Jedlicka 1988:213). Lopreato emphasized that although both cultural and biological factors join to produce this result in different societies and among different groups in societies, the biological elements are the *ultimate* causal forces. The preference that people typically exhibit for mates who are similar to themselves is then expanded, by a process of generalization, to include others of similar ethnicity; hence, the affiliative predisposition that helps to guide people in the choice of reproductive partners also "helps to explain such phenomena as ethnic conflict and ethnocentrism" (Lopreato 1984:310).

Whether or not one accepts a biocultural view of ethnocentrism, the idea that this universal phenomenon is a potent cause of prejudice is, like the other theories reviewed so far, quite plausible, and it easily fits many of the facts of everyday experience. But it, too, has shortcomings. For example, loyalty to one's ethnic in-group is frequently accompanied by an admiration for some specific accomplishments of the members of out-groups (R. Williams 1964:22). "We" may despise "them" and, at the same time, recognize that "they" are quite good at something. Even in the midst of war, for example, a hated enemy may be granted a grudging respect for his or her skill or daring. Such departures from perfect ethnocentrism, however, do not necessarily mean that an enemy out-group that is respected in some particular way is generally rated above the in-group. We may consider ourselves generally superior to them but still concede that they are very good in one particular way. Indeed, some such concession may even be expected to occur on the grounds that little glory is to be gained by defeating a markedly inferior foe. Furthermore, we sometimes admit that they are our superiors but seek, at the same time, to turn this fact to our advantage. For instance, when the Soviet Union successfully launched a space rocket before the United States did, the claim was frequently made that they had stolen the necessary ideas and technology from us. Finally, many cases exist in which in-group members have rejected their own group and joined another. As Robin Williams (1964:23) remarked, "history is replete with voluntary exiles, expatriates, out-group emulators, social climbers, renegades, and traitors."

Self-Hate

Another exception to the rule that ethnocentrism is automatic and universal in a group's members has attracted considerable theoretical attention. Even though in-groups usually react to out-group hostility by becoming prouder, more solidary, and more determined to maintain their social identities, domination by an out-group may lead a number of the in-group's members to accept the oppressor's evaluation of their group and, hence, of themselves. Despite the forces that usually operate to maintain group and individual pride, the effects of ethnocentrism are reversed and subordinate members look up to the dominating group and down on their own group. This condition, which is referred to as *self-hate* (or negative self-image) may begin to develop at an astonishingly early age.

Some very interesting discoveries were based on the use of a technique called the "dolls test," pioneered by Clark and Clark (1939). In the dolls test, children are shown two dolls that are identical except for their skin and hair color. To learn whether children have a color preference, they are asked to hand the researcher "the doll that is a nice color"; to learn whether children are aware of racial differences, they are asked to select "the doll that looks like a white child"; and to discover whether children have identified their own racial group membership, the researcher asks for "the doll that looks like you" (Clark and Clark 1958:602). In a study of 253 black children between the ages of three and seven, Clark and Clark

(1958:603) found, in regard to race awareness, that a large majority (93 percent) of the children could identify the "colored" doll. Despite their high ability to distinguish the two dolls correctly, however, many of the children, particularly the three- and four-year-olds, did not identify themselves as "colored." Among the six- and seven-year-olds, approximately two-thirds did so identify themselves.

Probably the most remarkable findings, though, concerned the children's skin color preferences. At every age level, and despite their own skin color, the majority of these children preferred the white doll to the brown doll. Most of them preferred to play with the white doll, thought that the white doll was "nice," and said that the brown doll "looks bad." These similarities among the different age groups, however, do conceal a difference of great possible significance. The greatest degree of "self-hate" appeared to be among the four- and five-year-olds. Beyond that point, the extent to which the children preferred the white dolls began to decline. When the seven-year-olds were asked to select "the doll that is a nice color," half of them chose the brown doll. This finding may be interpreted as showing that, at some point, self-hate begins to give way to the more "normal" feelings of group pride and self-esteem. It also may be interpreted, however, as showing that preschool children prefer the color white over brown, perhaps because the latter is associated with nighttime (Porter and Washington 1979:56).

A large number of subsequent studies generally supported the Clarks' findings, though many disagreements and contradictions arose in the process. It was confirmed, for example, that preschool children consistently display a strong preference for the color white (see, e.g., Asher and Allen 1969; Fox and Jordan 1973; Porter and Washington 1979).[11] It also was largely confirmed that black children begin to learn early in life that they are members of a despised group and that many of these children reject the symbols of their in-group and attempt to identify with symbols of the dominant white out-group; however, the age-related trend noted by the Clarks was not always found. Some studies found no age-related trend, while others found contradictory trends. Of special interest are findings indicating that the resurgence of efforts to generate "black pride" during the 1960s may sometimes have succeeded in reversing children's negative self-images. Roger Brown (1986:560) stated in this regard that "until 1970 no studies at all found black preference in American children whereas that result has been often reported since."

Although the dolls test has been used in many studies, it is not the only technique developed to study the self-images of black and white children. Horowitz (1936) and Morland (1966), for instance, used pictures of black and white children; more recently, Williams and his colleagues (see, e.g., Williams and Morland 1976) developed "a picture story format" to study this problem. Their main tool is the Preschool Racial Attitudes Measure (PRAM). The PRAM assesses children's racial attitudes by scoring their responses "to stories containing positive or negative evaluative attitudes," such as clean, dirty, good, bad (Williams and Morland 1976:101–102). On the basis of several studies in different parts of the United States, researchers using PRAM found that, on the average, both white and black children show a prowhite, anti-black bias. Taken altogether, the main thrust of much research on the self-esteem of black children supported the Clarks' (1958:608) judgment that children who learn they are members of an inferior group and accept that opinion may experience incalculable, possibly irreversible, damage to their personalities. The U.S. Supreme Court accepted this view in the famous school desegregation case, *Brown v. Board of Education of Topeka* (1954). The Court held that to segregate children "from others of similar age and qualifications solely because of their race generates a feeling of inferiority as to their status in the community that may affect their hearts and minds in a way unlikely ever to be undone" (Osofsky 1968:477).

By 1970, so much research had confirmed the idea that the self-esteem of black children is comparatively low that, as Heiss and Owens (1972:360) stated, it had come to seem "almost unassailable." Nevertheless, a growing body of research has raised questions about this view. McCarthy and Yancey (1971), for instance, suggested that the case for low black self-esteem is very weak. Following their lead, Heiss and Owens (1972:369) analyzed the results of two large-scale surveys and found no evidence "that Blacks are 'crippled' by low self-evaluations." Rosenberg and Simmons (1972) reached the same conclusion in a Baltimore study. Additionally, Lerner and Buehrig (1975:46), using open-end interviews rather than the forced-choice approach of the dolls test and PRAM, did not find that black children had negative self-attitudes. Some researchers believe, in fact, that one might make a stronger case for the idea that blacks have higher average self-esteem than whites (Drury 1980; Simmons 1978). After a thorough review of the literature, Stephan (1988:13) concluded that "four decades of research on self-esteem indicate that blacks do not have lower self-esteem than whites. . . . "

Some other questions raised concerning the earlier findings focused on variations among older and younger children, differences within the black group according to social class position, possible changes that have occurred since the 1960s, problems of research method, and problems of ambiguous concepts and theory (Broman, Neighbors, and Jackson 1988). In regard to the latter point, for instance, Porter and Washington (1979) argued that the concepts of self-hate and self-esteem have not been subjected to sufficient analysis. They also found, as noted previously, that the more recent studies show that adolescent and adult blacks now have a more favorable view of their blackness than was true at the time of the earlier studies. Hughes and Demo (1989:133) emphasized the importance of distinguishing the aspect of self-esteem that represents *personal worth* from the aspect that represents *personal control*.[12] They argued that feelings of high personal worth may coexist with feelings of low personal control and concluded that racial inequality has a much greater effect on the latter element than on the former (Hughes and Demo 1989:154). These newer findings may mean that the determinants of self-esteem have shifted during the past three decades, or they may mean that the methods of the earlier studies were invalid and led to mistaken conclusions (Bachman and O'Malley 1984). Clearly, a great deal more work on this important topic is needed before we conclude, with Adam (1978:48), that "the 1970s overturned the tradition epitomized by the Clarks."

Which Theory Is Best?

What conclusion may be reached from this brief review regarding the causes of prejudice? Evidently, many factors are at work. The culture of a society contains many ideas and beliefs concerning various racial and ethnic groups, and these ideas may be transmitted more or less intact from one generation to the next. Children learn these traditions as a natural and normal part of growing up. Moreover, since these traditions are indistinguishable in children's experience from the development of their own sense of self and are rooted in their basic sense of group membership or identity, children generally embrace the group's traditions as their own. Still further, many individuals regularly use the members of particular out-groups as scapegoats against whom their frustrations may be vented. Hence, one important conclusion regarding the diverse theories of prejudice is: "Each has something to teach us. None possesses a monopoly of insight" (Allport 1958:212).

For both intellectual and practical reasons, however, we wish to know more than this. Is prejudice best explained from a sociocultural perspective (as illustrated by the cultural transmission and group identification theories) or from a psychological perspective (as illustrated by the frustration-aggression theory)? Or is it the case that a given type of theory affords a better explanation in some contexts than in others? A study by Middleton (1976) illustrates one approach to answering these difficult questions. Middleton started with the fact that white southerners exhibit a much higher average level of prejudice against blacks than nonsoutherners but that the regions of the United States differ little in regard to prejudice toward Jews, Catholics, and immigrants. His analysis showed, first, that sociocultural factors are the most important determinants of the higher level of prejudice against blacks in the South; second, that these same factors play the greatest role in creating anti-black prejudice throughout the United States; but that, third, psychological factors operate in similar ways in each region to produce different levels of individual prejudice. These findings illustrate how *one* type of theory (sociocultural) may be shown to be the best explanation of *one* type of difference (between regions) for *one* type of prejudice (antiblack). In this way, the assumption that prejudice has many causes is refined, developed, and elaborated.

So far we have focused on prejudice and have assumed that (1) the reduction or elimination of discrimination requires an understanding of its causes; (2) prejudice is the cause of discrimination; and, therefore, (3) to reduce or eliminate discrimination, one must first attack prejudice and its causes. We did raise the question, however, of the extent to which prejudice is, in fact, the cause of discrimination, and now we must note that the pattern of causation depicted in Figures 6-1 and 6-2 is seriously deficient. Instead of placing all of our emphasis on the effect of prejudice on discrimination, we should place at least equal emphasis on the reverse pattern.

Figure 6-3 suggests two conclusions that run counter to the idea that prejudice is the sole cause of discrimination. First, three entirely new types of factors are now shown on the right side of the figure as causes of discrimination. This indicates that certain causal factors may generate discrimination directly rather than indirectly

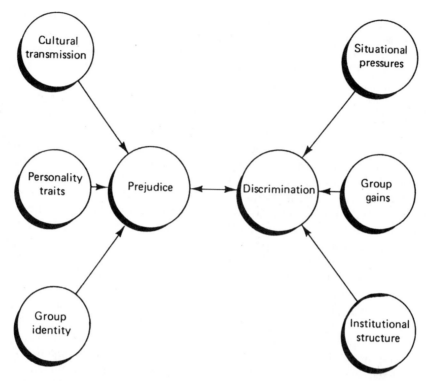

FIGURE 6-3   Major direct and indirect causes of prejudice and discrimination (arrows indicate the presumed direction of causation)

through a prior effect on prejudice. The second important feature is the arrow pointing from discrimination to prejudice. This suggests the interesting conclusion that discrimination is a cause of prejudice!

Theories of Discrimination

We have seen several ways in which prejudice, however generated, may lead to discrimination. But how can this process be reversed? A simple illustration from everyday life should help to clarify this idea.

Our discussion of cultural transmission emphasized that children just seem to absorb the "knowledge" that different ethnic groups possess specific traits and occupy different rungs on the ladder of social importance. Children also learn an enormous amount through imitation. They see their parents, older siblings, and neighbors performing certain acts, and they mimic those acts. In many of these cases, children literally do not know what they are doing. More important for our argument, though, is that in many cases children's actions are not accompanied by the same emotions and feelings that are present in the person they are imitating. Children "go through the motions," so to speak. They do not necessarily understand why the action is being performed and may have inner experiences during the act that are quite unlike those of the "model."

Applying this observation to the matter of prejudice and discrimination, we see that children frequently learn to hurl an epithet (or a rock) at members of an out-group *before* they know who they are attacking or why. The discriminatory act, in this instance, precedes the "appropriate" or expected internal condition. Only gradually, through direct and indirect instruction, does the child come to experience the prejudice he or she is "supposed" to feel. Once the prejudice is learned, the child may then experience it as coming before a given act of discrimination. The individual, thus, may say to others (and believe) that he or she has discriminated because he or she thinks or feels a particular way; however, from a broader perspective, the feeling of prejudice that precedes a given act of discrimination may itself have been preceded by certain acts of discrimination.

This is not the only (perhaps not even the main) way that discrimination may lead to prejudice. Discrimination by those who are wealthy and powerful may create other group differences that then foster prejudice. Myrdal ([1944]1964:1066) illustrated this point as follows. Assume, first, that the relationship of the white and black groups in America is determined *in part* by some degree of "racial prejudice" on the side of the whites directed against the blacks. Assume next that the standard of living among blacks is below that among whites and that this fact is itself due to discrimination by whites against blacks. Under these conditions, Myrdal contended, the lower standard of living among blacks stimulates and feeds "the antipathy of the whites for them." The discrimination of the whites, in this illustration, created conditions that generated prejudice which, in turn, afforded the foundation for further discrimination. Prejudice and discrimination formed a *vicious circle*. Whether one begins an analysis of race relations in America with prejudice or with discrimination, the result is the same. Each side of the prejudice-discrimination equation "feeds back" on the other side. Each side, then, "causes" the other in a circular and—from the standpoint of democratic values—vicious way. With these ideas as a background, let us move now to a consideration of the three types of theories of discrimination (which indirectly are also types of theories of prejudice) shown in Figure 6-3.

Situational Pressures Theories of Discrimination

This type of theory of discrimination is based on the well-known fact that people's "preaching" may not always correspond to their "practicing." There frequently is a discrepancy or gap between the creed and the deed. A common example of the *creed-deed discrepancy* arises when a person professes to have little or no ethnic prejudice but, in fact, discriminates in some situations. A familiar example of this point is the dominant group member who feels it is necessary for social reasons to avoid frequent, open association with members of minority groups. Such a person may confide, "I am not prejudiced, you understand; some of my best friends are _____ ; but what would my family and neighbors think?" This example illustrates a simple, but fundamental, sociological idea: *the social pressures exerted on individuals in different social situations may cause them to vary their behavior in ways that do not correspond to their inner beliefs and preferences*. When applied to racial and ethnic relations, this idea suggests that whether people discriminate or not may depend more on the characteristics and demands of the social situation than on their levels of prejudice. Once again we see that either to infer prejudice from a given act of discrimination or to infer tolerance from a failure to discriminate may be a mistake.

The type of creed-deed discrepancy in which people claim to be less prejudiced than they really are is what one would expect in a society in which the standards of fairness hold that people should be judged on merit; for that reason, many professions of tolerance in America are "taken with a grain of salt" (i.e., are considered to be hypocritical). Strangely enough, though, the gap between preaching and practicing also may arise in a second, and opposite, manner. People may actually claim in some situations to be more prejudiced than their actions would imply!

A seminal exploration of this second type of creed-deed discrepancy was conducted by LaPiere (1934). LaPiere and a Chinese couple traveled some ten thousand miles together in the United States, stopping at 66 hotels and other tourist accommodations and at 184 restaurants and cafes. Despite the high levels of prejudice and discrimination against the Chinese in the United States at that time, they were refused service only once in 251 instances. After the trip was over, LaPiere mailed questionnaires to all of the proprietors involved, asking whether they would accept as customers "members of the Chinese race." Among those who answered the questionnaire (51 percent), 92 percent of the hotel proprietors and 93 percent of the restaurant proprietors stated they *would not* accept Chinese as guests! In other words, the vast majority of a group of proprietors who already had demonstrated they would sometimes accept Chinese guests claimed they would discriminate if faced with the choice.

Why would some Americans wish to be thought less tolerant than they are? Perhaps the answer goes something like this: in the actual situations, many social elements came into play. The Chinese couple did not fit the prevailing negative stereotype, they were accompanied by a distinguished-looking white man, they were well-dressed, and they looked prosperous. Under these conditions, and despite the high levels of prejudice then prevalent against the Chinese, the travelers met almost no discrimination; but in the hypothetical situation described in the questionnaire, the proprietors' stereotypes, prejudices, and fears of dominant group disapproval were not restrained by concrete circumstances. The discrepancies between the proprietors' fair treatment of the Chinese guests and their statements that they would discriminate probably were due more to the characteristics of the actual and hypothetical situations than to the proprietors' individual levels of prejudice.

A number of other investigators pursued the problem raised by LaPiere's study: Why do people's attitudes and actions frequently fail to correspond? What other factors enter the picture to create this inconsistency? Lohman and Reitzes (1952:242), for instance, argued that in modern industrial society "attitudes toward minority groups may be of little consequence in explaining an individual's behavior." To test this idea, they studied the behavior of a sample of white workers in Chicago. The study was designed to compare the attitudes and behavior of workers who were members of a union that admitted blacks without reservation but who lived in a neighborhood where black residents were unwelcome. As members of the union, the workers were expected by other union members to ignore racial differences and to stand together on such common interests as wages and working conditions. As residents of the neighborhood, the workers were expected by their neighbors to act on the assumption that admitting blacks to the neighborhood as residents would lower property values. The results of the study showed that group membership was more important than individual attitudes. In the job situation, the workers seemed to agree with the official view of their union and to encourage all workers to unite for their common advantage, that is, to be unprejudiced; at home, however, the workers seemed to accept the official view of the neighborhood improvement association and to reject blacks as neighbors.

The studies by LaPiere and Lohman and Reitzes demonstrated that prejudice and discrimination do not necessarily go together. Discrimination may not occur when prejudice is present, and it may occur when prejudice is absent. In either case, a serious objection is raised to the presumption that prejudice is "the" cause of discrimination. To study this problem under more controlled conditions, several investigators performed social experiments concerning the relationship of prejudice to discrimination. In one influential study, DeFleur and Westie (1958) asked forty-six white students to participate in a nationwide campaign for racial integration. Twenty-three of the students had very unfavorable attitudes toward blacks, and the remaining twenty-three had very favorable attitudes. To test the extent of a person's willingness to act in a manner consistent with his or her prejudice level, the researchers asked the students to be photographed with a black person of the opposite sex and to sign release agreements to permit the pictures to be used in various phases of the campaign. The study showed that prejudice was positively related to discrimination (i.e., unwillingness to sign the releases); however, it also revealed that nine of the presumably unprejudiced students were less willing than the average to have their photographs used and that five of the presumably prejudiced students were more willing than the average to release their photographs. DeFleur and Westie interpreted these discrepancies in terms of differing peer group pressures.

A later study by Linn (1965) followed the method developed by DeFleur and Westie. He found, as had DeFleur and Westie, a large number of cases in which a person's verbal attitude did not match his or her willingness to sign a release to permit the photograph to be used under different circumstances. Linn (1965:364) agreed that different peer pressures were an important cause of these discrepancies but suggested that differences in role expectations were probably also important.

Green (1972) also used the photograph release approach and found that, regardless of their expressed racial attitude, white people's willingness to pose with a black person of the opposite sex diminished as the pose became more intimate. Green agreed with DeFleur and Westie that peer pressures in different social situations lead to inconsistencies between expressed attitudes and actual behavior. Warner and DeFleur (1969:154) proposed that although attitudes do play a role in causing behavior, such things as social norms, group memberships, and other situational factors also affect the relationship.[13]

These studies show that people who claim to be unprejudiced may, under some conditions, discriminate, but also that people who claim to be prejudiced may not discriminate. The specific social pressures arising in particular situations seem, in many instances, to outweigh personal prejudice as a cause of discrimination. This observation reveals a very interesting and important point about the way human beings (even social scientists!) reason about the causes of their own and other people's behavior. Most of us have a strong tendency "to underestimate the impact of situational factors and to overestimate the importance of internal dispositional factors" (R. Brown 1986:169). This tendency, called *the fundamental attribution error,* has been demonstrated in many studies (R. Brown 1986:176).

Since some of these ideas depart from common-sense reasoning, let us organize them in an illuminating way suggested by Merton (1949). Although people's levels of prejudice and discrimination actually range from extremely high to extremely low, for convenience we may think of them as being either high or low in each respect. By combining the two resulting dichotomies, any given individual may be classified or "typed" as (1) a prejudiced discriminator—high in prejudice, high in discrimination; (2) a prejudiced nondiscriminator—high in prejudice, low in discrimination; (3) an unprejudiced discriminator—low in prejudice, high in discrimination; or (4) an unprejudiced nondiscriminator—low in prejudice, low in discrimination. In the study by Lohman and Reitzes, the union workers who seemed to be low in prejudice but who nevertheless discriminated in the neighborhood setting appear to illustrate type 3, the unprejudiced discriminator. And in the study conducted by LaPiere, the proprietors who seemed to be prejudiced but did not discriminate in certain actual settings appear to illustrate type 2, the prejudiced nondiscriminator.

These observations are not intended to show that prejudice and discrimination never or seldom occur together. The existence of types 1 and 4 remind us, as is ordinarily supposed, that in many—possibly most—cases, people who are low in prejudice also are low in discrimination. But notice that the existence of people who actually are high in both prejudice and discrimination does not tell us the direction of causation. It is just as easy to assume in such cases that discrimination led to prejudice as it is to assume the reverse.

Situational pressures theories evidently differ from the three types of theories of prejudice discussed previously. Not only do they focus on behavior rather than on attitudes, they also emphasize the current determinants of behavior rather than those growing out of the socialization process. Nevertheless, they do share with the other types of theories one important characteristic. In each of the four types of theories considered thus far, our primary interest was the attitudes or behavior of *individuals*. Individuals learn stereotypes and social distance norms; individuals develop personality needs that may predispose them to becoming prejudiced; individuals respond to situational pressures and behave in discriminatory ways. As valuable as they are, these theories divert attention from the fact that people also are members of broad groups in a society that may be competing with one another for the possession of many desired ends—such things as property, prestige, and power. These intergroup conflicts arise from the fact that different groups occupy more or less favorable positions in the social order (or structure) and wish either to maintain or to improve those positions. Our two remaining types of theories focus on the consequences of *structural* factors as determinants of discrimination and, indirectly, of prejudice.

Group Gains Theories of Discrimination

In chapters 2 and 3 we noted briefly how the American Indians and Europeans struggled for possession of the land, and in chapters 4 and 5 we saw how the fear that immigrants would take jobs away from Americans was related to nativist movements and campaigns to restrict immigration. These conflicts between groups for the control of land and jobs, to name only two important resources, led to relatively fixed social arrangements in which the members of the more powerful groups enjoyed greater privileges and higher social standing than those of the less powerful groups. A system of ethnic domination and subordination (or stratification) had been born.

Noel (1968) argued that the combination of differences in group power, competition for scarce resources, and ethnocentrism invariably leads to this result. Presumably, moreover, such a system of stratification not only comes into existence but endures because the dominant groups "get something" out of it. To illustrate, if minority group workers are forced into the hardest, dirtiest, lowest-paying jobs, then majority group workers may occupy the "better" jobs and thereby realize an economic gain (Glenn 1966:161). Quite aside from any feelings of antipathy or hatred that the majority group workers may harbor or develop, they may discriminate because they, and perhaps all of the other members of their group, gain by such actions. Any feelings of antipathy or hatred that exist may themselves be understood as "secondary to the conflict for society's goodies" (Lieberson 1980:382).

Two issues are of special interest in regard to economic gains. First, the historical record we have reviewed leaves little room for doubt that the members of given minority groups (e.g., African and Mexican Americans) usually have received lower economic rewards than they would have in the absence of discrimination. One still may wonder, nonetheless, about the answer to the following question: "Do African Americans and Mexican Americans still 'pay a price' for being members of minorities?" If the answer to this question is "yes," then we may ask a second question: "If the members of the majority gain economically through discrimination, who benefits most—the employers or the dominant group workers?" Taken at face value, the answer to the first question seems obvious: "Yes, minority group workers do pay a price in the job market." For instance, the median[14] income of black families in the United States in 1990 was $24,089, while the median for white families was $35,811 (Barringer 1992:A1). The ratio of these two medians ($24,089/$35,811) is .63, which shows that, overall, black families received 63 cents for every dollar received by white families.

A moment's reflection will reveal, however, that this income difference, by itself, does not demonstrate the presence of discrimination by whites. There may be other pertinent differences between blacks and whites, such as in education or experience, that must be taken into account if we are to understand what produces the overall difference in family income. Several studies along this line have been conducted, and in chapters 9 and 11 we will consider some of their results. For the present, though, and in anticipation of the finding that there is still discrimination against blacks and Mexican Americans in the job market, let's focus attention here on the second question, "Who benefits most?"

Many writers have followed Karl Marx in asserting that the main beneficiaries of dominant group discrimination are the employers (the upper, ruling, or capitalist class). In a system of discrimination, the majority workers will receive higher pay than the minority workers, but the majority workers' belief that they are profiting from the system is an illusion based on short-term calculations. White employers encourage the hostility of the dominant group workers toward minority workers because the employers benefit in several ways. They apply the ancient maxim "divide and rule." They are enabled by the presence of a large, inexpensive labor pool to cut costs and increase profits. And they are afforded a "mask for privilege," a set of justifications for posing as the friends of the oppressed while not giving minority group workers a larger share of the economic pie (Simpson and Yinger 1972:127). The net result for the dominant group workers, the argument runs, is that their share of the pie is actually smaller in the long run than it would be if they united with the minority workers against their common oppressor. Hence, the white upper class deliberately promotes ethnic prejudices and racist ideas to separate the majority and minority workers and cause them to behave "irrationally," i.e., against their own best interests. By accepting the idea that the minority workers are their enemies, the majority workers do not perceive that their real enemy—the source of their own frustrations and low rewards—is the ruling class. Beck (1980:148) summarized this position as follows: "Racism in a capitalist society is an ideology fostered and maintained by employers to insure the fractionalization of the working class. . . ."

Many other writers reject the Marxian analysis and argue, instead, that high discrimination levels among white workers actually serve to increase their economic rewards, just as they suppose (Myrdal [1944]1964:68). This theme was pursued in a persuasive way by Bonacich (1972; 1973; 1975; 1976). She agreed with the Marxian writers that economic forces are at the root of ethnic antagonisms but disagreed that the conflict between white and black workers is economically "irrational." She attacked the Marxian notion that capitalists deliberately create a division between different groups of workers to subordinate them both. After all, if the employers of labor actually adopt such a strategy, then they must pay one group of workers (e.g., whites) more than is necessary, thus increasing their operating costs and reducing their profits. Why, Bonacich (1976:44) asked, would employers adopt such a "convoluted" strategy?

Her alternative theory stated that the antagonism of white workers toward black workers (among others) stems from the fact that the price of the workers' labor in the two groups differs *initially,* and that the capitalist class does not *create* but is *faced with* a "split labor market" (Bonacich 1972:549). A split labor market is characterized by conflict among three key groups: business people (capitalists), higher paid labor (e.g., whites), and cheaper labor (e.g., blacks) (Bonacich 1972:553). In these terms, the main economic interests of the two laboring groups are not essentially alike (as in the Marxian analysis), they are fundamentally different. Higher paid labor is genuinely threatened by the presence of cheaper labor. The latter may undercut the higher paid laborers by doing the same work at lower wages, as dominant group workers frequently claim. Since it is in the interest of the capitalist class to cut costs by hiring the least expensive workers, the capitalists may substitute the cheaper workers for the higher paid ones. Moreover, if the higher paid workers attempt to improve their wages and working conditions by organizing and striking, the employers may easily turn to the "reserve army" of the cheaper laborers to recruit strikebreakers. By using the cheaper laborers to undercut wages and to break strikes, the employers may undermine the position of the higher paid workers (Bonacich 1972:554; 1976:40; Boswell 1986:352–353).

How can the higher paid laborers control the quite real threat against them posed by the cheaper laborers? Two main methods are available. The first is simply to exclude the cheaper laborers from the territory in which the higher paid laborers work. This method frequently has been employed by workers all over the world. We have seen already, in chapter 5, that the United States excluded Chinese labor beginning in 1882, and we shall see in chapter 8 that the same strategy was used later against the Japanese. In both cases, the hostility of the white workers, rather than of the employers, provided the force behind the exclusionist efforts.

The second main method used by higher paid labor to combat cheaper labor in a split labor market is to "reserve" certain jobs for members of the higher paid group. Thus, certain jobs may become "white jobs," while others become "black jobs." If the higher paid group is sufficiently well-organized and powerful, it may be able to gain the employers' acceptance of this division of jobs and to permit the higher paid group to decide which jobs will be held exclusively by members of one laboring group or the other. Alternatively, the higher paid laborers may succeed in having the members of the two groups do the same work but at different rates of pay. By these methods, a rigid, castelike system of employment is developed.

A number of other studies have sought to discover whether the employers or the dominant group workers gain most by a system of discrimination (see, e.g., Semyonov and Cohen 1990). Although the researchers have adopted various approaches, sources of information, and techniques of analysis, the problem has proven difficult to solve; consequently our treatment of the complexities that have arisen in the process is necessarily greatly simplified. However, the logic of this type of inquiry may be illustrated through a brief description of studies completed by Glenn (1963; 1966) and Dowdall (1974) that covered two decades of experience in the United States.

To answer the question, "Do specific groups of whites gain from the fact that blacks are kept down and, if so, how?" Glenn and Dowdall examined data on a large number of cities in the United States for the years 1950, 1960, and 1970. The basic idea behind these studies is that if white people gain in various ways from the subordination of blacks, then the whites' advantage should be greater in cities having a relatively large black population. Where the black population is relatively large, whites should hold a higher proportion of high-prestige jobs, have higher incomes, and experience lower unemployment.

Glenn's analyses strongly supported the conclusion that in the middle of the twentieth century, urban white Americans still were gaining occupationally and economically through the subordination of African Americans. These effects were greater in southern cities, where the proportions of blacks were generally larger, than in northern and western cities. The gains to whites, however, were not evenly distributed. The groups that appeared to benefit most by the subordination of blacks "are middle-class Southern housewives and white workers in proprietary, managerial, sales, and upper-level manual occupations" (Glenn 1966:177). These advantages to whites, moreover, apparently were undiminished by the great efforts to create social changes during the 1960s. Dowdall (1974:181) reported, on the basis of data gathered in 1970, that "whites continued to benefit from the subordinate position of blacks by gaining higher occupational status, lower unemployment, and higher family income; Southern employers, overwhelmingly white, still seemed to gain from blacks in reduced labor costs."

The main results of Glenn's and Dowdall's studies agree, but it is not clear whether the findings strengthen the Marxian or split labor market interpretations of black-white economic conflict. While Glenn (1966:177) concluded that "the findings of this study do not support the Marxist view that discrimination . . . benefits the 'capitalist class' but hurts white workers," Dowdall (1974:182) maintained that both his and Glenn's analyses "seem completely consistent" with the view that "gains accrue more rapidly to those at the top."

The latter interpretation was supported in subsequent studies by Reich (1971) and Szymanski (1976) but not supported in studies by Beck (1980) and Semyonov and Cohen (1990). Reich and Szymanski found that although some aspects of black-white economic conflict serve to raise the earnings of white workers, these gains are, on balance, more than offset by the resulting weakening of the labor movement. Their studies showed that the more white workers discriminate against blacks, the more the white workers themselves are injured economically. Szymanski (1976:413) concluded that "the Marxist theory of the effect of racial discrimination of white workers is thus partially borne out." In opposition, however, Beck (1980:164) and Semyonov and Cohen (1990:113–114) presented evidence showing that dominant group workers do benefit by discrimination, though the latter study found (as had Glenn's) that the gains were greater for some dominant group workers than others.[15] Although the evidence is not decisive, it seems likely that the antagonism between majority group and minority group workers in the United States "is and will long remain partly a matter of realistic conflict" (Glenn 1966:178). Consequently, as shown by Burr, Galle, and Fossett (1991:844), as the relative size of the minority population increases (and becomes more visible) in a given location, dominant group discrimination and the levels of inequality between the groups also increase.

Most of the controversy regarding the possibility that whites gain through the subordination of blacks and other minorities has centered on the matter of economic gains, but the debate is not limited to this issue. In a pioneering analysis of white gains, Dollard (1957) argued that whites gained not only economically but in other ways as well. For instance, throughout most of the history of the United States, especially in the South, white men realized a "sexual gain" because they had sexual access to black women, while sexual relations between black men and white women were taboo. Citing still another advantage whites enjoyed over blacks, the "prestige gain," Dollard (1957:173–187) emphasized that the traditions of the South required black people to be completely submissive in the presence of whites. Indeed, the traditional southern "etiquette of race relations" (Doyle 1937) even required that blacks smother the whites in adulation. Any white person—no matter how young or unaccomplished—could address all black people—no matter how old or accomplished—by their first names. Blacks, on the other hand, always were required to address whites by titles of respect—they were expected to say "sir" or "m'am" and to show continuous agreement by saying "yes, Boss," "sho nuff," "well, I declare," and the like (Dollard 1957:180). Black people always were expected to defer to the wishes of white people and to praise their goodness, wit, and skill. Under these circumstances, the whites regularly received the satisfactions that come to human beings who believe themselves to be superior and are so treated. All of these requirements guaranteed prestige supremacy. No matter how low a white person was in the "pecking order," he or she was still above all of the blacks. Blacks who did not behave in the expected ways were regarded as "uppity" and "getting out of their place" (Dollard 1957:175). Such behavior was considered a challenge to the entire southern system of white supremacy.

Dollard's analysis seems quite compelling. But even here, as in the case of economic gains, it is not certain that the sexual, social, and psychological gains for whites of the white supremacy system completely outweighed their costs, especially in the long run. There are many noneconomic costs involved in maintaining a castelike system of subordination, and many of these costs are extraordinarily difficult to measure. To raise only one possibility, could it be true that the costs to the dominant group in feelings of guilt, fear, and anxiety have been so large as to counterbalance whatever satisfactions they may have received? This theme has been pursued in many works of literature, as well as in social science. For example, Lillian Smith (1963:28) stated in a moving passage: "I began to understand slowly at first but more clearly as the years passed, that the warped, distorted frame we have put around every Negro child from birth is around every white child also. . . . And I know that what cruelly shapes and cripples the personality of one is as cruelly shaping and crippling the personality of the other." The penetrating insight of the gifted writer thus suggests paths of understanding that the social scientist may, perhaps, only strive to walk upon.

Taken together, the results of the many studies and literary insights concerning the total effects of the system of white supremacy in the United States afford a basis for the claim that, however misguided they may be, the members of the dominant group have discriminated systematically against the members of subordinate racial and ethnic groups because the discriminators seem to gain by it. The prejudice generated by this intergroup conflict is then used to help explain and justify the fact that such social arrangements are, in a very broad sense, profitable for many, if not all, members of the dominant group.

Whether these conclusions are correct is a matter of considerable practical importance. If white workers or white employers do not truly gain by possessing ethnic prejudices and by discriminating, then they have, in fact, a strong incentive to discontinue such beliefs and practices. From this vantage point, one may argue that when people are properly educated so as to see correctly their own true interests, they may then cooperate to bring about needed social changes. On the other hand, if any substantial segment of the dominant group is realizing actual gains from the system of subordination, then they may be expected to resist changes tooth and nail.

Although the emphasis in group gains theories is on the relative gains and losses among groups that occupy different positions in the social structure, rather than on the attitudes and behavior of individuals, they nevertheless contain (in this form) the assumption that prejudice plays an important role as an accompaniment to and justification for discrimination. Moreover, from this perspective, the forms of intergroup discrimination are comparatively overt. One may locate specific individuals within the dominant group who refuse to hire or promote minority workers, who pay minority workers less than dominant workers for performing the same job, who demand sexual favors in return for employment, and so on. However, some scholars have argued that even if, miraculously, such "nonstructural" factors as individual prejudice and overt discrimination were to be completely eliminated, the normal operation of American society would still guarantee a high level of discrimination against subordinate racial and ethnic groups. Even if no one tried to discriminate, the argument runs, our traditional social arrangements—our institutions—would ensure discriminatory results.

We will illustrate the application of this version of "structuralist" thought to the problems of discrimination in our final type of theory—one which, if accepted, has profound implications for practical actions to reduce discrimination and prejudice.

Institutional Structure Theories of Discrimination

American racial and ethnic relations entered a critical period during the 1960s and, as the rioting in Los Angeles and other cities in the spring of 1992 reminded us, were still unsettled over a quarter of a century later. The events of both periods may have been generated to a considerable extent by an apparent inconsistency or paradox. By the mid-1960s, the Civil Rights Movement had scored numerous successes, especially on the legal front, symbolized by the 1954 Supreme Court school desegregation order in *Brown v. Board of Education of Topeka*. During the same period, national opinion polls showed that white Americans were becoming less prejudiced. A study conducted by scholars at the National Opinion Research Center (NORC), for example, found that public approval of school desegregation had risen from 30 percent in 1942 to 63 percent in 1963, and by 1982, 90 percent of all Americans accepted the principle of school desegregation (Schuman, Steeh, and Bobo 1985:75, 77). The NORC study also found that whites' approval of neighborhood desegregation had risen from 35 percent in 1942 to 64 percent in 1963 (Hyman and Sheatsley 1964:18–19). By 1976, 88 percent of the whites who were questioned in a study conducted by the Institute for Social Research (ISR) agreed that black people have a right to live wherever they can afford. In 1984, the overall level of anti-black prejudice had declined to the lowest level on record (Firebaugh and Davis 1988:261).[16] The paradox is that despite these many evidences of declines in prejudice, white Americans still seem generally unwilling to support "policies promoting racial economic equality" (Kluegel 1990:513).

These shifts in attitudes may have been part of a general shift among Americans in the direction of a greater tolerance of diversity.[17] Alternatively, the decline in prejudice revealed by public opinion polls may have been another illustration of the type of distortion, mentioned earlier, called social desirability bias. Several writers have emphasized that "old-style bigotry" now has "a disreputable image": expressions of racial and ethnic prejudice today are "generally more subtle, indirect and ostensibly nonracial" (Pettigrew and Martin 1987:46); "old-fashioned racism" may have been replaced by a much more guarded "modern racism" (Dovidio and Gaertner 1986). Dominant group members now are more likely to argue that the problems faced by African Americans are evidence of insufficient effort rather than a sign of genetic inferiority (Kluegel 1990:513).[18] Although majority group members generally reject global stereotypes and blatant forms of discrimination, they still oppose fundamental changes in race relations. The targets of their opposition have not changed, but these targets now are attacked indirectly rather than directly (Pettigrew and Martin 1989:171–172). For example, opponents of school desegregation may agree to the abstract principle that school desegregation is desirable but, at the same time, insist that this objective should be reached through neighborhood desegregation rather than through busing. In the meantime, most actual efforts to expand either busing or neighborhood desegregation are opposed; hence, the apparently nonracist acceptance of the goal of desegregating schools may be a "front" for continuing, more carefully veiled racism.

During this entire period of apparently decreasing prejudice and increasing opportunity, some members of minority groups (and in particular many African Americans, Mexican, and Native Americans) noticed that significant improvements were not taking place in their own lives. The rate of improvement seemed, at best, painfully slow,[19] and in many ways, after a period of improvement, there followed a period of decline. For example, a *Newsweek* poll published in April 1992 (Morganthau et al. 1992:21) found that 51 percent of African Americans felt that the quality of life for them had gotten worse during the preceding ten years. The article also repeated some generally known, but still sobering, figures concerning the very high rates among blacks of infant mortality, homicide, and imprisonment. An important question that loomed in the minds of many people was, "How can so many changes occur in the laws and in the attitudes of the majority but not be reflected in the actual living conditions of some of the members of minority groups?"

An intriguing answer to this question was presented by Carmichael and Hamilton (1967) in their influential book *Black Power.* The answer these authors suggested is that the ordinary operations of American institutions discriminate against subordinate groups. Schools, hospitals, factories, banks, and so on do not need to be staffed by prejudiced people to achieve discriminatory results. For example, most employers have certain formal educational requirements for hiring, such as a high school or college diploma. When these requirements are applied uniformly (and many would add "fairly") to all those who apply, the *automatic* result is to exclude those who have been deprived of an equal opportunity to gain the necessary credentials. If people have been subject to discrimination in the schools, then they are less likely to have graduated; therefore, they cannot qualify for a job that requires a diploma. Even if the people who conduct the hiring procedure are completely tolerant as individuals, the rules of the organization they represent will require them to accept only those who have proper diplomas, test scores, certificates, and so on. In this case, we see that the discrimination that occurs in one institutional setting may carry over into or have side effects on a related institutional setting (Feagin 1977). To carry the matter further, a father's difficulties in finding employment may lead his son to drop out of school to go to work. The son, too, may then later encounter the same employment problems as the father. Here we see how unintentional discrimination may place a vicious circle into operation both within and between generations.

Another type of institutional discrimination in employment arises because the members of a minority "lack some ability or qualification intentionally denied to them in the past" (Feagin 1977:189). If an employer requires that a person must have worked in one job for ten years to be qualified for another job, anyone who was deliberately excluded from the first job cannot possibly be qualified for the second. For instance, for a very long time, African Americans have had the experience of being "the last hired and the first fired." During periods of economic expansion, employers frequently have not hired black workers until no other workers were available. Then, during slack periods, the black workers frequently were the first to lose their jobs. Under these circumstances, it was very difficult for black workers to accumulate the years of seniority needed to qualify for many jobs. Therefore, wherever seniority rules are used in hiring and firing—even when such rules are applied uniformly—the black workers are at a disadvantage. The employers in this situation may be able to say truthfully that they are not prejudiced and are not discriminating, even though the application of the seniority rules may work to the disadvantage of the black workers. Just as an economic depression may be precipitated by millions of individual decisions that were not intended to produce a depression, this unintended outcome is caused, in Friedman's (1975:384) phrase, by "social laws no one passed." Consequently, as Ellison and London (1992:687) state, "Current struggles increasingly center on less obvious forms of institutional racism that injure more specific segments of the black population."

Note that the main claim of institutional discrimination theories is that current prejudice is not required to keep the system of discrimination intact. They acknowledge that prejudice initially may have played a key role in producing the existing system and do not deny that prejudice still produces some discrimination.[20] The central idea was expressed by Baron (1969:144) as follows: "There is a carefully articulated interrelation of the barriers created by each institution. Whereas the single institutional strand standing alone might not be so strong, the many strands together form a powerful web."

Both group gains theories and institutional discrimination theories emphasize that discrimination has important sources other than individual prejudice. This idea is exceptionally important in the present period. Many white Americans now recognize that their forefathers profited from discrimination against blacks and other minorities; some also acknowledge that the effects of past discrimination have not been entirely erased. It is not always easy to see, however, that even as prejudice levels decline, intergroup competition and traditional institutional arrangements may continue as before and may benefit all members of the dominant group. Consequently, the complaint frequently is heard, "I haven't discriminated against anyone, so why should I pay for the mistakes of the past?" The answer supported by "structural" theories is that white Americans still receive a direct "bonus" for being white even if they do nothing to "earn" it or are unaware they have received it.

We turn now, in chapter 7, to a consideration of actions that may be taken to reduce racial and ethnic prejudice and discrimination.

Key Ideas

1. Although prejudice (a negative attitude) is usually thought to precede and be the cause of discrimination (a negative action), discrimination may also precede prejudice and be a cause of it. Moreover, a person may be prejudiced but not discriminate and discriminate without being prejudiced.

2. Prejudice arises from several sources. Among the most important of these are:

   a. The transmission of specific attitudes and beliefs from one generation to the next—Children learn their group's stereotypes of different out-groups. They also learn which groups are to be admired and which should be held at a great social distance. In the United States, people from countries of the old immigration are socially least distant from the majority, while nonwhites are the most distant.

   b. The effort to manage the personal frustrations and problems of life—People frequently exhibit an exaggerated, seemingly "irrational" hostility toward members of out-groups. Such prejudices appear to have more to do with people's inner tensions and conflicts than with the characteristics of the members of the hated group(s).

   c. The sense of group identity, belongingness, and loyalty that people ordinarily develop toward their own group's members and culture—Pride in one's own group may easily shade into or stimulate prejudice toward others' groups.

3. Discrimination arises from several important sources, some of which do not directly involve prejudice:

   a. The social pressures that are exerted to ensure people's conformity to the norms of their group—Even when people do not personally desire to ostracize or harm the members of an out-group, they may be expected to do so by the other members of their own group. Those who violate the in-group norms may themselves be ostracized by the in-group members.

   b. The material and psychic gains that accompany social dominance—Whether or not it is owing to prejudice, discrimination confers advantages on at least some members of the dominant group. Dominant group members generally enjoy higher incomes, more desirable jobs, less unemployment, and more social deference than the members of subordinate groups.

   c. The normal operations of the society's institutions—Equal opportunity and fair play within a given institutional sector (e.g., the economy) may not lead to equal results. The lingering effects of past discrimination or the existence of discrimination in a related institution (e.g., education) may lead to the disproportionate disqualification of the members of minority groups. The rules of organizations may automatically discriminate.

4. Prejudice and discrimination are related to one another in an incomplete and circular fashion. Discrimination may be reduced by attacks on prejudice, and prejudice may be reduced by attacks on discrimination; however, declines in prejudice are not necessarily translated into reductions in discrimination, and vice versa.

Notes

1. This idea is so prevalent that in many cases discrimination is defined as the acting out of prejudice.

2. The term also has some obvious linguistic advantages. It certainly is easier to refer to beliefs, attitudes, or actions as "racist" than it is to say, for instance, that they "reflect prejudice founded on the idea that races may be ranked as superior and inferior."

3. This statement, of course, expresses a moral judgment rather than a sociological principle or fact of social organization.

4. Our classification and discussion of the main theories of prejudice and discrimination are particularly indebted to the outstanding presentations of Allport (1958) and of Simpson and Yinger (1972:63–164).

5. For a stimulating and enlightening discussion of the main issues, assumptions, and results of stereotype research, see Roger Brown (1986:586–609).

6. For reviews of the literature on stereotype research, see Bonjean, Hill, and McLemore (1967:163–168), Ehrlich (1973:20–60), Hamilton

and Trolier (1986), Lieberson (1982), and Arthur Miller (1982).

7. The authoritarian personality theory is one of the most influential of this type (see Adorno, Frenkel-Brunswik, Levinson, and Sanford 1950). According to this theory, highly prejudiced people are likely to exhibit a high level of frustration and displaced aggression as well as high levels of sexual repression, insecurity, and a "jungle philosophy" of life. For a good brief discussion, see Allport (1958:371–412). Behind this and many other personality theories lie the enormously influential ideas of Sigmund Freud.

8. The idea that people may "drain off" aggressive impulses by displacement is popular. Many people explain their enthusiasm for "contact" sports (such as football) or "striking" sports (such as bowling) by saying that it helps them to "get things out of their systems." The technical name for this process is *catharsis*.

9. Berkowitz suggested that hostile impulses will not disappear until the frustrated person actually injures the one who is responsible for the frustration.

10. Stephan stated in this regard that "one of the most intriguing consequences of categorization is that the mere division of people into groups leads to biased evaluations of the groups . . . and to discrimination . . . against out-group members" (Stephan 1985:613).

11. For a review of many of the earlier studies, see Proshansky (1966:311–371).

12. They also emphasize the importance of distinguishing these combined elements from *racial self-esteem* or ethnic pride (Hughes and Demo 1989).

13. For an excellent review of studies of the attitude-behavior relationship, see Schuman and Johnson (1976).

14. The median is the number that divides any set of numbers exactly in half, that is, the middle number.

15. The study by Semyonov and Cohen (1990) analyzes data on Jewish-Arab relations in Israel rather than black-white relations in the United States. Although the theoretical issue in both cases is the same, one may argue either that the results are more believable because they agree in the two settings or that they are less believable because the two settings differ in certain respects.

16. Although the statistics from attitude surveys are extremely valuable, the exact levels of a given attitude may vary with the wording of the questions and a number of other factors. In regard to the acceptance by whites of residential desegregation, for instance, NORC used a question that elicited a lower approval response (Schuman, Steeh, and Bobo 1985:60).

17. For an important study of this more general attitudinal shift, see Williams, Nunn, and St. Peter (1976).

18. Kluegel (1990:513) notes that although the modern type of racism does not focus on genetic inferiority it still attempts to explain group differences in individualistic terms. He refers to the modern type as *motivational individualism* and the older type as *traditional individualism*.

19. The question of the rate of change is a topic of the succeeding chapters. We may note in passing, however, that at the rates of change in effect between 1950 and 1960, the "gap" between white and nonwhite median years of schooling "would not close until the year 2022," while the gap in incomes "would not close until 2410!" (Broom and Glenn 1965b). See also Broom and Glenn (1965a:84–88, 155–222) and Lieberson and Fuguitt (1967:188–200).

20. If this position seems extreme, consider that in the eyes of some social learning or behavioral theorists, attitudes or opinions never cause actions. As Skinner (1974:10) stated: "Many of the things we observe just before we behave occur within our body, and it is easy to take them as the causes of our behavior. Feelings occur at just the right time to serve as causes of behavior." Hence, from a behaviorist perspective, prejudice is not a cause of discrimination! Please note that from this vantage point, although prejudices are not desirable psychic conditions, one should not attack them in the hope that this will lead to reductions in discrimination. For a critique of the institutional discrimination theory, see Butler (1978).

Chapter 7

Reducing Prejudice
and Discrimination

How can you change the opinions of men?
—*MARCUS AURELIUS*

It would be nice if we could make up for the disadvantages
that some groups have suffered without any inconveniences
to the advantaged group. I doubt whether this is possible. . . .
—*HOWARD A. GLICKSTEIN*

Privileged groups rarely give up their privileges without
strong resistance. —*MARTIN LUTHER KING, JR.*

155

The preceding chapter emphasized that the various types of theories of prejudice and discrimination are important sources of ideas concerning possible ways to attack these social problems. For example, if it is believed that prejudice and discrimination should be reduced and that these phenomena are rooted mainly in the dynamics of personality, then efforts may be made to reduce frustrations or other inner forces and to train people to "cope" with their personal problems. On the other hand, if it is believed that prejudice and discrimination are mainly products of America's normal operations, then only a substantial reorganization of the society's basic institutions will do. And if one holds with Allport (1958) and Myrdal ([1944]1964) that prejudice and discrimination result from multiple causes, then the "prescription" for a "cure" may involve a simultaneous attack on several— or, if possible, all—of the factors causing them. In this regard, Myrdal ([1944]1964:77) stated that "a rational policy will never work by changing only one factor."

There is not, however, a simple one-to-one correspondence between the theories and the various strategies of social change that may be implied by them. Consider, for example, some implications of cultural transmission theories of prejudice. One way to interfere with the transmission of racial and ethnic prejudice from one generation to another is to remove racial and ethnic stereotypes from children's school books. Minority group members may be portrayed in certain situations and roles that run counter to the prevailing stereotypes. But a cultural transmission theory of prejudice also suggests some more "militant" strategies. Stereotypes may be attacked by requiring children from different groups to attend the same schools and by removing barriers to neighborhood desegregation. From this standpoint, too, one may argue that required classes in multicultural education should be established in schools (at the primary levels to guarantee that the prejudices children learn at home will be challenged and in colleges and universities to combat intergroup tensions on campuses). These examples show that one's political stand, as well as one's theory of prejudice and discrimination, will have an important effect on the strategy of change one prefers.

Nevertheless, and despite many exceptions, a broad pattern of theoretical and strategic preferences is discernible. Dominant group members are more likely than subordinate group members to focus on the reduction of prejudice through methods derived from the cultural transmission and personality theories. They frequently propose such remedies for prejudice as courses in school to combat group stereotypes, books and films that portray sympathetically the plight of oppressed peoples, personal counseling for people who are filled with ethnic hatreds, and "get-togethers" that enable the members of different groups to become acquainted. Furthermore, the members of the dominant group are most likely to advocate methods of change that are gradual in their effects and not likely to result in open conflicts between groups.

Minority group members, in contrast, are more likely than majority group members to focus on the reduction of discrimination through methods derived from the group gains and institutional discrimination theories. They may think the "solutions" proposed by dominant group members are superficial or miss the mark entirely. Discrimination cannot be reduced effectively by attacking prejudice. Changes must be made in the society's organization—its structure. Minority group members, therefore, are more likely than those in the majority group to advocate methods that promise rapid social changes even though the risk of intergroup conflict may increase.

This broad pattern of theoretical and strategic preferences has been reflected in the studies conducted in this field. Most studies have focused on the reduction of prejudice through the use of various educational approaches. Gradually, however, the focus of attention has shifted toward the reduction of discrimination, especially through changes in the law and by means of organized social protest. We will illustrate these methods briefly, giving the most attention to the educational and legal approaches. Organized social protest will be treated more fully in the chapters that follow.

The Educational Approach

Factual Information

Many people believe that individual prejudice and discrimination reflect a lack of knowledge. But what constitutes knowledge? And how is knowledge best acquired? Differences of opinion concerning the answers to these questions have led to different educational methods for reducing prejudice.

A very common approach recommends simply that everyone should receive more education. This view rests on the belief that the more years of education people receive, the less likely they are to accept ethnic stereotypes or to express the wish to hold people of a different ethnicity at a great social distance. Fortunately for all who favor rational discourse in the treatment of human problems, there is considerable evidence to back up this belief. For example, in general, levels of education and prejudice are inversely related (Berelson and Steiner 1964:515). A more focused version of the assumption that ignorance leads to prejudice is that the more people learn about intergroup similarities and differences, the less prejudiced they will be (Hewstone 1986:10–12). This assumption lies behind many programs that require or encourage people in colleges and universities, in the military services, or in the workplace to take human relations training or courses in multicultural education. Here, again, there is some evidence that under specified conditions increases in people's knowledge about other groups leads to increases in intergroup cooperation and respect. But, regrettably for those who favor a largely cognitive approach to the problems of intergroup hostility, it is easy to overestimate the beneficial effects of this approach. The differences in levels of prejudice between educational groups may not be as large as the levels of prejudice associated with some other differences.

To illustrate, in a study of regional and educational differences in white Americans' attitudes toward African Americans, Taylor, Sheatsley, and Greeley (1978:45) found that in 1976 white southerners who had completed high school were only slightly more favorable toward racial integration than were white northerners with an elementary school education, and the northerners of lower education were noticeably more favorable toward integration than were white southerners who had attended but not completed high school. Moreover, white southerners who had attended but not completed college were less favorable toward integration than were white northern high school graduates. It should be said that there was a striking change in the pattern of regional differences during the first half of the 1970s, with southern college students and high school graduates showing a rapid acceptance of integration; but these findings still are consistent with the idea that reducing prejudice requires more than an increase in the level of formal education. Indeed, a skeptic might suggest that the apparent decreases in prejudice levels that are associated with increasing education levels reflect the shift from old-fashioned to modern racism (mentioned in chapter 6) more than they do authentic changes of people's basic attitudes. This skepticism finds support in the many studies showing that "stereotypic beliefs are extremely resistant to change" (Pettigrew and Martin 1989:186) and that information designed to counter such beliefs frequently is "explained away" (Hewstone 1989:37). For this reason, many researchers and practitioners feel that the effort to reduce prejudice and discrimination must rely upon, or at least incorporate, noncognitive elements.

Vicarious Experience

Instead of simply imparting specific facts to people, a program of multicultural education may be based on films, plays, television productions, biographies, and novels that present the members of all groups in a sympathetic way (Allport 1958:454). This approach attempts to "speak to the heart rather than to the head." The underlying premise is that exposure to such materials may help people to recognize and appreciate the humanness of the members of different groups, to sympathize with out-group members, and, thus, to reduce the tendency for people to see sharp differences between "them" and "us." Participants in such a program are encouraged to "take the role of the other," to see the world from another person's point of view, to "walk awhile in the other person's boots." Such a vicarious experience, it is assumed, should lead prejudiced people—members of minority as well as majority groups—to see themselves through the eyes of the targets of ethnic hatred, to dislike what they see, and, thereby, to stimulate changes in attitudes and behavior.

Several criticisms of the vicarious experience approach have been advanced. Some evidence suggests that prejudiced people frequently do not interpret accurately the films and books that run counter to their prejudices. They do not necessarily "get the message"; they may pay greatest attention to side issues and ignore the central point. It seems, too, that the effectiveness of a film or other dramatic presentation in reducing prejudice depends greatly on the skill with which the "message" of tolerance is presented. Some presentations actually create a "boomerang" or "polarization" effect, in which prejudices are heightened instead of diminished (R. Brown 1986:224). And one may reasonably argue that it is unrealistic to assume that something as superficial as a film or a book may seriously disrupt a deep-seated ethnic prejudice or lead forthwith to tolerant behavior.

An interesting attempt to test these ideas was conducted by Middleton (1960). This research was designed to counter the preceding criticisms. Two groups of university students were selected to participate in the study. One group of 329 subjects—the experimental group—was shown an award-winning commercial film, *Gentleman's Agreement,* while the other group of 116 subjects—the control group—was not shown the film. *Gentleman's Agreement* attempts to convey the twin messages that anti-Jewish sentiment (or antisemitism) is despicable and that it is perpetuated significantly by "fair weather liberals" (i.e., people who succumb to situational pressures to discriminate).

Middleton's primary findings were that (1) on the average, the anti-Jewish sentiments of the experimental group—those who saw the film—were significantly reduced following the showing, and (2) the same result—though not as pronounced—was found in regard to anti-black prejudice; hence, this study supports the idea that deeply ingrained ethnic prejudices may be significantly reduced by a particular kind of motion picture. It also supports the view that a good film aimed toward a particular ethnic prejudice (e.g., against Jews) may also reduce ethnic prejudices concerning other groups; thus the study affords some evidence in opposition to the main criticisms of the vicarious approach mentioned earlier.

This study is a fine example of the application of scientific reasoning in social research. It does not, however, prove that the best way to reduce ethnic prejudice is to arouse people's sympathies through dramatic or emotionally appealing presentations. As Middleton (1960:68) noted, there is no evidence that the reductions in prejudice observed in his experiment were permanent, and it is difficult to know to what extent the participants in the study surmised the researchers' intent and, as noted earlier, adjusted their answers in a socially desirable direction. Furthermore, even if the changes in prejudice were permanent and real, there is no evidence that these changes were translated into lowered levels of discrimination.

Intergroup Contact

So far, we have considered two main approaches to increasing the intercultural knowledge of prejudiced people: (1) exposing them to accurate information, especially concerning ethnic out-groups; and (2) assisting them "to place themselves in the other person's shoes." It is not easy to compare the effectiveness of these two approaches in reducing prejudice and discrimination. So far as attitude change is concerned, the informational approach generally appears to be weaker than the more emotional approach using novels, plays, films, and so on, but little evidence exists that either approach leads to permanent reductions in prejudice or to much change in behavior. It is possible, of course, that the changes take place over a long period of time and that they are difficult to detect. Still, it seems that other methods are required if much change is to be effected.

The drawbacks of the informational approach and the vicarious experience approach have led many people to favor a third approach to increasing the knowledge of prejudiced people about subordinate groups. The idea frequently is voiced that those who hate one another really do not know one another. A variation on this theme is that the parties to a conflict have experienced "a breakdown in communications." Consequently, one of the most common suggestions for improving intergroup relations is that people should "get together" so that they may establish communications, get to know one another, participate in various activities together, and discuss their differences. When people do things together, they have an excellent opportunity to discover what the members of different groups are really like. They are enabled to see that those in other groups have the same kinds of human emotions and problems they have. The opportunity arises in such a situation for people to learn how to judge the members of other groups on the basis of their individual merits and, in this way, to apply the same kinds of standards to others that they apply to people in their own group. Among scholars this idea is at the heart of what is known as *the contact hypothesis* (Allport 1958:250–261).

The idea that contact is an important avenue to the reduction of prejudice is certainly consistent with much everyday experience. "Few approaches to dealing with racial prejudice," Barnard and Benn (1988) observed, "have inspired as much hope and received as much attention as interracial contact." Practically everyone can name at least one person whom he or she disliked on sight but grew to like later on. Early students of the contact hypothesis concluded that such transformations are most probable if the people involved are of equal social status, if they are working cooperatively on something, if their activity is supported by people in positions of authority, and if the activity involves a relatively high level of intimacy (Stephan 1987:14). Intergroup contacts occurring under other circumstances, in contrast, seem likely to leave prejudices unchanged or even to intensify them. For instance, if the dominant members in the contact situation enjoy the higher status (e.g., in employer-employee relations), the contact may serve mainly to remind both parties of the dominant members' superior position, while if the minority members occupy the higher status (e.g., in police-citizen relations), the contact may increase the dominant members' resentment. In addition, equal-status contacts among people with only mild prejudices may be more successful than those involving people who hold strong prejudices. Moreover, many otherwise favorable contacts may not produce the desired result if those in positions of authority or social influence disapprove (Robinson and Preston 1976:911). For example, children involved in school desegregation programs may become more prejudiced unless parents, teachers, school administrators, and local elected officials make strong public declarations supporting desegregation. Everything considered, though, the work accomplished in this field "does seem to provide qualified support for the view that equal-status contact reduces prejudice" (See and Wilson 1988:228).[1]

Numerous factors in addition to those listed above have been shown to influence the outcome of contacts between the members of dominant and subordinate groups, including minimal competition, voluntary interaction, similarities in beliefs and values, and the way various types of information-processing biases influence perceptions (Barnard and Benn 1988:126; Hewstone 1986:37; Stephan 1985:643). In an effort to take these advances in knowledge into account, Stephan (1987:21–22) presented an inclusive conceptual model that has important implications for research and applications in this field.

A variety of social settings within which intergroup contacts occur have been investigated, but two settings have received special research attention. These are interracial housing and desegregated schooling.[2] Along with most other studies of intergroup contact, the basic assumption of housing and school desegregation research has been that contact (or even proximity) will lead to the reduction of prejudice and intergroup tension; however, after thorough reviews of the literature, Amir (1969; 1976) concluded that even under favorable circumstances changes in ethnic relations are not necessarily in the expected direction.

Let us consider Amir's generalization in light of some studies of interracial housing, beginning with some findings from the best-known study of racial desegregation in public housing (Deutsch and Collins 1956). These researchers compared two public housing projects in New York City and Newark, New Jersey, to see how desegregated housing affected relations between blacks and whites. In two of the projects, the tenants were assigned to apartments without regard to race. In the other two projects, the tenants were assigned to racially segregated buildings. It was, therefore, possible to study the reactions of people living in two situations that were highly similar except for the physical closeness of the members of the two races. The researchers were interested in such things as whether the black and white families had more frequent contact with one another in the "integrated" projects or the "segregated" projects, whether interracial contacts were more friendly in one of the two settings, and whether contacts between the members of the two races led to decreases in the tenants' prejudice levels.

The study showed that white housewives who lived in the two segregated projects had many fewer neighborly relations with blacks than did white housewives in the two integrated projects. In both of the segregated projects, in fact, there were almost no neighborly relations. Although the two integrated projects differed somewhat in their levels of neighborly relations, both were noticeably different from the segregated projects (Deutsch and Collins 1956:26–27). The study also showed that some white housewives in both types of projects became more favorable in their attitudes toward blacks, while some became more unfavorable; however, in both types of projects, more housewives changed in a favorable than in an unfavorable direction. Furthermore, the total number of favorable changes was much larger in the integrated than in the segregated projects (Deutsch and Collins 1956:42–43).

Although the main findings of Deutsch and Collins were strengthened and refined by a number of subsequent investigations (Ford 1973; Wilner, Walkley, and Cook 1955; Works 1961), some additional refinements were suggested. Ford (1973:1440), for instance, found that in an interracial housing project in which racial tension was present, a longer duration of residence in the project did not increase the tolerance of whites for blacks. He found, too (contrary to the findings of Works 1961), that equal-status contacts did not appear to reduce the prejudice of blacks for whites. Researchers also have extended the scope of the findings pertaining to residential contact through studies of middle-class neighborhoods (Meer and Freedman 1966).

Of particular importance here is a well-designed study by Hamilton and Bishop (1976). The study focused on middle-class residential neighborhoods in which desegregation did and did not occur. Because the researchers collected information before the desegregation of any of the neighborhoods took place, they were able to "follow" the changes in people's attitudes by gathering data at several different times. The study showed (unsurprisingly) that when whites learned a black family was moving into their neighborhood, this fact attracted much more notice than when another white family was moving in. The initial reaction to having black neighbors was frequently a concern that property values would decline. By the end of one year, however, most responses by the white neighbors toward the black families were positive. Moreover, the prejudice levels of the whites were lowered in the desegregated neighborhoods (Hamilton and Bishop 1976:65); however, the researchers found that the change toward favorable attitudes occurred whether the white residents actually had contact with the black neighbors or not. Hence, even though the attitudes of whites changed in the predicted direction, it does not appear that contact as such was responsible for it. Hamilton and Bishop (1976:66) suggested that perhaps the white neighbors were able to see that their fears had been groundless and that this "disconfirmation of expectancies" led to more favorable attitudes.

The evidence we have reviewed on the capacity of contact to reduce intergroup prejudice and discrimination was well summarized by Amir (1969:319): "At present there are conflicting views . . . regarding this problem." Obviously, intergroup contacts may not be hailed as *the* way to reduce prejudice, but, like the other "educational" methods we have considered, it surely has its place. Despite the limitations of attempting to reduce prejudice through interethnic contacts, the main point of the contact hypothesis has generally been supported by research: under appropriate conditions, personal contacts between majority and minority group members can lead to reductions in prejudice (Barnard and Benn 1988:133). The method seems to work best when people are, so to speak, "in the same boat," but even under apparently unfavorable conditions contact sometimes leads to reduced antipathy (Amir 1976).

Turning now to studies of school desegregation, we find an even larger and more varied literature. An important difference between studies of housing and school desegregation is that many of the former focused directly on the contact hypothesis. Studies of school desegregation, however, were concerned with a number of topics, including whether the "achievement gap" between black and white children is due to different values in the black and white communities (to which we return in chapter 11), whether "deficits" in achievement values (if they exist) are reversible, whether white teachers treat children alike regardless of ethnicity, whether the self-esteem of black children rises following desegregation, and so on (Gerard and Miller 1975:14–21). More generally, these studies were classified by St. John (1975:7) as focusing on academic achievement, motivation and self-confidence, and interracial attitudes and behavior. Although the effects of contact and proximity in each of these areas is a matter of considerable practical importance, we are interested here primarily in interracial attitudes and behavior.[3]

St. John's review of evidence relating to the contact hypothesis was based on forty-one studies conducted during a period of about thirty-five years in different regions of the country. They included sample sizes ranging from below one hundred to over three thousand and involved children of various ages, and they were based on a number of different research designs and data-gathering methods. St. John (1975:67–68) summarized the results of the studies by saying that "for either race positive findings are less common than negative findings and . . . [i]t is also apparent that the direction of the findings is as often contradictory as it is consistent for the two races. Sometimes desegregation is reported to have ameliorated the prejudice of whites but intensified that of Blacks, sometimes the reverse."

Even among the seven studies that focused most directly on desegregation's effect on racial attitudes and employed the best research methods, the pattern of findings was still conflicting. St. John (1975:80) concluded that "comparative studies of the racial attitudes of segregated and desegregated school children are inconclusive." She reminded us, nevertheless, that the conditions under which contact is theoretically expected to lead to changes in attitudes are seldom fully realized in actual desegregation programs and that when such conditions are met, the results are more promising. For instance, as expected under the contact hypothesis, "several of the studies reviewed found evidence that long-term desegregation had a beneficial effect on attitudes" (St. John 1975:98).

This conclusion received general support from the results of subsequent studies of the long-term effects of desegregation (Stephan 1986:196; 1988:19). Gerard and Miller (1975), for example, in a well-designed study of desegregation in the elementary schools of Riverside, California, gathered data on approximately 20,000 children's choices of friends, school work partners, and play partners, and they found some favorable changes in attitudes during the course of the study (Goodchilds, Green, and Bikson 1975). Although the observed attitude changes led to "little or no real integration . . . during the relatively long-term contact situation" (Gerard, Jackson, and Conolley 1975:237), studies covering still longer periods of time have shown that blacks who have attended desegregated schools are more likely than other blacks to attend college, to work in integrated settings, and to live in desegregated housing (Stephan 1988:19). We must recall, nonetheless, that the apparent long-term increases in occupational and residential integration following desegregated schooling may not be attributed unequivocally to changes in interracial attitudes or, in fact, to any other effect of school desegregation.

The results of survey studies of the type reviewed so far led some students of this problem to suggest that both desegregation programs and research concerning their effectiveness should be guided more closely by theoretical knowledge and that much more attention should be given to the actual school and classroom conditions under which children meet (St. John 1975:122; Mercer, Iadicola, and Moore 1980:294). It has been shown, for instance, that the equality of status among children within a desegregated classroom is often more apparent than real

(Schofield 1986:82; Schofield and Sagar 1979:169–173). Even in small groups in which children are expected to work cooperatively to accomplish a given task, white children frequently are more active and influential than minority group children (Cohen 1980:253–256). This finding led to systematic efforts to understand how the status rankings of the larger society are imported into the classroom and to devise various strategies to alter these rankings (Miller 1980:333–336; van Oudenhoven 1989:213; Webster and Driskell 1978); and several techniques have been developed to foster interdependence and cooperation among students in the classroom (R. Brown 1986:615–620; van Oudenhoven 1989:208–213). A review of some results of these efforts by The Committee on the Status of Black Americans (Jaynes and Williams 1989:81) stated that "interdependence in task performance in classroom learning groups appears to . . . support norms of equal-status interaction." Systematic efforts also have been devoted to understanding the extent to which the social-psychological processes that result in same-race friendships operate in situations of interracial contacts within schools. In an examination of the data from the High School and Beyond Survey, Hallinan and Williams (1989:76) found that of almost a million friendship pairs (dyads) "only a few hundred could be identified" as being cross-race, but the study also confirmed that children who do form cross-race friendships are likely to be in frequent contact and to be similar in their attitudes, values, and status.[4]

To the extent that "educational" methods of reducing prejudice are effective, discrimination also presumably is reduced. Remember, though, that this argument assumes that the most effective way to control discrimination is through an attack on prejudice; remember too that, as stated by Patchen et al. (1977:73), "the determinants of interracial behavior are different than those of opinion change." The practice of discrimination may be more or less independent of the existence of prejudice, and it may be possible, therefore, to reduce discrimination directly. Indeed, the institutional discrimination view implies that this is the only feasible approach.

Let us refer again to Merton's (1949) comparison of types of prejudice and discrimination. The prejudiced nondiscriminator fails to discriminate when an external restraint of some kind is encountered. The "external restraint" may be no more than the fear that the individual's friends may disapprove of discrimination. Or it could be a fear that one's business associates or clients will take their business elsewhere. Or it may be an awareness that discrimination is illegal and may, therefore, be punished. In addition to these fears, of course, the prejudiced nondiscriminator may hope that failing to discriminate will bring certain rewards. In short, many people who may harbor beliefs and feelings that seemingly could lead them to discriminate may, in particular social situations, behave in a nondiscriminatory way.

By the same reasoning, many people who do not discriminate in one social situation may do so in another. This fact means that when a person either discriminates or fails to discriminate, we cannot be sure whether the person is prejudiced. It means further that to predict whether an individual will discriminate, it may be more important to understand the features of the social situation than the individual's tolerance level, and in the effort to alter people's behavior "shaping situations" may be "more successful than direct attempts to change such deeply held attitudes as racism" (Pettigrew and Martin 1989:190). But to what extent can we rely on the restraints of particular social situations to control discrimination in America? Wouldn't it be better if Americans were always under restraint not to discriminate? Considerations such as these touch an old and controversial question: "If we wish people to stop discriminating (or anything else), why not pass a law against it?"

The Legal Approach

The Laws and the Mores

For more than a century, one of the most prominent features of interethnic conflict in America has been the effort to control intergroup relations through laws and judicial decisions. At the national level, in particular, many landmark laws and court cases afford a veritable outline of the fight to extend equal rights to all citizens. This approach has always received a substantial amount of support in America, at least at the verbal level. Americans generally claim to endorse the "American Creed" and to believe that its ideals should be inscribed into law (Myrdal [1944]1964:14). In practice, however, two currents of thought have tended to undermine this approach and to support opposition to it. The first current is that Americans seem generally to couple the statement "There ought to be a law" with a low degree of respect for law (Myrdal [1944]1964:14). As Berger (1968:1) stated, "Americans seem to want laws expressing high ideals but they seem also to want the convenience of ignoring or violating many of them with impunity." Hence, although many people appear to favor laws against discrimination in employment, schooling, housing, access to health care, and so on, such laws are not necessarily obeyed.

This fact is related to the second current of thought opposing the legal approach. It frequently is said that laws cannot enforce good conduct unless they are popular. Since laws that attempt to control private behavior or personal tastes are almost always unpopular, it is said that laws attempting to force equality cannot succeed. Of course, it may be conceded, laws may affect the blatant forms of discrimination, but such controls, at best, affect only the external form of lawful behavior. They cannot change the will to discriminate and cannot, therefore, prevent people from finding ways to circumvent the law. "Laws cannot change the hearts and minds of men," it is said. To support this view, people often cite the failure of the Prohibition experiment in America. Prohibition not only failed to prevent the manufacture, sale, and use of alcoholic beverages but also seemed actually to have encouraged it. It created a "backlash." Many people bought "bootleg" liquor and visited "speakeasies" during the Prohibition era partly because of the excitement that may accompany lawbreaking. People seemed attracted to drinking as a way to flaunt the law. Much the same sort of thing has accompanied efforts to increase the legal restraints on the use of other drugs and on such things as prostitution. The great lesson that seems to have been learned in these efforts to control socially disapproved behavior is that "you can't legislate morality!" Effective laws appear only to express what the people regard as legitimate and will accept.

This issue has been the source of a longstanding controversy in Western thought. Among social scientists, the view that unpopular legislation is doomed usually is traced to the influential work of William Graham Sumner (1906; Allport 1958:429–443). Sumner's arguments concerning the effort to change society through legislation rested on his analysis of the folkways and mores. Folkways, or customs, are the practices the members of a society have adopted as answers to life's problems (Sumner 1906:34). These methods of doing things gradually become traditions and, as such, define the kinds of behavior that are regarded as right or wrong. Every aspect of life is regulated by the folkways, ranging from how many spouses a person may have to what kind of clothing is acceptable. Those folkways having to do with the most serious social matters are called mores.

Sumner's discussion of the relationship of the laws to the mores is not easily summarized, but the most prominent portions of it appear to support the idea that laws are ineffective tools for bringing about social change. His commentary on the effects of the laws passed during the Reconstruction period following the Civil War is frequently quoted: "Vain attempts have been made to control the new order by legislation. The only result is the proof that legislation cannot make mores" (Sumner 1906:77). In another place, Sumner (1906:55) stated that since "acts of legislation come out of mores . . . legislation, to be strong, must be consistent with the mores."

Despite appearances, Sumner did not believe the laws could never have an effect on the mores. Indeed, as shown by Ball, Simpson, and Ikeda (1962), he believed that with proper planning laws definitely could be used to bring about fundamental changes. If laws are skillfully framed and rationally planned, he believed, then some portions of conduct could be altered, and if conduct were altered, then changes in thought and feeling would follow. However, he had little confidence that most legislators knew enough to use the law in this way (Sumner 1906:95). As a result, many people have relied on Sumner's authority to argue that laws cannot alter people's hearts and minds and, therefore, cannot alter behavior. Whether he intended it or not, Sumner's work has been interpreted by many readers to support the idea "that social change must always be glacier-like in its movement and that mass change in attitudes must precede legislative action" (Roche and Gordon 1965:332).

Let us acknowledge right away that there is a large element of good sense in this argument. Quite clearly, the enactment of a law cannot directly alter people's ideas and emotions. As Sumner emphasized, the "stroke of the pen" does not, in itself, produce changes in the morality of people; however, as this point ordinarily is understood, it contains two important errors. First, it misses the crucial distinction between attitudes and actions. Since most people assume that attitudes are the wellspring of action, the obvious difficulty of changing attitudes through legislation serves to discredit the idea that behavior may be altered in this way. Contemporary sociological thought on this matter, however, generally agrees with a statement by Martin Luther King, Jr. (1962:49): "While it may be true that morality cannot be legislated, behavior can be regulated," consequently, "the habits, if not the hearts, of people are being altered every day by Federal action."

The second important point that tends to be ignored by opponents of the legal approach is the possibility that actions—once they conform to the requirements of the law—may lead to a change in the attitudes that seem to underlie the previous actions. Recall, for example, our findings regarding desegregated housing. Very few of the white people living in interracial public housing may realistically be described as having voluntarily chosen these living conditions. For the most part, they accepted the apartments because they had to. As Deutsch and Collins (1956:22) described it, "Their intensive need for housing compelled them to move into a situation they would otherwise have avoided." But we saw that under the conditions studied, blacks and whites who were "forced" to live together did not generally become more antagonistic. In fact, the more closely the whites were required to live with the blacks, the more favorable their attitudes generally became. While this outcome runs counter to common-sense expectations, it readily may be interpreted (among other ways) in terms of the theory of cognitive dissonance introduced in chapter 6. If prejudiced people move into interracial housing, cognitive dissonance is produced. Since the fact of living in interracial housing cannot readily be denied or altered, the main route open to dissonance reduction is a change of attitude. Of course, our review of studies relating to the contact hypothesis has shown that many factors enter into most actual situations; so there is no guarantee that when people are "forced" to alter their discriminatory actions, they will experience a subsequent reduction in prejudice. Nevertheless, even when "their hearts are not in it," new ways of acting may lead people to new ways of thinking. As Pettigrew (1971:279) observed, "Laws first act to modify behavior, and this modified behavior in turn changes the participants' attitudes. . . . Behaving differently . . . often precedes thinking differently." Strange to say, therefore, perhaps the most effective way to reduce prejudice is first to reduce discrimination.

If we accept that some laws effectively alter behavior and that behavioral changes may then bring attitudes "into line," then the task of those who favor the legal approach is to estimate the probability that a proposed law to regulate discrimination will succeed. As was true in Sumner's day, there still is no scientific or mathematical solution to this problem. Although Sumner was surely right in his claim that laws are more likely to succeed if they "run with the mores," we now know something more about how they may succeed when the laws and the mores do not coincide. For instance, a number of studies of efforts to desegregate schools have discovered two important and related facts. First, if legal orders to desegregate are strongly and publicly supported by local government and school officials and other influential citizens, then the chance is greatly improved that the change will take place peacefully even when most people in the community are opposed to it. Second, officials should not be intimidated by a noisy opposition. Most people who protest a proposed change and hold up the specter of violence and retaliation will nonetheless accept the change once it has taken place. We should recognize, of course, that there are limits to the application of these ideas. The extent to which the opposition is concentrated and organized, the number of influential citizens who join the opposition, and the intensity of the opposition are a few of the factors that may contribute to the failure of a desegregation effort that is strongly supported by most of the community's leaders. But it is an advance in our thinking to see that the presence of such factors in a social situation do not necessarily mean that effective legislation is impossible.

Another important discovery in this regard is that a law prohibiting discrimination is much more likely to succeed if it is vigorously enforced. Public officials need not only to make public pronouncements of support for a new law, they also need to guarantee that those who violate the law—especially at the outset—are punished swiftly for doing so. The swift and certain punishment of violators has led, in many actual instances, to a rapid and generally peaceful acceptance of an initially unpopular law.

Still another significant point here is the capacity of public officials to enforce the law. For technical reasons, a law that is opposed only moderately may be more difficult to enforce than one that is opposed strongly; hence, some thought should be given to this point in advance of the passage of a law. We may speculate, for instance, that the Prohibition experiment might have failed even if it had been more strongly supported by the public. As Roche and Gordon (1965:336) observed, "Home manufacture of alcoholic beverages has . . . survived in the Soviet Union, and if the M.V.D. is incapable of banning private brew, there is little reason to suspect that a democratic society could handle the job."

Despite Sumner's emphasis on the general resistance of the mores to change, he also stressed that under some circumstances changes in them occur rapidly. One of these circumstances occurs when two or more sets of conflicting mores exist simultaneously in a society. This conflict generates a "strain toward consistency," and the law may tip the balance in one direction or the other. In modern societies, in particular, the law seldom is required to stand alone against a monolithic set of opposing mores. More often, the law chooses between competing moral codes (Berger 1968:219). In this way, the law is aided strongly by some existing ideas and beliefs to create a general social situation that favors obedience to the law once it has been adopted. Thus, the law, with the aid of an existing—though not necessarily predominant—moral code and strong official support and enforcement, may bring about a reduction in discrimination. Let us illustrate these ideas through further consideration of school desegregation.

We noted earlier that racial and ethnic prejudices among white Americans have declined markedly during the last several decades. Of special interest to us here is that a strong majority of whites in all regions of the country now agree that black children should attend school with white children; however, a large majority of those who say they accept the ideal of desegregated schools also reject the most prominent method of achieving this objective: "busing" (Orfield 1978:102).

School Busing

The use of buses to help children travel the distances between their homes and schools began in the United States several decades before buses were used for the purpose of desegregating schools. During the earlier period, school busing was widely hailed as a progressive tool to ensure that children—particularly rural children—would not be denied an education because they lacked transportation. Also during this period, busing was frequently used to maintain school segregation. When the nearest "neighborhood" school was a school for black children, white children often were bused to more distant schools that were designated for white children. Black children also were bused to schools for black children.

As we discuss more fully in chapter 10, the practice of assigning children of different races to different schools began to appear in the South immediately following the Civil War. The establishment of dual school systems became more widespread and rigid as the South adopted the legal system that came to be known as Jim Crow.[5] The Jim Crow system of legal segregation came into being in the South following the 1896 decision of the U.S. Supreme Court in *Plessy v. Ferguson*. As we explain more fully later, this case established that public transportation facilities (and, by implication, all other public facilities as well) could be "separate" as long as they were "equal." Under the protection of this ruling, the states of the old confederacy passed laws requiring separate schools for black and white children.

It quickly became obvious that the separate schools being established for blacks were not truly equal to those being established for whites—an inequality that had been predicted by Justice Harlan in a famous dissent in *Plessy*—so black people began to organize to fight Jim Crow. By the 1930s, one organization, the National Association for the Advancement of Colored People (NAACP), had selected segregation in education as the primary target of its efforts to establish the civil rights of black people.

The NAACP won a series of court victories that culminated in the momentous case *Brown v. Board of Education of Topeka,* 1954 (also called *Brown I*). Although the *Brown* decision officially ended the system of legal school segregation that had come into being following *Plessy,* it did not instantly bring about full school desegregation; nevertheless, a number of school districts in the South and the District of Columbia did begin to comply in 1955. Many other districts, however, offered strong resistance to desegregation through various pupil placement rules and "freedom-of-choice" plans. A "massive resistance" to desegregation in some states followed the second *Brown* decision in 1955 (i.e., *Brown II*), in which the Court stated that compliance must take place "with all deliberate speed." Whether the Court's language represented a prudent recognition that some delay was inevitable or was an unprincipled abdication of judicial responsibility has been a matter of vigorous debate (see, e.g., Graglia 1976:33–45). In any case, the effect was that "ten years after *Brown,* only 1.2 percent of the nearly 3 million Black students in the 11 Southern States attended school with white students" (U.S. Commission on Civil Rights 1976:4). One might well argue that this evidence shows the futility of a legal approach to social change.

Such a conclusion would be premature. Let us consider two complicating factors. First, the *Brown* decision was extraordinary in its scope. It led not only to a national effort to desegregate schools, but also to the formal desegregation of every institution in American life. As Graglia (1976:32) noted, "The *Brown* case was less a traditional law suit than a call for a social revolution. . . ." To effect such sweeping changes would be difficult under any circumstances, but in this case the difficulties were increased because many people thought the Court had exceeded its authority and had engaged in law making (Graglia 1976:44). Even so, one may argue that the low level of school desegregation during the period 1954–1964 reflected judicial hesitation more than it did judicial impotence (Graglia 1976:34–35). In the actual circumstances, however, *Brown's* place in American life remained ambiguous until Congress passed the Civil Rights Act of 1964. Through this act, Congress validated the prohibition of racial discrimination set forth in *Brown* and, in the process, created many official tools that could be used to help combat racial discrimination. For example, Title IV of the act authorizes the attorney general to bring school desegregation suits whenever private citizens cannot do so effectively, and Title VI permits the government to deny federal funds to school districts that discriminate (Osofsky 1968:571–572).

The second complicating factor is that after the Civil Rights Act was passed, the courts began to move with great vigor to desegregate schools. "Desegregation no longer progressed painfully from test case to test case. . . ." Glazer (1987:78) stated, "It moved rapidly as every school district in the South was required to comply . . . " with the law. In 1966, the Department of Health, Education, and Welfare (HEW) began to require statistical evidence that desegregation was occurring. In 1968, the U.S. Supreme Court ruled in *Green v. County School Board of New Kent County* that school systems could no longer have schools that were primarily for whites or for blacks, and in an especially important case, *Swann v. Charlotte-Mecklenburg County Board of Education* (1971), the Court ruled that busing might be used, where necessary, to eliminate segregation. In *Keyes v. School District No.1, Denver, Colorado* (1973), the Court made clear that busing could be used to bring about school desegregation outside of the South (Schuman, Steeh, and Bobo 1985:35–36). Of course, to repeat, busing children to schools was nothing new in American life, but never before had it been adopted by the Court as a means to ensure racial desegregation. This step initiated a prolonged and bitter controversy in American public affairs.

The objections to busing for the purposes of desegregation have been numerous. Indeed, it is difficult to find people of any race who positively like busing and think it is the best conceivable way to bring about desegregation. A survey conducted in 1972 found that 87 percent of the white people questioned were opposed to busing, and another survey conducted in 1983 found that 79 percent still were opposed to it. Although busing is more highly regarded among blacks, the level of opposition to it was, and has remained, fairly high. In both 1972 and

1983, 44 percent of the blacks questioned were opposed to busing, and in 1975 and 1977, more than half of the black respondents were opposed (Schuman, Steeh, and Bobo 1985:78, 147). Some critics in both races emphasize that busing takes children away from their neighborhoods and that this creates several kinds of disadvantages for the children; some emphasize the danger of accidents while traveling; some note the increased costs to taxpayers and the "ridiculous waste" of time and gasoline in the face of dwindling energy resources; some argue that even with this massive effort, school desegregation has "failed"; many state that they reject busing because it is "forced"; and some others argue that after 1964 the Court abandoned the goal of desegregation (i.e., school assignment without regard to race) and adopted forced integration (i.e., racial balance).[6]

Since our present discussion is focused on the relation of law to social change, the broad claim that desegregation has "failed" is particularly pertinent. Whatever one may think concerning the wisdom of attempting to achieve some form of racial balance in the schools, is it true that the orders of the courts and the other steps taken by the federal government under the Civil Rights Act have "failed"? If we take compliance with official orders as our criterion, the (short-run) answer to this question is an emphatic no! Based on the data collected in a survey of a large sample of school districts, the U.S. Commission on Civil Rights (1976:77–88) analyzed the role of the courts and the responsible executive agency—HEW—in effecting desegregation. The study focused on 615 school districts that had "taken substantial steps to desegregate" (U.S. Commission on Civil Rights 1976:78). Among these districts, 84 percent were desegregated between 1966 and 1975. Some 59 percent of the districts reported that either the courts or HEW had provided the most important impetus to desegregate. The remaining 41 percent stated that their programs were mainly initiated locally. During the period of heaviest intervention by legal bodies (1968–1972), the racial desegregation of school children rose sharply in the South (to 46 percent) while remaining nearly constant in the North and West (29 percent) (Pettigrew 1974:55; Jaynes and Williams 1989:75). By 1980, 70 percent of black students were attending schools in which at least 5 percent of the students were white (Stephan 1988:8).

In a separate analysis, Farley (1978) compared the levels of school segregation in large central cities. The index of segregation used by Farley, which is described more fully in subsequent chapters, ranges between 0 and 100. For example, if black students are represented in every school within a district in the same proportion as within the district as a whole, then the level of segregation is 0. From this standpoint, in 1954 the public schools of the South had an average index of segregation of nearly 100.

Using this approach, Farley (1978:30) found that between 1967 and 1974, school segregation declined in southern cities from 84 to 47. During the same period, the decline among northern and western cities was from 63 to 55. The pattern of a nationwide decline in segregation, with the South leading all other regions, continued throughout the 1970s; however, school segregation in the Northeast increased during the period for both black and Hispanic children. The increase in segregation in the Northeast occurred mainly in the "large, predominantly nonwhite school districts that have never been ordered to implement a major desegregation plan ... " (Orfield 1982:2). It is evident from these statistics that, although many children still attended schools in 1980 that were predominantly segregated, a substantial amount of desegregation of the public schools had taken place. It is also clear that most of this change occurred after 1967, mainly as a result of court orders and busing (Farley 1975:22; Orfield 1982:1).

To require a school district to desegregate and to require that it use buses to do so, of course, are not the same thing, and the studies cited do not tell us how extensively busing was employed during the period of greatest change. There can be little doubt, however, that busing was the leading tool used by school officials to meet the courts' definitions of compliance. The high degree of racial residential segregation in American cities (to which we return in later chapters) frequently forces the transportation of pupils if racial balance is accepted as a goal.

Even if one accepts the specific contention that official agencies have been able to effect school desegregation and to do so largely through busing, the broader argument concerning the reduction of discrimination and prejudice through legal means is hardly over. We noted earlier that even when children of different races are brought together, they may or may not relinquish prejudiced attitudes, depending on the operation of many other factors. Of special significance, too, is whether the legally enforced patterns of school desegregation can be maintained as long as residential segregation persists. For a long time, whites have moved more rapidly to the suburbs than blacks, and this trend (whatever its causes) has created many metropolitan districts that increasingly resemble white rings around a black core.[7] The U.S. Supreme Court ruled in the important case *Milliken v. Bradley* that it will not approve desegregation plans that attempt to cross school district lines to encompass an entire metropolitan area.[8] Hence, as long as the Court holds this view, it is possible that the large reductions in desegregation that have been achieved in many American cities may gradually be reversed by resegregation. Thus, the issue of housing segregation is intimately linked to the continuation of school segregation.

Affirmative Action

Another important and controversial legal approach to reducing racial discrimination was initiated soon after the NAACP turned its main energies to eliminating public school segregation. The focus of this second effort, however, was discrimination in employment. During 1941, as the United States prepared for entry into World War II, the black civil rights leader A. Philip Randolph launched a campaign to end racial discrimination in hiring in defense industries. He emphasized that black people had a legitimate stake in the nation's industrial and military defense efforts and demanded that they be included. He wrote letters to defense contractors requesting that black people be given a fair share of the jobs that were being created with federal dollars (Randolph [1941]1967a:392–399). And he wrote to government officials, including President Franklin D. Roosevelt, urging them to take official steps to ensure that black people would be received into job training programs and defense jobs. To give force to his efforts, Randolph organized a nonviolent, direct-action protest group called The March on Washington Movement. This organization, as its name suggests, was created to confront the federal government, if necessary, with the power of massive protest. Randolph argued that "an 'all-out' thundering march on Washington, ending in a monster and huge demonstration at Lincoln's monument will shake up white America" (Randolph [1941]1967b:398).

President Roosevelt responded in July 1941 with Executive Order 8802. This order affirmed that the policy of the federal government was the "full participation in the defense program by all persons, regardless of race, creed, color, or national origin" (Roosevelt [1941]1968:400). The order obligated defense contractors "not to discriminate against any worker because of race, creed, color, or national origin" and established a new Fair Employment Practices Committee (Roosevelt [1941]1968:401). This new FEPC, as it came to be called, was empowered to investigate complaints of discrimination that violated the provisions of the order and to recommend remedies for violations. Although Executive Order 8802 did not specify punishments for offenders or establish procedures to bring about compliance, it did state the government's position officially and in writing, and it did set into motion a chain of subsequent executive orders that were intended to curb discrimination in employment. For example, President Harry S. Truman continued the FEPC and, in Executive Order 10308, created the Committee on Governmental Contract Compliance to administer the nondiscrimination clauses in federal contracts (Benokraitis and Feagin 1978:9). In 1954, President Dwight D. Eisenhower expanded a bit further the government's effort to end discrimination in employment by issuing Executive Order 10557. This order required contractors to be nondiscriminatory "in recruitment, employment, promotion, and pay" and to see that subcontractors also adhered to these rules (Benokraitis and Feagin 1978:9).

The executive orders discussed represented a gradual increase in pressure on federal contractors to stop discriminating in the workplace. After about two decades of effort (and a number of executive orders we have not listed), many instances of overt discrimination by federally funded contractors had disappeared, but black workers still were very underrepresented in federally funded jobs and were still among "the last hired and the first fired." Some observers began to argue that the absence of racial discrimination could not by itself alter significantly the great inequalities in employment that had been created by centuries of prior discrimination. President Lyndon B. Johnson put it this way: "You do not take a person who for years has been hobbled by chains, and liberate him, bring him up to the starting line, and then say, 'You are free to compete with all the others'" (quoted by Hacker 1992:119); or as Sowell (1977:114), a critic of affirmative action, said, "If a firm has engaged in racial discrimination for years, and has an all-white work force as a result, then simply to stop explicit discrimination will mean little. . . ." To overcome the cumulative effects of discrimination, active, "affirmative" policies that go beyond sheer neutrality or "colorblindness" are required. Vice-President Richard Nixon, for example, stated that "the indifference of employers to establishing a positive policy of nondiscrimination" was the main obstacle to an increase in the hiring and promotion of minorities (Robinson and Spitz 1986–87:86). Although the federal government had attempted to redress past wrongs in the passage of the Thirteenth, Fourteenth, and Fifteenth Amendments to the Constitution, the development of Jim Crow had nullified those efforts. Now it was time, proponents of this view said, for the government to act again.

Such a policy was stated in Executive Order 10925, issued by President John F. Kennedy in 1961. This order stated that the government would encourage "equal opportunity for all qualified persons" through "positive measures" (Robinson and Spitz 1986–87:86) and that contractors would "take affirmative action that applicants are employed . . . without regard to their race, creed, color, or national origin" (Benokraitis and Feagin 1978:10). Executive Order 10925 marks the beginning of an extremely important shift away from a policy that assumes racial inequalities may be removed through an absence of discrimination and toward one that assumes that some positive assistance or preferential treatment is required to overcome the cumulative effects of past discrimination.[9] Since that time, actions by subsequent presidents, by Congress, and by the courts have defined, elaborated, and implemented this new policy. Also since that time, affirmative action policies have been extended to include women and members of some minority groups other than black Americans. In the process, these policies have become the focal point of a heated, complex, and frequently bitter debate. Although a brief treatment cannot grasp the legal and technical complexities of this debate, we will outline a few key events and arguments.

The long series of court cases resulting in *Brown* and the long series of presidential orders resulting in Executive Order 10925 established the legal basis for federal government actions to attack discrimination in education and employment. They were not, however, accompanied by penalties that school boards and contractors respected, by supporting laws, or by adequate administrative machinery. The 1960s brought significant changes in these conditions.

As noted previously, very important changes were embodied in the Civil Rights Act of 1964. In addition to enabling the government to bring school desegregation suits and to withhold funds to stop discrimination, Title VII banned "discrimination by employers or unions" and authorized "the Attorney General to sue" if he or she believes there is discrimination in employment (Osofsky 1968:372). The law also established an Equal Employment Opportunity Commission (EEOC) that was empowered to require remedial action if an employer was found to be guilty of intentional discrimination.

The Civil Rights Act was followed by a new series of presidential orders and court cases aimed at ending discrimination in employment. For example, Executive Order 11246, issued in 1965 by President Lyndon B. Johnson, continued the requirement that federal contractors must not discriminate and required that contractors must engage in affirmative action not only in those activities supported by federal dollars but also in all of their other business operations as well. By now, however, it was clear that exhortation alone would not have much effect in industries in which discriminatory practices had been the rule for many decades; therefore, Executive Order 11246 also created the Office of Federal Contract

Compliance (OFCC) to enforce the policy of affirmative action. The order required the low bidder for a federal contract to present "a specific proposal detailing the total number of employees he would use . . . and indicating how many of that number would constitute his 'goal' for minority employment" (Robinson and Spitz 1986–87:86–87). During this time, federal compliance officers increasingly required that affirmative action plans incorporate specific "timetables" and "goals" and that they produce "results." By 1971, an affirmative action plan was defined as "a set of specific and result-oriented procedures to which a contractor commits himself to apply every good faith effort" (Revised Order No. 4, quoted by Benokraitis and Feagin 1978:13).

Throughout this period, various lawsuits concerning discrimination in education and employment came before various courts. A particularly important case, *Griggs v. Duke Power Co.,* was decided by the U.S. Supreme Court in 1971. Duke Power Company had required applicants for a job or a promotion who did not have a high school diploma to pass a written test—one that whites passed more frequently than blacks. The plaintiffs argued that the test was too general and was not designed to test the specific abilities needed to perform the various jobs in question. The defendants argued that the same test was given to all job applicants and was, therefore, fair. The Court sided with the plaintiffs and ruled that employers must give tests that measure the abilities and skills that are pertinent to the job for which an application is being made. The tests were required to be fair not only in being the same for all applicants, but also in having a demonstrable relationship to job performance. Tests that routinely led to higher failure rates among the members of one race were suspect. This decision placed on the employer the burden of proving that employment procedures were fair, and it strengthened the argument that apparently "neutral" procedures might, nevertheless, be deemed to be discriminatory if they consistently produced unequal results.

Following the *Griggs* ruling, there was a sharp increase in the number of successful lawsuits that relied on statistical evidence to show that certain employment practices had a "disparate impact" on minority workers. Given these successes, and to avoid the costs of lawsuits, many employers began voluntary affirmative action programs aimed at removing racial and sexual imbalances in their work forces. For eighteen years, the Court's ruling appeared to be settled national policy; however, in 1989 the Court ruled in *Ward's Cove Packing v. Antonio* that employers no longer were required to shoulder the burden of proof in disparate impact cases. Instead, plantiffs were given the burden of showing that the practices they wish to challenge are not necessary (Greenhouse 1989:D6). This ruling, along with several others that narrowed the definition of racial harassment in the work place, reduced assistance to minority group contractors, simplified attacks on affirmative action, and created a widespread belief that many of the antidiscrimination programs of the preceding twenty-five years were in danger of being revoked.

Although nothing in the Civil Rights Act of 1964 or the executive orders we have reviewed required affirmative action in education, the similarities of the problems of discrimination in education and employment (and their legal remedies) served to bring together the conflict over principles in the two institutional arenas, and in 1972 Congress amended Title VII to extend coverage to educational institutions (Glickstein 1977:23). Though it may seem ironic, the application of affirmative action procedures has been fought as bitterly in the field of higher education as in any other segment of American society. For example, in the famous U.S. Supreme Court case *Regents of the University of California v. Bakke* (1978), Allan Bakke, a white applicant to the medical school at the University of California at Davis, argued that he had been discriminated against by the university because the medical school had established a quota for minority applicants. Although Bakke's grades were higher than those of some minority applicants who were admitted to the school, Bakke was denied admission. The Court ruled, in a complicated, closely contested decision, that Bakke was correct. The medical school could set a "goal" for the number of minority admissions, the ruling said, but it could not establish a rigid numerical "quota." The difference between a goal and a quota, in principle at least, is that a goal may be reached by showing "evidence of good faith and positive effort" (Pottinger 1977:44) and without compromising standards of merit and ability. Quotas, on the other hand, may be reached only by hiring a certain number of people in each target group even if standards of merit and ability are made to suffer. Critics maintain that, in practice, "numerical goals" and "precise timetables" are indistinguishable from quotas (Hook 1977:88).

The lines of argument surrounding desegregation in education and affirmative action in employment (including admissions and employment in higher education) have converged, and together they have presented American society with one of its most difficult ideological dilemmas. On the one hand, with the *Brown* decisions, the passage of the Civil Rights Act of 1964, and the passage of the Voting Rights Act of 1965, American society had fulfilled its political commitment to the civil equality of all persons without regard to "any individual's race, color, religion, sex, or national origin"; on the other hand, in the economic sphere, as well as in other social realms, the effects of past discrimination have continued into the present, even in the face of apparently "neutral," nondiscriminatory practices.

It is this continuation, of course, that fostered the belief that "something more" than simple neutrality, something "positive" and "affirmative," was required to assist the victims of discrimination to achieve economic equality. But how, critics ask, can we achieve a just society if we abandon the historic ideal of "colorblindness"? Isn't it a paradox that at just the historical moment when we had reached the goal of making it illegal to notice people's color, sex, and ethnicity in education and employment we then, in Glazer's (1987:4) words, "began an extensive effort to record the race, color, and (some) national origins of just about every student and employee . . . in the nation?" When we take note of color and deny a white person a job or admission to a professional school, is this an act of affirmative action or of reverse discrimination?

Critics of affirmative action often cite the language of the Civil Rights Act of 1964 and Executive Order 11246 to show that such action is, in fact, reverse discrimination and is unlawful. The Civil Rights Act, for instance, says that the law shall not "be interpreted to require any employer . . . to grant preferential treatment to any individual or to any group because of race, color, religion, sex or national origin because of an imbalance" in percentages or the total number of employees (Todorovich 1977:13). Executive Order 11246 states that although contractors "will take affirmative action," they "will not discriminate against any employee or applicant because of race, color, religion, sex or national origin" (Todorovich 1977:14).

The joint requirement that employers must avoid discrimination but, at the same time, must act affirmatively lies at the heart of the debate (Pottinger 1977:42). Defenders of affirmative action note that the courts have stated repeatedly that there is no contradiction in these requirements and that affirmative action is not reverse discrimination. One ruling stated, for example, that unless "affirmative relief against continuation of effects of past discrimination" is permitted, the stated purposes of the Civil Rights Act of 1964 would be completely nullified (Glickstein 1977:15).

The critics are unimpressed by such views. Court rulings stating that affirmative action is required by the Civil Rights Act of 1964, they argue, ignore the plain language of the law. They cite instances in which the phrase "without regard to race" have been interpreted to mean "with regard to race" (Todorovich 1977:20). Berns (quoted by Yarbrough 1985:v) warned that "if the laws may be used to discriminate against whites, there is no reason why . . . the laws may not once again be used to discriminate against blacks." Court rulings favoring affirmative action also ignore, critics say, the undeniable intent of the members of Congress who supported the law. Senator Hubert Humphrey, who was a strong supporter of the law, stated that the act "does not require an employer to achieve any kind of racial balance . . . by giving any kind of preferential treatment to any individual or group" (Sowell 1977:115).

Supporters of the law consider this criticism to be misleading. A simple recitation of the language of the law that prohibits preferential treatment neglects to note that this provision is inapplicable unless it is shown that there has been discrimination in the past. A neutral policy that is consistent with the language in question can succeed only when discrimination has not existed in the past or when the results of past discrimination have been overcome (Glickstein 1977:26; U.S. Commission on Civil Rights 1981a:15–37). Critics reply that, in fact, the requirement of showing past discrimination frequently has been ignored by the courts.

Another line of argument by supporters of affirmative action maintains that the relief afforded is intended to be only temporary. In upholding affirmative action in the *Bakke* decision, Justice Blackmun expressed his hope that such a policy would be unnecessary "within a decade at the most" (quoted by H. Graham 1992:51). Timetables, as well as goals, are a fundamental part of the remedy. Whenever the effects of past discrimination have been "sufficiently" removed, it is said, then we may return to the historic ideal of "colorblindness." In other words, affirmative action programs may be dismantled when their results have been achieved. Again, the critics of affirmative action find little consolation in such assurances. Although a few school systems and employers have been released from their obligations to continue their desegregation and affirmative action programs, most of these programs have by now become well institutionalized throughout the country, and it is by no means easy to foretell when they no longer will be necessary. On the other hand, the philosophy of affirmative action has not, as its critics feared, been able to drive out and replace the ideal of a colorblind society. Instead, we have reached what one scholar calls a condition of "stasis" (Glazer 1987:vii). On the whole, Americans seem neither to have accepted unconditionally the permanent necessity of affirmative action nor to have abandoned the idea that a just society requires individuals to be treated on their merits and without regard to their ascribed characteristics. Some critics, such as Glazer (1987:xviii), while maintaining that affirmative action is wrong in principle and should not be extended, nevertheless agree that the "massive machinery" of affirmative action is held in place because of "the condition of the Black population of the United States. . . . " Glazer went on to say that "the misery characterizing the mass of their poor stands as the great argument for affirmative action."

A most important consideration in all of this, of course, is whether affirmative action programs "work." Do they lead to increases in the hiring and promotion of minority and women workers? Do they lead to increases in the admission of minority students to graduate and professional programs? As we by now should expect, the evidence on these questions is mixed and controversial. For example, Robinson and Spitz (1986–87:88) cited several large-scale studies showing that affirmative action has "proven its effectiveness in increasing the employment of minorities and women while producing positive business results." And the Committee on the Status of Black Americans (Jaynes and Williams 1989:319) concluded that "while we cannot determine with the available data the precise numerical effect of antidiscrimination programs, the evidence does show positive effects."

Nevertheless, Sowell (1977:130) maintained that even if affirmative action programs do "here and there" help someone to get a job or be admitted to a college, the general effect of such programs has been "to destroy the legitimacy" of black achievements by making them "look like questionable accomplishments, or even outright gifts." He believes that the main beneficiaries of affirmative action have been the federal enforcement bureaucracies that have become "an administrative empire serving itself in the name of serving the disadvantaged" (Sowell 1977:131). Black (1977:176) also agreed that affirmative action undermines our basic concepts of social justice. Such programs may, for a time, appear to be desirable instruments of change, but in the long run, she argued, the "tribal logic of group discrimination" will backfire and the intended beneficiaries of the programs will be harmed. Kluegel and Smith (1982) found in this regard that the majority of white Americans believe that blacks and other racial minorities now have a much better than average chance to get ahead.

In a broader context, the consequences and life expectancies of affirmative action programs have created what Gordon (1981) referred to as "The New American Dilemma." Even if we have reached the condition of "stasis" described by Glazer, may we yet move permanently away from being a society that recognizes only the rights of individuals to become one in which the rights of groups also are acknowledged? If we do accept the latter goal (which Gordon called corporate pluralism), we accept a pattern that already exists to some degree in countries such as Belgium, Canada, and Switzerland and that existed in the former Soviet Union. In such societies, quotas are accepted in varying degrees and the ideal of economic justice is held to require that the distributions of income, power, and status of recognized groups shall be approximately equal (Gordon 1981:182–187).

There is, of course, much more to be said on the complex subject of legal approaches to the reduction of prejudice and discrimination. We conclude by noting that these approaches are consistent with the thinking of all those who emphasize the possibility and importance of direct methods of controlling discrimination, even though there are some important differences in the methods preferred by different theorists. Some who advocate direct-control methods, for instance, may place heavy emphasis on educational programs aimed at the reduction of prejudice, while others, such as the institutional discrimination theorists, may focus more attention on the way organizational rules are administered and on the laws passed by legislative bodies. Our discussion of affirmative action illustrates the point that the rules governing hiring and firing by corporations and those regulating all forms of licensing and certification play an enormously important role in the day-to-day lives of everyone in our society. Institutional discrimination theorists argue that strategic changes in the countless "laws" of the large bureaucracies of modern society are necessary before any attitudinal changes that may have taken place can be made effective.

Organized Social Protest

Although the role of organized protest in the reduction of discrimination is explored later, some preliminary comments are appropriate at this point. The discussion thus far has rested on the assumption that the majority's levels of prejudice and discrimination may be reduced with relatively little disharmony or open intergroup conflict. The usual expectation of those who favor education, intergroup contact, the passage of laws, and affirmative action is that, grumbling and complaining aside, the majority will respond to a program of change by easing its pressure on minorities and that the minorities, after some period of time, will become "equal" to the majority. Intergroup tensions will have been reduced with only moderate "dislocations" and "adjustments" along the way.

This assumption has been sharply challenged, usually by minority group members. It is argued, in keeping with the group gains theory, that equality will never be given freely by the majority. The majority is much more likely, in this view, to reduce its levels of discrimination in the face of a boycott, a strike, or a sit-in than in response to the usual kind of educational program or even to laws prohibiting discrimination. Indeed, the majority may be unwilling to adopt laws of this type unless it is pressured to do so by organized minority groups.

From this vantage point, it is possible to claim that whenever the legal approach succeeds, this result is largely due to the power of the minorities.

However desirable such things as educational programs, interracial contacts, and antidiscrimination laws may be, they must always be only a part of a larger program consisting of strong ethnic organizations and constant pressure on the majority. All efforts to reduce discrimination and to attain a social standing that is acceptable to the minority must involve some conflict. It is crucial to distinguish here, however, between nonviolent and violent conflict. Many who accept nonviolent conflict as a necessary part of social change are totally opposed to the use of violence and believe that it is, indeed, counterproductive.

Conclusion

We have seen that many students assume ethnic prejudice to be the sole or principal cause of discrimination and believe, therefore, that the primary question to be answered is, "What causes prejudice?" The underlying assumption here is that if the causes of prejudice can be discovered, then prejudice and, ultimately, discrimination can be reduced by attacking those causes. We have seen further, though, some evidence to suggest that discrimination has other roots. It may not arise mainly from prejudice; its reduction, therefore, may not require an attack on prejudice. Indeed, we have found that if discrimination is controlled first, a surprise extra benefit is sometimes a subsequent decline in prejudice.

The merits of these two opposing approaches—whether to attack prejudice or discrimination first—have led many observers to the view that a compromise is needed. A compromise approach emphasizes the reciprocal relationship of prejudice and discrimination and calls for a simultaneous attack at many different points in the causal chain.

From the standpoint of practical application, the main question is, "Are efforts to create social change aided more by theories that emphasize the role of prejudice, discrimination, or both?" The few illustrations presented show that various educational approaches can reduce prejudice. They do not tell us, however, whether these changes in attitude lead to less discrimination and toward equality among racial and ethnic groups. Our illustrations suggest, too, that discrimination may be reduced through legal means even though the prejudice levels of the dominant group have not been previously lowered. Laws against discrimination are aided by the open support of officials and other respected citizens. They also are aided by swift and certain enforcement. Nevertheless, the effort to control discrimination through law faces many obstacles and cannot be relied on as a sole solution to the problem.

Although we are very far indeed from being able to say exactly what measures are most effective in reducing prejudice and discrimination, our analysis supports the following conclusion: Given our present knowledge, it is probably best to assume that prejudice and discrimination form a vicious circle and must be attacked simultaneously. It is likely, however, that most people overestimate the role of prejudice as a cause of discrimination. Dominant group members, in particular, tend to ignore or play down the possible effectiveness of strategies that focus on the control of discrimination rather than the reduction of prejudice. Legal methods and some direct-action approaches not only may be the most effective ways to reduce discrimination but also may assist, through time, in the reduction of prejudice as well.

Key Ideas

1. Theories of prejudice and discrimination suggest ways to attack these problems. Dominant group members tend to focus on the reduction of prejudice, theories that emphasize cultural transmission and personality, and education as a tool of social change.

2. One important form of intergroup education is to expose people to information concerning out-groups; another is to assist people "to take the role of the other" through books, plays, films, and so on. Both of these methods appear to be useful but not powerful methods of reducing prejudice. The emotional approach seems to be somewhat more effective than the factual approach.

3. Intergroup contacts may be effective in reducing prejudice if the people involved are of similar social status and are engaged in an enjoyable or mutually significant activity. Under other circumstances, intergroup contacts may lead to increased prejudice.

4. Subordinate group members tend to focus on the reduction of discrimination, theories that emphasize group gains and institutional discrimination, and the law as an instrument of social change.

5. Many forms of discrimination may be reduced directly rather than by attempting first to alter people's prejudices. The passage and strict enforcement of antidiscrimination laws, even when these laws are not popular, may bring about rapid changes in behavior. Of course, attempts to "outflank" people's opinions and to require them not to discriminate may boomerang; under many circumstances, however, they do not. Furthermore, once people's discriminatory behavior has been altered, their prejudices are, in many instances, subsequently reduced.

6. Affirmative action has afforded one of the most important and controversial legal attacks on discrimination. Whether employers should or can take race and ethnicity into account in hiring and promotions without also compromising the nation's commitment to a colorblind society is at the heart of the issue.

7. Although America's contemporary policies and noblest ideals assume that prejudice and discrimination may be sharply reduced entirely through education and the passage of laws, history shows that changes in majority-minority relations typically have required the organized protest of minorities. While organized protest necessarily involves conflict, effective conflict may be limited to boycotts, strikes, lobbying, and other nonviolent tactics.

8. Since prejudice and discrimination form a vicious circle, it is best to attack them simultaneously. The exclusive or preponderant attention given in the past to the causes and reduction of prejudice rather than directly to discrimination is unwarranted.

Notes

1. An important effort to organize these ideas into an explanation of the effects of contact was presented by Robin Williams (1964:81–88).

2. Two other areas of special research interest are desegregation in the armed services (see, e.g., Buttler and Wilson 1978) and in the work place (see, e.g., Pettigrew and Martin 1989).

3. A review of the literature by Stephan (1988:13,16) supported the conclusion that in the short run "desegregation leads to small improvements in black reading achievement" and that in the long run "blacks who have attended desegregated high schools are more likely to finish high school, attend college, earn higher GPAs while in college, and are . . . less likely to drop out of college than blacks who attended segregated high schools." He also concluded that desegregation does not increase black self-esteem.

4. These researchers found, in an earlier study, that even though interracial friendships are rare, they are almost as stable as same-race choices (Hallinan and Williams 1987:662).

5. During the 1830s, after a white performer in blackface, Thomas D. Rice, presented a song that referred to Jim Crow, the term became a popular code word for the segregation of black people (Jordan and Litwack 1987:397; Woodward 1957:7).

6. For a spirited defense of the latter view, see Graglia (1976:46–66). Orfield (1978) presented arguments against each of the other claims.

7. The extent to which this trend reflects the "normal" forces of spatial mobility or was accelerated by school desegregation (the so-called "white flight" phenomenon) has been the subject of considerable debate and research. For reviews and interpretations of the findings, see Armor (1980), Jaynes and Williams (1989:83), and Sly and Pol (1980). Studies of the problems of desegregating housing, to which we return in chapter 11, show that white residents begin to leave a neighborhood if the number of black residents exceeds 8 percent of the total and that a "tipping point," beyond which all (or nearly all) whites will leave is reached when the percentage of black residents "is somewhere between 10 and 20 percent" (Hacker 1992:37). There are conspicuous exceptions, of course, and we need to know much more about them (see, e.g., Richardson 1992:A13; Ton 1992:A14).

8. For discussions of the implications of this important decision, see U.S. Commission on Civil Rights (1974).

9. Earlier examples of positive government action to combat discrimination, though they were not called "affirmative action," may be found. The Wagner Act of 1935, for instance, required both the cessation of discrimination and positive actions to reinstate some workers with back pay (Sowell 1977:114).

C h a p t e r 8

Japanese Americans

I am proud that I am an American citizen of Japanese ancestry . . . Because I believe in America . . . I pledge to do her honor in all times and all places. —MIKE MASAOKA

To create a truly fulfilling identity, Asian Americans realize they must redefine and articulate Asian American identity on their own terms. —AMY TACHIKI

Our discussions of immigration to America, nativism and racism, and prejudice and discrimination showed that the less the members of a group have resembled the Anglo-American ideal of an "American," the less acceptable they have been to the dominant group and the more prejudice and discrimination they have suffered. Those groups that are socially most "distant" from the dominant group's notion of the ideal American have been considered to be the lowest in "assimilative potential" or even to be "unassimilable."

Of all the many factors that affect the dominant group's reactions to a subordinate group, the factor of race has been most troublesome. We noted that during the colonial period, blacks and American Indians were defined as standing outside the developing Anglo-American society. As other racially distinctive groups have entered or been brought into the territory of the United States, they also have been viewed typically as being too distant from the American ideal to be included as full members of American society. They have been subjected, therefore, to levels of prejudice and discrimination resembling those directed toward the blacks and Indians. From this perspective, nonwhite people in America have had fewer opportunities and faced greater obstacles to material or worldly success than have white people. The possibility for these groups "to climb the ladder of success" (e.g., to achieve secondary assimilation) has been lower from the first and has remained so. Both the level of past discrimination and the extent to which that discrimination has been carried into the present are at issue.

Many Americans either reject this argument outright or accept only a modified form of it. Some believe that the obstacles standing in the way of the success of nonwhite groups is hardly different from those faced by their own forefathers. Others, who comprise the largest group, will agree that nonwhites have faced the highest levels of prejudice and discrimination, but they will not agree that these barriers have been large enough to explain why African, Mexican, and Native Americans have remained conspicuously outside the mainstream of American life. Probably, most white Americans believe that hard work, education, perseverance, and faith in the American dream are still the main ingredients of success in American society (Kluegel 1990:513). From this vantage point, even those who suffer the highest levels of prejudice and discrimination should be able to succeed if they will only try hard enough. Their battle may be more difficult, so the argument goes, but if they will quietly tend to their business, opportunities will appear and they will earn their place in American society.

The preceding contrast (differences in levels of discrimination versus differences in levels of effort) ignores the many other factors we have mentioned that affect the rate of assimilation of minorities and is, therefore, too sharp. The contrast nonetheless reflects real political differences in modern America and serves as a useful point of reference for further consideration of the experiences of all nonwhite groups in America.

This observation is especially true of Japanese Americans. While (as we discuss later) the largest nonwhite groups in America have been comparatively unsuccessful, materially speaking, Japanese Americans frequently have been singled out as an exception to the rule. A series of articles and books have proclaimed Japanese

Americans to be a "model minority," a nonwhite group that has overcome all obstacles through hard work and determination (Hosokawa 1969; Michner and Brinkley-Rogers 1971; Petersen 1971). One observer said, for example, that "no other immigrant group ever faced such difficulties as the Japanese encountered in this country" and "no group ever conducted themselves more creditably" (McWilliams 1949:155). Another contended that among those now alive, Japanese Americans have suffered more discrimination and injustice than any other of America's minorities (Petersen 1971:3). Despite the odds, however, in terms of many criteria of success and assimilation, the Japanese appear to have "made it" in America. They seem to vindicate the Horatio Alger stories of the American dream. For example, the average (mean) number of years of education among native-born Japanese Americans in 1976 was 13.2 years (Hirschman and Wong 1985:296). This level exceeded not only that attained by whites in 1976 but also the median level attained by whites in 1987 (12.7 years; U.S. Bureau of the Census 1989b:131).[1] Similarly, among white Americans who were employed in 1976, 14.2 percent of the males and 15.3 percent of the females were in occupations classified by the U.S. Bureau of the Census (1970:31) as "professional, technical, and kindred workers." Among Japanese Americans, 21.4 percent of the males and 15.9 percent of the females were classified in these high-prestige occupations.[2]

The extent, cost, and meaning of Japanese American success, however, has been the subject of debate. While most Japanese Americans appear to agree that theirs is a successful group, some others are not so sure. For instance, although in 1970 the average (mean) income was $9,159 for Japanese American men and $9,150 for their majority group counterparts (Kitano 1981:130), the respective average (median) incomes for families were $9,590 and $9,961. Since one might expect that the educational superiority of the Japanese Americans and their higher representation within professional occupations would have led to a clear earnings advantage for them, some observers interpreted the ambiguous standing of the two groups to be a reflection of continued discrimination against Japanese Americans. In addition, Kuo suggested that since most Japanese American professionals are in technical careers, the earnings difference may reflect an underrepresentation in positions of institutional power (cited by Hirschman and Wong 1985:303). These arguments have been weakened subsequently because by 1976, according to Hirschman and Wong (1984:594), the average income advantage of native-born Japanese American men over white men had increased substantially ($15,100 versus $13,500) and by 1988 Japanese American men were earning slightly more, on the average, than would be expected "given their educational levels and other relevant characteristics" (U.S. Commission on Civil Rights 1988:1).

The possibility that Japanese Americans may still suffer significantly from discrimination leads some members of this group to reject the idea that they are a modern American "success story." Many Japanese Americans, consequently, consider the "success story" characterization to be a self-serving stereotype through which the dominant group attempts to deny the continuation of discrimination against the Japanese Americans and to prove that a lack of effort—not discrimination—is responsible for the problems of African, Mexican, and Native Americans (Tachiki 1971:1).[3]

The Japanese Americans, then, present a puzzling and instructive picture. Despite their nonwhite racial identification, they appear in several important respects to have followed a path of assimilation resembling that of many of the new immigrants who were arriving from Europe during the same period. They surely have not disappeared as a group, however, and there is today a new questioning within the Japanese American community of its place in American society. Let us begin to explore this puzzle by examining some of the most important events that have affected the Japanese since their arrival in the United States. We return later to questions concerning the types and extent of Japanese American assimilation.

Japanese Immigration and Native Reactions

Anti-Asian Sentiment

The peak years of Japanese immigration occurred during the second immigrant stream from Europe. This period, please recall, was characterized by the growing hostility of native Americans to foreigners, by the development and popularization of racist ideas, and by the growth of legal efforts to restrict immigration; therefore, even though the Japanese immigration to America was comparatively small, many factors combined to create the impression that the United States was in grave danger of being overrun by "hordes" of "Mongolians" and must be constantly on guard against the "yellow peril." Although the phrase the "yellow peril" originally had been applied mainly to the Chinese, by 1905 it referred primarily to the Japanese.[4] In that year, a war between Russia and Japan ended in a resounding victory for Japan. For the first time since the Europeans had commenced to colonize the world during the fifteenth century, a "colored" nation had defeated a "white" nation. In so doing, Japan established a reputation as a first-rank military power. The belief that the United States was in imminent danger of being swamped in a sea of human waves from the East gained in popular acceptance, especially in California. This belief helped to revive those fears among California's working people that previously had been directed toward the Chinese, as we have seen in chapter 5, and to create a unified stand among them against the Japanese.

The extraordinary unity of California's white working people against the Japanese, as well as other Asian people, rested on a paradox. Although California has long been an important agricultural state, it has had a powerful labor movement from the very beginning. For such a movement to exist in a nonindustrial state, many different elements had to combine. Shopkeepers, rural people, and white-collar workers have all strongly supported labor unions. The glue holding this unusual coalition together, according to McWilliams (1949:140), has been an anti-Asian "emotional class consciousness." In addition, therefore, to the usual opposition laboring immigrants have faced from their direct native competitors,

Asian Americans in California have had to contend with a broadly based, powerful labor movement. In California, only the upper classes consistently have favored open immigration.

Practically none of the early criticism of "Asiatics" and "Mongolians" was directed toward the Japanese. From 1638 to 1868, the Japanese government had not permitted its citizens to emigrate; so until 1868 there had been no official Japanese emigration to the United States. Previous to that only a few castaways and government representatives had ever reached this country (Ichihashi 1932:47–48). Even after the Japanese government began to permit emigration, those granted passports were mainly students, who were expected to seek knowledge and come back home "so that the foundations of the Empire may be strengthened" (Ichihashi 1932:3). Laborers, in particular, were still forbidden to leave the country. The Japanese government did not wish to create the impression that Japan, like China, was a reservoir of coolie labor; consequently, until 1884, laborers did not receive permission to travel abroad (Ichihashi 1932:6).[5] Before 1890, hardly more than four thousand Japanese ever had traveled to the United States, and more than half of these had returned home (Ichihashi 1932:53). As a result, the U.S. census of 1890 showed only 2,039 Japanese in the entire country.

As noted previously, the Chinese Exclusion Act of 1882 marks the first time the United States acted either to restrict immigration on the basis of national origin or to bar members of a particular group from becoming citizens; however, since the act provided for the resumption of Chinese immigration in 1892, the supporters of Chinese exclusion continued to agitate, and the legislation was extended beyond 1892.[6] At just this time, the Japanese began to arrive in larger numbers. For example, in 1891 about fifteen hundred Japanese immigrants reached the United States. Although this was still an extremely small number compared to the population of the United States at that time or compared to the numbers of immigrants arriving simultaneously from several other countries, it represented a noticeable increase in Japanese immigration over the previous years. This increase, following as it did some forty years of anti-Chinese agitation, attracted the unfavorable attention of the San Francisco *Morning Call*. In a series of five articles, the *Call* launched a "crusade against Japanese contract labor" (Daniels 1969:20). The paper claimed the Japanese immigrants were taking work away from Americans and that by 1900 their immigration would reach a yearly level of 120,000. The number of Japanese arriving during the decade of the 1890s did, in fact, rise sharply over the 1880s: in 1900, there were over 25,000 Japanese in the United States (Table 8-1). But that number did not even come close to the dire predictions of the *Call*.[7]

Anti-Japanese Protest

The first large anti-Japanese protest meeting in California was organized in 1900, after labor unions gained partial control of the San Francisco city government (tenBroek, Barnhart, and Matson 1954:35). The meeting featured such prominent figures of the day as J. D. Phelan (later a U.S. senator) and E. A. Ross, a sociology professor at Stanford University. Phelan declared, in a speech to the group, that

TABLE 8-1 Japanese
Immigration to the United
States, 1861–1990*

Years	Number
1861–1870	149
1871–1880	186
1881–1890	2,270
1891–1900	25,942
1901–1910	129,797
1911–1920	83,837
1921–1930	33,462
1931–1940	1,948
1941–1950	1,555
1951–1960	46,250
1961–1970	39,988
1971–1980	49,775
1981–1990	47,085
Total	462,244

Source: U.S. Immigration and
Naturalization Service. *1990 Statistical
Yearbook* 1991:48–50.
*There is no record of immigration from
Japan before 1861.

"these Asiatic laborers will undermine our civilization" (tenBroek, Barnhart, and Matson 1954:35). He stated also, in a conspicuous display of poor judgment, that "the Chinese and Japanese are not the stuff of which American citizens can be made" (Daniels 1969:21). Ross advanced the familiar claim that Japanese immigration undercut native labor, a sentiment echoed in that election year by the platforms of both major political parties.

The charge that the Japanese were a threat to American labor deserves further comment. The small numbers of the Japanese plus the vigor of the native resistance to them have led writers to assume that the hostility toward the Japanese was totally or largely without foundation, that it was an "irrational" rejection based primarily on the fact of racial and cultural differences. This position was criticized by Bonacich (1972:551–554) on two grounds. First, she argued that Japanese workers for the most part were fortune seekers who intended to return home to Japan as soon as possible ("sojourners"); consequently, they were willing to work for lower wages than members of any other group and to work longer hours at the convenience of the employer. These characteristics served to reduce the overall cost of Japanese labor. Second, one should not assume that lower-cost labor must be present in large numbers to pose a genuine threat to native laborers. If the latter have reason to believe that a small group of lower-priced laborers are the vanguard of a larger flow, then they have a realistic basis for opposing that flow. Bonacich

(1972:555) argued therefore, as noted in chapter 6, that the movement to exclude the Japanese was an understandable reaction of higher-priced labor to the split labor market created by Japanese immigration.

After the anti-Japanese outbursts of 1900, things quieted down again until 1905. In that year, however, a sustained campaign against the Japanese was launched. The most conspicuous forces initiating this campaign were, as in 1892, a newspaper and, as in 1900, organized labor. The newspaper was the very influential, highly respected *San Francisco Chronicle*. Beginning in February 1905 and continuing for nearly a year, the *Chronicle* ran "scare" headlines and page-one articles attacking Japanese immigration. In its first broadside, the headline read: "THE JAPANESE INVASION, THE PROBLEM OF THE HOUR." Some of the subsequent headlines included "THE YELLOW PERIL—HOW JAPANESE CROWD OUT THE WHITE RACE" (Daniels 1969:25). In the articles accompanying such headlines, the paper repeated the old claims that the Japanese immigration would become a "raging torrent" that would inundate the West Coast. Repeated and embroidered, too, were the charges that the Japanese were unassimilable and were an economic threat to native laborers. In March 1905, the California legislature passed a resolution attacking the Japanese as "undesirable" and as a "blight" that would soon descend on our shores (Daniels 1969:27). It also asked Congress to restrict the further immigration of the Japanese. Every session of the California legislature for the next forty years considered measures against the Japanese.

The anti-Japanese barrage led to the formation, in May 1905, of the Japanese and Korean Exclusion League, which was later renamed the Asiatic Exclusion League (tenBroek, Barnhart, and Matson 1954:35). This league, comprised primarily of labor union representatives, was the first and most prominent organization founded for the purpose of excluding the Japanese from the United States. Its program listed both economic and racial reasons for exclusion. Among its principles, for instance, were listed the arguments, "We cannot compete with a people having a low standard of wages" and "It should be against public policy to permit our women to intermarry with Asiatics" (Daniels 1969:28). Although the Asiatic Exclusion League represented the conservative wing of the American labor movement, its main goal also was endorsed by many socialists. Jack London conveyed the prevailing mood in the following: "I am first of all a white man and only then a Socialist" (Daniels 1969:30). In 1907, the National Executive Committee of the American Socialist Party unanimously agreed to oppose the immigration of Asiatics.

The School Board Crisis

One of the first actions of the Asiatic Exclusion League was to endorse the segregation of Japanese pupils in the public schools of San Francisco. This idea was not new. In fact, the San Francisco Board of Education had announced only a few days before the league was formed that such a plan was being considered. In view of the fact that the "separate but equal" doctrine of public education had been in effect by this time for nine years, such an action does not seem too strange.[8] Moreover, since the segregation would affect only a small number of pupils in only one city, we might expect no more than local interest in it. Strangely enough, though, the conflict in San Francisco concerning the segregation of Japanese pupils spiraled into a tense confrontation between the governments of the United States and Japan.

The combined agitations of the *Chronicle* and the league were followed by a rapid increase in the number of incidents of interracial violence in San Francisco. Individual Japanese people were attacked. Rocks and eggs were thrown at and into places of business owned by Japanese. And a boycott instituted against Japanese restaurants was ended only after the restaurant owners agreed to pay for "protection." These incidents were accompanied by periodic demands that the board of education implement the segregation plan that had been mentioned. A year and a half after the league began its agitation, the board of education ordered all Japanese, Chinese, and Korean pupils to attend a separate school for Orientals. The board defended this action by referring to a California law that permitted school boards to take such steps.

This event received little public attention at the time, even in San Francisco, but it was destined to be amply noticed. Nine days after the order went into effect, various reports concerning it were published in Tokyo newspapers, and the Japanese government filed an official complaint with President Theodore Roosevelt. At this point, a problem that previously had been mainly of local interest became a matter of national concern and, possibly, of national security. President Roosevelt quickly announced his concern about the situation and authorized Secretary of State Elihu Root to use armed forces if necessary to protect the Japanese. A few weeks later, the president asked for more authority to protect the rights of aliens and, thereby, to prevent local mobs from committing acts "which would plunge us into war" (Daniels 1969:39).

The school board crisis set into motion a long and complicated series of negotiations between the governments of the United States and Japan, on the one hand, and the federal and California governments, on the other. President Roosevelt was sufficiently impressed by Admiral Togo's victory over the Russian fleet to believe that a solution must be reached that was in no way insulting to Japan. At the same time, he was eager to find some way to restrict Japanese immigration and to appease the anti-Japanese forces in California.

A compromise was achieved in two main steps during 1907 and 1908. The president agreed that he would move to restrict Japanese immigration if the school board would permit Japanese children, citizens or aliens, to return to the regular public schools. He also urged the California governor and state legislature to reject any further efforts to pass anti-Japanese legislation. On March 13, 1907, the board repealed the school segregation resolution, and on the next day the president issued an executive order saying that Japanese workers would no longer be permitted to enter the United States through Mexico, Canada, or Hawaii unless their passports specifically entitled them to do so (Ichihashi 1932:244–245).

The second part of the compromise was the celebrated "Gentlemen's Agreement" between the United States and Japan concerning the types of emigration the Japanese government would encourage. Under the terms of the agreement, to begin in the summer of 1908, the government of Japan would continue issuing passports to the United States only to nonlaborers; laborers who lived in America but had been visiting Japan; the wives, parents, and children of those who had settled in America; and those who owned an interest in an American farm enterprise (Ichihashi 1932:246; Petersen 1971:43). Additionally, on its own initiative, the Japanese government applied the terms of the Gentlemen's Agreement to Hawaii (which was now a U.S. possession) and sharply curtailed the issuance of passports to those who wished to go to Mexico. Thus, some eighteen months after the school crisis had erupted, the Gentlemen's Agreement appeared to have resolved a difficult set of problems. The anti-Japanese elements in California believed that the further immigration of the Japanese had been stopped even though no insulting restrictions had been placed by the United States on direct immigration from Japan. That matter had been handled "voluntarily" by the Japanese.[9]

The Gentlemen's Agreement had a dramatic impact on the number of Japanese aliens admitted to and remaining in the United States and Hawaii. The peak years of 1907–1908 were followed by sharp reductions in the number of admissions (Ichihashi 1932:58), and for the next two years departures actually exceeded admissions, resulting in a net decline of the Japanese population (Petersen 1971:197). These drastic changes ended what has been called the "frontier period" of the Japanese experience in America (LaViolette 1945:10; Miyamoto 1972:220).

The "Picture Bride" Invasion

As has been generally true of the vanguard among immigrant groups, most of the Japanese who came to America before 1908 were single men in search of a fortune; so at the beginning of this century there were in the United States nearly seven Japanese men for each Japanese woman (Petersen 1971:196). The Japanese community in America, consequently, contained few families and only the beginnings of ordinary institutional life. This situation changed rapidly, however, in the following decade. Since the Gentlemen's Agreement permitted those who were the wives of residents of the United States to enter, many of the men who decided to stay sent home to Japan for wives. This action was completely consistent with the Gentlemen's Agreement, but many Americans nevertheless saw it as treachery.

The traditional marriage customs of Japan became a topic of public discussion. In Japan, marriages were considered to be more a union of two families than of two individuals. When a young man was ready to marry, and an eligible woman was under consideration, a go-between who was respected by both families would investigate the backgrounds of the prospective partners. If both met all of the tests of eligibility, the go-between then would negotiate the wedding arrangements (Ichihashi 1932:293). Under normal circumstances, of course, the partners would meet at a specified place and time, and the wedding would be conducted. But what was to be done when the partners were, literally, oceans apart? A solution to this problem was the "picture bride marriage" (Miyamoto 1972:226). Under this arrangement, the prospective bride and groom exchanged photographs as a part of the agreement procedure. Then, after the go-between's work was over, the prospective bride would sail for America to conclude the marriage.

This practice of concluding marriages sight unseen struck many Americans as outrageous and uncivilized. Stories were circulated concerning fraudulent and "immoral" aspects of the process. It was said that the use of retouched photographs was common and that the Japanese men frequently "swapped" brides at the dock. More disturbing to many, though, was that the arrival of thousands of these "picture brides" seemed to confirm the view that the Japanese were determined to circumvent any measure intended to keep them from "overrunning" the country. If they were unable to accomplish this feat through immigration, it was said, then they would do it through high fertility rates!

The emotional character of the reaction to the "picture brides" created the impression that many more Japanese were arriving (and staying) than really were. During the period 1911–1920, however, so many Japanese left the country that the total gain of Japanese aliens was about seventeen thousand (Ichihashi 1932:292). The "picture bride" migration, nevertheless, greatly reduced the imbalance between the sexes in the Japanese community in America and created the conditions necessary for building families and developing institutionally complete communities. By 1920, there were less than two men for each woman, and the Japanese, like so many other immigrant groups, had formed numerous small communities and subcommunities that recreated, in many ways, the institutions and culture of the homeland.

The Japanese Family and Community in America

Family and Community Cohesion

Many immigrant groups to the United States have been clannish, have had families that (at least formally) were dominated by the father, have attached great importance to age, have given preference to male children (especially the first born), and have experienced a marked split between the first and second generations. While the Japanese were not unusual in possessing this cluster of characteristics, they exhibited them to an unusually high degree.

Consider the last point first. The different Japanese and Japanese American generations were so distinct from one another that they were identified by different names. The first-generation immigrants, the *Issei*, are primarily those who arrived before the legal exclusion of 1924. The second generation, the *Nisei*, are American-born citizens who generally reached adulthood before or by the outbreak of World War II. The third generation, the *Sansei*, were born mainly following World War II.[10]

The distinctiveness of the Japanese generations was created primarily by the interruption of the immigrant flow created, first, by the Gentlemen's Agreement and then, later, by exclusionary legislation. For this reason, the normal age gap that exists between generations became even more important than usual. The Issei did not continue to grow through the arrival of newcomers from Japan, so the age gap was not blurred by the presence of people of intermediate ages. Consequently, the Nisei seldom encountered a young person who recently had migrated from the old country. Nearly all of their peers were, like themselves, American-born. To a larger extent than is usually true of an immigrant group, therefore, the old-country experiences and ways of the Issei stood in sharp contrast to the American ways of the Nisei.

While the two-stage process through which the Issei immigration was halted generated special problems for them, it did not prevent them from developing in America, as in Japan, highly interdependent and cohesive communities. Within the ethnic community, a person could receive help in locating a job, finding a place to live, or starting a business. One could also speak the native language, eat familiar foods, and relax among relatives and friends. And, given the obvious hostility of so many Americans toward them, the ethnic community provided the Japanese some protection from the surrounding society. As has been true for other immigrant groups, the ethnic community was simultaneously a tool to assist the immigrant to adjust to the demands of the new setting and to sustain and embellish the way of life that had been left behind.[11]

Several aspects of Japanese family and community life are of special importance in understanding their adjustment in America both at the beginning and later on. As noted earlier, the traditional Japanese family was thought of not merely as a union of two people who were in love but as a union of two families. The extended family unit thus created was, in turn, connected in numerous ways through other marriages to the larger community. An important effect of this pattern of interrelationships was that everyone in the community had important obligations to many others within the community. The other side of the coin was that the family could call on the larger community for assistance and support. The Issei were extraordinarily eager to reestablish this traditional pattern of family and community relationships and to transmit its sustaining values to the Nisei. To a greater extent than most other immigrant groups of this period, the Issei identified with the homeland, took pride in its achievements, and, therefore, wished their children to have a strong tie to Japan. The open display of affection for Japan was frequently used against them in later years.

The Nisei were taught Japanese etiquette, which involves a high regard for obligation and authority. Children were expected to understand that they were members of a Japanese family and community, not just unfettered individuals, and that each member had numerous duties and responsibilities. The parents were obligated to the children, but the children were expected to reciprocate. In this way, the child learned that the acts of each individual are of significance to the entire group (LaViolette 1945:19; Miyamoto 1972:228–229).

In addition to the importance of politeness, respect for authority, attention to parental wishes, and duty to the community, the Issei also emphasized the traditional Japanese values of hard work, cleanliness, neatness, and honesty and the importance of education, occupational success, and good reputation. Although we turn later to an analysis of the importance of these values in the adjustment of the Japanese to American conditions, it is obvious that many traditional Japanese values are the same as many traditional values of the Anglo-Americans. We may presume even now, therefore, that their acceptance of these values has played an important part in the relations of the two groups.

As mentioned previously, the type of human relations stressed by the Issei within the family were synchronized with, and comprised an integral part of, the organization of the wider community. The main links between the extended family and the rest of the community grew out of the fact that people from the same areas of Japan tended to settle near one another in the United States. *Kenjin* (those from the same province or prefecture) felt especially close to one another and were preferred as friends, neighbors, business associates, and marriage partners. These bonds were so strong that associations based on them often were formed (*kenjinkai*). But the purposes of the *kenjinkai* went far beyond social, business, and recreational activities. They published newspapers, acted as employment agencies, provided legal advice, gave money to needy members, and paid medical and burial expenses (Light 1974:283). They also frequently sponsored a form of financial assistance known as the *tanomoshi-ko*. The *tanomoshi-ko* was an organization (usually of a few *kenjin*) through which money was pooled and then loaned in rotation to various members. This rotating pool of funds was loaned entirely on mutual trust and obligation (Light 1974:283; Miyamoto 1972:224; Petersen 1971:56–57). The success of the *tanomoshi-ko* frequently is cited to illustrate both the Japanese approach to worldly success and the strength of their interpersonal bonds.

Many of the functions of the *kenjinkai* were formalized in the Japanese Association, which, according to Kitano (1969:81), "was the most important Issei group." While the Japanese Association also provided numerous social and benevolent services, its main objective was the protection of the Japanese community. The Issei worked through this association to keep the Japanese community "in line" and, thereby, to reduce friction with the Americans. They also used the association to obtain legal services and police assistance. Whenever the police were unresponsive, the Japanese Association could turn to the Japanese consul and ask the Japanese government to intervene on their behalf. Everything considered, the Japanese Association has played an important role in establishing and maintaining traditional Japanese ways of life in the American setting and, consequently, of resisting cultural, primary, and marital assimilation (Kitano 1969:81–82). To the extent that the association promoted Japanese-owned businesses to serve an all-Japanese clientele, it also resisted secondary assimilation.

Another important form of association established by the Issei to build and strengthen the Japanese community in America was the Japanese Language School (Kitano 1969:24–25; LaViolette 1945:52–56; Petersen 1971:54–58). The Issei recognized that their ability to transmit the ideals of Japanese culture to their children required that the Nisei understand Japanese, so the main purpose of these schools was to teach Japanese to the Nisei. The schools also were expected to supplement the parents' efforts to instill the traditional ethics and values of Japan. Although the schools were not very effective in their efforts to transmit the Japanese language, they did symbolize the desire of the Issei to assure their children a Japanese education and, simultaneously, to prevent them from becoming "too American." The schools also brought the Nisei together after public school hours and on Saturdays, thereby strengthening the social ties among them and decreasing their contacts with other American children.

All of these factors combined to accentuate the differences between the Issei and Nisei. Each of the two generations was unusually homogeneous with respect to age, background, and general life experiences. The center of gravity within the Issei was the old country and its traditions. The Nisei, like most other second-generation groups, sought increasingly to break with the old ways.

Japanese Occupations and the Alien Land Laws

As stated earlier, the first Japanese to come to America after the Japanese government permitted it (in 1868) were not members of the laboring classes; they were students (the well-known "school boys") who took part-time jobs to help pay the costs of their stay. Most of these students worked as domestic servants. However, when the main body of Japanese immigration got underway during the 1890s, the new arrivals took a wide variety of jobs—in railroad construction, canning, lumbering, mining, fishing, seasonal farm labor, and so on. As the turn of the century approached, though, the Japanese moved increasingly into agricultural pursuits. During the first decade of the twentieth century, the number of Japanese in agriculture grew rapidly, especially in California, where they were most numerous; by 1908, agriculture was the leading form of employment among them (Ichihashi 1932:162–163).[12]

As the Japanese became more conspicuous in agriculture, native Americans began to complain that the Japanese were acquiring too much land and were "taking over" food production. As usual, a persuasive charge against the Japanese was they did not compete fairly. They were willing to work for less than white laborers and, in some instances, preferred payment in crops or land rather than in wages. In this way, they were gradually gaining a foothold in agriculture and driving out some of the native farmers.

The fear that the efficient Japanese would gradually acquire all of the farming land in California led to an increase in attempts to control them by legislation. Anti-Japanese land bills were introduced into the California legislature in 1909 and 1911. The first bill to become law, however, was the Alien Land Law of 1913. Although this law did not specifically mention the Japanese or any other nationality group, it was clearly aimed at the Japanese. Instead of saying that Japanese aliens could not own land, the law prohibited ownership by those who were "ineligible to citizenship."

This curious phrase rests on some equally curious facts about American naturalization law. When the first naturalization act was written in 1790, citizenship was made available to any "free white person," which excluded blacks and Indians; as noted in chapter 5, this prohibition was enlarged through the Chinese Exclusion Act of 1882. The ineligibility of the Japanese for citizenship, however, was based on a different circumstance. When Hawaii was annexed in 1898, "all persons who had been citizens of the Republic were given citizenship, and no others" (Petersen 1971:47). Since the Japanese had been denied citizenship in Hawaii, and since the Hawaiian rules of citizenship had been accepted by the United States, it was assumed when the Alien Land Law was enacted that the Japanese could not become citizens of the United States. As things turned out this position was correct, but the matter was not settled until 1922, when the Supreme Court ruled in *Ozawa v. United States* that the Japanese, indeed, were not eligible for citizenship.

The thinly veiled, discriminatory intent of the Alien Land Law was readily apparent in Japan. Once again, anti-Japanese activities in California precipitated an international incident. Many people in Japan favored war with the United States (Daniels 1969:61). When the law was signed, the Japanese government was very displeased and entered a vigorous official protest in Washington. The American government denied that the California law was intended to discriminate against the Japanese. Although the controversy stirred emotions on both sides of the Pacific, it was soon overshadowed by the gathering storm clouds of war in Europe. In the summer of 1914, World War I broke out. Japan quickly declared war on Germany and joined the Allies.

As matters developed, the Japanese were particularly successful in agriculture following the passage of the Alien Land Law. In the first place, the Issei soon learned ways to evade the law by registering their land in the names of their Nisei children (who were American citizens) or by placing their property in the hands of trusted American friends. Perhaps more important, though, than these legal evasions was that the outbreak of World War I sharply increased the need for agricultural workers. The Japanese were admirably suited to meet this sudden high demand. As a result, overt anti-Japanese activities in California were noticeably reduced.

Their traditional techniques of reclaiming land and farming it intensively served the Japanese well. "Their skill and energy," wrote Iwata (1962:37), "helped to reclaim and improve thousands of acres of worthless lands throughout the state . . . and made them fertile and immensely productive." Even though they controlled only about 1 percent of California's agricultural land, the crops they produced were valued at about 10 percent of the state's total. In Iwata's opinion (1962:37), the Issei were "a significant factor in making California one of the greatest farming States in the union."

When the war ended, the demand for agricultural products went down, and thousands of veterans came home looking for work. By then, too, it was obvious that the Gentlemen's Agreement had not stopped the growth of the Japanese population and that the Alien Land Law had not prevented the Japanese from increasing their land holdings. Hence, the agitation against the Japanese (whether Issei or Nisei) increased.[13] In 1920, an amended Alien Land Law was passed. This law attempted to close the loopholes of the earlier law. It even included a provision that prohibited the Issei from acquiring control of land by placing it in the names of their children. Since the Nisei were citizens of the United States, however, this provision was soon declared unconstitutional.

Exclusion

The Alien Land Law of 1920 represented the last major effort of the exclusionists to achieve their objective by working primarily at the state level. Their attention increasingly was centered on the idea of immigration restriction (or, if possible, exclusion) at the national level. And, as mentioned in our discussion of racism in chapter 5, the time was ripe for a national approach. The doctrine of white supremacy had become increasingly popular throughout the United States, as had the demand that the United States be protected against "the rising tide of color" through some form of federal restriction on immigration. Thus, the "California position" on the question of restriction, first articulated in opposition to the Chinese, had finally captured the sympathies of a national following.

The main thrust of the national movement was in the direction of some type of quota system rather than toward a system of exclusion. The Emergency Quota Act of 1921, as explained in chapter 5, established a quota system for many countries, but it also recognized the validity of the Gentlemen's Agreement and exempted Japan from the quota system. Nevertheless, when the Immigration Quota Act of 1924 (also discussed in chapter 5) was passed, the Gentlemen's Agreement was unilaterally repudiated and Japan was denied an immigration quota. At last, the dream of the exclusionists had been realized. Immigration from Japan had been stopped. This result is especially amazing when we consider that the number of Japanese who would have been eligible for admission each year under the quota system was 146!

Why did the United States accept the principle of exclusion for the Japanese (and thereby single Japan out for international humiliation) when the quota system would have reduced the number of Japanese immigrants to almost nothing? Surely what may be called the "racist climate of opinion" had something to do with it. Even some Americans who vigorously opposed a quota system for other nations were in favor of excluding the Japanese. Still, most leaders apparently favored a continuation of the Gentlemen's Agreement with the addition of a quota for Japan. The Japanese government apparently was ready to accept this new form of restriction since it applied to many other nations as well.

The crucial scene in this international tragedy was played primarily by Secretary of State Charles Evans Hughes, Ambassador Masanao Hanihara, and U.S. Senator Henry Cabot Lodge. At Hughes's suggestion, Ambassador Hanihara prepared a letter to Hughes that summarized the understandings of the Gentlemen's Agreement, expressed the Japanese government's willingness to modify the agreement if that pleased the United States, and briefly commented on the immigration bill then under consideration by Congress. The ambassador's comments concerning the immigration bill were guarded and very proper. He assured Secretary Hughes that the Japanese government in no way contested the right of the United States to regulate immigration but, in fact, wished to cooperate with the United States in doing so. He emphasized that Japan did not wish for its citizens to go where they were not wanted. He warned, though, that Japanese exclusion from the United

States would be "mortifying . . . to the Government and people of Japan" (Daniels 1969:101), and he closed by stating that exclusion would have "grave consequences." Instead of gaining the support of the Senate, as intended, this letter led Senator Lodge to speak in favor of Japanese exclusion on the ground that the phrase "grave consequences" was a "veiled threat" against the United States. Lodge's stand destroyed the support for a quota for Japan and led fairly directly to an exclusion provision in the new immigration law.

As Ambassador Hanihara had warned, the Japanese were very angry and resentful. The United States had, in their view, violated its own principles of equality and justice as well as the Gentlemen's Agreement. The primary issue was whether Japan was to be treated as an equal among nations. While it is impossible to weigh fully the consequences of these events, it is almost certain that the long-range relations between the two countries were damaged by them, and some scholars have suggested that it was an important link in the chain of events leading to the Japanese attack on Pearl Harbor in 1941 (Kitano 1969:28).

The Second-Generation Period

The cessation of Japanese immigration to the United States in 1924 and the continuing status of the Issei noncitizens left them in a very strange position. Like many other immigrant groups, they had come to America, established homes, started families, and filled various niches in the American economy. Indeed, in the latter respect, they had made quite a name for themselves. They were extremely industrious (to a fault, the natives thought), and by transferring many old-country skills they had become prominent in such fields as agriculture and landscape gardening. But despite the obvious ability of the Issei to adapt to American conditions, even in the face of the exaggerated hostility of the natives, their standing in this country at the end of the 1907–1924 "settlement period" was anything but secure.[14] To a considerable extent, the claims of the Japanese community to fair treatment in the United States rested on the fact that the Nisei were American citizens. This second generation of Japanese in America, then, represented an even bigger "bet" on the future than is normally the case. This generation would ensure the continuation of the Japanese community in America after the Issei were gone. The second-generation period, therefore, was one in which the Issei continued to build on the economic and community foundations established during the frontier and settlement periods. Their goal was to assist the Nisei to achieve the standing in American society to which their citizenship entitled them. At the same time, they continued to hope that their children would adopt and exemplify the traditional virtues of Japanese society.

As mentioned previously, the second-generation members of ethnic groups in America typically experience certain stresses and strains. They are "marginal," standing on the edge of two different cultures and societies. They are neither one nor the other, neither fully alien nor fully American. As the Nisei grew, they, too, encountered problems of this type. The ideas and ways of the Issei began to seem old-fashioned and inappropriate to American conditions. The children frequently were embarrassed that their parents could not speak fluent English and were often ashamed of their own Japanese appearance and manners. They resented being teased by other American children about their physical features and were hurt and angered when they were called "Japs." As the Nisei became aware that their parents were not and could not become citizens, they sometimes used this point to emphasize the difference between themselves and their parents (Ichihashi 1932:350).

The Issei did many things to aid the Nisei in bridging the gap between Japanese and American culture. They strongly approved of the Nisei attendance at public schools and constantly urged the children to study hard and bring honor to the family name. The Nisei were encouraged to participate in American-style youth organizations through the formation of Japanese Boy and Girl Scout troops, YMCAs and YWCAs, and all-Japanese baseball and basketball leagues. Also, as the Issei themselves underwent some degree of cultural assimilation, American ways of doing things were introduced into the home, the *kenjinkai,* and the Buddhist church.

As the Nisei began to reach adulthood, many of them felt that the older organizations established by the Issei did not meet their special needs. Even though they were Americans, they faced the same sort of prejudice and discrimination that was directed against their parents. Many natives, indeed, made no distinction between the two generations. They "all looked alike" to many natives and were considered to be aliens like their parents. Job discrimination was a particularly galling source of worry and frustration. The Nisei often asked themselves the questions, "What good is our American citizenship?" and "What can we do to claim our rightful place in this our native land?" (Hosokawa 1969:191,489).

During the 1920s, some young Nisei began to establish protective groups similar to the Japanese associations founded by the Issei. At first, these were local "loyalty leagues" or "citizen's leagues." By 1930, however, an umbrella organization of Nisei—the Japanese American Citizen's League (JACL)—was formed (Hosokawa 1969:194). The JACL made its appeal to all Nisei regardless of *ken,* religion, or political persuasion. The organization represented the Niseis' ambition and determination to rise in American society and be accepted as equals.

Although the JACL was originally formed to combat anti-Japanese activities, the organization quickly gave attention to such conventional matters as getting out the Nisei vote, electing Japanese Americans to public office, and working to gain citizenship for the Issei (Hosokawa 1969:197–200). These efforts were not very effective, but the JACL nevertheless provided an important rallying point for the Nisei and accelerated their cultural assimilation (Kitano 1969:82).

By 1941, the Japanese American community had been developing for about fifty years. The Issei had been notably successful economically and in raising their families, though they had experienced special hardships with the cessation of immigration and the denial of citizenship. The Nisei had undergone a high degree of cultural assimilation and were striving for secondary assimilation. Some members of the third generation, the Sansei, were now on the scene. It is true that anti-Japanese activities continued to exist, especially during election years. But neither these hostile activities nor any of those prior to this period may easily be compared to the events in the months following December 7, 1941.

War, Evacuation, and Relocation

The aerial attack on Pearl Harbor led to a declaration of war against Japan, to the establishment of martial law in Hawaii, and to the quick arrest of over twelve thousand German, Italian, and Japanese aliens. It also provoked a renewed attack in many newspapers against all of the Japanese, aliens and citizens alike. Many of the old hate slogans were revived and elaborated—"once a Jap, always a Jap," "all Japanese are loyal to the Emperor," "the Japanese race is a treacherous race"—and there were rumors that the Japanese were planning extensive sabotage. Once again, it was said that the language schools indoctrinated the Nisei in favor of Japan and that the other Japanese community organizations were fronts for Japanese patriotic fanaticism (tenBroek, Barnhart, and Matson 1954:93–94).[15] In the face of growing fears of an invasion of the West Coast, of espionage, and of sabotage, President Franklin Roosevelt issued, on February 19, 1942, Executive Order 9066 authorizing the military authorities as a national defense measure to prescribe military areas and to impose restrictions on the movements of all persons within those areas. Under this authority (supported by an act of Congress in March), Lt. Gen. John L. DeWitt, commander of the Western Defense Command, issued a long series of public proclamations and civilian exclusion orders beginning on March 2, 1942.[16] General DeWitt argued that the entire Pacific Coast was particularly vulnerable to attack, invasion, espionage, and sabotage and that, for this reason, certain groups of people would be excluded from some designated military areas as a matter of "military necessity." Under these orders, all people of Japanese ancestry, whether aliens or citizens, were required to leave the prohibited areas.

The first destination of the evacuees was a group of fifteen temporary "assembly centers." From the assembly centers, the evacuees were transferred to ten permanent "relocation centers." This movement was started in March 1942 and was completed in November. In the process, more than 110,000 people of Japanese ancestry—over 70,000 of whom were American citizens—had been forced from their homes and imprisoned without warrants or indictments.[17] All of this presumably was required by "military necessity." The individuals involved were not accused of any specific acts of disloyalty, and they were not tried for any crime in a court of law! Why, then, was the mass evacuation and internment of the Japanese and Japanese Americans a "military necessity"?

One of the most revealing commentaries on this subject is contained in General DeWitt's explanation of the decision to evacuate. The general wrote as follows:

In the war in which we are now engaged racial affinities are not severed by migration. The Japanese race is an enemy race and while many second and third generation Japanese born on United States soil, possessed of United States citizenship have become "Americanized," the racial strains are undiluted. . . . It therefore allows that along the vital Pacific Coast over 112,000 potential enemies, of Japanese extraction, are at large today. There are disturbing indications that these are organized and ready for concerted action at a favorable opportunity. The very fact that no sabotage has taken place to date is a disturbing and confirming indication that such action will be taken (quoted by Rostow 1945:140).[18]

It appears, therefore, that a very large group of people—most of whom were citizens of the United States—were arrested and imprisoned without trials purely and simply because of their race. It was assumed that while people from other nations may become Americans by birth, those of Japanese ancestry remain forever Japanese. And the "military necessity" for the evacuation and internment presumably was demonstrated by the fact that not one of the people so treated actually had engaged in sabotage! General DeWitt's line of reasoning amounted, in Daniels's (1975:25) words, to "playing 'Catch 22' with the Japanese Americans." Whether sabotage occurred or not, a foundation was laid for mass evacuation.

The national security questions raised here are complex. As we have seen, the Issei and Nisei were a highly organized, clannish group. They did work hard to maintain the Japanese language and traditional forms of family and community life. And since the Issei were ineligible for American citizenship, their ties with Japan frequently were quite strong. Consequently, one may agree, as several justices of the U.S. Supreme Court have, that the military threat to the West Coast in 1942 was real and that reason and prudence required that those of Japanese ancestry should be regarded in a special light. However, even if one were to agree that considerations of this type are reasonable, does it follow that the evacuation and relocation program was a suitable response?

Consider, for instance, the situation in Hawaii. There the Japanese population comprised over 30 percent of the total population, as compared to less than 2 percent of the population of the West Coast. Moreover, since Hawaii had been attacked once already, there was at least as much reason to believe that a planned invasion would strike there as at the West Coast. Hawaii, as mentioned earlier, was placed under martial law, and after a period of investigation, approximately 1,800 Issei and Nisei were sent to the mainland for internment. Of great significance, however, is that those taken into custody in Hawaii were arrested on the basis of individual actions and charges. There was no program to take people into custody on the basis of their racial or ethnic identity.

Consider, too, the way the problem of "presumed sympathy" was handled among the more than one million aliens of German and Italian descent. People included in this category had to abide by certain security regulations. They could not enter military areas, own or use firearms, travel without a permit, and so on. If German or Italian aliens were suspected of disloyal acts or were caught violating a regulation, they could be arrested, and if they were arrested they were required to appear before a hearing board. After hearing a case, the board could recommend internment, parole, or unconditional release. Here again, as in Hawaii, individual cases were treated individually. People were not arrested and interned simply because they were enemy aliens. Of even greater significance is that the security regulations did not apply in any way to *citizens* of German and Italian descent. It is difficult to escape the conclusion that "the dominant element in the development of our relocation policy was race prejudice, not a military estimate of a military problem" (Rostow 1945:142).

So far we have seen that over 110,000 people of Japanese ancestry were forced to leave their homes during 1942 and were placed in relocation centers on a plea of "military necessity." As will be shown later, the great majority of these people were still in the centers when the U.S. Supreme Court declared, near the end of 1944, that the relocation program had been illegal. For several years, then, tens of thousands of people who were completely innocent had been placed illegally in prison camps. What were these camps like? How did they affect the lives of those who were forced into them?

The Relocation Program

Approximately ten weeks after the attack on Pearl Harbor, the evacuation of the Japanese and Japanese Americans from the West Coast began. Both before and after the evacuation orders, there was great confusion. Each day brought new rumors concerning what was to be done. In January, Attorney General Biddle stated that there would be no "wholesale internment, without hearing and irrespective of the merits of individual cases" (Leighton 1946:17). Early in February, Biddle urged people not to persecute aliens, either economically or socially. He warned that such persecution could easily destroy the aliens' loyalty to the United States. But many people did not agree with Biddle. A few days after his warning, the mayor of Los Angeles called for the removal of the entire Japanese population to inland areas. In the following week, an opinion poll showed that there was widespread sentiment on the Pacific Coast (especially in California) favoring the internment of all Japanese aliens. There was some sentiment favoring the internment of Japanese Americans as well (Leighton 1946:21).

Throughout this period, numerous acts of hostility against the Japanese and Japanese Americans were reported: jobs were lost, credit was discontinued, "No Japs Allowed" signs appeared, Japanese women were attacked by men pretending to be FBI agents, and so on. Despite these problems, however, the government apparently still did not intend to carry out a mass evacuation. Tom C. Clark (later a justice of the U.S. Supreme Court) was quoted by the *Los Angeles Times* as promising "that there would be no mass evacuation, no transfer of people by the scores of thousands" (Leighton 1946:34). Even after the announcement of Public Proclamation No. 1, General DeWitt was quoted as saying that "no mass evacuation is planned for Japanese" (Leighton 1946:34). Nevertheless, only a short time later, a mass evacuation was underway.

Understandably, many Japanese Americans could hardly believe it. Everything they had been taught about the American system of democracy argued against such a possibility. They understood that, ideally at least, individuals are judged by their own acts. Even if every member of a person's family were a convicted felon, the person in question still must be regarded as innocent until proven guilty. The strong belief in the American system and the disillusionment that accompanied the evacuation are reflected in the following comments by a farmer's son, a social service student, and a Japanese American soldier, respectively (Leighton 1946:27):

> *I was very confident that there would be no evacuation on a major scale. . . . the American system of education . . . gave me faith that our government would not be moved by economic pressure and racial prejudice.*

> *It grieved me to think that evacuation had . . . set up a sharp line between a racial minority and the dominant group in a country which had spoken of equality of opportunity.*

> *They are evacuating all the Japanese from the Coast and even trying to take away our citizenship. I don't know why I am in the Army. I want to see democracy as it is supposed to be, but this is getting just as bad as Hitler.*

The evacuation proceeded in two main stages over approximately seven months. The first stage removed people from their homes to hastily prepared assembly centers in racetracks, fairgrounds, and livestock exhibition halls (tenBroek, Barnhart, and Matson 1954:126). Japanese and Japanese Americans of both sexes, all ages, and various socioeconomic categories were required to leave behind everything they could not carry. Many people sold their homes, businesses, and other possessions at cut-rate or "panic-sale" prices. Others stored their goods or simply left everything in locked houses hoping that they would be safe until their return. Many farmers were forced to leave fields in which their life's savings were invested. The economic cost alone to the Japanese and Japanese Americans was enormous. Of at least equal importance, however, was the incalculable cost in human misery. Probably only those who have experienced it can appreciate fully the emotional impact created when proud families and individuals are suddenly imprisoned even though they have committed no crime. Men and women who, on one day, were leading productive lives and planning for their children's futures were, on the next, assigned identification numbers and placed in guarded barracks with hundreds of others.

Most of those detained in the assembly centers gradually were moved to one of the relocation centers. These centers were placed away from the coastal areas and in climates that were "either too hot or too cold, too wet or too dry" (Hosokawa 1969:352), in California (Manzanar and Tule Lake), Arizona (Poston and Gila River), Arkansas (Rohwer and Jerome), Idaho (Minidoka), Utah (Topaz), Wyoming (Heart Mountain), and Colorado (Granada).[19]

The task of getting the camps ready for occupancy was very big indeed, and those who were given the job encountered numerous difficulties. Personnel, supplies, and equipment (all of which were scarce) had to be assembled in remote places. Moreover, since the army, the War Relocation Authority (WRA), civilian contractors, and other government agencies were all involved, there was no clear division of responsibility and authority. The result was that the camps were not finished when the first evacuees arrived. The new residents, therefore, were faced with various shortages and physical discomforts, and they had to do a substantial share of the construction work to complete the camps.

We noted earlier that the Japanese and Japanese Americans were bewildered by the evacuation and relocation program and that they generally felt it to be unjustified and undemocratic. There also was some concern within the government that this program—even given a serious external threat—might not be defensible in the full light of American traditions of justice. Many officials were eager, therefore, to distinguish the evacuation and relocation program from the concentration camp and forced-labor programs of the Nazis. Much of the language and planning for the relocation program seemed to be designed to put the entire matter in a pleasant light. For instance, the presidential order creating the WRA also created a War Relocation Work Corps. The Japanese who were leaving the prohibited military areas were invited to enlist "voluntarily" in the corps, which most of them did. This "enlistment" obligated the individual to accept whatever pay the WRA specified. The evacuees were referred to as "residents," and their barracks were called "apartments." Even the labels *assembly center* and *relocation center* might be called, as Justice Roberts suggested later, euphemisms for concentration camps (Tussman 1963:210).

Whether or not the relocation centers were, in fact, significantly better than the concentration camps of the Nazis, it does seem to be true that the WRA administrators generally wanted them to be better. This point may be illustrated through a brief description of the largest of the camps (Poston), which was located near Parker, Arizona.[20]

Life in the Camps

Poston consisted of three units of barracks and other facilities (recreation halls, latrines, laundries, hospitals, water towers, and so on). The three units were intended to house approximately twenty thousand people. The camp administrators were acutely aware that an effort should be made to organize it as democratically as possible under the circumstances. Their plan to achieve this goal was based on the idea that the camp should be modeled along the lines of a typical, self-governing, American community. This approach offered several possible advantages. First, it was hoped that a high degree of self-government would reassure the friendly aliens and, especially, the loyal citizens that the U.S. government recognized their rights and was concerned about their welfare. This may be viewed as part of an effort to persuade the Japanese to accept the "fact" that the evacuation was a military necessity. It also became, as time passed, part of an effort to show that the evacuation was a form of "protective custody." Second, if self-government were successful, then a much smaller force of outside guards and service workers would be needed. Third, it was hoped that the Poston community would soon be able to support itself through irrigation and farming the arid land of the Parker Valley. Not only would this decrease the government's expenses, but also it presumably would assist the Japanese in regaining their sense of independence and to feel that they were contributing to the war effort. Moreover, the reclamation of the desert would create a national asset that would endure beyond the war's end. Finally, if the administration's plan worked, the relocation centers might serve as an example of the differences between authoritarian and democratic responses to internal and external threats.

The first Japanese to arrive at Poston were volunteers; for the most part, they were Nisei who had decided to try to make the best of a bad situation. They responded favorably to the administration's plan to build Poston as a model community, and they provided numerous services for the thousands of evacuees who soon began to arrive. They registered the new arrivals, explained to them the camp's regulations, and acted as guides. They also worked in the hospital, established a community store, and assisted with the necessary clerical work involved in organizing the project.

The evacuees faced numerous problems related to housing, water, food, and other necessities. The "apartments" were flimsily constructed and small. Sometimes as many as eight people lived in one room. There was hardly any furniture. Mattresses were made of cloth bags stuffed with straw. The heat was intense in the summer, while winter temperatures occasionally fell below freezing. And then there were the armed guards and the barbed wire fences. It is little wonder that many people felt betrayed at having been sent to such a place and, therefore, either actively resisted or failed to cooperate fully with the administration's plans.[21] Nevertheless, a newspaper, police force, and fire department were established. A community council was elected, an irrigation canal was completed, gardens were planted, and various social activities were organized. By the end of August 1942, Poston's population had reached its peak of 17,867 people. By then, the more optimistic members of the administration were hoping that Poston soon would approximate a typical American community.

There were still many underlying problems, however. For example, there were internal divisions in the administrative group. Some officials felt that the efforts to encourage participation in the governing of the camp might lead to a loss of control over it. And among the evacuees there existed a strong difference of opinion concerning the desirability of cooperating with the administration. The conservatives, most of whom were Issei, did not trust the administration. Many of them were not even sure it would be good for them if America won the war. They also resented having the young Nisei volunteers in positions of authority. The volunteers were suspected of trying to be "big shots" who had rushed to Poston to "get in" with the administration. The liberals, most of whom were Nisei, were impatient with those who did not try to prove their Americanism. Many in this group were enjoying the new responsibilities and experiences camp life had made possible. They wished to work toward full acceptance as Americans.

As tensions mounted, there was an increase in stealing, name calling, and violence. Some evacuees believed there were FBI informers among them, and some of the suspected informers were assaulted. By the middle of November 1942, distrust and anger were widespread among the residents of Poston.

The dissatisfaction of the residents culminated in a demonstration and general strike in Unit I. The event that triggered the disorders was the arrest of two evacuees who were accused of having participated in a gang attack on a fellow resident. Following a series of demonstrations, protest meetings, and attempts to negotiate the release of the two arrested men, some members of the administration suggested that the strike was a pro-Japanese plot illustrating the need to shoot the "Japs" to show them their place. The ranking project administrator, however, did not turn matters over to the army. Rather, he chose to negotiate with an Emergency Executive Council (comprised almost entirely of Issei) that had been elected by the evacuees. After several days of negotiations, the Emergency Executive Council agreed to end the strike in return for the release of one of the two prisoners.

Although the strike in Poston ended on a cooperative note and without the use of military force, the form of self-government that emerged was not the one that the WRA had originally planned. Many officials were discouraged by the course of events in Poston and in most of the other relocation centers as well. For example, several weeks after the Poston strike, a "riot" at the Manzanar Relocation Center resulted in the killing and wounding of some of the evacuees. Consequently, the WRA abandoned the idea of developing the relocation centers as model communities. The decision was made, rather, that the best policy would be to resettle all loyal evacuees outside the centers as soon as possible. This new plan was strengthened when the War Department reversed an earlier stand regarding military service for the Nisei by announcing its intention to form an all-Nisei combat team. Eventually, over twenty thousand Japanese and Japanese American men were inducted following this change of policy. More than six thousand Nisei served in the Pacific theater, primarily as interpreters and translators. Most of the rest served in the 100th Battalion and the 442nd Regimental Combat Team. These units compiled an outstanding battle record in the European theater.[22] The decisions to resettle the evacuees and to enlist the Nisei for military duty led to a program of clearance and recruitment. Each evacuee was asked to answer a questionnaire concerning his or her background and loyalty to the United States. The registration program came as a surprise to the evacuees and resulted in anxiety, confusion, and resistance throughout the relocation centers.

The focus of controversy—around which several important issues revolved—was question 28: "Will you swear unqualified allegiance to the United States of America and . . . foreswear any form of allegiance to the Japanese emperor?" (Thomas and Nishimoto 1946:47).[23] Answering "yes" to this question was almost impossible for most Issei, who were, after all, ineligible for citizenship in the United States. If they now disclaimed allegiance to Japan, they would be "people without a country." Question 28, therefore, was revised as follows: "Will you swear to abide by the laws of the United States and to take no action which would in any way interfere with the war effort of the United States?" (Broom and Kitsuse 1956:28).

Although the revised question was acceptable to most Issei, the loyalty registration crisis was not settled.

As may well be imagined, many of the evacuees were extremely bitter and disillusioned by everything that had happened to them during the preceding year. Now, suddenly, they were asked to declare unswerving loyalty to the United States. Additionally, they correctly assumed answering "yes" to question 28 might mean they or some member of their family would be drafted into military service (or be pressured to "volunteer"). Many also accepted the government's argument that they were interned, at least in part, for their own safety; so they now feared they would be forced to leave the relocation centers to be resettled in some place where hostility toward them would make life uncomfortable or, possibly, unsafe. On the other hand, answering "no" or a refusal to answer certainly involved some risks. Would answering "no" interfere with the individual's efforts to recover property that had been lost in the evacuation? Would a presumably disloyal person be sent to a special prison camp? What effect would a declaration of disloyalty have on a person's job or educational opportunities following the war? The cross-pressures on the evacuees meant that a simple "yes" or "no" answer to question 28 could not easily be interpreted. It also sharpened the existing intergenerational conflict between the Issei and Nisei, adding to the general turbulence in the centers.

These complications interfered with the WRA's plan to grant leave clearances to the "loyal" Japanese (i.e., those who answered "yes") and to segregate the "disloyal" Japanese in a special camp (the Tule Lake Relocation Center). By November 1943—less than a year after the Poston strike—over eighteen thousand people had been segregated at Tule Lake.[24] However, as noted earlier, there was ample reason to believe that many of those at Tule Lake were not really disloyal. After further checking, in fact, over 8,500 of the segregants eventually were cleared.

The most surprising evidence of the deep-seated confusion among the Japanese was revealed by the effort to resettle those who were regarded as loyal. At first, the resettlement program seemed very effective. By the end of 1943, more than seventeen thousand people—most of whom were Nisei—had been cleared and released from the centers. As time passed, though, decreasing numbers of cleared residents chose to leave the confines of the camps. Despite an active effort on the part of the WRA to make resettlement attractive to the evacuees, nearly eighty thousand people remained in the centers at the beginning of 1945. Approximately half that number were still in the centers as the WRA moved to close them in the summer of 1945. It seems reasonable to conclude, as the WRA itself did, that the treatment of the Japanese in the United States during World War II had tended "to disintegrate the fiber of a people who had previous to evacuation, been unusually self-reliant, sturdy, and independent" (War Relocation Authority 1946).[25]

Legal Issues

The primary legal issues raised by the evacuation and relocation program were addressed by the U.S. Supreme Court in three different cases. The first of these

(*Hirabayashi v. United States*) reached the Court in June 1943, over a year after the relocation program had been set into motion. By this time, the situation that led to the creation of the program had been altered markedly. Various categories of people already had been released from the relocation centers. Most of these were Nisei students who were attending school in the Midwest and East. But as a result of the army's new recruitment effort among the Nisei, many of those who were released were people previously in the military services or their spouses. Nevertheless, most of the aliens and citizens of Japanese ancestry were still being held in the relocation centers, and those who had been released could not return to their homes. Moreover, it still was to be decided whether the government's treatment of the Japanese and Japanese Americans had been constitutional.

Gordon Hirabayashi was arrested, convicted, and jailed for violating two of General DeWitt's orders. He violated a curfew order by failing to stay in his place of residence between the hours of 8:00 p.m. and 6:00 a.m.; he did not report as ordered to register for evacuation. Hirabayashi's appeal to the Court maintained that the curfew and evacuation orders represented an unconstitutional delegation of congressional authority to the military and that the curfew should have applied not only to citizens of Japanese ancestry but to all citizens in the military areas.

In a unanimous opinion, the Court stated: "Distinctions between citizens solely because of their ancestry are by their very nature odious to a free people" (Tussman 1963:190) but ruled, nevertheless, that there had been a danger of espionage and sabotage and that the curfew order had been appropriate (Tussman 1963:192).

Although the opinion upholding the curfew order was unanimous, three justices expressed reservations. Justice Douglas agreed that "where the peril is great and time is short" (Tussman 1963:194) it may be necessary to make group distinctions, but he emphasized that the basic issue was loyalty, not ancestry. Justice Murphy noted that the restriction on the Japanese Americans "bears a melancholy resemblance to the treatment accorded to members of the Jewish race in Germany" (Tussman 1963:197), and Justice Rutledge feared the case might weaken the Court's power to review military decisions. But even with these reservations, the Court gave the appearance of agreeing with some of the charges (e.g., "a Jap is a Jap") that had long been the stock in trade of the most vocal anti-Japanese groups.

The second of the three cases under review here, *Korematsu v. United States,* concerned primarily the constitutionality of the evacuation of the Japanese Americans from the West Coast. Fred Korematsu was born in the United States, had never been out of the country, did not speak Japanese, and was not suspected of disloyalty. He had attempted to avoid the order to leave his home and had been convicted and given a suspended sentence. The Court upheld Korematsu's conviction. Unlike in *Hirabayashi,* however, the decision was not unanimous. Justice Roberts argued that Korematsu's constitutional rights had been violated. Justice Murphy stated that the exclusion resulted not from military necessity but from the mistaken ideas people had about the Japanese and that the episode "falls into the ugly abyss of racism" (Tussman 1963:213). Justice Jackson refused to accept the idea that a given act (in this case, refusing to leave home) could be a crime if committed by a citizen of one race but not by a citizen of another.

The reservations and disagreements that plagued the Court's members in their deliberations concerning the curfew and the evacuation reached full force in their consideration of *Endo v. United States*. Like Fred Korematsu, Mitsuye Endo was born in the United States, did not speak Japanese, and had committed no specific act of disloyalty. Endo challenged the right of the WRA to imprison her and other loyal Japanese Americans; on this, all of the justices agreed. The Court ordered that Ms. Endo and all other loyal Americans be set free unconditionally. Justice Murphy, who had only reluctantly agreed to the curfew and had rejected the evacuation, stated that the entire evacuation program had been discriminatory and was "utterly foreign to the ideals and traditions of the American people" (Petersen 1971:90). In one critic's opinion, "One hundred thousand persons were sent to concentration camps on a record which wouldn't support a conviction for stealing a dog" (Rostow 1945:146).

The full effects on the Japanese and Japanese Americans of the devastating experience of evacuation, relocation, and resettlement are beyond exact calculation. The dollar losses alone were estimated to be around $400 million in 1942 dollars (Hosokawa 1969:440). In 1948, an Evacuation Claims Act was passed and the internees were paid $38 million (in 1948 dollars!) as restitution for their losses. Debate concerning the adequacy of this payment continued, however, and in 1988 Congress passed a bill stating that a "grave injustice was done to both citizens and permanent resident aliens of Japanese ancestry" by the relocation program and that the relocation was a result of "racial prejudice, wartime hysteria, and a failure of political leadership." The bill agreed to award each of over sixty thousand surviving detainees a tax-free payment of about twenty thousand dollars (Leo 1988:70). The payments, accompanied by a formal apology by the president, commenced in October 1990 (*Time* 1990).

Another form of restitution also occurred during the decades following World War II. In 1983, Fred Korematsu was formally cleared of the charges leveled against him in 1942, and his conviction for refusing to obey a military order was overturned (*Time* 1983). In 1986, Gordon Hirabayashi won a court case establishing that government officials had withheld vital information during his trial in 1942. The court agreed that the government's claim that people of Japanese ancestry had been a threat to national security was false (Howery 1986:9).

Of course, no meaningful estimate may be made of the emotional costs suffered by the thousands of people who saw their hopes and aspirations destroyed and their families broken. What is plain in all of this is that the Japanese have been subjected in America to a level of discrimination similar to that encountered by the largest nonwhite minorities in the United States.

At the end of the second-generation period, the Japanese Americans had generally accepted the desirability of cultural and secondary assimilation. Many of them embraced the goal of primary and, perhaps, marital assimilation as well. What were the effects of the catastrophic events of World War II on their adjustment to American society?

Japanese American Assimilation

Cultural Assimilation

Our previous reasoning about rates of assimilation (in chapter 2) showed that it is necessary to think in terms of several subprocesses, such as cultural assimilation, secondary assimilation, and so on. We also saw (in chapter 1) the necessity of taking into account certain important factors that usually influence the course of assimilation, such as the size of the immigrant group, the social distance between the immigrants and the host society, whether the group entered voluntarily, the timing of the immigration, and the goals of the immigrants. In the case of the Japanese in America, the factor of intergenerational differences also assumed unusual importance. The Issei were even more clannish than most first-generation groups, and their level of cultural assimilation was generally low. The Issei's desire to maintain their own heritage, coupled with their resistance to adopting American ways, created barriers to the cultural assimilation of the Nisei. The Japanese Language Schools, as mentioned earlier, were designed to assist the Issei in transmitting their language and heritage and to prevent the development of a wide cultural gap between the generations; however, also as noted previously, the schools were not really very successful in this. Although the Nisei were restrained and "Japanesey" in the home, they apparently moved rapidly toward the American pattern of behavior in school and other public settings. The opposition between the Issei and Nisei also, as was shown, was increased by the evacuation and relocation experience. The effect of this increased intergenerational friction, though, may have differed among the older and younger Nisei. Those who were adolescents and young adults may have been propelled toward Anglo conformity by the evacuation and relocation.[26] Since the contacts of the children with Anglo-Americans were reduced during this period, however, and their contacts with other Japanese were increased, they may have become more Japanese in culture and thought than otherwise would have been the case (Broom and Kitsuse 1956:25).

Little has been said so far concerning the Sansei, but this third generation is of special importance in any effort to assess the rate of assimilation among Japanese Americans. According to the ideas of Park, the Sansei should be more assimilated than the Nisei. Their degree of cultural assimilation, in particular, should approach that of the Anglo-American majority.

The facts concerning cultural assimilation are far from complete and must be pieced together from several different sources. The evidence is generally based on studies of small samples, although some results from a national sample of Japanese Americans are available. The findings of these studies are not totally consistent, but they strongly suggest that the Sansei have assimilated culturally more than the Nisei, who, in turn, have assimilated culturally more than the Issei. Kitano (1969:156–157), for instance, examined differences in the way the members of the three generations respond to certain statements regarding traditional beliefs and attitudes. The expected pattern of intergenerational differences emerged clearly on matters of ethnic identity (e.g., "Once a Japanese, always a Japanese"), individual-group orientation (e.g., "A person who raises too many questions interferes with the progress of a group"), and realistic expectations (e.g., "Even if one has talent and ability, it does not mean that one will get ahead"). The pattern was either weak or not present, however, in regard to the respondents' views on means and ends, masculinity and responsibility, and passivity. For instance, although the Nisei and Sansei differed from the Issei on some points, they did not differ significantly from one another. In regard to some other views, the Issei and Nisei were more nearly in agreement and the Sansei were different.

Some of the inconsistencies found by Kitano may have been due to the small size of the sample, the geographical location represented, problems with the wording of the questionnaire, and so on, rather than to any real departure from the expected pattern of cultural assimilation. This interpretation has been strengthened, in general, by the results of four other studies. For example, Connor (1974:161) found in his study that the Issei were most likely to agree with statements reflecting traditional child-rearing ideas (e.g., "Parents can never be repaid for what they have done for their children"), the Sansei were least likely to agree, and the Nisei were intermediate in agreement. In a comparison of Nisei and Sansei, Feagin and Fujitaki (1972:18) found that although an individual's religious affiliation is a complicating factor, with Buddhism serving to support the traditional culture, some clear differences in cultural assimilation exist between the Nisei and Sansei. To illustrate, the Nisei were more likely to be comfortable speaking Japanese and to do so regularly in the home than were the Sansei. They also felt more strongly than the Sansei about the importance of maintaining Japanese customs and traditions.

Some pertinent results were presented by Matsumoto, Meredith, and Masuda (1973) in a study of sex and generation differences in ethnic identification among Japanese Americans in Honolulu and Seattle. Once again, the general pattern of increasing cultural assimilation by generation was discovered. The results of the latter study must be viewed with some caution, however, because there were some important differences between the Honolulu and Seattle findings. In Seattle, the Japanese identification of the Sansei was significantly lower than among the Nisei; in Honolulu, however, this difference was not significant. Even more important is that the fifty-item measure of ethnic identification used in this study included a broad range of topics touching on several aspects of the process of assimilation. It is possible, therefore, that a more detailed analysis might lead to somewhat different results. Finally, using the national sample (excluding Hawaii) of UCLA's Japanese American Research Project, Woodrum (1978:80) found that, in terms of English proficiency and religious affiliation, the Nisei were more culturally assimilated than the Issei. In terms of religious affiliation alone, the Sansei were more culturally assimilated than the Issei. With this evidence at hand, it seems reasonable to conclude that, as a rule, the Sansei are more assimilated culturally than the Nisei and that the Issei are less assimilated culturally than either of the other two generations.

Our interest so far has centered on the generational differences in cultural assimilation in the Japanese American group. The problem now to be considered concerns the extent to which the Sansei have become assimilated culturally in comparison to Anglo-Americans. Connor reported that the Issei and Nisei in his study believed the Sansei are "completely Americanized." Are they? Only two of the studies cited contain pertinent information. For example, although Connor found much less acceptance of traditional Japanese ideas among the Sansei than among the members of the other two generations, he nevertheless found more acceptance of these ideas among the Sansei than among a sample of Anglo-Americans. Kitano also found noticeable differences between the Sansei and Anglo-Americans in regard to certain beliefs and attitudes. In particular, the Sansei were between the Nisei and Anglo-Americans in their beliefs about masculinity and responsibility and in their beliefs about passivity.

A revival of cultural nationalism among the Sansei, beginning during the 1960s, affords some further evidence that they are interested in their Japanese heritage. As one would expect on the basis of Hansen's thesis (mentioned in chapter 1), a major theme of this revival is that Japanese Americans should reject the Anglo conformity of the Nisei and actively promote some form of cultural pluralism in which the valued traditions of Japan, as modified by the American experience, may be sustained and elaborated. The participants in this movement are extremely critical of the older generation's willingness to "make the most of a bad situation and push ahead" (Fujimoto 1971:207) or, even worse, to focus attention on the presumably "beneficial" effects of the wartime relocation. They view the historical experience of the Japanese minority in America as being essentially like that of the Chinese, Koreans, and Filipinos and quite similar to that of the African Americans, Mexican Americans, and American Indians.[27] As Ichioka (1971:222) stated in a critical review of Hosokawa's book *Nisei: The Quiet Americans,* "In this time of political, social, and moral crisis in America, old and new problems demand radical approaches, not tired orations. . . . We bid the old guard to retire as 'quiet Americans.'" Nevertheless, the militant and nationalist tone of the 1960s and 1970s had subsided sufficiently by the mid-1980s to permit Kitano and Daniels (1988:71) to remark that "the Sansei and Yonsei, or fourth generation, are the most 'American' of any Japanese group; many of them have never faced overt discrimination, and some have never had close ethnic ties or ethnic friends."

On the basis of these observations concerning the Sansei, we may offer the following generalization: Their level of cultural assimilation is higher than that of the two preceding generations, but they still exhibit some elements of the traditional culture of Japan and are, in some cases, actively attempting either to revive their ancient heritage or to construct a specifically Japanese American identity.[28]

Given the comparatively high degree of cultural assimilation among the Nisei and Sansei, how far have these groups moved toward the American pattern in terms of the other main subprocesses of assimilation? We saw previously that the Japanese Americans have attained, in some respects, a high degree of secondary structural assimilation (e.g., education, occupation, and income). Let us turn now to further evidence on this point.

Secondary Structural Assimilation

In addition to education, occupational attainment, and income, the main types of secondary assimilation are memberships in nonethnic formal organizations and movement into desegregated neighborhoods. Excellent evidence on organizational memberships for Japanese Americans may be found in several studies based on data gathered in UCLA's Japanese American Research Project (JARP). For example, Levine and Rhodes (1981:78–79) found that among the Nisei who belonged to only one organization (not counting church), 58 percent belonged to a Japanese American group and 42 percent did not. Even among "joiners" (Nisei who belonged to four or five organizations), 27 percent belonged to no Japanese organizations. The level of participation was lower still among the Sansei. Most of those in the third generation were not members of a Japanese organization. Among those who belonged to a noncollege organization, about half belonged to one that was not Japanese, and among the "joiners" most of the members' time was given to the nonethnic groups. Montero's (1980:60) analysis, also based on JARP data, showed that a majority of both the Nisei and Sansei (55 and 69 percent, respectively) who belong to groups name a non-Japanese group as their "favorite organization." In a different study, Fugita and O'Brien (1985:989) reported that, excluding church membership, over 69 percent of their sample belonged to non-Japanese organizations and almost 53 percent were members of Japanese organizations. Fugita and O'Brien believe, however, that the level of Japanese American participation in ethnic organizations is exceptionally high in comparison to other ethnic groups.

Another important measure of the extent to which secondary assimilation is occurring for a given ethnic minority is the degree to which the group lives in desegregated residential areas. We emphasized previously that American ethnic groups always have tended to congregate, as well as to be segregated, in certain areas and that these frequently have become known as "their" parts of town; however, to the extent that an ethnic group's members accept either the Anglo conformity or pluralist models of adaptation, we would expect that as assimilation occurred they would leave their old neighborhoods and move into less segregated neighborhoods, even if the initial segregation was largely voluntary (Zhou and Logan 1991:388). This expectation, called *the theory of spatial assimilation*[29] (Gross and Massey 1991:350) argues that "as a minority group's socioeconomic status increases, its members seek to improve their spatial position . . . [by] moving into neighborhoods with greater prestige, more amenities, safer streets, better schools, and higher-value homes" (Denton and Massey 1988:818). The initial residential segregation that was typical of European ethnic groups also has characterized the residential patterns of Japanese Americans. In most cities of the West, they have been noticeably segregated from other groups. The extent of this segregation, however, has varied greatly among the cities, reflecting the many factors that affect residential assimilation.

Sociologists frequently have studied the extent of residential segregation of different groups by calculating and comparing *indexes of dissimilarity*. The basic idea of an index of dissimilarity is this: If people were to move into neighborhoods without regard to their ethnicity, then people of different groups within a city would live in every neighborhood, and the proportion of each group living in each neighborhood would be the same as their share of their city's total population (Taeuber and Taeuber 1964:29). For instance, if 25 percent of the people in a given city were Japanese Americans, and if ethnicity had nothing to do with selecting a residence, then 25 percent of the people in each part of the city would be Japanese Americans; people would be spread evenly throughout the city, and there would be no segregation. On the other hand, if all of the city's Japanese Americans lived together, and there were no other ethnic groups represented among them, then there would be complete segregation. The index of residential segregation, therefore, ranges from a low of 0 (no segregation) to a high of 100 (complete segregation). Index values above 60 are considered high, those below 30 are considered low, and those between 30 and 60 are considered moderate (Kantrowitz, cited by Denton and Massey 1988:804). Although this way of estimating residential segregation has faults, it is extremely useful and easy to understand.[30]

Jiobu (1988a:114) presented valuable information on the residential segregation of Japanese Americans and the members of six other ethnic groups (each as compared to whites) in the twenty-one largest metropolitan areas of California.[31] For Japanese Americans, the average (mean) level of segregation (dissimilarity) was a moderate 46. The various SMSAs ranged from a high of 65 (in Visalia) to a low of 29 (in San Jose). The largest SMSA, Los Angeles, had an index of 54. The average level of segregation in the twenty-one SMSAs for Koreans, by comparison, was 69, and for Vietnamese the average was 76. In fact, the average segregation index for the Japanese was the lowest among the seven groups included in the study. These findings indicate that the level of residential assimilation among Japanese Americans in California is generally in the moderate range.

Some additional, broader information presented by Farley and Allen (1987:145) indicates that residential segregation among the Japanese is moderate throughout the United States. These researchers examined sixteen of the largest metropolitan areas in the United States and have found that the average level of residential segregation in 1980 for all Asians combined was 43, ranging from a high of 54 in New Orleans to a low of 31 in Washington. A study by Denton and Massey (1988), also of all Asian groups combined, supports the argument that as the Japanese have risen in socioeconomic status, they probably have become less segregated residentially. The study focused on the relationship of residential segregation to educational, occupational, and income levels among the twenty SMSAs in the United States that contained the largest populations of Asians in 1980. The results showed that the levels of segregation were substantially and uniformly higher among the least educated than they were among the most educated members of the Asian groups (Denton and Massey 1988:811).

While the findings of both the Farley and Allen and Denton and Massey studies just cited are based on analyses of all Asian groups combined, rather than specifically of the Japanese, it seems likely that they apply to the Japanese. Given that over 70 percent of Japanese Americans live in the Pacific Coast states (Lieberson and Waters 1988:59) and that among the seven nonwhite ethnic groups in

Jiobu's (1988:115) study "the Japanese are the least segregated and have the highest income . . . ," we may conclude that the residential segregation of Japanese Americans throughout the country falls generally in the moderate range and is low compared to that of other nonwhite ethnic groups.

In a different kind of study, Kagiwada (1972) adduced evidence for Los Angeles that is consistent with our conclusion.[32] Fewer than one-half of the Nisei and Sansei among his respondents claimed to live in a neighborhood in which more than 10 percent of their neighbors were Japanese. In contrast, more than half of the study participants indicated that at least 50 percent of their neighbors were white.

Taken together, these findings concerning organizational participation and residential segregation strengthen our earlier conclusions based on Japanese attainment in income, education, and occupation. By each of these measures, a substantial amount of secondary assimilation has occurred among Japanese Americans.

Primary Structural Assimilation

If Japanese Americans are participating less in all-Japanese organizations and are participating more in "mixed" organizations (including schools and businesses), then presumably some foundation has been laid for the more "social" activities that indicate the occurrence of primary structural assimilation. The studies based on UCLA's national sample supply important evidence concerning the extent to which the Nisei and Sansei interact with people of Japanese and non-Japanese ethnicity. For instance, in answer to questions concerning their two closest friends, a majority of the Nisei (53 percent) and a large majority of the Sansei (74 percent) reported that at least one of their two closest friends was non-Japanese (Montero 1980:60; see also Fugita and O'Brien 1985:993). With whom did the respondents associate after work? When other Japanese worked in the same place, the Nisei reported they were more likely to socialize with one another after work than with non-Japanese, but whether or not other Japanese Americans were present in the work place, the Nisei were more likely than not to see coworkers after work (Levine and Rhodes 1981:81). Finally, do Japanese Americans visit their neighbors more freely if they live in a mostly Japanese neighborhood? According to Levine and Rhodes (1981:83), "the Nisei are neighborly folk. Whatever the composition of their environs, about seven of every ten are on visiting terms with three or more neighbors." We conclude from these findings that the Nisei have reached a fairly high level of primary assimilation and (given the findings on the friendship patterns of the Sansei) that the Sansei are moving even further in that direction. This conclusion also is supported by the finding that 75 percent of the Nisei and 80 percent of the Sansei want their children to associate actively with Caucasians rather than sticking "pretty much with Japanese Americans" (Levine and Rhodes 1981:115).

Marital Assimilation

Marital assimilation, when completed, represents the end point among the subprocesses of assimilation we are studying. Intermarriage, therefore, is of special importance "because it can be understood as both an indicator of the degree of assimilation of ethnic and racial groups and an agent itself of further assimilation. . . . " (Lieberson and Waters 1988:162). It is, as Kennedy (1944:331) said, "the most infallible index" and "the surest means" of assimilation. Those who intermarry contribute to the blurring of ethnic boundaries. They decrease the homogeneity of their respective ethnic groups and increase the range of ethnic identities that their children may assume or be assigned. Some important factors that increase the rate of out-marriage (*exogamy*) are small group size, mixed ancestry, spatial nearness (*propinquity*), low social distance between ethnic groups, a long period of time in the United States, and religious similarity (Alba and Golden 1986; Stevens and Swicegood 1987).

Although the importance of studying intermarriage is clear, the solution of some research problems is less so, and the interpretation of statistics on intermarriage requires caution. For example, when a marriage occurs between a member of the dominant group and a member of a subordinate group, we ordinarily consider this to be evidence of marital assimilation by the partner from the subordinate group; however, if the friends of the married couple are drawn mainly from the subordinate group, if the couple lives in a neighborhood composed primarily of others in the subordinate group, and if the children of the marriage are raised in the religion and culture of the subordinate group, are we still to call this assimilation? Consider, also, this situation: Minority group members who marry-out frequently select partners from other minority groups. Does this represent assimilation? "Does a woman," as Spickard (1989:17) asked, "cease to be black or brown or yellow or white if she marries someone of another color?" And, finally, is the marriage of a person who is part Irish and part German to a person who is part Irish and part Italian an in-marriage (*endogamy*) or an out-marriage? With these questions in mind, let us examine some of the results of the available studies on intermarriage among the Japanese.[33]

Except in Hawaii, interracial marriages of all kinds in the United States have been low. This is due in large part, of course, to the fact that such marriages frequently have been illegal. Burma (1963) studied all forms of interethnic marriage in Los Angeles between 1948 and 1959 by analyzing information gathered from marriage licenses. Burma chose this period because before 1948 the laws of California prohibited intermarriages of whites with members of another race, and during 1959 it became illegal to require a marriage license to show an applicant's race. The study data, therefore, reflect what was happening during a crucial time span in an area possessing a comparatively large Japanese American population. Over 375,000 marriage applications were counted for the eleven-year period. More than three thousand of these involved some form of racial mixing, and six hundred of the racially mixed applicants were Japanese (Burma 1963:163). Burma calculated that by 1959 interracial marriages among all groups in Los Angeles County had become more than three times as frequent as in 1948. His data also show that out-marriages involving Japanese Americans rose from approximately 11 percent of all out-marriages in 1949 to nearly 23 percent of cases in 1959.[34]

A subsequent study of Japanese out-marriage by Kikimura and Kitano (1973) drew together the findings of several reports, including their own results from Los Angeles County during 1971 and 1972. Based on studies in Fresno and San Francisco reported by Tinker (1973), the trend in intermarriages between white Americans and Japanese Americans noted by Burma apparently has continued, especially among the Sansei. Tinker found that in Fresno in 1969–1971 half of all marriages involving Japanese Americans were out-marriages. Kikimura and Kitano discovered a similar level of out-marriage in Hawaii for 1970 and in Los Angeles during 1971 and 1972. The latter authors concluded that the various reports strongly suggest that out-marriages have become so frequent among Japanese Americans that the Sansei are approximately as likely to marry outside the group as within it.[35] Finally, Parkman and Sawyer (1967:597) compared intermarriage rates during the years 1928–1934 with those of 1948–1953 and found that the rate of Japanese out-marriage roughly tripled between the two periods.[36]

The trend toward increasing marital assimilation among Japanese Americans found in these geographically limited studies is generally confirmed by two more broadly based studies. On the basis of the national sample of the Japanese American Research Project, Woodrum (1978:80) found a steady increase in marital assimilation not only among the three generations under discussion but within the younger and older members of the Nisei and Sansei groups as well. Younger Nisei and Sansei are more likely to have married-out than the older members of their generations, while the younger Nisei are less likely to have married-out than the older Sansei. Similarly, on the basis of a national public use sample prepared by the U.S. Bureau of the Census, Gurak and Kritz (1978:38) analyzed intermarriage statistics for thirty-five ethnic groups and found that the Nisei marry-out more frequently than the Issei. This intergenerational trend should not be exaggerated, however. Gurak and Kritz also found that thirty-one of the thirty-five groups in the analysis have higher out-marriage rates than the Nisei. Moreover, the Nisei who marry-out are less likely to marry a member of the Anglo-American core group than were the Issei. Spickard (1989:119) noted that the intermarriage rate for each Japanese American generation has been higher in areas where the Japanese ancestry population was sparse.[37]

Though the case is far from proven, it seems reasonable to say that Japanese Americans have been moving rapidly in the direction of complete assimilation in regard to each of the four subprocesses we have examined. It is unclear, however, that the *amount* of assimilation in regard to each subprocess is what would be expected on the basis of Park's and Gordon's ideas. For instance, although it does seem that Japanese Americans are more assimilated culturally than either structurally or maritally, it is not clear that all types of structural assimilation are more nearly complete than marital assimilation.[38]

Our findings, then, are complicated and not entirely consistent. Despite the number of important questions that are still unanswered, though, it is easy to see why Japanese Americans frequently are mentioned as evidence that any group— regardless of their race, culture, or history of oppression—can move fully into the mainstream of American life, usually within three generations. It also is easy to see why controversy continues over the final outcome of this drama of association between two such apparently different groups. Much of the evidence seems to suggest that Park's and Gordon's analyses are correct and that complete or practically complete assimilation awaits Japanese Americans. Kitano and Daniels (1988:73) reported that the Sansei and later generations "overwhelmingly" accept interracial marriage. In their view, this belief "adds to the possible acceleration of assimilation . . . " (Kitano and Daniels 1988:73). But some of the evidence does not fit this interpretation, and it may be, as Petersen (1971:208) stated, "a false prognosis."

Japanese American "Success"

The success of the Japanese in American society, especially in terms of education and occupation, has raised the following question in the minds of many people: How have the Japanese Americans been able to overcome the stigma of a nonwhite identity and to do so in a comparatively short time against such great odds? Speaking quite broadly, the theories presented to explain this phenomenon have focused primarily on what may be called cultural and structural factors.[39]

The Cultural View

We stressed earlier that the Issei brought with them the traditional values of Japan. They believed in the importance of hard work, thrift, cleanliness, neatness, education, occupational success, the pursuit of long-range goals, politeness, respect for authority, mutual trust, perseverance, and duty to one's parents and community. The latter belief was at the center of family life. Marriages created not just unions of couples but unions of pairs of families. The extended family units that were formed thereby were connected, in turn, in numerous ways to the larger community. An important effect of this pattern of interrelationships was that everyone in the community had important obligations to many others in the community. Each of the individual families was embedded in a highly solidary network. Assistance and support were freely requested and freely given. Various traditions of organization, such as rotating credit groups, helped to strengthen community solidarity.

Value Compatibility
Advocates of the cultural view have emphasized two ways in which the family and community values just described have contributed to the success of the Japanese in America. The first focused on the idea that there is "a significant compatibility (but by no means identity) between the value systems found in the culture of Japan and the value systems in American middle class culture" (Caudill and DeVos 1956:1107). The argument is not that the Japanese and American middle-class cultures are similar in general, but that certain key values are common to these otherwise quite different cultures.

In a study of some twenty thousand Issei and Nisei who were resettled in Chicago during World War II, for example, Caudill and DeVos (1956) found that the Nisei quickly moved out of menial, unskilled, and poorly paid jobs into semiskilled, service, and managerial jobs. They also moved out of the undesirable residential districts and into more expensive housing. Not only were the Nisei accepted by employers, landlords, and neighbors, they generally were praised because they were well-groomed and courteous and showed respect for authority. Under these conditions, the Nisei were able to accomplish in less than five years a measure of secondary assimilation greater than that of several other ethnic groups that had been in Chicago for a much longer time. They had become, to a large extent, a middle-class group. From this perspective, the Nisei succeeded in Chicago because their values and behavior "meshed" well with those of the dominant group. Kitano (1969:76) expressed the point as follows: "All in all, Japanese reverence for hard work, achievement, self-control, dependability, manners, thrift, and diligence were entirely congruent with American middle-class perceptions."

A "meshing" of values, of course, also might have occurred as the Japanese, particularly the Nisei, became more assimilated culturally. This possibility has been explored by Montero and Tsukashima (1977) and by Connor (1975), with contradictory results. While Montero and Tsukashima found that those Nisei who were most culturally assimilated had a higher average level of education than those who were more traditional, Connor found that the more assimilated the Nisei became, the lower the value they placed on achievement.

Community Cohesion

The discussion so far has rested on the assumption that the Issei were the bearers of the traditional success values of Japan and that these values were transmitted substantially intact to the Nisei. This result, of course, is what one might expect in a closely knit family group. Please recall, however, that the generation gap between the Issei and Nisei was much larger in a number of important respects than has been true in most other ethnic groups in America. The average age of the Issei was higher than has generally been true for first-generation parents. And the Nisei rapidly turned to Christianity, while the Issei, in general, remained Buddhists. Petersen (1971:202–207) contended that the differences between the Issei and Nisei have led, in fact, to a high degree of intergenerational conflict over things such as dating, courtship, marriage, and politics. He emphasized, though, that the various forms of adolescent rebellion of the Nisei were not translated into the kind of general social rebellion that frequently has occurred among second-generation immigrants. Instead of high rates of delinquency, gang violence, and truancy, the Nisei have usually been considered to be "good" boys and girls by their teachers, law enforcement officers, and social welfare officials. Nevertheless, the intergenerational conflict that did exist was sufficiently serious to make us wonder how the Issei were able to perform the task of value transmission. How was this cultural miracle accomplished? Miyamoto (1939; 1972) and Petersen (1971) argued strongly that the transmission of traditional values to the Nisei and Sansei has been accomplished by the entire Japanese community. According to Miyamoto

(1972:218), "the Japanese minority maintained a high degree of family and community organization in America, and these organizations enforced value conformity and created conditions and means for status achievement."[40]

The emphasis on community solidarity in the transmission of values directs our attention to the high frequency with which other people in the Japanese community have supported the efforts of particular parents. If a child's parents emphasized the importance of being polite, for example, they could be assured that if the child were impolite other adults would be likely to admonish him or her or, at the very least, report the misbehavior to the parents. In this way the child grew up in a supportive community even when the generation gap in the immediate family was quite wide. In such a community, children had difficulty finding adult allies to aid their efforts to "go against" their parents. Little room was left for the argument that "all the other kids are doing it!" Children learned that their private goals were less important than the group's goals. They also learned to avoid actions that might bring dishonor to the group.

Kitano (1969:68) illustrated this point in the story of a Nisei child who broke his arm in an athletic contest. The child was told by a series of Japanese adults, including his scoutmaster, his parents, his doctor, and his schoolteacher, that "Japanese boys don't cry," and he was praised when he did not cry. In this way, the child was consistently rewarded in a wide range of social settings for not doing something that might bring shame to his ethnic group as well as to his family. Incidents of this sort were a daily reminder to the Nisei that they were Japanese and that the entire community expected them to behave as their parents had instructed them. More important, such incidents served to assure children that they would almost surely be rewarded for "good" behavior and punished for "bad" behavior. These experiences, it is assumed, molded the Nisei and prepared them for success in school and in later life.

Criticism

Few scholars have claimed that the culture of the Japanese has been irrelevant to their success in America. Still, as presented, the cultural view has attracted substantial criticism. We have alluded already to one of the most frequent complaints: When the achievements of the Japanese (or any other group) are recounted as a "success story," they present only one side of the tale. The resulting success stereotype then may be used by the majority as a "put-down" for other minorities, especially other colored minorities (Okimoto 1971; Tachiki 1971). The majority may point to the Japanese and ask, "They have made it; why can't you?" Since, apparently, success is the result of possessing the "right" values, the implied answer to the question is this: If a group is not "making it" in America, then they must not be transmitting the "right" values to their individual members. This implication, in effect, places all of the blame for the "failure" of the group on the group itself, and it diverts attention away from other factors in the situation that may be crucial. The opponents of cultural interpretations often state that such views "blame the victim" by asserting or implying that worldly success or failure is due mainly to individual differences in will power or effort.

Another related criticism is that the "success values" approach "has been made with respect to every ethnic group that has achieved a notable degree of affluence" (Steinberg 1981:84); consequently, unless an analysis is amplified to take into account other differences among these groups, nothing has been learned. It is, of course, true, as we emphasized, that an important difference between such successful groups as the Jews and Greeks, on the one hand, and the Japanese, on the other, is that the former two groups are classified as white.[41] But this argument loses force when it is noted that some other nonwhite groups, such as Chinese, Koreans, and Cubans, also frequently are cited as demonstrating the efficacy of success values. Steinberg (1981:87) summarized the requirements for an adequate analysis as follows: "Only by adopting a theoretical approach that explores the interaction between cultural and material factors is it possible to assess the role of values in ethnic mobility without mystifying culture and imputing a cultural superiority to groups that have enjoyed disproportionate success."

What we are referring to here as the structural view includes various attempts to explain group differences in terms of specific "material factors."

The Structural View

Discussions concerning the success of the Issei frequently note that despite their initial poverty they rapidly became established as the independent owners or operators of many small businesses and farms. Bonacich and Modell (1980:37–43) cited several studies showing that, even in the face of vigorous discrimination, the Japanese by 1930 were highly concentrated in small, family-owned businesses, as both owners and employees. From this vantage point, the general question, "How did the Issei succeed?" may be stated more specifically: "How did the Issei become so well-established in business?"

Several noncultural answers to this question have been proposed. Ikeda (1973:498), for instance, argued that the Japanese who came from the less impoverished districts of Japan and who had the highest literacy levels were the most successful in America. Daniels (1969:11–12) stated that the hostility of Americans toward the Japanese made their employment prospects so uncertain that the Japanese were practically forced to use their skills on an independent basis. Still another suggestion was that the Japanese reached the West Coast just in time to fill some empty niches in the economy of a rapidly expanding new region (Modell 1977). Lieberson (1980:381–382) argued that the cessation of immigration from Japan decreased direct competition between the natives and Japanese and created the opportunity for the latter gradually to occupy special niches.[42]

One influential noncultural explanation is the *middleman minority theory* mentioned in chapter 4. This theory was derived from the observation that, to a greater extent than has been typical of immigrants, the Japanese initially did not intend to settle permanently in America; they were, as noted earlier, "sojourners" who maintained a very strong attachment to their homeland. The condition of sojourning, according to Bonacich (1973:585–588), is a necessary ingredient in the development of a specific economic status known as the "middleman minority."

Such minorities, which have appeared throughout the world at different times in history, are referred to as "middlemen" because "they occupy an intermediate rather than low-status position" (Bonacich 1973:583). Such groups typically concentrate in commerce and trade. The main reasons for this appear to be that sojourners are strongly motivated (1) to work hard and be thrifty in order to amass capital as quickly as possible; (2) to take risks in the hope of great gains; and (3) to concentrate their funds in lines of work that permit easy liquidation (Bonacich and Modell 1980:30). These characteristics also promote high ethnic group solidarity. Since sojourners do not plan to remain in the new society, they cultivate ties with other members of their own group and avoid strong ties with those in the host group; hence, when sojourners have the requisite skills and values and are confronted by a hostile society, the chances are high that they will concentrate in small businesses of the middleman variety and will cooperate closely in economic and all other matters (Cobas 1985). Indeed, when the level of discrimination against a group's members is very high, such cooperation may be necessary if the group is to survive.

The strong solidarity and economic cooperation of the Japanese, from this perspective, enabled them to cut costs in a number of ways and, thereby, to compete very effectively not only with other small businesses but even with the giant firms that dominated the "center" of the American economy. For example, typically, the entire family worked long hours in the business without pay, and all earnings except those that were essential to life and health were "plowed back" into the business (Bonacich and Modell 1980:47). The businesses established and developed along these lines soon were able to provide employment for other Japanese who also were willing to work long hours at low pay; such employees commonly accepted room and board as a part of their pay, which further reduced the cost of running the business. Community solidarity encouraged business efficiency in yet another way. Businesses frequently were "integrated vertically" by agreements with kin who could help provide the business with supplies and help market its products, and they were "integrated horizontally" through cooperative agreements with kin who operated similar types of businesses. Through thrift and cooperation, the business holdings of the Japanese grew at a very rapid rate.

The middleman minority theory helps to explain not only the economic success of some immigrant groups but also how they provided the support their children needed to be able to enter that segment of the economy known as the *primary labor market*.[43] The primary labor market contains "good" jobs in the "center" of the economy—jobs that are stable, offer chances for promotion, and have high wages and good working conditions. Workers in this segment of the market receive earnings and promotions that are commensurate with their levels of education and skill. Most immigrants in the past, however, as well as large numbers of unskilled or undocumented contemporary immigrants, have been unable to find jobs that either were in the primary labor market or permitted movement into that market. These immigrants, instead, have been forced into the *secondary labor market*, which consists of "dead-end," unstable, poorly paid jobs in the "periphery" of the economy. Even people who assimilate culturally or possess high levels of education or skill may be trapped in this segment of the economy and be unable to move up occupationally.

This line of reasoning, known as *dual economy theory,* affords the point of departure for a competing explanation of the business success of certain immigrant groups.[44] Although many groups in history surely may be described as having played the role of middleman, Portes and Bach (1985:340) argue that the middleman theory "fits awkwardly" in some cases. They doubt, for instance, that it is a correct description of the experience of Japanese Americans, and they also question its application to the experience of Jewish Americans (who definitely were not sojourners) and Cuban Americans. They prefer instead the *ethnic enclave theory* suggested by Wilson and Portes (1980) (see chapter 4). This theory is based on the idea that immigrant workers who live in an ethnically enclosed labor market may be part of a special type of economy that provides routes of upward mobility for workers who might otherwise be trapped in the "ordinary" secondary labor market (Butler and Wilson 1988; Portes 1981; Wilson and Martin 1982). Such an economy is not a middleman economy, though it may resemble one in some ways. It does not necessarily function as an intermediary or link between those in the upper and lower reaches of the economy, but it is based on community solidarity, the presence of a pool of disadvantaged ethnic workers, and vertical and horizontal integration. It is a "distinctive economic formation characterized by the spatial concentration of immigrants who organize a variety of enterprises to serve their own ethnic market and the general population" (Portes and Bach 1985:203).[45] Ethnic enclave economies of this type—for example, the one developed by Cubans in Miami—thus present a third kind of labor market in which immigrant workers only *appear* to be participating in a secondary labor market located in the "periphery" of the economy (Wilson and Martin 1982:155). In fact, they occupy "good" jobs within the ethnic enclave resembling the "center" economy (Butler 1991:30).

There is general agreement that an enclave economy may enable immigrant businesspeople and workers to enjoy advantages similar to those of participants in the center of the economy and the primary labor market (Bailey and Waldinger 1991), but the way this "enclave effect" is produced is a subject of vigorous debate. One influential argument is that the secret lies in the enclave's ability "to reproduce . . . some of the characteristics of monopolistic control accounting for the success of enterprises in the center economy" (Wilson and Portes 1980:301–302; see also Wilson and Martin 1982:138–139). Another explanation of the "enclave effect" is the *theory of ethnic hegemony* presented by Jiobu (1988). This theory draws on the insights of middleman minority theory, dual labor market theory, and ethnic enclave theory, but it includes other elements as well. For ethnic hegemony to exist, a minority group's members must enter somewhat sheltered labor markets, have specialized knowledge or be willing to perform tasks that are avoided by the majority, have a large number of its members available for employment, be able to monopolize certain kinds of work, and produce goods and services that are in high demand among members of the majority. The success of the Japanese in America was possible, Jiobu (1988:357) states, because they were able "to establish ethnic hegemony over a narrow and important sector of agriculture."[46] Bailey and Waldinger (1991:435) agree with Jiobu that the Japanese agricultural businesses were very successful and were vertically linked, but they believe the answer to the puzzle lies in another direction. They argue that even though most immigrant firms resemble the small, high-risk establishments of the secondary sector, the immigrant firms are able to cut costs and reduce risks by relying on the informal training, information, and recruiting system that characterizes the ethnic enclave. According to this *informal training system theory,* employers are enabled to reduce the cost of finding the most suitable workers and the workers are enabled to reduce the risk of investing their time and energy in jobs that might otherwise have no future (Bailey and Waldinger 1991:435).

The Japanese business economy was destroyed by the relocation program during World War II, and although it was rebuilt in a modified form after the war, many of the Nisei found careers outside of the ethnic community. The high level of education among the Nisei opened up many opportunities in the mainstream economy.[47] The Nisei, as Montero noted (1980:85–86; 1981:835), were torn between their loyalty to the ethnic community and their desire to "get ahead" in the dominant society in occupations that require high levels of education and geographic mobility. There is some irony in the fact that the educational achievement that was so encouraged by the Issei and made possible by the solidarity of the Japanese community also made it possible for the Nisei to leave the ethnic community entirely (Bonacich and Modell 1980:152); on the other hand, as Butler (1991:244) proposed, the Issei's hope that their children would experience economic mobility in the broader society may have been an important reason for the parents' great efforts in business. Indeed, this pattern appears to be typical of entrepreneurial minorities. Portes and Bach (1985:346) concluded in this regard that the progress made by the immigrants is "consolidated into educational and occupational mobility, within and outside the ethnic enclave, by later generations."

In keeping with this view, the trend toward increased assimilation and decreased social ties to the Japanese community appears to be marked among the Sansei, though they still are prominent as entrepreneurs (O'Hare 1992:34). Their levels of education, occupational attainment, and out-marriage are even higher than among the Nisei. O'Brien and Fugita (1984) argued, however, that the increasing economic and social independence of the Sansei does not necessarily mean that their Japanese ethnicity is of diminished importance to them. These changes may mean, rather, that the basis of ethnic identification has shifted from one of mutual cooperation to one of psychological support; therefore, we should not conclude that the continued upward mobility of the Japanese necessarily will lead to the complete loss of Japanese identification and culture.

A Comparison of Success Theories

Our discussion has revealed a variety of factors that may help to explain the worldly success of the Japanese in America. For instance, they have lived by a code of values that appears to be related to achievement; they have exhibited a high degree of community solidarity that may be rooted both in the traditions of Japan and in their "middleman" adaptation to American society; and they have utilized the agricultural (and other) skills learned in Japan to fill special niches in the American economy. Each of these factors must be included in an adequate explanation of Japanese achievement.

We must neither ignore nor exaggerate the role of culture in our attempt to understand the Japanese experience in America. An exclusive emphasis on cultural factors, as noted earlier, tends to promote what Steinberg called "self-congratulatory sentimentalism" (1981:87); but it also is true, on the other hand, that situational and other "material" factors may be overemphasized. Are we to assume that *any* ethnic group that reached the West Coast of the United States at the time the Japanese did would have been equally successful? Most theorists recognize that the success values and group pride of the Japanese have played an important role in the outcome. As Hirschman and Wong (1986:4) stated, "The introduction of structural determinants does not eliminate the role of cultural influences."

The facts of Japanese success in education, occupational standing, and income levels, if not their causes, are generally uncontested. Hirschman and Wong (1985:304) cautioned, however, that to some extent Japanese American success, particularly in education, may signify that the group is being denied opportunities along other avenues of achievement. Kitano and Daniels (1988:74), similarly, noted that even with their worldly success, the Japanese are still physically visible and, therefore, are subject to certain kinds of limitations. For example, in television, movie, and stage productions, even Sansei who are highly assimilated culturally may still find that the roles they are asked to play are as an enemy soldier, gardener, cook, and so on. Evidently, as Kitano and Daniels (1988:74) observed, "the desired body type and physical image in America remains that of a Caucasian. . . ." Moreover, and despite the fact that large majorities of the Sansei believe they are well off in American society (Levine and Rhodes 1981:123), some Japanese American militants are not so sure about the human meaning of their success. Is the material success that has always lain at the center of the values of American society really a worthwhile goal for human beings (Takagi 1973:151)? In the view of some Japanese Americans, the answer to this question is an unequivocal "no!" Okimoto (1971:17) put it this way: "I doubt whether we have succeeded in any but the narrowest materialist definition of the word. For in a broader spiritual and human-istic sense we have failed abysmally, not only as a minority group but as compas-sionate human beings as well."

Evidently, these questions and observations plunge us headlong into the arena of conflicting value premises. They also illustrate in concrete terms the conflict between the ideology of Anglo conformity and such alternatives as cultural pluralism and separatism. Whether one prefers or rejects Anglo conformity, how-ever, it is generally agreed that the experience of Japanese Americans confirms the rule that nonwhite groups are especially subject to severe discrimination in the United States. It seems uncontested, too, that Japanese Americans have been exceptional in the extent to which they have undergone cultural and secondary assimilation. There is ample reason to believe, further, that both primary and marital assimilation are well underway; however, even though the evidence shows that the main trend for Japanese Americans is toward full Anglo conformity, it still is possible that the contemporary revitalization of ethnic consciousness among the Japanese is more than a passing fad (Levine and Rhodes 1981:152–154). Some form of pluralism, which previously was most popular among the Issei, has found new adherents among the Sansei and Yonsei.

Let us now pursue some of these issues further through a consideration of the experience of the Mexican Americans.

Key Ideas

1. Even though they have experienced exceptionally high levels of prejudice and discrimination, Japanese Americans are an exception to the generalizations that (a) nonwhite minorities in the United States have not attained high levels of education and occupation, and (b) second-generation immigrants exhibit high levels of social deviance.

2. An analysis of a group that has not responded to prejudice and discrimination in the usual ways may afford clues to why the usual responses arise and how they may be prevented.

3. The Japanese family and community in America have been highly cohesive.

4. Despite vigorous efforts to stop them, the Issei were very successful in small business enterprises, particularly in agriculture.

5. When Japanese nationals in the United States experienced discrimination, they could—and often did—turn to the Japanese government for assistance.

6. The Japanese generations in America have been unusually distinctive, largely due to the interference in immigration, beginning with the Gentlemen's Agreement and the cessation of immigration by the Exclusion Act of 1924.

7. The evacuation and relocation program during World War II resulted in the imprisonment of over seventy thousand citizens of the United States without any charges or criminal convictions.

8. An effort was made to organize the relocation centers along the lines of a typical American community. This largely unsuccessful attempt widened further the gap between the Issei and Nisei.

9. Cultural assimilation has been comparatively low among the Issei and comparatively high among the Nisei and Sansei.

10. The Sansei are not completely assimilated culturally, and some evidence supports the idea that pluralism is gaining in popularity among them.

11. More frequently than the Nisei, the Sansei have openly raised questions concerning the human costs of the worldly success of their group.

12. The Nisei and Sansei have moved substantially in the direction of secondary, primary, and marital assimilation.

13. It is not established that the *amount* of assimilation that has occurred in regard to each of the four main subprocesses of assimilation is consistent with Gordon's theory.

14. The history of the Japanese Americans generally supports the idea that disadvantages based on racial distinctiveness are not necessarily permanent in American society.

15. The cultural view of Japanese success in America emphasizes the role of their value system and traditional group solidarity. According to this view, Japanese achievement may be explained by the compatibility between certain key values in Japanese and middle-class American cultures and by various advantages stemming from Japan's tradition of group loyalty.

16. The structural view of Japanese success in America stresses the importance of various noncultural factors, such as the kinds of skills they possessed, their level of literacy, the level of economic development on the West Coast at the time of their arrival, their role as a "middleman minority," and their ability to establish ethnic enclaves and, through them, ethnic hegemony in certain markets.

Notes

1. Since the Immigration Act of 1965 gives preference to people of higher education, the educational mean of recent Japanese immigrants is even higher (14.8 years; Hirschman and Wong 1985:296).

2. These figures are elevated to some extent by the inclusion of the occupational levels of recent Japanese immigrants. In 1976, according to Hirschman and Wong 20 percent of the native-born and 41 percent of the foreign-born were professionals (Hirschman and Wong 1985:298; U.S. Commission on Civil Rights November 1988:2).

3. Some Japanese American scholars have concluded that it is seriously misleading even to consider the status of Japanese Americans as a question of assimilation. Takagi (1973) considers the concept of assimilation to be implicitly racist, while Kagiwada (1973) believes any study of assimilation processes necessarily strengthens the ideology of Anglo conformity.

4. The "yellow peril" was the central element in the stereotype of the Chinese. It signified their presumed hatred of America and their intention physically to conquer the United States following a period of "peaceful invasion." (See tenBroek, Barnhart, and Matson 1954:19–29.)

5. A small but famous group of so-called First Year Men did go to Hawaii in 1868—the year of the restoration of imperial rule. For an account of this immigration, see Marumoto (1972:5–39).

6. As noted in chapter 5, the Chinese Exclusion Act was repealed on December 17, 1943.

7. In 1990, the size of the U.S. population of Japanese ancestry was about 847,000, or 0.3 percent of the total population (U.S. Department of Commerce 1991).

8. This doctrine was put into effect in the historic U.S. Supreme Court case *Plessy v. Ferguson* (1896), which is discussed in chapter 10.

9. The American exclusionists had found allies beyond the borders of the United States. Many of the points of friction between the West Coast Americans and the Japanese existed also between the West Coast Canadians and the Japanese; so a Canadian branch of the Asiatic Exclusion League was formed in Vancouver, British Columbia, in 1907. During a mass meeting of the league to rally support for the exclusion of the Japanese and all other Asians from Canada, some members of the crowd began to destroy property in the Chinese and Japanese sections of the city. Fighting broke out between the exclusionists and the Japanese, and blood was shed. The rioting led to a deterioration of relations between Japan and Canada. Approximately four months later, Canada concluded a gentlemen's agreement along the lines of the one negotiated by the United States (Sugimoto 1972).

10. The terms *Issei, Nisei,* and *Sansei* mean literally the first, second, and third generation.

Two other frequently used generational terms are *Yonsei* and *Kibei*. The Yonsei are the fourth generation. The Kibei are Nisei who were sent to Japan as children to receive a traditional Japanese upbringing.

11. We should note that the Little Tokyo and Little Japan communities established by the Issei, like those of many other ethnic groups, were not simply replicas of those in the old country. The Issei adapted a number of Japanese styles, implements, and manners to the American setting. This is another instance of the process of ethnogenesis whereby new ethnic communities are created.

12. By this time the Japanese also had become prominent in rice farming in Texas (Walls 1987:39–80).

13. The well-known exclusionist Senator J. D. Phelan, for instance, stated that "the native Japanese are as undesirable as the imported" (Daniels 1969:83).

14. The names *settlement period* and *second-generation period* were used by Miyamoto (1972:220–221).

15. The Nisei were especially vulnerable to the charge of being loyal to Japan because of the difference between American and Japanese laws concerning citizenship. The United States is one of several nations that grant citizenship to those born in the country (the principle of *jus soli*), while Japan is among the several nations that grant citizenship on the basis of kinship (the principle of *jus sanguinis*). The Nisei, therefore, were citizens of both the United States and Japan.

16. For excellent presentations of the details of these events, see Daniels (1975), tenBroek, Barnhart, and Matson (1954:99–184) and Thomas and Nishimoto (1946:1–52).

17. In 1940, there were about 127,000 Japanese and Japanese Americans in the United States. Of these, 47,000 were aliens and 80,000 were American citizens. Approximately 90 percent of these 127,000 people lived in California, Arizona, Oregon, and Washington (D. Thomas 1952:3).

18. DeWitt was hardly the only notable person to argue that the absence of sabotage was evidence of disloyalty. The famous "liberal" columnist Walter Lippmann and the "liberal" Attorney General of California, Earl Warren, advanced the same idea (Walls 1987:145–146).

19. In addition to the relocation centers, the U.S. Immigration and Naturalization Service maintained at least fifteen "internment camps" in eight states. These smaller camps were designed to hold "potentially dangerous enemy aliens," among whom were included many Japanese (Walls 1987:175–176).

20. The following discussion of life in the Poston Relocation Center is based on the excellent study by Leighton (1946).

21. For a further analysis of this point, see the stimulating discussion by Grodzins (1956:105–131).

22. For a full discussion of the role of Japanese Americans in World War II, see Hosokawa (1969:393–422).

23. Question 27 also concerned the individual's loyalty and was prominent in the controversy. It read: "Are you willing to serve in the armed forces of the United States on combat duty, wherever ordered?" On the basis of their answers to questions 27 and 28, the evacuees were divided into "yes-yes" and "no-no" groups.

24. For a full analysis of the registration and segregation programs, see Thomas and Nishimoto (1946:53–361).

25. Quoted by Broom and Kitsuse (1956:32).

26. For a discussion of this point, see Kitano (1969:28).

27. Some evidence from the Japanese American Research Project indicates that at the time the data were gathered (1964 to 1966), these views were held by a minority of the Sansei. Levine and Rhodes (1981):123, 148) found in regard to the wartime relocation that eight of ten among both the Nisei and Sansei "believe that leaders who acted to make the episode orderly and comfortable used a better approach than those who protested." Similarly, the researchers found that a large majority of the Sansei were not at that time in favor of the black power movement. These authors do recognize, nevertheless, that the militant minority may persuade the majority to accept different views.

28. This revitalization effort appears to illustrate the workings of both Hansen's law and ethnogenesis. It involves an effort to construct a new ethnic identity that relates Japanese Americans to

all other Asians and to all other colored minorities as well as to their Japanese forebears.

29. Sanders and Nee (1987:745) refer to this idea as *the ecological hypothesis.*

30. Indexes of dissimilarity also are useful for estimating group differences in income, occupation, and education, and we will present information concerning such differences in later chapters. For a discussion of an alternative measure, the index of net difference, see Fossett, Galle, and Kelly (1986).

31. These areas are called Standard Metropolitan Statistical Areas (SMSAs). An SMSA consists of the population of a city containing at least fifty thousand residents plus all contiguous, functionally related, nonagricultural counties.

32. Kagiwada (1973:163) criticized his own study, among others, for having been conducted within an assimilationist framework. He concluded that "a more realistic framework would view these pluralistically oriented groups as struggling to maintain their religio-cultural integrity against the tremendous odds of assimilationist forces within our society." This criticism, however, appears to be directed toward the scope and interpretation of the findings reported here, and not their accuracy.

33. Problems of interpretation sometimes arise also from the way intermarriage rates are reported. Suppose there are six marriages in which both partners are Catholic and four marriages in which only one partner is Catholic. Since four of the ten marriages are mixed, we may say the rate *for marriages* is 40 percent; however, since there are sixteen Catholics in all, only four of whom are in a mixed marriage, we may say with equal logic that the rate *for individuals* is 25 percent (Rodman 1965:776–778). Either rate may be used, but confusion occurs when one is mistaken for the other.

34. Calculated form Table 6 in Burma (1963:163).

35. There is some evidence that this generalization may be less applicable to those who have a religious affiliation. In a study of 141 Buddhist and Christian Japanese Americans, Feagin and Fujitaki (1972:28) found no instance of out-marriage. It also is possible that the extent of marriage across racial lines overstates the degree to which Japanese Americans are pulling away from their ethnic group. Petersen (1971:224) argued that in Hawaii

the children of white-Japanese couples generally are identified as white or Japanese but not both and that, therefore, the Japanese group is maintaining its distinctiveness.

36. *Newsweek* reported in 1986 that more than half of all Japanese American marriages were outside of the group (Kantrowitz 1986:80).

37. Spickard (1989:119, 354) also noted that the Issei adhered to a "hierarchy of preferences both within and outside" of the Japanese American group and that these preferences weakened in particular ways among the younger generations.

38. This observation raises a crucial question that has been addressed by Williams and Ortega (1990:707). Is it possible, really, to determine whether one type of assimilation is more advanced than another? Are we trying to compare apples and oranges?

39. There is general agreement that one side of this dichotomy should be called *cultural;* however, several different terms are used to designate all, or only a portion of, the many factors described here as "structural." In addition to *structural,* some other common terms are *situational, contextual,* and *material* (Bonacich and Modell 1980:29–30).

40. The pattern of "enhanced striving" under adverse conditions that we have found among the Japanese has been noted also in other ethnic groups that typically have high levels of group solidarity. For an analysis of this pattern among the Jews and Chinese, see Eitzen (1968).

41. For discussions of Greek and Jewish mobility, respectively, see Moskos (1980:111–126), Rosen (1959), and Steinberg (1981:82–105).

42. This argument is an important part of Lieberson's (1980:381–383) answer to the question, "Why have Japanese Americans been more successful than African Americans?" An additional part of the answer is that even though the levels of discrimination against the Japanese have been very high, discrimination against blacks has been higher still. We return to this important question in chapter 11.

43. Hacker (1992:39) defines labor markets as "arenas where people and jobs are matched."

44. Dual economy theory has been expanded by some researchers into segmented labor market theory (Sanders and Nee 1987:745–748).

45. The emergence of ethnic enclaves, according to Portes and Rumbaut (1990:21), depends on three conditions: (1) immigrants with a knowledge of business; (2) access to sources of capital; and (3) access to labor. In their opinion the first requisite is the most important.

46. As noted previously, agriculture quickly became the main occupation of the Japanese, and in this category they became dominant in the specialized fields of truck farming and produce wholesaling. By 1940, with no more than 2 percent of California's population, nearly 40 percent of the members of this group "were directly involved in farming, wholesaling, or retailing truck produce" (Jiobu 1988:362).

47. Prior to World War II, however, even well-educated Nisei frequently were unable to find work outside the Japanese community (Jiobu 1988:364).

Mexican Americans

Despite great obstacles, this population as a whole is clearly moving further away from lower-class Mexican traditional culture and toward Anglo-American middle-class culture. . . . —FERNANDO PENALOSA

The North American culture is not worth copying: it is destructive of personal dignity; it is callous, vindictive, arrogant, militaristic, self-deceiving, and greedy . . . it is a cultural cesspool and a social and spiritual vacuum for the Chicano. —ARMANDO B. RENDON

The preceding chapters highlighted the point that the population of the United States has been built up mainly by successive waves of immigrants from various parts of the world and that these immigrants, broadly speaking, entered the society voluntarily. In the case of the Mexican Americans, however, we confront a second kind of situation.[1] Unlike the Irish, Germans, Italians, Jews, Chinese, Japanese, and nearly all other groups we have discussed, the Mexican Americans did not initially become "newcomers" to American society by leaving the old country and crossing oceans. Instead, like African Americans and Native Americans, they originally became a part of American society through conflict and coercion. The southwestern or "borderlands" region of what is now the United States, in which the Mexican American population still is concentrated, was settled by people of Spanish-Mexican-Indian ancestry long before it was settled by Anglo-Americans, and, along with the Native Americans, the Mexican Americans entered the society through the direct conquest of their homelands.

Some students believe this is a fact of overriding importance, a fact that makes totally inapplicable to the Mexican Americans the assimilationist ideas we have explored thus far. As Sanchez stated, "the Spanish Mexicans of the Southwest are not truly an immigrant group, for they are in their traditional home."[2] From this standpoint, the expectation that the experience of the Mexican Americans can be analyzed properly in terms of any or all of the three main ideologies of assimilation discussed previously is considered a serious mistake. It is argued, rather, that to understand the Mexican American experience we must employ an antiassimilationist ideology and framework. What basis is there for such a claim? What ideas does such a view contain?

The Colonial Model

The principal reasons to assume that something is wrong with a conventional assimilationist interpretation of the Mexican American experience may be most easily appreciated by considering again the predictions one would make on the basis of Park's race cycle theory. The Mexican American group has now been in existence since 1848, quite long enough to have passed through the conflict and accommodation stages and to be well into the final stage of complete assimilation. In terms of our modification of Gordon's concepts, we should by now have witnessed a high degree of cultural and secondary assimilation and a substantial degree of primary and marital assimilation. In fact, however, the relations between Mexican Americans and Anglos[3] in the borderlands have been marked by repeated instances of "falling back" into the conflict stage of Park's cycle. Considering the length of time that has elapsed since 1848, the levels of most forms of assimilation strike many observers as unexpectedly low.

We have seen that different ethnic groups have tried, with varying success, to preserve and elaborate their cultures and have been, in varying degrees, the objects of prejudice and discrimination. We have seen, too, that there are good reasons to question whether immigrant minorities ever have assimilated in precisely the way

Park's ideas would suggest. Nevertheless, we also have seen that as a guide to an understanding of the experience of many European groups in the United States—especially those from northern, western, and central Europe—the ideas of assimilationist theory are of considerable value. People of different heritages have been incorporated solidly into the society of the United States and have, for many purposes, come to view themselves mainly, if not exclusively, as Americans.

But how well would these ideas serve us if we wished to understand, say, interethnic relations in Africa? The colonized minorities of Africa generally have been in a very different situation from the immigrant minorities of the United States. In contrast to the more or less voluntary movement of the immigrant minorities to America, the colonized minorities of Africa generally were indigenous to the areas in which they became minorities and were forced to "join" the society of the colonizers. Furthermore, the colonized minorities of Africa typically were not numerical minorities. They were inferior in power, of course, which is why we call them minorities, but by sheer weight of numbers, if nothing else, they have been in a better position than immigrant minorities to maintain and elaborate their cultures in the face of the dominant group's efforts to establish its own culture as the only acceptable one (Blauner 1972:53).

The economic situation of the colonized minorities of Africa also has differed noticeably from that of the immigrant minorities in America. Although the American immigrant minorities usually have had to take whatever kind of work they could get, at least initially, they frequently have been able to move on to something more desirable after a while and to exercise some degree of choice in what they would accept. As we have seen, even their first jobs were likely to be ones that some Anglo-Americans were doing or had done recently. The complaint that "they" are undercutting us economically and are taking "our" jobs away has been heard monotonously in America. But this kind of labor difficulty did not arise in the African colonies. There the indigenous populations usually were required to engage in only the hardest, most menial kinds of tasks. The better jobs were reserved for members of the dominant group. Ordinarily, the opportunity to move around and compete freely with the members of the dominant group did not exist or was very limited (Blauner 1972:55).

Under these conditions, the colonized minorities in Africa did not usually come to think of themselves as French or Dutch or English, and they did not typically move into the mainstream of the dominant group's social life. The colonized minorities of Africa, instead, looked forward to the day when the European invaders could be annihilated or forced to leave and return to their own countries. The cycle of race relations here was not characterized by a steady movement forward, out of the stage of accommodation into the final stages of assimilation. Rather, it was primarily a back-and-forth movement between the stage of accommodation and the prior stage of conflict.[4] In its main or "classical" form, which was witnessed repeatedly in Africa after World War II, this oscillation continued until the dominant white group, in most instances, was thrown out of power and the previously colonized minorities became majorities. In many of these cases, of course, large numbers of the dominant white group fled or were driven out of the country. The final stage of relations between dominant Europeans and colonized Africans, then, was a conflict (usually violent) followed by separation rather than accommodation followed by assimilation.

Several observers have suggested that the kind of race relations existing between the invaders and natives in much of Africa affords a more understandable picture of the relations between Anglos and Mexican Americans than do the ideas of assimilationist theory. Moore (1970:464) stated that the concept of colonialism "describes and categorizes" the initial contacts of the Mexicans and the Americans. Similarly, Blauner (1972:119) argued that "the conquest and absorption of the Mexican population is an example of classical colonialism," while Acuña (1972:3) stated that "the conquest of the Southwest created a colonial situation in the traditional sense."

Mexican Americans, in fact, may be viewed as a people who have undergone classical colonialism not once but twice. The Indians of Mexico were first subdued by the Spaniards. Then, after Mexico became an independent nation, a portion of her population was subjugated by another migrant group. As in the case of African colonialism, one group (first the Spaniards and then the Anglo-Americans) invaded and occupied the territory of another group (the Mexicans). Thus, the original Mexican American population—what Alvarez (1985:37) called "the Creation Generation"—entered American society in a fundamentally different position from that of the Irish, German, or other ethnic minorities that were entering during the same period. "The Mexicans in the conquered territory," in Acuña's (1981:1) words, "became victims of a colonial process in which U.S. troops acted as an army of occupation."

The invaders have regulated closely the "place" within the dominant society of the conquered people, their descendants, and the more recent arrivals from Mexico. This regulation has been particularly apparent in the kinds of work that have been deemed suitable for people of Mexican ancestry. For most of the period since the borderlands became a part of the United States, Mexicans and Mexican Americans have been expected mainly to perform hard, menial, or "stoop" labor. In terms of the colonialist model, those of Mexican ancestry were viewed as meeting the same need for cheap, controlled labor as had African slaves. They were expected to "occupy positions at the bottom of the occupational structure. . . ." that "no free domestic labor can be found to perform. . . ." (Portes and Bach 1985:12); they were expected to fill permanently the dead-end jobs of the secondary labor market with no prospect of moving into those that permit people to be upwardly mobile (the primary labor market).[5]

Although the European groups we've discussed definitely displayed a certain resistance to Anglo conformity, as is seen in the rise of cultural pluralism, the solidarity (or clannishness) of the Mexican Americans generally has been more troublesome for the dominant group; consequently, the reactions of the Anglo-Americans—particularly in Texas—involved more force, more overt coercion, and a generally higher level of ethnic discrimination and racism than usually was true in the case of European minorities. Given the differences in the historical sequences, the colonial model proposes (in contrast to the immigrant model) that one should not expect the Mexican Americans to move into the mainstream of American life in three or four generations or to cease their existence as a profoundly distinctive group. One should expect, instead, that there will be constant tension in the direction of separation or even secession.

The colonialist perspective as we have discussed it has existed and been applied to the Mexican American experience for many years, though the frequent and explicit application of this view may be traced to the 1960s (Cuéllar 1970:149). As the protest activities of African Americans during this period gathered momentum, Mexican American protest became both more frequent and more visible. Many intellectuals in the group were critical in speeches and in print of the usual assimilationist interpretations of the condition of the Mexican Americans put forward by (mainly) Anglo-American scholars. An important result of these efforts has been the emergence and diffusion of an antiassimilationist interpretation of the Mexican American experience called *Chicanismo*.[6] Although Chicanismo is not a unitary, systematic philosophy (it is still being sharpened, debated, and modified), some version of the colonial model is a central element within it. Chicanismo usually emphasizes not only the unity of the Mexican American people but also their relationship to the Spanish-Indian peoples of Mexico and Central and South America. This much larger population, *La Raza*, is seen as sharing a very ancient and complicated heritage stemming not only from Spanish culture but also from the Aztec, Inca, Maya, and Toltec cultures. The Mexican American heritage, therefore, is a rich mixture of indigenous and Spanish civilizations. Its heroes include not only such courageous fighters against Anglo imperialism as Joaquin Murieta and Juan Cortina, but the illustrious Montezuma and the scholars and scientists of the Indian high civilizations (Murguía 1989:9). Chicanismo thus affords both an interpretation of how the Mexican American population came into being and emphasizes the antiquity and grandeur of Mexican American history. It serves to explain the troubles of the Mexican Americans and to increase their awareness of themselves as members of a distinctive and oppressed group (Moore and Pachon 1985:182). Those who espouse Chicanismo see themselves as a unique product of New World colonialism and, in some ways, as sharing the fate of other colonized minorities in the United States and throughout the world. They tend to reject "the cold and materialist Anglo culture" and to prefer, instead, the "family warmth and solidarity" (Murguía 1989:9) of Mexican American culture.

We now have considered some of the ways that an antiassimilationist perspective may differ from the more common assimilationist views, including cultural pluralism. Specifically, we have considered that three of America's minorities—Native Americans, Mexican Americans, and African Americans—have been forced to join American society and that two of these groups—the Native and Mexican Americans—have been conquered on their own land and have undergone a process of colonization quite similar to that experienced by the native populations of Africa.[7] We have seen that in the case of the Mexican Americans, some version of the colonialist interpretation has for some time been preferred by many members of the group itself and that, more recently, the colonial model afforded a focal point around which the ideology of Chicanismo was organized. Those who support the

Chicano view, therefore, sometimes suggest that the most desirable solutions to the problems of the Mexican American group lie in the direction of separation or secession. More often, however, the main aim is to combat Anglo conformity and to promote cultural pluralism.

Indian–Spanish Relations

To assess the competing claims of the assimilationist (immigrant model) and antiassimilationist (colonial model) interpretations of the Mexican American experience, let's begin with the landings of the Spaniards in Mexico during the second decade of the sixteenth century. Here, as in the case of the landings of the English in Virginia and Massachusetts approximately one hundred years later, a conquering European, Christian group established itself on lands previously occupied by indigenous American groups. In both instances, the dominant migrant group gradually expanded its frontiers to create an increasingly large colonial territory. The expansion of the English toward the west and of the Spanish toward the north were the processes that would one day bring these two enormous colonial developments together.

The specific course of colonial development in the English and Spanish territories differed in a number of significant respects. For one thing, the two powers' entire approaches to colonization were different. We described in chapter 3 the heavy reliance of the English on a private, profit-sharing method to promote exploration and colonization. The exploration and colonization of the Spanish territories, however, relied more strongly on the initiatives of the crown and the church. The Spanish monarchs were interested primarily in acquiring lands and precious metals, while the Roman Catholic Church wished to save the souls of the "heathens." The English, too, were interested at first in these very same things, but after a while it became clear that there was no gold and silver treasure on the Atlantic coast, and the efforts to Christianize the Indians proved to be largely futile.

These differences in colonization methods and experiences had one consequence of special importance for us: the relations between the conquering Europeans and the conquered Indians developed along significantly different paths in the two cases. As noted in chapter 3, the relations between the English and the Indians became predominantly hostile and were interspersed with warfare. The Indians soon were considered to stand in a completely different relation to the developing society than the Dutch, Irish, or Germans. The policy of the Anglo-Americans toward the Native Americans became one of exclusion and extermination. By and large, the Indians were forced to move west as the Anglo-American frontier advanced.

The relations between the Spaniards and the Indians in Mexico also were frequently hostile, but the Spaniards were much more successful than the Anglo-Americans in the matter of converting the Indians to Christianity, at least to many of its outward forms. Consequently, even though the Spaniards also took an enormous toll in human lives and misery, the cross as well as the sword marked the advance of the northern frontier of Mexico.[8] The policy of the Spaniards was to bring Christianized Indians into the colonial society they were building—peacefully if possible, but by force if necessary. The place of the indigenous people in Mexican society, to be sure, was at the very bottom. They provided most of the manual labor that was needed to construct and maintain the *haciendas* and to exploit the riches of the earth. They were the *peons,* who were bound to the Spanish masters and the land in a form of human slavery, but they also were human beings and Christians, and they were accepted as an integral, if lowly, part of Mexican society.[9]

The Spaniards' policy of counting the Indians "in" rather than "out" led, during a period of three centuries, to a much higher degree of marital (and other forms of) assimilation of the Indians with the dominant Europeans than was true on the eastern seaboard. Although the exact nature of this assimilation process lies beyond our scope, two things should be noted. First, just as the English subscribed generally to the Anglo conformity ideology of assimilation, the Spaniards adhered generally to what we may call the Hispano conformity ideology. The Indians were expected to do their very best to move toward a mastery of Spanish culture and ways of acting. Nevertheless—and this is the second point—by the time Mexico achieved independence in 1821, the culture and population of Mexico had become very much more "Indianized" than had the culture and population of the United States. Whatever may have been the intentions of the dominant Spaniards, the melting pot process of assimilation was more significant in Mexico than in the United States.

The Hispano-Indian society of Mexico and the Anglo-American society of the United States came into direct and continuous contact after the Louisiana Purchase in 1803. The line of contact between these groups was exceptionally long and blurred. Since the treaty through which the United States secured Louisiana from France did not give a detailed description of the boundaries of the territory, it stretched in a poorly defined way from a point west of New Orleans, through Texas to the Rocky Mountains, north along the Rockies, and then west to the Pacific. This helped to create and maintain an almost constant state of tension along the frontier, first between Spain and the United States and later between Mexico and the United States. Many Americans, including such illustrious figures as Thomas Jefferson and John Quincy Adams, seemed to believe that Texas definitely had been included in the purchase, but the Spanish and Mexican governments disagreed. Many other Americans believed that it was the "Manifest Destiny" of their country to span the continent and that the frontier should be extended to the Pacific, by force if necessary. In this way, a struggle began that led, by 1848, to the transfer of what we now know as the American southwest from Mexico to the United States and to the creation of the Mexican American minority group.

The Texas Frontier

The process through which the Mexican American group has emerged may be visualized more clearly by a consideration of some of the events that occurred in Texas after 1803. Spain's claim to the eastern portion of Texas was disputed openly by the United States until 1819, when Spain and the United States completed a treaty giving Florida to the United States and Texas to Spain. The treaty established the Sabine River as the boundary between Louisiana and Texas. In 1821, Mexico's long struggle to gain independence from Spain was successful, and all of Spain's North American territories then came under the control of the new nation. As the Americans attempted to push their frontier westward, consequently, they became involved in conflicts with Mexico.

The Mexican government worried from the beginning that it might be unable to secure its long, sparsely populated northern frontier from the encroachments of the Americans. Many people in the United States did not accept the treaty agreements that had been concluded with Spain. Many southerners, in particular, were eager to expand the cotton industry into the rich lands of East Texas. Furthermore, the United States recently had been flexing its muscles in international affairs (e.g., the Monroe Doctrine) and was clearly in a stronger military position than the young Mexican nation. Also, the Americans generally did not hide the fact that they regarded themselves to be racially superior to the heterogeneous population of Mexico. The majority of Mexico's citizens were either Indians or Spanish Indians (*mestizos*), and the heritage of the "pure" Spaniards was itself suspect in the Americans' minds because of the centuries of interaction between the Spaniards and various African populations (e.g., the Moors). Hence, racism played an important role in Mexican and American relations.

The Mexicans had some reason for optimism, however. They had established a form of government resembling that of the United States, and they hoped their northern neighbor would have a greater respect for the territorial integrity of a constitutional democracy than it had had for that of imperial Spain. In addition, the Mexican government decided to attempt to create a buffer zone between the two nations by colonizing Texas with Anglo-Americans. In one sense, this plan would merely promote Anglo-American dominance in the area, but since all of the Anglo-American settlers were expected to become citizens of Mexico and members of the Roman Catholic Church, the Mexican officials hoped to maintain control over them. They hoped that border relations would be improved and Texas would become a less tempting target for a forcible invasion.

This strategy ultimately failed. Less than fifteen years after Mexico gained her independence from Spain, Texas broke away from Mexico to establish still another independent republic.[10] Nevertheless, a basis for native Mexican (*Tejano*) and Anglo-American immigrant cooperation was created and maintained by able leaders from both sides. Stephen F. Austin, the leader of the first group of Anglo-American immigrants to Texas, was enthusiastic about the prospect of an independent Mexico and the development of Texas within it. He sincerely accepted Mexican citizenship and was a respected link between the native and immigrant groups. From the native Mexican side, such men as Ramón Músquiz and José Antonio Navarro worked energetically to assist the assimilation of the Anglo-Americans into Mexican society. But the good will and substantially similar interests of the native and immigrant leadership in Texas did not extend to Mexico City. In a way, the central authorities fell victims to their own plan. The colonization program was so successful that by 1835 the Anglo-American immigrants outnumbered the native Mexicans in Texas by about five to one; hence, as the talk of revolution spread, most of those who favored it were, simply as a matter of numbers, Anglo-Americans. When the revolution erupted, the Texan armies were comprised mainly of Anglo-Americans; nevertheless, a large proportion of the native Mexicans in Texas believed that various actions of the central government had been unjustified. Kibbe (1946:33) estimated that as many as one-third of those who opposed the government of Santa Anna were native Mexicans, and several all-native units participated in the actual fighting during the Texas revolution (Barker 1943:333).[11]

After the defeat of Santa Anna in 1836, Texas was established as an independent nation. The conflict between Texas and Mexico did not stop, however. Most of the Texans believed the boundary between the two countries was the Rio Grande, while still others thought Texas extended beyond the river to the Sierra Madre mountains. The Mexican government, on the other hand, did not officially concede that Texas was lost to them. Even those in Mexico who did recognize that Texas was now independent believed the boundary was the Nueces River. As a result, the large tract of land between the Rio Grande and the Nueces River continued to be an active battleground. Although the *Tejanos* were a numerical minority, they were not yet treated systematically as an ethnic minority. An ethnic line of distinction existed, of course, but it was a blurred rather than a sharp line. Paul Taylor (1934:21) described the situation as follows: "During the period of confusion some Texans were fighting with Mexicans. . . . other Texans were committing depredations against both Texans and Mexicans, while Mexicans could be found on both sides." Gradually, however, friendships between the *Tejanos* and the Anglo-American Texans became more difficult to maintain, and relations between the groups became more strained. Anglo-American Texans, in particular, increasingly failed to distinguish the *Tejanos* from Mexican nationals and came to regard the conflict in Texas as one of "Mexicans" versus "Americans" (Montejano 1987:26–30).

Many of the Anglo-American Texans did, in fact, still regard themselves as Americans and were eager to have Texas join the United States. This goal was shared by many people in the United States. As early as 1820, while Mexico was still a Spanish colony, Thomas Jefferson expressed the opinion that "Texas, in our hands, would be the richest state in the Union" (Rives 1913:23). It is hardly surprising, therefore, that after only some ten years of independence, Texas agreed to become part of the United States.

Conflict in the Borderlands

The annexation of Texas aggravated rather than ended the hostilities in the borderlands. President Santa Anna had warned in 1843 that "the Mexican government will consider equivalent to a declaration of war against the Mexican Republic the passage of an act for the incorporation of Texas with the territory of the United States" (Faulkner 1948:324). After the annexation, diplomatic relations between the two governments were broken, and both sides prepared for war. Since the United

States accepted Texas's claims concerning the boundary between the two nations, President Polk ordered General Taylor to occupy the land between the Nueces and the Rio Grande. The Mexicans, of course, considered this an invasion of their territory. In April 1846, a battle between Mexican and American troops occurred north of the Rio Grande, and in May President Polk asked Congress for a declaration of war against Mexico, claiming that Mexico "has invaded our territory and shed American blood on American soil" (Faulkner 1948:325). Abraham Lincoln was among those who did not agree with this explanation of the situation. His own view was that the war was "unnecessarily and unconstitutionally commenced by the President" (Faulkner 1948:325).

Constitutional or not, "one of the most obviously aggressive wars in American history" was underway (Jordan and Litwack 1987:315). The conflict involved not only the disputed territory between Texas and Mexico but all of Mexico. General Taylor moved south of the Rio Grande to Monterrey, Colonel Kearny directed the conquest of New Mexico, Arizona, and California, and General Scott invaded at Vera Cruz and captured Mexico City. In February 1848, Mexico surrendered under the terms of the Treaty of Guadalupe Hidalgo.

The treaty ceded to the United States nearly one-half of the territory of Mexico. The Rio Grande was established as the boundary of Texas, and the great bulk of the land that now comprises the southwestern region of the United States was acquired.[12] The "Manifest Destiny" of the United States to stretch from the Atlantic to the Pacific had now been achieved. The Spanish-Mexican-Indian group that was left behind as Mexico's northern frontier receded (75,000 to 100,000 people)[13] was now a conquered group. As individuals, they had the right either to "retain the title and rights of Mexican citizens, or acquire those of citizens of the United States" (Moquín and Van Doren 1971:246). Those who did not declare their intention to remain Mexicans automatically became citizens of the United States after one year. At this point, they were entitled legally to enjoy the same rights and privileges as all other U.S. citizens (del Castillo 1990). In practice, however, they generally were viewed as a defeated and inferior people whose rights did not need to be taken too seriously. They "gradually saw their property and influence dwindle as they faced . . . the flood of Anglo-Americans" (Burner, Fox-Genovese, and Bernhard 1991:387).

In this way, the Mexican Americans became a minority in the United States. Their entry into the society was by conquest and, to repeat, was quite different from that of the Irish and Germans who were arriving in large numbers in the East during the same period. The "Creation Generation" of Mexican Americans had not decided to leave their native land and go to the United States. They simply discovered one day that by a mutual agreement of the United States and Mexico (at gunpoint), the places where they lived were no longer in Mexico. In fact, to continue being Mexicans, they either had to leave their homes and move south of the new border established by the treaty or declare officially their intention to remain Mexican nationals within the United States. Acuña (1981:19) states that "About 2,000 elected to leave; most remained in what they considered *their* land."

The Treaty of Guadalupe Hidalgo did not end the physical violence between the Anglos and Mexican Americans in the borderlands. Although there is no accurate tabulation of the violent interethnic encounters that took place between individuals and groups, it has been reported that the number of Mexican Americans killed in the Southwest during the years 1850 to 1930 was greater than the number of lynchings of African Americans during that same period (Moquín and Van Doren 1971:253). In Moore's (1976:36) opinion, "No other part of the United States saw such prolonged intergroup violence as did the Border States from 1848 to 1925."

If the treaty did not end the violence, it did mark the point beyond which those of Mexican descent were subordinated to the Anglo-Americans. A system of ethnic domination and subordination had been born. We referred in chapter 6 to an important explanation of how such systems arise. Please recall that, as presented by Noel (1968), if one group has greater power than another, if there is competition for scarce resources, and if ethnocentrism is present, then a system of ethnic stratification invariably will arise. Our description of contacts between Mexicans and Americans in the borderlands strongly suggests that all three of these essential ingredients were present. The superior power of the Anglo-Americans was demonstrated, of course, by the outcome of the war with Mexico. The desire of the Anglo-Americans for the land, as we noted, was apparent for decades prior to the war. Though ethnocentrism was most conspicuous from the Anglo-Americans, feelings of superiority existed on both sides. We see, therefore, that the Americans had ample incentives to compete with the Mexicans for Texas, they had the power to seize it if necessary, and they typically had a low regard for the Mexican people. The combination of these ingredients created a highly unstable situation along all of Mexico's northern frontier, especially in the area of Texas.[14]

Many of the most spectacular conflicts took place or originated in the strip of land between the Nueces River and the Rio Grande. Numerous "filibustering expeditions" were launched by Americans in an attempt to extend U.S. territory even more deeply into Mexico.[15] The traffic was not entirely one-way, however. Between 1859 and 1873, the flamboyant Mexican leader Juan N. "Cheno" Cortina initiated a series of deadly raids along the Texas border (Acuña 1981:33–37; Rosenbaum 1981:41–45; Webb [1935]1987:173–193). Cortina, who was born near Brownsville, Texas, developed a deep hatred of *"gringos"* during the Mexican and American war. Throughout most of the 1850s, he lived on the Texas side of the river, gathered about him a band of roguish *vaqueros,* and was indicted for theft and murder (Lea 1957:159–160). He came prominently to attention in July 1859 in the first of a series of "Cortina wars." After rescuing a former servant from the Anglo-American marshal in Brownsville and wounding the marshal, Cortina brought together his men and captured Brownsville in an early morning raid. For the next two months, Cortina's force remained in the area between Brownsville and Rio Grande City, burning, looting, and killing. During the following years, Cortina's daring exploits won him labels ranging from "cattle thief" to "champion of his race" (Lea 1957:159). They also provoked continuous, bitter conflicts with military and law enforcement authorities on both sides of the Rio Grande.

The Cortina wars fanned the flames of ethnic hatred in Texas, and untold numbers of innocent people were their victims. The Anglo-Americans became increasingly suspicious of all "Mexicans" and were quick to punish anyone suspected of aiding Cortina. Similarly, Cortina did not waste time dealing with Mexican Americans who were suspected as informers. Obviously, the Mexican Americans were caught in the middle. Although some of them undoubtedly aided the Mexican raiders and admired Cortina, a large majority were loyal to the United States. Many of them, in fact, were active in the fight against Cortina; nevertheless, the mutual hatred of many of the Anglo-Americans and "Mexicans" became so intense that many on both sides of the ethnic line began to consider killing a representative of the other side to be a source of pride rather than a crime.

The interethnic violence in Texas reached a peak during the early 1870s, but by the end of 1875 the worst of the disorders was over. The combined actions of the authorities on both sides of the Rio Grande led to a reduction of border raiding. Cortina was commissioned as a general in the Mexican army and was stationed far from the border in Mexico City. By 1878, after more than forty years of almost continuous friction and warfare, the Anglo-Americans had established an uneasy control over the land between the Nueces River and the Rio Grande and over the Mexican American people who lived there.

The next three decades were relatively quiet along the Rio Grande. But if this period seemed to be one of accommodation, the hatreds and antagonisms smoldered at its very surface. Violent group conflict was always a possibility and was frequently a reality. Various incidents—shootings, lynchings, beatings, and so on—continued. Each incident usually led to some form of retaliation from the injured side, which, of course, aggravated the matter still further. Relations between the Mexican Americans and the Texas Rangers, in particular, were very poor (Acuña 1981:25–29). In the years to come, the rangers increasingly were viewed by Mexican Americans as an official expression of hatred against them.

The period of relative quiet was brought to an end by political and economic troubles. Employment opportunities for the ordinary Mexican citizen were declining in Mexico and increasing in the United States during the first decade of the twentieth century. At the same time, there was mounting opposition to the repressive regime of the dictator Porfírio Díaz. These factors encouraged the successful overthrow of Díaz by liberal revolutionaries in 1911. The new government was short-lived, however. The following period of conflict kept the border in a state of agitation.

When Francisco "Pancho" Villa crossed the border into New Mexico, raided Columbus, and killed a number of Americans, President Wilson sent General John J. "Blackjack" Pershing into Mexico to capture Villa. Pershing searched for Villa for nine months but returned home empty-handed. The years of revolution in Mexico and the border crossings by Villa and Pershing severely damaged the relations between Mexico and the United States, and they also fanned the flames of distrust and hatred that had existed for so long between the Mexican Americans and Anglos. As a result, an unknown number of innocent civilians—possibly as many as five thousand—were killed during this time (McWilliams 1973:111).

Quite clearly, the period of apparent accommodation between Mexican Americans and Anglos while Díaz was in power in Mexico had ended. It ended in open conflict not only between Mexico and the United States, but also between the two ethnic groups in the United States. This "reversion" to an earlier stage in Park's race cycle is a dramatic illustration of the point that the experience of the Mexican Americans has differed fundamentally from that of the European minorities. The periodic eruption of organized conflict between Mexican Americans and Anglos poses a serious challenge to the central ideas of the assimilationist perspective and suggests that a perspective that includes the colonialist view may be necessary for this analysis.

An important defense of the assimilationist view of the Mexican American experience, however, concerns the question of *when* the analysis actually should begin. While it is undeniable that the Mexican Americans were in the borderlands over three centuries before this territory was annexed by the United States, the critics of colonialist theory are more impressed by a series of events that coincided with the peak of the new immigration from Europe. These events laid the groundwork for arguing that the Mexican Americans, though initially Americans through conquest, are nevertheless similar in most essential respects to the Europeans of the new immigration. Let's turn to the basic ideas of this contention.

The Immigrant Model

How can a comparison of the Mexican Americans to the new immigrants possibly be valid? The basic argument is this: Although the Mexican Americans occupied the Southwest long before the Anglos, comparatively few of them resided on the American side of the border prior to 1900. For nearly fifty years after the signing of the Treaty of Guadalupe Hidalgo, relatively few Mexican nationals moved to the United States with the intention of becoming permanent residents. An unknown but probably large number of people did move back and forth across the border in search of work. At this time, however, such movements were mainly informal; few records were kept. For one period, in fact, between 1886 and 1893, there are no official records of immigration from Mexico into the United States.

In a way, this is not so strange. Please recall that the first major federal law restricting immigration was not enacted until 1882. America's policy had been to have an "open door" to the world, to encourage people to move to the United States and share the labors (and rewards) of developing the continent. Even when the attention of the nation did turn to immigration, the main focus of debate was the new immigration from Europe and the yellow peril from Asia. After the Chinese Exclusion Act was passed and the Gentlemen's Agreement was put into effect, there still was little concern about the immigration of Mexicans. U.S. policy toward Mexico remained unrestrictive. The border patrol did not begin operations until 1924, and its first efforts to control immigration from Mexico, strange to say, seem to have been directed primarily against the Chinese (Grebler, Moore, and Guzman 1970:519). Mexicans continued to cross into the United States legally and with ease.

For most practical purposes, a Mexican national could enter the United States (at a small fee) simply by obtaining permission at a border station. Still, as had been true since the end of the Mexican and American war, the flow of legal immigrants was only a trickle. Less than fourteen thousand entrants were counted during the entire last half of the nineteenth century.

Not until 1904 did the number of legal immigrants from Mexico in one year exceed one thousand (U.S. Bureau of the Census 1960:58–59). Beginning with that year, however, the number of entrants from Mexico began to rise substantially. The official count during this period appears greatly to understate the actual rate at which Mexicans were entering, and remaining in, the United States. One official report estimated that "at least 50,000 'nonstatistical' aliens" arrived in "normal" years (Gómez-Quiñones 1974:84). Another estimate suggested the figure may have reached 100,000 (Bryan 1972:334). No one can be sure, of course, how many of those who entered in a nonimmigrant status then became permanent residents of the United States, but it seems certain that a great many did.

The sudden sizable flow of immigrants from Mexico during the first decade of the twentieth century was greatly exceeded during the second decade, but a still greater wave of Mexican immigrants came during the period 1921–1930. From a purely official and numerical standpoint, then, the great period of Mexican immigration had hardly commenced when the peak of the new immigration was reached, and Mexican immigration did not crest until the new immigration was nearly over (Table 9-1).

During this period, the composition of the Mexican American population was transformed. Before 1900, most Mexican Americans either had been among those conquered in the Mexican-American War or were their descendants. From this standpoint, the Mexican immigrants of the period after 1900 were in many respects the first generation—entering more or less voluntarily and with the intention to become residents of the United States—of what has become the nation's second largest minority. From this standpoint, also, barely enough time has passed to test the three-generations hypothesis. The modern Mexican Americans are predominantly Mexican nationals who have entered the United States since 1900 or are their descendants. From an assimilationist perspective, therefore, they are, in the main, even "newer" than most of the new immigrants. The reason they have seemed slow to assimilate, so this argument goes, is that they are actually recent immigrants. They are not, strictly speaking, people who "got here first," and they have not had as long to adopt the American "way" as those who arrived in the United States before 1910. In short, the immigrant model downgrades the significance for the process of assimilation of the "historical primacy" of the Mexican Americans.

From the viewpoint of the colonial model, of course, the immigrant model misses the mark entirely. Even though, technically, the large population movement from Mexico to the United States since 1900 is an example of "immigration," is it reasonable to say that people who move from one side of a politically arbitrary (and mostly imaginary) border to the other are really "immigrants"? Is it reasonable to do this, in particular, when the "immigrants" are moving into a territory that previously had been a part of their homeland, with which they have maintained

**Table 9-1 Mexican
Immigration to the United
States, 1820–1990***

Years	Number
1820–1830	4,818
1831–1840	6,599
1841–1850	3,271
1851–1860	3,078
1861–1870	2,191
1871–1880	5,162
1881–1890	1,913
1891–1900	971
1901–1910	49,642
1911–1920	219,004
1921–1930	459,287
1931–1940	22,319
1941–1950	60,589
1951–1960	299,811
1961–1970	453,937
1971–1980	640,294
1981–1990	1,655,843
Total	3,888,729

Source: U.S. Immigration and
Naturalization Service, *Statistical Yearbook*
1990:48–50.
*There was no record of immigration from
Mexico between 1886 and 1893.

continuous contact, and in which their native culture still flourishes? Aren't such people more nearly "homecomers" than "newcomers"?

Alvarez (1985) believes it is more accurate to consider the people in this movement simply to be migrants rather than immigrants. In the first place, there is an obvious geographical difference between the immigration of the Irish or the Russian Jews and the immigration of the Mexicans. The latter could cross the border that separates the two countries so much more easily than the European immigrants could cross the Atlantic Ocean that the comparison of the effects of the two types of movement may seem a bit far-fetched. It is hard to believe that the psychological impact or meaning of moving across the border would be fundamentally similar to that of leaving Europe for America. In most instances, the European immigrants realized that they were leaving the old country for a long time, possibly for good; that they would arrive in a very different and strange land; and that their children would grow up under conditions differing radically from those they had experienced as children. Can the same things be said in general of the Mexican "immigrant"? Physically speaking, the territory of the United States and Mexico is continuous, and along most of the border, there is no prominent geographical feature to separate the two countries. As noted previously, Mexican workers frequently moved back and forth across the border prior to 1900 in search of work. Crossing the border was a familiar and fairly unimportant act. There is little reason to suppose that most of those who participated in the "immigration" from Mexico during the early part of the twentieth century thought of themselves as moving irrevocably from an old, familiar environment into a new and alien one.

There is another reason, closely related to the first, for rejecting the idea that Mexican Americans may be analyzed adequately as a fairly recent immigrant group. Not only are Mexico and the United States physically continuous, they are culturally overlapping. As we have seen, the Anglo-Americans established numerical and cultural dominance, as well as political and economic dominance, in much of the Southwest during the nineteenth century. However, in some parts of the Southwest, the Mexican American population has remained larger than the Anglo-American population, and throughout the borderlands the Mexican Americans have retained a strong and distinctive culture. This has been especially true in the cities, towns, and counties adjacent to the border, but it also is true in the many large concentrations of Mexican ancestry groups outside of the old borderlands. Even at considerable distances from the border, Spanish has continued to be the primary spoken language of many, if not most, Mexican Americans. Hundreds of Spanish place names dot the map of the American Southwest, and numerous Spanish words and terms have found their way into the vocabularies of the Anglo-Americans. In short, important elements of Mexican culture have been sustained in the United States. The presence of these familiar cultural elements almost surely has served further to modify the Mexican's "immigration" experience. It seems unlikely that the Mexicans have felt unalterably separated from their native land, as have so many other immigrants, or have felt so strange in the host country. It seems much more likely, rather, that many Mexicans have felt right at home in the Southwest and have not felt too strongly the usual pressure that is placed on immigrants to become "Americans."[16] Even if the pressure to assimilate was felt, it certainly could be more easily resisted than is ordinarily possible.

The final reason to be considered here for regarding those who moved from Mexico to the United States after 1900 as migrants rather than immigrants stems directly from the colonial model itself. Whatever one may conclude concerning the attitudes and reactions of the post-1900 Mexican newcomers, the relationship of this group to the host society was still strongly influenced by the fact that the Mexicans who had been "left behind" by the Treaty of Guadalupe Hidalgo were a conquered people in their own land. Even if we assume that the Mexicans who came to the United States after 1900 did regard the change as large and permanent, and even if they did feel that they were foreigners in the United States, they still could not assume the "normal" status of immigrants. The problem, according to this argument, is that the members of the host society did not distinguish between the "colonized" Mexicans and the "immigrant" Mexicans. The latter group could not function as immigrants because the host group did not recognize them as such. They were forced into the same kinds of jobs, housing, and subservience as the former. As Alvarez (1985:43) stated, "Socio-psychologically, the migrants, too, were a conquered people." From this perspective, Mexicans who have come to the United States since the Anglo-American conquest—even those who have come since 1900—have merely joined the ranks of the existing colonized Mexican American minority. Assimilation theorists may regard the large population movements of this century as "immigration" if they wish, but the similarities between the Mexican "immigration" and European immigration are, from this standpoint, largely superficial.

The comparison of the colonial and immigrant models shows that each emphasizes different aspects of the history of Mexican American and Anglo-American relations. Many of the most important facts are not in question. It is true, as is stressed in the colonialist account, that (1) the Mexicans occupied the borderlands hundreds of years before the Anglo-Americans arrived and, thus, may claim historical primacy; (2) the Anglo-Americans, through the annexation of Texas and the Mexican and American war, forced Mexico to cede the Spanish Southwest; (3) the relations between the Mexican Americans and Anglos in the borderlands have been even more filled with conflict and tension than usually has been the case for immigrant minorities; and (4) the processes of assimilation have not produced as much change among the Mexican Americans as one would expect to occur in an immigrant population during a period of over 140 years. But it also is true that the great majority of the Mexican American population is comprised of people who have entered the United States from Mexico since 1900 and their descendants. It may be possible, therefore, if one starts the analysis with the "Migrant Generation" (Alvarez 1985:39) of the early 1900s rather than with the "Creation Generation" of 1848, that the processes of assimilation may be operating among the Mexican Americans in a fairly "normal" way. To help evaluate these clashing interpretations, we now turn to some of the main features of the Mexican American experience since 1900.

Mexican Immigration and Native Reaction

We have seen that a combination of social turmoil in Mexico and economic opportunities in the United States led to a sharp rise in Mexican immigration during the first decade of the twentieth century.[17] The Mexicans' opportunities for work, to repeat, were mainly in the hard, dirty, and poorly paid jobs in railroading, mining, and agriculture. The work conditions experienced by large numbers of Mexicans and Mexican Americans in these three industries during the early portions of this century had a lasting effect on the Mexican American community. Railroad work, which was the main kind at first, helped to take significant numbers of Mexicans out of the Southwest into other parts of the United States. In many instances, railroad crews completed their jobs far from the border area and were forced to accept other jobs wherever they happened to be. Many Mexican American communities outside the Southwest started in this way (Gómez-Quiñones 1974:88; Kerr 1977:294).

Even more important in its effects was the way the Mexican labor force generally was organized. In each of these main industries, the work force was organized in gangs; frequently, the work gangs included all of the members of a family. This meant that entire families were intermittently on the move, living in temporary and frequently unsanitary housing. It meant also that the children of such families frequently engaged in unsafe, backbreaking labor and did not receive adequate schooling or health care. Additionally, migratory agricultural labor, which gradually became the primary source of employment for Mexican labor, is seasonal. Employers generally assumed and expected that the migratory Mexican workers would go "home" to Mexico when the work ran out.

The movement of Mexican labor into agricultural work was greatly facilitated by America's entry into World War I. In California, the demand for workers in the citrus, melon, tomato, and other industries increased sharply, encouraging Mexicans to come across the border to perform these necessary tasks. The other southwestern states were similarly affected. Workers were needed in Texas to tend the cotton, spinach, and onion crops, while in Arizona, New Mexico, and Colorado there was a shortage of workers to raise vegetables, forage crops, and sugar beets (Reisler 1976:77–100). From the beginning, these forms of labor were "seasonal, migratory, and on a contract basis" (Gómez-Quiñones 1974:89). To meet this increased demand for "stoop" labor, the Commissioner of Immigration and Naturalization approved, in 1917, some special regulations to permit Mexican farm workers to enter the United States in large numbers. Although the regulations soon were modified to permit temporary workers from Mexico also to fill jobs in railroad maintenance and mining, the "invasion" of agricultural work by both temporary and permanent immigrants from Mexico was the most prominent result.[18] Indeed, the events of this period served to stamp into the public's mind a stereotype of the Mexicans and Mexican Americans as agricultural workers.

As noted previously, the increasingly large migration of Mexicans to the United States during this time was not a topic of general concern or debate. Even though the Mexican migration reached its peak in 1924—the same year in which the Immigration Act established the quota restrictions on European immigration and excluded the Japanese—the open-door policy remained in effect for Mexicans. The new law, in fact, contained provisions that made it possible for a Mexican immigrant to work on the American side of the border during the day but to stay at his or her residence in Mexico during the night (Moore 1976:48). Moreover, as the open door began to close on people of many other nationalities, cheap labor from Mexico became even more attractive to employers in the United States; consequently, Mexican immigration jumped sharply during the 1920s both in absolute numbers and as a proportion of the total of all immigration to the country (Grebler, Moore, and Guzman 1970:64).

The mutual attraction of Mexican labor and American employers, however, began to subside shortly after the immigration restrictions on other nationalities had gone into effect. Both because the Mexican immigration had become so large and the agricultural sector of the American economy had gone into a downturn, Mexican immigration now became a subject of national controversy. Predictably, the demand now arose that the quota system established in 1924 be extended to cover Mexicans. To support this demand, some of the restrictionists used racist stereotypes to support their claims that the Mexicans were socially undesirable. A Texas congressman referred to them as "illiterate, unclean, peonized masses" who are a "mixture of Mediterranean-blooded Spanish peasants with low grade Indians" (Moore and Pachon 1985:136). As things developed, however, no extension of the restrictive legislation was needed.

The flow of Mexican immigration was dampened in the late 1920s when the United States discontinued the practice of issuing permanent visas at the border stations and instead required applicants to file at an American consulate, decreasing the chance that a permanent visa would be granted.[19] Under these circumstances, many people preferred to cross the border illegally to avoid the cost of waiting at the border, as well as the possibility that they would not be admitted. Of course, once these undocumented people reached the United States, they were fugitives and were in no position to insist on ethical treatment or to stand on legal rights. As a result, they frequently fell prey to the unscrupulous and discriminatory acts of labor contractors, employers, and underworld businesses. The life of the migratory or contract laborers also became harsher because they often were regarded with special hostility and suspicion by Mexican Americans, who feared that the uncontrolled entrance of Mexican laborers to the United States would depress working conditions for them.

The Great Depression

Although Mexican immigration appeared to be tapering off in the face of these control measures, a dramatic reduction in the flow followed the great financial crisis of 1929. The immediate and primary cause of this decline, of course, was the great reduction in employment opportunities. The prospects were so unattractive, indeed, that the Mexican immigration of 1931 fell below four thousand for the first time since 1907. The annual number of new arrivals fell even further in subsequent years and did not begin to recover noticeably until the beginning of World War II.

In addition to the fact that the Great Depression made the United States a less attractive destination for migrants, there was another development of special importance. Many groups and officials within the United States sought to decrease unemployment and the costs of government welfare by deporting Mexican aliens (Hoffman 1974). Some aliens, of course, as in the previous periods, had returned voluntarily to Mexico when their jobs dried up, but many had not, and the border patrol increased its efforts to locate and deport people who had become public charges or were in the United States illegally. At the same time, the authorities in many American cities found that it was much less expensive to pay the transportation and other costs of sending people to Mexico than it was to maintain them on welfare rolls.[20] These combined national and local efforts to save money by "sending the Mexicans home" were in some ways a preview of the evacuation of the Japanese and Japanese Americans nearly a decade later. As in the case of the later "roundup" of the Japanese, little attention was paid either to the preferences of the evacuees or to their legal status (Grebler, Moore, and Guzman 1970:524; Moore and Pachon 1985:137). Mexicans who were naturalized citizens frequently were "repatriated" along with Mexican nationals. Many native Americans of Mexican ancestry were scrutinized closely and were intimidated by the prospect of "repatriation." In some cases, families were broken apart when a Mexican parent was sent "home," while his or her American-born spouse and children remained behind.

The entire "charity deportation" program emphasized to the Mexican American community just how vulnerable they were to the actions, sometimes whimsical, of government officials. In some instances, the deportations spread panic within the *barrios*. People became afraid that if they applied for relief they would be sent to Mexico. As a result, it is quite possible that many people who were eligible for relief did not apply. Many others, apparently, concluded that they might be better off in Mexico than in the United States and voluntarily left the country. Whether willingly or not, uncounted thousands of U.S. residents of Mexican heritage were literally "shipped" to Mexico. McWilliams (1972:386) indicated that over 200,000 Mexicans left the United States during a twelve-month period of 1931–1932 alone, while Grebler, Moore, and Guzman (1970:526) stated that the Mexican-born population of the United States declined during the 1930s from 639,000 to around 377,000. More important, though, than the sheer number of deportations is that American citizens of Mexican heritage were shown dramatically that they were not necessarily considered full-fledged citizens. As long as there was a shortage of cheap labor, the "Mexicans" were welcomed and praised as cooperative, uncomplaining workers, but when economic times were bad, American officials wanted the "Mexicans" to go "home."

The Bracero Program

There was little need for additional cheap farm labor in the United States until World War II created a new shortage of workers. This time, however, the "cooperative" Mexican labor force was not so easily pulled across the border. For one thing, the war had also created a labor shortage in Mexico; for another, Mexico's government was no longer so easily persuaded that the United States was a "good neighbor." So instead of permitting an unrestricted out-migration of workers, Mexico agreed to allow *braceros* (farmhands) to enter the United States on certain conditions: the *braceros* were to receive free transportation and food; they were not to be given jobs currently held by American residents; they were to receive guarantees concerning wages, working conditions, and living quarters; and only a limited number of workers could be employed in a given year (McWilliams 1973:266). It was agreed, too, that specified Mexican officials could make inspections and investigate any complaints that might arise, and that the workers would be protected from discrimination (Reimers 1985:42–43). With these guarantees and protections, Mexican workers flocked to the *bracero* program. Between 1942 and 1945, over 167,000 agricultural workers were recruited under the plan.[21]

The *bracero* program is of special interest for two reasons. First, it provided some experience for both Mexico and the United States concerning the problems of planning and regulating the back-and-forth movement of temporary workers between the two countries. At the very least, the results of the program showed how difficult the task is. For example, as World War II progressed, employment opportunities for Mexican workers increased in the United States, and as they did the flow of undocumented temporary workers also increased. Many Mexican workers found it to be much more convenient and less expensive to be undocumented aliens than *braceros.* The American employers—chiefly growers and ranchers—also found that they could save time and money (and avoid "red tape") by hiring undocumented aliens; consequently, in many cases, the undocumented aliens and the *braceros* were receiving different wages and benefits while working together in the same fields (Grebler, Moore, and Guzman 1970:67). Needless to say, this situation produced many confusions and contradictions. It also produced an increase in the border patrol's efforts to locate, arrest, and deport undocumented migratory workers. This effort reached its pinnacle during 1954–1955 in a highly publicized roundup called "Operation Wetback" (Reimers 1985:56).

Even though hundreds of thousands of undocumented workers (and an untold number of legal entrants and American citizens) were returned to Mexico, many of them quickly came back to the United States either legally or, again, illegally. The existence of a mixture of legal and undocumented temporary workers of Mexican descent has continued to raise questions about the status of Mexican Americans in the United States. The dominant group's frequent failure to distinguish the Mexican Americans from the Mexican nationals has been made easier by the presence of so many of the latter. Both groups are easily considered by many members of the dominant group to be especially suited for hard manual labor and to be unsuited to possess all of the rights and privileges of American citizens. The idea also has been encouraged that Mexican Americans as well as Mexican nationals are "really" foreigners who may go "home" if they do not like conditions in the United States.

To complicate the picture still further, many members of the Mexican American community also have been ambivalent about the presence of many new arrivals from Mexico. On the one hand, the newcomers are often welcomed because they serve in important ways to replenish and strengthen the prized and distinctive culture of the Mexican Americans; at the same time, they constitute a deep pool of reserve laborers who may be called on by employers to keep wages low or to resist the efforts of American citizens to form strong and effective labor unions. Even though the law requires that domestic workers be hired in preference to immigrant workers, employers frequently attempt to get around this requirement (Dunne 1967:48). In many cases, though, little effort in this regard is needed because the work is so hard and the wages are so low that few domestic workers will accept the jobs (Portes and Bach 1985:62). Another threat posed for Mexican Americans by the newcomers is that they afford a continuous excuse for the border patrol and many other official agencies to pry into the private lives of those who "look Mexican." For this reason, as in the days of the welfare repatriations, Mexican

Americans still are much more exposed than most other Americans to the threat and the actuality of being deported illegally.

The *bracero* program is of special interest for another reason. As McWilliams (1973:269) suggested, it gave the Mexican government a firm basis on which to protest acts of discrimination not only against their citizens in the United States but also against Mexican Americans. For example, in October 1943, the Mexican government issued a formal protest "against the segregation of children of Mexican descent in certain Texas schools." The Mexican government also was aware of many other incidents of discrimination, particularly in Texas. One of these occurred when Sergeant Macario Garcia, a winner of the Congressional Medal of Honor, ordered a cup of coffee in a cafe in Sugar Land, Texas, and was refused service. A fight developed, and Sergeant Garcia was arrested on a charge of aggravated assault (McWilliams 1973:261). In another incident, a Mexican American PTA group in Melvin, Texas, was refused a permit to use a community center building. These and many other cases of overt or probable discrimination against Mexican Americans, as well as Mexicans, led the Mexican government in 1943 to halt the *bracero* program in Texas. This action led Governor Coke Stevenson of Texas to make a goodwill tour of Mexico, to proclaim a good neighbor policy for Texas, and to appoint a Good Neighbor Commission (McWilliams 1973:270). But these efforts, as well as others on the local level, failed to satisfy the Mexican government, and the *bracero* program was not resumed in Texas during World War II.

The Zoot Suit Riots

The problem of discrimination against Mexican Americans during World War II, however, was by no means restricted to Texas. Certain events that took place in the Los Angeles, California, area during this period were at least equally alarming and may have had a greater, more lasting, effect on the relations of Anglos and Mexican Americans. At about the same time the Japanese were being evacuated and interned, a number of incidents involving Mexican Americans, primarily young, second-generation males, were given wide publicity in the Los Angeles newspapers. Many, perhaps most, Mexican American youths living in the Flats of East Los Angeles and Boyle Heights belonged to or were associated with various juvenile gangs. There was nothing unusual about this. Beginning with the 1880s, the Flats had been occupied successively by Irish, Armenian, Russian Molokan, Slav, Jewish, and, finally, Mexican immigrant groups (Dworkin 1973:410). The Mexican juvenile gangs—like those that had been prominent in the preceding ethnic groups—varied in their size, chief interest, age composition, and so on. Many of these Mexican American gangs, however, were especially cohesive and troublesome to people in positions of authority. Whenever they were not actually engaged in delinquent behavior, they talked as if they soon would be. Probably of greater importance, though, they flaunted their distinctiveness, pride in their Mexican heritage, and resentment of the racism of the dominant group (Romo 1983:166). They called themselves *pachucos* and dressed in a manner that most members of the dominant group considered outlandish.

The most admired appearance among the *pachucos* required one to have a ducktail haircut and to be dressed in a striking costume called a "zoot suit." The zoot suit was distinguished by the trousers and the jacket. The trousers were tight at the ankles and the waist extended up over the chest. The main part of the trouser legs was very full. The jacket was long, full, and very broad in the shoulders. All of these features combined made the *pachuco* gang or the zoot suit gang very visible to other members of the community. They also served as a focus of criticism and ridicule by members of the dominant group.

The summers of 1942 and 1943 witnessed two particularly notable events involving pachuco "gangsters." The first of these centered on the mysterious death of a young Mexican American, José Díaz, following a fight between two rival gangs near an East Los Angeles swimming hole. Díaz's skull had been fractured, apparently in a fight, but an autopsy showed that he probably had been drunk when he died and that his injuries could have occurred in an automobile accident. The press coverage of this event was described by McWilliams (1973:229) as "an enormous web of melodramatic fancy." The gravel pit near which the gang fight occurred was referred to as "The Sleepy Lagoon," and it was emphasized in the newspapers that the case involved Mexican Americans. Twenty-two young men of the Thirty-eighth Street gang were arrested and charged with conspiracy to commit murder (Romo 1983:166). Following a trial that lasted several months, three of these young men were convicted of first-degree murder, nine were convicted of second-degree murder, five were convicted of lesser offenses, and five were acquitted (Romo 1983:166). The convictions were appealed by an organization of East Los Angeles citizens on the grounds that the trial had been conducted in a biased and improper way, in an atmosphere of sensationalism. The prosecution had played upon the fact that the defendants were of Mexican heritage, had ducktail haircuts, and wore zoot suits. These improper tactics were criticized by the appeals court, which overturned the lower court's decision. After nearly two years of imprisonment, the case was dismissed "for lack of evidence" (McWilliams 1973:231). While this outcome was viewed as a great victory for justice and the Mexican American community, the fact still remains that seventeen young men served prison sentences for a crime they were not proven to have committed. Their crime, it seems, was that they were Mexican Americans.

The Sleepy Lagoon trial, conducted as it was during the period of the Japanese internment and with generous press coverage, strengthened the impression held by many people that the Mexican Americans were "just naturally" criminals. The supposed natural link between Mexicanness and criminality seemed to receive official support shortly after the arrest of the Sleepy Lagoon defendants. Captain E. D. Ayres of the Los Angeles sheriff's office presented to the grand jury a report of the results of his investigation of what was considered to be the "problem of Mexican delinquency." Captain Ayres's suppositions, conclusions, and chain of reasoning sounded much like those presented by General DeWitt to justify the wartime treatment of the Japanese. In Captain Ayres's view, those of Mexican ancestry are more likely to engage in violent crimes than are those of Anglo-Saxon heritage because such behavior is an "inborn characteristic." Anglo-Saxon youths, said Captain Ayres, may use their fists or kick when they fight, but the "Mexican element" feels "a desire to use a knife or some lethal weapon . . . his desire is to kill, or at least let blood" (McWilliams 1973:234). Such opinions, presented by a police official during these tense days, could hardly have increased the dominant group's understanding of the underlying causes of the behavior of the *pachucos*. The answer lay in an entirely different direction. As noted by Sanchez (1972:410), the *pachuco* movement grew not out of the violent nature of the Spanish-speaking people but from the discriminatory social and economic situation in which the Mexican Americans lived. Nevertheless, the stereotype of the naturally violent *pachuco* gangster was apparently widely believed.

The publicity surrounding the Sleepy Lagoon trial, the presentation of the Ayres Report, and numerous contacts between the police and *pachuco* fighting gangs prepared the way for a second major series of incidents focusing primarily on the Mexican Americans. For approximately one week, from June 3 through June 10, 1943, the city of Los Angeles was rocked by what have come to be known as the "Zoot Suit Race Riots" (Mazon 1988). These disorders may be described as a series of mob attacks by off-duty police officers, U.S. sailors, and other servicemen directed mainly at Mexican Americans and people who wore zoot suits. The zoot suits, particularly when worn by those of Mexican descent, had gradually come to represent for many members of the dominant group an open defiance of constituted authority and a symbol of moral degradation. Consequently, those who wore them appeared to many to be enemies of the state who needed to be "taught a lesson."

There had been some intermittent fighting during this time between the "zooters" and sailors and marines who were stationed near the East Los Angeles barrio. The servicemen considered the *pachucos* to be draft dodgers, and the Mexican Americans resented the servicemen's frequent visits to their neighborhood (Romo 1983:167). Widespread violence between the servicemen and the "zooters" began when a group of sailors was beaten up, allegedly by a gang of Mexican Americans, while they were walking through the barrio area. On the following night, about two hundred sailors "invaded" East Los Angeles in a caravan of some twenty taxicabs. On their way, they stopped several times to beat severely at least four Mexican American youths wearing zoot suits. In the following days, the local newspapers featured reports concerning violence (and threats of violence) between servicemen and "zooters." By June 7, the number of people engaged in the disorders had swelled into the thousands. Throughout all of this, the Los Angeles police department reportedly took few steps to curb the activities of the servicemen and, for the most part, seemed to avoid the areas in which violence was occurring until after the conflict was over. In some cases, the police simply followed along behind the servicemen to arrest the Mexican Americans who had been attacked! The disorders were not brought under control until after military authorities intervened. Servicemen were ordered to stay out of downtown Los Angeles and the barrio, and the order was enforced by the shore patrol and military police.[22]

There can be little doubt that many members of the Anglo-American group subscribed to the theory of innate criminality among Mexican Americans and more or less openly approved of the efforts of the servicemen to "clean out" the "zooters." It seems clear, too, that the zoot suit itself became a hated symbol of Mexican American solidarity and defiance. In a large number of instances, the servicemen stripped the suits from their victims and ripped them apart. An official view of all this was illustrated dramatically when the Los Angeles City Council declared that it was a misdemeanor to wear a zoot suit (McWilliams 1973:245–250).

The repercussions of the Sleepy Lagoon trial and the zoot suit riots were felt throughout the United States as well as abroad. The disorders were headline news in newspapers all over the United States. Zoot suit and other race-related conflicts broke out in several other cities across the United States following the Los Angeles disorders. And just as the incidents of discrimination against Mexican Americans in Texas led the government of Mexico to end the *bracero* program, the ambassador from Mexico asked for an official explanation of the zoot suit riots. The explanation—that there was no prejudice or discrimination against people of Mexican ancestry—was hardly convincing. The war effort of the United States had been damaged; the allies of the United States had been given yet another reason to wonder about the strength of the country's commitment to racial and ethnic equality; and the enemies of the United States had been given a powerful weapon of propaganda that they did not hesitate to employ.

The Chicano "Awakening"

During this time, of course, Mexican American youths (and even some noncitizen aliens) were subject to the wartime military draft in the United States (R. Scott 1974:134). Considering the level of discrimination against these young men at the time, they seemed more eager to serve and fight for the United States than might have been expected. As in the case of the Nisei, the displacements and humiliations experienced by the Mexican Americans during the early war years appeared generally to heighten their desire to prove their loyalty and worth rather than the reverse. As a result, a disproportionately high number of Mexican Americans served in the armed forces; also, like the Nisei, they comprised a disproportionately high share of the casualty lists and were frequently cited for their outstanding fighting qualities and contributions to the war effort. The first congressional Medal of Honor awarded to a drafted enlisted man during World War II went to José P. Martínez of Los Angeles. Altogether, thirty-nine Mexican Americans received the congressional Medal of Honor (R. Scott 1974:140). The valor of the Mexican American fighting men earned the general respect and approval of their Anglo-American comrades in arms. Whereas in the early days of the war they frequently had been shunned or harassed by other servicemen as disloyal, undisciplined *pachucos,* they now generally were accepted on equal terms.

On this basis, they fully expected their position in civilian life after the war to be far better than it had been before the war. Their return to civilian life, however, was marked by bitter disappointment. They found mainly that the prejudices and the various forms of discrimination they had encountered before the war still remained. They still might be refused service in a restaurant, they still had difficulty obtaining work outside of the occupations traditionally assigned to them, and they still saw that the young people of *La Raza* typically attended segregated schools (R. Scott 1974:141). The reality of the continuation of prejudice and discrimination against them came as a severe shock to many returning veterans. Despite their loyal and costly services to the country, they still were second-class citizens. This discovery jolted not only the Mexican American veterans but their friends and families as well. The entire Mexican American community was affected, and an increased awareness of their collective problem as a minority group was stimulated. Hence, the period since World War II—and especially the 1960s—has been described by many observers as an "awakening" of the Mexican Americans. This awakening was marked by a sharp increase in organized political and protest activities by Mexican Americans in all of the main sectors of American life.

For roughly seventy-five years after the end of the war between Mexico and the United States, Mexican Americans in the Southwest typically did not engage actively in politics. Since the armed conflicts between Anglo-Americans and those of Mexican descent had continued to erupt during this period, any effort on the part of Mexican Americans to assert themselves was viewed with great suspicion by the members of the dominant group. Consequently, the first organizations that may be considered "political" in nature were very careful to adopt objectives that were likely to meet with the approval of Anglo-American leaders. For example, the most famous and successful organization of Mexican Americans—the League of United Latin American Citizens (LULAC)—was comprised mainly of people who emphasized assimilation into American society and felt it was their duty to develop "true and loyal" citizens of the United States (Cuéllar 1970:143; Marquez 1987). We should not be surprised to learn, however, that even this presumably uncontroversial goal aroused the fear in some Anglo-Americans that the "Mexicans" were forgetting "their place."

The years of World War II brought significant changes in the Mexican American community. In the first place, as noted earlier, a large number of Mexican Americans served in the armed forces. This experience permitted them to work side by side with Americans from different regions of the country and from different socioeconomic origins. In the process, they learned a great deal about the opportunities and privileges that most American citizens took for granted. They came to expect, also, that as equals in battle they were entitled to equal opportunities when they returned to civilian life. Many of these men felt "completely American." As such, they were unwilling to think of themselves as "Mexican" or to accept the inferior status generally accorded Mexicans. As expressed by Alvarez (1985:44), they were more likely to argue, "I am an 'American' who happens to be of Mexican descent. I am going to participate fully in this society because, like descendants of people from so many other lands, I was born here." In short, they accepted the immigrant model.

The war years did more than solidify the servicemen's acceptance of American identity, however. The events of the war accelerated the movement of Mexican Americans into the cities. As a result, this traditionally rural population was brought into more extensive and intimate contact with the Anglo-Americans. Large numbers of these migrants were exposed to even more overt forms of discrimination than they had learned was customary—for example, the zoot suit riots. They learned in this way that the opportunities of the city, attractive though they were in many cases, were nonetheless severely limited for "Mexicans."

The combination of continued, and even increased, discrimination against Mexican Americans on the home front and the new expectations of the returning servicemen set the stage for the emergence of new, more aggressive, political and social organizations following the war. In the immediate postwar years, one such organization, the Community Service Organization (CSO), was formed in California; another, the G.I. Forum, was formed in Texas. Both of these groups have sought to represent the interests of Mexican Americans on a wide social, economic, and political front (Allsup 1982; Cuéllar 1970:145–147). As the 1950s drew to a close, however, some Mexican Americans came to feel that organizations like LULAC, CSO, and the G.I. Forum were not pressing vigorously enough for equal rights. They thought, too, that the established organizations were not pursuing the correct strategy in the political arena. For these reasons, the Mexican American Political Association (MAPA), the Mexican American Youth Organization (MAYO), the Political Association of Spanish-Speaking Organizations (PASO), and the National Farm Workers Association (NFWA) were formed with the intention of putting direct pressure on the major political parties, including the nomination or appointment of their members to public office. A spectacular example of the success of this approach may be seen in the election of Mexican Americans to various offices in Crystal City, Texas.[23] These separate efforts were thought of as part of a larger movement, *La Causa* (Valdez 1982:271).[24]

We may summarize by saying that the prominent early Mexican American organizations moved in a gingerly way into the political arena. They took great pains to reassure the Anglo-Americans that they did not intend to create a disturbance but only to make themselves and their ethnic brethren into "better" (i.e., more Anglicized) citizens. As time passed, however, different organizations were formed for the purpose of placing greater pressure on the dominant society in an effort to gain more nearly equal treatment. In this way, a renewed emphasis on cultural nationalism emerged as a central feature of the Mexican American movement beginning in the 1960s.

This emphasis on cultural nationalism has brought into sharp relief many of the issues that are of greatest interest to us here. What are the goals of the Mexican Americans in American life? How important is it to Mexican Americans that their culture be strengthened and developed? To what extent are the processes of assimilation affecting the distinctiveness and solidarity of the Mexican Americans? The answers to these and other similar questions help to answer the larger question: "How useful are the colonial and immigrant models when applied to the Mexican American experience?"

Generation and Identity

Intergenerational Overlap

Our previous discussions of immigrant ethnic groups emphasized the importance of differences among the generations. Chapter 8, concerning the Japanese and Japanese Americans, in particular, showed that the generations were sufficiently distinct to bear different names. This distinctiveness was caused mainly by the immigration pattern experienced by this group. Most of the Japanese immigrants came during a period of roughly three decades (1890–1920). Thereafter, the Japanese population of the United States grew almost totally by natural increase until after World War II. For the most part, Issei men had married only Issei women. The Nisei children, therefore, were overwhelmingly native Americans born of foreign parents. It was very unusual for a Nisei to have only one parent who had been born in Japan.

This pattern, of course, has been common among nearly all immigrant groups to America, at least in the beginning. But among most other groups, the stream of foreign immigrants generally has continued in a fluctuating manner far beyond the original point of primary immigration. In this way, the foreign-born and native generations have continued to be mixed. An important result of this process is that many native-born Americans have had one parent who is an immigrant and one who is a native American. Obviously, whether one has two foreign-born parents, one foreign-born parent, or two native-born parents may have a significant effect on the type and extent of one's own assimilation in America. Also, the proportional size of these different groups within an ethnic group surely is a significant matter.

Both of these factors—the number of children of foreign, mixed, or native parentage and the proportion of the group that is foreign-born, mixed, or native— have played an especially important role in the Mexican American experience. The reason for this is fairly apparent. The nativity and parentage categories are unusually mixed for this ethnic group. In fact, no other American ethnic group presents such a variegated picture of nativity and foreignness.

The pattern through which the Mexican American population has developed affects the study of intergenerational differences in important ways. For example, among all ethnic groups in America, the category "natives of native parentage" includes the third and subsequent generations. But since among the Mexican Americans this category includes the descendants of the original settlers as well as those who have migrated to the United States since 1900, it is a more diverse category for this group than for the others we have studied. Nevertheless, since the Mexican immigration of the twentieth century (including the undocumented immigration) has continued at a high level, a large majority of the natives of native parentage are the descendants of relatively recent migrants. Consider, too, that the closeness of the mother country and the frequent movements back and forth across the border by some members of each of the nativity and parentage groups call into question the easy assumption that each generation should be more assimilated than the preceding one. In fact, this is one reason why those who regard the Mexican

Americans as a colonized minority believe that the intergenerational differences within their group will remain smaller than would be true for an immigrant minority. The crucial questions for us in this regard include, "Is the Mexican American culture being renewed and invigorated among the third and subsequent generations? Do the natives of native parentage exhibit levels of cultural assimilation that are consistent with the predictions flowing from the immigrant model? Has a new, emergent culture been formed?"

As was true in our discussion of Japanese Americans, the data needed to determine whether or in what ways the Mexican Americans are assimilating are far from complete. Although many different sources are of value, an indispensable body of information concerning this ethnic group has been compiled and tabulated by the U.S. Bureau of the Census. It is appropriate to consider at this point certain problems in the use of these data as well as some of the major things they reveal.

Census Identifiers

So far, we have referred to Mexican Americans or to those of Mexican ancestry without attempting to define exactly who the members of this group are. Because Mexican Americans are dispersed over a large geographical area, because they have come into American society both through conquest and through immigration, because their immigration has been heaviest during the twentieth century, and because legal immigration has been greatly exceeded by undocumented immigration (Frisbie 1975:4–5), they are an extremely heterogeneous group and present some special problems to anyone who wishes to make accurate general statements about them. The difficulties may be illustrated by considering the efforts of the U.S. Bureau of the Census to identify the members of this group.

The Census Bureau first attempted to count this population in 1930. Census enumerators were asked to classify people as "Mexican," whether they were foreign or native born, on the basis of their "racial" characteristics. This approach was found to be deficient, so in the 1940 census a question on mother tongue was presented to a 5 percent sample of the entire population. On the basis of the answers to this question, the Census Bureau was able to count the number of people in the sample who listed Spanish as their mother tongue. Although the effort to identify the Mexican American population in terms of the mother tongue criterion was discontinued after 1940, this approach did enable the investigators to divide the group into three nativity and parentage categories: foreign-born, natives of foreign or mixed parentage, and natives of native parentage. This method of classification, of course, "lumps together" foreign-born persons who have been in the United States for many years and those who arrived only recently, and it does not distinguish the native whose grandparents were immigrants from the native whose ancestors settled in the United States during the sixteenth century; nevertheless, it affords a crucial tool for the study of intergenerational differences.

In the 1950, 1960, and 1970 population censuses, the Census Bureau approached the identification of Mexican Americans in another way. In these years, lists of Spanish surnames were drawn up, and Mexican Americans were identified among those who were "white persons of Spanish surname." The use of Spanish surnames as a way to identify Mexican Americans also has been criticized. In the 1980 population census, a special "origin or descent" question was asked that permitted people of Hispanic origin to classify themselves as Mexican, Mexican American, Chicano, Puerto Rican, Cuban, or other Spanish/Hispanic (Bean and Tienda 1987:50).[25] Despite the imperfections of the various ways of classifying and counting the Mexican American population, the Census Bureau reports have made possible a number of highly informative (if not completely exact) analyses concerning the ethnic group of interest to us here. For instance, we may now examine the changes that are occurring through time in the occupations, incomes, and levels of education of the Spanish surname population, and we may compare these changes to those that are occurring in the Anglo-American population. In this way, we may determine in a broad way whether, or in what ways, the two populations are becoming more or less similar. The census tabulations also assist us in gaining an appreciation of some of the changes that are occurring from generation to generation in this ethnic group. Such comparisons assist us in estimating the level of secondary assimilation at various points in time and at various locations throughout the United States. Useful as these comparisons are, though, they do not reflect completely some of the kinds of diversity that exist among Mexican Americans. For this reason, we rely also on a number of other sources of information.

Let us first consider some basic points about this large, variegated ethnic group. Although substantial Mexican American groups are to be found in several states outside the Southwest—mainly in Illinois, New York, and Florida—in 1980 approximately 83 percent of the members of this group lived in the five southwestern states of Arizona, California, Colorado, New Mexico, and Texas (Bean and Tienda 1987:80); hence, the special reports of the Census Bureau focus entirely on these latter states. The reports show that the Spanish surname population has increased at each census period both in absolute size and as a proportion of the total population. By 1990, the Mexican American population had increased to about 13.5 million people (U.S. Department of Commerce June 12, 1991). California had the largest *number* of Mexican American residents, while New Mexico had the largest *proportion* of people of Spanish origin. A nonsouthwestern state, Illinois, has the third largest population of Mexican Americans (behind California and Texas).

Since it is widely known that the Mexican American population was for many years concentrated in various farm and rural areas, it may be something of a surprise to learn that during the last several decades this population has become predominantly urban. In 1979, over 80 percent of the Mexican American population was located in urban areas (Pachon and Moore 1981:116). We should note, however, that there are some substantial differences among the southwestern states in this respect. For instance, in California, nearly 91 percent of the Spanish surname population lives in urban areas, while the urban percentage in New Mexico is about 65 percent. Still, even in New Mexico, a large majority of those who live in rural areas do not live on farms.

In addition to the differences among the southwestern states in the proportion of Spanish surname persons who live in the cities and rural nonfarm areas, the cities themselves differ in the absolute and relative sizes of the Spanish surname population. For example, in terms of absolute size, the most "Mexican" metropolitan areas in the United States are Los Angeles-Long Beach (over 1.65 million), San Antonio (over 447,000), Houston (over 374,000), and Chicago (over 368,000) (Bean and Tienda 1987:150). Since there are large differences in the total populations of the cities of the Southwest, however, some smaller metropolitan areas have a decidedly visible Mexican American population and "atmosphere." Especially notable among these are El Paso, Brownsville-Harlingen-San Benito, McAllen-Pharr-Edinburg, Corpus Christi, and Albuquerque. These facts highlight again a basic characteristic of the Mexican American group: it is very heterogeneous. Our generalizations about this group, therefore, must be even more tentative than for most other American ethnic groups. With these limitations in mind, we turn to a brief consideration of the main subprocesses of assimilation.

Mexican American Assimilation

Cultural Assimilation

We have seen that ethnic groups in America, whether immigrant or colonized, typically have tried to maintain and elaborate their cultural heritages. The degree to which this has been true, however—as well as the group's success in doing so—has varied among ethnic groups. In regard to the maintenance of their heritage, the Mexican Americans have been one of the most successful ethnic groups in America. Consider again, for instance, what usually has happened in the important matter of language use.[26] Despite a great number of exceptions and local variations, the general pattern among American ethnic groups has been for the use of the ancestral tongue to diminish noticeably across the generations and for English to become the usual language among those in the third and subsequent generations. We should restate, perhaps, that this decline of the mother tongue sometimes has been hastened by the pressure to embrace the American way and sometimes has occurred because a particular group was too small or scattered to resist outside pressures effectively (Stevens 1992).[27]

Mexican Americans do not fit the usual pattern. Even though it is not possible to state even roughly what proportion of the Mexican American population has, over the years, preferred to maintain their native culture, it seems likely that the proportion has been high in comparison to most other American ethnic minorities. Whether this is true or not, it is clear that they have been the primary contributors to the maintenance of the Spanish language in the United States over a comparatively long period of time. For this reason, Spanish is more likely to survive in the United States than any other foreign language. In 1980, for example, Spanish was the language of the home for over 5 percent of people in the United States and was more commonly used in the home than all other non-English languages combined (Moore and Pachon 1985:119–120).

Grebler, Moore, and Guzman (1970:424) studied the extent to which Mexican Americans have retained the Spanish language. Their samples contained people from different income groups and different areas of residence in Los Angeles and San Antonio. Several findings are of special interest. First, the researchers found that a majority of the people they interviewed were bilingual but that a large majority were more comfortable in Spanish than in English. Second, the higher-income participants were more likely to be fluent in English than those .with lower incomes, and those who lived in neighborhoods containing a high proportion of Mexican Americans were more likely to use Spanish frequently than those who lived in less "Mexicanized" neighborhoods. Finally, income and minority concentration apparently affected the extent to which Mexican Americans prefer to use Spanish in conversation with their children. In both cities, between 33 and 73 percent of parents in the low-income groups reported that they used Spanish with their children all or most of the time, while between 10 and 22 percent of high-income parents reported a preference for Spanish as the language of the home.

How have Mexican Americans succeeded in maintaining the Spanish language in the face of pressure by the dominant group to adopt English? In general, of course, the answer to this question is to be found in the fact that this group is concentrated heavily in the borderlands near Mexico and has been steadily reinforced by continuing immigration. The language also in sustained by radio and television broadcasts. Grebler, Moore, and Guzman (1970:429) noted in this respect that Spanish-language radio stations in the United States play an important role in assisting people to maintain both their language and their ethnic identity. Over one-half of all foreign-language radio broadcasting in the United States is conducted in Spanish, and Spanish is the only foreign language that is used exclusively by any station. In the *barrios* of San Antonio and Los Angeles the Spanish-language radio stations are more popular than those using English. Between 1970 and 1980, according to Moore and Pachon (1985:122), the number of such stations increased from sixty to two hundred. Spanish-language television—including broadcasts for American audiences that originate in Mexico, Central America, and South America—also assists the Mexican American community to retain and strengthen its ethnic distinctiveness (Moore and Pachon 1985:122). There is evidence, too, that many commercial advertisers have learned the large Mexican American market may be approached profitably through Spanish-language radio and television broadcasts.

The high concentration of Mexican Americans at various points throughout the borderlands, the closeness of Mexico, and the success of Spanish-language radio and television stations all help to explain the preference for and frequent use of Spanish by most Mexican Americans. This preference and usage, in turn, afford strong evidence that cultural assimilation is not occurring among Mexican Americans in the same way it typically has among the European minorities. It is true, of course, that the older members of the group and those who are foreign-born rely most heavily on Spanish, and it is true that this pattern has been common among many other ethnic groups. There also is evidence, if one focuses on the native-born, that "language use and preference . . . shifts dramatically from Spanish to English within two generations" (Keefe and Padilla 1987:190). Nevertheless, the proportion of children in the group who learn Spanish as their first language and in whose homes Spanish is the preferred language continues to be high.

The high degree of bilingualism among Mexican Americans, perhaps even among natives of native parents, may illustrate the pluralist ideal of cultural assimilation discussed in chapter 2. The Mexican Americans, so far, may not be following the Anglo conformity pattern of cultural assimilation by substituting English for Spanish, though some scholars believe otherwise,[28] or, even if this switch is occurring, a change in only one cultural element (albeit a very important one) may not be sufficient to produce cultural assimilation in other respects. Keefe and Padilla (1987:16–18), however, present evidence that when cultural assimilation[29] is analyzed trait by trait one finds that as language loyalty declines among Mexican Americans, loyalty to the Mexican heritage nevertheless continues. Although many individual Mexican Americans have followed the traditional route to cultural assimilation and have given up the Spanish language entirely, a common pattern among the members of this group appears to be the addition of English to their language repertoire. Many members of this group wish to cultivate their language skills in both Spanish and English. Such factors as a person's educational level and the length of his or her residence in the United States affect this process (Grenier 1985).

More research along these lines must be conducted if we are to gain a better understanding of cultural assimilation. In addition, we need a more detailed picture of the views and day-to-day behavior of Mexican Americans, especially as these are expressed within the family. A vigorous, often heated, controversy has swirled around the subject of the characteristics of the Mexican American family. It has been described as patriarchal, religious, cohesive, and traditional. Men, particularly older men, have been portrayed as regulating family life in a strict and austere way (much has been made of the notion of "machismo"), while women have been portrayed as subordinate, religious, and patient sufferers. Many critics of such portrayals have agreed with Norma Williams's (1990:2) assessment that some influential scholarly works have been affected by the stereotypical definitions of Mexican Americans held by the majority group.

Williams (1990) has conducted a valuable study of continuities and changes within the Mexican American family during the last several decades. Through a series of in-depth interviews with seventy-five Mexican American couples, primarily in three Texas cities,[30] she gathered information on the rituals that surround the important life-cycle events of birth, marriage, and death.[31] She asked the respondents questions concerning the way these important life-cycle events were handled in the past and in the present. She pieced together from the interviews the ritual patterns that commonly were followed in the period from the 1920s through the 1950s, and these patterns were taken for study purposes to represent the "traditional" practices against which the "current" practices were contrasted.[32] With this information, she was able to describe the standard practices for each time period as seen through the eyes of the study participants, to compare the traditional and current cultures of Mexican Americans in each of the two social classes, and to show that the practices varied within each time period.

The study's conclusions showed, among other things, that the cohesion of the extended family declined during the period under study, with funeral ceremonies remaining "as the last bastion for sustaining extended kinship arrangements" (Williams 1990:138).[33] The results showed, too, that the power of men in the past was indeed greater than that of women (though never as great as the stereotypes suggest) and that although the power of men declined during the decades studied, it continued to exceed that of women in the later period.

The findings were interpreted within a broad framework concerning the general effects of industrialization, urbanization, and bureaucratization on family life in America. Williams argued that during the last several decades Mexican American families (on the whole) have become more like Anglo-American families but that this trend toward convergence does not mean Mexican Americans "are attempting to become like Anglos." Despite appearances, she maintains, the increasing similarity of Anglo and Mexican American families does not lend support to the "assimilationist model" (Williams 1990:145). Her thesis, instead, is that the increasing similarity is occurring because both sets of families "are responding to major changes on the societal and global levels" (Williams 1990:148). This interesting argument deserves additional scholarly attention. It illustrates how the principles behind the models of assimilation presented in chapter 2 may be tested against specific research findings.[34]

In another important study of family structure and ethnicity, Keefe and Padilla (1987) examined generational differences among Mexican Americans and also compared the family structures of Mexican Americans to those of Anglo-Americans. The analysis was based on interviews and reinterviews with samples of Anglo and Mexican American respondents in three California cities.[35] One major part of the research focused on the interactions of the respondents with their primary kin (parents, siblings, children) and secondary kin (other relatives) within and outside of the local community.

Among the many (and complicated) findings, three stand out. First, primary kin ties were the most significant for both Anglos and Mexican Americans, but Anglos had fewer primary kin close at hand and Mexican Americans maintained closer ties. Second, Mexican Americans were more likely than Anglos to have a local extended family and to maintain contact with its members. These two findings lead to a third that is of special importance in relation to cultural assimilation: Mexican Americans had a larger and more integrated extended family system than did Anglos, as is widely supposed, but the difference existed only in the comparison between *native-born* Mexican Americans and Anglos (Keefe and Padilla 1987:136–139). First-generation immigrants resembled Anglos in this respect more than either group resembled native-born Mexican Americans. In short, even though Mexican Americans in the second and third generations appeared to be assimilating culturally in some important respects, the effect of these changes was to strengthen, rather than weaken, the extended family. Even though the native-born Mexican Americans were highly urbanized and exposed to many sources of family breakdown, "The Chicano family," as Keefe and Padilla (1987:144) stated, "is far from being a declining institution."

We conclude, therefore, that the kind of cultural assimilation we might expect on the basis of Park's and Gordon's theories—a substitution across the board of Anglo for Mexican American culture—seems not to be occurring. Movement toward assimilation in some respects has not been accompanied by changes in all of the other aspects of culture; however, if the ideas of assimilationist theories seem inadequate to explain what is occurring among Mexican Americans, the ideas of colonialist theory also fall short. Although Mexican Americans reject many facets of Anglo-American culture, the two groups appear nevertheless to be moving toward one another in some important ways, which, as Williams (1990) maintains, may not mean that the former are adopting the culture of the latter. Mexican Americans appear to accept the necessity, if not the desirability, of secondary structural assimilation (i.e., "integration"). Let's examine some facts in this regard.

Secondary Structural Assimilation

Our exploration of secondary assimilation among Mexican Americans focuses on their occupational distribution, incomes, educational attainments, and residential location.

As noted previously, Mexican Americans have from the beginning played a distinctive role in the American labor force. By 1920, Mexican American workers were much more likely to be employed as farming, mining, or railroad laborers than in any other capacity. And they were far more likely to be found in these occupational pursuits than were Anglo-American workers. This concentration in certain types of work has not, of course, been complete. Especially since the beginning of World War II, Mexican Americans have been moving out of "their" customary occupations and into many different jobs that pay more and carry with them a higher level of pay and social prestige. For example, the proportion of native-born Mexican American men engaged in "professional" occupations rose steadily from over 3 percent in 1960 and to nearly 9 percent in 1990 (Bean and Tienda 1987:328; U.S. Bureau of the Census 1991a:12), while the number engaged in farming fell below 4 percent.

Before we conclude that Mexican Americans soon will be completely assimilated occupationally, several cautions are in order. For instance, the rate of increase in the proportion of Mexican American men working in the professions seen in the 1960s slowed noticeably during the 1970s. Moreover, although Mexican American men, as compared to Anglo men, experienced a relative gain in professional work between 1960 and 1980, the actual gap between the two groups increased from 6.0 percent in 1960 (3.3 versus 9.3 percent) to 6.4 percent in 1980 (5.7 versus 12.1 percent) (Bean and Tienda 1987:329).[36] In addition, despite the higher rate of increase in professional employment among Mexican American than Anglo men, the level of professional employment among Mexican Americans in 1980 still had not reached the Anglo level for 1960.[37] The levels of professional employment among native-born women of both ethnic groups are generally higher, but a comparison of Mexican American and Anglo women leads to the same conclusions as for men (Bean and Tienda 1987:334–335).

We should note also in this connection that even when Mexican Americans gain access to the more "desirable" occupations, they frequently are in the lower paid positions within them. Combining this fact with the continuing differences between the occupational distributions of Anglos and Mexican Americans, we should not be surprised to find a continuation of income differences between the two groups. And this is, indeed, the case. Although Mexican Americans showed a steady improvement in income during the 1960–1980 period, the ratio of personal income for Mexican Americans to that of Anglos hovered around .67.[38] This means that even during a period of rising occupational standing and increased income, the average (mean) income for Mexican Americans remained about two-thirds that of Anglos.

When median family incomes for 1980 and 1989 are compared, however, a somewhat different picture emerges. The median family incomes of non-Hispanic and Mexican American families in 1980 were $21,235 and $14,510, respectively (Bean and Tienda 1987:346–347). While the ratio of these averages (.68) is slightly higher than that reported previously for personal income, the ratio of the family medians for 1989 ($33,915 versus $21,025) had declined to .62 (U.S. Bureau of the Census 1991b:38, 40); therefore, despite a rise in the dollar income among Mexican American families in the latter period, their relative position declined. Moreover, the absolute gap between the two groups in this respect increased between 1980 and 1989 from $6,725 to $12,890. We may conclude, therefore, that although the real economic situation of the Mexican Americans may be improving gradually, the relative and absolute gaps between the Mexican American and Anglo groups are still growing. We should note, too, that a much higher percentage of Mexican American families than Anglo families live in poverty (25 versus 8 percent; (U.S. Bureau of the Census 1991b:38, 40).

Whether people find it possible to move out of low-prestige, poorly paid jobs into jobs that are thought to be more desirable may depend to a considerable extent on the educational levels of the people involved. It is of special importance, therefore, to know whether the educational level of the Mexican American population has been increasing over time. Such increases would be expected if this ethnic group has been moving in the direction of secondary assimilation.

Past research has emphasized that Mexican American children have been faced with severe discrimination in the schools and, as a consequence, have had lower achievement levels than Anglos (Fligstein and Fernandez 1985:164; Valdivieso and Davis 1988:6). Although Mexican Americans still lag far behind the Anglo population, the available evidence nevertheless suggests strongly that they are becoming more assimilated in regard to education. For example, the average (median) level of education among Mexican Americans increased from 6.4 years in 1960 to 9.1 years in 1980. Among the native-born portion of the group, the average rose from 7.6 years in 1960 to 11.1 years in 1980. The foreign-born group also showed a marked average increase, from 3.6 years in 1960 to 6.1 years in 1980. By 1987, the proportion of Mexican Americans completing four years of high school or more had risen to 46 percent, the highest level ever recorded, and the median level of education among those between twenty-five and thirty-four years of age had reached 12.1 years (U.S. Bureau of the Census 1989a:8). In addition, college enrollments among all Hispanics had risen almost 50 percent since 1978 (*Chronicle of Higher Education* 1988).

We must be cautious in interpreting this evidence of increases in schooling among Mexican Americans, however. Even though the successive generations of Mexican Americans seem to be achieving higher levels of education, one careful analysis (Bean, Chapa, Berg, and Sowards, forthcoming) shows that within younger age cohorts the third generation generally has not reached the educational level of the second generation. To illustrate, the mean level of education among second-generation men between the ages of twenty-five and twenty-nine was 12.3 years, but among third-generation men the average was 12.2 years. Similarly, among second- and third-generation women between the ages of twenty-five and twenty-nine, the mean levels of education were 11.9 and 11.7, respectively. These findings call into question the adequacy of the view, based on the overall statistics, that each generation of Mexican Americans is attaining a higher level of education than its predecessors. A second problem that continues to be particularly prominent among Mexican American youths is that the rate at which they "drop out" (or are "pushed out") of school before reaching high school graduation is high. For example, among native-born Mexican Americans between the ages of eighteen and twenty-five in 1980, slightly more than 30 percent had not completed high school, and among the foreign-born the level of noncompletion was about twice as high (Bean and Tienda 1987:272). An important factor affecting these levels is the frequency with which Mexican American children are required to repeat grades (Fligstein and Fernandez 1985:165).

The broad figures we have presented concerning the occupations, incomes, and educational levels of Mexican Americans conceal many underlying differences of interest. For example, since Anglos on the average have higher levels of education and hold better-paying jobs than Mexican Americans, some of the difference in median incomes is due to these factors. It is accurate to say, therefore, that some of the income inequality between Mexican and Anglo Americans arises from the educational and occupational differences between the two groups.

In chapter 6 we mentioned that one way of assessing the extent to which the dominant group discriminates against minority groups is to calculate the pay of similar workers in different ethnic groups to discover whether it "costs" to be a member of a minority group.[39] The methods used in these studies are too advanced to be considered in detail, but the underlying idea can be illustrated simply. In 1959, the mean income for male Mexican American workers who had completed four years of college or more was $7,207, but at the same time the mean income for Anglo workers with the same level of education was $8,458.[40] Similarly, Anglos who had completed less than eight years of school earned more, on the average ($4,642), than Mexican Americans who had attended high school for up to three years ($4,563). In other words, *so far as education alone* is concerned, it appears that Mexican Americans "pay a price" in the job market because of their group membership.

If nothing else were considered, this conclusion would be premature because factors other than education affect income. To illustrate, it is likely that the average age of Mexican Americans with college degrees is lower than for Anglos with a similar level of education. Since older, more experienced people generally have higher incomes, some of the income differences we have noted may be due to the experience differences between older Anglo and younger Mexican American workers. Our comparison, consequently, should be restricted at least to Anglos and Mexican Americans who have degrees and are of similar ages. When the groups have been "matched" in several important respects, it is reasonable to suppose that any remaining income difference is due largely to discrimination. By a similar method, Poston and Alvírez (1973:708) showed that in 1959, approximately $900 of the average difference between Mexican American and Anglo workers may have been a result of discrimination. Moreover, some subsequent analyses (Cotton 1985; Poston, Alvírez, and Tienda 1976) found that the economic "cost" of being a Mexican American worker increased during the 1970s despite the increasing levels of education among Mexican Americans![41]

As we noted previously, another important measure of the extent to which secondary assimilation is occurring for a given ethnic minority is the degree to which the group lives in the same residential areas as the members of the dominant group. In most cities of the United States, Mexican Americans long have been, and still are, noticeably segregated, not only from Anglos but also from African Americans. However, the extent of this segregation, as we saw for Japanese Americans, varies greatly among cities and regions of the country. For example, the lowest regional index of residential segregation (dissimilarity) of Mexican Americans and Anglos in the United States in 1980 was 48.3 (the South) and the highest was 62.3 (the Northeast). Among ten SMSAs with large Mexican American populations, the lowest level of residential segregation was 39.1 (Riverside, California) and the highest was 66.0 (New York City). Intermediate levels were found in such cities as Chicago (64.0), Los Angeles (61.1), San Antonio (58.9), and Houston (50.4) (Bean and Tienda 1987:174). The levels of residential segregation between Hispanics and Anglos in some smaller SMSAs with relatively large Mexican American populations include Fresno (45.4), Phoenix (49.4), and Corpus Christi (51.6) (Massey and Denton 1987:815–816). Most of these residential segregation indexes lie within the moderate range, though the average for the cities of the Southwest is higher than the average for the nation (Lopez 1981:53–54); hence, although there are large and important differences among cities, the typical situation is a moderate degree of Mexican American-Anglo residential segregation.

The extent to which Mexican Americans and Anglos are segregated residentially may be decreasing over time and, if so, this would indicate that secondary assimilation is taking place. If, on the other hand, the level of residential segregation has remained unchanged for several decades or has increased, this would indicate strongly that a full merger of the ethnic groups is hardly just over the horizon. Massey and Denton (1987) calculated the changes in residential similarity between Hispanics and Anglos between 1970 and 1980 for sixty SMSAs.[42] Thirty-three of the SMSAs studied showed a decline in Hispanic-Anglo residential segregation and the remaining twenty-seven showed an increase. More to the point, however, is that the changes in some of the SMSAs with a very high percentage of Mexican Americans showed an average increase. In thirteen SMSAs having more than 100,000 Mexican Americans who comprised at least 80 percent of the Hispanic population, an increase in residential segregation occurred in nine, and the average decline in the remaining four SMSAs was comparatively small (+5.4 versus −1.9).[43] Some findings for the period 1980–1990 suggest that this general pattern of residential segregation may have continued through that period (Harrison and Weinberg 1992).

To interpret these facts, it is helpful to have a standard of comparison. Although the extent of black-white residential segregation will be discussed more fully in chapter 11, we may note here that in 1980, the average Hispanic-Anglo index in the sixty SMSAs studied by Massey and Denton (1987:816) was 43.4, while the black-white index was 69.4. The fact that Mexican Americans are less segregated from Anglos than are blacks is not due simply to socioeconomic differences between the two minority groups. The evidence points strongly to the conclusion, consistent with the spatial mobility hypothesis, that segregation among Mexican Americans declines sharply with rising socioeconomic status, suburbanization, and the number of generations spent in the United States (Massey and Denton 1987:803, 819). However, higher-status blacks and suburban blacks are approximately as likely to live in a segregated neighborhood as are those who are less affluent (Clark and Mueller 1988; Massey 1979; Massey and Denton 1987). It is probable, therefore, that the slight average increase in residential segregation of Mexican Americans during the 1970s may be attributed to the fact that the rapid immigration of Mexicans to the United States has led, at least temporarily, to an increase in the relative size of urban Mexican communities.[44] The apparent increases in education, socioeconomic status, and suburbanization for the native-born are consistent with the view that secondary assimilation is underway.

Primary Structural Assimilation

The evidence reviewed shows that, in general, Mexican Americans have been moving out of rural areas and into the cities, and that within the cities they are less segregated from Anglos than are blacks. It shows, too, that native-born Mexican Americans more nearly approximate the educational level of Anglo-Americans than do foreign-born Mexican Americans and that Mexican Americans are more likely now to be working in jobs that previously were almost exclusively held by Anglo-Americans. Each of these forms of secondary assimilation favors an increase in the amount of equal-status interaction that will occur between Mexican Americans and Anglos, and thereby raises the probability that friendships will develop across the ethnic line. We would expect, therefore, an increase in the number of

Anglo-Mexican American friendships on the job, in the neighborhood, and among those of similar education and income. We also would expect more friendships to form between Anglos and Mexican Americans of native parentage than between Anglos and Mexican Americans of mixed or foreign parentage.

Although little is known concerning the trends in Mexican American-Anglo friendship formation, some valuable evidence was provided by the work of researchers in UCLA's Mexican American Study Project (Grebler, Moore, and Guzman 1970). The researchers gathered information on the friendships of Mexican Americans in three large cities during various periods of the respondents' lives. The study participants in Albuquerque, Los Angeles, and San Antonio were asked about the ethnicity of their friends when they were children, about the ethnicity of their present friends, and about the ethnicity of their children's friends. Thus, each person was asked to report on three generations of experience. In all three cities, the participants reported that the extent of out-group friendship relations had increased through time (Moore 1970:134).

For example, while 45 percent of the participants in Albuquerque said that all of their childhood friends had been Mexican Americans, only 22 percent of them said this was still true, and only 12 percent of these same participants said that all of their children's friends were Mexican American. In other words, the extent of friendly relations with non-Mexican Americans appears to have increased markedly for these people and for their children. The same pattern of increasing out-group friendships was found in Los Angeles and San Antonio. In Los Angeles, those claiming exclusively Mexican American friends for themselves as children and for their own children fell from 52 percent to 18 percent; in San Antonio, the decline was from 70 percent to 39 percent.

As expected, this overall pattern differed for those who lived in more or less desegregated neighborhoods, and it also varied by income level. For example, in Los Angeles and San Antonio, the Mexican Americans who lived in neighborhoods having relatively few Mexican Americans ("frontier" or desegregated areas) were more likely to have predominantly Anglo friends than were those living in neighborhoods having a relatively large number of Mexican Americans ("colony" or segregated areas). And, for the most part, those of higher income who lived in frontier areas were more likely to have predominantly Anglo friends than were those of lower income (Grebler, Moore, and Guzman 1970:397). The income differences discovered in the desegregated neighborhoods, however, did not hold up in the segregated areas. People of higher income in the colony areas were hardly more likely to report a predominance of Anglo friends than were those of lower income in those areas.

Taken together, these findings from three of the main centers of Mexican American culture suggest that, with the passage of time, Mexican Americans decreasingly have only Mexican American friends. Although this generational trend is much more pronounced among those living in desegregated neighborhoods and among those of higher income, it suggests that if the occupational, educational, and residential assimilation of Mexican Americans continue, primary assimilation also will increase.

We emphasized previously that when a dominant and subordinate group are brought together by conquest, the groups frequently react to one another with greater mutual hatred and rejection than if the minority arose through immigration. For this reason, Mexican Americans frequently have been described as having a low assimilative potential. Despite the forces working toward ethnic separateness, however, we have seen that Mexican Americans and Anglos are in some respects coming closer together. Let us turn now to that "most infallible index" of assimilation—intermarriage (Kennedy 1944:331).

Marital Assimilation

Several studies of Mexican American intermarriage have been conducted, the majority of them focusing on Los Angeles, Albuquerque, and San Antonio. Three main findings stand out. First, the occurrence of out-marriage for Mexican Americans is much lower in some places than in others. For instance, in the early 1960s, the rate of out-marriage for marriages (see Note 33, chapter 8) was 20 percent in San Antonio (Alvírez and Bean 1976:285), 33 percent in Albuquerque, and 5 percent in Edinburg, Texas (Murguía and Frisbie 1977:384). Second, there has been a gradual long-term increase in the rate of out-marriage. For example, in a study comparing rates of out-marriage in San Antonio, Bradshaw and Bean (1970:393) demonstrated that the rate for marriages in 1850 was about 10 percent. One hundred years later, the rate had approximately doubled. This general trend may be seen even in some small, comparatively isolated communities that have a tradition of high levels of social distance. Cazares, Murguía, and Frisbie (1985:399), for instance, compared out-marriage rates for Mexican Americans in Pecos County, Texas, for the periods 1880–1960 and 1970–1978 and found that out-marriage (for marriages) had increased from .043 to .155. Some studies, however, show that the rise in out-marriages is not rapid or that a rise may be followed by a decline. In Corpus Christi, for instance, the rate hardly changed between the early 1960s and 1970s, rising from 15 to 16 percent (Alvírez and Bean 1976:383). By 1988, the rate had reached 18 percent (Sherwood 1988:14D). In Albuquerque, a rapid rise from 33 percent in 1964 to 48 percent in 1967 was followed by a sharp decline to 39 percent in 1971 (Murguía and Frisbie 1977:384), and in California there was a gradual decline from 55 percent in 1962 to 51 percent in 1974 (Schoen, Nelson, and Collins 1978).

The third main finding of interest here is that Mexican Americans who are natives of native parentage are more likely to marry-out than are Mexican Americans of mixed parentage, who, in turn, are more likely to marry-out than are those born in Mexico (Grebler, Moore, and Guzman 1970:409; Moore and Pachon 1985:108). Also, those in the second and third generations who marry-out are more likely to marry Anglos than to marry immigrants from Mexico (Mittlebach and Moore 1968:54). In short, whether one examines the overall out-marriage rates at different points in time or the rates for those in different generations, the main conclusion appears to be the same: Mexican Americans are moving slowly toward marital assimilation (Murguía 1982:50).

Some writers believe the evidence on out-marriage supports the immigrant model. Mittlebach and Moore (1968:53) stated that in Los Angeles, at least, the rate of Mexican American out-marriage "is roughly that of the Italian and Polish ethnic populations in Buffalo, New York, a generation ago," and in a reanalysis of these data, Schoen and Cohen (1980:365) agreed that the assimilation of the Mexican Americans "appears to be very much in the tradition of earlier American immigration." Similarly, Penalosa (1970:50) concluded that many contemporary changes among the Mexican Americans suggest they are coming to resemble "a European immigrant group of a generation ago."

Schoen and Cohen (1980) also touched on the important theoretical question of how well the sequence of assimilation processes outlined by Gordon (1964) (i.e., cultural, structural, marital, and so on) describes the actual experience of different ethnic groups. They found that high levels of cultural assimilation may have a more important effect on marital assimilation than do high levels of occupational assimilation, which suggests that the levels of assimilation exhibited by a group may not always correspond to the order of the subprocesses of assimilation indicated by Gordon's theory. In an important direct test of this portion of Gordon's theory, Williams and Ortega (1990:707) concluded "that different ethnic groups have substantially different patterns of assimilation." For example, they found "that Mexican Americans are much less acculturated than African Americans, but they are more assimilated structurally" (Williams and Ortega 1990:708).

Mexican American "Success"

What does the evidence on the various forms of assimilation among Mexican Americans tell us about the success with which they have adapted to American life? How, for instance, do they compare with Japanese Americans? Although Mexican Americans have been moving toward the American mainstream, they have not been as successful (from the perspective of Anglo conformity) as Japanese Americans. In nearly every—if not every—aspect of assimilation, Mexican Americans less nearly approximate the Anglo-American ideal than do Japanese Americans. They have not relinquished their culture as rapidly; they have not attained equal levels of occupation, education, and income; and they appear to be more segregated in their friendship and marital patterns. Why is this true?

This question lies at the very heart of the ideological issues we have discussed throughout this book. In some respects, the comparative "failure" of the Mexican Americans in terms of Anglo conformity may, with equal force, be seen as "success" from the perspective of cultural pluralism. Mexican Americans have been more successful than Japanese Americans in their efforts to maintain and develop their own distinctive heritage, the desirability of which seems clearly to be acknowledged by many Japanese Americans, particularly among the Sansei and Yonsei. Please recall, though, that ideal cultural pluralism (as sketched in chapter 2) calls for a high level of secondary assimilation, as does Anglo conformity; hence, in this regard, Mexican Americans still have not reached the goal of ideal pluralism. The trick, of course, is to be successful in worldly ways without failing in the cultural, social, and marital spheres of group life.

But what if worldly success can be purchased only at the price of cultural failure? What if the maintenance of the culture is itself an obstacle to the attainment of worldly success? What if the pluralist ideal of cultural assimilation by addition is unrealistic? These explosive questions have been in the forefront of the frequently bitter debate concerning public policies relating to Mexican Americans.

Consider, for example, the question of the use of Spanish in the schools. The dominant group insisted until the latter part of the 1960s that only English was the legal and proper language of instruction in the schools. Mexican American children have been said to suffer from a language "barrier" that must be "surmounted." From this point of view, teaching the children in Spanish only retards their assimilation into the mainstream of American life. Even when the desirability of bilingual education has been acknowledged, the curriculum usually has been designed to "phase out" Spanish as early as possible.

The assumption underlying this stand is that the possession of a Mexican heritage is a handicap in the modern world. From the Mexican American point of view, however, this assumption is simply part of a broader struggle between the Mexican American and Anglo cultures. A frequent observation concerning classical colonialism is that oppressor groups not only conquer the territories of the groups they subordinate but attempt to destroy the native cultures as well; thus, many Mexican Americans consider the insistence that they give up Spanish and undergo full cultural assimilation to be an example of "cultural imperialism." The complexity of the disagreement between those who insist that Mexican culture retards secondary assimilation (i.e., achievement and success) and those who oppose this view may be illustrated by a very brief consideration of some studies of Mexican American culture conducted by Anglo-American social scientists.

Two early studies on this subject were very influential. Beginning in the 1940s, Florence Kluckhohn, an anthropologist, initiated a series of studies of the Spanish Americans (Hispanos) of northern New Mexico. Her basic idea was that all human cultures contain values that specify the approved solutions to five inevitable human problems. For instance, each culture will tend to emphasize the importance of the past, the present, or the future; consequently, one may say that the members of a given society tend to share a past, present, or future "orientation" (Kluckhohn 1956:346). She also believed that the dominant value concerning time in American society is an orientation toward the future. Members of the dominant group place a high value on such things as planning ahead and "saving for a rainy day." In contrast, she argued that the Spanish Americans of northern New Mexico emphasized the present and do not expect the future to be better than the past or present. In addition to a future orientation, the Anglo-American culture was found to stress individualism, accomplishment, mastery over nature, and the perfectibility of humans. The Hispano culture, in contrast, was found to stress the present, collective goals or familism, being rather than doing, fatalism, and the imperfectibility of human beings. Although Kluckhohn stated that these cultural differences are not absolute, she argued that they are largely responsible for the slow rate and degree of assimilation of Spanish Americans. The resemblance of this explanation for the "failure" of those of Spanish heritage to that of the cultural explanation for the "success" of the Japanese Americans (discussed in chapter 8) is apparent.

The second influential early study of interest to us here was conducted by Saunders (1954). He, too, was interested in the major features of the Spanish-American and Anglo-American cultures. More specifically, he was interested in the health and illness behavior of these two groups and the possibility that the differences in their health behavior were produced by the underlying differences between the culture patterns of the two groups. He noted, for instance, that Spanish Americans were more likely to resist or refuse hospitalization than Anglo-Americans, and he argued that this difference arose, in some measure, because placing people in the hospital when they are sick is contrary to the Spanish Americans' belief that a sick person should have his or her family near the bedside.

Another value or attitude that makes hospitalization objectionable to the Spanish Americans, according to Saunders, is their emphasis on the present. This value conflicts with the desire of hospital personnel to schedule visits and treatments rigidly in advance. Also, the apparent faith of hospital personnel in an activistic, scientific approach to the curing of illness is vastly different from the presumably more passive, semireligious approach that has been traditional among some Spanish Americans. Among the people studied by Saunders, the belief was widespread that a number of common diseases such as *mal de ojo, susto,* and *empacho* are not understood by scientifically trained Anglo-American health personnel and, therefore, cannot be treated by them. Only a traditional healer, such as a *curandero,* can diagnose and treat them. Saunders hoped this analysis would help scientific healers to bridge the cultural gap between themselves and their Spanish-speaking patients (Spector 1985:164–165).

The studies of Kluckhohn and Saunders stimulated the interest of a number of other researchers in the question of the value differences between Anglos and Mexican Americans, particularly as these differences affected the groups' health beliefs and practices.[45] Although some students, including Saunders (1954:169), recognized that at least some of the presumed cultural differences between the two ethnic groups might be a reflection of the fact that most of the Mexican Americans who had been studied lived in isolated rural communities and were below the socioeconomic average of most Anglo-Americans, the idea was widely accepted that many of the Mexican Americans' health problems were due to their "passivism." Improved health, from this perspective, depended on the acceptance by the Mexican Americans of Anglo-American values and beliefs.

Mexican American scholars launched a scathing critique of the "cultural determinism" exemplified by Kluckhohn, Saunders, and their followers. Romano (1968), for example, maintained that such concepts as "present orientation," "fatalism," and "familism" have been used by Anglo-American scholars to label Mexican Americans as passive recipients of whatever fate may thrust upon them. Such ideas, Romano contended (1968:24), are simply social science stereotypes that strengthen the popular notion among Anglos that Mexican Americans are largely responsible for their own unfortunate circumstances—a situation that can be changed only through full cultural assimilation. In a similar vein, Vaca (1970:26) argued that the attack on the values of Mexican American culture is only a mask for the Anglo conformity ideology. Cultural analysis, he said, presents a "vicious," "misleading," and "degrading" portrait of Mexican American culture. It is a portrait that distorts reality and implies that Mexican American culture should not continue to exist within contemporary American society. Norma Williams (1990:22) pointed out that the characteristics noted in the earlier studies, such as fatalism, are common in all traditional societies and, therefore, are not *particularly* characteristic of Mexican Americans.

In keeping with a more positive view of Mexican American culture, several studies in the health field failed to support the main implications of the value orientations approach.[46] Of greater importance, however, has been an increasing emphasis on noncultural explanations of the socioeconomic position of Mexican Americans. We noted earlier, for example, that a substantial portion of the average difference between the incomes of Mexican American and Anglo workers may be caused by discrimination. We noted, too, that documented and undocumented immigration to the United States has been intimately related to changing economic circumstances (Portes and Rumbaut 1990:14). And we emphasized that both Mexican immigrant workers and native Mexican American workers typically have entered a "split" or "dual" labor market in the United States. One set of jobs, historically "reserved" for Anglo workers, has offered good pay, security, and the possibility of advancement. The second set of jobs, into which "cheap" labor typically has been funneled, has consisted of the backbreaking, seasonal, and "stoop" work that Anglo workers ordinarily have refused to perform (Barrera 1979:114, 209; Pachon and Moore 1981:118–119; Portes and Bach 1985:69). The latter jobs have offered little hope of advancement even when the workers were educated and experienced. When minority workers are routinely allocated to dead-end jobs, according to this line of criticism, no amount of "activism" or "future orientation" will lead to significantly improved economic circumstances.

As in the case of the worldly "success" of Japanese Americans, our discussion strongly suggests that a strictly cultural explanation of the comparative "failure" of Mexican Americans is inadequate. To assume that whatever problems Mexican Americans have are the fault of their culture is to ignore the effects of structural factors that exist in the surrounding society. Both critics of the cultural explanation and its defenders agree, of course, that Mexican American culture is different from Anglo-American culture in certain respects (Moore and Pachon 1985:122–131). Indeed, were that not the case, all talk of Mexican American culture would be pointless. It is the determination of Mexican Americans to maintain a distinctive culture that is a source of conflict with the dominant group. But to agree that Mexican American culture is *different* is by no means to acknowledge that it is *deficient*. As Barrera (1979:180) argued, "The cultural apparatus of any people is so complex that presumably negative traits can always be found. . . . " But unless a bipartisan comparison is conducted of the "negative" and "positive" traits in both the dominant and subordinate groups, Barrera believes, no valid inferences concerning the relation of values to success are possible.

Most Mexican Americans seem to be determined to find a middle way wherein the "positive" features of their culture and their pride in *La Raza* will move side by side with increasing secondary assimilation, but some members of this ethnic group appear to have concluded that separation or secession may be the only solution to the problem of cultural survival. They have rejected the value orientations analysis of their situation and are engaged in constructing a stronger, more nearly independent community.

The evidence we have reviewed concerning the cultural, secondary, primary, and marital assimilation of Mexican Americans may be interpreted as lending partial support to either the immigrant or the colonial models. Neither interpretation seems to fit all the facts. Mexican Americans appear to be statistically, as they are in reality, both a conquered and an immigrant minority. We will return to this puzzle in chapter 14.

Key Ideas

1. The relations between Mexican Americans and Anglos represent a second kind of intergroup contact. Like Native Americans and African Americans, Mexican Americans orginally entered the United States through force rather than through voluntary immigration.

2. Some social analysts think a sequence of intergroup relations that is initiated through forced entry cannot be understood in terms of the theories of Anglo conformity, the melting pot, or cultural pluralism. They believe, instead, that a variation of colonialist theory (e.g., internal colonialism) affords a more accurate picture of the relations between Mexican Americans and Anglos.

3. Colonized minorities, in contrast to immigrant minorities, usually remain in their homeland, are especially committed to the preservation of their native culture, and are prevented by the dominant group from moving about freely to compete for jobs with members of the dominant group. Under these conditions, the sequence of race relations does not move steadily "forward" toward full intergroup merger; it is characterized, rather, by a back-and-forth movement out of conflict into accommodation and back again into conflict. This sequence is interrupted by the expulsion or annihilation of one group or the other.

4. The Spanish approach to colonization differed from that of the English. A key difference was that the Spanish included the indigenous people in the developing colonial society, while the English excluded them. As a result, the Indians of Mexico have moved much further toward full assimilation than have the Indians of the United States.

5. The Mexican American group emerged out of a long series of conflicts between the United States and Spain and between the United States and Mexico. Although the Texas revolution was not based on ethnic differences, the ethnic cleavage gradually deepened following Texas's independence. The Mexican American group emerged as a distinct minority group at the end of the Mexican-American War.

6. The Treaty of Guadalupe Hidalgo did not end hostilities between the Mexican Americans and Anglos in the borderlands. Continuous struggle, marked by intermittent open conflict, was a conspicuous element of border life well into the twentieth century.

7. Although the Mexican American group was created when the United States forcibly occupied the southwestern and western lands previously owned by Mexico, most present members of the group are not the descendants of that "creation generation." The Mexican American population of the United States has grown overwhelmingly through immigration from Mexico since the beginning of the twentieth century.

8. Since Mexican immigration reached its peak later than the peak of the new immigration, many social analysts think of Mexican Americans as being even "newer" to America than the new immigrants. Their apparent slowness to assimilate, therefore, may be due to their comparatively recent arrival in the United States.

9. Advocates of the colonial model dispute the claims of those who prefer the immigrant model. It is said that Mexicans who move to the United States are better thought of as migrants than as immigrants. From this viewpoint, the movement of Mexicans across an arbitrary political boundary into an area that is both geographically and culturally similar to their homeland is not to be compared to movements of Europeans across oceans into a country with a much different culture. Moreover, when Mexican nationals have reached the United States, the members of the dominant group typically have greeted them with even higher levels of prejudice and discrimination than has usually been directed toward European immigrants.

10. Three widely publicized examples of dominant group discrimination against Mexican Americans are the "charity deportations" in the 1930s, the "Zoot Suit Race Riots" in the 1940s, and "Operation Wetback" in the 1950s. In each of these cases, some officials of the dominant group demonstrated that they made no real distinction between Mexican American citizens and Mexican nationals. They also revealed their belief that all people of Mexican ancestry are innately inferior. As in the case of the evacuation and internment of Japanese Americans, many citizens were illegally punished, in this case through deportation, intimidation, and physical assault.

11. The bracero program illustrates how the relations of the dominant group in America to its minorities may be altered by international events.

12. World War II and the Mexican Americans' active participation in it increased the group's commitment to Anglo conformity and led many of its members to expect a sharp decline in prejudice and discrimination following the war. When the expected changes did not occur, the Mexican American group commenced an "awakening" that has been expressed in a higher degree of formal social and political organization and in a sharp increase in interest in the goals of cultural pluralism. There also has been an increase in interest in separatism and secession.

13. Today, although Mexican Americans, in general, show higher levels of cultural, secondary, primary, and marital assimilation than they did in 1950, it seems unlikely that the differences between Mexican Americans and Anglos will soon disappear.

Assimilation in jobs and income, for example, is not occurring rapidly and, in fact, may have been halted during the 1970s and 1980s.

14. A popular explanation of the comparative lack of worldly success by Mexican Americans has focused on the way their values differ from those of Anglos. It has been claimed that such things as their "present orientation" and "familism" are obstacles to success. From this perspective, Mexican Americans must hasten to rid themselves of their culture if they wish to get ahead in American life.

15. The value orientations approach has been vigorously attacked as a form of cultural imperialism that works in the service of the Anglo conformity ideology. Mexican Americans do not believe that their heritage is defective or is a handicap to achievement. They believe, instead, that dominant group discrimination and the traditional allocation of Mexican Americans to dead-end jobs are the biggest barriers to secondary structural assimilation.

16. Neither the colonial model nor the immigrant model fits all the facts of the Mexican American experience. Their history includes both colonization and immigration, and an adequate account of their present and future social reality must reconcile these facts.

Notes

1. Probably no other American ethnic group has been more absorbed by the questions "Who are we? What shall we call ourselves?" The members of the group vary widely in their specific histories, geographical locations, and social characteristics, and each term of identification adopted by one segment of this population has been considered inaccurate or offensive by those in some other segment. In addition to *Mexican American,* the terms *Chicano, Latino, Latin America, Spanish American, Hispano, Spanish surname,* and *Mexicano* have been prominent as identifiers, and each has a fairly specific connotation that sets it apart from the others. Some people prefer the broad term *Hispanic,* but it refers not only to Mexican Americans but also to Puerto Ricans, Cubans, and all other people of Spanish ancestry. The term *Mexican American* appears currently to be the most widely accepted and is used in this book to designate all people who trace their ancestry to Mexico, either before or after the Spanish conquest. For discussions of different terms of self-reference in this group, see Garcia (1981), Nostrand (1973), and Romo and Romo (1985:318–321).

2. George I. Sanchez, quoted by Grebler, Moore, and Guzman (1970:545).

3. The term *Anglo* refers to all non-Hispanic whites.

4. Lieberson (1961:908) showed that this pattern has been typical in situations in which the migrant group has been dominant.

5. See Edwards, Reich, and Gordon (1975) for an influential statement of this view.

6. In Vigil's (1980:202) opinion, "the development of Mexican Americanzaje (or Chicanismo, as it is sometimes called) is the most pervasive sign of the altered consciousness of Mexican-Americans."

7. The terms *internal colonialism* and *the third world perspective* often are used to emphasize that there are some differences between the experience of classical colonialism and that of nonwhite people in America (Blauner 1971:54, 70). For discussions of the concepts of colonialism, internal colonialism and neocolonialism and the situations to which they apply, see Barrera (1979:188–204) and Moore (1976).

8. Diseases also, as we note again in chapter 12, played a very important role in the conquest. Crosby (1972:52) stated in this regard that "we have so long been hypnotized by the daring of the conquistador that we have overlooked the importance of his biological allies."

9. Had the official policy of Spain been followed in general practice, the status of the Indians would have been higher. The Laws of the Indies, promulgated in 1542, stated that "Indians are free persons and vassals of the crown. . . . Nothing is to be taken from the Indians except in fair trade" (quoted in McNickle 1973:28).

10. Some observers have argued that an armed conflict in Texas was the inevitable result of the confrontation of rival and clashing cultures. This argument ignores the fact that to a considerable extent the main cleavage in Texas during the colonial period was not between Mexican natives and Anglo-American immigrants but, rather, between those who favored a strong central government and those who preferred greater provincial autonomy. It is true that the Anglo-Americans were overwhelmingly in the latter category, but it is also true that a large proportion of the native Mexicans joined them in opposing the central government. There was, of course, some hostility between individuals in the two groups (see, e.g., DeLeon 1983, Paredes 1978).

11. Nine of the defenders killed in the Alamo were *Tejanos*.

12. An additional 54,000 square miles along the southern border of the New Mexico Territory was bought from Mexico in 1853. Moore and Pachon (1985:19) stated that "as it happened (and no Mexican thinks it accidental), the Gadsden Purchase . . . included some of the richest copper mines in the United States."

13. Pachon and Moore (1981) stated there were around 75,000 Mexicans in the Southwest in 1848, while del Castillo (1990) estimated 100,000. Terry Jordan (1981:276) estimated there were around 83,000 Mexican Americans in Texas by 1887.

14. For a discussion of the attitudes of Anglo-Americans toward Mexicans during the nineteenth century and an application of Noel's theory to this situation, see McLemore (1973).

15. (P. Taylor 1934:29) referred to the period 1848–1878 as "The Golden Age of Anglo-American filibustering."

16. The rate of naturalization among Mexicans has been, in Moore's opinion, "extraordinarily slow" (Moore 1976:49; see also Moore and Pachon 1985:135).

17. For an analysis of some of the specific forces lying behind these broad currents, see Acuña (1981:194–206) and Barrera (1979:67–75).

18. Portes and Rumbaut (1990:17) point out that these "invasions" occur because employers in the host society are willing to hire new workers.

19. The consular officers began to apply strict standards to determine whether an applicant for a visa was likely to become a public charge in the United States (Moore and Pachon 1985:136).

20. Although Mexican labor had been brought to the United States initially to perform mainly rural tasks, by 1930 the majority of the Mexican origin population lived in cities (see, e.g., Romo 1983).

21. Calculated from Table 4-3 in Grebler, Moore, and Guzman (1970:68).

22. These orders were given after the Mexican government protested and the U.S. State Department ordered the Navy to act (Romo 1983:167).

23. For accounts of the Mexican American movement in Crystal City, see Camejo (1973) and Gutierrez and Hirsch (1973). Perhaps less spectacular, but of greater general importance, has been an increase in the number of Mexican Americans elected to public office. Pachon and Moore (1981:123) showed, for example, that between 1950 and 1979 the total number of Mexican American state legislators in the Southwest climbed from twenty to eighty-two.

24. For further discussion of this point, see, for example, McLemore and Romo (1985:20).

25. The problems of using different identifiers have been discussed by Hernandez, Estrada, and Alvírez (1973).

26. For a broader discussion of the measurement of cultural assimilation, see Hazuda, Stern, and Haffner (1988).

27. See Stevens and Swicegood (1987) for an analysis of the relationship of language persistence to the survival of an ethnic group.

28. See, for example, Fishman, "Language, Ethnic Identity, and Political Loyalty," cited by Moore and Pachon (1985:120).

29. These researchers prefer the term *acculturation* and consider this process to be a prereq-

uisite to assimilation rather than its initial subprocess (Keefe and Padilla 1987:15).

30. The cities were Austin, Corpus Christi, and Harlingen.

31. Thirty-eight couples represented the "working class" and thirty-seven represented the "business/professional class."

32. An important feature of this study is the researcher's care in constructing a standard to use for comparison. To supplement the information gained from the seventy-five couples concerning the baseline practices, Norma Williams (1990:155) also interviewed a supplementary group of people in their sixties, seventies, and eighties.

33. Even here, many changes were found. For example, the announcements of a person's death that were printed and distributed to friends and relatives (*esquelas*) have disappeared—as have the practices of displaying the body in the home and conducting all-night wakes (Williams 1990:56).

34. Williams's (1990) critique of assimilation theory strikes directly at the Anglo conformity model; however, if the Anglo and Mexican American cultures are becoming more alike, then her findings may provide support for a version of the melting pot theory (even if the increasing similarity is not a result of the emulation of Anglos by Mexican Americans). The implications of her findings for cultural pluralism remain to be explored.

35. The cities were Santa Barbara, Santa Paula, and Oxnard. The largest of three surveys included interviews with 626 respondents.

36. This seemingly paradoxical result arises because a low rate of increase when applied to a large number may yield a larger absolute increase than a higher rate of increase that is applied to a small number.

37. Since foreign-born Mexican men have lower levels of professional employment than the native-born, and since foreign-born Anglo men have higher levels than the native-born, a comparison based on these combined groups would reveal an even greater gap.

38. Calculated from Table 10.6 in Bean and Tienda (1988:368–369).

39. See, for example, Farley and Allen (1987: 335–342); Mindiola (1979); Poston and Alvírez (1973); Poston, Alvírez, and Tienda (1976); Siegel (1965); and Williams, Beeson, and Johnson (1973).

40. Calculated from Poston and Alvírez (1973:707, Table 1).

41. There also is evidence that among Mexican Americans, the "costs" are greater for those whose appearance is darker and more Indian than for those who are lighter, more "European-looking." For analyses and discussion, see Bohara and Davila (1992) and Telles and Murguía (1990; 1992).

42. The sixty SMSAs were the fifty largest SMSAs plus ten others having large Hispanic populations.

43. Calculated from Bean and Tienda (1988:150, Table 5.8) and Massey and Denton (1987:815–816, Table 3).

44. An increase in the size of an ethnic community may occur as long as the stock of houses permits it. When the areas in which various groups traditionally have settled are filled, further rapid immigration leads to a "spillover" into the surrounding neighborhoods and to a decrease in residential segregation (Massey and Denton 1987:818).

45. For a review of these studies, see Weaver (1973:85–102).

46. Several studies have found that in some respects Mexican Americans are as receptive or more receptive to scientific medicine than are Anglos, especially when those compared are of a similar social class level. (See, e.g., Angel 1985; Hoppe and Heller 1975; Karno and Edgerton 1970; McLemore 1963; Sheldon 1966; Weaver 1973.)

African Americans:

From Slavery to Segregation

The Negro must have a country and a nation of his own.
—Marcus Garvey

To those of my race who depend on bettering their condition in a foreign land . . . I would say "Cast down your bucket where you are." —BOOKER T. WASHINGTON

The equality . . . which modern men must have in order to live is not to be confounded with sameness. On the contrary, in our case, it is rather insistence upon the right of diversity. —W. E. B. DUBOIS

We seek . . . the inclusion of Negro Americans in the nation's life, not their exclusion. This is our land, as much as any American's. —ROY WILKINS

The analysis of chapter 9 revealed several important parallels between the history of Mexican Americans and that of many colonized peoples throughout the world. Chief among these is that, through conquest, the Mexican Americans lost lands to which they had had a longstanding claim. Initially, they did not enter the United States voluntarily; consequently, many members of this ethnic group have felt they are conquered people in their own land.

Mexican Americans, of course, are not alone among American minorities in this respect. Native Americans were undeniably natives in their own land, and they most assuredly have not become a part of American society either voluntarily or through immigration. As discussed in chapter 2, the primary contacts between the two groups took place within a framework of conflict. The Native Americans were more interested in repelling the invaders than they were in becoming part of their society, and the Anglo-Americans were more interested in expelling or annihilating the Native Americans than they were in assimilating them. The overall result was that the Native Americans were forced off nearly all of the lands that the Europeans considered desirable.

With these ideas and examples as a background, we turn to a consideration of America's largest, most conspicuous racial minority—black or African Americans. Unlike the European minorities, African Americans did not migrate voluntarily, and unlike Native Americans and Mexican Americans, they were not present on American soil when the English and Anglo-Americans arrived. Like the Mexican American experience, therefore, the black experience does not fit neatly either the colonial or immigrant perspectives. As a result, both viewpoints have been prominent in the arguments concerning the place and future of African Americans in American life.

The Period of Slavery

In chapter 3 we learned that the first Africans to arrive in Jamestown in 1619 were purchased as bonded or indentured servants and, as such, were not of a significantly different status than many white servants in the colony. We learned also that only gradually did the English, who were struggling to survive and to learn how to turn a profit for the colony's investors, shift from whites to blacks as the main source of cheap labor. During most of the seventeenth century, the main source of labor was the pool of paupers, convicts, adventurers, and those "spirited away" (kidnapped) from the British Isles. In addition, during the early decades the Africans were viewed not just as laborers, but also as people who possessed valuable knowledge that could help the colonies to survive and prosper. Their knowledge of rice cultivation, animal husbandry, basket making, and fishing, for instance, contributed to the survival of the English colonies (Burner, Fox-Genovese, and Bernhard 1991:80). Under these conditions, white labor was as inexpensive as black labor, and the number of black slaves increased slowly. For example, Virginia's non-Indian population in 1650 was around fifteen thousand; of that number "there were only about 300 blacks, and not all of these were slaves"

(Burner, Fox-Genovese, and Bernhard 1991:79). During the last half of the century, however, changes in the laws and the methods of tobacco cultivation in the colonies led to the acceptance of black slavery as the solution to the labor problem. The numbers of black slaves then mounted rapidly and the practice of indenturing whites declined. By 1720, "In every colony south of Maryland, African slaves outnumbered white servants. . . " (Morison 1972:207). By 1760 there were between 120,000 and 140,000 African slaves in Virginia, of a total population near 300,000 (Burner, Fox-Genovese, and Bernhard 1991:81; Morison 1972:207).

As blackness became, in Bennett's (1966:38) phrase, "a badge of servitude," the rules of servitude themselves became much more restrictive. The system of slavery that emerged in the United States during the eighteenth century to replace the earlier system of indenture deprived its victims of all human rights. It is no wonder that individual flight and organized rebellion among the slaves increased during this time, as did the level of vigilance among the masters. Nevertheless, many observers have felt that the slaves' response to their predicament was slight in relation to the oppressiveness of the regime. Even if one accepts the highest estimates of the numbers of runaways and insurrections, one may still wonder "Why were the numbers not much larger?"

The interest surrounding this question has generated a wide-ranging and complex modern debate concerning slavery. Though it involves oversimplification, we may gain some appreciation of the relationship between the various interpretations of slavery—as well as their relation to the efforts to solve modern problems of racism—by considering very briefly four leading points of view.

The first viewpoint challenges the question's basic assumption and argues that the resistance of black slaves was much greater than is usually supposed. Please recall, as discussed in chapter 3, that many Africans vigorously resisted enslavement. As they were transported through the terrifying and deadly "Middle Passage" to the New World, the slaves sometimes overcame the crews and captured the ships on which they were imprisoned, and when no other forms of escape or attack seemed possible, many slaves committed suicide. The unwillingness to be slaves involved the use of every form of resistance imaginable and continued throughout the long period of American slavery. From the first, individual slaves fought the system by running away. After the Underground Railroad was organized, their chances were greatly improved, leading to the establishment of many "maroon communities" of fugitive slaves.

Individual forms of resistance were supplemented by organized resistance. As noted previously, the leaders of the Georgia Colony recognized slave insurrections to be a distinct possibility and tried to regulate the number of slaves that could be imported. The same fear existed in the other colonies, and many precautions were taken to keep the ratio of black slaves to whites below a certain level. Slaves could not associate freely with one another, use their native languages, travel freely, or learn skills that the whites thought might threaten the established order. All of these forms of interference and regulation made difficult the black's efforts to organize rebellions. Rebellions, and conspiracies to rebel, were organized nevertheless. In 1739, for instance, seventy-five people of both races were killed in one uprising, and in 1741, New York City experienced a panic with racial overtones "which, for cruelty and sheer terror, surpassed the Salem witch-hunt" (Morison 1972:207). The panic started after some fires broke out and ended with the burning of thirteen black people and the hanging of eighteen blacks and four whites.

During the nineteenth century, many free black people participated actively in the abolitionist movement and the work of the Underground Railroad. Men like David Walker, Martin Delany, and Frederick Douglass issued ringing denunciations of slavery and encouraged black slaves to resist and, if possible, to escape. Women such as Sojourner Truth and Harriet Tubman also became famous as abolitionists. Tubman, "The Moses of Her People," is reported to have made nineteen trips to the South and to have assisted 200 to 300 slaves to escape (Frazier 1957:98; Burner, Fox-Genovese, and Bernhard 1991:402). Since the operations of the Railroad were conducted with the utmost secrecy, the exact number of slaves whose escape was aided is unknown. Some authorities believe, however, that between 1810 and 1860 the South may have lost as many as 100,000 slaves in this way (Franklin and Moss 1988:172). It is certain that the number had swelled during those years to such proportions that southern politicians demanded strong federal legislation to help stem the flow. In 1850, a strict Fugitive Slave Law was passed as a part of a larger congressional compromise concerning slavery. This law required citizens of the northern states to return fugitive slaves to their owners. It also placed many free blacks in the North in danger of being kidnapped or falsely accused as runaways, leading abolitionists to refer to the act as the "Man-Stealing Law" (Ducas 1970:112–113).

Despite these efforts and the often cruel punishment of those involved in such plots, at least two hundred insurrections, and possibly as many as twelve hundred, were planned between 1664 and 1860 (Jacobs and Landau 1971:100), and at least fifteen were actually carried out (Davie 1949:44). At least fourteen others were on the verge of erupting at the time they were discovered, although none of the revolts was very large or successful.

Three uprisings during the nineteenth century attracted widespread attention. The first of these was led in 1800 by Gabriel Prosser, a slave who worked as a blacksmith in the vicinity of Richmond, Virginia. This man apparently used Biblical quotations to persuade other slaves that their situation was similar to that of the Israelites under the pharoahs and that God would help them to gain their freedom (Bardolph 1961:35). Although many slaves were involved in Gabriel's insurrection plan, a torrential rain and the betrayal of the conspiracy by two slaves brought the effort to a quick end. Gabriel was captured and hanged.

A second notable slave insurrection was organized in 1822 by Denmark Vesey in Charleston, South Carolina. Vesey had been permitted to purchase his freedom in 1800 and, therefore, had had the opportunity to move about and to gain a knowledge of current events. For instance, he apparently knew something about the French Revolution and the successful slave revolt in Haiti. He used this information to inspire the slaves he contacted to organize and rebel. Whenever he observed slaves behaving subserviently toward whites, he would chide them. Vesey's conspiracy was revealed by a loyal house slave, and the authorities arrested

136 of its leaders (Ducas 1970:108). Vesey and thirty-four others were hanged; the remainder were deported from the United States.

The most famous uprising was led by Nat Turner in 1831 in Virginia. Unlike Vesey, Turner was not free, nor was he a careful planner. His approach to insurrection was mystical. He claimed to hear voices from heaven and to be "called" to free his people. The revolt began when Turner and a handful of followers killed all the whites in his master's household. After that, the group moved from place to place, killing a total of fifty-five white men, women, and children. Local whites and the state militia quickly scattered Turner's band. After a six-week search, he was captured and later hanged.[1]

The willingness of slaves to protest their treatment increased with the onset of the Civil War. White southerners became ever more fearful that the slaves, especially the field hands, would rebel. A number of additional steps were taken to control them. For instance, the patrol laws were strengthened, slave rations and supplies were increased, and picket lines were doubled to discourage escape attempts. But as the Union Army invaded various portions of the Confederacy, and as the prospects increased that the slaves in those areas would soon be freed, many of them were encouraged to raise objections to the way they were treated. According to Davie (1949:45), many slaves refused to accept punishment, were insolent to their masters, frequently assaulted whites, informed for the Union armies, and joined the Union armies as recruits. As the plantation system approached its zenith, the masters' control methods were "fine-tuned." On the legal side, the system became more precise and rigid than ever before, although on the interpersonal side the masters may well have exhibited more of the legendary paternal concern than in previous periods.

The second interpretation to be considered here was presented by Elkins. In his view, the resistance of the black slaves in the United States was less than one would have expected because the U.S. slave system was even more oppressive than slave systems usually are. Elkins (1968:52–80) compared American and Latin American slavery and argued there were some important differences between them. In the United States, slavery gradually became much more precise, definite, all-inclusive, and severe than in Latin America. In the United States, black people were presumed to be slaves unless proven otherwise, and the term of servitude was for life. Also, in the United States, marriages between slaves, even when conducted by ministers, were not legally binding. Furthermore, in the United States, slave masters had the power of life and death over slaves. None of this is meant to suggest that a slave's life in Latin America was easy. Elkins did argue, though, that slaves in Latin America could more easily become free and, once free, were more easily accepted into the dominant society. Social distinctions based on color did not become as sharp as they did in the United States. For example, in modern Brazil residential segregation by color exists but "By U.S. standards . . . is generally moderate" (Telles 1992:194).

Elkins maintained that the differences between American and Latin American slavery arose because the quest for profit in the latter was restrained by the power of the church and the state. This restraint enabled the black slaves of Latin America to maintain an essentially human status. In the United States, the slave experience was so shocking, so total, so brutal, that it not only stripped away traditions, but also reduced the slaves personally as well as legally to a subhuman condition.

Elkins pursued this thesis in a fascinating way. He suggested that the American system of slave control resembled the total control of the twentieth-century concentration camp. Just as prisoners who are exposed to absolute power in concentration camps become psychologically debilitated, docile, and childlike, African American slaves also experienced profound personality disintegration. The psychological effects of slavery, indeed, afford a realistic underpinning for the so-called "Sambo" stereotype of the slave. This image of the typical personality of the black slave assumes he or she "was docile but irresponsible, loyal but lazy, humble but chronically given to lying and stealing" (Elkins 1968:82).

This explanation not only appears to account for many of the facts of African American slavery but (as we note again later) also is congruent with some arguments that some of the modern problems of African Americans may be traced to the continuing effects of slavery. It is not settled, however, that African American slaves were as genuinely submissive as Elkins suggested, nor that slavery of Africans in America was worse than any other kind. Mintz (1969:30–31), for instance, pointed out that during its earliest and latest periods, Spanish slavery in the West Indies was at least as bad as American slavery. Patterson (1977:415) also considered it an error to believe that American slavery was especially pernicious. He argued that the "Sambo" personality type may be found among slaves of any time or place.[2]

Probably the most startling and controversial attack on Elkins's thesis (and the third viewpoint to be considered here) was presented by Fogel and Engerman (1974), whose analysis has, so to speak, stood Elkins on his head. Instead of viewing the slave system as purely repressive and psychologically destructive, Fogel and Engerman assembled evidence to show that the masters used the carrot as well as the stick, that they made many efforts to reward the slaves whose personal and family behavior followed the dominant pattern and who worked diligently to help make the farm or plantation prosper. The result of the masters' efforts to motivate the slaves more by rewards than by punishments, claimed Fogel and Engerman, was that the typical slave was a vigorous and productive worker. They were not at all the "Sambos" portrayed by traditional historians and folklore (Fogel and Engerman 1974:231). Rather, because the masters gave careful attention to such matters as slave management, diet, family stability, bonuses, and promotions, the slaves were much more efficient workers than either northern farm workers or free southern laborers (Fogel and Engerman 1974:192–209). Instead of being "Sambo," the slave laborer became the type of well-motivated worker portrayed in the books of Horatio Alger (Gutman 1975:165). From this perspective, the problems experienced by modern African Americans cannot be explained as a continuation of the damage done to their personalities and families during the ordeal of slavery.

Even though the interpretations of Elkins and of Fogel and Engerman reach opposing conclusions concerning the effects of slavery on the motives and actions of the slaves, both interpretations have been attacked by advocates of a fourth interpretation. In the opinion of Gutman, for example, despite their many differences, the approaches of Elkins and of Fogel and Engerman share a common flaw. Both see the slaves essentially as passive beings who can only have been what the master class wanted them to be. As Gutman (1975:166) stated, "Sambo and the slave Horatio Alger are very different men. But the model which has created the archetypal enslaved Afro-American remains the same. In both models, the enslaved are 'made over' by their owners."

In contrast to the views that portray the beliefs and behaviors of slaves purely as reactions to the requirements of the masters, Gutman stressed the active role played by the slaves in charting their own course despite the heavy restrictions placed on them by the masters. Ralph Ellison (1964:316) encapsulated this view as follows: "Are American Negroes simply the creation of white men, or have they at least helped to create themselves out of what they found around them? Men have made a way of life in caves and upon cliffs, why cannot Negroes have made a life upon the horns of the white men's dilemma?"[3]

The simplified description we have presented of different interpretations of black slavery focused only on the central thrust of the system for the oppressed group. In fact, however, the system had many different effects, and the debate concerning it has ranged over a very broad spectrum of issues. Of special importance has been the analysis of the effects of slavery on the black family, to which we return later in the chapter.

Immigrant or Colonized Minority?

The experience of black people in America up to the time of the Civil War resembled, in some respects, that of both an immigrant and a colonized minority. They were an "immigrant" minority in the sense that they had traveled from their native lands and entered the host American society as members of a subordinate group; unlike European immigrants, however, their subordinate position was not regarded as something temporary, something to be left behind as the process of assimilation worked its magic. As Philpott (1978:117) stated, "The process of arrival and adjustment was harsh and bitter for everyone . . . but only blacks suffered the special strains of contending with the color line." Blacks also resembled a "colonized" minority in the sense that they had been physically "conquered" and, subsequently, had not been accepted as suitable candidates for full membership in the society of the conquerors. But they were not a conquered people in their own land. The very structure of the relations between the native, dominant whites and the "immigrant" but enslaved Africans was such that neither the immigrant nor the colonial perspective seems completely applicable.

Although some black people became highly assimilated culturally during the slave period, they were very unusual. The majority of blacks, and especially slaves, were deliberately kept from learning any more of white people's ways than was absolutely necessary. At the same time, and partly as a result, little structural assimilation occurred during the long ordeal of slavery. Even free blacks were subject to a high degree of discrimination and were not readily accepted into the mainstream of American institutional life.[4] On the other hand, the classical solution of the colonized minority's dilemma—throwing the invaders out—was hardly possible; however, the goal of ending the domination of the whites by leaving the United States and, perhaps, returning to Africa was the subject of serious discussion and concrete actions.

The most notable example of a secessionist solution to the "Negro problem" during this period began in 1816 when the American Colonization Society was founded. This organization was founded primarily to assist free blacks in leaving the United States. It was supported by some blacks and by many whites who feared the free blacks would spread unrest among the slaves. In 1822, the American Colonization Society established a colony for free blacks on the West Coast of Africa. In 1824, the colony was named Liberia, and the main settlement, Monrovia, was established. The colony grew slowly during the next twenty-five years and, in 1847, was declared a republic.

Although Liberia still exists today as the second oldest black republic in the world (after Haiti), the return of African Americans to this African state was not successful as a solution to American race problems. First, fewer than three thousand colonists from America were present in the colony at the time it became a republic. Second, some influential black leaders in America—even some, like Martin Delany (1971), who favored some kind of separatist solution—did not support the Liberian experiment.

While neither an assimilationist nor a colonialist interpretation seems truly congruent with the situation of blacks in America before the Civil War, it seems clear that the essential character of the relations between the races during that period is most nearly captured by the colonialist view. For example, even if it were granted that the relations between blacks and whites in most instances were basically humane and mutually considerate, it still is true that the blacks (whether slave or free) were not on the road to full assimilation. Among the slaves whose ancestors had arrived during the colonial period, many more than three generations had passed, but the black experience up to the Civil War was in no important respect comparable to that of the colonial Dutch, Irish, or Germans. On the other hand, one can find significant parallels between the condition of the blacks and the Indians. Both peoples had been subjected to a tremendous cultural shock. Their customary ways of living had been shattered. Their primary choices in life were reduced to extreme subordination, annihilation, or flight. As Blauner (1972:54) asserted, "Whether oppression takes place at home in the oppressed's native land or in the heart of the colonizer's mother country, colonization remains colonization."[5]

The relative superiority of the colonialist interpretation of the antebellum period does not assure us, however, that it is the proper tool for analyzing events in the twentieth century. That question must wait until we have reviewed the major features of the black experience in America since the Civil War.

Emancipation and Reconstruction

As the Civil War approached, the popularity of abolishing slavery waned. Lincoln himself favored deportation as a solution to the "Negro problem," and even after the war was underway, he stated clearly that his main purpose in fighting it was to save the Union rather than to affect the status of slavery. Some time passed before he was convinced that freeing the slaves was essential if the southern rebellion was to be crushed. Moreover, many people in the North shared the opinion of white southerners that black people were naturally suited to servitude and should not be encouraged to seek equality. This opinion was sufficiently common during the early years of the war that northern officers were generally unwilling to accept blacks as soldiers. There were even reports of northern officers who returned runaway slaves to their southern masters! This situation was altered, however, when Lincoln issued the Emancipation Proclamation on January 1, 1863. Among other things, the order proclaimed the southern slaves to be free and authorized the armed forces of the United States to enlist freedmen. Black regiments from Massachusetts, New York, and Pennsylvania were soon organized, and when the North began to draft military recruits, blacks were included. Altogether, around 180,000 African Americans fought against the Confederacy, winning fourteen Congressional Medals of Honor (Butler 1991:199). But, as usual, the inclusion of blacks did not mean they were treated equally. They did not at first receive the same pay as the white troops, and white officers were embarrassed to be assigned to command them.

By the end of the war, a Freedmen's Bureau had been established to assist all former slaves to assume their new status as free people (Franklin and Moss 1988:208–210). There were between 3.5 and 4 million freed slaves, and most of them had no way to earn a living (Davie 1949:21). In addition to the sheer size of the task, the bureau labored under constant criticism. Nevertheless, until it expired in 1872, the bureau made a substantial contribution to the welfare of the former slaves and to many white people as well.

The task of providing for the freed slaves, however, was only a part of the broader task of rebuilding or reconstructing the economic and political systems of the South. The outcome of the war had determined that the federal government was supreme, but it had not determined what the status of the defeated Confederate states would be. In President Lincoln's view, the southern states had never really left the Union; therefore, they continued to exist as states and the job of reintegrating them did not require massive reorganization. His Proclamation of Amnesty and Reconstruction in 1863 offered a pardon to nearly all southerners who would pledge allegiance to the United States and agree to support the abolition of slavery.

Lincoln's ideas concerning Reconstruction were bitterly opposed by a group of Republican leaders in Congress, the so-called Radical Republicans. This group argued that the southern states had committed suicide, so to speak, and should be forced to meet stiff requirements to be readmitted to the Union on an equal footing with the loyal states. They also argued that the seceded states should have the status of a conquered province and come under the jurisdiction of Congress.

After the assassination of President Lincoln in 1865, President Andrew Johnson adopted a Reconstruction plan similar to Lincoln's. On the basis of this plan, Johnson quickly recognized the governments of Louisiana, Arkansas, Tennessee, and Virginia. By the end of 1865, the Thirteenth Amendment had been ratified, all of the Confederate states had been recognized by the president, and all except Texas had held conventions and elected representatives and senators to Congress. In only a few months, President Johnson apparently had achieved the political restoration of the South. But some new southern laws, called "Black Codes," severely restricted the rights of blacks, and these laws gave the Radical Republicans the political leverage they needed to fight the president's program (Franklin and Moss 1988:206).[6] They led the fight to pass the Civil Rights Act of 1866.

This law, based on the Thirteenth Amendment and passed over Johnson's veto, declared blacks to be citizens of the United States, gave them equal civil rights, and gave the federal courts jurisdiction over cases arising under the act (Faulkner 1948:401). Soon after this, Congress approved the Fourteenth Amendment and four sweeping Reconstruction bills. The governments of the South were declared illegal, and the states themselves were divided into five military districts. The general in charge of each district was ordered to hold new elections in which the freed slaves could participate equally. The new state legislatures created by these elections were to write new constitutions to ensure all citizens the right to vote. An acceptable constitution and the approval of the Fourteenth Amendment were required for the readmission of a state to the Union. By 1870, these conditions had been met by all eleven former Confederate states, and they were again represented in Congress.

Congressional Reconstruction infuriated the members of the old planter class and nurtured a hatred that has been slow to die. In the elections creating the Reconstruction legislatures, 703,400 black and 660,000 white voters were registered (Franklin 1961:80); for the first time, black legislators were elected to public office. Among the whites, many who were elected were "carpetbaggers" from the North and "scalawags" (Union loyalists) from the South. The composition of these conventions and the widespread bribery, fraud, and theft that became common in the governments established by them led quickly to charges that "Negro-carpetbag-scalawag" rule was the result of a "conspiracy to degrade and destroy the Southern way of life" (Franklin 1961:103). Such charges ignore certain pertinent facts. In regard to composition, only in South Carolina did black legislators outnumber whites, and only in Mississippi and Virginia did northern whites outnumber southern whites (Franklin 1961:102). In regard to honesty, the graft and corruption emerging in the southern Reconstruction governments was often small by comparison with that occurring in the North during this same period. In Franklin's (1961:151) opinion, "the tragedy of public immorality in the Southern states was only part of a national tragedy." It should be said also that despite the unfavorable conditions under which they labored, the Reconstruction governments succeeded to some extent in placing political power in the hands of the common people. For the first time, many poor whites were able to vote and to participate directly in the affairs of government.

Many blacks soon began to express the new freedoms granted by the Emancipation Proclamation, the Civil Rights Act, and the Reconstruction acts. The assertion of their rights violated the traditional "etiquette of race relations" that symbolized and helped to maintain the whites' position of dominance. Whites were further provoked to untold instances of retaliation against blacks by the fact that blacks were now competing directly with them for jobs.

The whites also developed direct, organized, secret methods to intimidate and punish blacks who attempted to exercise their new rights. The most spectacular of the organizations attempting to force blacks back into their traditional servile position and, simultaneously, to restore political power to the whites was the Ku Klux Klan, formed in 1866.[7] The initial purpose of this organization was to provide amusement to white gentlemen, but it was soon discovered that the Klan's peculiar costume and symbols could be used to frighten many of the blacks. Accordingly, the Klan's purpose soon became the destruction of the Reconstruction governments and the return of black people to their traditional subordinate status. The main tactics of the Klan involved mysterious incantations, cross burnings, and somber warnings delivered in full costume at night. But when these methods seemed insufficient, house burnings, floggings, and murder were added. The Klan quickly became a convenient "cover" for anyone (whether members or not) who wished to punish or intimidate black people. Such tactics were so effective that black people soon found it expedient to show no interest whatever in political matters. They found it was safer to proclaim that politics was "white man's business." This protective reaction, adopted during the Reconstruction period, was to last for many decades.

As the Klan's campaign against blacks became increasingly terrorist, some states and the federal government passed anti-Klan laws. Even some members deplored the violence and felt that things had gotten out of hand. But the efforts to control the violence against blacks and to prevent intimidation were not successful.

The repressive methods of the Klan became somewhat less common as the whites found other ways to regain control of the state governments. For example, with the closing of the Freedmen's Bureau, blacks lost an important source of economic aid and, thereby, became more dependent on local landowners for assistance. When political privileges were restored to the Confederate veterans and the Supreme Court struck down some portions of the laws designed to enforce Congressional Reconstruction, the whites were aided in reestablishing political control. The Democratic Party became the main instrument for the "redemption" of the South, ensuring for decades that the southern states would vote "solidly" in that party's column. The disputed presidential election of 1876 led in 1877 to the complete withdrawal of federal troops and the end of Reconstruction.

The Restoration of White Supremacy

Race relations in the South had been dramatically and irrevocably altered by war, emancipation, defeat, and Reconstruction. The successful campaign of the old planter class, with the aid of poor whites and many business people, to end Radical Republican Reconstruction and recapture political control of the South did not put everything back into its prewar place. It is true that in many cases the freed slaves returned to their original plantations as laborers or tenants. In such cases, the old master-slave relationship was hardly altered. Even in such cases, though, neither whites nor blacks could forget that the latter had openly challenged white dominance during the Reconstruction years. Neither could they ignore the fact that blacks were now free to move about and, where possible, to sell their labor in the open market. Having succeeded in recapturing the state governments and bringing about the withdrawal of federal troops, the whites wished to reestablish fully their dominance over blacks; as a part of this effort, they insisted the racial problem was a southern problem that should be resolved by southerners without "interference." The northerners, in turn, had been left in a state of exhaustion by the efforts that had gone into assuring the freedom and civil rights of blacks. Their general response to the white southerner's demands to be given a free hand, therefore, was to "wink and look the other way."

The economic and legal weapons used by the whites to return the blacks as nearly as possible to a condition of slavery are of considerable interest. On the economic side, there developed a new system of agricultural production that reduced many blacks to a state resembling slavery. On the legal side, the folkways of southern race relations were extended and enforced by law to include almost every aspect of race relations.

The planters still retained most of the productive land, but they generally were bankrupt. They had lost their slaves without compensation and generally were unable to pay wages for labor. These circumstances gave rise to a new system of agriculture to replace the old plantation system. The new system worked in the following way. Banks and other lenders advanced money to the planters for a certain (usually large) share of the planter's next crop. The planters, in turn, advanced money and supplies to tenants for a certain share (also usually large) of their portion of the next crop. This system of crop sharing by tenants and landowners had a number of consequences. While it did permit the South's agricultural economy to resume production, it created a vicious circle of borrowing and indebtedness. Because cotton was the cash crop in greatest demand, this method of financing also led to the overproduction of cotton and the rapid depletion of the soil's nutrients. Each of these elements helped to drive large numbers of landowners out of business. Large numbers of tenants and owners no longer could earn a living in agriculture and were, thereby, forced to migrate to the cities (Davie 1949:63–67).

The tenancy and "sharecropping" system worked to the disadvantage of practically everyone but the lenders, but the greatest disadvantage was to the black tenants. Many white landowners did not make public exact records of the amounts they received for their crops or the amounts of credit they had extended to their tenants for food, clothing, and supplies during a given year. Since many tenants could neither read nor write, they had no effective way to challenge the owner's statement of what they were entitled to from the sale of the crop or what they owed the owner for supplies. Moreover, black tenants soon learned they were in no position to insist that they be given an accurate statement of their earnings and debts. For a black person even to hint that he or she was being cheated by a white was regarded by the whites as the height of insolence and was sure to be punished; consequently, the tenants could do little or nothing when they learned, after the sale of the crops, that their backbreaking labor was to be rewarded by an increase in their debt. The tenants, especially the black tenants, were kept by these devices in a condition of peonage hardly better than the slavery from which they presumably had recently escaped.

The process of lowering the social standing of blacks from the pinnacle reached during Reconstruction involved legal as well as economic weapons. The primary areas of conflict for many years were the right to vote and segregation in public transportation. Following the Civil War, many railroad and steamship lines refused to permit blacks to purchase first-class accommodations. And as a part of the Black Codes regulating the movements and privileges of the freedmen, Mississippi, Florida, and Texas each passed laws restricting the use of first-class railroad cars by blacks (Woodward 1957:xiv–xv). The laws were the first of many Jim Crow laws passed by southern legislatures to segregate blacks from whites. When the Lincoln-Johnson governments in the South were overturned and the congressional Reconstruction governments were established, these first Jim Crow laws were repealed. But as the quest to reestablish white supremacy grew, Jim Crow legislation began to reappear. At first, only the right to vote and to use public transportation were very much affected. In time, however, every aspect of life—schooling, housing, religion, jobs, the courts, recreation, health care, and so on—was included.

The repeal of the first Jim Crow laws did not reflect the sentiment of most southern whites and did not mean that they were ready to accept racial equality in "social" matters. Even before the end of the Reconstruction period, in fact, both the churches and the schools had become almost completely segregated without any legislation whatever. Although the whites gave indications they intended to keep the races largely apart, the end of Reconstruction did not herald an all-out legislative campaign to reenslave blacks. Numerous observers of the situation in the South during the years immediately following the end of Reconstruction were surprised to see many instances in which black people received equal treatment in public places (Woodward 1957:16–26). Nevertheless, the influence of those who favored the complete segregation of blacks in every sphere of life increased each year. Interracial violence was extremely common. And, increasingly, the whites—especially those of the lower or "cracker" class—sought to prevent blacks from participating in elections. Also during this period, the rate at which blacks were being lynched by whites began to rise dramatically (Frazier 1957:160).

Gradually, the pressure mounted to separate the races in every way, to disfranchise blacks, and to place them in a position of complete subordination. The campaign to bring these results about generally centered on the right of blacks to vote and on segregation in public transportation. To prevent blacks from voting, it was necessary to devise a scheme that would circumvent the Fifteenth Amendment. In 1890, Mississippi set the trend by enacting provisions in its constitution that created certain requirements for voters. During the succeeding twenty-five years, all of the old Confederate states changed their constitutions or their laws to reduce the number of blacks who voted. The methods employed relied on three main ideas, usually used in combination.

In some states, voters were required to pass "literacy" tests or to be property holders. In some states, the voters were required to pay a poll tax, usually months in advance of an election. And in some states, the procedure for nominating people to office was restricted to whites (the white primary) on the ground that the nominations were not elections and were, therefore, a "private" matter. These qualifications also had a deterrent effect on many white voters; however, several loopholes in the laws were created to decrease their effects on whites. For instance, to meet the literacy test, a person might be required to show an "understanding" of some portion of the federal or state constitution. Since white officials were in charge of these "tests" and decided who passed, only black people were ever found to be "illiterate" and to be unqualified to vote.

Another technique to permit whites only to evade the other voter qualifications was the notorious "grandfather clause." Under one type of grandfather clause, people could qualify as voters only if their ancestors had been eligible to vote in 1860 (Frazier 1957:157). Since practically no southern blacks could meet this type of test, and many whites could, a grandfather clause disqualified many more blacks than whites. Some idea of the efficiency of these methods may be seen from the records in Louisiana. In 1896, there were over 130,000 black voters in that state; in 1904, there were less than 1,400 (Lawson 1976:14–15; Woodward 1957:68).

The other main focus of the segregationists' efforts—public transportation—led to a momentous decision by the U.S. Supreme Court affecting the civil rights of all Americans. In 1890, Louisiana passed a law requiring separate rail car facilities for whites and blacks. The law stated that "all railway companies carrying passengers . . . in this state shall provide equal but separate accommodations for the white and colored races" (Tussman 1963:65). Under the law, whites and blacks were not permitted to sit together in a coach or a section of a coach. Criminal charges could be filed for a violation of the law.

In 1896, this law was challenged in the Supreme Court in the famous "separate but equal" case *Plessy v. Ferguson*. Plessy, who was stated to be "seven-eighths caucasian," had been ordered to leave a coach assigned to members of the white race and had refused to comply. He had been arrested and jailed for violating the law. The main legal point in Plessy's case was that he had been deprived of his rights under the Fourteenth Amendment to the Constitution. The majority of the Court argued that even though the amendment was intended to achieve the absolute equality of the races, neither the amendment nor any other law could abolish social distinctions based on color.

The majority opinion was eloquently challenged by Justice Harlan, who argued there were two main reasons for declaring the Louisiana law unconstitutional. First, in his opinion, it violated the personal freedoms of all of the people of Louisiana. It was the purpose of the Thirteenth, Fourteenth, and Fifteenth amendments to make the Constitution colorblind and to remove the race line from the American system of government. But if the logic of the Court's majority were accepted, the possibility would be opened for the states to regulate the relations of the races far beyond the sphere of public transportation. For example, if a state may prescribe separate railway coaches, then it may also insist that whites and blacks must walk on opposite sides of the street or sit on opposite sides of the courtroom or be segregated in public meetings. By this reasoning, Justice Harlan pointed out, the state could require the separation in railway coaches of Protestant and Catholic passengers or of native and naturalized citizens.

Justice Harlan also believed that, in the long run, the decision would stimulate racial resentment and hatred. The real meaning of the Louisiana law, he argued, is that whites consider blacks to be so inferior that it is degrading to mingle with them in any way. The statute was not intended to guarantee that blacks would not be forced to associate with whites but that whites would not be forced to associate with blacks. Such an approach to race relations is a serious mistake, Harlan believed. "The destinies of the two races in this country," he wrote, "are indissolubly linked together, and the interests of both require that the common government of all shall not permit the seeds of race hate to be planted under the sanction of law" (Tussman 1963:81). The result of attempting to segregate the races by law would be to ensure that racial conflict would continue and be a threat to the security of both races.

Harlan's fear that the result of *Plessy* would be the extension of racial segregation not only in railroad coaches but in many other spheres of life was clearly justified. Within three years, every southern state had adopted a law segregating the races aboard trains. By 1910, most of the same states had extended segregation to include the waiting rooms in railway stations; by 1920, racial segregation in the South (and a few adjoining states) had become the normal practice in almost every public matter. In time, signs proclaiming "whites only" or "colored" were displayed at drinking fountains, restrooms, theaters, swimming pools, libraries, public telephones, bathing beaches, hospital entrances, restaurants, and so on. In many instances, the laws regulating the permissible behavior of the members of the two races stated exactly, in feet and inches, how far apart their separate entrances into public buildings or places of amusement must be and how close together they were allowed to sit or stand. Of course, in all of these situations, the separate facilities for blacks were supposed to be equal to those for the whites. In fact, this was almost never the case. In only a few short years, the white southerners had succeeded by law in creating a caste system similar to the one in India. All black people, regardless of their attainments or personal qualities, were beneath all white people. Once again, as in the period of slavery, the black people had no rights the white people were bound to respect.

In some ways, the Jim Crow system that emerged after 1890 was an even more efficient instrument of subordination than slavery had been. It is true that blacks under Jim Crow were no longer legally the property of the whites, but it is also true that the whites no longer had as strong an incentive to be concerned about the welfare of blacks. Under slavery, at least some of the blacks were in close daily contact with some of the whites, and those contacts were frequently friendly and compassionate (though it is easy to exaggerate this). The Jim Crow system made many forms of friendly and understanding contacts between the races practically impossible. Residential segregation *increased* as the Jim Crow system became more pervasive. Blacks increasingly were pressured into slum "darktown" or ghetto areas occupied solely by blacks.

In some ways, the system of enforced racial segregation also may have been as difficult to bear psychologically as slavery had been. During the period of slavery, a major source of emotional sustenance for blacks was the hope, however faint, that someday they might be free, that laws would be enacted to release them from bondage, to give them full legal standing and civil rights. Emancipation, the Thirteenth, Fourteenth, and Fifteenth Amendments, and Reconstruction all seemed to fulfill this dim and ancient hope. For nearly three decades, there was some reason to believe that these legal changes were going to be substantially effective. Black people voted, were elected to office, moved about fairly freely, mingled with whites in public places, and owned property. Interracial conflicts and violence were present throughout the period, to be sure, but formal slavery had been irrevocably abolished. It did not seem that most whites actually wished to reestablish white supremacy or that they would be able to do so if they tried. Gradually, however, the majority of whites, north as well as south of the Mason-Dixon line, lost interest in the struggle to ensure that the changes effected by the Civil War would be thoroughgoing and permanent. The Supreme Court's decision in *Plessy* cleared the way for the rise of Jim Crowism and the virtual reenslavement of black people in many southern and adjoining states. Although under the Jim Crow system black people still retained significant freedoms, such as the right to attend schools (albeit inferior ones) and to own property, the laws permitted under *Plessy* had practically neutralized the *intent* of the post-Civil War amendments to the Constitution.

We should note in passing that although legal segregation, with only a few exceptions, was established primarily in the South and in some border states, many forms of racial discrimination, including some segregation, occurred in other parts of the country. Even in states that had enacted special civil rights laws attempting to guarantee the rights contained in the Constitution, many discriminatory practices existed. For example, hotels were suddenly "filled" when black guests tried to register, or theaters were "sold out" when black patrons arrived. Cases have been reported in which blacks were served "doctored" foods in restaurants to discourage them from returning (Davie 1949:290). Moreover, socially enforced residential segregation, as we note next, became the rule throughout the United States.

Nevertheless, the Jim Crow laws of the southern states helped create and strengthen a system of racial discrimination that went far beyond the extralegal discrimination that has been prevalent in many parts of the United States.

Migration, Urbanization, and Employment

Immediately after the Civil War, some black people began to exercise their new freedom to move about. At first, this movement took place almost entirely in the South and consisted primarily of migration from the Atlantic seaboard to the more westerly states of the South and from rural areas into the cities. For instance, the number of blacks in Kansas increased from seventeen thousand in 1870 to forty-three thousand in 1880 (Farley and Allen 1987:110) while in the previous decade, the black population of fourteen southern cities had increased by roughly 90 percent (Frazier 1957:190). Many social and economic forces favoring migration out of the South were at work. As we have seen already, the newly created Jim Crow system reduced the black masses to second-class citizenship, and this legal attack was accompanied by economic woes. In the rural areas, crop failures, the boll weevil, and soil depletion were crippling the cotton industry. In the cities, many jobs that traditionally had been "Negro jobs" either were being displaced by machines or were being taken over by whites. At the same time these "push" factors were operating in the South, the "pull" factors in the North were comparatively weak. For example, despite the need for labor in the industrializing areas, and despite the general hostility of employers toward foreign laborers, the hostility of both white northern workers and their employers against black workers was even greater (Lieberson 1980:5, 383).[8] Moreover, both federal immigration policies and the desires of southern leaders to maintain a cheap labor pool conspired to make it difficult for blacks to take advantage of any opportunities that might have awaited them in the North (Farley and Allen 1987:110–112).

Conditions in the North changed sharply, however, with the outbreak of World War I. The war suddenly halted the supply of cheap labor that had been provided by European immigration, and it was stopped just at a time when the demand for labor to produce war materials was rising. Northern employers looked to the South for a new supply of cheap labor, and during the period 1910–1920 more than a half-million black people headed north (Farley and Allen 1987:113).[9] This movement is of special interest not only because it was the largest mass migration of blacks from the South up to that time, but also because it originated mainly in the Deep South rather than in the border states. Most of the migrants sought jobs in New York, Chicago, Philadelphia, and Detroit. The black population of these cities increased during the decade by nearly 750,000 (Frazier 1957:191). The newcomers found jobs in iron and steel mills, automobile construction, chemical plants, and other industrial settings. They received much higher wages than they were accustomed to in the South, and northern employers, for the most part, found them to be competent and easier to work with than immigrant laborers from foreign countries.

The urbanization of blacks in the cities of the North, though greatly aided by industrial jobs and high wages, was hindered by the prejudice and discrimination of whites. In the workplace, whites struggled to prevent blacks from gaining union membership and the better training and jobs that accompanied such membership. In the broader community, whites fought to force blacks into segregated neighborhoods. Prior to this time, blacks, along with other poor people, had been concentrated in areas of low-rent housing, but if they wished to and could afford it blacks were able to live in various parts of the cities. Now, however, real estate agents catered to the preferences of whites and "steered" black customers into all-black neighborhoods (Farley and Allen 1987:136–137). Increasingly, cities passed laws requiring blacks and whites to live in segregated areas, and in some places—conspicuously in East St. Louis and Chicago—bloody attacks on black people took place (Farley and Allen 1987:115).[10]

Just as the great migration of Mexicans into the United States in the twentieth century has caused many observers to believe the immigrant model applies to them, the great migration of African Americans to the North has been compared to the European immigrations. From this perspective, although African Americans have been physically present in the United States for centuries, their entry into the American industrial economy as "immigrants" actually has been underway for only three generations; hence, even though their experience up to the time of World War I may properly be characterized as colonial, their experience since that time increasingly has been that of recent immigrants (Kristol 1972).

The end of World War I and the onset of the Depression years of the 1920s and 1930s greatly reduced the migration of southern blacks to the North and West, but the movement was by no means stopped. The black population of these regions continued to rise throughout the period, and at a much faster rate than in the South. For example, from 1920 to 1940, over twice as many blacks left the South as had departed during the period 1910–1920, while the black population of the South rose only slightly (Farley and Allen 1987:113).

The next great surge of black migration accompanied World War II. As in the case of World War I, many African Americans moved to the war plants in the cities of the North and West. Again, Chicago, Detroit, New York, and Philadelphia received large numbers of these migrants. By this time, however, the South also had become far more industrialized than previously; so many migrating blacks moved to southern cities, such as Birmingham, Houston, Norfolk, and New Orleans. And for the first time, western cities, such as Los Angeles, Portland, and San Diego, drew sizable numbers of blacks out of the South.

The favorite single destination for migrants was Harlem, in New York City. This African American community grew during the period under discussion into the largest urban black population in the world (Davie 1949:100). Although Jim Crow laws continued to dominate the lives of black southerners, many of their brothers had escaped to other regions of the country, had learned to live in cities, and were working in industrial occupations. These migrants were still subjected to many types of informal, extralegal discrimination. Nevertheless, northern blacks enjoyed a greater degree of formal and legal equality, and this legal advantage afforded a basis from which to launch an energetic, if excruciatingly slow, judicial and legislative offensive against all forms of discrimination affecting blacks and—by extension—all other minority groups in America. This offensive, generally referred to as the Civil Rights Movement, may be dated from the period in which Jim Crowism was becoming established in America.

The Civil Rights Movement

Tuskegee and Niagara

The Supreme Court's decision in *Plessy v. Ferguson* marks the point at which black people in the South officially had lost the battle to retain most of the advantages won in the Civil War. As we noted, however, the decision in *Plessy* was not only a signal to the South that it might go ahead on a state-by-state basis to reduce African Americans to the position of second-class citizens, it also was a ratification of many changes that already had occurred in the relations between the races. The level of white violence against blacks had risen sharply, the doctrine of innate black inferiority was gaining in strength (as discussed in chapter 5), and many blacks feared that to continue open resistance to white supremacy was foolhardy. Even before *Plessy* made it official, therefore, black people had been forced into an inferior status, and some black leaders had concluded that the wisest course of action was to accept the fact that whites were not going to permit black equality, at least not in the short run. Many believed a better course of action was to declare publicly the willingness of blacks to stay in their "place," to attempt to "measure up" to white standards, and perhaps thereby to "win" white approval and acceptance.

The most influential statement of the view that blacks should accept a new accommodation with whites on the whites' terms was voiced by the black leader Booker T. Washington. Washington, the founder and principal of Tuskegee Institute, voiced his opinion on this subject in a speech at the Atlanta exposition of 1895. Washington's famous "Atlanta Compromise" was carefully designed to assure white people that blacks were ready to accept their inferior status in the political arena. He stated: "In all things that are purely social, we can be as separate as the fingers yet one as the hand in all things essential to mutual progress" (Washington 1959:156). He argued further that blacks were still too recently removed from slavery to take their place as equals among whites. He emphasized that blacks must adopt an economic program of manual labor and self-help as the best means to win their full rights as citizens, rather than engaging in political action. They must be content, he said, with the gradual achievement of recognition. The Atlanta speech implied that the "deficiencies" of black people, rather than the discrimination of whites, was responsible for the generally deplorable conditions among blacks. Washington advocated agricultural and industrial training rather than higher education for blacks. Needless to say, these views were very flattering to the whites and were immediately praised by them. It has been reported that many of the white people who heard Washington's speech leaped to their feet in a standing ovation, while many blacks in the audience sat silently weeping.

Washington became a celebrity almost overnight. Until his death twenty years later, he was the most influential and powerful speaker for black America. His views on race relations were central to the so-called Tuskeegee point of view, which stressed appeasement of the whites, segregation, and the importance of self-help. He presented both a program (the "gospel of wealth") and an organization (The National Negro Business League) to help attain it. At the center of his strategy was the development of black business enterprise and economic solidarity among blacks (Butler and Wilson 1988:136–137).

Washington's approach to the race question was widely accepted among blacks as well as whites, but its acceptance was not universal. For example, in 1902, Monroe Trotter (1971:35) attacked Washington as a "Benedict Arnold of the Negro race." In 1903, W. E. B. DuBois established himself as Washington's leading critic. DuBois, the holder of a Ph.D. degree from Harvard University, called Washington's teachings propaganda that was helping to speed the construction of a racial caste system. In 1905, a small group of black "radicals" under the leadership of DuBois formed the Niagara Movement to express opposition to Washington's program. They disagreed with him emphatically on many major issues. Their "Declaration of Principles" stated that black people should protest the curtailment of their political and civil rights. They pointed out that the denial of opportunities to blacks in the South amounted to "virtual slavery." And they proclaimed their refusal to accept the impression left by Washington and his followers "that the Negro American assents to inferiority, is submissive under oppression, and apologetic before insults." In contrast to Washington's strategy of political submission coupled with economic development, the members of the Niagara Movement insisted that agitation and complaint is the best way for blacks to escape the "barbarian" practices of discrimination based on race (Meier, Rudwick, and Broderick 1971:58–62).

Given the time at which it was made, the Niagara Declaration seemed very "radical." Jim Crowism was reaching full fruition. In the minds of most people, blacks as well as whites, the segregation of the races in the South would remain the "solution" to the race problem until blacks were able to "live up" to white standards and "earn" gradual acceptance as equals. It should be observed, though, that for all their differences the Washington "conservatives" and the DuBois "radicals" agreed that blacks should strive to establish economic independence, that they should join together to attempt to solve their problems, and that the ultimate goal of any strategy should be the full acceptance of African Americans as first-class citizens of the United States (Meier, Rudwick, and Broderick 1971:xxvi). They disagreed sharply on whether the proper means to the attainment of their ends should be humility, subservience, and patience or an aggressive, indignant demand for the immediate recognition of their rights.

The Niagara group was not large or immediately very influential, but its declaration revealed dramatically that not all blacks accepted Washington's policies. More important, however, is that, in 1909, most of the Niagara group's members merged with a group of white liberals to form the National Association for the Advancement of Colored People (NAACP). The NAACP was, in the words of a later report, "the spiritual descendant of the Abolitionist Movement" (Meier, Rudwick, and Broderick 1971:178). The leaders of the NAACP opposed "the ever-growing oppression," "the systematic persecution," and the disfranchisement of black people. They demanded that everyone, including blacks, be given free public schooling that would focus on professional education for the most gifted—what DuBois had earlier called "the talented tenth"—as well as industrial training for all who wished it; however, this goal could not be achieved unless blacks received equal treatment under the law. Consequently, the NAACP adopted a legal and legislative strategy. It called on Congress and the president to enforce strictly the Constitution's provisions on civil rights and the right to vote, and it urged that educational expenditures for black children be made equal to those for whites (Meier, Rudwick, and Broderick 1971:65–66).[11]

The NAACP soon began to make its presence felt. As editor of the organization's official magazine, *The Crisis,* DuBois was able to place his ideas before a large audience. In 1915, the organization's legal efforts helped to bring about a Supreme Court decision declaring the "grandfather clause" unconstitutional. After Booker T. Washington died later that year, the NAACP became the leading organization devoted to the civil rights of African Americans.

The acceptance of the NAACP by blacks, however, was never total. At the very time of its inception, in fact, certain events were forcing many blacks to conclude that no amount of legal action could guarantee them first-class citizenship. Although the recent black migrants to the cities were finding many new lines of work and receiving better pay than ever before, they soon discovered that the cities—even the northern cities—were not the promised land. In the North, there was competition between the races for jobs, housing, the use of public recreational facilities, and space for the establishment of business enterprises (Butler and Wilson 1988:152). In the South, blacks were hemmed in on every side by Jim Crow restrictions. As a result of these conditions, many cities became powderkegs of racial resentment and unrest.

Three types of interracial violence were prominent during this period. Lynchings, especially of blacks by whites, had been an important form of violence for several decades and was still a source of great concern. Although the actual number of lynchings was somewhat lower between 1910 and 1920 than in the two previous decades, the circumstances under which they occurred and the publicity they received led to more open and angry denunciations by black spokespersons than in the past. Many lynchings were conducted in an especially sadistic way and in a carnival atmosphere. Some victims were tortured and burned at the stake, and some newspapers issued invitations to whites to come to witness a lynching or a burning. Between "Emancipation and the Great Depression," according to Beck and Tolnay (1990:526), "about 3,000 blacks were lynched in the American south." Unsurprisingly, some militant black leaders advocated armed resistance as a solution to these problems (Franklin and Moss 1988:318–321; Meier, Rudwick, and Broderick 1971:96–98).

Another main form of violence during these years consisted of mob attacks by whites on the property of black people and on the people themselves. This type of violence was most common in the cities of the South. For the most part, in these outbreaks, blacks were unorganized and defenseless, but in some cases they fought back. For example, in 1921 between fifty and seventy-five armed blacks confronted a white mob of fifteen hundred to two thousand people in Tulsa, Oklahoma. In the conflict that followed, over fifty people died and "the entire section known as Black Wall Street—over one thousand homes and businesses—lay in ruins" (Butler and Wilson 1988:147). In several outbreaks in cities of the North, blacks also organized and retaliated against whites.

The summer following the end of World War I was filled with such a large number of mob attacks by whites, and so much blood was shed, that James Weldon Johnson (1968:304), head of the NAACP, referred to it as "the Red Summer." Approximately two dozen outbreaks occurred in American cities in the summer of 1919. Fourteen blacks were publicly burned, eleven of them alive (Lincoln 1961:56). These conflicts were of the type usually described as race "riots."

Two other points were of special significance at this time. First, the rise of white nativist sentiment was expressed in a revival of the Ku Klux Klan after a "slumber of half a century" (Osofsky 1968:314). Second, all of these things—lynchings, burnings, mob attacks by whites, race riots, and the Klan revival—had occurred during or immediately following a great war "to make the world safe for democracy." Between 350,000 and 400,000 African Americans had served during World War I. The inconsistency between the nation's lofty international ideals and the actual conditions at home was not lost on many blacks.

All of these elements combined following the war to give a large number of blacks a new sense of their racial identity, and this new awareness was accompanied by an upsurge in expressions of black pride. This "Black Renaissance" was visibly furthered by a group of writers and artists in Harlem. At the same time, many blacks were more convinced than ever before that the prospects of black people in America were very poor. Under these conditions, the legalistic approach of the NAACP did not seem sufficiently direct or vigorous to many blacks. The situation seemed to call for statements, plans, and actions that would effectively express the deeply felt anger of the black community and mobilize the community's efforts in relation to a common goal. In the minds of hundreds of thousands of African Americans, the program offered by a new leader, Marcus Garvey, seemed the answer to a prayer.

Separatism

Garvey, a dark-skinned man, was born in Jamaica in 1887. He came to the United States during World War I and organized the Universal Negro Improvement Association (UNIA). The UNIA's major long-range goal was to enable African Americans to leave the United States and settle in an independent nation in Africa. As Baker said, "Garvey's UNIA was an effort to have black Americans vote with their feet" (1970:8).

Somewhat ironically, Garvey's colonization program had been inspired by a reading of the "conservative" Booker T. Washington's *Up From Slavery*. Garvey admired Washington's emphasis on racial separation and self-help. His ideas concerning the eventual solution of America's racial problem, though, were radically different from Washington's. While Washington saw separation as a tool to be used to gain eventual acceptance by white Americans, Garvey visualized the renunciation of American citizenship and the permanent separation of the two races.

The idea of recolonization, of course, was not at all new, but Garvey's "back to Africa" movement represented the first time a black man had attempted to organize such a venture. Moreover, the effort came at a time when large masses of African Americans were congregated in urban ghettos and were ready to listen. Garvey lashed out at most black leaders for "aping white people" and for exhibiting "the slave spirit of dependence" (A. Garvey 1970:25). These so-called leaders, he said, were "Uncle Toms" who could not be trusted. He argued that the time had come for blacks to be self-reliant, to have a country of their own in Africa. The purpose of the UNIA was to inspire "an unfortunate race with pride in self and with the determination" to take its place as an equal among races (M. Garvey 1968a:295).

The philosophy of independence preached by Garvey fired the imagination of black people not only in America but throughout the world. In America, his message appealed mainly to the lower-class, urban masses. Middle-class or professional and business people were offended by his attacks on them and their acceptance of white standards. They were offended, too, by his contempt for those, like DuBois, who were of mixed ancestry and had light-colored skin. Garvey's heroes were men like Denmark Vesey, Gabriel Prosser, and Nat Turner.

In August 1920, the First International Convention of the UNIA met in New York. Twenty-five thousand delegates from all over the world—including an African prince and several tribal chiefs—gathered to hear Garvey's opening address (Cronon 1968:64). The convention drafted a "Declaration of Rights of the Negro Peoples of the World" containing twelve major complaints and fifty-four demands (M. Garvey 1968b:296–302). The declaration protested lynchings, burnings, Jim Crow laws and practices, inferior schools, exclusion from labor unions, exclusion from elective offices, discrimination in wages, unfair treatment in the courts, and so on. Among the demands cited in the declaration were the insistence that blacks be given the right to be governed by people of their own race and the right to repossess Africa. The convention elected Garvey as the provisional president of the African republic. It also declared the colors red (for the blood shed by black people), black (to symbolize their racial pride), and green (for the fresh hope of a new life) to be the colors of the black race. Finally, they adopted an international anthem (Cronon 1968:67–68).

Under Garvey's leadership, the UNIA established a number of black-run business enterprises, including the Black Star Steamship Line. This line was intended to link black people throughout the world and to provide the transportation they would need to return "home." The UNIA also established the Universal African Legion, the Black Eagle Flying Corps, the Universal Black Cross Nurses, and some other organizations designed to promote self-reliance and black pride. These organizations—with their members dressed in smart uniforms—dramatized Garvey's ideas and attracted widespread attention and admiration.

Garvey's tactics also earned him the enmity of most other influential black leaders in America and of various governments at home and abroad. For example, the U.S. Department of Justice and a committee representing the state of New York attempted to prove that Garvey was a radical agitator and a threat to the government. The governments of Britain and France attempted to force the Republic of Liberia in Africa to cancel its plans to permit the UNIA to send colonists there.

Garvey's numerous enemies slowly closed in on him. Both the NAACP, which by comparison seemed "conservative," and the socialists, under A. Philip Randolph, agreed that Garvey must be stopped. They were assisted in their efforts by Garvey's own shortcomings as an administrator. In 1922, Garvey's black opponents assisted in having him indicted for mail fraud; in 1923, he was convicted and imprisoned in the federal penitentiary in Atlanta. Although his sentence was commuted in 1927, he was deported to Jamaica as an undesirable alien. After his deportation, the UNIA no longer had an inspiring leader, and the influence of the largest mass movement among African Americans to that date waned. The scandal and suspicion created by the trial, imprisonment, and deportation of Garvey discredited the idea of recolonization for some time to come and led to a rapid decline of the UNIA. The organization did not disappear entirely, though, and its nationalistic message has had an enduring influence among African Americans.

Two direct descendants of the UNIA have been very prominent. The first of these, the Lost Nation of Islam, came into existence less than five years after Garvey's deportation. The second, to which we turn later, did not arise until the mid-1960s.

The Lost Nation of Islam (or Black Muslim) group was launched by two inspiring leaders. The first of these, W. D. Fard, was a man of mystery. Little is known about him. He appeared in the black community of Detroit in 1930 and then mysteriously disappeared just four years later. His primary doctrine was that the white race was the devil on earth, that African Americans were the lost tribe of Shebazz, and that the salvation of blacks lay not in the white man's religion, Christianity, but in the black's true religion, Mohammedanism (Lincoln 1961:72–80). Fard founded the Temple of Islam and assembled a devoted following. Chief among his disciples was Elijah Poole, who became known as Elijah Muhammad. After Fard's sudden disappearance in 1934, Elijah Muhammad assumed the leadership of the movement and took the title "Messenger of Allah" (Lincoln 1961:15–16).

The teachings of Elijah Muhammad, like those of Marcus Garvey, advocated race pride, self-help, and the separation of the races; however, his views differed from Garvey's in at least two important respects. First, although Garvey stated that Jesus had been black and that black people should renounce Christianity and its white symbolism, religion had been secondary to politics in the UNIA. Among the Black Muslims, however, religion has been the dominant element. They have developed an extremely demanding moral code that is quite puritanical. It forbids the use of tobacco or drugs as well as extramarital sexual relations, racial intermarriage, dancing, attendance at movies, participation in sports, laziness, lying, and a host of other things.

Second, the political goals of the Black Muslim movement also differ from those of the UNIA. Garvey's main goals were to return black people to Africa and Africa to black people. Elijah Muhammad, however, was neither so explicit about his political objectives nor so determined to leave the United States. The Muslims have called at various times for a separate nation in the United States and have suggested that several states should be set aside for this purpose.

The most important difference between the Garvey movement and the Black Muslim movement, however, is that the latter has gradually gained in strength and influence over the years. The number of official members of the Black Muslim organization is unknown, though it may not exceed 200,000; but the effect of the movement extends far beyond its membership. Certainly, the teachings of Elijah Muhammad and his famous convert Malcolm X have been widely circulated in the United States and overseas. Many people who do not belong to the Muslim church or subscribe to all of its teachings nevertheless have developed respect for the Muslims' high standards and strict discipline. They have developed respect, too, for the effects the standards and discipline have had on the lives of their members. The Muslims have been notably successful in the rehabilitation of ex-convicts and drug addicts and in their efforts to build a strong economic base. The strict moral code and philosophy of economic independence have had an especially powerful appeal to the many victimized black people who reside in the urban ghettos of America. It has played a significant role in "revitalizing" the lives of many people who previously had given up in the face of seemingly overwhelming difficulties.

The importance of the Black Muslim movement cannot be measured solely in terms of its official size. After the collapse of the Garvey movement, it served as a valuable repository of black separatist philosophy and as a continuing reminder to African Americans that there was a genuine alternative to the goal of "integration." Nevertheless, Garvey's imprisonment and deportation effectively halted large-scale nationalistic activities among blacks for over three decades.

Strategy, Tactics, and Conflict

The NAACP, of course, had maintained its legal warfare against discrimination throughout the period under discussion. But with the onset of the Great Depression in 1929, the association was increasingly criticized for its relative inactivity in economic matters. The Depression struck hard at all American workers, to be sure, but its effects on black workers were particularly devastating. They had been systematically excluded from most units of the leading labor organization, the American Federation of Labor (AFL), and, as usual, they were "the last hired and the first fired."

These circumstances led to significant developments in the strategy and tactics of African Americans. We noted previously, for example, the rise of the Black Muslims. By the mid-1930s, the NAACP felt compelled to announce some changes in its economic policies. Also during this time of economic catastrophe, the Socialist and Communist parties were actively trying to recruit blacks into their ranks, though with little success. Of special interest, though, was the organization of a number of new protest groups whose main objective was more and better jobs for black people. These organizations were part of a widespread effort to persuade African Americans to use their substantial economic power as a lever to improve conditions. The common slogan of these organizations, "Don't Buy Where You Can't Work," emphasized that their primary weapon was the economic boycott. The boycott was supplemented by another of organized labor's standard weapons, the picket line.

One of the new organizations to employ this direct-action approach was the New Negro Alliance, Inc. The alliance grew out of a spontaneous protest occurring at a hamburger grill in Washington, D.C. (Bunche 1971b:122). This grill was located in a black residential area and depended entirely on black customers. Early in 1933, the black workers at the grill were fired, and white workers were hired to replace them. Several onlookers were outraged by this act of blatant discrimination and formed a picket line at the grill. This tactic quickly led to the reinstatement of the black workers and the establishment of the alliance. This form of protest was so successful that many other groups, including the NAACP, adopted it. The NAACP's new willingness to address the economic problems of black people, however, continued to be a secondary aspect of its program. Its legal approach was still primary. Increasingly, the NAACP's main efforts focused on the issue of school segregation.

The beginning of World War II signaled the close of the Great Depression. The demand for labor rapidly increased as armaments production rose. The boom spread to construction, service industries, transportation, and other sectors of the economy, but the sudden increase in the demand for labor served mainly to put the huge force of unemployed whites back to work. Before the United States entered the war, blacks were practically excluded from government-funded war production. The main jobs that opened up for blacks were as service workers and farm laborers (Myrdal [1944]1964:409–412).

The continuation of conspicuous discrimination in the midst of still another global war "to make the world safe for democracy" enraged many African Americans. Two forms of discrimination were particularly galling: discrimination in war production and in the armed forces. Both of these areas involved federal dollars and, therefore, seemed to represent national policy. One leader, A. Philip Randolph, established, in 1942, the March on Washington Movement, which sought to organize millions of black people "so that they may be summoned to action over night and thrown into physical motion." He argued that "mass power" used in an orderly and lawful way was "the most effective weapon a minority people can wield" (Randolph 1971a:230). Although the United States still had not entered the war at the time Randolph issued his first call to march, President Roosevelt was eager to prevent any large demonstration of unrest. In June 1941, the president issued an executive order (No. 8802) prohibiting racial discrimination in defense industries, in government, and in defense training programs. The order also established a Fair Employment Practices Committee (FEPC) to investigate possible violations of the order.

The principle of nonviolent direct action had broad appeal. Some leaders, however, felt that the March on Washington Movement's application of the principle left much to be desired. Specifically, they objected to the exclusion of whites from participation in the movement and to the absence of a program to prevent mass protest from becoming violent. Consequently, still another protest organization, the Congress of Racial Equality (CORE), was formed to further the use of nonviolent direct action. CORE leaders were afraid that many embittered African Americans were ready to employ violence in a desperate attempt to force the dominant group to grant them civil and social equality. Bayard Rustin observed, in 1942, that some blacks had concluded it would be better to die to gain victory at home than to die on a foreign battlefield in defense of white Americans. He also reported that many blacks even hoped for a Japanese victory "since it don't matter who you're a slave for" (Rustin 1971:236).

CORE's philosophy represented an attempt to apply the methods of Jesus and Gandhi to the racial situation in America. It rested on the conviction that social conflicts cannot really be solved by violent methods, that violence simply breeds more violence, and that "turning the other cheek" has the power to shame the evildoer. This approach was later adopted and refined by Martin Luther King, Jr.

The practical expression of these beliefs involved a carefully graduated set of steps. In a conflict situation, the first step was patient negotiation. If this effort failed, the next step was to attempt to arouse public opinion against the opponent's discriminatory actions. Only after these remedies were exhausted did CORE advocate the use of boycotts, picket lines, and strikes.

In addition to patient negotiations, agitation, and the use of labor's protest methods, however, CORE developed a new technique of nonviolent direct action that appears to have been first used in 1942 following an incident of discrimination in a cafe against two CORE leaders, James R. Robinson and James Farmer. After nearly a month of negotiation, including several attempts to talk with the restaurant's managers by telephone and in person, the CORE leaders sent the last of several letters to the cafe's management saying that unless the management agreed to talk with them, they would be forced to take some other course of action. More than a week later, an interracial group of twenty-five people entered the restaurant and took seats. The white people among the group were served promptly, but the black people were not served at all; however, the white people did not eat. Instead, they told the manager that they did not wish to eat until their black friends also had been served. The manager angrily refused; so the group simply continued to occupy a large number of the restaurant's seats. When customers who were waiting to be served saw they would be unable to be seated, they left. After a period of fuming, the manager had all of the protesters served. Thus ended successfully the first "sit-in," a technique of protest that became increasingly popular during the next two decades (Farmer 1971:243–246).

The protest tactics of organizations such as the March on Washington Movement and CORE were only part of the complicated interracial situation that existed in the United States during World War II. We saw previously that the tense early years of the war were marked by numerous open confrontations and violence between ethnic groups. Mexican American "zoot suiters," the reader will recall, had been attacked in Los Angeles and other American cities; Mexican Americans in the armed forces had been discriminated against both inside and outside the service. We have seen, too, that intense anti-Japanese sentiments supported the fateful evacuation and illegal internment of the Japanese from the West Coast. During this period, various forms of violence involving blacks and whites also erupted. Confrontations reminiscent of the "Red Summer" of 1919 occurred in Mobile, Alabama, in Beaumont and El Paso, Texas, in Philadelphia, Pennsylvania, and in Newark, New Jersey. The largest outburst took place in June 1943 in Detroit, Michigan. Racial tensions in Detroit had been building over a long period of time as both white and black southerners moved there to work in the automobile industry. According to one account, twenty-five blacks and nine whites were killed, and over seven hundred other people were injured (Osofsky 1968:420).

These confrontations and the memory of the interracial violence following World War I raised fears that a similar bloody period might follow World War II. Two prominent forces acted to reduce the likelihood of violence. The first of these was the decline of European colonialism. The Allies in World War II had fought not only against fascism but also, officially, against the doctrine of white supremacy. During the course of the war, large numbers of nonwhite peoples in the United States, including Mexican Americans, Japanese Americans, Native Americans, Chinese Americans, and African Americans, became more aware of their kinship to the nonwhite peoples of the entire world. They also had become aware that many of these colored and oppressed peoples, like themselves, were fighting and dying to save the very nations that had been historically the main representatives of the white supremacy theory. Certainly, the experiences of many men and women in uniform emphasized the disparity between the official principles of the United States and the actual practices within it. The way the military services were organized supplied daily examples of the discrepancy. Throughout the military services, Jim Crow practices were common. And since many military training camps were in the South, black servicemen faced segregation when they left the camps. They were frequently in danger of physical assault not only by local citizens but by officers of the law as well. For instance, a black soldier was shot in Little Rock, Arkansas, because he would not tip his hat and say "sir" to a policeman. Another black soldier was shot by two police officers because he had taken a bus seat reserved for a white in Beaumont, Texas (Rustin 1971:235). In Centerville, Mississippi, a sheriff obligingly shot a black soldier in the chest merely because a white MP asked him to (Milner 1968:419).

As the old colonial empires were dissolved following the war, and as new independent nations arose in their place, incidents such as those described became increasingly embarrassing to American leaders. How could the United States explain to the peoples of other nations the discrepancy between its ringing declarations of human rights and the treatment of its own minority groups at home?

The external pressures on the American government were accompanied by a series of important changes in its official domestic policies. The patient legal work of the NAACP and the direct-action methods of the March on Washington Movement and CORE had begun to show some dramatic results. For example, in 1948, as President Truman and Congress considered the advisability of instituting a peacetime military draft, the leader of the March on Washington Movement, A. Philip Randolph, took a strong stand against segregation in the armed forces. Randolph stated that unless the military services were desegregated, he would lead a nationwide campaign to encourage young people to disobey the law. He stated further, "I personally will advise Negroes to refuse to fight as slaves for a democracy they cannot possess and cannot enjoy" (Randolph 1971b:278). Later that year, President Truman acted to end all segregation in the U.S. armed forces (Osofsky 1968:465.)

Victories in the Courts

The NAACP's battle to end segregation in public education had gradually gained strength through an impressive series of court victories. As early as 1938, the Supreme Court ruled that the State University of Missouri was required to admit a black applicant to its law school. Similar rulings were handed down in cases affecting the law school of the University of Oklahoma (1948), the law school of the University of Texas (1950), and the graduate school of the University of Oklahoma (1950). These rulings led to an all-out effort by the officials of segregated school systems to improve facilities for black students and, if possible, to make them physically equal to those for whites. These victories also laid the groundwork in 1954 for one of the most important court cases in the history of the United States: *Brown v. Board of Education of Topeka.*

Brown differed from the other cases just mentioned in a very important respect. The earlier cases had not called into question the "separate but equal doctrine" approved in the Court's *Plessy* decision in 1896. Now, however, the Court brought this doctrine directly under review. The question of central importance was this: Even if the separate educational facilities for the minority group are equal in buildings, libraries, teacher qualifications, and the like, do these "equal" facilities provide educationally equal opportunities? The Court ruled that they do not. Chief Justice Warren, speaking for the Court, argued that to separate children "from others of similar age and qualifications solely because of their race generates a feeling of inferiority as to their status in the community that may affect their hearts and minds in a way unlikely ever to be undone. . . . We conclude that in the field of public education the doctrine of "separate but equal" has no place. Separate educational facilities are inherently unequal" (Clark 1963:159).

Segregation in public schools was unanimously held to violate the "equal protection" clause of the Fourteenth Amendment and, therefore, was declared unconstitutional. In a separate ruling on the same day, the Court also declared segregated schools to be a violation of the "due process" clause of the Fifth Amendment.

In its *Brown* ruling in May 1954 (*Brown I*), the Supreme Court recognized the difficulties that would be encountered in the effort to desegregate public schools; consequently, as explained in chapter 7, the Court issued another decision in 1955 (*Brown II*) on the question of *how* the transition from segregation to desegregation was to be achieved. The Court emphasized that variations in local conditions had to be taken into account in planning for the change and that the primary responsibility for implementation of the 1954 ruling rested with local authorities and the lower courts. The Court insisted, however, that local school systems must "make a prompt and reasonable start toward full compliance" with its decision and racial discrimination in school admissions must be halted "with all deliberate speed" (Tussman 1963:45–46).

The *Brown* rulings ushered in a new era of hope among blacks and of heightened resistance to "integration" among whites. White citizens councils, described by some blacks as "the Klan in gray flannel suits" (Osofsky 1968:479), were formed throughout the South to find ways to prevent school desegregation. The KKK itself underwent another revival. All of the old charges of the white supremacists were again brought forward. And many southern politicians searched frantically for the legal grounds needed to overturn the Court's school desegregation decisions. Although school desegregation was initiated promptly and successfully in many southern communities, the general intensity of white reactions to desegregation efforts began to make clear to African Americans that change "with all deliberate speed" might, in fact, be very slow. The growing pessimism among blacks was fueled by numerous incidents of intimidation and violence throughout the South.

An important episode in the struggle to desegregate the schools occurred in Little Rock, Arkansas, during the 1957–1958 school year. The Little Rock school board had begun work on a school desegregation plan in 1954, almost immediately after the first *Brown* decision. While the board was developing its plan, Arkansas state officials were attempting to "nullify" the *Brown* decisions. The central feature of the Arkansas nullification plan was an amendment to the state constitution declaring the *Brown* decisions to be unconstitutional. Despite the state of Arkansas' stand, the school officials of Little Rock moved ahead to desegregate. Nine black school children were selected to attend Central High School beginning in September 1957. On the day before school opened, the governor of Arkansas, without notifying the school officials, assigned units of the Arkansas National Guard to Central High School and declared the school "off limits" to black children. When the nine black students attempted to enter school the next day, the national guardsmen, on the governor's orders, prevented them from entering. Each day for the next three weeks, this performance was repeated. At the end of this time, President Eisenhower sent federal troops to Central High, and the students at last were admitted. Federal troops remained at the school for the rest of the school year, a year filled with tension and disturbances. The threat to law and order was so serious that by the end of the year the school board begged the courts to permit them to discontinue their plan.

These events raised some very serious questions. Could a state nullify a Supreme Court decision? Who was responsible for the chaos surrounding the effort to desegregate Central High? Should a desegregation effort be discontinued or delayed if it threatens to lead to racial conflict? The Court reviewed these questions and concluded that: (1) No state can nullify a decision of the Court. The state of Arkansas, therefore, acted unconstitutionally in preventing black children from attending Central High; (2) The actions of the governor and other officials of the state of Arkansas had been, in the Court's view, largely responsible for all of the turmoil surrounding the desegregation effort. The governor's actions had increased opposition to the desegregation plan and encouraged people to oppose it; (3) The Court refused to accept the idea that desegregation attempts should be carried out only if no violence or disorder were threatened. The importance of public peace was recognized, of course, but black children's rights to an equal education were not to be sacrificed in the name of law and order.

Despite the Court's unwavering stand on the correctness of its *Brown* decisions, it could not arrest the declining faith of many black people in the law's unaided power to bring about a swift end to the many forms of racial discrimination they faced (of which school segregation was only one). The conviction grew that some further action was needed, something bolder and more direct. The "something bolder" produced a dramatic shift in the direction of the civil rights movement.

Key Ideas

1. Some scholars have argued that the slave system of the United States was essentially different from and more oppressive than the slave systems of Latin America. A controversial argument favoring this thesis maintains that the "unbridled capitalism" of the United States turned plantations, in effect, into concentration camps. The result was complete dehumanization of the slaves. Both the thesis of greater oppression and the thesis of complete personality destruction are still under review.

2. After the Civil War, southern whites were unwilling to accept the freed slaves as equals. The whites developed, therefore, a number of techniques to intimidate blacks and to restore control of the southern governments to the whites. There was not, however, an extensive system of laws regulating the relations of the races. The Jim Crow system of legal segregation developed mainly between 1890 and 1920—during the period of the new immigration. The development of the Jim Crow system was strongly encouraged by the Supreme Court's "separate but equal" doctrine in *Plessy v. Ferguson*.

3. As the Jim Crow system developed, African Americans were organizing to resist it and to claim their full rights as American citizens. The NAACP, the leading protest organization for decades to come, demanded full equality for blacks and launched a legal battle to attain it.

4. Like Mexican Americans, African Americans appear to be in some ways a colonized and in some ways an immigrant minority. Up to the time of World War I, the black experience was so marked by oppression that the colonial model seems quite apt. The great northward "immigration" of World War I, however, laid a foundation for arguing that African Americans resemble a recent immigrant group.

5. World War I was followed by numerous episodes of black-white conflict and the emergence of a mass secessionist movement under the leadership of Marcus Garvey. Garvey emphasized race pride, self-help, and the unity of black people everywhere.

6. During the Great Depression, African Americans began to adopt the boycott and other weapons of the labor movement as tactics to force equal treatment. The NAACP began to focus on the issue of school segregation.

7. The years during and immediately after World War II produced changes in federal policies aimed at reducing discrimination in employment, in schools, and in the armed forces.

8. In 1954, the Supreme Court ruled in *Brown v. Topeka Board of Education* (*Brown I*) that public school segregation was unconstitutional and was psychologically damaging to the segregated children. In a second *Brown* decision (*Brown II*), the Court declared that desegregation should occur with "all deliberate speed."

Notes

1. The largest slave insurrection to take place in the United States occurred in Louisiana during 1811. According to Genovese (1974:592), "between 300 and 500 slaves, armed with pikes, hoes, and axes but few firearms, marched on New Orleans with flags flying and drums beating." The rebels were engaged by a force of militia and regular troops and were rapidly defeated.

2. Patterson (1977:416) noted, however, that even if Elkins is correct concerning the personality effects of slavery, it is not necessary to assume that these effects prevented slave revolts.

3. Quoted by Horton (1966:712).

4. Martin Delany described the situation in these words: "The slave is more secure than we; he knows who holds the heel upon his bosom— we know not the wretch who may grasp us by the throat" (quoted by Jacobs and Landau 1971:149).

5. The identification of colonization with extreme oppression, whether an actual colonial system is established or not, was explained by William J. Wilson as follows (1972:262): "Fundamental to the colonial model is the distinction between colonization as a process and colonialism as a social, political and economic system. It is the process of colonization that defines experiences which are common to many non-white people of the world, including Black Americans."

6. The Black Codes, which resembled the antebellum "Slave Codes," nevertheless gave some recognition to the new status of blacks. In some states they could now acquire, own, and sell property; enter into contracts; and be legally married (Davie 1949:46–47; Jordan and Litwack 1987:378). But some of the new laws restricted the freedom of blacks in so many ways that they could, in effect, be forced back into slavery (Binder and Reimers 1988:312–314).

7. The name is based on the Greek word for circle (*kyklos*). Some other secret societies that were formed during this period were the Knights of the White Camelia, the Constitutional Union Guards, and the Pale Faces (Franklin and Moss 1988:226).

8. The rise in immigration during this period led to both increased racial and ethnic competition

for jobs and the organization of labor unions to fight competition. According to Olzak, the rise of labor unions increased "the rate of violence against blacks" (1989:1328).

9. The "pulls" of jobs and higher wages in the North were assisted by "pushes" from the South. Blacks were at the bottom of the plantation economy; jobs were lost as the boll weevil attacked the cotton crops; and violence against blacks—particularly lynching—encouraged migration (Tolnay and Beck 1992:104).

10. The laws requiring residential segregation were struck down in *Buchanan v. Warley* (1917).

11. Another important organization consisting of both blacks and whites was formed soon after the NAACP. The National Urban League, started in 1911, was an interracial effort to help blacks who were migrating to the cities to find jobs and get established. The Urban League has always been considered much more conservative than "protest" organizations like the NAACP.

Chapter 11

African Americans:

Protest and Social Change

Power concedes nothing without demand.
—FREDERICK DOUGLASS

When you are forever fighting a degenerating sense
of 'nobodiness'—then you will understand why we
find it difficult to wait. —MARTIN LUTHER KING, JR.

If . . . the lower class . . . were overnight to acquire the
attitudes, motivations, and habits of the working
class—the most serious and intractable problems of
the city would all disappear. . . . —EDWARD C. BANFIELD

315

The Rise of Direct Action

At the very time when the complete legal liberation of African Americans seemed to have arrived, there was a sharp increase in unemployment among them. The serious, visible decline in the economic circumstances accompanying this reversal produced renewed bitterness. Something more specific, however, served to precipitate a new phase in the effort to ensure the civil rights of African Americans. On December 1, 1955, in Montgomery, Alabama, Mrs. Rosa Parks refused to yield her bus seat to a white person and was arrested. As the news of Mrs. Parks's arrest spread, black people in the city, at the urging of E. D. Nixon, a NAACP leader, began to call for a boycott of the local buses. In less than a week, nearly all of the more than forty thousand black citizens of Montgomery had rallied around the dynamic young pastor of the Dexter Avenue Baptist Church, Martin Luther King, Jr., in a massive boycott of the buses. At first, the boycott was intended to last only one day, but various incidents of harassment and intimidation by whites led to a decision to continue the boycott indefinitely. This decision was followed by further, more violent acts of intimidation. For instance, on January 30, 1956, King's home was bombed; two days later, the home of E. D. Nixon also was bombed. On February 22, twenty-four black ministers and fifty-five others were arrested for nonviolent protesting (King 1971a:297).

The confrontation between blacks and whites over segregation in Montgomery ended in the desegregation of the buses more than a year later. During that time, the bus boycott became a symbol of nonviolent resistance throughout the South and the entire world. Martin Luther King, Jr., became the leading voice for the philosophy of nonviolent protest and the most prominent figure in what rapidly became a new phase of the relations between whites and blacks in America. The events in Montgomery and Little Rock contributed to a growing conviction among African Americans that, in King's (1964:80) words, "privileged groups seldom give up their privileges voluntarily." To promote the philosophy and practices of nonviolent protest, King founded the Southern Christian Leadership Conference (SCLC) in January 1957.

The decade following the Montgomery bus boycott was filled with many new and dramatic developments in American race relations. Although the legal approach continued to play an indispensable role, direct action became a far more popular tactic, especially among young people. A sit-in by college students at a Woolworth's lunch counter in Greensboro, North Carolina, in February 1960, set off a veritable chain reaction of student sit-ins throughout the South and of white reactions to them. These events led rapidly to the formation of yet another organization devoted to nonviolent direct action, the Student Nonviolent Coordinating Committee (SNCC). Although the members of the new organization accepted the philosophy of nonviolence espoused by CORE and SCLC and were clearly inspired by Martin Luther King, Jr., they believed their goals could not be pursued vigorously enough within any of the existing organizations. The many lines of cleavage within the black community became prominent once again, in a more complicated way than ever before. The older organizations, such as the once "radical" NAACP, were now regarded by many as "too conservative." Simultaneously, however, the older organizations were being changed by the "radical" tactics of direct action.[1]

Amidst charges of excessive "conservatism" and "radicalism," nearly all of the main black protest groups adopted some combination of legal and direct-action methods, although the new organizations were in the vanguard (McAdam 1982; Morris 1984). In this process, the entire Civil Rights Movement became more militant. It also became increasingly critical of white liberals, who seemed too quick to counsel delay and patience in the face of injustice. The battle cry "Freedom Now!" gradually gained acceptance even among many black "conservatives." The NAACP, for example, sponsored many demonstrations during this period, and CORE pioneered still another new protest tactic by conducting an interracial "Freedom Ride" on a bus headed for New Orleans. Here, for the first time, white people joined in the protest. This ride ended when the bus was fire-bombed in Alabama, but many others were to follow (Burns 1963:55). The representatives of the different protest organizations found that whatever their legal rights were supposed to be, sit-ins, kneel-ins, lie-ins, boycotts, picket lines, and freedom rides might each be met by mob violence, tear gas, police dogs, arrests, jail terms, and, in some cases, death.

The tempo of direct action increased during the spring of 1963. The number of demonstrations in the South reached a new high, and the nonviolent technique was frequently used in the North as well. Two events of 1963 merit special attention.

The first of these took place in Birmingham, Alabama. Birmingham at this time was a symbol of southern white resistance to desegregation; its commissioner of public safety, Eugene "Bull" Connor, was an open and committed opponent of any form of interracial compromise. In this setting, black people still lived in almost total segregation, and the safety of their property and persons was uncertain. In the spring of 1963, a coalition of black leaders, under the direction of Martin Luther King, Jr., decided to join in and expand an ongoing nonviolent protest campaign in Birmingham. The protests began mildly early in April 1963, with well-organized demonstrators going to jail for conducting sit-ins at lunch counters (King 1964:60). But before the protest campaign ended over a month later, thousands of demonstrators had been jailed and physically assaulted by police. On April 12, Good Friday, two of the protest leaders—King and Abernathy—were placed in jail, where they remained for eight days. After their release, the tempo of protest increased. Hundreds of young people were recruited and trained in nonviolent protest methods. On May 2, more than a thousand of them went to jail (King 1964:99). The next day's marchers were met with clubs, high-pressure water hoses, cattle prods, and police dogs. This attack on unarmed, unresisting men, women, and children aroused enormous national and international support. One week later, a formal truce was reached with a committee of Birmingham's business leaders. It was agreed, among other things, that lunch counters, restrooms, and so on would be desegregated and that immediate efforts would commence to improve the employment opportunities of blacks. The Birmingham protests had demonstrated dramatically that, in King's (1964:46) words, "the theory of nonviolent direct action was a fact."

The second event was the huge (approximately 250,000 people) March on Washington. Reviving the technique he had pioneered during the early years of World War II, A. Philip Randolph called for a massive protest march on the nation's capital to dramatize the problem of unemployment. The march, in August 1963, captured the attention of the entire country. For millions of people, Martin Luther King's famous "I Have a Dream" speech encapsulated the aspirations of the Civil Rights Movement. The march showed that the movement was beginning to look beyond direct-action protest toward a new focus on political action, beyond civil rights to a heightened concern for economic opportunity, and beyond appeals to the conscience of white people to a demand for equality.

The effects of the direct-action protests between 1956 and 1964 were mixed. In most southern states, nonviolent direct action had achieved rapid changes in desegregating restaurants, theaters, buses, hotels, and so on. Even the old etiquette of race relations with all of its humiliations and deference rituals required of blacks was crumbling. Black men and women increasingly could expect to be addressed by titles of respect and to be served courteously. The protests had been far less successful, however, in states such as Alabama and Mississippi. They were less successful, too, in bringing about changes in segregated schooling, poor housing, and discrimination in law enforcement in both the North and the South. Moreover, throughout 1964, instances of violence increased. For example, three voter registration workers (James Chaney, Andrew Goodman, and Michael Schwerner) were killed in Mississippi. Members of the KKK were suspected, and in 1967 seven of the suspects were convicted on civil rights charges (Bullard 1991:21–22).

The escalation of violence by whites led to a gradual weakening of the allegiance of many blacks to the philosophy of nonviolent resistance. Increasingly, blacks fought back (National Advisory Commission 1968:230–231), but as the limitations of direct action became apparent, black leaders began to turn in different directions. The political pressure mounted by the March on Washington was increased through voter registration and "get out the vote" drives. With the strong support of President Johnson, President Kennedy's civil rights program was passed as the Civil Rights Act of 1964. This legislation prohibits discrimination in voting, public accommodations and facilities, schools, courts, and employment; however, official violations of the voting rights section of the law (Title I) occurred in the South soon after the law was passed. Opposition to these violations was expressed in a nonviolent demonstration in Selma, Alabama, led by Martin Luther King, Jr. Shortly thereafter, Congress passed the Voting Rights Act of 1965. This law suspended all literacy tests for voters and permitted the federal government to station poll watchers in all of the states of the South (Osofsky 1968:570–581).

In a formal sense, the major goals of the civil rights "revolution" had been reached. The legislation of 1964 and 1965 marked the end of official segregation in America. Yet something was clearly wrong. The laws had not, in fact, ended all forms of discrimination, and, like the direct-action demonstrations that preceded them, they had had little visible effect on conditions in the black ghettos of the cities. After a decade of notable victories, most of the African Americans' basic problems still remained. In addition to pervasive unemployment, underemployment, and poverty, the black ghetto was characterized by high "street" crime, poor health and sanitation, poor housing, inferior schools, poor city services, high divorce and separation rates, low access to "city hall," demeaning and inadequate welfare services, high prices for inferior goods and services, and poor relations with the police. What now was to be done? Should the Civil Rights Movement continue to rely mainly on nonviolent protest and the power of the ballot in the fight for equality? An answer from the past attained renewed popularity.

Black Power

We mentioned earlier that the *Brown* decisions encouraged most African Americans to believe the end of school segregation and other forms of inequality was near. We saw, however, that these "rising expectations" were soon dampened by the strong evidence—as in Montgomery, Little Rock, and Birmingham—that many whites intended to resist the Court's rulings in every way possible, including the use of violence. The primary reaction among blacks to the massive resistance of the whites, as noted earlier, was nonviolent protest. This was not the only reaction among blacks, however. Not since the days of Marcus Garvey had so many African Americans appeared to be ready to listen to those who doubted the possibility or desirability of "integration" and who urged, instead, some form of separation. The organization that was best able to capitalize on this renewed interest in a separatist solution was the Lost Nation of Islam (the Black Muslims).

The Black Muslims, please recall, had been led since the mid-1930s by Elijah Muhammad. The Muslims had been hard at work during the intervening years but had not attracted many converts; however, during the late 1950s and early 1960s, they attracted many new converts and a great deal of attention from the mass media of communication. A new and dynamic Muslim leader, Malcolm X, was a particularly effective advocate of the black nationalist philosophy.

Malcolm, who substituted "X" for the surname his grandparents had received from their slave master (Little), became the minister of the large Muslim temple in Harlem. Like his teacher, Elijah Muhammad, Malcolm X emphasized that black people must organize to regain their self-respect and to assert their collective power. Consequently, he and his followers sought some form of separation from white America. If the U.S. government would not pay the costs of sending blacks to Africa, then, Malcolm X argued, the United States should set aside some territory within its borders so African Americans could move away from the whites. Malcolm believed that such a separate territory should be given as payment for the long period during which black slaves worked without pay to help build America. Malcolm X also emphasized that he was not in favor of separation for its own sake but as the only way for African Americans to gain freedom, justice, and equality (Malcolm X and Farmer 1971:390). He stated that integration was unacceptable only because freedom, justice, and equality could not be obtained in this way. Perhaps tokens of equality could be achieved through this method (e.g., "an integrated cup of coffee"), but not true equality.

Malcolm X's view of the race problem took into account conditions throughout the world. He was very interested in Africa and believed strongly that black people worldwide were interdependent and shared a similar destiny. In time, Malcolm X and Elijah Muhammad came into conflict over various matters; in March 1964, Malcolm X left the Black Muslim organization. He founded a rival group, the Organization of Afro-American Unity, which stressed the unity of all people of African descent throughout the Western Hemisphere and in Africa. Although all people of African descent were eligible for membership, its main purpose was to unify African Americans. The organization's charter emphasized the right of Afro-Americans to defend themselves against violence in any way necessary. Nonviolent protest could succeed, he argued, only when the oppressors were basically moral, and in the United States they are not (Malcolm X 1971).

Malcolm X was by no means the only African American who contended during the early 1960s that violence should be met with violence. As the violent reactions of whites to nonviolent protest became widespread, many blacks came to feel that violence was, in some cases, necessary. In addition to this "defensive" use of violence, however, some African Americans began to think in terms of attack. The most militant members of the group began to use the word "revolution" as more than a metaphor.

The clearest evidence of a shift among some blacks away from the acceptance of only "defensive" violence and toward the acceptance of "offensive" violence began to appear in 1964. For example, on July 16, an off-duty New York City police lieutenant intervened in a dispute between some black youths and a white man. When one of the youths attacked with a knife, the officer shot and killed him. Two days later, a rally called by CORE to protest the lynchings of civil rights workers in Mississippi led to a clash with police in which one person was killed. In the following days, a crowd attacked the police with Molotov cocktails, bricks, and bottles in Harlem and Bedford-Stuyvesant in New York; the police responded with gunfire (National Advisory Commission 1968:36).

The change in the mood of African Americans was unmistakable by the following summer. On a hot evening in August 1965, a California motorcycle patrol officer stopped a young black man for speeding near the Watts area of Los Angeles. After the driver failed a sobriety test, he was arrested. The officer radioed for assistance while a crowd of people gathered. Within ten minutes, the crowd numbered more than 250 people. At this point, the prisoner's brother and mother arrived and began to struggle with the police. They, too, were arrested. By now, the crowd had more than tripled in size and had become very angry. The police also arrested a young woman whom they mistakenly believed had spat on them; as they departed, the crowd threw stones at the police car (McCone 1968:608).

Rumors that the police had beaten the intoxicated driver, his family, and a pregnant woman spread throughout the area. Later, groups of black people stoned and overturned passing automobiles, beat up white motorists, and harassed the police (National Advisory Commission 1968:37). The next evening, three cars were set on fire, snipers opened fire on the firefighters, and people began burning and looting stores and buildings owned by whites. On the following day, the burning, looting, and sniping spread into the Watts area. Two city blocks on 103rd Street were burned out while firemen were held off by sniper fire (McCone 1968:615). Late in the day, the governor of California ordered nearly fourteen thousand national guardsmen into the area to restore peace. Burning and looting spread into other parts of southeast Los Angeles, and the fighting between rioters, police, and guardsmen continued for two more days.

The Watts area rioting was the worst in America since the 1943 outbreak in Detroit. Thirty-four people were killed and over 1,000 were injured, 118 with gunshot wounds, and more than 600 buildings were damaged or totally destroyed. Estimates of the property damage ranged from $35 to over $40 million. The pattern of burning and looting strongly suggested that the black rioters had intentionally focused their attacks on food, liquor, furniture, clothing, and department stores owned by white people. To many, perhaps most, white Americans, the violence seemed incomprehensible. After all, the preceding decade had been marked by momentous court decisions and legislative victories, and the Jim Crow system had been undermined by legal and nonviolent protest actions. The Watts explosion intensified public discussion of the question, "Why are African Americans rioting now, just when things are getting better?"

This question has given rise to some fascinating theories of collective violence. One of the most popular ideas is that people become dissatisfied as they compare their present circumstances with some possible or anticipated future condition. We have alluded, for instance, to the idea that as conditions improve, people begin to believe that real change is possible, and their hopes rise; however, since actual social changes may well occur more slowly than people desire or expect, they begin to perceive a gap between what they believe is possible and what actually exists. This discrepancy between hopes and reality produces discontent and may generate collective action to speed change. This theory is called the *rising expectations hypothesis* (Geschwender 1968).

Two other closely related theories are the *relative deprivation hypothesis* and the *rise and drop hypothesis*. The former focuses on how people determine whether change is occurring rapidly enough. Even when social changes are proceeding rapidly, discontent may be generated if the subordinate group compares their progress with that of the dominant group and sees that the gap between the groups is not narrowing. Objectively, the subordinate group's circumstances may be improving, but if their subjective experience is one of "no progress," they will feel deprived relative to the dominant group. The rise and drop hypothesis suggests that "revolutions are most likely to occur when a prolonged period of objective economic and social improvement is followed by a short period of sharp reversal" (Davies, quoted by Geschwender 1968:7). When a period of improvement is followed by a sudden decline, even if the individual is still better off than previously, the expectations that were aroused during the former period turn to frustration and anger. Such a state of mind may easily lead to violent outbursts.[2]

Whatever the reason, the level of black protest increased during 1966. According to the National Advisory Commission (1968:40), forty-three major and "minor disorders and riots" occurred during that year, including a new outburst in Watts. Two of the major disorders, in Chicago and the Hough section of Cleveland, involved extensive looting, rock throwing, fire bombing, and shooting at the police. In each case, the disorders and riots were preceded by a history of dissatisfaction among blacks in regard to police practices, unemployment, inadequate housing, inadequate education, and many other things (National Advisory Commission 1968:143–144), and they were usually precipitated by some seemingly minor incident, frequently involving the police. For example, in Chicago, the rioting commenced after police arrested a black youth who had illegally opened a fire hydrant to cool off with water.

Shortly after the Chicago violence had subsided, another event served to dramatize the heightened militance of many African Americans and their impatience with the rate of social change. The event was a speech delivered by Stokely Carmichael (1966), chairman of SNCC, late in July. Like many black leaders before him, Carmichael urged black people to "get together," to organize in their own behalf. He rejected the idea that African Americans could "get ahead" through individual ambition and hard work. What was needed, he said, was "Black Power." Carmichael argued that black people had to recognize that they were not the inferior beings whites had portrayed them to be. Black people are able to take care of their own business. Furthermore, as the Muslims have taught, black people must take pride in their physical features. They must learn that black is beautiful. The slogan "Black Power" was not completely new, nor were the ideas of race pride and self-help it suggests; however, the use of this phrase at this particular time took on special significance. The phrase was vague enough to encompass a wide range of perspectives. It symbolized the frustration of many integrationists as well as black nationalists. In the minds of many white people, though, the slogan was identified primarily with black revolutionaries and separatist organizations.

The increasing willingness of African Americans, especially young adults, to demand an immediate end to racial inequalities and to back their demands with violence, if necessary, ushered in still another new phase in black-white relations. Just as the legal approach had been made secondary by the advent of widespread nonviolent protests, the use of violent methods moved to the fore. As in the earlier shift, organizations, leaders, and methods that had at first seemed "radical" now seemed "conservative" by comparison. The level of violence was escalated again during 1967, with most of the disorders occurring in July. According to the National Advisory Commission (1968:112), there were between 51 and 217 disorders during the first nine months of the year, depending on one's definition of a "disorder." The commission focused on 164 disorders in 128 cities, 8 of which were judged to be "major" and 33 of which were judged to be "serious."[3]

The violent protests declined after 1968.[4] Many factors probably contributed to "taking the steam out" of the Black Power Movement. Such factors as the declining coverage by the media and the changing tactics of law enforcement agencies are frequently mentioned in this regard. Probably important, too, is that some of the most influential black leaders had never accepted the principles of separation or violent protest. For example, shortly before his assassination on April 4, 1968, Martin Luther King, Jr. (1971b:586) argued that "the time has come for a return to mass nonviolent protest." The continuation of violent tactics, he believed, would only stimulate increased white repression. Under these circumstances, it was foolhardy for blacks to continue such measures. Rather, in his view, nonviolence was more relevant as an effective device than ever before: "Violence is not only morally repugnant, it is pragmatically barren" (King 1968:585). Apparently, most African Americans soon accepted this assessment. By 1973, legal and political approaches to the solution of the problem of racial inequality had once again become the primary weapons of the African Americans.[5]

Civil rights activities by African Americans during the 1970s and 1980s were, in Brisbane's words (1976:575), "calmer, more sober, more conservative." Global economic and political problems during the 1970s thrust such issues as inflation and military spending to the forefront. These changes were joined in the 1980s by a shift to the political right during the administrations of Presidents Ronald Reagan and George Bush. These social and political trends were reflected in a decreased willingness by the dominant group to support the social spending needed to maintain the levels reached during the 1960s. Even though many other groups—including women, homosexuals, the elderly, and the physically handicapped—also organized to combat discrimination and gain equal rights, the 1970s and 1980s witnessed what Tabb (1979:349) called a "dramatic loss of momentum." The U.S. Commission on Civil Rights (1981a:35) expressed concern that in such matters as school and job desegregation, police protection, voting rights, housing, and affirmative action, the federal government's civil rights enforcement effort was not adequately funded and coordinated. In some cases, according to the commission (U.S. Commission on Civil Rights 1979a), changes in the laws have "aided and abetted the obstructionists." Numerous court rulings during the 1980s served to restrict the scope of effective minority action against civil rights violations. Even though the Civil Rights Act of 1991 reversed the effects of some rulings of the U.S. Supreme Court concerning discrimination in employment, the fact that the rulings had been made still increased the concern of many African Americans that their civil rights were in jeopardy.

Later in this chapter, we will examine evidence that even though a considerable segment of the African American population benefitted from the legal and social changes instituted in the 1960s, the life circumstances of many others have improved little or have gotten worse. For example, as noted in chapter 6, a *Newsweek* poll published in April 1992 (Morganthau et al. 1992:21) found that 51 percent of African Americans felt the quality of life had gotten worse during the preceding ten years. The article cited figures concerning the very high rates among blacks of infant mortality, homicide, and imprisonment. These and other facts have led an increasing number of observers to express the fear that the most disadvantaged of the inner-city ghetto dwellers, white and Hispanic as well as black, are now so separated from the rest of the society that there is a danger their condition will become permanent. This group of individuals who seem to be completely outside the occupational and other structures of society frequently are described as an *underclass*.[6]

Even during the "quiescent" 1980s, there were numerous signs that the gains of the 1960s and 1970s were under attack. There were various "incidents," often involving conflict with police officers, and these incidents sometimes exploded into major urban riots. For instance, in Miami, Florida three large disturbances took place during the 1980s. In May 1980, eighteen people were killed and over four hundred were injured in the Liberty City section; in December 1982, two people were killed and more than twenty-five were injured in the Overtown section; and in January 1989, six people were injured and thirty buildings were burned, again in Overtown, after a policeman killed a black motorcyclist (Reinhold 1992:A12). These and many other events were reminders that America's racial problems had not been solved.

These problems returned to national prominence and a higher place on the political agenda in the spring of 1992. Earlier, in March 1991, a black man named Rodney King had been arrested for traffic violations by four white Los Angeles police officers. The arrest was videotaped covertly by a citizen who was observing nearby. The videotape, shown repeatedly on television and seen by people throughout the United States, showed Mr. King writhing on the ground while being kicked and beaten with a baton by the officers. According to press and television accounts, most viewers of the tape, white as well as black, thought that the arrest and beating of Mr. King was a clear case of police brutality and that it involved an excessive use of force; consequently, people all over the country were keenly interested in how the authorities would respond to the apparently improper behavior of the officers.

Over a year later, following a change of venue from Los Angeles County to Simi Valley in suburban Ventura County, the officers came to trial primarily on charges of "assault with a deadly weapon" and "excessive use of force as a police officer." The trial received wide press coverage, and evidently most people expected the officers to be found guilty of criminal conduct.[7] Instead, the nation was "stunned" (as many newspapers reported) by the acquittal of all four officers on the first main charge and of three officers on the second.[8]

The response to the news of the acquittals was in some cases violent. Major urban disorders erupted in several American cities, with the largest and most severe rioting of the twentieth century occurring in Los Angeles itself. The violence started in the Florence-Normandie area of South Central Los Angeles and spread southeast into Watts and north into Koreatown. As in the case of the Watts riots in the 1960s, nonblack people were the main targets, but in this case Hispanic people were also prominent among the rioters and Asian people, principally Koreans (but also some Cambodians), were among the targets. City, state, and federal officials called for the rioting to end. Mr. King, in a halting yet eloquent appeal for peace, asked the crucial question: "Can we all get along?" Again, as in the 1960s, thousands of troops were rushed to the scene, and by the end of the first week in May, the explosion was over.[9] Estimates of the deaths and damage vary, but at least fifty-one people were murdered (*New York Times* May 17 and August 13, 1992), hundreds more were injured, and burning and looting were responsible for millions of dollars in damage. Twenty-seven of the victims of the rioting were black.

A *TIME/CNN* poll taken during this period made clear some of the differences between the views of black and white Americans concerning the state of race relations in the United States. Consider, for example, the answers to the following questions: "Have prejudice and discrimination against blacks become more prevalent in recent years?"—54 percent of the blacks and 31 percent of the whites answered "yes" (Kramer 1992:41); "Would the verdict [in the King trial] have been different if the police and the man they had beaten had all been white?"—82 percent of the blacks and 44 percent of the whites answered "yes" (Lacayo 1992:32); "Which makes you angrier, the verdict or the violence that followed?"— twice as many blacks as whites said the verdict made them angrier, while almost three times as many whites as blacks said the violence made them angrier (Ellis 1992:28); and when asked to give "the reason for the jury's not-guilty verdict," 45 percent of the blacks and 12 percent of the whites said "racism" (Church 1992:25).

The racial disagreement seen in these answers (and dramatized in the riots) certainly shows that the long road of change traveled by black and white Americans since 1619 has not yet produced the levels of merger called for by the various ideologies of assimilation. Many African Americans are disappointed, angry, and bitter and do not believe that they yet have achieved equality as citizens.[10]

Our sketch has traced the slow and painful movement of African Americans out of slavery to citizenship and out of rigid segregation and the denial of equal rights to a legal and official form of equality. But the many evidences that "old-fashioned racism" has been replaced to some extent by "modern racism," and the widespread belief among African Americans that the gains of the 1960s have been eroded, make the careful analysis of social and economic changes and trends all the more important. We turn, therefore, as we have in the cases of Japanese and Mexican Americans, to the question of the extent to which the movement toward intergroup merger (i.e., assimilation) has occurred between black and white Americans.

African American Assimilation

Cultural Assimilation

Each ethnic group we have considered so far has faced the question, "As we adopt American culture, what shall become of our own culture?" We saw that, although there are important group differences in this respect, each group has made an effort to retain and transmit a portion of its heritage. The tendency of an ethnic group to attempt to retain its heritage has been shown to be intimately related, among other things, to whether a group has entered the country voluntarily. As a rule, groups that have come into the United States voluntarily have been more willing to undertake cultural assimilation than have Mexican Americans and Native Americans. From this perspective, we should expect that African Americans would have been very resistant to cultural assimilation. Even though they were separated from their homelands, like many other immigrants, the separation was forced. It did not arise in any way from a dissatisfaction with life in the old country or the desire to start anew in another land; thus, like Mexican Americans and Native Americans, Africans initially did not wish to undertake cultural assimilation. Apparently, however, they had little choice in the matter. Those who survived the horrors of being captured, bought, and transported to America were in an extremely poor position to retain or transmit their heritage. The entire system of American slavery was constructed, as noted in chapters 3 and 10, to strip the slaves of their cultures and to replace these cultures with ways of thinking and acting that were deemed appropriate for slaves. People from many tribes and kingdoms, people who spoke different languages, and people with highly different levels of education and prior social status were thrown together and treated as if they were alike. They were assigned new "American" names and were required to learn the rudiments of English. Every effort was made to force the slaves to discontinue the use of their own languages and customs. In this way, the link to the African past was severely disrupted. Frazier (1957:3–4), for instance, stated that this process was so effective that significant elements of African culture have survived only in certain isolated areas.

This view is not only defensible, but it also has seemed to many to be inescapable. Nevertheless, the question of the persistence and influence of the African heritage may not be dismissed so easily. Although generally it is agreed that the disruption of African culture was greater in the United States than in any other part of the New World, it also generally is agreed that African Americans do possess some distinctive modes of speech, family life, religious observances, music, folklore, and so on. Myrdal ([1944]1964:930) conceded in this respect that black patterns of living do contain some "peculiarities" that may indicate the presence of a distinctive culture, but he denied that these differences may be traced to Africa.[11]

A number of scholars believe both that there is a distinctive African American culture and that this culture is strongly related to the African traditions brought to America by the slaves; consequently, they have sought to reveal the importance of African "survivals" to various aspects of African American life. In regard to language, for instance, Herskovits (1958:281–291) presented evidence that in certain areas of the United States many African words, names, and phrases used by African Americans have been translated from African languages into English. Herskovits argued further that the high prevalence of common-law marriage among African Americans represents an adjustment of the polygynous family form to the American setting. And he suggests that mothers and grandmothers play an unusually important role in the families of African Americans, just as they did in the traditional life of West Africa. A similar argument pertains to certain religious rituals. Herskovits believed that the popularity of the Baptist church among African Americans is probably due to the similarity of its rituals to those of the river cults of West Africa.

Each of these points was disputed by Frazier (1957). Although there is clear evidence of language survivals in a few isolated African American communities, such as the Gullah communities on the coasts of Georgia and South Carolina, such survivals do not seem to be widespread. Frazier argued also that the similarities between the family and religious lives of African Americans and those of West African tribes are more easily explained as having arisen within the United States than as being survivals of African customs. In general, Frazier (1957:7) maintained that in the United States black slaves were so scattered throughout the South and were so thoroughly dominated on the plantations that they had little chance to preserve or transmit their African heritage.

The debate over African American culture has continued to attract scholarly attention, and, no doubt, the final word has not yet been spoken. An important, if unsurprising, result of the exchanges so far is that the terms of the inquiry gradually have been redefined. It has become increasingly accepted that an African American culture does exist, even though its main elements may not have been transmitted intact from their African origins. To illustrate, Lawrence Levine (1977:6), in an analysis of slave songs, found that their "style . . . remained closer to the musical styles and performances of West Africa . . . than to the musical style of Western Europe." He found that a number of the characteristics of African cultures, such as the high praise given to verbal improvisation, have remained central features of African American songs. Levine argued that it is a mistake to assume that cultural elements must be unchanged to be "survivals" of African tradition. Such a view, he maintained, misinterprets the nature of culture itself. "Culture is not a fixed condition but a process. . . . The question is not one of survivals but of transformations" (L. Levine 1977:5). Gutman (1976:212) expressed a supporting but somewhat more restrained view. He suggested that too little is currently known to allow one to trace important elements of African American culture to their origins and that perhaps Herskovits did lay too much stress on the direct transmission of African traditions. Nonetheless, he believed Herskovits demonstrated some important continuities between the lives of the plantation slaves of the early nineteenth century and those of rural Mississippi blacks in the third decade of the twentieth century.

As noted previously, the answers given to questions of this type imply a certain view of how the problems facing African Americans should be solved, and they usually are associated with some social policy position. Myrdal ([1944]1964:928), for instance, stated that the distinctive traits of African Americans are primarily the result of reactions to the discrimination of whites and the requirements of white society; hence, the distinctive traits of African American culture (to the extent they exist) are considered to be "distorted" and "pathological" reflections of American culture. This view implies that such problems as poverty and unemployment, high street crime rates, and teenage pregnancy result from improper and distorted cultural assimilation and will disappear as African Americans are aided to complete that process. What mainly is needed, from this perspective, is for African Americans to give up the remnants of their African heritage and adopt the standard American culture. An important implication of this suggested "solution" is that African Americans should not be proud of their distinctive characteristics and should strive to abandon all traces of their African heritage.

The idea that African American culture is "pathological," that it has not served as a "positive" way to help African Americans to adapt to their environment, has enjoyed wide acceptance. A well-known version of this belief holds that the "deficiencies" of black culture may be seen in the "breakdown" of the black family. Although this view has been common, at least since the influential work of Frazier (1939), its direct political impact is generally traced to an explosive document prepared by Daniel P. Moynihan (1965) to help shape the federal government's War on Poverty during the 1960s. This document, commonly called the Moynihan Report, was based on the assumption that "at the heart of the deterioration of the fabric of Negro society is the deterioration of the Negro family" (Moynihan 1965:5). The "deterioration" of the black family was judged, in turn, to be the lasting result of the indescribable oppression experienced during slavery. The inability of black slaves to contract legal marriages, the inability of the black man to act as breadwinner and family protector, and the frequent separation of family members at the auction block all led to the development of a matrifocal (mother-centered) family pattern. These conditions led also to a general acceptance among blacks of sexual promiscuity, plural "marriages," and illegitimacy. The main result of the general "weakness" of the black family in America is what Moynihan (1965:29–45) referred to as a "tangle of pathology" that may be seen in the "reversed roles of husband and wife," lowered levels of education and school attendance, lowered income, lowered IQs, and high rates of arrest, delinquency, unemployment, and narcotics use. The proper goal of government action, therefore, is to enhance "the stability and resources of the Negro American family" (Moynihan 1965:48). Please notice that this analysis is consistent with Elkins's view, discussed in chapter 10, that the modern problems facing African Americans are a lingering consequence of the extraordinary harshness of the slavery period.

A storm of protest broke as the results of Moynihan's analysis became generally known. Although his description of the severity and immediate effects of the slavery period was generally accepted, his conclusions concerning their modern effects were not. Critics have attacked the idea that the problems of African Americans stem from the presumed weaknesses and failures of the black family. They have emphasized, instead, the many strengths, resources, and achievements of the black family (see, e.g., Billingsley 1968; J. Jackson 1991; Rainwater and Yancey 1967; Wilkinson 1978). Hill (1971), for instance, argued that in black families there are stronger kinship bonds than among whites, that there is a strong emphasis on work and ambition, and that there is an equalitarian (rather than a "matriarchal") authority pattern. Moreover, accumulating evidence supports the idea that the extended family, rather than the nuclear family, is the proper unit of analysis for studies of the strengths and weaknesses of the black family (Hatchett, Cochran, and Jackson 1991:49). The net result of many studies has been to cast grave doubts on Moynihan's thesis that there is a "tangle of pathology" in black families arising from a failure of African Americans to overcome the "disorganizing" effects of the slavery experience. Such a view, many critics have noted, emphasizes the effects of past discrimination but ignores or minimizes the effects of present discrimination. In this way, the modern social problems of blacks appear to result from failures in the black group to overcome the legacy of the past—a view that, to many observers, seems to "blame the victim"—rather than from the contemporary actions of the dominant group.

Although most of Moynihan's critics apparently accept his analysis of the historical effects of slavery on black family life while rejecting his "tangle of pathology" conclusion, some reject both his analysis and conclusion. For example, Gutman (1976) unearthed considerable evidence showing that the inability of African Americans to form strong and lasting families during slavery has been greatly exaggerated. By studying the records of the Freedmen's Bureau, population censuses, marriage and birth registers, letters written by both blacks and whites, and so on, Gutman discovered that, despite the great hardships of enslavement, most slaves lived in households headed by men as well as women and that many slave couples had enduring relationships. Consequently, children frequently grew up in a home with two parents—parents who had gone through some accepted ceremony of marriage. The members of slave families were quite conscious of, and influenced by, their ties to kinfolk. For example, children usually were named for members of their blood kin group. Also, marriages to close blood relatives were discouraged. Although premarital intercourse was accepted, marriage was expected to follow if a pregnancy resulted. And once married, husband and wife were expected to remain faithful to one another. Gutman (1976:95–100) concluded from his analysis of slave marriages and families that despite the undeniable hardships and restrictions of slavery, black slaves were not simply disorganized, atomized individuals. They placed a high value on family stability and responsibility. A subsequent study comparing black and white family structure in Philadelphia in 1850 and 1880 found that roughly three-quarters of the families in both groups consisted of two parents and their dependent children. The study found also that the households of former slaves were more likely than other black households to be headed by couples (Furstenberg, Hershberg, and Modell 1985).[12] Slavery surely narrowed the choices available to the slaves, but these downtrodden people apparently were able, nonetheless, to create a distinctive culture and social identity that was rooted in and transmitted by families. These families were struggling, with discernible success, to cope with the obstacles to family unity presented by the slave system. The presumption does not seem justified, therefore, that the contemporary problems of African Americans are mainly a reflection of their failure to develop a family pattern during slavery that was capable of transmitting "positive" values from one generation to the next.

What, however, has happened to black and white family organization during the twentieth century? Is it still true that the families of these groups are about equally likely to be headed by couples? The evidence on these questions shows clearly that "there has been a more or less steady shifting away from the 'conventional' family model among black families" (Farley and Allen 1987:186). Families headed by husbands and wives have declined in recent decades among both black and white families, but they have declined more rapidly among blacks (Eggebeen and Lichter; 1991:803; Glick 1988). By 1990, couple-headed families comprised about 59 percent of white households and 36 percent of black households. At the same time, female-headed family households comprised about 9 percent of the white total and about 31 percent of the black total (U.S. Bureau of the Census 1991b:46). While these changes in family organization leave us still with the problem of attempting to understand the relative contributions of culture and living conditions in bringing them about, they do not, taken alone, support the view that black family life is a "distorted" or "deviant" form of white family life. In the view of most contemporary scholars of family life, the answer to the question raised earlier—"Are American Negroes simply the creation of white men, or have they at least helped to create themselves out of what they found around them?" (R. Ellison 1964:316)—appears to be that African Americans have for a very long time been in the process of constructing a resilient new culture based on their experiences in the past and in the present. We thus encounter again the process of ethnogenesis discussed in chapter 4. Cultural assimilation involves not only the acceptance of new cultural elements and the rejection of old ones; it includes, also, the creation of new elements of culture.[13]

We may acknowledge the reality of black culture and view its development as positive, however, without claiming African Americans are low in cultural assimilation. Indeed, most students believe that blacks and whites of the same social class levels are more alike than different in their values, behavior, and family organization (e.g., Gordon 1964:173).[14] To illustrate, Farley and Allen (1987:174–175) found that among both whites and blacks the prevalence of traditional couple-headed families increases as income levels rise. About 86 percent of white families with annual incomes of $50,000 or more in 1980 were headed by husband-wife pairs, and about 78 percent of blacks in the same income category were headed by husband-wife pairs. They also found, though, some evidence of differences between the races in household organization that could not be attributed to economic status. Of special interest was that, regardless of income level, African Americans are significantly more likely than white Americans to have extended family members living in the household (Farley and Allen 1987:178). This finding fits well with the thesis that some of the differences between black and white families are cultural creations rather than "pathological deviations" from the white pattern. We conclude, therefore, that although African Americans are not simply and totally identical to middle-class Anglo-Americans in culture, their level of cultural assimilation is high.

Secondary Structural Assimilation

There can be no doubt that since emancipation African Americans have moved in many important ways toward the goal of full secondary assimilation; however, it is equally clear that a number of gaps still exist between the levels of whites and blacks in such significant matters as jobs, income, education, and housing. Moreover, as we shall see, if contemporary trends continue, the differences in these areas will not disappear soon.

Whites, of course, always have been more heavily concentrated than blacks in the higher-prestige, better-paying jobs, and they still are. For example, although the proportion of black men in professional jobs increased almost sixfold between 1940 and 1980, their proportion was still lower than that among white men in 1960 (10.7

versus 11.4 percent) (Farley and Allen 1987:264), and by 1984 the proportion of black professionals had *declined* to 8.0 (Jaynes and Williams 1989:273). A similar situation exists among black male proprietors, managers, and officials. Despite a more than fivefold increase in jobs in these categories, the proportion of black men in these high-prestige positions in 1980 still had not equaled that of white men in 1940 (6.7 versus 10.7 percent), and the percentage for black men had shrunk by 1984 to 6.3 percent. The pattern among black and white women is similar. Despite a more than threefold increase in professional jobs and a more than fivefold increase in jobs as proprietors, managers, and officials, black women in 1980 had not reached the levels of white women in 1940 (14.8 versus 14.9 percent and 3.7 versus 4.4 percent, respectively). Contrary to the general trend, however, black women had by 1984 surpassed the 1940 level of white women in the proprietors, managers, and officials category class (5.2 percent).

The overall occupational distribution of blacks, nevertheless, has become more similar to that of whites. Between 1940 and 1980, the index of occupational dissimilarity for black and white men fell from 43 to 24, showing a large movement in the direction of occupational assimilation (Farley and Allen 1987:265).[15] This movement was not uniform within the various regions of the country, however. Based on a different measure of occupational assimilation, Fossett, Galle, and Kelly (1986) showed that occupational inequality *increased* in the South during the 1940s and 1950s. Two subsequent studies showed that although the aggregate reductions in occupational inequality for the nation during the 1940s and 1950s were produced by the movement of blacks out of the South, there were real improvements in employment opportunities for blacks during the 1970s (Burr, Galle, and Fossett 1991; Fossett, Galle, and Burr 1989).

An even greater change occurred among women. The index of occupational dissimilarity for women declined from 63 in 1940 to 18 in 1980. This means that even though the occupational distributions of black and white women were further apart in 1940 than the men's, by 1980 the women's distributions were closer together than the men's. Two other points are of particular interest here. One is a dramatic change in the proportion of black women working in domestic service. In 1940, 60 percent of employed black women were household workers. By 1984, only 5.9 percent of employed black women held such jobs. The second point of interest is that black women who were employed in 1980 were almost as likely to hold professional jobs as white men, though both were less likely to be employed as professionals than white women (Farley and Allen 1987:264–265).

Although the occupational "upgrading" revealed by these statistics is encouraging for those who favor secondary assimilation as a goal, four additional considerations are in order. First, since blacks are more likely than whites to occupy the lower positions of pay and prestige within each occupational category, occupational assimilation probably would still be incomplete even if the index of occupational dissimilarity were zero. Second, on the basis of more refined occupational data, Farley and Allen (1987:270–274) found that the rate at which blacks were moving into high-prestige jobs during the 1970s slowed during the 1980s. Third, rapid technological and economic changes, such as increasing automation and the transfer of unskilled jobs to other countries, are permanently displacing black workers who are concentrated in the secondary labor market (Bowman 1991:159). Finally, the apparent reductions in occupational inequality cited before are based on figures for blacks who are a part of the employed labor force, but large numbers of blacks are unemployed, underemployed, or employed at substandard wages. For most of the years between 1955 and 1975, the unemployment rate for black men was roughly twice as high as for whites, and after 1975 the gap widened. Furthermore, during this time, unemployment among black teenagers was exceptionally high. Among eighteen- and nineteen-year-olds, 60 percent of whites but only 39 percent of blacks were in the labor force, and among those in the labor force unemployment was twice as high among black youths as among whites (Farley and Allen 1987:214, 238). It appears, therefore, that while black males are now more likely to get jobs that previously were "reserved" for whites, they still are much less likely to get a job at all.

There has been a definite increase in black incomes during the past four decades, both in dollars and in purchasing power, but there still are large gaps between the incomes of blacks and whites. The U.S. decennial census of 1990 showed that, overall, the median incomes of black households (families) increased more rapidly during the 1980s than the median family incomes of whites but that the overall gap between the groups changed little during the decade (Barringer 1992:A1). The ratio of the median incomes at the beginning of the decade was .62, and at the end it was .63 ($24,089/$35,811). This means that, on the average, for every 63 cents received by African American families, white American families received one dollar. The size of the gap between black and white median family incomes, however, varied with the region of the country, ranging from a high of over .75 in the West to a low of about .60 in the South. In the Midwest, the ratio actually declined during the 1980s from about .68 to about .63. Blacks were hit hard in the Midwest by the closing of many entry-level factory jobs that previously helped to open the door to upward mobility (Barringer 1992:A10).

The picture is similar if we compare per capita incomes rather than median family incomes, except that black women have fared better in the cross-race comparison than have black men. In 1949, for instance the ratio of the per capita incomes of black and white men was .57 and in 1985 it was still at that level. For women the ratio was .66 in 1949 and by 1985 had risen to .88, though it reached a higher level (.91) in 1969 (Farley and Allen 1987:300).[16]

These comparisons, taken together, suggest only a modest movement toward the income assimilation of African Americans. In two of the four main regions of the country (West and Northwest), the gap in median family incomes decreased noticeably during the past decade, but in the South the income gap remained the same and in the Midwest it grew larger (Barringer 1992:A1). In general, the modest improvements in the ratio of black incomes to those of whites from 1949 to 1979 was halted during the 1980s.[17] Perhaps even more revealing is a comparison of the total average wealth (or total assests) of black and white Americans. U.S. Bureau of the Census figures released in 1990 showed that the estimated median net worth of African American households was $4,169, as compared to $43,279 for white households (O'Hare, et al. 1991:30).

As shown in our comparisons of Mexican American and Anglo incomes in chapter 9, the general figures we have presented conceal many specific differences of importance. For instance, since women typically have lower incomes than men, and since more black than white families are headed by women, then more poor black than poor white families are headed by women. Also, as in the case of the Mexican American-Anglo comparison, some of the differences in per capita incomes between blacks and whites is due to the higher educational level of the whites. For instance, Smith and Welch (1978:3) found in a study of black-white income changes that if only full-time workers were compared, the income ratio in 1975 was 77 percent instead of the 62 percent that applied to all workers (Smith and Welch 1978:3). Once again we see (as in chapter 9) that to estimate the income "costs" of discrimination against a minority group, it is necessary to "match" the groups being compared in many (or, if it were possible, all) important respects.

Through an approach of this type, Farley and Allen (1987:354) showed that in 1985, even when the employed workers of the groups were matched in several pertinent ways, there still was a substantial difference in earnings between black and white males (over $3,000) that may have been the result of discrimination. This difference, moreover, represented the reversal of a trend toward greater similarity between the earnings of black and white men that had been underway for four decades (Smith and Welch 1986); therefore, for black men at least, it would appear that the effect of discrimination on earnings increased during the early 1980s. The results of the analysis for women, however, contained a surprise. To begin with, employed black women earned an average of about $650 *more* in 1980 and about $800 more in 1985 than did white women, and had the black women been identical to white women in the respects considered in this study, then the gaps *in favor* of black women would have increased to around $900 in 1980 and $1,100 in 1985; but as Hacker (1992:96) observed in a similar type of study, "The comparative status of women warrants only a muted cheer. . . ." because women of both races are underpaid. For both sexes, however, educational gains (especially at the college level) appear to make a substantial difference in the incomes they receive (Farley and Allen 1987:347; Smith and Welch 1978, 1986).[18] Therefore, estimates of black progress in the area of income usually focus on changes in the level of education and on changes in the pattern of schooling (i.e., desegregation).

Prior to emancipation, the vast majority of blacks were given no formal schooling; consequently, changes in the level of education among blacks since the Reconstruction period have been enormous. In 1870, 80 percent of African Americans were illiterate; in the same year, illiteracy among whites stood at 12 percent. By 1970, these levels had fallen to approximately 4 percent of all blacks over fourteen years old and to less than one percent for whites of the same age group (Goff 1976:422). Also by 1970, practically all children of both races between the ages of seven and thirteen were enrolled in school. Before the completion of high school and college, however, a larger proportion of blacks leave school, especially once they pass the age of compulsory attendance. In 1970, among those eighteen to nineteen years old, 40 percent of blacks and 49 percent of whites were enrolled. These figures had increased by 1989 to 50 percent for blacks and 56 percent for whites (U.S. Bureau of the Census 1991b:137). By 1989, the median level of education for black and white adults aged twenty-five and older had reached 12.4 and 12.7 years, respectively (U.S. Bureau of the Census 1991b:139).

As in the case of occupational and income trends, indexes of dissimilarity afford a convenient indication of the overall pattern of the relative educational changes occurring among blacks and whites. Between 1940 and 1975, for instance, the index of educational dissimilarity for black and white men aged twenty-five and older dropped from approximately 44 to 24 (Farley 1977:191). Among women, the indexes declined from around 43 to 24. These findings show that the educational patterns of black and white Americans are moving in the direction of complete educational assimilation.

These findings do not show, however, that the trend toward educational assimilation is steady or inevitable. For instance, although the rate of college *attendance* among black high school graduates had reached 28 percent by 1980 (compared to 32 percent for whites), the rate for college attendance among white high school graduates continued to rise during the next five years to 35 percent, while the rate for blacks declined to 27 percent. While this decline occurred among both women and men, it was most pronounced among men (U.S. Bureau of the Census 1991b:158). After 1985, however, the college enrollment rates for blacks, both men and women, resumed an upward course, reaching about 32 percent in 1989 (compared to 39 percent for whites) (U.S. Bureau of the Census 1991b:157). As we have noticed in some other contexts, however, even though there was a noticable rise in college enrollments among blacks during the 1980s, the gap between blacks and whites in this respect actually increased. A similar observation applies to a comparison of the rates of college *completion* by blacks and whites. For instance, between 1940 and 1989 the percentage of blacks who completed college rose from 1.3 to 11.8, more than a ninefold increase. By contrast, during the same time, the percentage of all adults who completed college rose from 4.6 to 21.1, less than a fivefold increase; nevertheless, the absolute difference in college completions between the two groups rose from 3.3 percent in 1940 to 9.3 percent in 1989 (U.S. Bureau of the Census 1991b:138. As in the case of income gains, black progress, though real, is a part of a general increase in American society. Such an increase within a given group may or may not keep pace with that of the total population. Even when it does keep pace in a relative sense, the absolute differences may actually widen (Darden 1974).

Educational levels, of course, reveal little concerning educational quality. But if, as the *Brown* decisions state, segregated schooling is damaging to those who are set apart, then the continuation of segregated schools reduces the quality of education for blacks. From this standpoint, educational assimilation is incomplete as long as the schools are segregated, even if the indexes of educational dissimilarity used so far were to reach zero.[19]

In our discussion of school desegregation in chapter 7, we noted that a substantial amount of school desegregation occurred between 1968 and 1973, primarily because of court-ordered busing. This approach to desegregation was adopted, despite its unpopularity, largely because there has been a strong trend toward the concentration of blacks in the neighborhoods of central cities and of whites in the suburbs (Farley 1978:42). Given this trend, and the continued unpopularity of busing, will further movements toward school desegregation depend on the desegregation of housing?

In some areas of the South, housing patterns still reflect the effects of slavery and the plantation economy. In the antebellum South, slaves and their families commonly lived in the backyards of the white masters (Taeuber and Taeuber 1969:48). Following the Civil War, cities in both the North and the South followed a similar pattern of low residential segregation. Although whites typically enjoyed superior dwellings, blacks and whites were found side by side in various parts of the cities (Farley and Allen 1987:136–137); consequently, the level of residential segregation throughout the country was typically less than it is in most parts of the United States today. Even when the Jim Crow system of deliberate, legal segregation came into being between 1890 and 1920, the southern pattern of interracial housing was not much affected. In the "Southern Plan" of segregation (Pettigrew 1975:36), it was unnecessary to force blacks into racially separate geographical areas. Both tradition and the Jim Crow system created such a vast social distance between the races that residential closeness did not threaten the respective social "places" of the two races. As African Americans began to stream out of the South during World War I, however, they entered northern states in which they were, in most respects, legally equal to whites. Certain facts of northern life, nevertheless, prevented blacks from dispersing throughout all parts of the cities.

There was, first of all, an economic barrier. Like the European immigrants before them, most blacks could afford to live only in the least expensive "slum" areas of the cities. But also of great importance, as noted in chapter 10, was that black people faced an enormous amount of legal and extralegal housing discrimination. Even when black people could afford housing outside of the ghettos, they usually were unable to purchase it (Philpott 1978:213–214)—a condition that has continued into the latter part of the twentieth century (Jaynes and Williams 1989:145).[20] Since 1917, when legal housing segregation was struck down, the "Northern Plan" of segregation has relied primarily on housing segregation rather than legal segregation to keep the races apart in other respects. A comparison of the Southern and Northern Plans to achieve racial segregation illustrates an interesting principle: physical and social distance are to a degree interchangeable. As long as a dominant group's social position is unassailable, it may permit subordinates to be physically close; however, when the dominant group's efforts to maintain social distance begin to crumble, it may erect physical barriers "as a second line of defense" (van den Berghe 1967:30).

Comprehensive, detailed studies of trends in housing segregation in the United States prior to 1940 are unavailable. Some studies of selected cities have been conducted, however. These studies suggest that in northern and southern cities residential segregation increased gradually from emancipation to World War I and then accelerated sharply until 1930 (Taeuber and Taeuber 1969:43–55). Since 1940, the U.S. Bureau of the Census has published housing information on a large sample of American cities. Using this information, Taeuber and Taeuber (1969:32–41) calculated residential segregation indexes (indexes of dissimilarity) for 207 American cities in 1960 and for 109 cities during 1940–1960. Their analysis established two important points. First, the average level of residential segregation of blacks and whites in American cities by 1940 was very high in every region of the country. No city in the Northeast, for instance, had a residential segregation index lower than 74.3, while most cities of this region had indexes between 80 and 89. One city (Atlantic City) had an index of 94.6. A similar pattern existed in the other regions, with the South having the highest average. Second, although there was a slight decline in residential segregation between 1940 and 1960 in most of the 109 cities studied, the amounts were usually small, and the patterns within the cities were varied. For instance, some cities had an increase in residential segregation during one or both of the two decades studied. In any event, by 1960, the average level of residential segregation in American cities was still nearly as high as it was in 1940. The national average in 1960 was 86.2, and the lowest regional average (for the Northeast) was 79.2. Indeed, the lowest single city (San Jose, California) registered the high segregation score of 60.4, while some cities (e.g., Orlando and Fort Lauderdale, Florida, and Odessa, Texas) approached complete residential segregation.

What has happened to residential segregation in U.S. cities since 1960? Because the cities have continued to grow and change, certain problems of comparison have arisen. As mentioned previously, blacks have continued to move into the central cities, and whites have continued to form suburban rings around them. To what extent, then, must the analysis of residential segregation focus on the metropolitan area rather than on the central city? Questions of this type have led to controversy concerning the direction of residential segregation. For example, a study by Sørensen, Taeuber, and Hollingsworth (1975) extended the Taeubers' earlier study of 109 cities. This study found a small average decrease in residential segregation in the United States between 1960 and 1970, bringing the average level below that of 1940. A different study by Van Valey, Roof, and Wilcox (1977:842), based on metropolitan area as well as central city comparisons, however, showed that the average level of residential segregation existing in 1970 was almost the same as in 1960.

The legal battle to overturn segregation in education, employment, voting, public accommodations, and so on also has been waged in regard to housing. For example, restrictive covenants have been declared illegal, rules requiring segregation in federally funded housing have been removed, and open housing laws have been passed. In 1968, Congress passed the Fair Housing Act, barring "racial discrimination on the part of any parties involved in the sale, rental, or financing of most housing units" (Farley and Allen 1987:139).[21]

Data indicating the effects of these efforts in some American cities and metropolitan areas with large black populations in 1980 were presented by Farley and Allen (1987:140–146). These authors showed, for instance, that among the twenty-five central cities with the largest black populations, all but two (Philadelphia and Cleveland) experienced some decline in black-white residential segregation between 1970 and 1980. The declines ranged from −13 index points in Dallas (96 versus 83 percent) to −1 in Chicago (93 versus 92 percent). Overall, declines during the decade occurred in twenty of the twenty-five cities, with an average of −6.

In a similar study of all metropolitan areas in the United States using 1990 data, Harrison and Weinberg (1992)[22] found decreases in the residential segregation of blacks in most of the metropolitan areas. The declines were substantial in eighteen large areas, most of which are in Florida and Texas. Especially notable in comparison to the segregation levels of 1960 were the declines in Orlando and Odessa. The average decline of −5.8 in the index of dissimilarity between 1980 and 1990 nearly matched that of the decline for the period from 1970 to 1980 (Harrison and Weinberg 1992:22–35). During the period 1960–1990, the average residential segregation of African Americans declined in American cities from 86.2 to 69.4.[23]

These findings suggest that racial residential segregation in American cities declined noticeably during the 1970s and 1980s. Other findings, however, cast doubt on that conclusion. In a study of suburbs in forty-four metropolitan areas, Logan and Schneider (1984:877) found that the suburbs were hardly less segregated in 1980 than they were in 1970. To explain the apparent contradiction of the results of these two studies, Farley and Allen presented the following idea: A study by Lake (1981, cited by Farley and Allen 1987:143–144) showed that although African Americans have indeed been moving to the suburbs more frequently than in the past, this movement generally has been into neighborhoods that either already have comparatively large black populations or are near such neighborhoods. Such a pattern of suburbanization among African Americans could create an appearance of residential desegregation that would not adequately reflect the real social situation. Instead of bringing middle-class blacks and whites into more frequent contact in desegregated suburban settings, this pattern would lead to the replacement of whites by blacks and to the reproduction of residential segregation. Even if such a process were at work, however, a study by Barrett Lee (1985) showed that it is not universal. In a study of census tract changes during the 1970s, he showed that "significant percentages of tracts . . . remained racially stable during the decade" (Lee 1985:361).

Whether residential segregation is declining or is continuing in a new guise, certain points seem to be beyond dispute. Although black people, like white people, attempt to turn improvements in occupations and incomes into improvements in housing (as predicted by the spatial mobility hypothesis), it is clear that the gains scored by blacks since World War II have not been translated commensurately into residential assimilation (Hwang et al. 1985). High-status blacks are much more likely than high-status whites to live in "poorer, more dilapidated areas" that are "characterized by higher rates of poverty, dependency, crime, and mortality" (Massey, Condran, and Denton 1987:29). There are, of course, some conspicuous departures from that pattern. Many affluent black families do live in mostly white suburbs and some—perhaps an increasing number—elect to live in expensive all-black suburbs (Dent 1992; O'Hare et al. 1991:31). Another important implication of continuing residential segregation is that since it "is the major cause of racial segregation in public schools" (Farley and Allen 1987:157), many people will continue to be forced to choose to some extent between their desire to have neighborhood schools and their desire to maintain segregated housing.

What, then, are we to conclude concerning the secondary assimilation of African Americans? Our consideration of changes in occupations, incomes, educational levels, and housing patterns suggests that, on the average, African Americans have been moving slowly during recent decades toward the pattern found among whites, though there are significant differences in the experiences of men and women in these respects, and the movement toward assimilation was halted or slowed during the 1980s. When compared to an ideal of perfect secondary assimilation, all of the changes we have discussed are small. For this reason, most observers appear to agree with Farley (1988:24) that, although gains among blacks "are widespread," blacks "will not soon attain parity with whites. . . . "

Primary Structural Assimilation

The gains previously discussed have increased the chance that blacks and whites will have social contacts in different situations. Desegregation in schools alone has brought hundreds of thousands of students, teachers, and parents together in new ways. And there is good evidence of an increase in cross-racial contacts in other settings, too. Between 1964 and 1974, researchers at the University of Michigan's Institute for Social Research found an increase in contacts between blacks and whites in neighborhoods and on the job as well as in schools (ISR 1975:4).[24] Throughout this same time, too, as mentioned in chapter 7, the attitudes of white people became more favorable toward desegregation, a fact that presumably should have helped turn many of the personal contacts into friendships. The Michigan studies reported, in fact, that this has happened. The proportion of whites who had no black friends declined from about 80 percent in 1964 to about 60 percent ten years later.

The extent to which whites have contacts with blacks, however, is not identical to the contacts of blacks with whites. Since there are so many more whites in America than blacks, blacks are much more likely to interact with whites than the other way around. For this reason (if no other), the amount of segregation may seem different to members of the two groups. An interesting illustration of this point is that more than 75 percent of the blacks included in the Michigan samples said they had some white friends.

We must observe again, though, that important as these reported changes are, they are modest in relation to the ideal of complete primary assimilation. From this standpoint, whites and blacks are still mainly separated in their personal relations everywhere but in the schools. Even there, patterns of friendly association still tend to be largely with members of the same race. For example, as noted in chapter 7, a study by Hallinan and Williams (1989) of over a million high school friendship pairs revealed only a few hundred cross-race friendships, and in colleges and universities, it is common for black students to form their own sororities, fraternities, and political organizations. The reason usually given by black students for the latter phenomenon is that "such activities make predominantly white campuses more hospitable" (Collison 1988:A39). We need not accept that explanation at face value to conclude that the level of primary assimilation among African Americans, though rising, is still low.

Marital Assimilation

The marriage of blacks outside their group—especially with whites—has long been a subject of interest.[25] An understanding of this process, though, has been complicated by laws in many states prohibiting black-white intermarriage, by differences in record-keeping procedures, and by a trend toward removing racial identifications from marriage records. In 1967, when the Supreme Court ruled that laws prohibiting interracial marriages were unconstitutional, sixteen states still had them. At that time, too, only three states (Hawaii, Michigan, and Nebraska) published official records on interracial marriages (Heer 1966:263). By 1976, the effort to remove racial identifications from marriage records had been successful in seven states and the District of Columbia (Monahan 1976:224).

Despite the technical problems created by these conditions, some excellent studies have been conducted.[26] Three of the main findings of these studies are that (1) out-marriages among blacks have been much less common than out-marriages among other racial and ethnic groups; (2) the rate of black-white intermarriage went up rapidly during the 1960s in both the North and the South; and (3) the number of black-white intermarriages is higher in the North than in the South, but the rate of black-white intermarriages is higher in the South than in the North.

Given the social and legal pressures opposing black-white marriages in the United States, the infrequency with which they occur is not surprising. In a study of interracial marriages in Los Angeles during 1948–1959, Burma (1963:160) found that black men were much less likely to marry outside of their group than were Japanese, Chinese, Filipino, or Indian men, and black women were even less likely to marry-out than were black men. After all the turmoil and change of the 1960s, blacks were still found to be the least likely of thirty-five different American racial and ethnic groups to marry-out (Gurak and Kritz 1978:38). Lieberson and Waters (1988:173, 176) showed that although black women seem less likely to marry within their group now than in the past, the probability of such marriages is still *very much* higher than among any of the twenty-one other groups included in their analysis.[27] To be more specific, almost 99 percent of black women in their first marriages had married black men. Among the next most in-married group, Puerto Ricans, the comparable figure was about 79 percent.

Even though the level of black out-marriage is still extremely low when compared to other racial and ethnic groups, the rate of change has jumped noticeably since 1960. Monahan (1976) conducted a nationwide survey of black-white intermarriage and found that the total proportion of mixed marriages rose from 1.4 per one thousand marriages in 1963 to 2.6 in 1970. By 1990 the rate was nearly 4 per one thousand marriages (Wilkerson 1991:A1). Throughout this period, the proportion of black-white intermarriage was three to four times higher in the North than in the South, though the rate of increase was much faster in the South than in the North.

In their analysis of data from the 1980 census, Lieberson and Waters (1988:176) found that although the first marriages of black women under the age of twenty-five were still very likely to have been with black men, the younger women were much less likely to have married within the group than had older black women. For example, those under twenty-five were less than half as likely to have married-in as had those between the ages of twenty-five and thirty-four, and they were less than one-tenth as likely to have married-in as had those between the ages of fifty-five and sixty-four.

It seems unlikely that the increasing rate of black-white intermarriage will soon produce a very large overall effect. In addition to the fact that the level of marital assimilation of blacks was extremely low to begin with and that the levels of primary assimilation of blacks are still low, there is the further fact that white opposition to marital assimilation has always been high and is still noticeable (Spickard 1989:341). Indeed, although the opposition of whites to intermarriage with blacks appears to be declining, it is still greater than against any other group. For example, in 1972 two in five whites interviewed believed that intermarriages between blacks and whites should be illegal; this proportion fell to one white in five nearly two decades later (Wilkerson 1991:A1). If that many whites still believe cross-racial marriages should be illegal then, presumably, a much higher proportion believes such marriages are not a good idea. A Gallup Poll in 1983 also found that 22 percent of blacks expressed disapproval of interracial marriages (Schuman, Steeh, and Bobo 1985:75, 145). These considerations all suggest that the level of marital assimilation among blacks in America will probably remain low for the foreseeable future.

Whether it is their intention or not, African Americans appear to be moving toward the goal of ideal pluralism. They appear simultaneously to be mastering Anglo-American culture and developing their own distinctive culture, and their level of secondary assimilation is generally rising. But while blacks and whites seem to be coming together in cultural and secondary structural ways, they appear to be remaining largely apart in their private relations. This broad assessment must not blind us to the continuing problems African Americans face in jobs, incomes, education, and housing. The remaining gaps in these areas give little assurance that the past separation of the races will not continue or deepen. As stated in one report, even middle-class blacks "speak again and again of 'living in two worlds' " (McCarroll, McDowell, and Winbush, cited in Lacayo 1989:58). On the other hand, for those who seek pluralism, there is no assurance, if secondary assimilation accelerates, that the culture of blacks and their separate social lives will survive the pressures of Anglo conformity.

African American "Success"

One of the great questions of our time is: "Why haven't African Americans been more 'successful' in worldly ways?" We indicated earlier that in very broad terms a split has long existed between those who favor hereditarian and those who favor environmental answers to this important question. With the ostensible decline of the popularity of the hereditarian position—or, at least, in open expressions of it—public and scholarly debate increasingly has occurred among various groups of environmentalists. We have encountered this situation previously in our discussions of the worldly success of Japanese Americans and Mexican Americans, and we have seen in our discussion of the problems of African Americans so far that alternative environmental explanations also are competing here.

In chapter 10, for instance, we discussed different perspectives on the reactions of African Americans to slavery, none of which assumed African Americans to be inherently inferior to whites. We observed, too, that the differing environmental perspectives on the effects of slavery are associated with differing interpretations of the experiences and strengths of the black slave family. Taken together, we saw that these perspectives have played a highly visible role in the analysis of the modern social problems that are prevalent among blacks. Please recall that, in general, we have classified the various environmental explanations as either cultural (i.e., those that attribute group differences primarily to the different norms, values, and motives of their members) or structural (i.e., those that attribute group differences to such "material factors" as income differences and the social forces that help create those differences).

During the 1960s, the view that blacks had been psychologically crushed under slavery (as expressed, for example, by Elkins) and the view that the African American family is a "distorted" and "pathological" remnant of the slave period (as expressed, for example, by Moynihan) were joined by a similar, overlapping view designated *the culture of poverty thesis*. This term, usually attributed to Lewis (1965), quickly became popular in discussions of poor people in general and of blacks in particular.

The basic idea of the culture of poverty thesis is that poor people develop a particular pattern of values and ways of coping with their difficulties and that this pattern is passed down essentially intact from one generation to the next. The children of the poor learn in their homes and neighborhoods ways of thinking and acting that middle-class people consider to be "deviant" and "maladaptive." Important among the values of the poor are an emphasis on the present that, when translated into behavior, results in an "inability to defer gratification." The poor live for the here and now, taking little thought for the future. Such values and behavior, according to this thesis, prevent poor people from taking school seriously or from working hard when they get a job. They do not succeed in these activities, therefore, and do not climb "the ladder of success." Since these "failure" responses are passed on to each succeeding generation, a vicious circle of poverty is created. The poverty of one generation breeds and ensures the poverty of its successor, resulting in socially inherited welfare dependency.

Among African Americans, this poverty cycle may be traced back to the slavery period, as argued by Frazier, Elkins, Moynihan, and others. From this perspective, poor blacks live in families that are "culturally deprived" and are characterized by the "tangle of pathology" noted by Moynihan. Unless the poverty cycle is broken, the children of such families are destined to learn the same "defective" pattern of behavior exhibited by their elders and, inevitably, to remain as dependents on the welfare rolls. Black people, in this view, must be taught success values and behaviors like those of the Japanese and Anglo-Americans. Otherwise, even when opportunities for advancement arise in society, they will be unprepared to take advantage of them.[28]

A heated controversy arose over this thesis. Indeed, the argument quickly overlapped and reinforced the existing cleavages concerning the effects of the slave experience on blacks and fed on the growing public interest in the Moynihan Report. Each of these foci of debate was strongly related to the federal government's policies in the War on Poverty. Millions of tax dollars were committed to programs based on the assumption that the black family and culture were "defective" and must be replaced with the "healthy" or "normal" culture of the Anglo-Americans. Until this cultural transformation can be accomplished, it was said, poor blacks are doomed to go on perpetuating the culture of poverty and to remain trapped at the bottom of the socioeconomic ladder.

The culture of poverty debate has now filled the pages of numerous books, government publications, and scholarly articles, and it is much too far-reaching to be adequately summarized here. We saw previously, though, that many observers doubt the black family, either now or during the slave period, is as weak or lacking in adaptive capacity as the culture of poverty thesis assumes. Moreover, most of the research conducted to determine whether poor people do, as claimed, possess a specific, distinctive culture has not supported this idea.[29] For example, the belief that poor black males do not take seriously the matter of getting and keeping jobs because they possess a "present orientation" (and are interested, therefore, only in the gratification of their many immediate desires) has been vigorously challenged by Elliot Liebow (1967). Instead of viewing the black worker as the carrier of "defective" values, Liebow (1967:64–65) maintained that what looks like a "present orientation" to the middle-class observer is, in fact, a "future orientation." The poor black worker is no less aware of the future than is his or her middle-class critic, but, said Liebow, these two people are looking at very different futures. The black worker is facing a future "in which everything is uncertain except the ultimate destruction of his hopes and the eventual realization of his fears. . . . Thus, when Richard squanders a week's pay in two days it is not because, like an animal or a child, he is 'present-time oriented,' unaware or unconcerned with his future. He does so precisely because he is aware of the future and the hopelessness of it all" (Liebow 1967:66).

Many critics see in the culture of poverty thesis, as in the Moynihan thesis, an elaborate way to shift the responsibility for social change away from the majority and onto the shoulders of the minority. From this perspective, the culture of poverty thesis is just a "nice," "liberal" way of saying that if they can't succeed, something must be wrong with *them*. The implication of this thesis for public action is clear: we must assist black people to become more like white people. On a broader scale, this is the central argument of Anglo conformity.

The debate over the problems facing African Americans focused more sharply, beginning in the 1970s and continuing into the 1990s, on the causes of rapidly rising rates of out-of-wedlock births, teenage pregnancies, welfare dependency, female-headed households, unemployment, drug addiction, and street crime among ghetto blacks. Although these phenomena also afforded the basis for the debates of the 1960s, their rates of occurrence were substantially lower at that time. The critics of the culture of poverty thesis were able to make a plausible case that the black ghetto family and community, despite appearances, were basically sound. Many of the differences between the mainstream population and black ghetto dwellers, as we said, were viewed primarily as evidence of the resilience and adaptability of people in distressing circumstances, as "functional" rather than as "pathological" But after the civil rights victories of the 1960s in the courts and Congress and after the social programs and infusions of money that comprised the War on Poverty, most Americans—including those who supported these measures and critics of the culture of poverty thesis—believed these changes should go a long way toward erasing the legacy of past discrimination and that, therefore, the rates of joblessness, poverty, out-of-wedlock births, and so on, among blacks would begin a noticeable, perhaps steady, decline.

It is true, as our review of the evidence has shown, that African Americans as a group have moved slowly toward secondary assimilation in occupations, in-comes, and education, but the social deterioration in many urban ghettos has continued despite substantial efforts to reverse the trends. One consequence is that the income gap between husband-wife families and female-headed families has grown larger among both blacks and whites, but since female-headed families have increased in prevalence more rapidly among blacks than whites (Farley 1988:24–25),[30] black children are much more likely than white children to live in female-headed households and, therefore, are more likely to live in poverty (Eggebeen and Lichter 1991:803). To illustrate, the median family income of black two-parent households in 1989 was about 3.3 times as high as the median for black female-headed households ($31,757 versus $9,590) (O'Hare, et al. 1991:20). These facts have led an increasing number of observers to express the fear that the most disadvantaged of the inner-city ghetto dwellers, the "hard-core" poor or underclass, white as well as black, are becoming so separated from the rest of the society that there is a danger the condition will become permanent.[31]

The evidence that differences *within* the black community have been increasing as cultural and secondary assimilation has occurred among some segments of the black population served as the springboard for William J. Wilson's (1978) controversial presentation of the thesis that race itself is declining in significance as a factor affecting socioeconomic status.[32] Stated very briefly, the reasoning behind this thesis is as follows: Throughout the long years between the beginnings of African American slavery and the end of World War II, practically all blacks were members of an oppressed lower caste. Under these conditions, black people's racial affiliation rather than their economic circumstances determined their chances for occupational advancement; therefore, the inequalities between blacks and whites were, strictly speaking, *racial* in nature. Since World War II, however, the forces of industrialization (discussed in chapter 1) have led to the creation of a significant black middle class, among whom occupational advancement depends more on *class* location than on racial membership. The result is a growing cleavage within the black community in which socioeconomic classes have become more visible than previously (Wilson 1978:2–4; see also Featherman and Hauser 1978:381–382). In short, well-educated blacks increasingly have the same opportunities for occupational advancement as whites, while the uneducated members of all groups, including whites, increasingly descend into a multiethnic underclass. From this perspective, the object of modern programs to change the lives of poor blacks should focus specifically on those aspects of industrial life that create class inequalities. Such programs should not continue to operate on the assumption that racial oppression is still the *paramount* problem (Wilson 1978:154).

Wilson's conclusions angered many scholars and stirred a debate that has not yet been settled. The Association of Black Sociologists (ABS) published a denunciation (*Footnotes* 1978) of Wilson's book and accused him of omitting significant facts "regarding the continuing discrimination against blacks at all class levels," of misinterpreting some of the facts presented, and of drawing unwarranted conclusions. The ABS stated further that its members were "outraged over the misinterpretation of the Black experience" and "extremely disturbed over the policy implications" of the book. Stanfield (1988) charged that such concepts as "the underclass" and "truly disadvantaged" are "faddish, simplistic" extensions of "obsolete" theories that do not explain what is taking place among blacks.

In another critique, Gans (1990:271) states that the term *underclass* is "value-laden" and has become "the newest buzzword for the *undeserving* poor" (cited by Wilson 1991:4). From this viewpoint, the term *underclass* stigmatizes the very poor and, in the process, implies the correctness of the culture of poverty thesis. Wilson, of course, was aware that in such matters as public school education, residential segregation, and full political participation racial antagonism is still very much alive. His argument, however, was that "there is every reason to believe that talented and educated blacks, like talented and educated whites, will continue to enjoy the advantages and privileges of their class status" (Wilson 1978:153).[33]

Wilson (1987) expanded his analysis of the underclass or *ghetto poor*[34] in another, and also controversial, book. He acknowledged that during the fifteen years following the Moynihan Report (1965–1980), and despite the Great Society programs, the proportion of black births occurring outside of marriage rose from 25 to 57 percent, and the proportion of black families headed by women rose from 25 to 43 percent; he acknowledged too that welfare dependency, violent crime, and increased joblessness among blacks had reached "catastrophic proportions" (Wilson 1987:21). In the minds of many, the continuation of these "pre-War on Poverty" trends undercut the argument that the problems of ghetto blacks were primarily a result of continued disadvantages stemming from slavery. Instead, they strengthened the argument that these problems are mainly the product of individual moral and behavioral failings.

This latter idea was given a greater circulation and acceptance than it deserved, in Wilson's opinion, because many scholars who opposed narrow versions of the culture of poverty thesis but who nonetheless believed cultural elements should be included in a proper analysis of ghetto problems were silenced by the fear that if they described the behavior of racial minorities in terms "that could construed as unflattering or stigmatizing" then their work would be laid open to "the charge of racism or of 'blaming the victim'" (Wilson 1991:5). A growing reluctance on the part of liberal scholars to explore the role of individual values and morality in ghetto problems left them without "a convincing rebuttal to the forceful but erroneous arguments by conservative scholars and policy makers that attribute these problems to the social values of the ghetto underclass" (Wilson 1989:135).

In Wilson's view, the problems of poverty, unemployment, street crime, teenage pregnancy, and so on cannot be explained fully either as the result of the effects of the culture of poverty or as a simple consequence of racial discrimination. He argued that only a complex explanation that includes "societal, demographic, and neighborhood variables will suffice" (Wilson 1987:30). Such an explanation must include not only cultural elements and well-recognized structural elements, such as the effects on African Americans of the dual labor market and the decline in industrial jobs, but it also must include a consideration of the consequences of rising joblessness among black men on the structure of the black family. He stated that "the sharp rise of black female-headed families is directly related to increasing black male joblessness" (Wilson 1987:105). In a symposium on his work (Newby 1989),[35] some of Wilson's critics construed his emphasis on male joblessness to mean that he believed the problems of female heads of families to be of secondary importance.[36] Wilson (1989:138) replied that by showing the increase in female-headed households to be due primarily to broad social forces that result in male joblessness, he challenged the "argument that the increase . . . was due primarily to . . . welfare generosity. . . . "

We have seen in this brief summary that many questions concerning the "success" of African Americans are still unanswered. Some of the evidence reviewed so far shows that in the important areas of occupations, income, and education, racial differences have declined substantially. These findings show that as a group African Americans *are* succeeding in some ways and that the gains are significant. As Farley (1988:24) expressed it, "This is not tokenism. Throughout the economy and in all regions, racial differences on the most important indicators are now smaller than before." The result has been the development of what frequently is referred to as "the new black middle class" (Landry 1987). But we also saw that in some ways the gaps between the achievements of blacks and the rest of the population are growing. It is possible, as Wilson contended, that better-educated blacks have taken advantage of the opportunities created by the Civil Rights Movement and have moved out of the inner cities, leaving behind in the ghetto an increasingly visible group of poor blacks. In addition, the income gap between husband-wife families and female-headed families has grown larger among both blacks and whites, and female-headed families are increasing in prevalence more rapidly among blacks than whites (Farley 1988:24–25). About 30 percent of the difference between the poverty rates of the two groups may be accounted for by the fact that more black families have female heads (Eggebeen and Lichter 1991:803). As a consequence of these changes, about 75 percent of children under the age of six who live in female-headed black families are living in poverty (U.S. Bureau of the Census 1991b:463).[37]

Before leaving this perplexing subject, let's briefly reconsider some ideas raised earlier concerning entrepreneurial minorities. We noted in chapters 4 and 8 that many minority groups in the United States and throughout the world have reacted to dominant group hostility by becoming middleman minorities or by developing a secure economic base within an ethnic enclave. We may now wonder, "To what extent have black Americans relied on self-employment as a response to hostility?" O'Hare (January 1992:34) reported U.S. Bureau of the Census findings showing that while the number of black-owned firms was less than 15 per 1,000 population, these figures were over 102 for Korean Americans, about 76 for Asian Indian Americans, over 66 for Japanese Americans, and about 63 for Cuban Americans.[38] The figures also showed, however, that the number of black-owned businesses grew in the years 1972–1987 from over 187,000 to over 424,000 (O'Hare et al. 1991:26). Nevertheless, this mode of adaptation to out-group threat was still comparatively low among African Americans. But why was this true?

Our review of some of the explanations of the business success of Japanese Americans revealed that a number of different factors may lead a group into an entrepreneurial mode of adaptation, and it showed also that the matter is very controversial. Lieberson (1980:381–382), for instance, listed several important factors to be considered in comparing the economic success of Asian Americans and African Americans, including a greater opportunity for "Asian groups to occupy special niches," an even higher level of hostility by whites toward blacks than Asians, and the higher level of economic competition presented to whites by blacks. Portes and Bach (1985:45–48) described various explanations of group differences in business success and concluded, as stated previously, that one way "up" is the development of an ethnic enclave economy whose component firms function in ways that resemble those at the "center" of the economy rather than those at the "periphery." They agreed with Frazier (1957) that to develop an enclave economy a group must possess "'a tradition of enterprise' based primarily on experience in 'buying and selling'" (Portes and Bach 1985:46). In a comparison of Cuban-owned and black-owned businesses in Miami, Wilson and Martin (1982:155) found that "the black business community appears to be merely an extension of the periphery economy. . . . " while the Cuban community had created an enclave economy.

The question of the business success of African Americans has concerned many thinkers and has been analyzed further by Butler (1991). A major objective of Butler's analysis was to challenge the belief that African Americans do not have a strong tradition of business and self-help. He argued that (1) beginning during the colonial period, a noticeable segment of the black American population followed an entrepreneurial path similar to that of the middleman minorities; (2) a substantial black middleman economy was constructed before 1900; but (3) with the development of the Jim Crow system, segregation forced black business development to detour from the usual path of middleman groups and to develop, instead, as a *truncated middleman group* (Butler 1991:143, 228). As black entrepreneurs were separated from white consumers, they became dependent on "Protected markets in personal services catering to other blacks. . . . " (Boyd 1991:411). Meanwhile, the massive migration to the North and the cities commenced as many African Americans sought economic security through competition for jobs in the open market.

An important consequence of this historical pattern, Butler argued, is that black Americans have followed two routes to wordly success in American society, one of which is largely unrecognized. The first route to success, described in our discussion of the secondary assimilation of the new black middle class, resembles what one would expect on the basis of the immigrant model (Butler 1991:242–244). Despite the extremely high levels of discrimination against them, the new arrivals in the northern and southern cities, like many immigrants before them, worked hard to establish themselves in the society's mainstream and to make a place in the world for their children. Many third- and fourth-generation descendants of this group are now "making it in America," but, as William J. Wilson's (1987) analysis shows, many others are being left behind, and there is no consensus concerning the steps that should be taken to prevent the ghetto poor from remaining hopelessly at the bottom of the American heap.

The second route to success, in Butler's view, stems from a strong, misunderstood, and greatly underestimated tradition of business enterprise among African Americans. He argued that the modern-day descendants of African Americans who engaged in business have inherited a philosophy of life and a way of adapting to extreme hostility resembling that of the descendants of middleman minorities, and with similar socioeconomic consequences (Butler 1991:258, 314). In his view, "Afro-Americans today who find themselves locked into poverty and despair in the core central cities" should look to the experiences of the truncated middleman group of black Americans for clues concerning how to adapt successfully to contemporary circumstances (Butler 1991:322). He stated that, with appropriate adjustments for new conditions, the example of the truncated African American middleman group may afford a blueprint for adjustment for many of those who do not wish to follow, or are unable to follow, the three-generations model.

All of the arguments presented concerning the worldly success of African Americans are hotly contested and are of great public importance. As we emphasized previously, positions taken in the public debate over what should be done to promote the assimilation of minority groups are closely connected to competing social policy views. Liberals, generally, stress the role of past and present discrimination in creating and maintaining group differences and are critical of arguments, such as the culture of poverty thesis, that attempt to locate the source of success in the cultural values and motives of group members. Conservatives, on the other hand, focus strongly on the role of cultural differences as important causes of group differences in success. William J. Wilson (1991:1) argued that his approach transcends the "simplistic either/or notions of culture versus social structure. . . . " by showing some of the links between these notions. Butler (1991:324), too, argued that his approach "is neither conservative nor liberal" but, rather, is one that encourages African Americans to consider "a path which has been followed for centuries by oppressed and outcast groups."[39]

Regardless of the extent to which increases in the worldly success of African Americans depend on changes in black culture, on a greater similarity of opportunities, or on "the dynamic interplay between ghetto-specific cultural characteristics and social and economic opportunities" (W. Wilson 1987:18), it is probable that this issue will continue to animate political debates for some time to come. The disagreement over the question of the causes of African American success may serve to remind us that social scientific theories and evidence frequently suggest certain practical steps that may be taken to solve social problems. It should remind us, too, that the various ideologies of group adjustment lie just beneath the surface of public debate over what should be done regarding the assimilation of minority groups.

In chapter 12, we consider the relationship of these issues to the experience of Native Americans.

Key Ideas

1. Massive resistance by whites to the *Brown* decisions was met by a sharp increase in the use of nonviolent protest tactics by African Americans. Racial confrontations in southern cities such as Little Rock, Montgomery, Greensboro, and Birmingham crumbled the structure of Jim Crow segregation in public places and accommodations and paved the way for the passage of the Civil Rights Act of 1964 and the Voting Rights Act of 1965.

2. All of these changes ensured the legal equality of African Americans. They did not, however, alter noticeably the living conditions of most African Americans. During this period many African Americans, especially young African Americans, turned away from non-violent protest toward the use of violence. For several years the cities of the United States were torn by racial violence.

3. Many observers have stated either that African Americans are culturally "nothing but" Americans or that their culture is a "distorted" variant of mainstream American culture. It seems more accurate to say that African Americans have developed and possess a distinctive culture of their own but that they, like Mexican Americans, are moving toward an additive form of cultural assimilation.

4. African Americans, especially women, appear to be moving toward secondary assimilation in jobs. There also has been secondary assimilation in incomes, again especially among women; but the trend among men slowed during the 1970s. The evidence on the education gap also is mixed, with the overall trend pointing toward educational assimilation (both in the years of schooling and in desegregated facilities), but there are several indications of slowed change in this respect. Finally, practically no change is occurring in the sphere of residential segregation.

5. While the rate of primary and marital assimilation has increased markedly, the total amount of these forms of assimilation is still very low, and the gap between blacks and whites will remain (at present rates of change) for a long time to come. The continued primary and marital separation of whites and blacks, along with the visible changes in cultural and secondary assimilation, suggests that blacks are moving toward the goal of cultural pluralism.

6. Although the hereditarian thesis concerning African American achievement is still debated, public policy in the last three decades was more affected by a disagreement within the ranks of the environmentalists. Just as the comparatively high achievement of Japanese Americans and the comparatively low achievement of Mexican Americans have been interpreted by some to be a consequence of particular values within their cultures, the culture of poverty thesis maintains that most blacks possess and transmit to their children values that are obstacles to success. This thesis plays down the role of majority group discrimination as a barrier to minority group achievement.

7. Business enterprise is increasing rapidly among African Americans, though this mode of adaptation to out-group threat is still comparatively low. The role of self-help in the lives of African Americans has received renewed scrutiny.

Notes

1. During this period, many new organizations came into being. The scholars of the Committee on the Status of Black Americans (CSBA), who prepared the comprehensive study *A Common Destiny,* reported that more than eleven hundred organizations were founded between 1965 and 1987 (Jaynes and Williams 1989:186).

2. Davies combines in this hypothesis the insights of Marx and Engels, on the one hand, with those of Tocqueville, on the other. The former writers favored the view that revolution should occur when people's life circumstances become so deplorable that they can't take it anymore. Tocqueville, in contrast, proposed an early form of the rising expectations view.

3. The major disorders involved a combination of four factors: (1) many fires, looting, and reports of sniping; (2) more than two days of violence; (3) large crowds; and (4) the use of National Guard and federal forces along with local law enforcement agencies. Among the eight cities having major disorders, those in Detroit and New-

ark were the largest and most damaging. The fighting in some cities included the use of tanks and machine guns. In Detroit alone, there were forty-three deaths, and property damage exceeded $40 million (National Advisory Commission 1968:107–116).

4. Some observers believe the peak was reached later (see, e.g., Feagin and Hahn 1973:105–106).

5. Did the urban riots by blacks affect the extent to which welfare programs were expanded? In the opinion of Isaac and Kelly (1981), the riots did lead to an expansion of several major welfare programs.

6. Many people object to the term *underclass,* regarding it as one that distorts the analysis of poverty to fit the ideology of political conservatives. We return shortly to some of the criticisms.

7. In a *TIME/CNN* poll 79 percent of white and 78 percent of black respondents said they expected a verdict of guilty (Church 1991:23).

8. Two of the officers also were acquitted on charges of "filing a false police report" and one was acquitted as an "accessory after the fact to a felony."

9. Disorders in other places, for example Las Vegas, Nevada, continued for some time thereafter. According to Dirk Johnson, (1992:A10), violence erupted on sixteen of the eighteen nights following April 30.

10. The depth of disillusionment among African Americans is revealed in some startling findings concerning the extent to which they believe the AIDS epidemic represents a genocidal plot. A New York Times/WCBS-TV news poll found "that 1 black in 10 believes the AIDS virus was 'deliberately created in a laboratory in order to infect black people' and and additional 2 in 10 thought that might be so" (*New York Times* May 12, 1992:A14). ·

11. Myrdal ([1944]1964:928) stated that the institutions of African Americans "show little similarity to African institutions."

12. Some later studies have not fully supported Gutman's view. See, for example, Agresti (1978:697–706).

13. An excellent illustration of this process is the establishment of the Kwanzaa holiday period by Mavlana Ron Karenga. The seven-day holiday is celebrated each year, beginning on December 26. Each day is devoted to one of the seven cardinal principles of the Black Value System (Monsho 1988).

14. Gordon (1964:76) agreed that lower-class blacks are still not assimilated culturally but maintained this is not due to African cultural survivals.

15. See chapter 8 for a description of indexes of dissimilarity.

16. These figures comparing individuals are based on constant 1984 dollars.

17. The largest political subdivision in the United States in which income parity between the races has been reported is the borough of Queens in New York City. Some demographers believe that even this degree of parity is "nothing short of astonishing. . . . " (Roberts 1992:A1).

18. Hacker's (1992:95) comparisons show that this result may not hold for men.

19. Also, even if all schools were segregated, it still would be possible to have segregated classrooms *within* the schools.

20. The question "Do blacks prefer to live in segregated housing?" frequently arises. A series of national polls shows that they do not and that their preference for desegregated housing is rising (Farley and Allen 1987:150–155; Goldman 1970:171; Jaynes and Williams 1989:143).

21. Schuman and Bobo (1988:295) found that some of the opposition to open housing laws may reflect a general opposition to federal coercion, but they found also that "personal prejudice against blacks" is an important element.

22. I wish to thank the authors for sending me a copy of their report. I wish also to thank Teresa A. Sullivan for calling the study to my attention.

23. Among twenty-five of America's largest metropolitan areas in 1990, the lowest segregation score for African Americans was Anaheim-Santa Ana's 44. The highest was Detroit's 89 (O'Hare and Usdansky 1992:7).

24. For a full description of these surveys, see Schuman and Hatchett (1974).

25. Our discussion is limited to legally defined marriages. Over the centuries, of course, there has been a great deal of biological "mixing" or "miscegenation" (Herskovits 1928).

26. For references to this literature, see Monahan (1976:223–231).

27. See also Alba and Golden (1986).

28. Some of the key elements of the culture of poverty are the same as those suggested by Kluckholn as central to the value orientations of the Spanish Americans, but there are some differences (Kluckholn 1956:342–357). For a comparison of the two cultures, see Burma (1970:17–28).

29. See for example, Coward, Williams, and Feagin (1974:621–634), Jaynes and Williams (1989:540–544), and Van Til and Van Til (1974: 313–321).

30. The proportion of female-headed households is much larger among blacks than whites, but the ratio of black-to-white female-headed households was the same in 1990 as in 1950. In

1950 the ratio was 17.2:5.3 (3.2 percent); in 1990 it was 56.2:17.3 (3.2 percent) (Hacker 1992:68). "This raises the possibility," Hacker (1992:69) states, "that what we have . . . are . . . concurrent adaptations to common cultural trends."

31. Sawhill (1991:177) stated that based on a broad definition, the underclass includes about 8 million people; based on a narrow definition it includes about 2 to 3 million people.

32. This argument has appeared in several different analyses during the past century. For incisive comments concerning a number of these, see Wilhelm (1983:117–119) and Boston (1988:1–21).

33. The extent to which middle-class African Americans may enjoy their status is a matter of controversy. Feagin (1991) has shown that, despite all of the legislation designed to prevent discrimination, middle-class African Americans still encounter a substantial degree of discrimination in public places.

34. William J. Wilson (1991:6) adopted the term "ghetto poor" in an effort to shift attention away from the pejorative connotations of the term *underclass* and toward a focus on research issues.

35. I wish to thank Gideon Sjoberg for calling this symposium to my attention.

36. For other examples of analyses that relate to Wilson's work, see Massey and Eggers (1990), Moore (1989), Schoen and Kluegel (1988), and Thomas and Hughes (1986).

37. The percentages of children who live in poverty in black married-couple families and white female-headed families were (in 1987) about 12 and 43 percent, respectively.

38. The level of self-employment among non-Hispanic whites was just over 67.

39. Butler notes that the debate over self-help has been confused unnecessarily with the separatist (or conservative) views of Booker T. Washington, citing Harold Cruse's remark that "integrationists would rather be tarred and feathered than suspected of the nationalist taint" (Butler 1991:274).

Native Americans

We told you a little while ago that we had an
uneasiness on our minds, and we shall now
tell you what it is; it is concerning our land.
—*MOHAWK SPEAKER, ALBANY CONGRESS, 1754*

The thinking Indian . . . asks that he be treated as
an American. . . . —*SOCIETY OF AMERICAN INDIANS*

For the sake of our psychic stability as well as our
physical well-being we must be free men and
exercise free choices. —*CLYDE WARRIOR*

*The Indian people are going to remain Indians
for a long time to come. —MELVIN THOM*

They were called "the vanishing Americans." After three centuries of contact with
Europeans, the indigenous people of what is now the continental United States had
declined in number from at least two million to less than one-eighth of that (Snipp
1989:10, 63). The whites' diseases, bullets, alcoholic beverages, and industrial
civilization had taken their appalling toll. Whole tribes, bands, or nations—perhaps
fifty altogether—had disappeared (Spicer 1980a:58). Although the extent of the
depopulation from diseases varied considerably among different tribes and locations, McNeill (1976:190) estimated that, overall, more than 90 percent of the Native
American population was decimated by epidemic diseases. Deneven concluded in
this regard that "the discovery of America was followed by possibly the greatest
demographic disaster in the history of the world" (quoted by Snipp 1989:15). But
in the present century, the American Indians have failed to "vanish" as anticipated.
Instead, their population has increased rapidly, and today they are one of the fastest
growing groups in the United States. Their amazing increase has produced a
population that may be approaching in size the one existing in 1600.[1]

Even at the time of the American Revolution, the Indian population still may
have been large enough for a unified stand by the tribes in direct contact with
the Europeans to have brought the colonization effort to a halt—at least for a
while. But the onset of the Industrial Revolution in Europe in the last quarter
of the eighteenth century created a force that was irresistible. The swelling
population in Europe was reflected in an enormous emigration to America, and the
developments in machine technology radically altered the terms of the competition
between the Americans and the Indians. These developments set the stage for
the military conquest that took place during the last half of the nineteenth
century. It was the completion of this conquest that seemed to spell the end for
the indigenous people as bearers of distinctive cultures. In fact, as stated earlier,
many tribes have vanished. But in 1981, the U.S. government still recognized 283
tribes, and an additional 175 groups sought official recognition (Olson and
Wilson 1984:180). More than 150 Native American languages are still in use, not
counting dialects (Stewart 1977a:501). American Indians, as Spicer (1980a:59)
observed, "were not and have not become a single . . . people justifying a single
label . . . as most Americans believe. They comprise at least 170 peoples with
different cultural backgrounds, different historical experiences, and . . . different
senses of identity."

In chapters 2 and 3, we examined briefly the relations between some of the
coastal tribes and the English during the seventeenth century to help explain the
origin of the Anglo conformity ideology and to illustrate the scope of its application.
Now we enlarge our inquiry to trace in broad outline some of the key events,
people, and social processes that help to explain the present circumstances of the
diverse people called American "Indians" and "Native Americans."

English Penetration of the Continent

Decades before the English founded Jamestown and Plymouth, French explorers and fishermen were active along the St. Lawrence waterway and the eastern coast of Canada. By 1600, it was apparent that the greatest profits in this part of the New World would come from animal furs and skins. The Indians were willing to trade many valuable pelts for relatively small returns in guns, gunpowder, alcoholic beverages, clothing, costume jewelry, and other European goods.

The French established stable trade relations with the large Huron tribes near the Great Lakes and, despite the small number of the French, initiated a vigorous effort to convert the Native Americans to Christianity. When the Puritan population of New England had reached fifty thousand there probably were less than five thousand representatives of France in Canada. French fur trappers, explorers, and priests rapidly expanded their alliances with various tribes and extended French claims to the entire Mississippi River Valley and portions of the Gulf Coast. They hoped to dominate the fur trade and pin the English colonists to the Atlantic seaboard. The English, of course, were eager to prevent French dominance, and to achieve this they needed Native American partners in the interior who could supply pelts either as trappers or as "middlemen" between the English and the tribes still further west. For example, after the English seized New Netherland, they assumed control of the active fur trading network that the Dutch had established with the Iroquois (in particular, the Mohawks) along the Hudson River Valley (Nash 1974:93, 99).

This new relationship between the Iroquois and the English increased England's ability to compete for the western fur trade, but it also had other consequences. The Iroquois, in search of pelts, invaded lands under the control of rival tribes, some of whom were trade allies of the French. These invasions led to bloody conflicts among the tribes and to enormous changes in their relative sizes and strengths. They also were accompanied by a wide variety of changes in the cultures of all the tribes in contact with the French and English. The struggle between these European powers and their respective Native American allies for the control of Canada, the Mississippi Valley, and the fur trade continued for nearly one hundred years. During most of this time, the English were able to depend on either the assistance or the neutrality of some or all of the powerful Five Nations of the Iroquois.[2]

Given their small numbers, how were the French able to sustain this conflict? First, the English colonies were very divided among themselves, which made planning and organizing any military undertaking difficult. Second, the French were careful to send as traders men who knew something of the Indians' customs and who, consequently, could interact with them in an agreeable way. It was said that the French traders became "more Indian than French," while the English traders frequently were "despised and held in great Contempt by the Indians as liars and Persons regarding nothing but their own Gain" (McNickle 1973:38–39). Of special significance was the fact that the French government adopted as its official policy the view that interracial mixing was desirable (Nash 1974:104) (though such an open and accepting approach to the Indians did not mean the French lacked ethnocentrism). The Indians preferred to do business with the usually nonviolent and friendly French than with the frequently haughty and unpredictable English.

Why, then, were the French unable to establish a lasting alliance with the Iroquois? Both France and England realized that the League of the Iroquois was of pivotal importance in the effort to gain control of the continent. A French observer marveled "that three or four thousand souls can make tremble a whole new world," while an English commentator stated that the Iroquois "will cast the balance" in the conflict (Nash 1974:240–241). Two great advantages of dealing with the English in this tug of war were that they offered the Iroquois higher prices for their furs and the trade goods they supplied were of a higher quality than those the Iroquois could get from the French.[3]

These advantages did not cause the Iroquois to recognize English sovereignty over their territory. Throughout these years, the sharp business practices of the English traders and land speculators continued to create frictions, and the Iroquois became ever more contemptuous of the English and their culture. A famous illustration of their opinion of English civilization occurred in 1744. In answer to an invitation to send some of their young men to be educated in Virginia, the Iroquois replied, "If the English Gentlemen would send a Dozen or two of their children to Onondaga, the great Council would take care of their Education, bring them up in really what was the best Manner and make men of them" (Nash 1974:260).

The showdown between France and England came in the French and Indian War, which was fought mainly between 1754 and 1761.[4] During the first several years of this conflict, the Iroquois were primarily neutral, though the Mohawks sometimes supported the English and the Senecas sometimes supported the French. However, as it became increasingly clear there was a real danger that the French and their allies would drive the English colonists into the sea, the English counter-attacked with a large fighting force and soon reversed the trend of the war. At this point, the Iroquois threw their full weight to the side of the English (Nash 1974:267–268). Within two years the war in Canada and the upper Mississippi region was over and an avalanche of new settlers poured into the Ohio Valley.

At this moment an Ottawa chief named Pontiac and an evangelist called the Delaware Prophet attempted to convince the American Indians that they should give up the white man's trade goods, return to the old ways, and create an intertribal military organization to combat the whites (Josephy 1961:110–112). Through a series of councils, Pontiac gained the support of the Hurons, Potawatomis, Chippewas, Delawares, Kickapoos, Shawnees, and a number of other tribes. Starting with a siege of Fort Detroit in May 1763, warriors from many tribes commenced an attack against the English. As the fighting spread and intensified, the frontier was hurled back toward the Atlantic coast. By September, however, the English were being reinforced steadily by fresh troops. When Pontiac received word that the French, Spanish, and English had signed a treaty in Europe, he sued for peace.[5]

Anglo–American Indian Policies

Pontiac's uprising failed to drive the English out of North America, but it did demonstrate that a concerted effort on the part of united tribes still could pose a substantial threat to the colonies. It also served as a final argument for those in England who believed the colonies should be required to follow a uniform policy toward the Indians. Such a policy, The Proclamation of 1763, was promulgated by the king in October. This famous proclamation declared that (1) all land west of the crest of the Appalachian mountains was "Indian country," (2) any settlers west of the Appalachians who had not acquired a legal title to their land from the Indians must return to the colonies, and (3) all future land purchases from the Indians must be conducted in public meetings attended by representatives of the king (McNickle 1973:43).[6]

The Proclamation of 1763 recognized that the government of England was obligated to attempt to control trade between the Indians and the colonists and, in particular, was obligated to prevent the swelling colonial population from invading Indian country. But there were too many colonists and too few soldiers and Indians. At a time when the colonists were already in the process of rejecting royal authority, there was no way for the English to prevent the colonists from moving onto tribal lands and taking possession of them by fair means or foul.

The proclamation, nevertheless, had far-reaching consequences. For example, during the American Revolution, the Continental Congress took steps to observe the provisions of the royal policy and to establish friendly relations with the Indians. An early note from Congress to the Iroquois stated, "Brothers! This is a family quarrel between us and Old England. . . . We desire you to remain at home, and not join on either side, but keep the hatchet buried deep" (McNickle 1973:49). In 1787, the proclamation's lead was followed further in the famous Northwest Territory Ordinance, which promised that: "The utmost good faith shall always be observed toward the Indians; their lands and property shall never be taken from them without their consent: and their property, rights, and liberty, they shall never be invaded or disturbed, unless in just and lawful wars authorized by Congress" (Jackson and Galli 1977:3).

In principle, then, Congress decided to follow the policies established by the English; however, the practical problems of regulating contacts between the frontiersmen and the Indians were as great as ever. George Washington lamented that the frontiersmen, "in defiance of the proclamation of Congress . . . roam over the Country on the Indian side of the Ohio, mark out Lands, Survey, and even settle them. This gives great discontent to the Indians . . ." (Prucha 1962:35).

After Washington became president, he and Henry Knox, his secretary of war, set out to establish, in Knox's words, "a firm peace" based on the "principles of justice and moderation" (Prucha 1962:41). Their main tool was a series of laws (Trade and Intercourse Acts) to enforce the treaties already concluded with the major tribes of the North and South, as well as all future treaties that might be made. The existing treaties with such tribes as the Iroquois, Delawares, Wyandots, Chippewas, Ottowas, Shawnees, Cherokees, Choctaws, and Chickasaws were being widely violated. The basic problem was "the presence of . . . tribesmen in the path of aggressive and land-hungry whites" (Prucha 1962:3). The traders and settlers were by now masters of several effective methods of separating the Indians from their lands.

Consider, for example, some of the events following the Greenville Treaty of 1795, through which twelve Indian tribes ceded around 50 million acres of Ohio to the United States. As usual, the Indians received a certain quantity of goods and a promise of future annual payments for their land and a line was drawn on the map to separate Indian country from white country. However, as the white population in the Ohio Valley grew, many traders and settlers tried to gain concessions from the Indians beyond the established frontier line; as in the past, one of their major trade offerings to the Indians was liquor. Huge quantities of liquor were given to them in return for their land and other possessions. The effects were felt by the tribes throughout the Northwest Territory. Josephy (1961:147) stated that "almost overnight large segments of once proud and dignified tribes became demoralized in drunkenness and disease."

A new leader, Tecumseh, and his brother, Tenskwatawa (called the Shawnee Prophet), came forward at this time to resume Pontiac's call to turn away from the white man's way and unite to prevent the whites from acquiring any more land. In a council meeting with Governor William Henry Harrison, later a president of the United States, Tecumseh argued: "No tribe has a right to sell, even to each other, much less to strangers, who demand all and will take no less. . . . Sell a country! Why not sell the air, the clouds and the great sea, as well as the earth? Did not the Great Spirit make them all for the use of his children?" (Josephy 1961:155).

Harrison rejected Tecumseh's view of land ownership and made clear that he would continue to make treaties and acquire tribal lands.[7] Tecumseh, therefore, renewed his efforts to weld a broad alliance of tribes to resist any further advances by the whites. As a part of this massive project, Tecumseh returned to the South to meet with the leaders of the strong tribes throughout the region and to urge them to join him in a pan-Indian uprising against the United States. Although Tecumseh's oratory was eloquent, most of the older chiefs were not convinced they should now become the allies of some of their traditional tribal enemies. Many also were receiving annual gifts from the whites and were reluctant to give these up.

When he returned home, Tecumseh found that his warriors had violated his orders and attacked Harrison's forces on Tippecanoe Creek. Soon after this engagement, the War of 1812 between England and the United States erupted, and Tecumseh threw all of his weight into the conflict on the side of the English. He believed this was the last chance the Native Americans would have to stop the expansion of the United States. Perhaps if the English won the war, he reasoned, then the rights of the tribes would be respected; but if the United States won, he stated, "it will not be many years before our last place of abode and our last hunting ground will be taken from us, and the remnants of the different tribes . . . will all be driven toward the setting sun" (Josephy 1961:163). The English lost the war; Tecumseh lost his life in battle, and the American Indians never again had the active support of a European power against the United States.

Indian Removal

Legal Issues

In 1802, the state of Georgia and the federal government faced one another in a land dispute. A compromise was reached whereby Georgia ceded its western lands to the United States in return for a promise that the federal government would extinguish the land claims of the Cherokees in Georgia "as early as the same can be peaceably obtained, on reasonable terms" (Hagan 1971:54). In the effort to fulfill this promise, the federal government, through a series of treaties, forced the Cherokees to give up most of the 60 million acres of land involved. This pressure on the Cherokees was particularly ironic because these people were making a determined effort to adjust to the whites' ways and were widely celebrated as one of the most "civilized" of all the tribes.[8] Their nation was organized as a loosely federated republic. They had a written constitution, a bicameral legislature, and an appellate judiciary. One of their members, Sequoyah, devised a system of writing based on syllables that permitted the Cherokee language to be written, and this invention led to the spread of literacy among the Cherokees (Spicer 1980a:84). Nevertheless, the Georgians believed the agreement of 1802 had assured them complete control of the Cherokees' land, so in 1828 and 1829, Georgia annexed the Cherokees' land and asserted that the Cherokee people were subject to the laws of Georgia rather than to Cherokee laws. The Cherokees rejected Georgia's claim to jurisdiction and presented their views before the U.S. Supreme Court in the cases *Cherokee Nation v. Georgia* (1831) and *Worcester v. Georgia* (1832). The judgments in these cases, with Chief Justice John Marshall speaking for the Court, established the basic principles that have guided the Indian policies of the United States ever since (McNickle 1973:52).

These cases dealt with different aspects of the general question, "Are Indian tribes sovereign nations?" The main issue in *Cherokee Nation* was whether an Indian tribe, like other foreign nations, has the constitutional right to bring a court action against a state. The Court ruled that the Cherokee tribe was not a foreign nation and, therefore, could not sue Georgia. Although Chief Justice Marshall stated that American Indians "are acknowledged to have an unquestionable . . . right to the lands they occupy," he stated further that "tribes which reside within the acknowledged boundaries of the United States . . . may more correctly, perhaps, be denominated domestic dependent nations" (Chaudhuri 1985:24).[9] This ruling, while agreeing that Native American tribes are sovereign nations, nevertheless placed limits on their sovereignty.

The main issue in *Worcester* was whether Georgia could pass laws that superceded the laws of the Cherokees, and on this score the Court ruled in favor of the Indians. "The Cherokee Nation," Marshall wrote, "is a distinct community, occupying its own territory . . . in which the laws of Georgia can have no force . . ." (McNickle 1973:55). This decision established the principle that although tribal sovereignty has limits (as shown in *Cherokee Nation*), the remaining sovereignty is great indeed. Tribal powers include the right to make treaties, to be protected from state encroachments, and to enjoy certain basic immunities with respect to the United States (Chaudhuri 1985:23, 26). Taken together, the *Cherokee Nation* and *Worcester* rulings conveyed an ambivalent view of the limits of tribal authority that has continued to the present.[10]

Even though the Cherokees won in the *Worcester* case, they had the bad fortune to do so while Andrew Jackson was president of the United States. For many years Jackson had favored a policy of forcing the Indians to move west of the Mississippi, and as president he sponsored the Indian Removal Act of 1830. Since this act was designed to force all of the Indians in the southeastern states to move west of the Mississippi, Jackson was unimpressed by the Court's rulings. He made it clear, rather, that he would enforce the Indian Removal Act.[11] During the next six years, Jackson concluded ninety-four treaties with the tribes to induce them to move to new homes in Indian Territory (now Oklahoma) to make room for the thousands of white settlers who were eager to move onto Indian lands (Faulkner 1948:202). All of the usual tactics, including bribery, threats, and misrepresentation, were employed to bring these treaties into existence, and most of the tribes were reluctant to agree to them. Even though many of the Indians' white friends saw removal as a way to help protect the Indians from the whites, the Indians no longer believed the government's promises (Lurie 1982:138). When Jackson sent a message saying that the Indians were to receive "an ample district west of the Mississippi River . . . to be guaranteed to the Indian tribes as long as they shall occupy it," the leaders of the Chocktaws replied: "The red people are of the opinion, that in a few years the Americans will also wish to possess the land west of the Mississippi" (McNickle 1973:72).

The Indians were not given a choice. The removal process, which continued into the 1840s, is widely regarded as one of the most dishonorable chapters in American history. Removal shattered the lives of tens of thousands of people who were rapidly adopting many elements of white culture. Many of these people owned their own homes, earned their living through farming, and sent their children to school as did their white neighbors. In some cases, they also owned slaves. Despite their level of cultural assimilation, they did not receive the protection of the federal government. The Indians felt that by adopting the policy of removal, the U.S. government was violating its own principles of fairness and justice. One appeal to the conscience of the citizens of the United States read as follows: "Our cause is . . . the cause of liberty and justice. It is based upon your own principles, which we have learned from yourselves; for we have gloried to count your Washington and your Jefferson our great teachers" (Josephy 1961:179).

The Trail of Tears

Faced with the calamity of losing the last of their ancestral grounds, some tribes decided to fight; others decided to petition Congress and seek protection from the courts. In the end, nearly all of them were moved hundreds of miles along what has become known as "The Trail of Tears."[12] Of the "Five Civilized Tribes" in the Southeast (the Cherokees, Choctaws, Creeks, Chickasaws, and Seminoles), the

Choctaws were the first participants in a tragedy that, in Mooney's opinion (quoted in Van Every 1971:30), "may well exceed in weight of grief and pathos any other passage in American history." In return for 6 million acres of land, the tribe received a "perpetual" land grant in Indian Territory and annual payments of $6,000 per year. On these terms, twenty thousand Choctaws agreed to move. The ordeal of removal took three years. Approximately five thousand people died of famine and disease along the way (Spicer 1980a:85).

The army was sent against the Creeks in 1836, and more than seventeen thousand people were forced into a two-year march. Over 2,000 died of disease, starvation, and exposure during the journey, and an additional 3,500 died within three months after arriving in Indian Territory (Spicer 1980a:86). The Chickasaws resisted removal through lengthy negotiations, but during a period of over thirteen years, approximately one thousand Chickasaws died on The Trail of Tears.

The Cherokees chose to continue the legal fight they apparently had won in the *Worcester* decision, but after gold was discovered in the Cherokees' territory the pressure to open their land to the whites became irresistible. Finally, in the winter of 1838, the army was ordered to escort seventeen thousand Cherokees to Indian Territory. The agonizing march over The Trail of Tears claimed four thousand Cherokee lives (Spicer 1980a:84).[13]

The Seminoles, an offshoot of the Creek Nation, had fought against the United States in the War of 1812 and again in 1818 when Andrew Jackson invaded Florida in a move against the Spanish. Another source of friction was the fact that many blacks either had fled from the United States or been purchased there and were now living among the Seminoles. The Seminoles also were angry over the deceptive practices that had been used in attempting to arrange their removal to the West; consequently, the Indians showed increasing signs of discontent over the plan and, in December 1835, killed an Indian agent and attacked a group of soldiers. The war thus started lasted for nearly seven years. It led to the deaths of between fifteen hundred and two thousand American soldiers and cost the United States at least $20 million (Josephy 1968:324).

By the early 1840s, approximately a hundred thousand Native Americans had been moved from their homes east of the Mississippi into Indian Territory. While most of these refugees had come from the southeastern portion of the United States, such tribes as the Delawares, Kickapoos, Miamis, Ottawas, Peorias, Pottawatomies, Sacs, Foxes, Shawnees, and Wyandots also were removed from their homes in the North and East. The only large tribes to remain in the Northeast were members of the Iroquois League; however, even among the Iroquois, elements of the Cayugas, Oneidas, and Senecas were moved to Indian Territory (Spicer 1980a:61).

The great influx of people into Indian Territory created numerous new problems. The U.S. government had pledged to provide rations, weapons, and tools, but these necessities frequently did not arrive or did not arrive in sufficient quantities. Additionally, the United States had promised protection against the "wild tribes" who already lived in or near Indian Territory, and this promise also was not kept. The Comanches, Osages, and Pawnees, for example, were outraged that the newcomers were moving into their territory, competing with them for buffalo, and generally interfering with their established ways of living. As buffalo became more difficult to find, these Plains tribes raided the livestock of the Indian refugees, and the newcomers were forced to defend themselves (Hagan 1971:85–87).

By the latter part of the 1840s, only scattered fragments of once great tribes still remained east of the Mississippi River, but even before the removal process had ended, wagon trains from the United States were crossing Indian country headed for Oregon. After gold was discovered in California, the Plains tribes who, without their permission, had fallen under the jurisdiction of the United States, could not be protected from this westward movement. Finally, it was becoming clear that the idea of drawing a line on the map that would give the eastern portion of the country to the whites and the western portion to the Indians could not work. White traders, hunters, trappers, farmers, ranchers, and miners could not be kept on the eastern side of the frontier line. Nevertheless, the various western tribes had not abandoned the idea of maintaining control of their homelands, and their efforts to resist have given modern people much of the imagery, romance, legend, and tragedy associated with the saga of "the winning of the West." But behind the saga lies the reality that already had been experienced by the tribes of the East in the previous two hundred years. The pattern in the two cases was very similar. Treaties with individual tribes were followed by the encroachments of the white frontiersmen. The encroachments led to attacks, and the attacks led to retaliation. No matter how valiantly the Indians fought, they were outmanned and outgunned. In the end, they were forced to accept new treaties that were even less favorable than before. In a span of less than four decades, the experience of the western tribes recapitulated that of the eastern tribes.

Plains Wars and Reservations

The federal government tried to preserve the frontier boundary by building a line of forts running from Canada to Mexico near the ninety-fifth meridian. The soldiers garrisoned in these forts were expected to keep unlicensed traders and travelers out of Indian country, to prevent or punish Indian attacks on white settlements and caravans, and to protect the eastern Indians from the Plains Indians.

The Plains Indians who now faced the forts and frontiersmen of the United States practiced a way of life that has captured the imagination of people throughout the world. Consider the familiar image of the Indian warrior: he is dressed in fringed and beaded buckskins, mounted on a dashing charger, wearing a war bonnet of flowing eagle feathers. This image, which is frequently held of all Native Americans, derives principally from the cultures of the Plains tribes, especially those of the Sioux (Dakota or Lakota). Moreover, this complex of traits, also including certain styles of dancing and singing, has been most influential in the popular pan-Indian culture of modern Native Americans (Wax 1971:149).

This exciting and dramatic style of life, which has had such a profound influence on non-Indians and Indians alike, did not begin to take shape until near the beginning of the eighteenth century, when the Plains Indians acquired horses and firearms from the Spanish. Until then, the Plains had not been a very hospitable place to live, and the human population consequently had been small.[14] As the tribes near the Plains learned the arts of horsemanship, two important cultural changes occurred. First, many tribes began to mold their entire way of life around the use of the horse and the buffalo. Mounted and with guns, they now found the buffalo to be not only a reliable source of food but also a source of materials for housing, clothing, tools, and many other useful articles (Lurie 1982:133). Under these new conditions, many tribes deserted their previous localities to take up a nomadic existence. In addition to those who were being lured onto the Plains, many tribes were being pushed onto them by the "domino effect" of the westward expansion of the French and English colonizers.

The second major cultural change associated with the emergence of the horse-buffalo complex was a sharp increase in intertribal warfare. The competition among the tribes for hunting grounds frequently led to conflict, while the scarcity of horses led to a thrilling and conflict-filled pattern of raiding and theft. Fighting skill and prowess in war were highly valued as warfare became a central feature of the Plains culture. The young men clamored for opportunities to "count coup"—to touch the living members of hostile tribes. The more numerous and daring the warrior's coup, the higher his social status became in the tribe (Hagan 1971:106).

The development of the horse-buffalo and war complexes is well illustrated by the Arapahos, Blackfeet, Cheyennes, Comanches, and Crows, among others, but no tribes exceeded the Sioux as examples of the new life style. At the end of the seventeenth century, three major divisions of the Dakota-speaking peoples (Teton Sioux, Yankton Sioux, and Santee Sioux) lived in the forests of what is now Minnesota. As the Chippewas, who were allied with the French in the fur trade, moved into their territory, the Dakotas were forced to move westward. Spicer (1980a:92) noted that they became the dominant peoples of the northern Plains and the most thoroughly adapted as horse-riding buffalo hunters. Various bands among the Tetons—for example, the Brulés, Oglalas, Minneconjoux, and Hunkpapas—were particularly respected for their horsemanship and feared for their fighting abilities.

When the whites began to cross the Plains, the tribes were "in the very midst of their great cultural fluorescence and were formidable and enthusiastic warriors" (Lurie 1982:139). But the whites' diseases immediately began to take a terrible toll. In 1837, the Mandan tribe, one of the few farming tribes of the Plains, was decimated by smallpox. Their population fell from around 1,600 to less than 100 (Hagan 1971:94; Wax 1971:32–33). Over a period of years, cholera and smallpox took about one-half of the Crow tribe's four thousand people (Spicer 1980a:93), and in 1849 the Pawnees lost a fourth of their population to diseases (Hagan 1971:94). These catastrophes were intensified by the rapid depletion of the buffalo. White hunters slaughtered the herds, making it much more difficult for the Indians to maintain a proper diet.

Soon after the signing of the Treaty of Guadalupe Hidalgo, Oregon, New Mexico, Utah, Kansas, and Nebraska were organized as territories, and California was admitted to the Union as the thirty-first state. Each of these steps stimulated traffic across Indian country, bringing about increasing contacts and conflicts between Indian and white people.

To regulate these interactions, the army quickly extended to the western tribes the tried-and-true system of treaties and reservations that had been so successful in dispossessing the Native Americans of the East. At Fort Laramie a treaty was signed in 1851 in which approximately ten thousand Plains Indians agreed to permit the whites' wagon trains to cross their territory (D. Brown 1973:68). In return, the United States agreed to make annual payments of food and other supplies and also to provide protection from the white people traveling west. In the same year, the Santee Sioux ceded most of their territory in return for a guaranteed reservation on the Minnesota River (Josephy 1968:336). Shortly thereafter, treaties were signed by several tribes in the eastern portion of the Plains ceding over 90 percent of their lands and accepting reservations (Hagan 1971:98).

As had been true in the East, the government's inability to prevent violations of the treaties and its (or its Indian agents') frequent failure of the government to provide the rations and supplies guaranteed to the tribes led to renewed and expanded conflicts. As a result, the thirty-year period during and following the Civil War was a time of frequent, widespread warfare between Indians and whites. The events of many of these conflicts were well publicized and dramatized both at the time of their occurrence and subsequently. The names of the Indian war chiefs and their white opponents became well known. One need only mention chiefs such as Red Cloud, Sitting Bull, Gall, Crazy Horse, Spotted Tail, Joseph, Little Crow, Cochise, Geronimo, Little Wolf, and Quanah or white military leaders such as Kit Carson, Phillip Sheridan, William Sherman, George Crook, Alfred Terry, O. O. Howard, John Gibbon, and George Custer to be reminded of the tragedies that took place and the blood that was spilled across the West during these years.

The events surrounding the efforts of the Sioux to defend the last of their hunting grounds are of special interest. The end of the Civil War brought a renewed effort by the whites to build roads and railroads across Indian country. To protect caravans passing through the land of the Sioux, the federal government attempted to complete a treaty with the Sioux that would grant them a trainload of presents and an annual payment of supplies thereafter. At the very time the treaty was being negotiated, however, the army sent a regiment of troops into Sioux country to build a chain of forts along the Powder River. The Sioux chiefs, led by the Oglala Chief Red Cloud, were enraged by this action and broke off the negotiations. Red Cloud gathered the warriors of the various Sioux tribes and sought the assistance of the Arapahos, Cheyennes, and even his enemies, the Crows. After several months of guerrilla warfare, a small group of decoys led by Crazy Horse lured a detachment of soldiers under Captain William Fetterman into a trap. All eighty-one soldiers were slain.

After this battle, called the Fetterman Massacre by the whites, a new commission was sent from Washington to meet with Red Cloud and the other Sioux chiefs. Red Cloud refused to meet with the commission. Soon another commission, led by General William T. (for Tecumseh!) Sherman, came west and, again, Red Cloud refused to meet with them. Instead he sent this message: "If the Great Father kept white men out of my country, peace would last forever, but if they disturb me, there will be no peace. . . . The Great Spirit raised me in this land, and has raised you in another land. . . . I mean to keep this land" (Brown 1972:140). The following year Sherman tried to meet with Red Cloud, but the Oglala chief would not meet with the commission unless the soldiers were withdrawn from the forts along the Powder River. Finally, in 1868, the forts were abandoned and a treaty was signed in which both sides promised to keep the peace. The Treaty of 1868 also established the Great Sioux Reservation, comprising most of what is now North and South Dakota.

The peace did not last long. White miners, in violation of the Treaty of 1868, moved into the *sacred* Black Hills to mine gold. The Sioux were infuriated by this renewed invasion of their precious land and protested strongly to Washington. The government replied by offering to buy or lease the Black Hills so the gold could be mined. When the Sioux refused to permit mining on any basis, the government decided to dispossess them by force. All of the tribes in the area were ordered to report to the reservation agencies, but large groups of Sioux led by Sitting Bull, Crazy Horse, and their allies did not report. In addition, numerous "treaty" Indians left their reservations to join the "hostiles"; so in 1876, Generals Crook and Terry and Colonels Gibbon and Custer were ordered into Sioux country to "whip the hostiles" into submission (Brown 1972:367–372; Josephy 1968:340).[15]

General Sheridan organized a three-pronged offensive in the summer of 1876—the centennial summer of American independence. According to the plan, Crook would lead a column from the south, Gibbon would approach from the west, and Terry, with Custer in command of the Seventh Cavalry, would move from the east. Crook's forces, however, were stopped on June 17 at Rosebud Creek by a thousand Sioux and Cheyenne warriors led by Crazy Horse and Two Moon.[16] The general was surprised by this attack and concluded that prudence dictated a retreat back into Wyoming. Crook, therefore, no longer provided the anvil against which the hammers of Terry's, Custer's, and Gibbon's forces could strike.

With Crook's column out of action, the Sioux and Cheyenne warriors returned to their main camp, now on the Little Bighorn River, Montana Territory. Four days after the Battle of the Rosebud, but with no knowledge of the battle, Terry, Custer, and Gibbon joined forces and devised a new plan of attack. Gibbon would proceed south along the Little Bighorn and Custer would follow a parallel route on the Rosebud. On June 26, the two columns would turn toward one another and attack from two sides. However, on June 25 Custer marched on the encampment.[17] This apparently premature advance may have been precipitated by the belief, which Custer shared with many of the army's commanders, that the Indians would "skedaddle" as soon as they discovered the approaching troops. The army's main concern, therefore, was to prevent the Indians' escape. The Indians, however, had decided to make a stand and had amassed an army of between 1,000 and 2,500 warriors, depending on who's estimate one accepts.[18] As his Seventh Cavalry units approached the village, Custer divided the cavalrymen into three groups and attacked.[19] One group of three companies (between 160 and 200 men), led by

Captain William Benteen, was sent to the left to block an escape in that direction. A second group of three companies, under Major Marcus Reno, was ordered to proceed toward the southern end of the camp and attack. The remaining group of perhaps 265 men, led by Custer, swung to the right to approach the northern end of the camp. Custer's detachment was soon surrounded by warriors led by Crazy Horse, Two Moon, and Gall.[20] Every member of Custer's group was killed, and the remaining two groups of the Seventh Cavalry suffered heavy losses.[21]

The stunning victory of the Indians over the U.S. Army on the Little Bighorn River was, in fact, one of the last gasps of a people fighting frantically to preserve their independence. Some of the warriors who helped to destroy Custer's units on the Little Bighorn were survivors of an earlier surprise attack and slaughter by Custer of a group of Southern Cheyennes on the Washita River. Others were the friends or relatives of the Southern Cheyennes and Arapahos who were murdered in what is known as the Sand Creek Massacre.

The unprovoked and shameful attack at Sand Creek occurred in the winter of 1864. Two Southern Cheyenne chiefs, Black Kettle and White Antelope, and an Arapaho chief, Left Hand, were ordered by the governor of the newly formed Colorado Territory, John Evans, to report to their reservation agent at Fort Lyon. The chiefs obeyed this order and shortly afterward established a winter camp on Sand Creek, about thirty miles from the fort. Since the chiefs had obeyed the order to report to their agent, they felt completely safe. Nevertheless, on November 29, a force of about seven hundred Colorado militia, commanded by Indian-hating Colonel J. J. Chivington, fell upon the camp without warning. The shocked and helpless Indians gathered under an American flag flown by Black Kettle to show the soldiers they were at peace, but nothing could stop Chivington's troops. At least 130 men, women, and children were killed, scalped, and mutilated (Brown 1972:68–98).[22] Connell (1984:176) reconstructed the grisly scene from first-hand reports: "Cpl. Amos Miksch . . . testified that he 'saw some men unjointing fingers to get rings off, and cutting off ears to get silver ornaments.' Lt. James Connor testified that . . . he did not find a single Indian corpse, regardless of age or sex, that had not been scalped. 'I heard of numerous instances in which men had cut out the private parts of females. . . .' " In the opinion of General Nelson A. Miles, who later fought against the Sioux, the massacre at Sand Creek was the "foulest and most unjustifiable crime in the annals of America" (Hagan 1971:108).[23]

The memory of such atrocities by whites against the Native Americans did nothing to still the outburst of anger among white people as the news of "Custer's last stand" spread. The federal government claimed the Indians had violated the Treaty of 1868 and, therefore, must now sign a new agreement under which they would cede to the whites all rights to the Black Hills and the Powder River country. The Indians were told that if they did not sign, their rations would be discontinued and they would be sent south to Indian Territory. Without the rations supplied at the agencies, many would starve, and none of them relished the thought of being forced to move far away from their beloved Black Hills. With great reluctance, Red Cloud and Spotted Tail signed the agreement and then were placed under virtual arrest at their agencies in Nebraska.

Gradually, the chiefs of most of the other Sioux tribes signed the new agreement to give up the Black Hills. Sitting Bull, however, had taken his people and fled to Canada. Crazy Horse's people spent the winter of 1876–1877 searching for food and fighting soldiers. When General Crook sent word to Crazy Horse that he could have a reservation in the Powder River country if he would surrender, the great Sioux war chief marched into the Red Cloud Agency in Nebraska to become a reservation Indian (Brown 1972:290–294).[24]

With the surrender of Crazy Horse and, later the same year, Chief Joseph and his Nez Perces, armed resistance to American dominance in the territory acquired from Mexico had nearly ended. Several other famous confrontations occurred during the next ten years, including an "escape" by the Northern Cheyennes from Indian Territory, the so-called Ute War, and the last-ditch efforts of the Apaches in the Southwest. Irresistibly, however, the forces of the rapidly industrializing American giant stripped away the means whereby an open fight could be sustained. The buffalo had been slaughtered, and the Native American population had declined precipitously during the nineteenth century from approximately 600,000 to less than half that number, primarily as a result of disease and famine.[25] Most of the survivors had been assigned to reservations and, under military guard, were required to live on them. No further military resistance was possible. The words of Chief Joseph's widely publicized surrender speech reflected the situation in eloquent, tragic phrases: "Our chiefs are killed. . . . It is cold and we have no blankets. The little children are freezing to death. . . . Hear me, my chiefs. I am tired; my heart is sick and sad. From where the sun now stands, I will fight no more forever" (Josephy 1961:339–340).

From Separatism to Anglo Conformity

We have seen that from the earliest days of the American republic, the primary thrust of the official policy of the federal government embodied the idea that Indians and whites should be kept apart. This policy was responsible for the sharp distinction that was created between Indian country and white country. Ultimately, it also led to the great expansion of the reservation system. Throughout this time, however, many people had doubted the wisdom of separatism and had urged, instead, that the Indians be assisted to become "civilized"; consequently, a secondary, seemingly contradictory, thrust of official policy embodied the idea that the Native Americans could "be absorbed into American society" if they were given the tools, animals, seeds, and information needed to become farmers (Prucha 1962:214). The Indian Trade and Intercourse Act of 1793 empowered the president to "promote civilization" among "friendly Indians" and to expend twenty thousand dollars a year for two years for this purpose (Jackson and Galli 1977:63). Various additional laws continued this policy until 1819, after which time the amount of the annual "civilization fund" was reduced to ten thousand dollars, but the payment was then placed on a permanent basis.

The Bureau of Indian Affairs

The actual work of administering these activities relating to the American Indians had been entrusted to the secretary of war in 1789. As the years passed, however, the burden of Indian affairs became much greater. Secretary John Calhoun, in 1824, created a new branch in the War Department, which he named the Bureau of Indian Affairs (BIA). Among the duties of the head of the bureau was "the administration of the fund for the civilization of the Indians . . ." (Jackson and Galli 1977:43). The work of the BIA commenced immediately, although until Congress approved the plan, the duties assigned to the head of the BIA were still legally the responsibility of the secretary of war. The legal status of the BIA and the scope of its authority were clarified by the Indian Trade and Intercourse Act of 1834. Through this act, the commissioner of Indian affairs was placed atop an organization that, in Deloria's (1972:52) words, has exercised "immense power . . . over the lives and property of the Indian people . . ." from that time to this.[26]

At the bottom of the BIA's hierarchy of authority were the Indian agents and subagents, employees who lived on the reservations and were responsible for distributing annuities (either in money or in goods) and for carrying out the program to civilize the Indians. As the reservation system expanded and increasing numbers of Native Americans became dependent on the BIA and its agents, the question of the relationship between the federal government and the tribes grew more perplexing. The idea that the tribes were separate nations and could remain so began to give way to the idea that they were "wards" of the government, their "guardian." Simultaneously, the idea that no further treaties should be signed with the tribes grew in popularity.

The End of Treaty Making

The question "Are Indian tribes nations?" was answered by Congress, oddly enough, in the Appropriations Act of 1871. A rider to this act stated that Indian tribes would no longer be recognized as powers "with whom the United States may contract by treaty" (Hertzberg 1971:3–4). All treaties previously established would continue in force, but all new arrangements between the federal government and the tribes would be decided by Congress through legislation rather than by negotiation.

This sweeping change in the legal status of the Native American tribes greatly strengthened the hand of those who thought the government's traditional separatist policy should be discontinued. If the tribes were not nations and could not negotiate treaties, then why should they continue to live on reservations apart from other people? Land speculators and potential settlers wondered why the Indians should continue to occupy more land than they were "using"; political conservatives, forgetting the agreements to pay the Native Americans for their earlier land cessions, wondered why the government should continue to pay out "doles" to support them; and reformers wondered if the "civilizing" process would not be hastened if the reservations were divided up so each family would have its own specific plot of land. Thus, both greed and humanitarian concern combined in support of legislation to break up the reservations, end the established policy of separatism, and institute a policy of Anglo conformity.

The legislative battle over this issue was heated and prolonged. Critics of the plan to divide the reservations into individual allotments of land argued that it would "despoil the Indians of their lands and . . . make them vagabonds . . ." (McNickle 1973:81). Advocates of the plan, in contrast, argued that the allotment of reservation lands to individuals would help instill in the Indians a pride of ownership, encouraging them to give up their tribal past and adopt the American way of life.

The Dawes Act

The break with the past came in February 1887 with the passage of the General Allotment (Dawes) Act.[27] The law provided that the reservations were to be surveyed and divided into tracts. The tracts then were to be allotted to the members of the tribes in parcels of 160 acres (for family heads), 80 acres, or 40 acres. Any land left over after each tribal member had received his or her allotment would be declared "surplus" and could be sold to the United States. The money a tribe might receive for any surplus land that was sold would be held in trust by the U.S. Treasury, and the interest from the funds could be used to support activities that would hasten the movement of the tribes toward Anglo conformity. As an added inducement to give up their tribal heritages, each Indian who accepted an allotment and adopted "civilized" ways also then could become a citizen of the United States. If after a twenty-five-year trial period an individual allotee had proven to be capable of managing his or her own affairs, that person could receive a "certificate of competency," a title to his or her land, and citizenship. At this point, presumably, the individual would have become a well-motivated, self-reliant farmer and, therefore, would be no longer a ward of the federal government (McNickle 1973:82–83; Spicer 1980b:116). If the plan worked, then in one stroke the tribal life of the Native Americans would be disrupted and individual members of the tribes would be transformed into ordinary citizens.

The tribes, of course, were unable to do much to stop this legal attack on their way of life. The Five Civilized Tribes, nevertheless, organized protests against the Dawes proposal. As a result, the Dawes Act was not applied to the Five Civilized Tribes, the tribes of Indian Territory, or the New York Indians (Hoxie 1984:72). The government expected, though, that allotments still would take place on the basis of negotiations with the excluded tribes. When it became clear that these tribes simply did not intend to accept the allotment policy, the government replied with further legislation. In 1898 the Curtis Act stated that the tribal governments that had refused allotment no longer existed and, henceforth, tribal chiefs would be appointed by the president. The termination of these tribal governments removed the last organized resistance to the allotment of the reservation lands.

Did the Indians who received individual parcels of land adopt the white model and become self-sufficient farmers? Generally, they did not. The main effect of the

Dawes Act was to transfer most of the plots of land held by individual Indians into the hands of white people. As the opponents of the act had feared, the desire of the whites for land and the Indians' ignorance of American law led to the widespread use of deceitful and fraudulent practices in real estate transactions. During the period 1887–1934, the Native Americans lost over 87 million acres of land—approximately two-thirds of their collective holdings before the passage of the Dawes Act (Jackson and Galli 1977:95). Most of the land that remained to them was arid and barren. It was predominantly land that white people considered worthless and did not want.

Another important effect of the Dawes Act was to increase greatly the power of the BIA and its control over the individual lives of Native American people. To carry out the provisions of the act, the BIA had to hire more people and have them intrude in unprecedented detail into the lives of tribal members. For instance, the BIA was charged with developing membership rolls for the recognized tribes to determine who was and was not eligible for government services (Snipp 1989:33).[28] As the various initial tasks of surveying and allotting were completed on a reservation, other subsidiary tasks were discovered to be necessary. For the allotees to farm their lands, for example, irrigation systems sometimes were needed; so the BIA entered into the contracting business. Some allotees were physically unable to farm their lands; so the BIA arranged for the lease or rent of the lands and investment of the collected funds. In doing these and many other things, the agents of the BIA exercised decision-making powers that traditionally were the prerogatives of the chiefs and the tribal councils. But now, even the rations to which the tribes were entitled by the terms of existing treaties were sometimes withheld if they did not seem to their agents to be making satisfactory progress in the direction of Anglo conformity.

Beyond the losses of land and the decline in the Native Americans' ability to control their lives were other, still broader, effects of the law. The Dawes Act was the centerpiece of the general effort to bring the Indians into the mainstream of American society. Please recall that this was the early period of the new immigration, with its heightened nativism and renewed emphasis on the importance of the Anglo conformity assimilation of foreign elements in the American population. The Dawes Act was consonant with this developing mood. It strengthened various policies designed to separate the tribes from their heritages and, at the same time, force upon them the culture of the dominant group.

Indian Education

The forces that helped move the U.S. government to adopt an Indian policy favoring Anglo conformity were also at work in the field of education. The attempt to "civilize" the Native Americans had always included educational programs, and schools for this purpose were established in colonial times. But as the nineteenth century advanced and the tribes increasingly were confined to reservations, building and operating schools for them became an important function of the BIA. At first the BIA established two kinds of schools—day schools and boarding schools—

both of which were located on the reservations. Students who did well in the day schools, which were located near their homes, became candidates for "advancement" out of their homes and into the boarding schools. The boarding schools removed Native American children from their families and increased their exposure to the English language and Anglo-American ways of thinking and acting. Yet, in time, the conviction grew that something further was needed "to equip the Indians with necessary competencies and to update them to their changed situation in the world" (Jackson and Galli 1977:75). The Native American child, it was argued, needed to be removed not only from the family but from the reservation as well. To accomplish this, the off-reservation boarding school came into existence.

The BIA authorized Richard H. Pratt, an army officer, to convert an abandoned army barracks at Carlisle, Pennsylvania, into a boarding school for Indians.[29] The famous Carlisle School, thus founded, was definitely based on the Anglo conformity ideology. Pratt believed the Native Americans' heritage should be replaced with the skills and attitudes of the larger society, and the best way to do this, he thought, was permanently to remove the children from their tribal surroundings (Hertzberg 1971:16–17; Hoxie 1984:54–60). As an extension of this idea, Pratt also developed the "outing system." Under this system, Native American children from Carlisle attended public schools while living in the homes of selected American families. In this way, each child was separated not only from his or her family and tribe, but from all other Native Americans as well.

In the decades following the passage of the Dawes Act, the BIA expanded the off-reservation boarding school system. The curriculum at the off-reservation schools was mainly a mixture of the "three Rs" and a number of vocational arts and crafts. Still, they were considered to be a step above the reservation boarding schools, from which they drew most of their students. Whatever their academic merit may have been, they definitely represented an intensive effort to employ schooling as a device to transform American Indian children into ordinary citizens of the United States.

The Ghost Dance and Wounded Knee

The attempt to "civilize" Native Americans through education was intimately tied to various programs to Christianize them. Beginning with the early contacts among the English and Native Americans, missionary schools were established and supported by various Christian groups. Indeed, by 1819 the missionary effort was so well established that when Congress appropriated the "civilization fund" referred to earlier, the president approved grants to missionary societies to assist in their educational work (Jackson and Galli 1977:69). Of course, the primary effort of the missionary schools was not simply to teach the Native Americans but to convert them, and to be satisfactorily converted they were expected to give up all vestiges of their native religious beliefs and practices. This goal of the missionary schools also was adopted by the government-supported schools as a part of their general Anglo conformity policy. Any sign that reservation Indians were not accepting

Christianity or, worse yet, were retreating from Christianity was viewed with suspicion.

The whites' fear of a resurgence of tribal religious beliefs and practices was revealed by a tragic and infamous episode in the winter of 1890. During the latter part of the 1880s, a spiritual revival called the Ghost Dance Religion swept over the Plains. This religion, like several others of the time, promised Native Americans that by practicing certain rituals, dances, and songs, they could harness the supernatural power of their ancestors and thereby cause the white men to vanish from the earth. The dead people of all tribes would be resurrected, the buffalo would return to the Plains, and the land would resume its original splendor.

The Messiah of the Ghost Dance Religion, Wovoka, was a member of the Paiute tribe of Nevada. He urged Indians of all tribes to participate in the Ghost Dance, to lead good lives, and to await peacefully the promised day of the resurrection of the ancestors. The rituals and ideas of the Ghost Dance combined Christian and indigenous elements. For example, the Messiah taught that "you must not fight. Do right always" (Brown 1972:409). At the same time, the Native Americans wore special Ghost Shirts that many believed to be bulletproof.

The Ghost Dance reached the Sioux in the fall of 1890 and quickly spread on the Sioux reservations. Ghost dancing rapidly became so common that "almost all other activities came to a halt" (Brown 1972:409). The strange behavior of the Indians frightened the whites. Calls went out for military protection and the arrest of the Ghost Dance leaders. One of the leaders to be arrested was Sitting Bull, the famous medicine chief of the Hunkpapa Sioux. Sitting Bull had returned to the United States from Canada almost ten years earlier, had become a celebrity while touring with "Buffalo Bill" Cody's Wild West Show, and was now living with his people at the Standing Rock reservation. Shortly after the order went out, Sitting Bull was arrested and, in a tragic sequence of events, killed by two of the Native American officers who took him into custody.

Another leader to be arrested was a Minneconjou named Big Foot. When news of Sitting Bull's death reached Big Foot, he and about 350 others, most of whom were women and children, fled toward Red Cloud's Pine Ridge reservation. On the way, he was apprehended by units of the Seventh Cavalry (Custer's former regiment) and was ordered to an army tent camp at Wounded Knee Creek, South Dakota. The Native Americans camped that night at Wounded Knee. The soldiers were deployed around the camp, with their big guns placed on high ground overlooking the entire area. Early the next morning the army commanders ordered the warriors, most of whom wore Ghost Shirts, to turn in their guns and other arms. As the search neared its end, one young warrior raised his rifle over his head and, according to some reports, fired. The soldiers' reaction was immediate. A withering blast of rifle fire, soon followed by the shells of the big guns, cut through the surrounded and practically defenseless Native Americans (Brown 1972:413–418). At the end of the "battle," at least 40 percent of the Native Americans were dead (Spicer 1980a:93).[30]

The death of Sitting Bull and the U.S. Army's actions at Wounded Knee snuffed out the Ghost Dance Religion and, with it, the hope of the rebirth of tribal independence. It became clear to the Native Americans that the Ghost Shirts could not stop bullets. It also became clear that the whites had no intention of permitting the open practice of the Ghost Dance and were prepared to use violent methods, if necessary, to suppress it. The carnage at Wounded Knee, which occurred in the year that the frontier officially was declared closed, has served ever since as a symbol of the appalling quality of European-Indian relations in the period from 1607 to 1890. For almost three centuries, the white people had encroached upon the tribes' lands and had insisted either that the Indians be driven away or be made over in the image of white people. The Native Americans' resistance to either of these demands frequently had led to attempts to annihilate them.

Alternations between Anglo Conformity and Cultural Pluralism

As the twentieth century approached, the policy of Anglo conformity was in full sway. The number of Native Americans had declined to around 250,000, their lands were being allotted and sold, and the idea that they would soon vanish reached new highs in popularity among the whites. Many thought that the end of the "Indian problem" was in sight; however, one conspicuous legal barrier still prevented the disappearance of the Native Americans into the mainstream. Although the allotment procedure of the Dawes Act created a path to citizenship for American Indians, as late as 1924 at least one-third of them still were not citizens of the United States. The noncitizen Native Americans were in legal limbo—"their status was neither that of a citizen nor that of an alien. They were prisoners of war when no state of war existed" (McNickle 1973:91). As a show of gratitude to the thousands of Native Americans who had volunteered to fight in the American armed forces in World War I, Congress passed the Indian Citizenship Act in 1924. Many Indians were far from pleased to have received this gift, however. They were suspicious that this was yet another of the whites' tricks to escape their treaty obligations and detribalize the Native Americans.[31]

Some Native American voters, nevertheless, soon became involved in political matters, and their activities helped to initiate a thorough analysis of the effects of the federal government's trusteeship of Native American people. The results of this analysis, known as the Meriam Report, were published in 1928.[32] The report showed in detail that the land allotment policy had failed in its basic purpose. Individual allotments had not aided the Native Americans to overcome the problems of ignorance, poverty, and disease and to move into the American mainstream. On the contrary, by the time the Meriam Report was undertaken, most of the allotees had lost control of their lands and, in the process, their best chance to become self-sufficient. In the meantime, those who had continued to live on unallotted reservations actually had been fairly successful in giving individuals the responsibility of using specified plots of land for their own support. Paradoxically, the "magic" of individual ownership appeared to be working best among those who owned their lands communally. This difference may have arisen because, unlike the allottees, the individual proprietors of tribal lands could not sell them (Jackson and Galli 1977:99).

The Indian Reorganization Act

The Meriam Report came at a time when many people were calling for a radical change in the government's approach to Indian affairs. This call was answered by the Indian Reorganization Act (IRA), or Wheeler-Howard Act, of 1934. By this act, the federal government abandoned the effort to require Native Americans to adopt the dominant group's life style and embraced instead a pluralist policy. Generally speaking, the new policy sought to assist (not force) them to "lead self-respecting, organized lives in harmony with their own aims and ideals, as an integral part of American life" (McNickle 1973:93). More specifically, the IRA restored the right of the tribes to govern themselves *provided* they were willing to adopt the American model of representative democracy. The IRA also afforded the tribes the right to organize themselves as corporate business enterprises.

The acceptance of these two important new rights was itself a matter of choice and was to be decided by a majority vote of the adult members of each tribe. As in the case of citizenship, many Native Americans were suspicious of the government's motives and feared that reorganization concealed some new effort to destroy the tribes. Regional conferences were held to explain reorganization and allay the Native Americans' fears. Altogether, 258 elections were held, and around two-thirds of the tribes voted to accept the IRA (Wax 1971:57). Ninety-two tribes wrote constitutions, and seventy-two tribes agreed to draft charters of incorporation (Philp 1986:18). Eventually, the right to self-government was extended even to the tribes that voted against the IRA.

In addition to stimulating democratic self-government and an active participation in the American business economy, the IRA also aimed to encourage Native Americans to maintain and develop their identities as Native Americans. Under the policies of the Dawes Act, all things Indian had been denigrated or suppressed. Native American children in government schools had not been permitted to wear long hair, to dress in their tribal costumes, to engage in tribal rituals, or to speak their native languages. There was a constant fear that the newly civilized youngsters would "go back to the blanket" (Hertzberg 1971:18). The new policy no longer viewed tribal life as an alien leftover from a savage past—as something totally incompatible with contemporary American life. Instead, Native Americans were encouraged to develop their arts and crafts, to revive and transmit their ancient rituals and ceremonies, and to participate in community life on an equal footing with other Americans.

The reorganization of most of the tribes under the provisions of the IRA did not launch a dramatic increase in their educational level and standard of living; however, under the leadership of Commissioner John Collier, the management of Indian affairs definitely took a new direction. Programs were initiated to enable the tribes to recover some of their lost lands and to consolidate lands that had been reduced to numerous tiny fractions through the application of inheritance laws.

Loan funds were established to help finance a college education for qualified Native American students and to help the new tribal corporations to develop and market new products or exploit the reservations' natural resources. More than in any previous period of their lives on the reservations, Native Americans began to participate in the planning and execution of the various programs intended to assist them.

Throughout this period of reform, however, the BIA was still very much in control of reservation life. The bureau still received the annual appropriations from Congress, of course, and its scope now was expanded to include certain new duties, such as assisting the tribes to organize representative governments, some of which appeared to represent the interests of the BIA more than those of their respective tribes. The BIA also continued to play a strong role in the determination of tribal memberships and the administration of justice; consequently, many Native Americans disliked the IRA and did not approve of the way it was administered.[33] Despite the efforts of many people, a large discrepancy was maintained between the ideals of the IRA and the realities of Native American life.

The "Termination" Policy

The discrepancy between ideals and reality was encouraged by many members of Congress and other government officials who did not agree with the new pluralist Indian policies. The opponents of the IRA still had not abandoned the entrenched belief remaining from an earlier time that the government should "destroy tribal relations" and deal with Native Americans "not as nations or tribes or bands, but as individual citizens" (Svensson 1973:27).

Champions of the Anglo conformity policy regained the upper hand during the two administrations of President Eisenhower. In 1953, Congress adopted a resolution, House Concurrent Resolution 108, declaring that the Indians "should be freed from Federal supervision and control" (Bahr, Chadwick, and Day 1972:485). To set Native Americans "free," HCR 108 suggested that all laws and treaties then binding the United States to the tribes should be nullified. This new policy, which became known as "termination," seemed to be a direct assault on the idea that the tribes were entitled to payments and services for the land they had assigned to the government through treaties.[34] The Native Americans viewed this change as another shocking example of a unilateral action by the government to avoid completing its part of the treaty bargains (Svensson 1973:32).[35]

Congress hoped the termination policy would get the government "out of the Indian business" (Spicer 1980b:119). The termination of the services to a tribe could occur only if the tribe were sufficiently assimilated, willing to sever its tie with the federal government, and able to survive economically with local and state help. Few tribes were found to meet these standards.

The termination experience of the Klamath tribe of Oregon illustrates why the policy was so unpopular among Native Americans. The Klamaths, with a tribal membership of around two thousand people, owned nearly one million acres of land containing forests valued at approximately $50,000 per person (McNickle

1973:106). The government's plan gave the tribal members, many of whom did not understand the alternatives, no more than three years to decide what to do with their collective wealth. They could either form a corporation to manage their property or sell the land and timber and divide the money among the members of the tribe. Either way, the government's trusteeship would be terminated.

The issue was settled by a tribal vote in favor of selling and dividing the money. The Klamaths understood that the federal government would buy their land, establish a national forest, and pay each member of the tribe $43,500. As matters developed, the government disbanded the Klamath Tribal Council and ended the trust relationship but certified only a fraction of the tribe's members as "competent." Ten years later over one-half of the members had not received their payments and continued to be wards of the government. The main result of termination for them was the destruction of tribal government and the disorganization of tribal life (Spicer 1980a:106). This policy, according to a U.S. Senate report, created a high level of personal disorganization among the Klamaths (McNickle 1973:107). It also increased poverty and deepened further the Native Americans' distrust of the federal government in general and the BIA in particular. As Olson and Wilson (1984:138) laconically observed, "a government check could hardly compensate for a way of life."

The experience of the Menominees and, to a lesser extent, the other tribes that were terminated paralleled that of the Klamaths (Peroff 1981).[36] By the end of the second Eisenhower administration, it was apparent that the termination policy, as had been true of the earlier allotment policy, would not liberate Native Americans to participate fully in the mainstream of American life. Both of these policies sought to end abruptly the special relationship of Native Americans to the U.S. government; they served, in fact, only to take away from the tribes the resources they needed to create the very independence the policies tried to enforce.

It is vital to note here that the resistance of Native Americans to the termination policy did not mean they wished to continue forever as dependents of the federal government. Most of them endorsed the IRA goal of "the ultimate disappearance of any need for government aid or supervision" (McNickle 1973:93), and they would surely have loved to be free of the interference and regulation of the BIA. But in addition to the understandable fear that termination would deny them their treaty entitlements, there was the even greater fear that an abrupt end to their special status would mean an end to tribal life and their existence as Indians. The policy of termination did not take into account the strong wish among American Indians to fashion a mode of participating in American society without sacrificing their distinctiveness as Indians.

Governmental actions to effect termination had been brought to a standstill by 1961.[37] As the War on Poverty came into being, the termination policy, in Deloria's (1985c:251) words, "simply evaporated." Native Americans began to participate in various new government programs designed to expand their role in planning and controlling their own destiny. Near the end of the decade, President Johnson affirmed the right of Indians "to remain Indians while exercising their rights as Americans" (McNickle 1973:124), and in 1968, the Indian Civil Rights Act was passed. President Nixon, in 1970, attacked the idea that the federal government had the right to terminate unilaterally its special relationship to American Indians. He stated that the Indians were entitled by treaties and other agreements to the provision of numerous community services. The goal of national policy, the president said, must be to encourage self-determination among the Indians and "to strengthen the Indian's sense of autonomy without threatening his sense of community" (Jackson and Galli 1977:134). He also called for the renunciation of HCR 108. The intent of this presidential message was enacted into law by Congress in 1975 with the passage of the Indian Self-Determination and Educational Assistance Act. This act established a new relationship between the tribes and the federal government that, Olson and Wilson (1984:204) stated, represents "the greatest victory for pan-Indian activists in American history. . . ." A Federal Acknowledgement Program, under which terminated and unrecognized tribes may apply for federal recognition, was adopted in 1978. Since that time, federal budgets for Indian affairs have been reduced, but no new broad national policies have been adopted (Deloria 1985c:255).

Pan-Indian Responses and Initiatives

Protest Organizations

The rejection by the federal government of the Anglo conformity policy implied by termination and the return to the pluralist policy implicit in self-determination was, in part, a reflection of an unprecedented level of Native American political organization and activity. Throughout history, as we have seen, the basic social unit of Native American life has been the tribe. Native Americans generally were not organized at a level above the tribe, and when they were—as in the Powhatan, Wampanoag, and Iroquois Confederations—the organizations were loose. One's loyalty to the tribe still was primary. The tribal groups, nevertheless, did realize the advantages of acting together in broader groups. The efforts of such men as Metacom, Pontiac, Tecumseh, and Sitting Bull serve to remind us that the idea of organizing to resist the common foe is not new. As noted earlier, however, intertribal enmities and factionalism within the various tribes helped to prevent any of these efforts from achieving lasting success. Gradually, the Native Americans were divided, defeated, and concentrated on reservations. By the time the tribes' treaty-making powers were revoked in 1871, the federal government had assumed complete control of their lives. They became "wards" of the government—incompetent and dependent children whose "parent" had to see to their every need and make all of their decisions.

As the last pitiful remnants of the previously proud and self-sufficient tribes were forced onto the reservations, various "friends of the Indians," most of whom represented Christian groups, began to agitate in their behalf. The early 1880s produced a number of actions intended to ameliorate the conditions among Native Americans. The Women's National Indian Association was formed to protest the forced removal of the Poncas to Indian Territory. A stinging indictment of the way the United States had treated the Indians, *A Century of Dishonor,* was published by Helen Hunt Jackson. The Indian Rights Association was formed, and a series of annual conferences to coordinate various efforts to assist the Indians was instituted at Lake Mohonk, New York (Hertzberg 1971:20). All of these groups were formed by white people, and, of course, their ideas of what would be good for Native Americans molded the various programs and projects that were undertaken.

Please recall that the activities of such well-meaning groups and individuals were partly responsible for the passage of the Dawes Act in 1887. At a time when the question of how to dissolve foreign elements into the main body of American society was becoming ever more pressing and the Anglo conformity ideology was beginning to gain greater strength, the idea that Native Americans could best be assimilated by forcing them to abandon their ancient heritages and adopt the culture of the dominant society seemed to many white supporters to be quite humane and sensible. Few whites thought to consult the Indians to ask what *they* thought or wanted. Nevertheless, the Indians did have opinions, and, as mentioned earlier, the Five Civilized Tribes led a lobbying effort to prevent the passage of the Dawes Act, which managed to limit its application for a time.[38]

The various strategies of the whites, whether friends or foes, to civilize the Indians gradually helped to create a comparatively large group of Indians who were highly educated in the white fashion. These Native Americans moved easily between the white and Indian worlds. They also usually had friends and acquaintances in more than a single tribe. Many in this marginal position believed that their people must recognize that the white-dominated industrial American society would destroy all things Indian unless the Indians joined together, accepted the reality of the changed conditions, and attempted to fashion a new "Indian identity beyond the tribe and within the American social order" (Hertzberg 1971:300). Representatives from this Native American elite came together during the early years of the twentieth century to devise a plan through which Indians could become full participants in American society. In 1911, on Columbus Day in Columbus, Ohio, an organization was founded exclusively by and for Indians. The Society for American Indians (SAI) adopted a constitution to promote "the advancement of the Indian in enlightenment," "citizenship among Indians," and "the right to oppose any movement which may be detrimental to the race" (Hertzberg 1971:80).

Among the leaders of the new organization were several people who were well known and respected in both the Indian and white worlds. Dr. Charles Eastman (Ohiyesa), a Sioux, learned to read both English and Lakota as a child. He later graduated from Dartmouth and Boston University Medical School and was a physician at the Pine Ridge Reservation at the time of the Wounded Knee Massacre. Dr. Carlos Montezuma (Wassaja), the fiery Apache, worked his way through the University of Illinois and the Chicago Medical College. He practiced medicine at several reservations, at Carlisle, and in Chicago. Dr. Arthur Parker (Gawasowannah), a Seneca, graduated from high school in White Plains, New York, and was educated as a Presbyterian minister and as an anthropologist. He became famous for his studies of the Iroquois. Although the leaders of the SAI shared the stated objectives of the organization, they differed in certain ways that later led to friction among them. Like many other Americans of the period, the SAI leaders spoke in terms of the melting pot metaphor. Their opinions ranged, in fact, between pluralism and Anglo conformity (Hertzberg 1971:39–57, 63, 156, 195).

The active life of the SAI was approximately thirteen years. The organization gradually came to represent two principal goals: the abolition of the BIA and the extension of citizenship to all Indians. The first of these seemed so nearly impossible to many of the members that it became a point of vigorous disagreement. The latter goal, as we have seen, was attained in 1924. The importance of the SAI, however, went beyond its specific accomplishments. The SAI demonstrated that some Indians were interested in organizing to pursue Indian goals within the framework of American society. The idea that Indians could adjust to the dominant society was now seen as a foundation on which to erect intertribal cooperation and to build a pan-Indian identity.

After the decline of the SAI and the passage of the IRA, the impulse to construct a pan-Indian organization at the national level was weakened. As a part of President Franklin Roosevelt's "New Deal," the IRA promised Native Americans a new set of options, including various opportunities to take command of their own tribal affairs. Further organizational efforts seemed unnecessary. The experiences of many Native Americans during World War II, however, and the gradual rise in congressional opposition to the pluralist philosophy underlying the IRA, led once again to the formation of a national pan-Indian organization.

The National Congress of American Indians (NCAI) was formed in 1944 by a group of World War II veterans. Like the Mexican American and black war veterans, these men were exposed to many different influences as they traveled around the country and abroad. They came to believe that as citizens of the United States who had risked their lives defending the country, they were entitled to equal treatment and a "fair shake" in economic matters. They were unwilling simply to return to the reservations to live under the authority of the BIA or to be relegated quietly to the slums of the cities. The main objective of the NCAI was to seek national legislation favoring Native American interests while preventing legislation that would be harmful to those interests. The organization sought to make the promises of the IRA, then beginning to fade, a reality. They wished to promote the interests of all Native Americans but, simultaneously, to permit each tribe to pursue its own particular objectives within the framework of its agreements with the United States. When the termination policy was initiated by HCR 108, the NCAI was in the forefront of the opposition. The leaders of the organization did not wish to see any radical change in the relationships of the tribes with the federal government. They certainly did not love the BIA, yet they feared that any marked change was likely to make matters worse. The fight against termination, therefore, became a focal point of NCAI activities during the 1950s.[39]

This was a time of intellectual and spiritual ferment among Native Americans. Many war veterans and their children were completing high school and entering college in unprecedented numbers (Steiner 1968:31). As had been true a half-century earlier for those who founded the SAI, these new young intellectuals were uncertain of their place in American society. Were they leaving their tribal lives irrevocably behind to enter the American mainstream? Were they to return to the reservations when their formal education had ended? Or were they to shuttle back and forth in a kind of marginal no-man's land?

The New Tribalism

A young Navajo, Herbert Blatchford, and some of his friends at the University of New Mexico invited their parents to visit with them in 1954 to consider their questions. The elders told the students that they should complete their education in white ways and then bring their knowledge back to the reservations (Steiner 1968:33). From this beginning, a small group of Native American university students commenced to organize and struggle to formulate a new policy in Indian affairs. The new policy they created—variously called the new tribalism, tribal nationalism, or Red Power—was given its first full expression in 1961 following a very influential gathering, the American Indian Chicago Conference.

The Chicago conference started as a convention of the "Indian establishment" comprised of influential tribal leaders and noted students of Native American life (Olson and Wilson 1984:158–159). Several uninvited young intellectuals also were there. In addition to Herbert Blatchford, Mel Thom (Paiute), and Clyde Warrior (Ponca), nine others were present. These young people attended various conference sessions and grew increasingly impatient with the proceedings. To express their dissatisfaction with what they saw as the excessive caution of their elders, they formed a youth caucus, began to participate actively in various committee meetings, and finally played a major role in drafting the Declaration of Indian Purpose issued by the conference. Shortly after the conference, the youth caucus met again—this time in New Mexico—and established a new pan-Indian organization, the National Indian Youth Council (NIYC).

The Declaration of Indian Purpose stressed the Indians' "right of sovereignty," their agreement with Chief Justice Marshall's view that the tribes' treaties with the United States are binding, their determination to maintain their identity, and their need for technical assistance to regain "the adjustment they enjoyed as the original possessors of their native land" (Bahr, Chadwick, and Day 1972:485–486). These points represented a broad base of agreement between the members of the older NCAI and the newer NIYC. The two organizations diverged, however, on the matter of tactics. The NIYC wished to become more active in pressing Native American claims, but they did not wish simply to adopt the confrontation tactics of black activists. The older leaders were generally opposed to any direct confrontation, such as a sit-in, because such behavior was "un-Indian." They did not consider American Indians to be just another minority group demanding to be treated like all other Americans. The younger leaders, however, considered their fight to be in some ways a part of the larger fight between the dominant society and all other oppressed groups, and they argued that, along with the other nonwhite groups (and whatever the "Uncle Tomahawks" might think), "Indians must exercise their rights" (Steiner 1968:304).

In 1964, the young militants got their first chance to apply their ideas. The Supreme Court of the State of Washington nullified eleven federal treaties that had guaranteed the fishing rights of Native Americans in that state. The Makah tribe, which included Bruce Wilkie, a founder of the NIYC, called upon the NIYC to organize a protest concerning the loss of these fishing rights. The NIYC's president, Mel Thom, agreed to lead a nonviolent protest action.

At first the conservative leaders of the twenty-six tribes in Washington did not favor a protest. They feared that by violating the court's order they might go to jail, which is "undignified" and not "the Indian way." Nevertheless in March 1964, several hundred people representing different tribes gathered for a fish-in on the Quillayute River. The Indians were hesitant in the beginning, but then, as Thom recounted, "the tensions broke" and the "Indians began to enjoy it" (Steiner 1968:50). The fish-in idea spread rapidly. Native Americans from all over the United States rushed to the Northwest to support the Washington State tribes. The idea also was elaborated. There were "treaty treks," "canoe treks," and war dances in the state capital building.[40]

The next several years were marked by a sharp increase in organized Indian actions to protest various conditions or violations of civil rights. Most of these actions were conventional, nondisruptive efforts to improve the lives of Native Americans; however, the number of actions involving direct nonviolent confrontations—what Day (1972:515–516) called "obstructive tactics"—was an increasing proportion of the total. For example, in 1969, a group of young Native Americans, most of whom lived in the San Francisco Bay area, seized Alcatraz Island in an effort to "hold on to the old ways" (Indians of All Tribes 1971:200; James 1986:230). They took this action on the basis of a federal law that gave Native Americans the right to reclaim lands that were no longer being used. Although it did not achieve the avowed purposes of establishing title and a pan-Indian cultural center, the occupation of Alcatraz did succeed "in dramatizing the Native American demand for self-determination, tribal lands, and tribal identities" (Olson and Wilson 1984:170).

In the following year, the American Indian Movement (AIM) was established in Minneapolis, Minnesota. This militant new body quickly grew into a national organization that argued for Indian sovereignty, insisted on the protection of the Indians' treaty rights, and challenged the validity of the tribal governments formed under the IRA (Bonney 1977:215). The AIM's first major action, organized in 1972 in cooperation with some other Native American groups, was a protest march in Washington, D.C. called "The Trail of Broken Treaties." This protest action climaxed with a six-day seizure and occupation of the BIA's offices (Olson and Wilson 1984:171). Then, in 1973, to protest violations of the Sioux Treaty of 1868, AIM members led by Russell Means and Dennis Banks seized Wounded Knee village on the Pine Ridge Reservation. The occupation of Wounded Knee, which lasted for seventy days, led to an armed face-off that attracted widespread media attention. The occupation ended when federal officials agreed to send a team of investigators to discuss the problem of broken treaties (Kifner 1979; Olson and Wilson 1984:172–174).[41] Subsequently, AIM members have protested the operations of several corporations on reservations (Bonney 1977:215–217).

The underlying issue of Native American sovereignty is revealed in many court cases relating to tribal land claims, water rights, fishing and hunting rights, religious and burial rights, and contract disputes (*NARF Legal Review* 1991; 1992). In some cases the Native Americans have won; in other cases they have lost; and many cases are still in the courts. An important victory for Native Americans occurred in 1980, when the Pasamaquoddy and Penobscot tribes of Maine claimed thousands of acres of land and won a judgment of over $81 million (Wagar 1992:92).

In a case regarding fishing rights, the Supreme Court of the State of Vermont ruled in 1992 that members of the Abenaki tribe were required to pay for licenses to fish on land that they claim as their own. The court stated that the Abenaki's title to the land (an area of about 150 square miles) has "been voided by the 'increasing weight of history' . . ."(*New York Times* June 18, 1992). The Abenaki rejected this doctrine and promised to carry the fight into the federal courts. Other legal battles concern the Native Americans' ability to collect fees and be exempted from taxes. This source of friction is illustrated by a struggle between the Seneca and the state of New York. As a sovereign people, the residents of the Cattaraugus Reservation have been able to sell cigarettes and fuel to non-Indians at prices that do not include the state's sales tax, but the state estimated it was losing about $50 million a year in this way and imposed restrictions on the amount of tax-free selling the Indians may conduct (Gruson 1992).

Another illustration of the jurisdictional conflicts between particular tribes and outside legal entities concerns the operation of games of chance. During the past two decades, Indians have increasingly turned to gaming as a source of income (*Americans Before Columbus* 1992:3); by 1992 there were more than two hundred tribes throughout the country with gambling businesses that were generating an estimated $2.5 billion per year (D. Johnson 1992). The gaming industry, thus, became a very important source of money and jobs on many Indian reservations (Clines 1993). Consider the following: the Eastern Band of Cherokees earned about $850,000 per year between 1982 and 1992, and they spent the money on government services for tribal members; the Santee Sioux helped tribal members buy homes or cars or go back to school; the Yankton Sioux Tribe's casino employed over 175 tribal members, about 80 percent of whom had been on unemployment; and unemployment in the Sandia Pueblo in New Mexico was reduced to 2 percent (*Americans Before Columbus* 1992).

A conflict developed because federal legislation enacted in 1988 stated that certain types of gambling could be offered on the reservations only if they were legal in the state outside of the reservation. To offer any other type of gambling, Native Americans had to negotiate with state officials and gain their approval. One of the difficulties the tribes faced was that in many instances the state officials were unwilling to grant the permission needed to operate some games, and matters grew worse after new federal rules went into effect in 1992. The new rules placed electronic gambling machines in the category that required Native Americans to gain the approval of state officials. Arizona officials refused to permit the Yavapai-

Apache to continue offering some popular games that had been producing an estimated $1.4 million per year in revenue for the tribe. The Yavapai-Apache refused to discontinue the games on the ground that the state had refused to negotiate in good faith (*Americans Before Columbus* 1992). The day after the new rules took effect, F.B.I. agents raided several reservations across Arizona to seize game machines. At one of the sites they were blockaded by a group of Native Americans, and a five-hour standoff ensued. The governor of Arizona negotiated an agreement with the tribal chairman and declared a ten-day "cooling-off" period (*New York Times* May 13, 1992). The F.B.I. raids triggered angry reactions throughout the Indian nations. Mr. Tim Giago, editor of *The Lakota Times,* was quoted as saying, "The Indian nations are sick and tired of being treated like children. . . . Why in hell should these lands need the state's permission?" (D. Johnson 1992).

Issues and incidents such as these serve to heighten Native Americans' awareness of their shared characteristics and, thus, to promote the emergence of a new concept of "Indianness." An important, but in some ways fragile, framework of agreement has developed from these beginnings. On the one hand, this framework sometimes appears to be "only a thin veneer over reservation communities deeply divided by competing groups who often work at cross purposes" (Buffalohead 1986:270)[42]; on the other hand, it has enabled Native Americans to act in concert to protect their treaty rights and enlarge the powers of their tribal governments. As Deloria (1985a:4) expressed it, "the *process* of formulating the federal government's posture toward Indians has changed substantially and definitely for the better in almost every instance."

Immigrant or Colonized Minority?

As noted in chapter 9, the Mexican Americans originally entered the United States as a conquered group in their own homeland. In chapter 10 we saw that although African Americans did not remain in their homeland, they nonetheless may be described as a conquered group. In each of these discussions, we observed that the early relations between the minority in question and the dominant American society seemed to fit closely the pattern described by the colonial model. Like both African and Mexican Americans, Native Americans clearly entered American society as members of conquered groups; and, like Mexican Americans', their homelands were invaded and occupied by outsiders. The colonization of their lands was followed by political and economic domination and by numerous efforts to exploit their labor (Jacobson 1984).

In our consideration of contemporary Mexican Americans, we argued that the large migration of Mexicans to the United States since 1900 affords a basis for applying the immigrant model to that group. Our consideration of African Americans, similarly, focused on their large twentieth-century migration since 1915 from the rural South to the urban-industrial North. In both instances—while acknowledging the earlier condition of these groups as conquered peoples—one may make the case that applying the immigrant model to them advances our understanding of contemporary events. But given the special relationship of the Native Americans to the federal government and the continuation of reservation and tribal life into the last decade of the twentieth century, is there any basis whatsoever for considering Native Americans to be similar to the immigrant minorities?

This attempt to apply the immigrant model encounters more obstacles than in the cases of the Mexican and African Americans. Indeed, such an effort may at first seem far-fetched. Once again, however, the possibility of such an application rests on the consequences of rural-to-urban migrations. In 1887, when the Dawes Act was passed, nearly all Native Americans lived on reservations or in rural communities; however, by 1980, more than half of them had left the reservations and were living in cities and towns.

As we saw, many "friends of the Indians" argued that the passage of the Dawes Act would help Indians to become independent farmers, but the law actually caused many Indians to lose their land, frequently leaving them with no alternative but to move to nearby towns or more distant cities. In the process, their ties with those who remained on the reservations were weakened; they were forced to take town and city jobs, usually as unskilled workers; and they were required to take into account in their daily lives the language, ideas, manners, and ways of acting that predominated in the urban centers. Under such circumstances, some Native Americans, especially those who attended the boarding schools, moved rapidly in the direction of cultural and secondary assimilation. Many others clustered together in small colonies or ghettos where they clung uncertainly to the bottom rung of the economic ladder. In both cases, however, the urban Indians were subjected to the same broad forces of modernization as their contemporaries who were reaching the cities from Europe, Asia, Mexico, and the rural South.

Until the onset of World War II, the proportion of Native Americans who lived mainly or permanently in urban centers was comparatively small; however, during the war, the number of Native Americans moving to towns and cities increased sharply. Approximately forty thousand Native Americans were attracted to the cities, primarily on the West Coast, by new employment opportunities created by the war. The migration was stimulated, too, because many of the approximately twenty-five thousand Native Americans who were drafted into the armed forces were stationed in or near cities (Stewart 1977b:524).[43] At the end of the war, approximately eighty thousand Native Americans lived in urban places (Spicer 1980b:110).

The primary surge in the urban Indian population, however, came after that time. Despite the hopes aroused by the IRA, at the war's end most people on the reservations were still living under conditions of abject poverty. Their populations were increasing more rapidly than their economies could support, and unemployment on the reservations was extremely high. These were among the circumstances that helped to move the federal government toward the policy of termination, with its underlying ideology of Anglo conformity. Rather than attempting more vigorously to develop the reservations and strengthen tribal life, the BIA launched a new program to help Native Americans "relocate" in cities. This kind of assistance was by no means new, but the effort became much more important after 1950, when

Dillon S. Meyer, who directed the program to relocate the Japanese and Japanese Americans during World War II, became the commissioner of Indian affairs (Officer 1986:122). In 1952, the relocation idea became the foundation for a greatly expanded nationwide effort called the Voluntary Relocation Program.

The purposes of the relocation program included various types of job training, counseling, and job creation. Those who were selected for the program were provided transportation to a designated Employment Assistance Center in cities such as Chicago, Los Angeles, and Denver; since the program's directors wished to make it difficult for the participants to return home, they usually were sent to cities fairly far from their reservations. The idea of solving the "Indian Problem" by forcing the Indians into the mainstream again became dominant; so the relocation and termination programs reflected, to some extent, the same general ideological climate. The message communicated to Native Americans was "either conform to the Anglo way and move several hundred miles away from the reservation or stay . . . and live at substandard levels" (Bahr, Chadwick, and Day 1972:408). Between 1953 and 1972, over 100,000 Native Americans were relocated in American cities under this program.[44] In addition, during the same period of time, more than 200,000 other Native Americans moved away from their reservations without help from the program.[45]

The tremendous growth of the urban Indian population in the last three decades affords a basis for arguing that, like Mexican Americans and African Americans, Native Americans too are now on the road to higher levels of assimilation. This argument implies that if Native Americans seem to be less assimilated than the other groups, this difference may be explained by their later movement to the cities and the lower proportion of Native Americans now living in cities. Implied, also, is the belief that as Native Americans become more urbanized they will move more fully into the mainstream. Price (1972:438) stated the case in this way: "Conditions in the city lead the Indian away from tribal patterns. The reservation offers a very narrow range of occupational, religious, political, and recreational alternatives. The range of possible choices is vastly increased in the city."

We will return to this argument shortly, but first one additional point concerning the urban experience of Native Americans should be mentioned. Many Native Americans who *reside* in cities do not, in a certain social sense, *live* there. Some Native Americans, as Bahr (Bahr, Chadwick, and Day 1972:408) expressed it, are only temporary migrants who "raid" the city, "take" city resources, and then return to the reservation or small off-reservation community to "live." This practice resembles that of the "birds of passage" and "sojourners" we noted among various American immigrant groups, but the nearness of the reservations and the strength of the tribal ties may mean that the intention to return home is more easily put into practice by Native Americans than by members of most other groups. This particularly may be the case of urban Indians who plan to return to the reservations when they retire from their city jobs. Even those who are not temporary migrants or do not plan to return to the reservation permanently may still maintain a strong sense of Indian identity and may do everything in their power to relate themselves to urban life as Indians. This point may be amplified by a brief consideration of the extent to which Native Americans have been affected by the main subprocesses of assimilation.

Native American Assimilation

The preceding discussion suggests that the level of assimilation among Native Americans is, in general, comparatively low. Indeed, as we saw, they have clung tenaciously to their tribal heritages and currently are struggling to amplify a pan-Indian identity as well. Also suggested in the previous discussion of the migration of Native Americans to urban areas is the view that the reservations are repositories of the traditional cultures and therefore those who remain on reservations are likely to live in a more traditional way and to preserve their tribal heritages than are off-reservation Indians. Ideally, therefore, to assess the levels of cultural, secondary structural, primary structural, and marital assimilation of the Native Americans, one would wish to be able to state the current level of each type of assimilation among each of the distinct Native American groups, taking into account the differences between reservation and off-reservation residents within each tribe. Such a complete approach cannot be attempted here. We must rely, rather, on (1) general comparisons that tend to submerge the important differences that exist among the tribes and (2) a few specific examples chosen to illustrate some contemporary variations among the tribes.

Cultural Assimilation

We saw that several dozen Native American languages are now extinct. For example, the Narragansetts of New England and the Luisenos of California have not spoken their native languages for at least a century. In addition to the languages that are no longer used, several other Native American languages may be nearing extinction. The Sac and Fox people of Oklahoma, for instance, are mainly English speakers. Among the Omahas, less than 10 percent of those under the age of forty speak only the native tongue. By 1980, in fact, in only one census region (the Mountain States) did a majority of Native Americans (62 percent) speak their native language in the home. The next highest region of native language use was in the West North Central region (21 percent) (Snipp 1989:176).

Nevertheless, to repeat, more than 150 different Native American languages still exist and are used in varying degrees on a daily basis. In some cases, these languages are spoken by a majority of the tribal members who, usually, also speak English, Spanish, or French. For example, most Oklahoma Cherokees, Iroquois, and Penobscots are bilingual. Furthermore, many Native Americans also speak more than a single Native American language or dialect. In some cases, where the Native American languages already are in general use in a tribe, the number of native language speakers is growing. Among the Navajos—the largest and one of the fastest growing tribes in the United States—a majority (at least thirty thousand people) of those on the reservation use the mother tongue in the home. Navajo is also a language of instruction in schools such as the Rough Rock School and the Navajo Community College. Among the Apaches and many other tribes there is renewed interest in learning and using the mother tongue (Olson and Wilson 1984:202–204; Spicer 1980a:67–104).

What, then, are the general prospects for the survival and growth of the Native American languages? Since, presumably, a language community is easier to maintain in comparative isolation, we should expect native languages to fare better on or near reservations; and since children are more likely to be affected by exposure to alien languages than are adults, we should expect older people to report a greater use of Native American languages. An analysis by Gundlach and Busch (1981), for instance, showed that Indians who were twenty-five years or older were more likely than those under twenty-five to report that Native American language was used in their home when they were children. This finding was true for both reservation and off-reservation people; however, the percentage who reported a Native American mother tongue was much higher for both age groups among those on the reservations. Snipp's (1989:178) analysis confirmed that native language speakers are generally found in nonmetropolitan and reservation areas. For instance, in the East South Central region of the country, around 90 percent of those living on or near a reservation speak a native language in the home, while in the same region only about 5 percent of those in metropolitan areas do so.

Snipp (1989:180) also reported some interesting findings concerning age differences in language use. Older people are more likely than children to be among those who speak a native language but little English, though the proportions in both cases were low. Among those between the ages of sixty-one and seventy, for instance, around 5 percent spoke little English. Among those between the ages of eleven and twenty, less than 2 percent spoke little English. Of special interest is the finding that young people were slightly *more* likely than older people to speak a native language and also to be fluent English speakers. Over 24 percent of those between the ages of eleven and twenty and over 23 percent of those between the ages of sixty-one and seventy were in this category.

These data suggest that although those who live on or near reservations and in nonmetropolitan areas are more likely to have a Native American mother tongue than those who live in metropolitan areas, English is nevertheless the primary language of most Native Americans. They also indicate, however, that approximately 25 percent of Native Americans are fluent in both English and a native language, and that the younger people are slightly more likely to be bilingual than the older. So far as languages alone are concerned, then, the Native American cultures seem very unlikely to disappear within the next generation or two. The actual conditions among Native Americans may well be more nearly consistent with the pluralist conception of cultural assimilation (i.e., by language addition) than with the Anglo conformity conception (i.e., by language substitution). The critical point here, of course, is the extent to which Native Americans continue to become or remain bilingual and multilingual.

Although language is an extremely important part of culture, there also are other significant cultural elements that may continue, be modified, or die whether a native language exists or not. Religious preferences, housing styles, hair and dress styles, recreational patterns, and so on also reveal whether, or to what extent, one way of life has been added to or exchanged for another.

Consider briefly the matter of religious preferences. Our historical sketch has shown that an enormous effort has been made by many different religious bodies to Christianize Native Americans. The resulting pattern of religious affiliations is very complex. Many Native Americans have accepted Christian beliefs, many practice both Christian rites and those of an indigenous religion, and many adhere solely to an indigenous religion. In the latter case, as we saw in the Ghost Dance Religion, some elements of Christianity also may be included. In many cases, an adherence to Christian or native religious ways parallels a person's general level of "Indianness," which, in turn, tends to be related to whether a person is considered to be a "full-blood" or "mixed-blood." In general, the "full-bloods" are culturally more conservative, more likely to live on a reservation, and more likely to practice a native religion.[46]

Several native religions are closely identified with particular tribes. The Silas John Religion of the Apaches and the Handsome Lake (or Longhouse) Religion of the Iroquois are illustrative. Probably the best known, and certainly the most controversial, of the Native American religions is practiced by members of the Native American Church (NAC). The NAC is a pan-Indian religious movement that is nevertheless closely related to traditional tribal life (Hertzberg 1971:239). Its religious beliefs are compatible in several important respects with those of most Christian denominations. The church emphasizes brotherly love, close family ties, self-reliance, and the avoidance of alcohol. The controversial element, however, arises from the ritual use by NAC members of peyote, which contains several psychedelic substances. The use of peyote is a formal part of the sacrament; the recreational use of it is prohibited (Wax 1971:142–144).[47]

A variety of Christian denominations and native religions may be found among most tribes. For example, the Comanches are mainly members of the Methodist and Dutch Reformed churches, but a substantial number also belong to the NAC or practice their tribal religion; the Kiowas are divided among the Catholic, Methodist, Episcopal, and Baptist churches, as well as the NAC; the Pawnees include Catholics, members of the NAC, and adherents to their tribal religion; and the Sioux are mainly Episcopalians, Catholics, or members of the Church of God. They, too, include many members of the NAC and their tribal Yuwipi cult. In some cases, an individual may belong to more than one religious organization (Spicer 1980a:88–92). This crisscross pattern of religious experiences and affiliations frequently has been the basis of conflict in some tribes. The Nez Perces, for instance, long have been split between rival Presbyterian and Catholic groups, while the Prairie Band of the Potawatomis have been torn between conservatives, who adhere largely to the native religions, and liberals, who are mainly Christians (Spicer 1980a:79, 95).

The variety and complexity that exists among Native Americans in regard to language and religion extends to every other sphere of life. In many cases, the members of a given tribe may live in a manner that is largely indistinguishable from that of their white neighbors, although even in such cases of high cultural assimilation certain distinctive native elements may still be present. The variety of cultural "mixes" also extends to differences within various tribes. Consider the Oklahoma Cherokees, for example. This nonreservation group is located principally in a five-county region of northeastern Oklahoma, and the people who are considered, or consider themselves to be, Cherokees vary markedly in culture. Wax (1971:92–93) distinguished broadly between the "tribal Cherokees" and those "of Cherokee lineage." The tribal Cherokees live in old, distinctively Cherokee communities that have Cherokee names, and among these groups the main language of the home and church is Cherokee. Those of Cherokee lineage, however, may maintain only the most superficial connection with their heritage. They may have no social relationships with the tribal Cherokees, may live entirely in the white way, and may be unable to speak Cherokee. This same general pattern of variation within specific tribes may be found throughout the United States.

What, then, are we to conclude concerning the cultural assimilation of Native Americans? First, all tribal cultures have been drastically changed by their long period of contact with the dominant American culture[48]; hence, a large majority of Native Americans today speak English as one of their languages and exhibit greater or lesser degrees of acceptance of Anglo-American ways. Second, the number of people who bear a particular Native American culture, in many cases, either has stabilized or now is increasing. Third, in addition to the maintenance and elaboration of the many tribal cultures, pan-Indian culture continues to develop. Although traditional rivalries and factionalism are still prominent, increasingly these are being subordinated to the larger concerns that affect all Native Americans. Simultaneously, Native American people are emphasizing ways in which the many tribes share certain values. These pan-Indian values—which Steele (1982:287) called "the informal credentials of 'Indianness' "—include such things as an acceptance of obligations to the extended family, the importance of mutual aid among Indians, noninterference in the affairs of others, a reverence for nature, and pride in a knowledge of native languages. Pan-Indian values also include a rejection of acquisitiveness and some types of competition.

As the urban Indian population grows, pan-Indianism is likely to increase in importance. Active all-Indian associations have been formed in urban areas with large Indian populations. The Bay Area American Indian Council of San Francisco, representing around one hundred tribes, and the Chicago American Indian Center, also representing nearly one hundred tribes, are prominent examples of this trend (Spicer 1980a:113). Additionally, there are numerous all-Indian powwows, dances, and ceremonies, such as the annual American Indian Exposition at Anadarko, Oklahoma, which encourage Native Americans to travel and associate with one another.

Finally, the maintenance of the tribal cultures and the development of a pan-Indian culture both serve to assure that the American Indians will have the option to remain American Indians even as they continue to assimilate the dominant culture. As Stewart (1977a:521) observed, "eventually, Indian cultures may fade away . . . ," but in the meantime "Indians believe they can function with competence in modern society as Indians."

Secondary Structural Assimilation

The long period of conflict with the dominant society, the unwillingness of most tribes to adopt the dominant American ways, and the continuation of prejudice and discrimination into the present all have conspired to keep Native Americans from participating equally in the educational, occupational, and financial systems of American society. For many decades, they have lived in poverty, been ravaged by poor health and early death, and been inadequately clothed and sheltered. Native Americans long have been, as Josephy (1971:15) stated, "the poorest of the poor."

No simple statistical accounting can do justice to the suffering the Native American peoples have endured. The authors of a 1969 report of the U.S. Senate's Special Subcommittee on Indian Education (Josephy 1971:168) commented on this point as follows: "We are shocked at what we discovered. . . . We have developed page after page of statistics. These cold figures mark a stain on our national conscience, a stain which has spread slowly for hundreds of years. They tell a story . . . but they cannot tell the whole story. They cannot . . . tell of the despair, the frustration, the hopelessness, the poignancy, of children who want to learn but are not taught; . . . of families which want to stay together but are forced apart; or of . . . children who want neighborhood schools but are sent thousands of miles away to remote and alien boarding schools."

If we consider a bit further the matter of schooling, two points stand out. First, there have been definite increases in the educational levels of Native Americans during recent years; but, second, their educational attainments still lag noticeably behind those of whites. For example, by 1980 over one-half of all Native Americans over the age of twenty-four had completed high school. At the same time, over two-thirds of the comparable white population had completed high school. Between 1970 and 1980, the percentage of Native Americans who had completed four or more years of college rose from 3.8 to 7.7, but during this same period the percentage of whites to complete this level of education rose from 11.3 to 17.1 (Snipp 1989:188–190). As we have seen in some of our comparisons of Mexican and African Americans with whites, the rates of increase have been higher among Native Americans than among whites but the absolute size of the gap between them has grown.

We emphasized previously that the range of social variation among Native Americans is wide, and this point certainly applies to differences in educational attainment. Probably the most noticeable differences are between those who live in nonmetropolitan or reservation areas and those who live elsewhere, but there also are large differences between the young and the old. In general, for both sexes, those who live in metropolitan areas and those who are younger have higher average levels of educational attainment. For example, among metropolitan residents over twenty-four years old who live in various regions of the country, the percentage of those with twelve or more years of education ranges, roughly, between 57 and 71, while among those in nonmetropolitan areas the range is 37 to 60 percent. When people of different ages who live in various regions and have completed twelve or more years of education are compared, the range for those between the ages of twenty-five and thirty (including both sexes and both types of residential location) is, roughly, 71 to 79 percent, and for those over age seventy the range is between 13 to 29 percent (Snipp 1989:196–198).

There are substantial educational differences, too, among those who are over twenty-four and reside on one of the sixteen largest reservations. To illustrate, in 1970 almost 36 percent of those over twenty-four years of age on the Wind River reservation in Wyoming graduated from high school, while less than 13 percent graduated on the Papago reservation in Arizona. In 1980, these levels were over 39 and 25 percent, respectively. During the decade, however, the relative ranking of the reservations changed. In 1980, the Fort Peck reservation in Montana had the highest proportion of graduates (almost 50 percent), while the Rosebud reservation in South Dakota had the lowest (almost 20 percent) (Snipp 1989:202–203).

These figures attest to a general and rapid rise in the educational levels of Native Americans—levels that now approximate those of Mexican and African Americans—but they tell us nothing concerning the quality of the schooling Native Americans receive, nor do they answer the question, "What does the educational experience of Native American children mean to them?" One devastating answer to that question may be found in the most extensive study of American education, the famous Coleman Report (1966). This study revealed that in answer to the question, "How bright do you think you are?" Native American children ranked themselves below all other groups.

We referred earlier to the schools operated by the BIA and their role in the attempt to force Native Americans to adopt Anglo conformity. In the early days of this system, a comparatively small number of children attended public schools. Today, however, over two-thirds of Native American children attend public schools, and the role of some of the government-operated schools has changed markedly. Many Native Americans now view the BIA reservation schools as their best chance to mold the education of their children along the lines they desire. In some instances, when the BIA has attempted to close reservation schools, Native Americans have protested and stopped the closings (Washburn 1973:103–104).

The trend toward greater control by Native Americans of the content and style of their education also has extended into higher education with the establishment of such institutions as the Navajo Community College (mentioned earlier), the Lakota Higher Education Center, and Sinte Gleska College (*Newsweek* 1973:71–72). Although the continued movement of Native Americans toward higher levels of educational attainment seems almost certain, one may well doubt whether the remaining gap between Native Americans and the dominant group will close rapidly.

Along with higher levels of education, the jobs of Native Americans who are employed have become more like those of the dominant group, but, both on and off the reservations, unemployment among Native Americans is high and economic hardship is common. The overall unemployment rates among men and women between the ages of twenty-one and twenty-five, for instance, are over 18 percent and 14 percent, respectively, and these rates are substantially below those for men and women between the ages of sixteen and twenty (over 25 and 21 percent, respectively). The levels of unemployment on the reservations are even more unfavorable than the overall pattern, and on the sixteen largest reservations the rate increased during the 1970s. To illustrate, at the Pine Ridge reservation in South Dakota, the unemployment rate rose between 1970 and 1980 from over 16 percent to nearly 36 percent; during the same period, the unemployment level at the Gila River reservation in Arizona rose from 13 percent to over 29 percent. These increases in unemployment occurred when the number of people in the labor force also was increasing, suggesting that the increasing education and skill levels of Native Americans were not matched by employment opportunities on the reservations (Snipp 1989:220, 226, 227).

Among Native Americans who have jobs, to repeat, the pattern of employment has become more similar to the dominant white pattern. In 1970, for instance, roughly 64 percent of white women and 43 percent of Native American women were employed in nonmanual jobs. By 1980, these figures had become 70 percent and 56 percent, respectively. Among men, the comparable figures were 41 and 22 percent in 1970 and 45 and 28 in 1980. We should note, also, that employed female and male Native Americans in both 1970 and 1980 were more likely to hold nonmanual jobs than were African Americans (Snipp 1989:231).

Another way the jobs of Native Americans differ from those of whites is that Native Americans are more likely to be employed by federal, state, or local governments. Native American employment by governmental agencies rose between 1970 and 1980 from around 24 percent to over 28 percent, while the employment of whites by government rose only slightly, to remain between 15 and 16 percent. African Americans have become more similar to Native Americans in this respect. During the same period, government jobs for African Americans increased from about 15 percent to about 27 percent (Snipp 1989:238).

Although Native Americans still are plagued by high unemployment and the accompanying economic hardships, and although their general pattern of employment more nearly resembles that of blacks than of whites, there is clear evidence that their increasing educational levels lead to higher-paying, higher-prestige jobs. In 1980, for example, 59 percent of Native American women and 55 percent of Native American men who had received a college education were employed in managerial and professional jobs, while an additional 28 percent of the women and 18 percent of the men in this group held technical, sales, and administrative support jobs (Snipp 1989:246). It is nonetheless true, though, that Native Americans have much more difficulty translating high school graduation into college attendance than do whites. Snipp (1989:190) calculated that of every additional one hundred white high school graduates, an additional forty-one people graduate from college; but among Indians, one hundred additional high school graduates produces only twelve additional college graduates. Furthermore, there is some evidence that the probability that a Native American between the ages of twenty-five and thirty will have completed four or more years of college is now *lower* than for those between the ages of thirty-one and seventy (Snipp 1989:200).

The improved educational and employment levels of Native Americans have been accompanied by some improvement in income levels. As an example, in 1970 the ratio of the median family income of Native Americans to that of whites was .57, which was less than 90 percent of the comparable figure for African Americans (U.S. Bureau of the Census 1973a). By 1979 this ratio had risen to .66, which was, at that point, *higher* than the ratio of the median family income of blacks to whites (.60). During the same period, the proportion of Native American families below the poverty line (24 percent) also declined to a point below that of African Americans (26 percent), but both of these groups still have much larger proportions of poor families than do whites (7 percent) (Snipp 1989:249).

Health care is an area in which the efforts to close the gap between Indians and whites appears to be having marked success. To illustrate, consider the change in the infant mortality rates among Native Americans. From 1950 to 1983, this sensitive indicator of the general health level of a population declined from an extremely high eighty-two infant deaths per one thousand Native American births per year to about eleven deaths per one thousand births (Snipp 1989:352).[49] This large decline within such a short period of time is remarkable. Not only is the Native American infant mortality rate rapidly approaching the white level (9.7 per 1,000 in 1983), it has fallen well below the rate for African Americans (19.2 in 1983) (U.S. Bureau of the Census 1991b:77).

The improvement in infant mortality, as important as it is, does not mean that the general health and mortality experience of Native Americans is no longer a matter of concern. They still are much more likely than all Americans combined to die fairly early in life. Davis, Hunt, and Kitzes (1989:271) reported that in 1982, "37 percent of the deaths among American Indians occurred before age 45, compared with 12 percent of deaths in the same age group in the U.S. population." Native Americans also still suffer a disproportionate number of deaths from causes that reflect some of the broader problems they face. For example, although accidental deaths among them have declined dramatically since 1970, Native Americans still are more than twice as likely to die in an accident as are members of the general population. Suicide rates among Native Americans, though also lower than in 1970, are still over 11 percent higher than the rate for all Americans (Snipp 1989:350); and Native American teenagers are about four times as likely to attempt suicide as other teens (Brasher 1992). Native Americans also are about twice as likely to be murdered, about four times as likely to die of alcoholism, and about nine times as likely to die of tuberculosis as are other Americans (Snipp 1989:350–358). As is true of the American population as a whole, however, Native Americans are more likely to die of heart disease than of any other single cause (Rhoades et al. 1988:622).

The statistics concerning the status of Native Americans in various areas of life may be viewed, from different perspectives, either as encouraging or discouraging. If one emphasizes the recency of serious attention to the development of the reservations and to integrating Native Americans into urban life and industrial occupations, then the size of the "lags" in these areas may be viewed in some ways as being relatively low. But when the lags are seen absolutely—in terms of human privation and misery—it is evident that much remains to be done. Even though it may now be true, after many decades of effort, that Native Americans, collectively, are no longer the "poorest of the poor," it also is true that they still are far from having the standard of living enjoyed by whites and still "are one of the most disadvantaged racial/ethnic groups in the United States" (Sandefur and Scott 1983:44).

Primary Structural Assimilation

Throughout the centuries, Indians and whites have enjoyed few opportunities to be genuinely friendly. Some members of each group, of course, have had large numbers of friends in the other group, but the ordinary state of affairs has been for most of each Native American's friends to be others of the same tribe.

Given the long history of conflicts between Native American and European peoples, and given the effort to contain Native Americans by segregating them in Indian country and on reservations, this outcome is hardly surprising. The historically low level of primary assimilation among Native Americans has been extended into the present. Reservation Indians, by both choice and circumstance, are unlikely to have very many contacts with non-Indians. Urban Indians, on the other hand, may have numerous opportunities to form friendships with non-Indians in schools and colleges, at work, in various social organizations, and in their neighborhoods. How do Native Americans react to these possibilities?

Some valuable information on this question was presented by Ablon (1972) in a study of Native Americans who lived in the San Francisco Bay area. Most of those studied had come to the area under the BIA's relocation program. Ablon interviewed fifty-three Native Americans concerning many aspects of their lives in the city, including such things as who their early social contacts in the city were, how those contacts were made, whether they preferred Indian or white friends, how they felt about themselves, and so on. She found, first, that Native Americans most frequently established their social contacts at gatherings sponsored by various intertribal organizations founded by or for Native Americans. The next most common form of early contacts was with friends or relatives from the reservations. The participants reported that after they had been in the city for a while, an increasing proportion of their social contacts were with people from work and in their neighborhoods. Most stated that they had white friends as well as Indian friends. However, in all of these contexts, their friendships with whites tended to be superficial. Only three of fifty-four Native Americans who participated in the study stated they had more white than Indian friends.

Ablon (1972:422–423) argued that two prevalent attitudes among Native Americans toward whites are suspicion and a fear of rejection. Whites who attempt to be friendly toward them are suspected of wishing to take advantage of them; they also fear that whites will look down on them if they learn the details of the Native Americans' poverty-stricken reservation lives or their tribal beliefs. Moreover, aside from their reasons for wishing to avoid whites, Indians have a strong, positive wish to be with other Indians. This view accords with One Feather's (1986:171) observation that "the people who moved to urban areas formed their own Indian communities. Indian centers became a focal point for the people that lived in cities."

As usual, of course, we should expect that the behavior pattern just described would vary among tribes. In a study of Native Americans in Los Angeles—the city with the largest Native American population—Price (1972) compared members of the three major tribal groups in the city (the Navajo, Sioux, and Five Civilized Tribes). He found that the Navajo were least likely to establish extratribal ties to life in the city and members of the Five Civilized Tribes were most likely to do so. The Sioux were intermediate. For example, 64 percent of the Navajo, 33 percent of the Sioux, and 26 percent of the members of the Five Civilized Tribes revealed that they "associate entirely or mostly with Indians" (Price 1972:437). In general, the Navajo also maintained the strongest ties to the reservations, while members of the Five Civilized Tribes maintained the weakest ties. From these findings, Price (1972:436) argued that the Navajos probably would "shift over time to patterns of life exemplified by the Five Civilized Tribes."

While the occurrence of such a shift would imply a parallel increase in primary assimilation for those involved, there is little reason to suppose that urban Native Americans will soon reach a point at which associations with other Native Americans will become unimportant. Liebow (1989:67) found in Phoenix, for instance, that the Native Americans there—representing many tribes—"have set about self-consciously creating a collective identity that is primarily tied to their adoptive metropolitan home." As Price (1972:439) noted, "the great majority of Indians in the city clearly are ideologically and emotionally affiliated with pan-Indianism." The maintenance or growth of this commitment among Native Americans may well exert a continuing pressure against full primary assimilation.

Marital Assimilation

The romantic courtship and marriage of John Rolfe and Pocahontas during the earliest years of the Jamestown Colony did not foretell a high level of marital assimilation of the Native Americans into English society. Although we lack the information needed to discuss these matters precisely in the present, much less in the distant past, it appears that until recently the levels of marital assimilation among Native Americans have been low. This is what we would have expected on the basis of our discussion of the generally low levels of primary assimilation. To be sure, various circumstances have produced higher levels of intermarriage at some times and places than others. For example, during the early years in the southern colonies, where white women were scarce and Native American women were plentiful, there were numerous white male-Indian female marriages. According to Gary Nash (1974:282), Thomas Bosomworth, who was a chaplain in the Georgia colony, "found it respectable to marry a Creek woman . . . and many others followed his example."

As in the case of African Americans, of course, the actual levels of sexual relations between Indians and whites always have been higher than the rates of legitimate intermarriage; consequently, the level of amalgamation after almost four centuries of contact is quite high. The proportion of Native American "full-bloods" in the 1980s varied among tribes and was, in general, higher on the reservations than in the cities. In both locations, however, only a minority of Native Americans now qualify as biological "full-bloods," and many millions of Americans who do not profess a Native American identity claim some degree of Native American ancestry.[50] We should note again that the terms *full-blood* and *mixed-blood* frequently refer to a person's cultural commitment rather than strictly to biological ancestry. Large numbers of mixed-bloods in the past and present have been, or now are, "completely Indian" in the way they think of themselves and live. On the other hand, numerous biological full-bloods have adopted the white man's way of life and have been regarded by themselves and other Indians as no longer Indian. Our claim that the levels of Indian-white intermarriage have been low, therefore, is based only on those marriages in which one of the partners considers himself or herself to be an Indian. Most instances in which one partner acknowledges some degree of mixed ancestry are not examples of Indian-white intermarriage.

Roy (1972:233), for instance, found that among twenty-eight Spokane couples living on a reservation, twenty marriages in which both partners were Native Americans included at least one member who was not a full-blood. Roy (1972:233) did note, however, that "people with a high percentage of Indian ancestry tended to select mates with a high percentage of Indian ancestry . . . ," suggesting there is a relationship between the Indians' cultural and biological identities. A subsequent study of the Spokanes by White and Chadwick (1972:246) found that urban Indians were more likely than reservation Indians to consider their identities to be mainly a matter of ancestry. The explanation of this finding appears to be that urban Indians suffer more discrimination because of their physical appearance and, therefore, feel "Indian" if they look "Indian."

Despite the paucity of research on Native American intermarriage, at least two generalizations seem well-founded. First, and despite generally low levels of primary assimilation, even among urban dwellers, the levels of marital assimilation among Native Americans appear to have risen sharply in recent times. Between 1960 and 1970, the proportion of Indian men who married non-Indian women rose from 15 percent to 33 percent, and the proportion of Indian women who married non-Indian men rose from 24.2 to 39.0 (Heer 1980:519; Sandefur and McKinnell 1986:348). Taken at face value, these findings suggest a strong surge among Native Americans toward the mainstream of society. Given all of our other findings, however, it seems possible that the apparently large increase in intermarriage may be "related to an increased desire among persons with mixed white and Indian ancestry to identify themselves as Indian Americans" (Heer 1980:519). Adding strength to this view are the findings of Passel and Berman (cited by Sandefur and McKinnell 1986:348) that as many as 358,000 people in the United States changed their self-identification from white to Indian during the 1970s.

A second generalization is that exogamy is much more common among Native Americans than among African Americans. For example, Sandefur and McKinnell (1986:357) showed that in states that traditionally have had large numbers of people who define themselves as Native Americans (states where pressures toward endogamy, presumably, are strong), 37 percent of Native American men nevertheless marry women of different races. Exogamy is even higher in states that traditionally have had comparatively small Native American populations. In these states, about 62 percent of Native American men marry women of other races. These researchers also found, however, that endogamous Native American couples are likely to be poorer and less educated than endogamous African American couples.

These broad generalizations, of course, leave many questions unanswered. Are the rates of intermarriage among some tribes remaining steady or falling in contrast to the general trend? Are the rates of intertribal intermarriage increasing? If so, what is the social and cultural significance of these changes? These and other questions invite further study. For the moment, however, we must be content to note that the rates of Indian-white intermarriage appear to have risen sharply, which may signify an historic change in the relations of the two groups.

Native American "Success"

We have noted that since the time of the first contacts in North America, some European peoples have attempted to "civilize" the Native Americans; however, the primary approach of the whites throughout most of the centuries since then has been to attempt to separate the two groups of people. Native Americans, for their part, have responded in a complementary fashion. Some of them have more or less willingly accepted "civilization," but far more common has been the attempt to remain apart, to accept only certain elements of European culture, and still to maintain their traditional ways of life.

Until the end of the nineteenth century, the Native Americans experienced only sporadic pressures to "succeed" within American society, but with the passage of the Dawes Act in 1887 the U.S. government adopted as its official and exclusive policy a program to force them to accept the ways of the dominant society. This change, to repeat, did not cause Native Americans to alter their traditional policies. If they could not regain their lost lands and means of subsistence, then they still wished at least to become "dependent domestic nations"—self-governing groups within the boundaries of American society.

Once again, perhaps more sharply than previously, we see an illustration of the close link between a group's ideology and the question of assessing its success in American society. Even though the tribes have varied in their willingness to accept certain elements of white culture, there can be little doubt that the central impulse among Native Americans has been to resist being drawn into American society. From this perspective, any step toward assimilation that involved the substitution of white for Native American ways has represented some measure of failure.

While it has seemed clear to most white Americans that their civilization—at first agrarian but now urban-industrial—is superior and worth adopting, Native Americans have largely disagreed. To a considerable extent, American ethnocentrism has been matched by Native American ethnocentrism. The Native Americans' conviction that their way is best has been bolstered by the increasing problems confronting industrial civilization. Problems relating to air and water pollution, soil erosion, energy exhaustion, ecological imbalance, and widespread feelings of loneliness and powerlessness are all interpreted by many Native Americans, and some non-Indians as well, as a sign of the impermanence and inferiority of white culture. From this perspective, Native Americans always have had a great deal to teach the whites about life, and soon, perhaps, the whites will be forced to listen. Deloria (1972:506) argued the point as follows: "At the present time everyone is watching how mainstream America will handle the issues of pollution, poverty, crime and racism when it does not fundamentally understand the issues. . . . It just seems to a lot of Indians that this continent was a lot better off when we were running it."

The outcome of the Native Americans' struggle against the worldly success of white society is unclear at present. They appear now to have become predominantly an urban people, but many hope that "tribalism can be incorporated with modern technology in an urban setting" (Deloria 1972:506). This hope is counterbalanced, however, by the unquenched fear that the ancient tribal values will be lost before they can become ascendant. As Deloria (1981:149) stated subsequently: "While tribal traditions provide a bulwark against the consumer society, continued contact may well mean the end of Indian uniqueness in a world increasingly homogenized. The pervasive fear of Indians is that they will in the years ahead move from their plateau of small nationhood to the status of another ethnic group in the American melting pot."

We have described in several of the preceding chapters some of the dramatic changes that have occurred in American racial and ethnic relations during recent decades. In chapter 13 we consider further some of the ways white Americans have reacted to these changes, and we present additional information concerning the new immigration.

Key Ideas

1. France, England, Spain, and Holland each attempted to gain control of portions of North America. Prior to the American Revolution, the conflict was waged mainly between France and her Native American allies, England and her Native American allies, and the tribes that at any given moment refused to form an alliance with either of these European powers.

2. The greater numbers of the English and the timely support of the Iroquois led to the defeat of France and her allies.

3. Pontiac's uprising was an intertribal effort to stop the westward expansion of Anglo-American society. It showed the power of a concerted Native American resistance and led the King of England to issue the Proclamation of 1763. This important document laid the foundation for the separatist Indian policies adopted later by the new American republic.

4. Land-hungry traders, settlers, and politicians devised numerous methods to persuade Native Americans to sell or cede their lands. Although many land transactions were conducted in "the utmost good faith," many also involved deception, fraud, bribery, and threats of violence. The pressure of the whites on the Indians led to continuous friction and the transfer of enormous tracts of land to the whites.

5. Like Pontiac before him, Tecumseh attempted to form a pan-Indian military alliance to stop the advance of the whites. Tecumseh's plan included many more tribes spread over a much larger area. It was the most ambitious military effort ever attempted by the Native Americans.

6. The Indian Removal Act led to the forced evacuation to Indian Territory of most of the Indians east of the Mississippi River.

7. During the eighteenth and nineteenth centuries, the Plains Indians had developed a way of life based on the horse, the buffalo, and raiding. The removal of the eastern Indians to Indian Territory and the movement of white Americans across the Plains precipitated several decades of bitter, tragic, and widely publicized warfare between the western Indians and the Americans.

8. The United States government continued the system of making treaties with Native American tribes until 1871. In that year, Congress declared that the United States would honor all existing treaties but would no longer recognize the tribes as treaty-making powers. By this time, most of the tribes had been assigned to reservations and placed under the direct supervision of the Bureau of Indian Affairs.

9. Through the General Allotment (Dawes) Act of 1887, the federal government abandoned its long policy of separatism and adopted a policy of Anglo conformity. Native Americans were to be forced to accept "civilization" and enter the mainstream of American life.

10. The Meriam Report showed that few Native Americans became independent, self-sufficient farmers under the provisions of the Dawes Act. The main effects of the act were to place most of their lands in the hands of white people and to increase their levels of poverty.

11. The Indian Reorganization Act of 1934, which replaced the Dawes Act, was based on the ideology of cultural pluralism. The Indians were encouraged to remain Indians and to participate as fully as they wished in the life of the broader society. The "termination" policy of the 1950s represented a brief return to the Anglo conformity policy. The Indian Self-Determination Act of 1975 marked the resumption of a policy of cultural pluralism.

12. A number of national pan-Indian organizations have been formed to promote the interests and welfare of Native Americans. These organizations have been based on varying ideologies of adjustment, but in general they have expressed the wish that the American Indians be permitted to retain their cultural heritages.

13. Since the middle of the twentieth century, Native Americans have migrated in large numbers to urban areas, and they are now predominantly an urban people.

The urban Indians appear to be moving more rapidly toward cultural assimilation than are those on reservations. This observation affords a basis for attempting to interpret the contemporary experience of Native Americans in terms of the immigrant model; however, among both reservation and off-reservation Indians, cultural addition is more conspicuous than cultural substitution.

14. The movement of Native Americans toward secondary assimilation in education, occupations, incomes, and health care has been very rapid during recent decades, especially among urban dwellers. Despite the rapid rates of change, however, Native American averages still lag behind those of American society in general. Native American income levels have come to approximate those of African and Mexican Americans. The average educational level among the Native Americans, however, now is higher than among Mexican Americans, and the rate of infant mortality among Native Americans is lower than among African Americans.

15. Historically, primary and marital assimilation of Native Americans into white society have been low. Although the levels of primary assimilation may be rising somewhat faster in the cities than on reservations, the levels still appear to be generally low. Marital assimilation, on the other hand, appears in recent years to have risen sharply. This puzzling finding suggests either that the levels of primary assimilation also are rising sharply or that the higher rates of intermarriage represent the assimilation of spouses of Native Americans into Native American society.

16. Since the end of official separatism in the nineteenth century, the dominant society has alternated between an Indian policy of Anglo conformity and cultural pluralism. Throughout this time, Native Americans as a whole have rejected the dominant culture and have defined success mainly in terms of tribal and cultural survival. From this perspective, the Native Americans have been very successful.

Notes

1. The official statistics on Native Americans are difficult to interpret. For example, on the basis of the race item in the 1980 census, there were over 1.4 million Native Americans, but on the basis of the ancestry item, there were only 6.7 million Native Americans. Moreover, the racial identification of those who claimed Native American ancestry was mixed, with approximately 77 percent of those claiming Native American ancestry also identifying themselves as white. For the purpose of his analysis, and after an illuminating discussion of the problems involved, Snipp (1989:58) defined the Indian population as *"persons who identified their race as American Indian, Eskimo, or Aleut in the 1980 census. . . ."* On the basis of the race item in the 1990 census, there were 1.96 million people in the category

"American Indian, Eskimo, or Aleut," of whom 1.88 million were classified as "American Indian" (U.S. Department of Commerce 1991).

2. During this period, the Tuscaroras were driven out of the South and were accepted into the Iroquois League. The League then became the Six Nations of the Iroquois.

3. Of special significance in this regard was the higher quality of English rum. For an illuminating brief discussion of the role of alcoholic beverages in the life of the Indians, see Nash (1974: 252–255).

4. In Europe this conflict was known as the Seven Years' War.

5. In 1769, Pontiac was killed by a Peoria whom he believed to be a friend (Josephy 1961:128).

6. The Proclamation of 1763 outraged the colonists who were eager to settle on Native Americans' lands. It frequently is mentioned as an important factor leading to the American Revolution.

7. During the entire treaty-making period, which lasted for nearly a century, the white Americans concluded 645 treaties with various tribes (Jackson and Galli 1977:26).

8. One critic, Jedidiah Morse, wrote in 1820 that "to remove these Indians from their homes . . . can hardly be reconciled with the professed object of civilizing them (Dennis 1977:24).

9. Justice Marshall went on to describe the relation of Native Americans to the United States as "that of ward to his guardian . . ." (Jackson and Galli 1977:59). The use of the term *ward,* with its implication of dependency and close supervision, later created numerous problems for Native Americans.

10. A third, earlier, ruling by Marshall (*Johnson v. McIntosh*) denied that Indians had title to the land they occupied, confusing matters still further (Chaudhuri 1985:24–25).

11. Legend insists that on hearing about the decision in *Worcester,* Jackson retorted, "John Marshall has made his decision. Now let him enforce it!"

12. The term *The Trail of Tears* originally applied specifically to the removal experience of the Cherokees. Since then it has become generalized to describe the entire removal process.

13. About a thousand Cherokees fled from Georgia to North Carolina, where they established a separate tribe. The contemporary Eastern Band of the Cherokees, their descendants, still live in North Carolina.

14. Some of the sedentary farming tribes, such as the Mandans and Hidatsas, lived along Plains rivers before the rise of the horse-buffalo complex.

15. Although Custer was at this time a Lt. Colonel, he had held the rank of brevet (temporary) Major General during the Civil War. He continued thereafter to expect people to address him as "General" and, in fact, most did.

16. Although Crook lost only ten men in this battle, it was "undoubtedly his least successful Indian fight" (Connell 1984:89).

17. The literature on Custer and his conduct of the battle of the Little Bighorn is large and controversial. Many of his critics have maintained that this "early" approach to the Native American camp was just another example of "Iron Butt's" reckless determination to seek glory and enhance his reputation as an inspiring and flamboyant leader. His defenders have pointed out that Terry's written order to Custer did not specify that a coordinated attack would take place on the 26th. For first-hand accounts by both Indians and whites, as well as subsequent analyses and commentaries, see W. Graham (1953); for a keen appraisal of Custer and many of the other men involved in the Plains wars, see Connell (1984); and for an account of modern archaeological research at the Custer battleground, see Scott and Connor (1986). I am indebted to Symmes C. Oliver for calling these sources to my attention.

18. Dr. Charles Eastman (Ohiyesa) presents the former figure and Lieutenant (later General) Godfrey presents the latter (see W. Graham 1953:97, 151).

19. Custer's command included about 650 cavalrymen, 145 infantrymen, and 40 "Ree" (Arikara) Scouts. Connell (1984:383) stated that "certain historians will profess to know just how many men followed the Son of the Morning Star into that arid cul-de-sac, but most will not cut it quite so fine."

20. Some other chiefs present at the battle were Low Dog, Crow King, Hump, and Iron Thunder. Sitting Bull was a medicine chief rather than a war chief, so he was not on the battlefield.

21. Both Major Reno and Captain Benteen were later accused of cowardice for failing to go to Custer's aid. A court of inquiry, convened at Major Reno's request in 1879, concluded that "the conduct of the officers throughout was excellent . . ." (W. Graham 1952:92, 157).

22. Josephy (1968:337) reported that the number of Native American dead was near three hundred.

23. Chiefs Black Kettle and White Antelope escaped at Sand Creek but were killed later (1868) in Custer's attack at the Washita.

24. The government showed no sign of keeping its promise to Crazy Horse, and he soon be-

came unhappy and troublesome. General Crook attempted to have him arrested. Crazy Horse resisted and was killed on September 5, 1877 (Josephy 1961:306–309).

25. In 1860, it was estimated that there were approximately 20 million on the Plains. In 1890 there were fewer than six hundred.

26. The BIA was transferred in 1849 from the War Department to the Department of the Interior.

27. Perhaps it is more exact to think of the Dawes Act as the culmination of a gradual shift toward Anglo conformity policy, rather than as the starting point of the new policy (Hoxie 1984:70).

28. To make these assignments, the BIA relied heavily on the blood theory of racial membership discussed in chapter 1. Despite the impossibility of an accurate determination of a person's degree of "Indian blood," the BIA still relies on the outdated "blood quantum" approach and requires that a person be at least a "1/4 blood" to receive certain government benefits (Snipp 1989:34).

29. This idea was pioneered by Pratt at Hampton Institute in Virginia in 1878.

30. Brown (1972:417) stated that of the original 350 men, women, and children, 153 are known to have died. Since many others died later of their wounds and from exposure, some have estimated the total dead at nearly three hundred.

31. Although this act conferred U.S. citizenship on Native Americans, several states refused to recognize them as citizens of the state. A number of court cases were fought over this issue during the next several decades (McCool 1985:107–112).

32. Meriam et al. (1928).

33. Some Indians referred to the Wheeler-Howard Act as the "Wheel-law" and claimed that the wheel was rolling the wrong way (Old Person 1986:107).

34. The ominous word *termination* does not appear in the resolution (Officer 1986:114).

35. Public Law 280, passed during the same summer, also had an important effect on the status of Native Americans. PL 280 extended to certain states jurisdiction over civil and criminal matters on federal Indian reservations, thus attacking the principle of sovereignty established in *Worcester* (Svennson 1973:33–34).

36. The Menominees were restored to their tribal status in 1974 through the passage of the Menominee Restoration Act.

37. One hundred nine bands and tribes had been terminated by this time (S. O'Brien 1985:44).

38. A council of Indians representing nineteen tribes in Indian Territory sent the president of the United States a resolution attacking the Dawes Act. The resolution stated that "like other people, the Indian needs at least the germ of political identity, some governmental organization of his own . . . in order to make true progress in the affairs of life. This peculiarity in the Indian character is elsewhere called patriotism, and the wise and patient fashioning . . . of which alone will successfully solve the question of civilization" (Hertzberg 1971:9).

39. An important legislative victory for NCAI occurred in 1946 when Congress established an Indian Claims Commission. The purpose of the commission was to hear cases involving damages to Indian tribes and to attempt to compensate the tribes fairly. By the time this program was ended in 1978, according to Olson and Wilson, 285 tribal claims had been settled (among 850 filed) and over $800 million had been awarded. Some critics argue, however, that the commission was largely a failure (S. O'Brien 1985:52) and, "despite some good intentions . . . was soon another monument to . . . European values . . . " (Olson and Wilson 1984:137, 142).

40. This type of protest had been adopted a few years earlier by the Tuscarora leader Mad Bear Anderson (Bongartz 1972). About two years after the Washington state fish-in, representatives of the U.S. Department of Justice appeared before Washington State's Supreme Court *in behalf of the Indians,* arguing that the federal treaties signed with them were "solemn obligations of the government" (Steiner 1968:61).

41. Most discussions of this event have interpreted it as an Indian-white confrontation. Some scholars, however, view it primarily a a struggle between traditional and nontraditional Indians (Holm 1985: 137–144).

42. In the matter of gambling casinos, for example, there is intertribal and intratribal conflict as well as conflict between the tribes and state and

federal officials (*Americans Before Columbus* 1992).

43. The most famous of the veterans were the "code talkers" (most of whom were Navajos), whose native languages were not understood by enemy interceptors (Jacobson 1984:167).

44. The program was renamed the Employment Assistance Program in 1962 (Olson and Wilson 1984:163)., Steward (1977b:526) stated that is was renamed because the original name was too reminiscent of the War Relocation Authority, which carried an undesirable connotation. Nash (1986:166) commented that "relocation was an underfunded, ill-conceived program with a negative name."

45. In 1980, Los Angeles-Long Beach was the metropolitan area with the largest Native American population (60,893 people). Some other areas with large populations were New York-Jersey City-Newark, San Francisco-Oakland, Seattle-Tacoma-Everett, Tulsa, Oklahoma City, Phoenix, Minneapolis-St. Paul, San Diego, Detroit, and Chicago (Olson and Wilson 1984:164, 209). Native American urban populations may be growing rapidly and now may greatly exceed the 1980 figures.

46. For an excellent discussion of the "blood quantum" approach to racial identification, see Snipp (1989).

47. Despite a congressional joint resolution called "The American Indian Religious Freedom Act" (passed in 1978), the U.S. Supreme Court has held that tribal religions are not constitutionally protected. This situation has led to a pan-Indian effort in support of new legislation to guarantee religious freedom to Indians (*NARF Legal Review* 1991).

48. Snipp (1989:20) observed that since the white man's diseases generally preceded the actual arrival of many white people, the "traditional" tribal societies that were found by the whites *already* had been markedly altered.

49. These figures reflect only the experiences of the approximately 850,000 Native Americans who in 1980 lived within the boundaries of the eighty-eight service units of the Indian Health Service (IHS).

50. One of the most frequently heard claims by whites in this regard is that they are descended from an Indian "princess," usually a Cherokee on the grandmother's side (Svensson 1973:7). Deloria (1969:11) speculated in this connection that since apparently no one wants to claim a male Indian as an ancestor most tribes must have been "entirely female for the first three hundred years of white occupation."

A Renewal of Ethnicity and Immigration

Ethnic diversity is an opportunity rather than a problem.
—ANDREW M. GREELEY

For the third generation, the . . . ethnic cultures . . . are now
only an ancestral memory . . . to be savored once in a while
in a museum or at an ethnic festival. —HERBERT J. GANS

It doesn't take much to become a refugee. Your race or
beliefs can be enough. —UNHCR WALL POSTER, BANGKOK

> *English is under attack in America. . . . Our ancestors*
> *had to overcome great hardships just to get here. . . .*
> *Yet they understood that learning English was the*
> *key to success in America. —S. I. HAYAKAWA*

The experiences of the groups we have discussed in the five preceding chapters—Japanese Americans, Mexican Americans, African Americans, and Native Americans—reveal some of the social consequences of the main types of intergroup contact at different periods in American history. Japanese Americans were voluntary immigrants during the second great immigrant stream, were prevented from continuing to immigrate by the Immigration Act of 1924, and have been able to resume voluntary immigration since 1952. Mexican Americans were created through conquest but have been prominent in both the second and third great immigrant streams. African Americans were a part of the colonial immigration but, since the overwhelming majority of the group came as slaves, were "immigrants" only in the Pickwickian sense. Native Americans were gradually subjected to the rule of Europeans and their descendants over a long period of time. We reviewed a number of ideas concerning the factors that have encouraged members of these groups to adopt or reject one or another of the ideologies of group adjustment discussed in chapters 2 and 3, as well as the factors that have facilitated or impeded the groups' efforts to attain their objectives. We turn now to a brief consideration of the way domestic and international events since 1965 have combined to highlight, and also to challenge, the ideas we have explored thus far.

An Ethnic Revival

The 1960s generally are remembered as a period of social turbulence and rapid change. The outstanding events associated with this image—interracial violence, the war in Southeast Asia, civil rights and antiwar protests, major legislation and court rulings in the field of civil rights, and a revival of racial and ethnic consciousness—have been mentioned in previous chapters. We now examine more closely the way these events were intertwined with an increase in the competition among the various ideologies of adjustment and the emergence of the third great immigrant stream during this time.

The year 1965 provides a convenient point of departure. This was the year of the interracial violence in Watts, the passage of the Voting Rights Act, and the passage of the Amendments to the Immigration and Nationality Act. It also was the year President Lyndon Johnson began sharply to increase the commitment of U.S. troops to the Vietnam War. The Voting Rights Act marked the formal conclusion of decades of efforts to establish the legal equality of the races in America, but the other events signaled the early stages in a new period of racial and ethnic turmoil. As we saw in chapter 4, the major changes in the basic immigration laws of the United States occurred as the supply of Third World workers and refugees was increasing. At the same time, there was a growing disillusionment among African,

Mexican, and Native Americans with the idea that they could reach their objectives by relying on civil rights laws and court rulings. Their disenchantment coincided with (and almost surely contributed to) a very surprising aspect of that turbulent period—a phenomenon referred to in such phrases as "the rise of the unmeltable ethnics" (Novak 1971), "the new pluralism" (Feldstein and Costello 1974:414), and "the resurgence of ethnicity" (Glazer and Moynihan 1970:xxxi).

Just at the moment when most observers were anticipating the rapid extinction of the remaining significant differences among white ethnic groups, these distinctions seemed to revive with startling intensity. Many white ethnics suddenly became more aware of, or more vocal about, their cultural roots. New organizations were formed by Polish Americans, Lithuanian Americans, Slovakian Americans, Arab Americans, and many others. Television programs, shirt signs, and bumper stickers burst forth with commentaries announcing an awareness of, and pride in, an ethnic identification.[1]

Why was the revival of ethnic consciousness, or open discussion about ethnic attachments, a surprise? For one thing, there seemed to be abundant evidence that those who had come in the second immigrant stream and their descendants had accepted the goal of Anglo conformity and were well advanced in cultural and secondary assimilation. World War I and the quotas of the Immigration Act of 1924 had combined to reduce the number of immigrants reaching the United States, and this reduction, in turn, had weakened the bonds between the newcomers and their homelands. Then World War II served to emphasize to all Americans that despite their various origins, their sole allegiance now was to the United States. German Americans, Italian Americans, and Japanese Americans were called on to fight against the home countries of their grandparents or parents. Rates of enlistment in the military services and rates of naturalization among the foreign-born were high. Popular novels and movies portrayed white ethnics of the second immigrant stream as the equals of the descendants of the colonial and first-stream immigrants (Alba 1988:143). After the war, Americans of Hungarian, Czech, Lithuanian, Latvian, Estonian, Polish, and other eastern European ethnicities were torn as they watched the "iron curtain" of communism descend between them and many loved ones in their ancestral homelands.

Not all of the evidence, it is true, supported the view that Anglo conformity assimilation was taking place in a simple, straightforward way. A new interpretation of assimilation in America was proposed by Kennedy in 1944. She found, in a study of intermarriage trends in New Haven, Connecticut, that the rates of out-marriage (exogamy) had steadily increased among seven ethnic groups. She concluded that, as predicted by the Anglo conformity theory, ethnic lines were indeed fading; however, her analysis revealed that the out-marriages were clustered along religious lines. When the members of three Protestant groups—British, German, and Scandinavian Americans—married-out, they were most likely to select partners from one of those same Protestant groups. The members of three Catholic groups— the Irish, Italians, and Poles—preferred Catholic partners if they chose to go outside their own ethnic group. Throughout the seventy-year period studied by Kennedy, Jewish exogamy remained low. Even when out-marriages crossed religious lines,

Kennedy found religion was still an important consideration. Catholics, in particular, were unwilling to marry non-Catholics unless the wedding ceremony was Catholic. On the strength of these findings, Kennedy suggested that America's assimilation was occurring not in one but in three melting pots. Even though ethnic endogamy is loosening, "groups with the same religions tend to intermarry." Kennedy (1944:332) predicted, therefore, that "the future cleavages will be along religious lines."

Kennedy's "triple melting pot" thesis has been the focal point of subsequent analysis. Hollingshead (1950:624), for instance, agreed with Kennedy and concluded that "we are going to have three pots boiling merrily side by side with little fusion between them for an indefinite period." Alba and Kessler (1979) also have presented evidence that is consistent with Kennedy's thesis. These researchers have reported that, within the American Catholic group, there has been a sharp increase in intermarriages among the nationality groups, suggesting that the ethnic boundaries within the Catholic group gradually are eroding. Peach (1981), on the other hand, has criticized the triple melting pot view by noting that since spatial proximity, as well as religion, has a strong effect on the selection of marital partners, the patterns of residential segregation in American cities may work, in many cases, to weaken the influence of religion on mate selection. For instance, if Irish Catholics live in largely Protestant neighborhoods that are highly segregated from Italian Catholics, then the spatial proximity of Protestants will increase the probablity of Irish-Protestant marriages and decrease the probability of Irish-Italian marriages. The findings of Lieberson and Waters (1988:232–236) also showed that both religion and spatial proximity affect marital choices. The extent to which the three religious melting pots remain distinguishable, therefore, may depend strongly on the levels of residential segregation among the groups.

Kennedy's interpretation, as well as her findings, also has been questioned, notably by Herberg. In Herberg's (1960:34) view, "it would be misleading to conclude that the old ethnic lines had disappeared or were no longer significant." In the past, he argued, the nationality groups had considered religion to be a part of their ethnicity. But with the passage of time, religion has become the main instrument through which essentially ethnic concerns are preserved and expressed. The demands by the dominant group that minority groups conform to the Anglo-American pattern have focused more on language and general behavior than they have on religion. The three major religious groups, therefore, gradually have become equally "American" entities. As Herberg (1960:258) expressed it, "to be a Protestant, a Catholic, or a Jew are the alternative ways of being an American." For this reason, people of Polish, Italian, or French Canadian ancestry, for instance, find it much easier, and more American, to represent their ethnic concerns as Catholic concerns.

Glazer and Moynihan (1964:314) addressed the same issue in their influential analysis of ethnic groups in New York City and found, as Kennedy did, that the distinctions between the Irish, Italians, Poles, and German Catholics were being reduced by intermarriage. They agreed with Herberg, too, that as the specifically national aspect of ethnicity was declining, it was being replaced by religious affiliations and identities. Glazer and Moynihan also emphasized, however, that the triple melting pot did not include blacks and Puerto Ricans.[2] Despite the many changes in race relations that already had been effected by the Civil Rights Movement and the bright promise of further changes, the authors argued that the next stage of evolution in American society would maintain strong racial as well as religious distinctions. From this vantage point, the dramatic confrontations between whites and nonwhites that developed during the 1960s may seem understandable.

The idea that religious identities were replacing ethnic affiliations was soon challenged, however, by the revival of ethnicity after 1965. Indeed, at the end of the decade, Glazer and Moynihan (1970:xxxvi) themselves noted that ethnicity was being reasserted in its own right by numerous white ethnic groups. Pride in one's ethnicity as well as in one's religion was becoming more acceptable. But much more than pride was involved. The new groups being revived (or formed) were very concerned about the rapid changes taking place in American life and the effects of these changes on their lives. This concern was particularly visible among white ethnics of lower-middle-class status, those who worked mainly in blue-collar jobs.

The large-scale changes of the 1960s were perceived by many working-class ethnic Americans as threatening to undermine their hard-won gains. Many white ethnics feared that the rules of "making it" in America had been changed. The War on Poverty, the apparent success of confrontation politics, and the growing opposition to the war in Vietnam all created the impression that hard work, obedience to the law, and patriotism were no longer highly valued in America. They felt betrayed and cheated.[3] When they protested the apparent abandonment of the traditional American virtues and insisted that *their* parents and grandparents had "made it" in America without a handout, they were described on television and in newspapers as "flag wavers," "hard hats," "pigs," and "racists."

The latter charge arose because many of the efforts to expand employment, housing, and educational opportunities for blacks, especially in the large urban centers of the north central and northeastern states, were openly and vocally opposed by working-class whites, many of whom were not Anglo-Americans. The interracial conflict was not simply a "white backlash." It had economic and political roots, and it involved the continued existence of many of the ethnic neighborhoods that had been created during the years of the new immigration.

Ethnic neighborhoods, as noted previously, were formed as places of refuge and protection in an alien world. The immigrants needed the support and assistance of others like themselves to establish a foothold in the new country. The ethnic neighborhood provided an economic base for the struggling newcomers. It also facilitated their efforts to organize and to participate collectively in the American political system. In the neighborhood, they could exchange information concerning the location of jobs and the views of various candidates for political office. Through neighborhood organizations, they could combine their forces to combat discrimination in employment or to negotiate with "city hall." In the neighborhood, they could engage in deeply satisfying human relationships with others who shared their language, religion, cuisine, and memories of the old country. The ethnic American neighborhood, in short, has been a device to enable immigrants to come to grips with the new while preserving many of the psychological satisfactions of the old. Mikulski (1974:441) described these neighborhoods as "genuine urban villages. Warmth, charm, and zesty communal spirit were their characteristics."

Viewed in this way, the ethnic neighborhood has many "positive," desirable features. It may, in fact, be cited as an excellent example of what is meant by cultural pluralism; however, ethnic neighborhoods (as described in chapters 4 and 5) have long been viewed with suspicion by native Americans. They are the "slums," the source of organized crime and many other social pathologies. The ethnic neighborhood is a living reminder that Anglo conformity has not been completely successful. Their continuance, especially into the third generation, strikes many people as "downright un-American." Certainly any effort to *strengthen* such neighborhoods to ensure their continued existence flies in the face of the expectation that "the ethnics" will adopt full Anglo conformity and disperse into the broader society as quickly as possible. Efforts to reassert one's ethnicity, consequently, frequently have been condemned or ridiculed. They have been seen as an attempt to continue something "negative" and undesirable.

The rapid, large-scale social changes of the 1960s brought these "positive" and "negative" images of white ethnicity to the forefront of public discussion. Since in the large northern and eastern cities many white ethnic neighborhoods were close to black neighborhoods, the attempt to expand housing opportunities for blacks and to desegregate public schools had a large and immediate impact on the nearby white neighborhoods. When the residents protested that desegregation was being achieved at the expense of their distinctive traditions, their resistance was taken by some critics to be a "cover" for racism—a reaction inspired less by devotion to pluralism than by a desire to protect their socioeconomic position. Steinberg (1981:255), for instance, expressed skepticism concerning the motivations of many of pluralism's advocates and argued that "the idea of cultural pluralism has intrinsic appeal to groups who stand to benefit from maintaining . . . ethnic boundaries." The main problem here is that emphasizing neighborhood maintenance is different from emphasizing the exclusion of people of different ethnicities though, as Glazer and Moynihan (1970:xxxix) expressed it, "the acts that serve one aim are hard to distinguish from the acts that serve the other."

Both private and governmental forces pressed against the white ethnic neighborhoods. These forces were closely related to the desegregation effort but went beyond it. On the private side, the "blockbusting" tactics of real estate brokers and "redlining" policies of lending agencies each contributed directly to the disintegration of the neighborhoods. "Blockbusting" refers to the racially tinged methods used by real estate dealers to frighten whites into selling their homes for less than the true value. Many whites fear that the movement of blacks into their neighborhoods spells doom not only for the area's ethnic integrity but for its economic value as well. Playing on these fears, real estate brokers may arrange the sale of one home on a city block to a black family. Once the block has been penetrated, the "blockbuster" may buy a number of other homes cheaply from the remaining whites. The dealer then may turn a neat profit by selling the homes at much higher prices to middle-class blacks.

"Redlining" (or "blacklisting") does not necessarily lead to the replacement of white residents by blacks, but it does contribute to the deterioration of neighborhoods. As residential neighborhoods age, lenders at some point may become convinced that the housing there is no longer a safe investment. They may fear the area is on the verge of becoming a slum. When this happens, they may refuse to grant home improvement loans to homeowners, thus ensuring that the property will not be maintained and that the area will indeed become a slum.[4]

The private pressures on the white ethnic neighborhoods have been multiplied by government policies. For example, the Veterans Administration and the Federal Housing Administration frequently have followed the same policies as private lenders, refusing to make loans on old houses or houses in so-called marginal areas. Moreover, since World War II, the federal government has pursued a vigorous policy of urban renewal. This policy has required that dilapidated areas in cities be cleared to make room for public housing, highways, civic centers, and so on. The administrators and planners of urban renewal programs, of course, follow certain guidelines to determine which areas of the city are slums or likely to become slums. Old and rundown houses, a high population density, and mixed land use are accepted as the most important signs that an area is "falling apart" and should be cleared for other purposes. These signs may be quite misleading, however. Many working-class white ethnic neighborhoods share these characteristics but are by no means "falling apart" (Krickus 1974:434). Although they may appear to the casual eye to be decaying, they are many times places of hidden social strength (Kriegel 1974:419). Such neighborhoods are direct descendants of the "urban villages" created by the immigrants to meet life's challenges; for many people, they still serve this purpose.

The frequent inability of white ethnics to prevent the physical destruction of their neighborhoods reflected some of the other problems that stimulated their resurgence as distinctive groups. In the first place, they had been subjected to a severe economic "squeeze." Many of them were struggling to make a living, keep their homes, pay their bills, and, perhaps, send a child to college. Although they were seriously pressed by inflation and unemployment, they were "too rich" to qualify for many of the government and private programs established to assist poor people. As Mikulski (1974:442) stated, "Colleges make practically no effort to provide scholarships for kids named Colstiani, Stukowski, or Klima."

Another important factor contributing to the growing anger of the white ethnics was a marked shift in the American political process. The formation of Franklin Roosevelt's New Deal during the Great Depression of the 1930s represented an alliance of labor, white ethnic groups, and liberal intellectuals. During the 1960s, labor and liberal leaders shifted their attention to the nonwhite minorities, especially African Americans (Feldstein and Costello 1974:417). The ability of white ethnics to be heard sympathetically in the halls of government was suddenly and sharply reduced. By the beginning of the 1970s, consequently, white ethnics increasingly were looking for ways to translate their many grievances into effective political action. They sought to ensure that government programs for the victims of discrimination did not ignore their needs and problems. They felt forced to compete with African, Mexican, and Puerto Rican Americans for space, jobs, and federal dollars. At the national level, they strongly supported candidates who seemed likely to resist desegregation (such as Richard Nixon and George Wallace); in local elections, candidates openly sought the "Polish vote" or the "Italian vote" in a way that had not been seen for many years. In this process, the white ethnics inevitably appeared to be opposed to progressive social change and to reducing discrimination against nonwhite Americans.

Some of those who have defended the demands of white ethnics insist that their critics have failed to understand that the social changes of the 1960s were being accomplished disproportionately at the expense of white ethnics who lived in the centers of large cities. Novak (1971:14) observed that the white ethnics wished to know "why the gains of Blacks should be solely at *their* expense. They themselves have so little and feel so constricted." Anglo-Americans who lived in the suburbs, worked in professional jobs, and sent their children to private schools were to a considerable extent insulated from the direct costs of desegregation programs and could afford, therefore, to see the resulting interracial conflict in purely moral terms. It was for them, to cite Novak (1971:14) again, "a moral gravy train."

To interpret the resurgence of white ethnic awareness exclusively in terms of anti-black sentiment or the rational defense of group interest would be to miss another very important point. It seems almost certain that the white ethnics had never stopped being aware of their old-country identities. They had subdued regular displays of ethnic consciousness because, as Greeley (1971:18) noted, "it was not considered good form in the larger society to talk about such subjects, save on approved days of the year like Columbus Day or St. Patrick's Day." But as black militance and consciousness grew stronger during the 1960s, and as American institutions began to recognize and accept the right of blacks to proclaim and celebrate their blackness, people of many other groups saw no reason to continue to hide their own ethnic pride. "What the Blacks have done," Greeley (1971:18) argued, "is to legitimate ethnic self-consciousness."

The New Immigration

The rise of pluralism as an acceptable alternative to Anglo conformity served, in effect, to increase the ethnic heterogeneity of American society. The assumption that the white ethnics of the second immigrant stream were rapidly moving toward full Anglo conformity assimilation was suddenly viewed as questionable. But the mounting strength of the pluralist view was not the only force working to increase ethnic heterogeneity in America during this period. As we discussed in chapter 4, the demise of the national origins quota principle in 1965, the increasing volume of refugees being created by warfare in Indochina (i.e., Vietnam, Cambodia, and

Laos), and the increasing numbers of Third World workers who wished to enter the United States combined to trigger the largest stream of immigrants to America since the first two decades of the twentieth century (see again Table 4-1).

One consequence of the changes that stimulated the third great immigrant stream—the latest new immigration—is that Europe's contribution to the total number of immigrants declined sharply, while the contributions from Mexico, other countries of the Western Hemisphere, and Asia rose very rapidly. Another characteristic of the third stream is that many of these newcomers settled in different parts of the country. New York is still a popular destination, but California, Texas, Florida, Louisiana, and Pennsylvania are among the states now receiving large numbers of immigrants. These most recent newcomers also represent a much wider range of social, educational, and occupational backgrounds than was true of those in the first and second streams.

An especially important characteristic of this new immigrant stream is that it contained a disproportionately large share of refugees. With the conspicuous exception of the African slaves, those who came to America during the colonial period and as a part of the first and second immigrant streams were, to repeat, voluntary migrants. The "refugee problem" of the latter half of the twentieth century, however, has been created by internal and international conflicts in which millions of people have fled their homelands fearing for their lives. These people have not sought resettlement in the United States or some other country primarily to improve their economic or religious opportunities but, rather, to avoid execution, imprisonment, or persecution for political reasons.

The expulsion of people from their lands of residence, of course, is nothing new in world history, but, as noted briefly in chapter 4, the problems associated with refugee movements have increased since the seventeenth century. As the world became organized into nation-states, and as the human population skyrocketed, governments increasingly sought to control the composition of their populations by welcoming some groups and driving out others. This tendency has increased until, by the twentieth century, the problem of what to do with the rising number of refugees has become an important international question.[5]

Following the end of World War II, the number of refugees increased even more rapidly than before. In the United States, this increase generated new tensions between the national origins quota principle of admission and America's view of itself as a place of asylum for refugees. Under the Displaced Persons Act of 1948 and the Refugee Relief Act of 1953, many people who were displaced by World War II or were refugees from communist countries were admitted to the United States. The Hungarian Revolution of 1956, for instance, led large numbers of the defeated anticommunist "freedom fighters" to seek admission to the United States. President Eisenhower set a precedent by admitting thousands of Hungarians above Hungary's quota through a provision of the McCarran-Walter Act that enabled the government to grant asylum to people under the "parole" authority of the U.S. attorney general (Reimers 1985:26). The parole provision also was used by President Kennedy in 1961 to circumvent the quotas to aid anticommunist refugees who fled Cuba following Fidel Castro's successful revolution (Reimers 1985:27). Following the failed Bay of Pigs invasion of Cuba, the Migration and Refugee Assistance Act of 1962 was passed to grant refugee status to resident Cubans.

The refugee issue resurfaced in dramatic fashion as the Vietnam War drew to a close in 1975. Indochina had become the scene of a protracted and complicated series of civil and international wars stretching from the 1930s through the 1970s, and, as we shall see, the United States became progressively involved in the most intense portion of the fighting during the latter half of the 1960s. When the war ended, many people left Indochina and came to the United States. Since the largest group of Indochinese immigrants have been from Vietnam, we turn now to a closer examination of these representatives of the new immigration.

The Vietnamese

Very few emigrants from Indochina had entered the United States before 1961. Between 1951 and 1960, for example, the number of entries was 335 from Vietnam, 14 from Laos, and 11 from Cambodia (U.S. Immigration and Naturalization Service 1986:4). The situation changed noticeably, however, during the period 1961–1970 and changed dramatically during the period 1971–1980.

The people of Indochina have long histories and ancient cultures. They carved for themselves distinctive places in a land that has been vulnerable for millenia to the influences and domination of China and India. Despite over a thousand years of Chinese rule (111 B.C. to 939 A.D.), the Vietnamese were able to fashion their own unique culture and to maintain it in the face of intense external pressures. For approximately nine hundred years after the Chinese were driven out, the Vietnamese maintained an independent government, but beginning in 1535 they were brought into contact with Europe through the activities of Portugese traders and missionaries. Soon thereafter the Dutch, English, and French followed in the commercial and religious paths opened by the Portugese; in this way, the Vietnamese were introduced to the forces of European expansion already at work in the New World (Montero 1979:12–15).

We saw in chapter 12 that France and England struggled during the last half of the eighteenth century for control of North America. This struggle had its counterpart in Asia, and France sought to bring Vietnam—consisting (from north to south) of Tonkin, Annam, and Cochin China—under its control. During the first half of the nineteenth century, the French tried to accomplish this goal primarily through trade, diplomacy, and the conversion of the people to Catholicism, but later they resorted to armed force. For example, in 1787 a French missionary arranged an agreement between Louis XVI of France and Nguyen-Anh of Cochin China that gave France trading privileges in return for assisting Nguyen-Anh to gain control of Annam and Tonkin. Nguyen-Ahn was successful, but his successors in office withdrew France's privileges during the first half of the nineteenth century. Throughout this time, Catholic missionaries from France were at work converting Vietnamese people to Christianity. When the rulers of Vietnam became alarmed by the success of the missionaries and issued orders that they be killed, France (in 1861) initiated a military conquest. In 1883, all of Vietnam and most of Indochina

TABLE 13-1 Vietnamese Immigration to the United States, 1951–1990*

Years	Number
1951–1960	335
1961–1970	4,340
1971–1980	172,820
1981–1990	280,782
Total	458,277

Source: U.S. Immigration and Naturalization Service, *Statistical Yearbook* 1991:48–50.
*There was no separate listing for Vietnam before 1951.

became unwilling colonies of France (Montero 1979:16; Morse and Hendelson 1972a:262–263; Strand and Jones 1985:23–24).

Our previous discussions of the relationship between dominant invading groups and colonized minorities would lead us to expect that the French conquest of Vietnam probably would result in long-term conflict, and that is exactly what happened. The Vietnamese rankled under French rule. The French built highways, railroads, canals, and port facilities; but most of the wealth that was created went into the pockets of the French, while the Vietnamese people were rewarded with heavy taxation and sometimes brutal treatment. They also were denied freedom of speech, were unable to move freely from place to place, and were subject to detention and imprisonment without cause (Strand and Jones 1985:24). Two opposing groups of nationalists were organized following World War I, one favoring a communist approach to Vietnamese independence and the other favoring an anticommunist system. Both aimed to end foreign domination of Vietnam, and both initiated unsuccessful revolutionary uprisings during the 1930s (Morse and Hendelson 1972a:263).

When France surrendered to Germany early in World War II, Japan demanded and received military and trade privileges in the region. Although the Vichy government in France maintained nominal authority, the Japanese became the virtual rulers of Indochina. The dissatisfaction among the people that led to the prewar uprisings against the French became greater still during the Japanese occupation, and several resistance groups fought against them. Following Japan's surrender to the Allies in 1945, the Vietnamese people were in no mood to have the French return to power; so before the French reinvaded the country the nationalist groups formed a coalition party, the Vietminh, and established the Republic of Vietnam, with Ho Chi Minh as its president. With U.S. and British support, however, the French did come back. Eight years of bitter struggle with the Vietminh led to the Geneva Agreements of 1954, whereby Vietnam was partitioned at the seventeenth parallel.[6] The partition acknowledged the temporary existence of two Vietnams, one in the north and one in the south. The forces of France and the former Emperor of Annam gathered in South Vietnam, while those of the Vietminh gathered in North Vietnam (Morse and Hendelson 1972a:265–266).

In 1955, with the support of the U.S. government, a relatively unknown Catholic leader, Ngo Dinh Diem, proposed that South Vietnam become an independent country. Following a questionable referendum (in which Diem won 605,000 of a possible 450,000 votes in Saigon!), South Vietnam was established as a separate republic, with Diem at its helm (Strand and Jones 1985:25). In 1956, Diem canceled elections that had been scheduled to select a president for a reunited Vietnam. After the elections were canceled, the National Liberation Front (or Vietcong) launched a guerrilla war in South Vietnam, supported by North Vietnam. The United States continued to support the government of South Vietnam and gradually was enmeshed in a full-scale war with both the Vietcong and the regular military forces of North Vietnam. As the casualties mounted, the war became increasingly unpopular in the United States and among the people of South Vietnam, and in 1969 President Nixon began to withdraw U.S. troops. The war ended suddenly in 1975, when the South Vietnamese army collapsed in the space of a few weeks under the combined attacks of the Vietcong and the Vietminh (Wright 1980:509).

The Indochinese War lasted thirty years beyond the end of World War II. Although it was centered on Vietnam, it also included Cambodia (Kampuchea) and Laos. In the process, hundreds of thousands of people were uprooted. Their villages became battlefields, and they fled to escape death or mutilation (Kelly 1977:13). The extent of the unrest and fear was clearly evident following the Geneva Accords of 1954. Under these agreements, people were allowed to choose within six months whether they wished to live above or below the seventeenth parallel. In response, between 800,000 and 1 million Vietnamese (most of whom were Catholics) migrated from the North to the South (Kelly 1977:13; Morse and Hendelson 1972b:317; Nhan 1979:xiii). When the fighting resumed in the South, literally millions of people again fled from the combat areas and sought asylum first in the cities[7] and neighboring countries of Asia (such as Thailand, China, Hong Kong, Malaysia, and Indonesia) and later in second countries of asylum, such as the United States and France.

Most of those coming to America during the 1960s were the wives and children of U.S. citizens, but as the end of the war approached the U.S. government announced that some refugees from Vietnam would be evacuated and resettled in the United States. Exactly who would be evacuated, how many, and what their status in America would be was not clearly explained. Presumably, the dependents of American citizens, Vietnamese who were or had been employed by the U.S. government, and those who would be targets of reprisal by the North Vietnamese would be the main evacuees (Kelly 1977:18–19). But the planning did not keep pace with events. No one anticipated the rapidity of the South Vietnamese army's collapse, so in April 1975, as the communist troops approached Saigon, a hastily arranged and panicky evacuation of more than sixty thousand Vietnamese was set into motion. Most refugees were flown to the Philippines and then to a holding center at Guam (Kelly 1977:30). Amidst the chaos of the evacuation, an additional seventy thousand Vietnamese people left the country on their own initiative within the same week (Wright 1980:509). One way or another, by the middle of May approximately 130,000 refugees had entered U.S. territory. Nevertheless, many people whom the Americans had wished to evacuate were left behind and many whom the government had not planned to evacuate were included (Kelly 1977:22; Montero 1979:2). Within a few months, an additional sixty thousand refugees had reached camps in Thailand and Hong Kong, and these were only the vanguard of many thousands more to come during the next few years.

This massive evacuation brought into play several types of social machinery that had been created to handle refugee problems. In 1951, the United Nations High Commission for Refugees (UNHCR) was created for this very purpose, and its facilities were mobilized to assist in solving the human problems generated by the Indochinese crisis. The UNHCR works primarily through other UN agencies, individual governments, and charitable international organizations to provide support for refugees and places of permanent asylum for them (Strand and Jones 1985:3–5). Several countries agreed to accept some of the refugees, but the countries that agreed to receive the largest number were those that were seen as being most responsible for the debacle—the United States and France. Within two years of the collapse of South Vietnam, the United States accepted over 148,000 people, while France accepted over 37,000.[8]

In the United States, there were questions concerning the legal status of the newcomers. In the last days of the Vietnamese conflict, the attorney general's "parole" authority was invoked (as it had been earlier for Hungarians and Cubans) to enable the resettlement to the United States of up to fifty thousand Vietnamese refugees who would have been at "high risk" under the new communist regime in South Vietnam (Kitano and Daniels 1988:137; Montero 1979:73–74; Strand and Jones 1985:36). The existing laws and authority were supplemented in 1975 by the Indochina Migration and Refugee Assistance Act, which provided funds to pay for the transportation and resettlement of the refugees. A permanent Refugee Resettlement Program was put into place in the Refugee Act of 1980. This act recognized America's continuing role in the world as a place of asylum and created special agencies to oversee and coordinate the resettlement of refugees (Kitano and Daniels 1988:137; Strand and Jones 1985:38–39).

The basic responsibility for managing the evacuation from Vietnam in 1975 was assigned by President Ford to the Interagency Task Force for Indochinese Refugees (IATF). The IATF set up the initial receiving station at Guam, but as that island's facilities quickly became overcrowded four mainland refugee camps were established in California (Camp Pendleton), Pennsylvania (Fort Indian Town Gap), Arkansas (Fort Chafee), and Florida (Eglin Air Force Base) to assist the refugees to begin life anew in the United States. The camps were intended to serve as temporary stations for "processing" and relocating the newcomers. Their main purpose was to provide each person or family the assistance they needed to enable them to move into American life as self-supporting members of society. They were expected to assist the newcomers, in Kelly's (1977:2) phrase, to make "the transition from refugee to immigrant. . . ."

When the refugees reached a particular camp, they received security interviews and physical examinations and were assigned to living quarters in a tent or barracks. At this point, the comparatively few people who received security clearances and could prove they had cash reserves of at least $4,000 per family member were permitted to leave the camps. The large majority, however, were required to register with one of nine accredited voluntary agencies that had agreed to arrange the refugees' resettlement. The agencies had contracted with the IATF to find individual or group sponsors who would, in Montero's (1979:26) words, "assume fiscal and personal responsibility for the refugee families for a period of up to two years." The IATF awarded the agencies $500 for each refugee who was placed with a sponsor. Since over 60 percent of the refugees arrived in family groups of five or more, these grants provided $2,500 or more to assist in the resettlement of most families; nevertheless, since the average cost of resettling one family was around $5,600, most of the cost of resettlement was borne by the refugees' sponsors (Montero 1979:24, 28).[9] Under these circumstances, most refugees were sponsored by groups rather than by individual Americans.

The first of the four original mainland refugee centers, at Camp Pendeleton, California, opened on April 29, 1975, the day before Saigon fell. By December of that year, approximately 130,000 people had been released from the reception centers into the United States. Over 121,000 of these had been matched with sponsors through the efforts of the voluntary agencies, and the remainder had been released after proving they did not require assistance (Strand and Jones 1985:33). Through this massive and rapid program, Vietnamese refugees were dispersed (though unevenly and in the face of some criticism) to every state in the United States. California received more than one-third of the refugees, while Texas, Pennsylvania, Louisiana, Virginia, Washington, and Florida (in that order) together received another one-third. The remaining refugees were scattered throughout the country, ranging from a few thousand in Illinois, New York, and Minnesota, to less than a hundred in Vermont and Wyoming (Montero 1979:8). This generally successful operation was only the prelude, however, to a second wave of refugees from Indochina.

The fall of South Vietnam in 1975 brought to a close America's direct participation in the fighting in Indochina. But the "end of the war" did not mean conflict and turmoil in that region had ceased or that people were no longer homeless or in search of places of refuge. While the Vietminh and Vietcong were successfully establishing a communist government in Vietnam, the Pathet Lao, a communist resistance group in Laos, was enjoying similar success in Laos. The new Laotian government waged war against the Hmong people of the mountain regions and harassed many of the ethnic Chinese who dominated the merchant and professional occupations. As a result, thousands of Laotians fled to neighboring Thailand in search of protection.

Also in 1975, an insurgent group called the Khmer Rouge successfully toppled the American-backed government of Cambodia. Like Vietnam, Cambodia had been heavily bombed during the early 1970s and millions of people had been driven from their homes. Now the new Khmer Rouge rulers of Cambodia, led by Pol Pot, instituted a shocking relocation and slaughter that, in the words of Kitano and Daniels (1988:147), "ended with the murder of at least one million Cambodians by Cambodians and the forced relocation of many others."[10] This carnage, which ranks among the leading disasters of human history, created new refugees in Cambodia and helped drive them out of the country. More than 100,000 Cambodians fled to Thailand in 1978 and 1979. These refugees were then joined in 1980 by an additional 150,000 Cambodians who were victims of famine. Most of these people were jammed into refugee camps that the Thai government had erected along the Thai-Cambodian border (Strand and Jones 1985:19–21, 34). Dislocated people were on the move throughout Indochina, a testament to indescribable human misery and suffering.

During the last years of the 1970s, conditions in Vietnam were still very unsettled. The government of the Socialist Republic of Vietnam was involved in the conflicts in Cambodia and Laos and also was engaged in border conflicts with China. In addition, the government was pressing to restructure Vietnam's economy along communist lines. As part of the latter effort, large numbers of people who were engaged in private business or the professions (including many of the ethnic Chinese) were subjected to various reprisals, "reeducation programs," confiscations of property, conscriptions to forced labor, and threats of worse to come. Under these circumstances, tens of thousands of people were gripped by panic and fled the country by sea in frail, untrustworthy boats. The flight of these frightened, horribly vulnerable "boat people" captured the attention, and occasionally the sympathy, of observers throughout the world.[11]

Thousands of people, of course, had used small boats in 1975 to reach rescue vessels from the United States and other nations waiting off the coast of Vietnam. But this was different. There were no rescue vessels awaiting them this time and, indeed, the refugees were far from certain they would arrive safely at any destination. The main objective was to get out, to escape before it was too late. Once they were at sea, however, the dangers they faced were formidable. Many overloaded boats were swamped and the occupants drowned; the motors on many boats failed, leaving the occupants to drift until they starved or died of thirst or disease; and perhaps as many as 80 percent of the boats were attacked by pirates (Kitano and Daniels 1988:141). Even when the refugees succeeded in reaching land or a possible rescue vessel, they often were refused sanctuary or were physically attacked, killed, or driven away (St Cartmail 1983:87–97).

There is no exact count of the Indochinese (including Vietnamese) boat people. St Cartmail (1983:89–90) estimated that by 1982, over 493,000 people had arrived by boat in countries of first asylum. This figure does not include the tens of thousands of people (possibly more than 200,000) who were drowned or died of other causes in their attempt to find safety. Among those who did reach a safe shore, however, the largest number (over 158,000) were accepted, temporarily at least, by Malaysia. The next largest number of boat people (over 101,000) were received in Hong Kong.[12] Indonesia and Thailand also each received over sixty thousand. Since the facilities of the first asylum countries generally were inadequate for dealing with such large numbers of refugees, the UNHCR has continued to work to find permanent asylum for them. By 1981, over 197,000 of the boat people had been accepted by the United States (Strand and Jones 1985:9), but, obviously, many thousands of people were still displaced and awaiting new homes.

An Involuntary Immigrant Minority?

We emphasized previously that the circumstances under which groups make their first contacts with one another continue long afterward to influence their interrelations and that whether a given group's entrance into a society is largely voluntary or involuntary is of special importance. A voluntary entrance, we assumed, reflects mainly the "pulls" or attractions of the new society for immigrants and suggests a desire on their part to join the new society. This positive psychological state presumably sets the stage for the movement of the group's members through the various subprocesses of assimilation. Although voluntary immigrants may be expected to offer various forms of resistance to the pressures to assimilate (as discussed previously), they usually do so less fiercely than members of groups that were forced to join the host society.

Our previous discussions also have noted, however, that for most people, even "voluntary" emigration from óne's homeland will have been precipitated in part by "pushes" as well as "pulls." Contented people seldom are willing to endure the hardships that attend relocating in a new society. Indeed, in the cases of the Scotch-Irish, the Colonial Irish, and the Russian Jews, to name only three, the "pushes" from the homeland were very strong. Many people in these instances were forced to choose between leaving their homes and misery or an early death where they were. Emigration under such circumstances is not completely "voluntary"; nevertheless, despite the presence of "push" factors in these emigrations, we did not refer to the people involved in them as refugees and were not surprised that they accepted the prospect of at least certain forms of assimilation.[13]

Should we have the same expectations concerning the contemporary refugees who now reside in America? Is there any reason to suppose that the reactions of these newcomers will differ substantially from those of their many predecessors who also fled from starvation and life-threatening oppression? One difference of possible importance between the earlier and present cases is that the former usually could choose among a much wider range of *destinations*. The expansion of Europe's colonial empires opened up (usually over the bitter opposition of the indigenous peoples) vast new territories for settlement; so emigrants wishing relief from the various threats and miseries of European societies often could decide which one of several new societies they would join. The third-stream refugees, in contrast, not only have been victimized by numerous "pushes" in their home societies but have had little choice in selecting their destinations. Their fates, in general, have been decided by the joint actions of the UNHCR, the appointed agencies of the U.S. government, the contracting voluntary agencies, and the willingness of sponsors to oversee and support their resettlement. Moreover, the

Vietnamese refugees who entered the United States in the immediate post-war wave realized after they reached the refugee camps on the U.S. mainland that they probably would not return to their homelands (Kelly 1977:2–3).

Whether the narrowing of the range of choices available to refugees of the third stream has affected the course of their adaptation to American society remains to be seen. Their restricted choices may have created feelings of entrapment and resentment that will interfere with a full acceptance of American life by the refugees, and the deliberate dispersion of the refugees throughout the United States may have deprived them of the family and community support that has been of inestimable value to so many previous immigrant groups. On the other hand, the resettlement program may have helped, on balance, to cushion the shock of the refugees' rapid, largely unplanned, evacuation and may have been partially successful at least in transforming "refugees into immigrants." Consider, for example, that despite their primitive character, the camps that were set up to receive the refugees *did* exist and they *did* provide temporary shelter, food, clothing, and medical care for the refugees. The camps also provided, through the voluntary agencies, certain social services such as child care classes, college placement services, and English language training. The Vietnamese also received information about life in America and instructions concerning how to handle typical problems they would encounter. After leaving the camps, the refugees' various sponsors continued to provide life's necessities, to help them find jobs and enroll their children in schools, and to assist them to understand the basics of American life (Kelly 1977:83–89; Montero 1979:27). Even though the Vietnamese refugees did not seek such a dependent position, and even though there were some instances of coercion and exploitation in the resettlement process, one may nevertheless entertain the idea that the aid the refugees received served to moderate the effects of evacuation and may have put them on a footing resembling that of previous immigrants who also were more "pushed" from their homelands than they were "pulled" to America.

As we stressed in previous chapters, assimilation is a long-term process; hence, the studies needed to answer fully the questions raised here must await the passage of time. We are extremely fortunate, though, in already having available the results of a few major studies that shed some light on the subject of the early course of assimilation among the Vietnamese in America which may provide some clues concerning their future prospects. We turn now to the results of these studies.

Vietnamese American Assimilation

In previous discussions, we mentioned several factors (in addition to a largely voluntary or forced entrance into the host society) that may influence the rate of assimilation for a particular group. Among the most important of these factors are the group members' command of English, their educational levels, their work skills and employment opportunities, the extent to which a group organizes along family and ethnic lines for mutual aid and support, and the economic conditions in the host society at the time the group arrives. Although all of these factors may come into play immediately and simultaneously the moment the immigrants arrive, they represent different aspects of the assimilation process and will be more or less prominent at various times. Let us begin, as before, with cultural assimilation.

Cultural Assimilation

The extent to which English is used and understood by the members of an immigrant group is the key indicator of the occurrence of cultural assimilation in the group. The group's level of cultural assimilation, in turn, influences every aspect of its members' interactions with those in the host society and affects the probability that other types of assimilation will occur. Immigrants need to know the language to communicate effectively with those around them. They must find and keep jobs—jobs they hope will be commensurate with their educational levels and occupational skills. They must arrange for places to live, enroll their children in schools, and, in general, negotiate their way through a new and strange society—in this case, the complications of a large, modern, urban, bureaucratic society. The central questions to be raised here, then, are: "How proficient were the Vietnamese refugees in the English language at the time of their arrival? To what extent has their level of English proficiency risen since then?" The answers to these questions should help us make some assessment of the rate at which cultural assimilation is taking place among Vietnamese Americans.

Information concerning the Vietnamese refugees' command of English was gathered in each of four valuable studies of differing scope. The first of these, by Montero (1979), describes and analyzes a series of studies conducted under the sponsorship of the U.S. Department of Health, Education, and Welfare (HEW) following the opening of the four mainland resettlement camps in 1975. The second study, by Jiobu (1988a), is a careful analysis of the data gathered in the 1980 census pertaining to eight ethnic groups (including the Vietnamese) for the entire state of California. Third, we rely on a study by Strand and Jones (1985) that reports the results of a sample survey of the Indochinese who were living in San Diego, California, in 1981. Finally, we draw on a study by Caplan, Whitmore, and Choy (1989) based on two sample surveys of Indochinese boat people conducted in 1981 and 1984 in five locations in the United States.[14]

The HEW reports analyzed by Montero (1979) included data on the entire population of refugees who went through the camps between 1975 and 1977 and on five special samples studied to ascertain how well the refugees were adapting to American life. The sample surveys were conducted in five waves (or steps), by telephone, with random samples of Vietnamese household heads who had been resettled in various American communities (Montero 1979:33–55). The five waves of the study included various numbers of participants, and waves two through five included various numbers of household heads who had participated in one of the earlier waves.[15]

In four of the surveys, the participants were asked whether the members of their household could understand, speak, read, and write English and to answer "not at all," "some," or "well" in relation to each category. For example, the second survey, which was based on interviews of a national probability sample "of all refugees who had left the camps on or before October 15, 1975" (Montero 1979:35), revealed that between 18 and 19 percent of the respondents said they could understand, speak, read, and write English well, while about half that proportion said they could not understand, speak, read, or write English at all.[16] It is apparent, therefore, that the remainder of the Vietnamese refugees (roughly 72 percent) who were released from the resettlement camps during the first few months had some ability to understand, speak, read, and write English.

Estimates of the English proficiency of the resettled Vietnamese rose rapidly in the first two years following their arrival. Survey five, conducted in 1977, found that those reporting they could understand or speak English well had risen to 34 percent and those reporting they could read or write English well had risen to about 30 percent. At the same time, those saying they could not understand, speak, read, or write English at all had fallen to between 2 and 4 percent. Although the differences observed between surveys two and five could be the result of sampling biases, it nevertheless seems probable that between one-fifth and one-third of the Vietnamese refugees who fled to the United States after the fall of Saigon had a good command of English at the time of their arrival or had acquired such a command during the initial months of their resettlement.

Further information on the English proficiency of the Vietnamese was gathered in the 1980 decennial census enumeration. Jiobu (1988a:16) presented some of the findings as part of a detailed analysis of eight California ethnic groups. The questionnaires used by the census takers asked the household head to say whether each member of the household could speak English "very well," "well," "not well," or "not at all." For the purpose of his analysis, Jiobu (1988a:102–103) combined the first two levels of English proficiency and found that 54 percent of the Vietnamese in California appeared to be able to speak English very well or well. Taken at face value, such a comparison shows a sharp rise from the 34 percent who said they spoke English well in HEW's fifth survey to 54 percent who said they spoke English well or very well in the census survey. Since the Census Bureau's proficiency levels do not correspond directly to those used in the HEW surveys, we must be cautious in making a comparison between the results of the two studies (even assuming that self-reports in different situations represent the same thing). It nevertheless seems reasonable to suppose that a substantial rise in English proficiency among the Vietnamese did occur during the three-year interval, even if it were not so large as 20 percent.[17]

Still further information on the question of English language skills was reported by Strand and Jones (1985) from a sample survey of the approximately forty thousand Indochinese refugees who lived in San Diego, California, in 1981. Questionnaires were administered to the primary breadwinner in eight hundred households. As was true in the HEW and census surveys, the questionnaire sought information on all members of the household. The final sample consisted of 800 people, 430 of whom were Vietnamese. The respondents were asked, among other things, whether they were able to read and write English. Almost 53 percent of the Vietnamese said they could.[18] Unlike the HEW and Census Bureau surveys, though, no information was gathered on the level of the respondents' reading and writing skills; so, again, we cannot make a direct comparison of the results of this study with those of the other two.[19]

Finally, a study by Caplan, Whitmore, and Choy (1989:39) focused on samples of Indochinese boat people, including 690 Vietnamese households. The initial and current levels of the refugees' competence in English was assessed using three measures of reading, speaking, and performance. The researchers found that most of the adults initially had little or no command of English, though in some Vietnamese households (more than one-third) "the majority of adults knew at least some English when they arrived" (Caplan, Whitmore, and Choy 1989:31). By the time the interviews were conducted, there had been substantial improvements in the refugees' ability to conduct their daily affairs in English. Consider the following comparisons of the percentage of refugees who felt able to perform certain tasks in English at the earlier and later times, respectively: shop for food (32 versus 92 percent); apply for aid (13 versus 45 percent); hold a job as a salesperson (6 versus 23 percent) (Caplan, Whitmore, and Choy 1989:220).[20] Although the four studies we have cited concerning the English language skills of the Vietnamese are not strictly comparable, a cautious reading of the combined findings of these studies suggests that no less than one-third of the Vietnamese refugees, and possibly as many as one-half, were fairly proficient English speakers after no more than five years in the United States.

What do these estimates of the linguistic assimilation of Vietnamese Americans tell us about their cultural assimilation? Is it occurring slowly or rapidly? As the reader may expect, no unqualified answer can be given to these questions. As we stressed previously, one must have some basis of comparison to say whether any form of assimilation is occurring slowly or rapidly. For example, although we have little systematic information concerning the English language proficiency of the Issei who entered the United States between 1890 and 1924, it seems certain that of these two groups the Vietnamese who arrived in the 1970s were by far the more proficient. This difference should not surprise us, of course, given the extensive contact between Americans and Vietnamese in Vietnam between 1950 and 1975 and the general spread of the English language throughout the world. Regardless of the explanation, however, it certainly would appear that the cultural assimilation of the Vietnamese is proceeding more rapidly than it did among the Issei. Similarly, Strand and Jones (1985:102–103) showed that the Vietnamese in San Diego were much less likely than the Lao, Hmong, and Cambodian refugees to perceive English communication as a group problem and were much more likely to report that they could read and write English, which again suggests that the Vietnamese are undergoing comparatively rapid cultural assimilation. On the other hand, Jiobu's (1988a:103) comparison of the English proficiency of the Vietnamese with that of six other nonwhite groups, including such recent Asian arrivals as the Koreans and Filipinos, showed that the Vietnamese, as a group, are the least proficient in English. Jiobu (1988a:103) did stress, however, that "even among the Vietnamese, the group with the most recent immigration history, somewhat more than one-half are proficient in English." In short, we may claim that when compared to many immigrants of the past, as well as to some other recent arrivals, the linguistic (and, hence, cultural) assimilation of the Vietnamese appears to be occurring at a rapid rate.

Secondary Structural Assimilation

Our principal indicators of secondary assimilation among Vietnamese Americans are education, occupation, income, and residential segregation. We examine each of these briefly.

Information on the educational level of the Vietnamese refugees is very good because it was gathered as a routine part of each person's induction into the resettlement camps, and the general result is quite clear. The statistics released by the federal government show that "nearly 50 percent of the heads of household have at least a secondary school education, and more than 25 percent are college and university graduates," leading Montero (1979:22) to conclude that "the Vietnamese refugees are relatively well-educated by any standard. . . ." Stated differently, the average (median) educational level of the Vietnamese refugees by 1980 was approximately fourteen years (Jiobu 1988a:92), which equaled the educational level of white Californians.[21] We should note, however, that the educational levels of the boat people—those comprising the second wave of immigration after 1978—were generally lower than that of those who arrived immediately following the evacuation of 1975 (Caplan, Whitmore, and Choy 1989:24).

Of special interest in regard to education is the experience of the refugees' children. The researchers gathered information concerning their grade point averages (GPAs) in school and their scores on standardized tests that are used throughout the nation. On both counts the children in this sample scored well. For example, almost three-fourths of the children had overall GPAs in the A or B grade range, and on the standardized California Achievement Test, over 60 percent scored in the top half (Caplan, Whitmore, and Choy 1989:70). Taken together, these findings add strength to the idea that the high level of education among the Vietnamese helps to explain why their cultural assimilation appears to be proceeding fairly rapidly. It also suggests the hypothesis that their occupational assimilation in the adult generation should be comparatively rapid.

We have good information concerning the occupations of the Vietnamese in their homeland. As one would expect on the basis of their high educational level (especially in the first wave), there was a strong representation of doctors, managers, and other professionals. Indeed, although they had had many different kinds of occupations, the largest single category was professional, technical, and managerial pursuits (24 percent) (Montero 1979:23).

How have the Vietnamese fared in the American occupational system? Two points stand out. First, in general, the longer a person has been in the United States the more likely it is that he or she will be employed. Montero (1979:43–44) showed that the employment rate among male heads of household rose from 68 to 95 percent between surveys one and five, while the employment rate among female heads of household rose from 51 to 93 percent.[22] Strand and Jones (1985:116–117) found that, in San Diego, the employment level rose from 20 percent among those who had resided there less than one year to 93 percent among those who had resided there for six years. Caplan, Whitmore, and Choy (1989:53) found that unemployment declined rapidly from about 88 percent shortly after the refugees' arrival to about 28 percent after 40 months in the United States. The second point of note, however, is that the occupational talents and skills exercised by the refugees in their native land frequently did not carry over directly into the American setting. The fifth HEW survey, for instance, showed that although 95 percent of the male heads of household and 93 percent of female heads of household had found some kind of employment, the kinds of jobs the refugees held often were of lower pay and prestige than the jobs they had held in Vietnam. To illustrate, almost 61 percent of the household heads who had held white-collar jobs in Vietnam were in blue-collar jobs at the time of the fifth survey (Montero 1979:38–44). In a general comparison of the level of occupational assimilation among the Vietnamese in California as a whole, Jiobu (1988a:87) found that the index of occupational dissimilarity among the Vietnamese was higher than that among Filipinos, Chinese, Koreans, and Japanese.[23] This comparison shows that the job distribution of Vietnamese workers did not resemble that of white workers as much as did the job distributions of the other groups named; however, the job distribution of the Vietnamese was slightly *more* similar to that of the whites than was the distribution of blacks (14 versus 15 percent), and it was *very much more* similar to the white distribution than was the distribution of Mexican Americans (14 versus 34 percent).

These comparisons showed that the Vietnamese achieved a high level of employment within a few years of their arrival in the United States but, nevertheless, experienced a general decline in their occupational standing. The overall prestige level of the occupations they undertook in the United States was lower than those they held in Vietnam and lower than one might expect on the basis of their educational level. Kelly (1977:179) reported, for instance, cases in which the director general of the South Vietnamese Ministry of the Interior was employed working in yards, an air force colonel was delivering newspapers, a medical doctor was a dishwasher, and the chief of staff of the South Vietnamese Army was a waiter. We should note, too, that although the level of employment was high among those in the labor force, refugees are consistently less likely to be in the labor force than are most Americans (Bach and Carroll-Seguin 1986:401). It is not surprising, therefore, to find that the Vietnamese were not as highly paid as the workers in many other groups and that they considered money problems to be of special importance. Strand and Jones (1985:134–135) reported, indeed, that among twenty problem areas, the Vietnamese ranked "not enough money" as of greatest importance. Montero (1979:51) stated that in 1977 "the typical annual income of refugee households" was about $9,600, as compared to "a median household income of $13,572 for the United States as a whole." And Jiobu's (1988a:96) analysis showed that a higher proportion (23 percent) of Vietnamese earned less than $5,000 per year than was true of any of the other seven groups with whom they were compared. Nevertheless, if we focus on household, rather than individual, income, the Vietnamese have made notable progress. For instance, Caplan, Whitmore, and Choy (1989:62) found that after one year in the United States, the household incomes in their sample had exceeded the official poverty level and after forty or more months they had exceeded that level by 71 percent.[24] It is abundantly clear, therefore, that although their income levels at the time of these studies was still comparatively low, the Vietnamese Americans nevertheless have found a place in the American occupational structure and have achieved a high level of economic self-sufficiency.

We turn now to the last of the four indicators of secondary assimilation under review, residential assimilation. As noted in chapter 8, Jiobu (1988a:107–148) presented a thorough description and analysis of the extent to which the seven nonwhite ethnic groups in his study were residentially segregated in the twenty-one SMSAs in California. The main finding of this study for our present purpose, though, is simply that among the seven nonwhite groups, the average level of residential segregation was higher for the Vietnamese than for any other group (Jiobu 1988a:114). This finding is much easier to state than to explain. Jiobu's analysis focused on a number of hypotheses involving the relative contributions to segregation of such factors as the absolute and relative size of the minority populations and the relative economic status of the minority groups. For example, although the Vietnamese (the most segregated group) had the lowest income level and the Japanese (the least segregated group) had the highest income level, Jiobu (1988a:142) nevertheless showed that noneconomic factors (such as the relative size of the minority) were more important causes of residential segregation.

What conclusion concerning the secondary assimilation of the Vietnamese follows from this brief review of their education, occupations, income, and residential segregation? As was true in the case of cultural assimilation, we cannot say definitely whether the secondary assimilation of the Vietnamese has proceeded slowly or rapidly. Certainly it seems clear that the Vietnamese, as a group, underwent an immediate decline in occupational and social position when they arrived in the United States. One might suppose that, to some extent, such a phenomenon would be inevitable. Problems with a new language, the customs of the host society, arranging the most suitable locations in which to live and work, and so on could easily prevent any immigrant group from immediately becoming established at their previous social level. It also is true that the Vietnamese reached the United States during a period of economic recession, and this circumstance played an important role in leading the federal government to adopt the policy of dispersing the refugees throughout the country. Government officials believed that heavy concentrations of refugees in a small number of locations during a time of economic recession would increase the difficulty of finding jobs for the newcomers (Kelly 1977:184). They also feared that the competition between U.S. citizens and refugees for scarce jobs would heighten prejudices and trigger acts of discrimination by the natives. Perhaps these concerns were justified. It is not clear, though, that the dispersion strategy actually improved the economic prospects of the Vietnamese, because it interfered with their ability to maintain and develop the kinds of family and community ties that have aided many other immigrant groups in their struggles to adapt to new social conditions (e.g., as discussed in chapter

8, an ethnic economic enclave or ethnic hegemony). This interference may have had especially important consequences in the case of the Vietnamese because of what has been referred to as the "unconditional nature" of kinship in Vietnamese society (Haines 1988:3).

Studies focusing on the psychological and interpersonal consequences for the Vietnamese created by the shock of a rapid, unplanned entry into the United States, an unanticipated period of dependence, and a sharp downturn in economic standing have found widespread psychological distress, depression, and marital conflict among the refugees (see, e.g., Kinzie 1981; Lin, Tazuma, and Masuda 1979; Montero 1979:30–31). We do not know whether the reported levels of distress and conflict were greater than those experienced by most other immigrants in the past or whether the refugee experience has had an extraordinary effect on the adjustment of the second generation (see, e.g., Eisenbruch 1988:282–300). If so, the process of secondary assimilation may be impeded.

Primary Structural Assimilation

We noted previously that immigrant groups to America commonly have considered the freedom and development of the individual to be less important than the welfare of the family. Certainly the Vietnamese have been described in these terms. Discussions have emphasized that the family is "an entity by itself, an irreducible value and the only way of life for the Vietnamese" (Phung thi Hanh, quoted by Haines 1988:3) and have suggested that the family is, perhaps, even more important among the Vietnamese than among most other groups. Whether or not the latter claim is warranted, it is true that the resettled Vietnamese have attempted to maintain contacts with family members and compatriots in other parts of the country and, in many cases, have moved from their initial locations to other places having larger Vietnamese populations, particularly to California. For example, at the end of the resettlement program in December 1975, 27,199 Vietnamese were in California, but by July 1976, their numbers had risen to over 30,000 (Kelly 1977:200). While family reunification provided the primary impetus for this migration, some of the movement has been stimulated by the deliberate efforts of Vietnamese leaders to help reorganize the community within the new social context (Kelly 1977:202). This regrouping to achieve family and community cohesion resembles the earlier formation of ethnic enclaves by the Chinese and Japanese immigrants of the late nineteenth and early twentieth centuries (Montero 1979:61).

The focus of the Vietnamese on the maintenance and reunification of their families and community, along with the great demands of cultural and secondary assimilation, presumably has left them with little time or inclination to establish and develop primary relationships with native Americans. Certainly, little systematic information concerning this process is available. The Vietnamese have worked closely with their resettlement sponsors, of course, and an unknown number of lasting friendships may have emerged from these relationships. Even here, though, the relationship between the American sponsors and the Vietnamese was mainly one in which the dominant Americans were making decisions for the subordinate Vietnamese in an effort to "resettle" them and to bring an end to the financial responsibilities of sponsorship (Kelly 1977:159). Such an arrangement does not encourage the formation of the friendly, equalitarian types of relationships that we have described as primary.

Marital Assimilation

Given the brief period of time the Vietnamese have been in the United States, the extent to which they arrived in family groups, and their apparently low level of primary assimilation, there is little reason to expect a high level of marital assimilation among them. It is true, of course, that many of the first Vietnamese to come to the United States during the 1960s were the spouses of Americans, but this group is now a relatively small proportion of the total Vietnamese American population. Our interest centers on how much exogamy has occurred among the entire group.

The best available evidence on this point comes from Jiobu's (1988a:159–162) analysis of 241,102 couples, and the pertinent findings may be stated succinctly. Of the eight ethnic groups represented in this study, the Vietnamese had a very low rate of intermarriage and the lowest rate observed in the comparison. We conclude, therefore, that comparatively little marital assimilation has occurred among the Vietnamese. The data do not permit us to describe the intermarried couples, but we may speculate that a substantial proportion of the existing intermarriages occurred in Vietnam, primarily between Vietnamese women and American men, and that the rate of exogamy among the refugees in the United States has been, so far, extremely low.

Conclusion

We emphasized that statements concerning the speed of assimilation of any group must be made with reference to the rate at which other groups have assimilated. Too little time has elapsed and too little is known to enable us now to make confident assertions about the Vietnamese experience in America, but the research findings we reviewed do afford some basis for tentative generalizations in this regard.

In comparison to most earlier immigrant groups, the Vietnamese appear to be undergoing a fairly rapid cultural assimilation. Their knowledge of the English language and of American society appears to have been unusually high at the time they arrived and to have increased noticeably during their early years here. Their familiarity with American society and culture was promoted by the decades of contact in Vietnam prior to the evacuation. Moreover, the presence of a comparatively large proportion of educated and professional people in the group may be an additional factor favoring rapid cultural assimilation. Of special importance, the children of the boat people (including the Vietnamese) are reported to be succeeding very well in American schools (Caplan, Choy, and Whitmore 1992).

The high initial educational and occupational levels of the Vietnamese adults did not, however, prevent them from undergoing rapid downward mobility as they moved into American society. The initial jobs available to them were not, on the average, commensurate with their educational and occupational backgrounds; consequently, their income levels have been comparatively low. Residential segregation among the Vietnamese has been high despite efforts of the American government to disperse them throughout the population. Indeed, the Vietnamese, like so many before them, have worked hard to construct their own distinctive communities and institutions, and they may have done this in the face of above-average levels of psychological distress and family conflict.

Primary and marital assimilation appear to be occurring slowly among the Vietnamese Americans, although we cannot say whether the rates in these respects are unusually slow. In any event, there is little reason at present to suppose the Vietnamese Americans will undergo these forms of assimilation in a particularly rapid way.

If we must be cautious in generalizing about the degrees of assimilation among Vietnamese Americans thus far, we must be doubly so in forecasting their probable future. On the basis of the available evidence, however—and despite the unquestionably unique hardships this group has faced—the events we outlined suggest the Vietnamese are following a sequence of adaptation to the American setting that will produce results resembling those found among Chinese and Japanese Americans. Caplan, Whitmore, and Choy (1989: vi, 136) stated that the refugees in their study "were moving out of economic dependency, finding jobs, and climbing out of poverty at a steady pace" and exhibit many of the same value commitments that have been found among successful Asian American groups. Montero (1979:58–63) and Strand and Jones (1985:138) proposed that although the Vietnamese (unlike the Chinese and Japanese) have gone through receiving camps, involuntary dispersion, and sponsored resettlement, they will, nevertheless, construct ethnic enclaves that will serve as a foundation for later socioeconomic achievement. Montero (1979:62) suggested, moreover, that assimilation among the Vietnamese will occur more quickly than among the other Asian groups (Montero 1979:62).[25] Strand and Jones (1985:138) cautioned, however, that the same group cohesion that may foster the individual's self-development and capacity to move into the broader society may also serve to restrict that movement, and Martin, Hammond, and Hardy (1988) found evidence in one Vietnamese business community of both enclave formation and individual entrepreneurial resistance to such a development.

Clearly, the unfolding experience of the Vietnamese in America has much to teach us about the human meaning of immigration and adaptation to new circumstances, as well as the resilience of American society and its capacity to continue to serve as a place of asylum for at least some of the world's dispossessed people.[26]

Resurgent Nativism?

In chapter 5 we learned that scientific racism gave a strong intellectual underpinning to the movement to restrict immigration and that it served to justify discrimination against groups that were the least acceptable to nativists. The success of the restrictive legislation of the 1920s led to a long-term decline of popular concern about immigration and of the activities of nativist groups. However, the contemporary period of rising immigration has produced, as we have seen, a broad-ranging public discussion of its effects on the United States and many signs of a possible upswing in nativism. Numerous newspaper and magazine articles have appeared describing certain nativist organizations and their activities. Organizations such as the Ku Klux Klan, the Nationalist Movement, and the White Aryan Resistance appear to have increased their activities and memberships. A number of guerrilla warfare training camps have been established by the KKK in preparation for an expected "race war" (*Klanwatch* 1981). A nativist group called the National Socialist White People's Party has been active in an effort to stem the flow of undocumented workers from Mexico (Bustamante 1980:142), an another, the Bruder Schweigen Strike Force Two, has been implicated in a bombing attack on a Roman Catholic priest (Salholz and Miller 1988:29).[27]

Still another neo-Nazi group called the "skinheads" (because of their close-cropped hair or shaved heads) has attracted substantial media attention.[28] This group, which encourages violence against minority groups, appears to be connected in various ways to the KKK and other "Aryan" white supremacist groups, and they appear to be responsible for a sharp increase in violent attacks on minority-group members (Bullard 1991:54). In 1989, for instance, the skinheads attempted to organize an "Aryan Woodstock" in California's Napa Valley. Soon thereafter, four members of this organization attacked a black man and a couple they believed to be Jewish (*Austin American-Statesman* 1989a; 1989b). In 1992, following the murder of a homeless black man in Birmingham, Alabama, and a series of disputes and disturbances surrounding the Rodney King verdict in Los Angeles, a neo-Nazi rally took place in Birmingham to "call attention to the fact that 'Alabama has been designated as a white homeland' " (*New York Times* June 14, 1992:21).

A report by the Anti-Defamation League of B'nai Brith stated that anti-Semitic harassment and vandalism had risen, and a number of reports have surfaced concerning bigotry and interethnic violence on college campuses (U.S. Commission on Civil Rights June 1989; May/June 1992:3). For instance, in April 1992, Olivet College, a liberal arts college in Michigan with a tradition of racial harmony, erupted in open conflict between white and black students (Martinez 1992). Numerous incidents have been reported of hostility directed toward Asian groups, which has increased the fears of many Asian Americans (Mura 1992; Mydans 1992). A study published by the U.S. Commission on Civil Rights showed that "Asian Americans are the victims of widespread bigotry, discrimination, barriers to equal opportunity, and even violence. . . ." (U.S. Commission on Civil Rights March/April 1992:1). In national public opinion polls, Americans have expressed fear and resentment concerning the job competition created by Asian refugees and the preferential treatment they are believed to have received (Kitano 1981:136). Both of these concerns have played a role in violent episodes in Texas between Vietnamese immigrants and native fishermen (supported by the KKK) in regard to coastal fishing rights. They also may have contributed to violence and unrest in Miami during the 1980s, the port of entry for many refugees and undocumented aliens from Cuba and Haiti, and to the violence directed toward Koreans and Cambodians in the Los Angeles riots in May 1992.[29] Rising xenophobia also may be inferred from the fact that by the end of 1988, seventeen states had amended their constitutions to make English their official language, and twenty-three other states were considering a similar step (Elias 1988:D8).

These and other related events have focused attention on many of the issues that were prominent at the time of the earlier great immigrant streams. There is a widespread fear that many of the Hispanic and Asian immigrants of the third stream are too different and will prove to be unassimilable. National debates over the questions of illegal immigration and bilingualism have prompted "declarations that the nation will create another 'Quebec' in California, New York, or Miami" (Reimers 1985:xi), and one widely circulated magazine (*Esquire*) has published an article (cited by Reimers 1985:252) entitled "The Latinization of America: What Does It Mean When You Walk the Streets of Your Own Country and You Don't Understand a Word of the Language?"[30] In 1992, the Republican Party approved a plank in their national platform urging that a fence be built along the Mexican border to keep out undocumented aliens (Rosenbaum 1992:A12).

Amidst these indications of a resurgent nativism, however, are signs of resistance to the rise of racism and xenophobia. The attempted "Aryan Woodstock" rally, for instance, was attended by about one hundred skinheads, but it also was attended by about five hundred jeering protesters and two hundred police officers. The skinhead attack on the Jewish couple and black man led to the arrest and jailing of four members of the group—an action that was applauded by onlookers. At about the same time, the U.S. Justice Department opened a criminal investigation of the Confederate Hammer Skins, a skinhead group in the Dallas, Texas area; an all-white jury in Alabama convicted a member of the KKK for the murder of a black teenager (*Austin American-Statesman* 1989a; 1989b); and five members of the Bruder Schweigen group were convicted of illegal violence and other infractions of the law (Salholz and Miller 1988:29). The presence of neo-Nazi groups in Birmingham also was greeted by an outpouring of protest (*New York Times* June 14, 1992:21), and city officials in Athens, Georgia refused to allow a Klan march immediately following the King verdict in Los Angeles (Smothers 1992). Bullard (1992:52) states that "Between 1979 and 1989 . . . the U.S. Justice Department prosecuted at least 114 white supremacists for acts of racially motivated violence." In addition, some nationally circulated magazines have published articles that focus on the positive contributions of minorities to the culture and economy of the United States (e.g., *Time* July 11, 1988, March 13, 1989; *U.S. News & World Report* 1989).

These events illustrate the continuing conflict between the ideologies of Anglo conformity and cultural pluralism in American life. The ethnic revival and the third immigration have added to the heterogeneity of American society and have strengthened the forces of pluralism, but it is apparent, too, that for many native Americans, Anglo conformity is still considered to be the only true route to Americanization. What is the probable outcome of this continuing struggle? Chapter 14 suggests some answers.

Key Ideas

1. The decline in the importance of ethnic identities in twentieth-century America may have been more apparent than real. Ethnic concerns frequently may have been presented as religious concerns.

2. During the 1970s, the right of Americans to have and maintain an ethnic heritage other than the Anglo-American heritage was increasingly defended.

3. Considerable conflict has been generated around the issue of the preservation of ethnic neighborhoods. Government and business policies that have tended to identify such neighborhoods as slums have been vigorously attacked. White ethnics also frequently have fought desegregation of schools and neighborhoods on the ground that such efforts place an unfair burden on them.

4. The third immigrant stream (or new immigration) has consisted mainly of people from Mexico, other Western Hemisphere nations, and Asia. Many of these newcomers have been refugees seeking asylum in the United States.

5. The Vietnamese have been an especially visible refugee group. The collapse of South Vietnam in 1975 led to a large evacuation of Vietnamese people and their resettlement in the United States.

6. The sudden emigration of the Vietnamese and the U.S. government's resettlement program for those who came to America combined to create a unique immigration experience for this group of people.

7. The cultural assimilation of the Vietnamese appears to be taking place rapidly. Although their secondary assimilation may be occurring slowly, there are reasons to believe it gradually will accelerate and reach a high level. Primary and marital assimilation appear to be very low.

8. There were many indications during the 1980s that xenophobia and racism in the United States were rising, but there also were indications of a substantial resistance to this resurgence.

Notes

1. In Gans's (1985:429) opinion, "there has been no revival. . . ."

2. Justice Thurgood Marshall made the point as follows: "The dream of America as the great melting pot has not been realized for the Negro; because of his skin color he never even made it into the pot" (*Board of Regents of University of California v. Bakke,* 438 U.S. at 299, 1978).

3. Brink and Harris (1966:135) found that in the middle 1960s low-income whites were more alienated than low-income blacks.

4. The practice of redlining, long under attack by federal agencies and community groups, appears to be on the decline. According to Wayne (1992:1), "banks . . . across the country have started making mortgage loans in neighborhoods they have traditionally avoided."

5. For a general treatment of this question, see the special issue of *International Migration Review* 20 (Summer 1986).

6. During this time, the French created the noncommunist State of Vietnam (under the former Emperor of Annam). The United States officially recognized the government of South Vietnam in 1950.

7. The population of Saigon, for example, rose between 1961 and 1975 from 300,000 to over 3 million (Kelly 1977:15).

8. Canada and Australia together accepted approximately eleven thousand more, and an additional seven thousand were accepted by fourteen other countries (calculated in Table 1.1 in Montero 1979:3).

9. The sponsors' costs were increased further by the fact that the voluntary agencies were entitled to keep between $50 and $500 of the resettlement grants to cover administrative costs (Kelly 1977:133).

10. Some writers present much higher estimates of the numbers murdered. St Cartmail (1983:90) stated that more than two million died, while Strand and Jones (1985:21) said that "millions" were killed.

11. Refugees tend to come in two flows: the "notables" and the "mass" fleeing from "economic exactions and hardships imposed by the same regimes" (Portes and Rumbaut 1990:25).

12. Government agencies often try to determine whether an immigrant actually is fleeing political persecution or is mainly seeking improved economic circumstances. Those who are judged to be "economic" migrants may be returned to their home countries. On this basis, Great Britain agreed in 1989 to send many of the boat people in Hong Kong back to Vietnam.

13. Kunz (1973) argued that the people in "anticipatory" refugee emigrations (as opposed to "acute") are able to plan their departure and are more likely to adjust satisfactorily to new circumstances. As Montero (1979:58) noted, however, "both the acute and anticipatory refugee patterns" may be found among the Vietnamese.

14. The five locations were Boston, Chicago, Houston, Orange County (California), and Seattle.

15. For example, the first wave led to 1,570 completed interviews. The second wave consisted of 1,424 completed interviews, including 446 interviews with people who had participated in the first wave. Since the household heads reported information on all of the members of their households, the total number of people represented in the various waves was substantially larger than the number of interviews completed (Montero 1979:35).

16. Calculated from Table 4.6 in Montero 1979:48.

17. A partial explanation of the apparent rise may be found in the fact that many Vietnamese who were originally resettled in other states have subsequently migrated to California (Jiobu 1988a:15). It is possible that the migrants to California have possessed an above-average ability to speak English and that their added presence has helped to create an exaggerated impression of the rapidity with which the Vietnamese are learning to speak English.

18. They also were asked how serious a problem English language communication was within their group. Approximately 66 percent of the Vietnamese respondents said the problem was "very serious" (Strand and Jones 1985:102), but these findings refer to various people's *perceptions* of their group's language abilities rather than to their *own* abilities.

19. Although our discussion may suggest that the Vietnamese are fairly homogeneous, this group, like all of the others we have discussed, is quite heterogenous (Bach and Carroll-Seguin 1986:402). Important differences existed between the ethnic Vietnamese and the ethnic Chinese of Vietnam. In a sample survey study of these two components of the Vietnamese population, Desbartes (1986:414, 416) found that the ethnic Vietnamese were substantially higher in the percentage who understood English, had attended a university, were Catholic, and were in higher-prestige occupations. The ethnic Chinese were higher in the percentage who were in business.

20. Although these findings include the results for the entire Indochinese sample, they appear to reflect the Vietnamese experience at least as well as they do the experience of the Chinese-Vietnamese and Laotians in the sample.

21. The median level of education for both the Vietnamese and whites was one year below that of the Chinese and Japanese and two years below that of the Filipinos and Koreans.

22. Twenty percent of those employed worked less than forty hours per week.

23. See again chapter 8 for a discussion of indexes of dissimilarity.

24. They also found that " 'Arrival English' had the greatest consequence for economic progress" (Caplan, Whitmore, and Choy 1989:77).

25. Although Montero forecast "complete" assimilation, his discussion focused on indicators of cultural and secondary assimilation.

26. In Reimers's (1985:250) opinion, "the United States can probably absorb the current rate of immigration, about 550,000 annually, without excessive negative economic effects."

27. According to Bullard (1991:59), "there were more than 350 known white supremacist groups in the United States" in 1991.

28. Paradoxically, some people who are called skinheads are antiracists.

29. African American unrest in Miami and Los Angeles undoubtedly also reflects other, probably more important, causes, such as police-community relations, as discussed in chapter 11. (See also U.S. Commission on Civil Rights March 1989:1–2).

30. An additional, less sensational, sign of rising xenophobia (and possibly racism) may be seen in the concern that many people express over increases in the foreign ownership of American companies and property (Norton 1989:45).

Chapter **14**

The Future of
Ethnicity in America

*The question poses itself: how to restore the balance
between* unum *and* pluribus? —ARTHUR M. SCHLESINGER, JR.

*Well, how does a nation of no one culture, no one
language, no one race, no one history, no one ethnic stock
continue to exist as one, while encouraging diversity?*
—MICHAEL NOVAK

*. . . ethnicity may be turning into symbolic ethnicity,
an ethnicity of last resort. . . .* —HERBERT J. GANS

> *The American nationality is still forming: its*
> *processes are mysterious, and the final form, if there*
> *is ever to be a final form, is as yet unknown.*
> —*NATHAN GLAZER AND DANIEL P. MOYNIHAN*

The combined forces of the ethnic revival and the third great immigrant stream gave rise to a debate over the future of racial and ethnic groups in America that is still underway. Will the white ethnics of the first and second immigrant streams follow the path of the colonial Scotch-Irish and Germans and, for all practical purposes, soon disappear into the American mainstream? Or will they persist as distinct groups? Will nonwhites follow the path of the colonial whites but at a slower rate? Or will they continue indefinitely as more or less separate groups? Will some form of pluralism be accepted by all groups, even the Anglo-Americans, thus encouraging many groups to maintain and elaborate their distinctive heritages? Or will the Anglo-Americans insist on Anglo conformity?

When Is Soon?

Any meaningful speculation about these important matters requires further consideration of a prior question. When we say that an ethnic group will "persist" or that it will "soon disappear," what periods of time are involved? We saw earlier that the main point of reference in most discussions of group adjustment in America is the three-generations process. We saw, too, that by this standard very few, if any, American groups have achieved Anglo conformity assimilation in the expected period of time. Even the colonial Scotch-Irish and Germans did not undergo primary and marital assimilation within three generations. The Germans, in particular, maintained their language and other cultural elements well beyond that time (see chapter 3). Indeed, it still may be possible in the last decade of the twentieth century to find distinctive patterns of behavior among some of the descendants of these colonial immigrants. For example, a number of people in the United States still report that they are of Scotch-Irish ancestry. This group, therefore, may be said to have at least a nominal sense of ethnic identity other than American and may, in this respect, be said to "persist" (Lieberson and Waters 1988:13–14).[1] Additionally, if the conditions were right, it is still possible that these traces of group identity could serve as the foundation for some sort of ethnic group revival or mobilization.

It is true, nonetheless, that the present levels of merger between the colonial immigrant groups and the Anglo-American core are so high as to be virtually complete, and it is very likely that these levels of merger were reached before the end of the nineteenth century. Since the colonial Scotch-Irish and Germans began entering in force during the early part of the eighteenth century, we may say that the full Anglo conformity assimilation of a northwestern European group in America may occur in less than 200 years, possibly in less than 150 years. Although this estimate extends the three-generations idea to as many as six or eight generations, it gives evidence that the Anglo conformity merger of some groups does occur, as Park said, "eventually." Moreover, if one adopts the cultural pluralists' definition of full assimilation, it is likely that the colonial immigrants approximated that goal in three or, at most, four generations.

Turning from the colonial immigrants to those who formed the first immigrant stream, we find little to alter the conclusions just reached. Many of the descendants of these immigrants have been in the United States for as long as six generations, and few for less than three. The level of cultural and secondary assimilation between them and the Anglo-American core is unquestionably high, though not necessarily as high as that of the colonial immigrants. The first-stream immigrant Irish and Germans in New York, for instance, still may be more distinguishable than their colonial counterparts (Glazer and Moynihan 1964), but there is no reason to suppose that the first-stream immigrants are less assimilated at this point than the colonials were after a similar period of time. On the contrary, there is every reason to suppose that with the further passage of time these nineteenth-century immigrants will move toward higher levels of Anglo conformity. Again, this judgment must be tempered with the realization that a number of events could revive and strengthen the ethnic bonds that still exist or that new ethnic groups might arise from the remnants of the old.

The status of the white ethnics of the second immigrant stream, however, as discussed briefly in chapter 13, continues as a topic of contemporary debate. Why after three or, in some cases, four generations are these groups still, or again, so much in evidence? What is going to happen to them? Are the white ethnics "on the threshold of disappearance" (Dinnerstein and Reimers 1975:140), or will they continue to play an important role in the future (Greeley 1971:167)?

Such questions reveal clearly why it is essential to be specific about the time periods under discussion. Curiously, the prediction that the white ethnics will "soon disappear" is not necessarily inconsistent with the prediction that they will "continue to be significant for some time to come." It all depends on what these phrases mean. For example, in historical terms, "soon" may easily mean another generation or two, and "continue to be significant" may mean a level of merger similar to that currently exhibited by the nineteenth-century Irish and Germans.

White Ethnic Assimilation

Let's explore these issues briefly by comparing, in certain respects, the immigrants of the first and second streams with each other and with the members of the host American group. Our discussion draws heavily on (and greatly simplifies) the illuminating research of Alba (1985; 1988), which focuses on Italian Americans as "a strategic test case," and of Lieberson and Waters (1988), which compares a number of different white ethnic groups. Following our usual order, we consider some evidence relating to cultural, secondary, and marital assimilation.[2]

As discussed in chapter 4, the Italian immigrants of the second stream did not seem to be good prospects for Anglo conformity assimilation. They were, comparatively speaking, poor, ignorant, unskilled birds of passage. Their continued allegiance to the family and the Italian community and their suspicion of American education combined to maintain a high level of ethnic distinctiveness well beyond the decline in immigration after 1924. As Alba (1988:141) stated: "By the end of the 1930s . . . the group's . . . cultural and occupational background would seem to have doomed Italian Americans to a perpetual position of inferiority and separateness in American society."

The changes that have taken place since then, however, have not confirmed that expectation. In regard to cultural differences, for instance, Alba (1985:135; 1988:146–147) marshaled evidence from the General Social Surveys of the National Opinion Research Center for the years 1975–1980 to compare certain values of the Italian Americans with those of a group of Protestants of British ancestry. When such factors as the respondent's sex and age, the education and occupation of his or her parents, and the region of the country in which the person now lives or was raised were taken into account, Italian Americans were found to be very similar to WASPs. To illustrate, they did not differ significantly in their opinions on abortion, feminism, premarital sex, adultery, homosexuality, and divorce. Two items that suggested the Italians still had a greater allegiance to family values were that they were more likely than WASPs to reside where they had grown up and they more frequently agreed that children's elders should teach them what is right.

Lieberson and Waters (1988:95) presented findings concerning changes that have taken place in the fertility levels of the women of the first and second immigrant streams (the "old"/"new" distinction of chapter 4) that may suggest changes that have taken place in people's values concerning family size. In 1910, the fertility rates of women from four south-central-eastern (SCE) European countries of the second stream were all higher than those of five northwestern (NW) European first-stream countries, and the women of both streams were characterized by higher rates than the women of the host group. By 1940, the average fertility levels of the women of both immigrant groups had declined sharply, but the two groups were still distinguishable. The NW European women still had lower fertility rates than did the SCE European women. By 1980, however, the fertility differences among all women of European ancestry between the ages of forty-five and fifty-four were much lower than previously, and the distinction between the first and second streams had "essentially vanished" (Lieberson and Waters 1988:100). To the extent that changes in fertility patterns reflect changes in cultural values and beliefs, we may interpret the great reductions in fertility rates, and the resulting similarity among the ethnic groups, as an important indication that cultural assimilation among these groups now is high. In Alba's (1988:153) opinion, "among virtually all white ethnic groups, one can observe a progressive, if gradual, dampening of cultural distinctiveness."

How do the NW and SCE European groups compare on such measures of secondary assimilation as occupation, education, and income? We again draw on, and simplify, the analyses of Lieberson and Waters (1988) and Alba (1988). Our previous discussions showed that such factors as the skills immigrants have brought with them, their time of arrival in the United States, and the geographical location of their points of entry have resulted in higher and lower concentrations of different groups in particular occupations. For example, in 1900, in comparison to the remainder of the white male work force, male Irish immigrants were more than four times as likely to be police officers or firefighters, German men were nearly nine times as likely to be be bakers, Russian men (a majority of whom were Jews) were over thirty times as likely to be tailors, and Italian men were over nine times as likely to be barbers and hairdressers (Lieberson and Waters 1988:124–126).

An important question of interest to us here is this: Have the earlier patterns of occupational concentration and avoidance continued into the latter part of the twentieth century? For each of thirteen ethnic groups examined by Lieberson and Waters, there has been a "leveling" of their characteristic occupational patterns, but there still are some "significant remnants" of the patterns found for 1900. To illustrate, the probability that Russian men would be tailors, as compared to all other white men, declined from over thirty in 1900 to less than three in 1980. Nevertheless, they were still more likely to be tailors than to be in any of the other specific occupations being compared. On the other hand, they were no longer the leading ethnic group in this regard. Italian men, by 1980, were more than three times as likely to be tailors as were all other men and were slightly more likely to be tailors than to be barbers and hairdressers. Nevertheless, in a general comparison of the occupational distributions of Italians and WASPs conducted by Alba (1985:122–123), no significant overall difference was found when the groups were matched for age, place of residence, and family background. Lieberson and Waters (1988:127) summarized their findings as follows: "In general . . . there is a reduction of the distinctive ethnic occupational dispositions found in 1900 for immigrant men. This is to be expected under normal assimilative processes. However, these early immigrant occupational patterns still have significant vestiges 80 years later. . . ."

In a further analysis of the 1980 occupational patterns for men—this time using indexes of dissimilarity—Lieberson and Waters (1988:129–135) found that, except for Jewish men, the occupational distributions of white men are fairly similar. The main reason the Jewish pattern is different is that this group is more heavily concentrated in professional occupations than are white men in general. Of special importance, though, is that the general occupational patterns of those in the first and second immigrant streams were, by 1980, no longer significantly different, even when Jewish men were included. The general occupational patterns of first- and second-stream women also were no longer significantly different.

The immigrants of the first two streams also differed in their average levels of education, with those from NW Europe showing much higher levels of literacy. Has this distinctiveness been maintained? Lieberson and Waters (1988:112–115) compared the changes among twelve groups, and the results for these groups are clear. The educational differences among the groups have declined sharply. This conclusion is consistent with Alba's (1988:145) detailed comparison of the extent to which Italian Americans and Anglo Americans have attended or completed college. For example, among both second- and third-generation Italian men and women born after 1950, the levels of college attendance and graduation are very similar to those of Anglo Americans of the same age. This similarity represents a large change from the differences found when earlier age groups—for instance, those born between 1915 and 1935—are compared.

Direct census information on the income differences of the various ethnic groups for the early decades of the century is not available; however, on the basis of estimates of group differences in income, Lieberson and Waters (1988:140–142) believe there is little reason to think that the earlier pattern of inequalities exists today. Indeed, they found that, by 1980, the NW European groups did not have an income advantage over the SCE European groups. Therefore, in regard to three crucial indicators of secondary assimilation—occupation, education, and income—the level among European ancestry groups appears to be high.[3]

Turning now to intermarriage, the "cardinal indicator" of shifts in ethnic boundaries (Alba 1988:148), the findings support four important conclusions. First, the trends among Italians and all white groups taken together show declines in within-group marriages (Alba 1988:149–152; Lieberson and Waters 1988:197). For example, among third-generation Italian men of unmixed ancestry who were born before 1920, about 43 percent were married to women who also were of unmixed Italian ancestry. Among the Italian men of unmixed ancestry who were born after 1949, however, 20 percent—less than half as many as before—were married to women who were of unmixed ancestry. The figures pertaining to Italian women showed a similar pattern. Second, because of the increase in intermarriages among white ethnics, the number of people of European ancestry in the United States who are products of ethnic intermarriages has grown steadily larger (relatively as well as absolutely). Among Italian Americans, for instance, the proportion of those with mixed ancestry has risen from around 6 percent among those over sixty-five years of age to over 81 percent among those under five years of age. Third, people of unmixed ethnic ancestry are still somewhat more likely to choose mates from their own ethnic group than are those of mixed ethnic ancestry. Fourth, though the boundaries among white ethnic groups are steadily being eroded by intermarriage, even those of mixed ancestry are still more likely to marry someone of their own ancestry than to marry someone of any other given ancestry.[4] In short, although the marital assimilation of Europeans and their descendants is well underway, it is still incomplete.

On the basis of these considerations, the following speculations seem reasonable. The white ethnics of the new immigration have not disappeared in three generations, but neither did the colonial or old immigrants.[5] As Neidert and Farley (1985:849) concluded, "if assimilation means that third-generation ethnic groups will be indistinguishable from the core English group. . . ," then these groups still have not assimilated; however, they go on to say, "if assimilation means that ethnic groups are neither favored nor at a disadvantage in the process of occupational achievement, then there is strong evidence to support the theory."

While three generations may be long enough to permit a high degree of cultural and secondary assimilation among white European groups, the remaining forms of assimilation may take much longer. Even when the host and immigrant groups are similar in race and culture, full Anglo conformity assimilation may require as many as eight generations. On the assumption that members of the second immigrant stream are moving toward an Anglo conformity merger with the dominant group, they should become decreasingly distinctive as time goes on. Within three more generations, they may be no more distinctive than the nineteenth-century Irish and Germans are now. Perhaps, given another two generations beyond that, they may be no more distinctive than the colonial Irish and Germans are now.

In short, the sheer fact that the second-stream groups have not disappeared within three generations is not really too surprising. The expectation that they would disappear has rested on a misunderstanding of the group adjustments that have occurred in the past. Since the speed of Anglo conformity assimilation among the colonial and first-stream immigrants has been much slower than is generally recognized, the belief that the merger of the second-stream immigrants with the host group is unusually slow has not yet been put fully to the test. Indeed, on the basis of the evidence we have reviewed, one can argue that the speed with which the SCE Europeans have assimilated culturally and in the secondary arena constitutes, in Greeley's (1985) phrase, an "ethnic miracle." Paradoxically, pluralist *principles* appear to have been gaining force just when *ethnic differences* themselves have been, as Steinberg (1981:254) argued, "on the wane." In his view, the United States has "never before . . . been closer to welding a national identity out of the melange of ethnic groups that populated its soil."[6] Perhaps, to use Alba's (1985; 1988) engaging expression, the white ethnics are entering the "twilight" of their ethnicity.

The twilight metaphor is compelling but requires some comment. As would be true of objects in a planetary twilight, this view "acknowledges that ethnicity has not entirely disappeared . . . but, at the same time, it captures the reality that ethnicity is nonetheless steadily receding" (Alba 1985:159). The evidence that we presented favoring this view may be bolstered still further by the important analyses of "unhyphenated whites" presented by Lieberson (1988). Although the U.S. Bureau of the Census discouraged people from giving the response "American" to the ancestry question in the 1980 Census, 13.3 million people (nearly 6 percent of the population) could not, or would not, specify any other ancestry (Lieberson 1988:171).

As applied to ethnicity, however, the twilight metaphor has one flaw. Except in certain seasons in certain latitudes, earthly twilights give way to nightfall, but in Alba's lexicon (1985:162) the twilight of ethnicity "will not in the near future, and may never, turn into night." Even if ethnicity among Europeans and their descendants is moving toward, or has reached, a point beyond which it will no longer serve reliably as an authentic basis for group cohesion and economic support, valued ethnic identities nevertheless may serve as social insulation—what Handlin called "contexts of belonging"—to prevent the anonymity and bewilderment that frequently develops in urban-industrial settings.[7] What may survive is a new form of ethnicity that Gans (1985) referred to as "symbolic ethnicity." Symbolic ethnicity arises "as the functions of ethnic cultures and groups diminish and identity becomes the primary way of being ethnic" (Gans 1985:434). Gans predicted that this form of ethnicity, especially when it also reflects religious differences, may easily persist into the fifth and sixth generations and beyond. Waters (1990:166) also argued that symbolic ethnicity "will continue to characterize the ethnicity of later-generation whites." In her view, symbolic ethnicity has a strong appeal to white Americans because it helps to reduce the tension between the individual's desire to be, simultaneously, both special and a part of a community (Waters 1990:147–150). Identification with an ethnic group carries for whites many rewards and few penalties; for nonwhites, however, "the consequences of being Asian or Hispanic or black are not symbolic. . . . They are real and hurtful" (Waters 1990:156).[8]

Whether the continuation of white ethnic distinctiveness and identity will be "a living, breathing reality of everyday life" (Alba 1985:1) or an expression of "a nostalgic allegiance to the culture of the immigrant generation" (Gans 1985:435) remains to be seen. Either way, however, one would expect a continued prominence of white ethnicity in American life for at least one or two more generations and a continued or growing acceptance of cultural pluralism as the principal view of the way immigrants and their descendants should become Americanized.

While this conclusion seems reasonable in regard to white ethnics, how well does it fit the situation of nonwhite Americans? Please recall that some observers have interpreted the conflict between the Anglo-Americans and nonwhite American minorities in terms of the colonial model. Under this interpretation, the initial relations between the dominant group and the colonized minorities establish a pattern that does not lead toward Anglo conformity. This pattern leads, rather, to an attempt by the minority to decolonize, perhaps through the establishment of separate nations, by overthrowing the invaders, or by leaving the territory altogether. The dominant group, for its part, prefers either that the nonwhites leave the territory or assimilate culturally while remaining apart and subordinate in all other ways. Since in this view both the dominant group and nonwhite minorities resist the full merger of the groups, one would expect the continuation of friction among them, resulting after a time in separation or secession.

The main criticisms of the colonial model rest on an effort to show that some nonwhite groups (e.g., Japanese Americans) have achieved a high level of cultural and secondary assimilation and that the recent historical experiences of Mexican, African, and Native Americans resemble in essential ways those of the second-stream immigrants from Europe. This argument—the immigrant model—does not claim that the immigration experience of the Japanese and the migration experiences of the other groups are identical to that of European immigrants. The nonwhite groups have faced, as Kristol (1972:205) conceded, "unique and peculiar dilemmas of their own." Lieberson (1980:383), in an extensive analysis of the differences between African Americans and new immigrants, concluded that "the situation for new Europeans in the United States, bad as it may have been, was not as bad as that experienced by blacks at the same time." Glazer (1971:451) maintained, however, that "the differences are smaller and the similarities greater" than the colonial model suggests. From this standpoint, most African Americans in the northern cities have not yet been there three generations, and while they have met less favorable conditions and greater discrimination there than previous immigrants, their future experiences may nevertheless resemble those of the white ethnics.

The immigrant model does not deny the validity of the colonial model as an interpretation of some of the experiences of nonwhites in America (e.g., slavery, the conquest of Native and Mexican Americans, the relocation centers). It does assert, however, that in different ways the nonwhites are moving toward some form of assimilation, perhaps cultural pluralism, and are moving away from separation and secession. From the standpoint of national unity, the immigrant model is evidently more optimistic than the colonial model. Which of these views, then, gives us the best basis for forecasting the probable course of race relations in the United States? As we have seen, the answer to this question is still a matter of keen debate. But it is possible, as frequently happens, that the wrong question has been asked. Since the histories of African, Mexican, Japanese, and Native Americans contain certain elements that may justify either the colonial or the immigrant view, we may conclude (as people frequently do in such arguments) that both views are to some extent correct. Perhaps only time will tell which view most nearly describes the future. This is really not a very satisfactory conclusion, however; so let us consider an alternative idea, proposed by Francis (1976), that may help to clarify the issue.

Primary and Secondary Ethnic Groups

We have stressed throughout that the conditions surrounding the initial contact between groups are extremely important in understanding the subsequent course of their relations. We have observed in general that (1) a conquered minority is likely to be hostile for a long period of time and to have separatist and secessionist tendencies, and (2) an immigrant minority is likely to exhibit hostility for a shorter period of time and to prefer some form of assimilation. There is a substantial amount of evidence, drawn from racial and ethnic contacts throughout the world, to support these generalizations. It is their strength, indeed, that sustains the debate over the colonial and immigrant models. For this reason, the alternative view we will consider does not question the accuracy of these generalizations. It attempts, instead, to explain why the conquest sequence and the immigration sequence usually, rather than always, result in tendencies toward secession and assimilation, respectively. In so doing, we may see the facts of conquest and assimilation in a new light.

As mentioned in chapter 2, Francis suggested that, in the modern world, contacts between racial and ethnic groups lead to the formation of two main kinds of groups, which he called, simply, *primary* and *secondary*.[9] The members of primary ethnic groups enter a society as entire units; the members of secondary ethnic groups enter individually or in small bands.

Since primary ethnic groups are complete social units at the outset, their relationship to the host society is mainly political. The group's members "remain firmly embedded . . . in a web of familiar relationships" (Francis 1976:169). The primary ethnic group seems to be a "fragment" of its "parent" society. It is a "viable corporate unit" (Francis 1976:397) that is able to "continue functioning in the host society in much the same way as . . . in the parent society" (Francis 1976:170). The members do not wish equal treatment with the majority and do wish to be a separate group. Therefore, they resist vigorously any efforts that the host society might make to bring about any aspect of assimilation.

The conditions leading to the formation of a secondary ethnic group are quite different. Its members are, at the outset, completely dependent on the host society for the satisfaction of all their needs, economic as well as social. There are no established ethnic institutions; therefore, there is no web of familiar relationships. The ethnic group itself remains to be formed within the host society in response to the conditions there. The group's respective members possess little in the way of resources and cannot continue to function as they did in the parent society. The social pattern that the group develops represents a mixture of the cultures of the parent society and the host society. It is identical to neither but is in some sense a variety of each (Francis 1976:223). The members of a secondary ethnic group desire equal treatment with the majority and are more willing to undergo assimilation than are those of a primary ethnic group (Francis 1976:397).

This comparison of primary and secondary ethnic groups gives us an important clue concerning why colonized minorities are more likely to develop along nationalistic lines and to be more resistant to assimilation than are immigrant minorities. When minorities arise through conquest, they are more likely to form primary than secondary ethnic groups. When minorities arise through immigration, on the other hand, they are more likely to form secondary than primary ethnic groups. Since the primary ethnic group is a complete social unit from the beginning, an important objective is to protect what it has. Its relationship to the host society, therefore, is likely to be one of resistance to assimilation. The secondary ethnic group, in contrast, is formed in part as a response to discrimination by members of the host group. An important goal of the secondary ethnic group, therefore, is to protect its members from discrimination in such areas as work, education, and political participation.

Let us now apply this reasoning to the debate over the colonial and immigrant models. Although colonized minorities are *likely* to form primary ethnic groups, and immigrant minorities are *likely* to form secondary ethnic groups, these outcomes are not inevitable. Primary ethnic groups may arise through migration, and secondary ethnic groups may arise through conquest. Knowing whether a group has entered the society by conquest or immigration enables us to guess what type of ethnic group *probably* has been formed. Useful as this information is, it may lead us to miss a central point: whether a given ethnic group has been conquered or has come from elsewhere, the fundamental issue is whether the group actually did become primary or secondary after coming into contact with the host society. It is the *result* of contact rather than the *process leading to it* that has the greatest effect on subsequent relations of the dominant and subordinate groups.

The primary-secondary distinction clarifies another point that is hidden in the debate over the colonial and immigrant models. Whether the original contact between two groups leads to the formation of a primary or a secondary ethnic group, this situation is not fixed for all time. A group that initially forms a primary ethnic group may, at a later time, be transformed into a secondary ethnic group or vice versa. This view of the outcome of contact between a dominant and a subordinate group, therefore, is more dynamic than either the colonial or immigrant models.

Conclusions

What does this alternative view tell us about the present and future relations of whites and nonwhites in America? Consider, for example, Mexican Americans. As we emphasized, this group clearly was created through conquest. The fact of conquest itself, however, is not so crucial to our understanding of the present and future condition of this dominated group as is the fact that, following the Treaty of Guadalupe Hidalgo, the Mexican Americans became a primary ethnic group. They did not seek to enter the mainstream of the larger society and did not depend on its economy or other institutions for the satisfaction of life's needs. They maintained this position well into the twentieth century. Nevertheless, as the forces of industrialization and urbanization became strong in the Southwest, not only Mexican Americans but Mexican nationals as well began to move into the American economy. The vast social changes accompanying the immigration of large numbers of Mexicans to the United States did not mean that Mexican Americans had somehow stopped being a colonized minority or that the history of conquest between them and the dominant group could be erased or disregarded. These changes meant, rather, that this group was beginning the prodigious transformation from a primary to a secondary ethnic group. Despite the efforts of many, probably most, Mexican Americans to resist this transformation, the process has predominated throughout the twentieth century.

Since the end of World War II, the majority of Mexican Americans have moved into urban settings and have become dependent on the industrial economy for their livelihoods. At the same time, they increasingly have accepted their status as American citizens and have expected and demanded that they be accorded the rights and privileges of other Americans. In short, *they have become predominantly a secondary ethnic group.* It is this fact, rather than the movement of large numbers of Mexicans to the United States since 1910, that justifies the expectation that Mexican Americans now are moving toward the American mainstream. Most Mexican Americans appear to desire "the best of both worlds." While this formula for group adjustment is somewhat vague, the specific demands presented in behalf of the group (even by militants) generally imply an acceptance of cultural pluralism.[10] It seems likely that this perspective will continue to gain support in the years to come.

This judgment concerning the goals of Mexican Americans must be accepted only tentatively. While they now are mainly members of a secondary ethnic group, and thus desire to be treated like other citizens, they may not remain so. Their proximity to Mexico and the continuation of discrimination against them in the United States are forces that favor their possible retransformation into a primary ethnic group. Unless these citizens are permitted to advance (as compared to the dominant group) in income, education, political participation, health care, police protection, and housing, they may at some point reject pluralist goals and seek separatist or secessionist solutions instead. While such an occurrence is improbable, it certainly is not impossible. As noted in chapter 11, Mexican Americans are having more difficulty than blacks and Native Americans in gaining occupational prestige that is commensurate with their educational levels (Neidert and Farley 1985:848), and there is little reason to suppose they will continue to bear the burden of this inequity in perpetual silence. Even less likely, however, is the opposite possibility—that the Mexican American group will soon embrace Anglo conformity. There is every reason to believe that Mexican Americans will remain, and will wish to remain, a distinctive ethnic group in American life for several generations to come.

Like Mexican Americans, Native Americans clearly entered American society through conquest, and they afford many illustrations of the formation of primary ethnic groups. The various Native American societies obviously were viable social units before they were conquered. Afterward, the Native Americans did not desire to be treated as citizens; they preferred instead to be permitted to reconstruct their own independent societies. Most tribes have steadfastly resisted assimilation into the dominant society for more than three centuries. Since they became citizens in 1924, however, Native Americans have shown increasing signs of being transformed from a large number of primary ethnic groups into one loosely federated, secondary ethnic group. Like most other Americans, they have been unable to resist completely the pressures of urbanization, industrialization, and bureaucratization. To a much greater extent than generally is recognized, as stated in chapter 12, Native Americans have moved into urban centers in search of employment. They have not, though, readily broken their ties to the reservations or to other members of their tribes in the cities. In general, their movement toward the status of a secondary ethnic group has not been as great as among the Mexican Americans, though, as noted previously, there are wide differences among the various tribes in this regard. The tribes generally are quite cool toward the prospect of full Anglo conformity; they continue to be ambivalent about secondary assimilation, and they continue to resist all efforts to terminate their treaty rights. Nonetheless, they seem to continue to move toward the goal of being admitted into American society on an equal footing with other citizens while maintaining the right to live as Native Americans.

Although African Americans were not conquered in their homeland, as were Mexican and Native Americans, there can be no question that under slavery this group was cruelly treated and endured unbelievable suffering. These facts surely do suggest strong parallels between the experiences of African, Mexican, and Native Americans. We may, therefore, with considerable justification, view African Americans as a colonized minority; however, and this is crucial, *African Americans did not form a primary ethnic group.* How could they? They were not a fragment of a parent society. They represented many different nationalities and did not share a common culture. They were not independent of the host society; they were totally dependent upon it. Indeed, even the formation of a secondary ethnic group was greatly hindered by the slave system, with its vigilance and deliberate interference with the efforts of slaves to communicate with one another and to organize. Only slowly and with great care were African slaves able to construct institutions of their own within the host society. This process, if not its rate of change, resembled the experience of many other immigrant groups.

Our sketch of African American history in chapters 10 and 11 does not furnish the evidence needed to determine just how popular the various ideologies of group adjustment—ranging from Anglo conformity to secession—have been. We know only that their popularity has varied through time. Even without systematic evidence—and with all due respect to Garveyism—it seems safe to say that, during most of the twentieth century, African Americans have been mainly divided between cultural pluralism and Anglo conformity (Jaynes and Williams 1989:195). The NAACP, the Urban League, CORE, the March on Washington Movement, SCLC, and many other organizations have centered their efforts on improving jobs, education, income, housing, health care, and so on (i.e., on increasing secondary assimilation). Since these goals are common to both Anglo conformity and cultural pluralism, it is not clear which of these ideologies has been most favored.

The 1960s brought about noticeable changes in the perspectives of African Americans. They increasingly doubted that Anglo conformity was a desirable goal and that cultural pluralism was feasible; separatist ideas again gained a more sympathetic hearing. Separatist sentiments seemed to decline during the 1970s and 1980s, but some signs of a revival began to appear in the early 1990s. The continued inability of many African Americans to gain better jobs, housing, police protection, and representation in the councils of government is sure to strengthen the hand of separatists and to create pressures favoring the formation of a primary ethnic group (Lieberson and Waters 1988:155; Neidert and Farley 1985:848). In any event, however, African Americans will continue to be a distinctive ethnic group in American society for many additional generations.

Given this information, the following tentative conclusions are offered. The main quarrel between the Anglo-Americans and white ethnics concerns cultural pluralism. The strength of Anglo conformity is greater among the former, while the strength of pluralism is greater among the latter. There is virtually no support in either group for separatism or secessionism.

The picture is different when whites are compared to nonwhites, but not drastically so. There is definitely some support in both sets of groups for separatism, with the strongest support being among the whites. For instance, many whites want blacks to be kept out of their neighborhoods and feel they have the right to keep them out (Schuman, Steeh, and Bobo 1985:97; Taylor, Sheatsley, and Greeley 1978:269). In both sets of groups, however, the predominant ideology in regard to the other set is cultural pluralism.

The increasing support for cultural pluralism among both whites and nonwhites suggests that a foundation is being constructed for a broad agreement on ethnic group goals. Although the popularity of separatism may not be ignored, pluralism has emerged as the chief alternative to Anglo conformity in American thought concerning racial and ethnic relations. This point is frequently obscured by criticisms of assimilationist theory. For example, many critics conclude their attacks on assimilationist theory by advocating cultural pluralism. Despite its rejection of full Anglo conformity, cultural pluralism (we have tried to show) is best understood as a form of assimilation that is competing for acceptance in American society as a legitimate alternative goal.

To insist that Anglo conformity and cultural pluralism are both legitimate forms of assimilation, however, may obscure another important point. We must emphasize again that the differences between these two are by no means trivial. Quite different social policies and tactics of change are sometimes suggested by these two assimilationist ideologies. One of the clearest illustrations of this point is the example of bilingual-bicultural education. Most people who favor Anglo conformity are opposed to programs of bilingual-bicultural education. Although the opposition is strongest to public school programs of this type, it extends also to private programs. We have seen, for example, that Anglo-Americans objected to the language schools of the Japanese. They also objected to the Talmud-Torah schools of the Jews, and there has always been some suspicion that Catholic parochial instruction—even when conducted in English—is designed to maintain foreign ways in our midst.

The pursuit of Anglo conformity, nevertheless, is not logically inconsistent with some versions of bilingual-bicultural education. For instance, some liberal Anglo conformists are willing to support bilingual-bicultural programs in the public schools for a comparatively short period of time. The aim of such programs is to act as a "bridge" between the culture of the home and the culture of the larger society. The expectation in this case is that minority children will be most successfully "weaned" from the parent culture if their primary instruction is conducted in the language of the home. As is usual under Anglo conformity doctrine, however, children taught in this way are expected, after a few years, to complete the crossover to the English language and Anglo-American ways and to leave their ethnic cultures permanently behind.

It is here that Anglo conformity and pluralist policies differ. Cultural pluralists may agree that bilingual-bicultural education should give children a full command of English and the customs and values of the dominant society. They will not agree, though, that the object of such an education should be to wean the children away from the parent culture. On the contrary, from the perspective of cultural pluralism, bilingual-bicultural education should ensure not only that minority children will master the dominant culture but also that they will be assisted to preserve and elaborate their heritages in a full and appreciative way.

These differences in the educational policies favored by Anglo conformists and cultural pluralists should dispel any notion that the debate between them is purely academic. The public schools in America, as traditionally operated, clearly are instruments of Anglo conformity. Furthermore, it does not follow that just *any* program of bilingual-bicultural education is pluralistic. The implementation of an educational program in the public schools that would genuinely meet the criteria of pluralism would require significant changes in the curriculum, teaching materials, teacher training, and allocation of funds. Beyond this, of course, would be numerous smaller problems such as those encountered in the assignment of students and teachers to schools and classrooms. At what point should non-English speakers be placed in desegregated classrooms? If desegregation begins in kindergarten or first grade, should dominant group children also be required to become bilingual? When should minority children be shifted to classes taught exclusively in English? These and many other problems are certain to appear in any practical effort to pursue the goal of cultural pluralism.

But these changes, while large, controversial, and difficult to effect, are quite modest compared to the demands of the advocates of separatism. Under this doctrine, minority group children would not be required to master the language and customs of the dominant group. Indeed, in areas in which ethnic groups are a majority, the schools would be under their separate control, and any child of the dominant group who might attend such a school would be expected to conform to the standards of the given minority. Quite clearly, the aim of such a program would be "a transformation of American institutions rather than an inclusion into them" (Skolnick 1975:573). Quite clearly, also, it would be extremely difficult to muster the support necessary to introduce such changes into education in modern America. Both Anglo conformists and cultural pluralists consider such far-reaching proposals extreme and unworkable. As Schlesinger warned "History is littered with the wreck of states that tried to combine diverse ethnic or linguistic or religious groups within a single sovereignty" (1992:129–130).

Another example of the different social policies preferred by Anglo conformists and cultural pluralists may be found in the controversy surrounding the preservation of ethnic neighborhoods. As noted earlier in this chapter, Anglo conformists tend to view the continuation of white ethnic neighborhoods with suspicion. People who live there and struggle to maintain a distinctive ethnic culture are considered to be something less than full-fledged or "real" Americans. These "hyphenated" Americans, Anglo conformists believe, should be strongly encouraged by government policies covering such things as VA and FHA loans, urban renewal, and highway construction to move out of their neighborhoods and disperse throughout the cities.

We have seen that many minority group members take a very different view of the matter. To them, the ethnic neighborhood does not represent a restraint on assimilation. It represents, rather, the way in which a group of people have chosen to express their Americanism. The neighborhood is a source of social morale and is the main link through which the individual is "plugged into" the society. The individual receives social and psychological support from family and friends in the neighborhood. The destruction of the neighborhood, therefore, does not signify the end of an alien culture and the complete adoption of American culture. It may signify, instead, the destruction of a specific way of being an American.[11] It is not surprising, therefore, that many white ethnics object to the assumption by government officials that the old neighborhoods are slums or that they oppose policies that further the neighborhoods' deterioration.

This brief comparison of the social policy preferences of Anglo conformists and cultural pluralists should suffice to show that they do indeed differ—and in ways that most Americans consider to be of great importance; however, their disagreements, though large and significant, take place primarily in a mutually accepted economic and political framework. This does not mean that cultural pluralists are uncritical of the American economic and political system, nor does it mean that the conflicts arising between Anglo conformists and pluralists in this connection are minor. It does mean that cultural pluralists believe the operating principles of American life afford, in Glazer's (1972:174) words, "enormous scope for group diversity." Although the dominant group has long wished to convert the ideas of Anglo conformity into the law of the land—to *require* that everyone become "Americanized" along the lines they prefer—the official policy of the country in the long run always has rejected this approach as "un-American."

It is true, as our historical review illustrates, that official discrimination has occurred against many of the ethnic groups in the United States, especially against the nonwhite groups. But the courts and legislatures have declared (even if slowly) that all of these acts are opposed to America's basic principles. Slavery was, at last, ended; the relocation of the Japanese was declared illegal; African, Japanese, and Native Americans have become citizens; and discrimination on the basis of race, color, and national origins has been declared unconstitutional (Glazer 1972:175). The basic faith of the cultural pluralists is that the consensus on the principles of American economic and political life does not require abject submission to the will of the dominant group. Even though the amount and severity of dominant group discrimination in U.S. history must give even an optimist pause, the main ethnic group conflicts of the past have been settled on the side of the rights of minorities. Stated differently, the "tyranny of the majority," which Tocqueville ([1835]/1988:250) warned might be the fatal flaw of democracy, has, so far, been forestalled, and cultural pluralists believe American institutions are sufficiently flexible to permit this pattern of group adjustments to continue.

The right to maintain a pluralist pattern, however, does not ensure a group's actual success in doing so. Regardless of the desire of a group's members to have "the best of both," may it not be true, as discussed in chapter 1, that the forces behind the historical shift away from tradition and toward modernity gradually will erode the distinctiveness of the ethnic groups in American society? Will these groups, as Park's cycle theory insists, finally be "melted" into the dominant society?

Our analysis supports two basic conclusions. First, America's shift from an agrarian to an urban-industrial society has made it extremely difficult for primary ethnic groups to survive or be generated. During the twentieth century, Mexican Americans have become much more nearly a secondary than a primary ethnic group and Native Americans are being pressed in the direction of secondary group formation. Our second conclusion, however, is that the adjustment of the colonial, old, and new immigrants from Europe demonstrates that industrialization does not inevitably undermine racial and ethnic groupings (See and Wilson 1988:236). While many groups have undergone a high degree of cultural and secondary assimilation within three generations, the third and subsequent generations frequently have experienced a renewed interest in revitalizing their ethnic heritages and ties. In time, nevertheless, even the secondary ethnic groups may well succumb to the homogenizing pressures of America's industrial civilization. No one knows how long this outcome may take. Unless there are catastrophic changes in the world order, it seems almost certain that the white ethnics will disappear before the nonwhites; but taking history as our guide, some of the former could sustain themselves for several additional generations, especially symbolically, and the disappearance of the latter could take centuries.

Taken together, these two conclusions suggest a third. While primary ethnic groups may be "obsolete" in modern societies, a "leftover" from times gone by, secondary ethnic groups are compatible with an urban-industrial society. Indeed, as most critics of Anglo conformity fondly note, America's great industrial might could not have been developed without the enormous contributions of racial and ethnic minorities. Although the continued existence of these minorities may pose a problem for national unity, they also may help to sustain a sense of individual and social purpose for many Americans.

Although the problems of national unity that may be posed by the existence of racial and ethnic cleavages are of great importance, more pressing is the continuing failure to afford an equal opportunity for secondary assimilation to every American who wishes it. As Wrong (1977:488) stated, we must "increase the opportunities for individuals to escape from their ethnic communities, if they so wish, and improve the levels and quality of living in the ethnic communities themselves." Increasing the individual's opportunities to leave the ethnic community or remain in it, however, requires additional reductions in the existing levels of racial and ethnic discrimination. Needed, also, are further, genuine reductions in racial and ethnic prejudices. We must learn, as Voltaire urged, to "pardon reciprocally each other's folly." Each of these measures reflects the best traditions and highest aspirations of the American people.

Key Ideas

1. The occurrence of full Anglo conformity assimilation has been much slower than is generally recognized. Very few American groups have achieved full merger with the dominant group within three generations; however, virtually complete merger has occurred for practically all white ethnic groups within eight generations. Hence, groups from the countries of the new immigration are unlikely to disappear in less than four generations, and they may continue for eight. This means that some new immigrant groups currently in the United States will persist in some respects for at least one more generation and perhaps for as many as five. It is not known whether the period of ethnic distinctiveness can be extended beyond this point.

2. Since no nonwhite group has experienced full Anglo conformity assimilation, no one knows whether this process can occur; however, some nonwhite immigrant groups (e.g., Japanese Americans) have experienced a high level of cultural pluralism, demonstrating that under some circumstances this assimilationist goal may be approximated by nonwhites within three generations.

3. Francis (1976) presented a theory that relates conquest and immigration to ethnic group formation. According to Francis, primary ethnic groups are viable corporate units whose members seek to maintain their group rather than to be accepted as equal members of the dominant society. Secondary ethnic groups form within the host society and serve, among other things, as instruments to assist the group's members to attain equal treatment. Primary ethnic groups are more likely to be formed through conquest, while secondary ethnic groups are more likely to arise through immigration.

4. Francis's analysis of primary and secondary ethnic groups may explain why heavily oppressed groups such as Mexican, African, and Native Americans may nonetheless adopt cultural pluralism or Anglo conformity as goals. For example, although Mexican Americans originally were conquered and formed a primary ethnic group, their subsequent experiences have, for the most part, transformed them into a secondary ethnic group. However, even though cultural pluralism is now widely accepted among Mexican Americans, the continuation of discrimination against them could lead to their retransformation into a primary ethnic group.

5. Like the Mexican Americans, Native Americans were conquered and have formed primary ethnic groups and, with substantial variations among the tribes, some groups have shown definite movement toward the acceptance of cultural pluralism. An increased resistance to this movement by the dominant group, however, could easily halt it and strengthen Native Americans' demands for autonomy.

6. The main line of division between Anglo-Americans and white ethnics concerns cultural pluralism. Anglo conformity is stronger among the former, and cultural pluralism is stronger among the latter.

7. Although separatist sentiment is stronger across the white-nonwhite line, the main division here also is between those who favor cultural pluralism or some alternative.

8. In many cases, Anglo conformity and cultural pluralism, though both ideologies of assimilation, lead to noticeably different social policies and tactics of change. These differences nevertheless occur within a framework of broad agreement.

9. America's shift from an agrarian to an urban-industrial society has made it extremely difficult for primary ethnic groups to survive or be generated. Secondary ethnic groups nevertheless may persist within American society for many generations.

10. While ethnic groups, even secondary ethnic groups, may pose a problem for national unity, they also help to give meaning and purpose to people's lives.

11. The failure to grant equal opportunity to achieve secondary assimilation is a more pressing problem for America than the existence of ethnic divisions. Higher levels of secondary assimilation among minorities require further reductions in the levels of prejudice and discrimination.

Notes

1. Whether people who report a particular ancestry actually are of that ancestry is, of course, a different issue (see, e.g., Lieberson and Waters 1988:22–25).

2. We are even less able here than usual to present evidence concerning primary assimilation. No analysis of changes in primary relations among ethnic groups since the beginning of the twentieth century is available. We may presume, however, that the observed levels of secondary and marital assimilation in any given case may serve as a reasonable basis for conjecture concerning the probable levels of primary assimilation.

3. In an earlier study based on information from the National Opinion Research Center, Greely (1985:272) found that although the family income of Italian and Polish Catholics was not as high as that of Irish and German Catholics, all four Catholic groups were above the British Protestants and the national average for American whites.

4. Some of these conclusions rest in part on inferences based on differences in age cohorts in 1980. The information needed for direct comparisons with earlier periods is unavailable.

5. Many *individuals* have lost their ethnic identities. The speculations here refer entirely to groups.

6. An apparent paradox, discussed by Alba and Golden (1986:218), is that although the rates of intermarriage have gone up, the tendencies toward intermarriage appear to have remained stable. The authors observed that the rates have risen because the tendencies to marry-out are

higher in the mixed-ancestry groups and because these groups have increased in size.

7. Quoted by Herberg (1960:43).

8. Waters (1990:155–164) argued further that people who experience ethnicity as a trait that they may choose either to ignore or to accentuate may greatly underestimate the extent to which an ethnic identity creates obstacles in American society for those who are racially distinctive. As a result, being "an ethnic" may reduce, rather than increase, a white person's understanding of the problems facing nonwhites.

9. Although we find here another example of the primary-secondary distinction used to divide structural assimilation into subprocesses, the terms here apply to groups rather than subprocesses.

10. For example, one presentation of the aims of the Chicano movement stresses the need for various forms of education and the recognition of Chicano culture by the dominant group. The list of priorities adopted by the first convention of La Raza Unida Party includes improvements in the areas of jobs, education, housing, health, and the administration of justice (Forbes 1973:292–294). La Raza Unida's goals also include, however, such separatist policies as community control of law enforcement, the schools, and the economy.

11. The disappearance of ethnic neighborhoods does not necessarily mean the ethnic community will disappear. In this connection, see Parenti (1967:717–726).

References

Ablon, Joan. "Relocated American Indians in the San Francisco Bay Area: Social Interaction and Indian Identity," in Howard M. Bahr, Bruce A. Chadwick, and Robert C. Day, eds. *Native Americans Today* (New York: Harper & Row, 1972), 412–428.

Abrams, Franklin. "Immigration Law and Its Enforcement: Reflections of American Immigration Policy," in Roy Simon Bryce-Laporte, ed. *Sourcebook on the New Immigration* (New Brunswick, N.J.: Transaction Books, 1980), 27–35.

———. "American Immigration Policy: How Strait the Gate?" in Richard R. Hofstetter, ed. *U.S. Immigration Policy* (Durham, N.C.: Duke University Press, 1984).

Acuña, Rodolfo. *Occupied America* (San Francisco: Canfield Press, 1972).

———. *Occupied America,* 2nd ed. (New York: Harper & Row, 1981).

Adam, Barry D. "Inferiorization and 'Self-Esteem,'" *Social Psychology* 41 (March 1978):47–57.

Adamic, Louis. *A Nation of Nations* (New York: Harper and Brothers, 1944).

Adams, Romanzo. "The Unorthodox Race Doctrine of Hawaii," in E. B. Reuter, ed. *Race and Culture Contacts* (New York: McGraw-Hill, 1934), 143–160.

Adorno, T. W.; Frenkel-Brunswik, Else; Levinson, Daniel J.; and Sanford, R. Nevitt. *The Authoritarian Personality* (New York: Harper and Brothers, 1950).

Agresti, Barbara Finlay. "The First Decades of Freedom: Black Families in a Southern County, 1870–1885," *Journal of Marriage and the Family* 40 (November 1978):697–706.

Alba, Richard D., ed. *Italian Americans* (Englewood Cliffs, N.J.: Prentice-Hall, 1985).

———, ed. *Ethnicity and Race in the U.S.A.* (New York: Routledge, 1988a).

———. "The Twilight of Ethnicity Among Americans of European Ancestry: The Case of Italians," in Richard D. Alba, ed. *Ethnicity and Race in the U.S.A.* (New York: Routledge, 1988b), 134–158.

Alba, Richard D., and Golden, Reid M. "Patterns of Ethnic Marriage in the United States," *Social Forces* 65 (September 1986):202–223.

Alba, Richard D., and Kessler, Ronald C. "Patterns of Interethnic Marriage Among American Catholics," *Social Forces* 57 (June 1979):1124–1140.

Allport, Gordon. *The Nature of Prejudice* (Garden City, N.Y.: Doubleday, 1958).

Allsup, Carl. *The American G.I. Forum: Origins and Evolution.* Center for Mexican American Studies Monograph no. 6 (Austin: University of Texas Press, 1982).

Alvarez, Rodolfo. "The Psycho-Historical and Socioeconomic Development of the Chicano Community in the United States," in Rodolfo O. de la Garza, Frank D. Bean, Charles M. Bonjean, Ricardo Romo, and Rodolfo Alvarez, eds. *The Mexican American Experience* (Austin: University of Texas Press, 1985), 33–56.

Alvírez, David, and Bean, Frank D. "The Mexican American Family," in C. H. Mindel and R. W. Habenstein, eds. *Ethnic Families in America: Patterns and Variations* (New York: Elsevier North-Holland, 1976), 271–292.

Americans Before Columbus. "Stakes Are High as Tribes Take a Gamble," (winter 1992):3.

Amir, Yehuda. "Contact Hypothesis in Ethnic Relations," *Psychological Bulletin* 71 (May 1969):319–342.

———. "The Role of Intergroup Contact in Change of Prejudice and Ethnic Relations," in P. A. Katz, ed. *Toward the Elimination of Racism* (New York: Pergamon Press, 1976), 245–308.

Anderson, Charles H. *White Protestant Americans* (Englewood Cliffs, N.J.: Prentice-Hall, 1970).

Angel, Ronald. "The Health of the Mexican Origin Population," in Rodolfo O. de la Garza, Frank D. Bean, Charles M. Bonjean, Ricardo Romo, and Rodolfo Alvarez, eds. *The Mexican Ameri-*

can Experience (Austin: University of Texas Press, 1985), 411–426.

Anzovin, Steven, ed. *The Problem of Immigration* (New York: H. W. Wilson, 1985), 129–131.

Armor, David J. "White Flight and the Future of School Desegregation," in Walter G. Stephan and Joe R. Feagin, eds. *School Desegregation* (New York: Plenum Press, 1980), 187–226.

Asher, Steven R., and Allen, Vernon L. "Racial Preference and Social Comparison Processes," *Journal of Social Issues* 25, no. 1 (1969):157–166.

Austin American-Statesman. "500 Protest Lightly Attended 'Aryan Woodstock' Rally," March 5, 1989a.

———. "Skinheads Are Target of Investigation," May 14, 1989b, p. B5.

———. "Skinheads Jailed in California Attack," May 30, 1989c, p. A4.

———. "White Alabama Jury Convicts Klansman in Black's Murder," May 19, 1989d, p. A7.

Bach, Robert L., and Carroll-Seguin, Rita. "Labor Force Participation, Household Composition and Sponsorship among Southeast Asian Refugees," *International Migration Review* 20 (Summer 1986):381–404.

Bache, R. Meade. "Reaction Time with Reference to Race," *Psychological Review* 21 (September 1895):475–486.

Bachman, Jerald, and O'Malley, Patrick M. "Black-White Differences in Self-Esteem: Are They Affected by Response Styles?" *American Journal of Sociology* 90 (November 1984): 624–639.

Bahr, Howard M.; Chadwick, Bruce A.; and Day, Robert C.; eds. *Native Americans Today* (New York: Harper & Row, 1972).

Bailey, Thomas, and Waldinger, Roger. "Primary, Secondary, and Enclave Labor Markets: A Training Systems Approach," *American Sociological Review* 56 (August 1991):432–445.

Baker, Ross K., ed. *The Afro-American* (New York: Van Nostrand Reinhold Company, 1970).

Ball, Harry V.; Simpson, George Eaton; and Ikeda, Kiyoshi. "Law and Social Change: Sumner Reconsidered," *American Journal of Sociology* 57 (March 1962):532–540.

Baltzell, E. Digby. *The Protestant Establishment* (New York: Vintage Books, 1964).

Bardolph, Richard. *The Negro Vanguard* (New York: Vintage Books, 1961).

Barker, Eugene C. "Native Latin American Contributions to the Colonization and Independence of Texas," *Southwestern Historical Quarterly* 46 (April 1943):317–335.

Barnard, William A., and Benn, Mark S. "Belief Congruence and Prejudice Reduction in an Interracial Contact Setting," *The Journal of Social Psychology* 97 (February 1988):125–134.

Baron, Harold M. "The Web of Urban Racism," in Louis L. Knowles and Kenneth Prewitt, eds. *Institutional Racism in America* (Englewood Cliffs, N.J.: Prentice-Hall, 1969), 134–176.

Baron, Robert A. *Human Aggression* (New York: Plenum Press, 1977).

Barrera, Mario. *Race and Class in the Southwest* (South Bend, Ind.: University of Notre Dame Press, 1979).

Barringer, Felicity. "White-Black Disparity in Income Narrowed in 80's, Census Shows," *The New York Times* (July 24, 1992):A1, A10.

Bean, Frank D.; Chapa, Jorge; Berg, Ruth; and Sowards, Kathryn. "Educational and Sociodemographic Incorporation Among Hispanic Immigrants to the United States," in Barry Edmonston and Jeffrey S. Passell, eds. *Immigration and Ethnicity: The Integration of America's Newest Immigrants* (Washington, D.C.: The Urban Institute, forthcoming).

Bean, Frank D.; Espenshade, Thomas J.; White, Michael J.; and Dymowski, Robert F. "Post-IRCA Changes in the Volume and Composition of Undocumented Migration to the United States: An Assessment Based on Apprehensions Data," in Frank D. Bean, Barry Edmonston, and Jeffrey S. Passel, eds. *Undocumented Migration to the United States* (Santa Monica and Washington: Rand Corporation and The Urban Institute, 1990), 111–158.

Bean, Frank D., and Frisbie, W. Parker, eds. *The Demography of Racial and Ethnic Groups* (New York: Academic Press, 1978).

Bean, Frank D.; Schmandt, Jurgen; and Weintraub, Sidney; eds. *Mexican and Central American Population and U.S. Immigration Policy* (Austin, Tex.: Center for Mexican American Studies, 1989).

Bean, Frank D., and Tienda, Marta. *The Hispanic Population of the United States* (New York: Russell Sage Foundation, 1987).

Bean, Frank D.; Vernez, George; and Keely, Charles B. *Opening and Closing the Doors* (Santa Monica and Washington: Rand Corporation and The Urban Institute, 1989).

Beck, E. M. "Discrimination and White Economic Loss: A Time Series Examination of the Radical Model," *Social Forces* 59 (September 1980):148–168.

Beck, E. M., and Tolnay, Stewart. "The Killing Fields of the Deep South: The Market for Cotton and the Lynching of Blacks, 1882–1930," *American Sociological Review* 55 (August 1990):526–539.

Becker, Gary S. *The Economics of Discrimination* (Chicago: University of Chicago Press, 1971).

Benedict, Ruth. *Race: Science and Politics* (New York: Viking Press, 1961).

Bennett, Lerone, Jr. *Before the Mayflower,* rev. ed. (New York: Penguin Books, 1966).

Benokraitis, Nijole V., and Feagin, Joe R. *Affirmative Action and Equal Opportunity: Action, Inaction, Reaction* (Boulder, Colo.: Westview Press, 1978).

Berelson, Bernard, and Salter, Patricia J. "Majority and Minority Americans: An Analysis of Magazine Fiction," *Public Opinion Quarterly* 10 (Summer 1946):168–190.

Berelson, Bernard, and Steiner, Gary A. *Human Behavior: An Inventory of Scientific Findings* (New York: Harcourt, Brace & World, 1964).

Berger, Morroe. *Equality by Statute,* rev. ed. (Garden City, N.Y.: Doubleday, 1968).

Berkowitz, Leonard, ed. *Roots of Aggression: A Re-examination of the Frustration-Aggression Hypothesis* (New York: Atherton Press, 1969).

Bernard, William S. "Immigration: History of U.S. Policy," in Stephan Thernstrom, Ann Orlov, and Oscar Handlin, eds. *Harvard Encyclopedia of American Ethnic Groups* (Cambridge, Mass.: The Belknap Press, 1980), 486–495.

Berns, Walter. "Affirmative Action vs. the Declaration of Independence," *New Perspectives* 1 (Summer 1984):21, 27–28.

Berry, Brewton. *Race and Ethnic Relations,* 3rd ed. (Boston: Houghton Mifflin, 1965).

Bierstedt, Robert. *The Social Order,* 3rd ed. (New York: McGraw-Hill, 1970).

Billingsley, Andrew. *Black Families in White America* (Englewood Cliffs, N.J.: Prentice-Hall, 1968).

Binder, Frederick M., and David M. Reimers, eds. *The Way We Lived,* vol. 1 (Lexington, Mass.: D. C. Heath, 1988).

Black, Virginia. "The Erosion of Legal Principles in the Creation of Legal Policies," in Barry R. Gross, ed. *Reverse Discrimination* (Buffalo, N.Y.: Prometheus Books, 1977), 163–183.

Blau, Zena Smith. *Black Children/White Children* (New York: The Free Press, 1981).

Blauner, Robert. *Racial Oppression in America* (New York: Harper & Row, 1972).

Block, N. J., and Dworkin, Gerald, eds. *The IQ Controversy* (New York: Pantheon Books, 1976).

Blumer, Herbert. "Industrialisation and Race Relations," in Guy Hunter, ed. *Industrialization and Race Relations: A Symposium* (London: Oxford University Press, 1965).

Bodnar, John. *The Transplanted* (Bloomington: Indiana University Press, 1985).

Bogardus, Emory S. "A Social Distance Scale," *Sociology and Social Research* 17 (January-February 1933):265–271.

———. *Social Distance* (Yellow Springs, Ohio: Antioch Press, 1959).

Bohara, Alok K., and Davíla, Alberto. "A Reassessment of the Phenotypic Discrimination and Income Differences among Mexican Americans," *Social Science Quarterly* 73 (March 1992):114–119.

Bolino, August C. *The Ellis Island Source Book* (Washington, D.C.:The Catholic University of America, 1985).

Bonacich, Edna. "A Theory of Ethnic Antagonism: The Split Labor Market," *American Sociological Review* 37 (October 1972):547–559.

———. "A Theory of Middleman Minorities," *American Sociological Review* 38 (October 1973):583–594.

———. "Abolition, the Extension of Slavery, and the Position of Free Blacks: A Study of Split Labor Markets in the United States, 1830–1863," *American Journal of Sociology* 81 (November 1975):601–628.

———. "Advanced Capitalism and Black/White Race Relations in the United States: A Split Labor Market Interpretation," *American Sociological Review* 41 (February 1976):34–51.

Bonacich, Edna, and Modell, John. *The Economic Basis of Ethnic Solidarity* (Berkeley: University of California Press, 1980).

Bongartz, Roy. "The New Indian," in Howard M. Bahr, Bruce A. Chadwick, and Robert C. Day, eds. *Native Americans Today* (New York: Harper & Row, 1972).

Bonjean, Charles M.; Hill, Richard J.; and McLemore, S. Dale. *Sociological Measurement* (San Francisco: Chandler, 1967).

Bonney, Rachel A. "The Role of AIM Leaders in Indian Nationalism," *American Indian Quarterly* (Autumn 1977):209–224.

Borjas, George J., and Tienda, Marta, eds. *Hispanics in the U.S. Economy* (Orlando: Academic Press, 1985).

Boston, Thomas D. *Race, Class, and Conservatism* (Boston: Unwin Hyman, 1988).

Boswell, Terry E. "A Split Labor Market Analysis of Discrimination Against Chinese Immigrants, 1850–1882," *American Sociological Review* 51 (June 1986):352–371.

Bowman, Phillip J. "Joblessness," in James S. Jackson, ed. *Life in Black America* (Newbury Park, Calif.: Sage Publications, 1991), 156–178.

Boyd, Robert L. "A Contextual Analysis of Black Self-Employment in Large Metropolitan Areas, 1970–1980)," *Social Forces* 70 (December 1991):409–429.

Boyer, William H., and Walsh, Paul. "Innate Intelligence: An Insidious Myth?" in Edgar A. Schuler, Thomas Ford Hoult, Duane L. Gibson, and Wilbur B. Brookover, eds. *Readings in Sociology,* 5th ed. (New York: Thomas Y. Crowell, 1974), 55–62.

Bradshaw, Benjamin S., and Bean, Frank D. "Intermarriage Between Persons of Spanish and Non-Spanish Surname: Changes from the Mid-Nineteenth Century to the Mid-Twentieth Century," *Social Science Quarterly* 51 (September 1970):389–395.

Brasher, Philip. "High Risk of Suicide Found in Native American Youths," *Austin American-Statesman* (March 25, 1992):A4.

Brigham, Carl C. *A Study of American Intelligence* (Princeton, N.J.: Princeton University Press, 1923).

———. "Intelligence Tests of Immigrant Groups," *Psychological Review* 37 (March 1930):158–165.

Brink, William, and Harris, Louis. *Black and White* (New York: Simon & Schuster, 1966).

Brisbane, Robert H. "Black Protest in America," in Mabel M. Smythe, ed. *The Black American Reference Book* (Englewood Cliffs, N.J.: Prentice-Hall, 1976), 537–579.

Broman, Clifford L.; Neighbors, Harold W.; and Jackson, James S. "Racial Group Identification Among Black Adults," *Social Forces* 67 (September 1988):146–158.

Broom, Leonard, and Glenn, Norval D. *Transformation of the Negro American* (New York: Harper & Row, 1965a).

———. "When Will America's Negroes Catch Up?" *New Society* 6 (March 25, 1965b):6–7.

Broom, Leonard, and Kitsuse, John L. *The Managed Casualty* (Berkeley and Los Angeles: University of California Press, 1956).

Brophy, William, and Aberle, Sophie D. *The Indian: America's Unfinished Business* (Norman: University of Oklahoma Press, 1966).

Brown, Dee. *Bury My Heart at Wounded Knee* (New York: Bantam Books, 1972).

Brown, Roger. *Social Psychology,* 2nd ed. (New York: The Free Press, 1986).

Bryan, Samuel. "Mexican Immigrants on the Labor Market," in Wayne Moquin and Charles Van Doren, eds. *A Documentary History of the Mexican Americans* (New York: Bantam Books, 1972), 333–339.

Bryce-Laporte, Roy Simon, ed. *Sourcebook on the New Immigration* (New Brunswick, N.J.: Transaction Books, 1980).

Buffalohead, W. Roger. "Self-Rule in the Past and the Future: An Overview," in Kenneth R. Philp, ed. *Indian Self-Rule* (Salt Lake City: Howe Brothers, 1986), 265–277.

Bullard, Sara, ed. *The Ku Klux Klan: A History of Violence and Racism,* 4th ed. (Montgomery, Ala.: Klanwatch, The Southern Poverty Law Center, 1991).

Bunche, Ralph J. "A Critical Analysis of the Tactics and Programs of Minority Groups," *Journal of*

Negro Education 4 (July 1935):308–320; reprinted in August Meier, Elliott Rudwick, and Francis L. Broderick, eds. *Black Protest Thought in the Twentieth Century,* 2nd ed. (Indianapolis and New York: Bobbs-Merrill, 1971a), 183–202.

———. "The Programs, Ideologies, Tactics, and Achievements of Negro Betterment and Interracial Organizations," unpublished memorandum, 1940; in August Meier, Elliott Rudwick, and Francis L. Broderick, eds. *Black Protest Thought in the Twentieth Century,* 2nd ed. (Indianapolis and New York: Bobbs-Merrill, 1971b), 122–131.

Burma, John H. "Interethnic Marriage in Los Angeles, 1948–1959," *Social Forces* 42 (December 1963):156–165.

———. "A Comparison of the Mexican American Subculture with the Oscar Lewis Culture of Poverty Model," in John H. Burma, ed. *Mexican Americans in the United States* (Cambridge, Mass.: Schenkman, 1970), 17–28.

Burner, David; Fox-Genovese, Elizabeth; and Bernhard, Virginia. *A College History of the United States,* vol. 1 (St. James, N. Y.: Brandywine Press, 1991).

Burns, W. Haywood. *The Voices of Negro Protest* (New York: Oxford University Press, 1963).

Burr, Jeffrey A.; Galle, Omer R.; and Fossett, Mark A. "Racial Occupational Inequality in Southern Metropolitan Areas, 1940–1980: Revisiting the Visibility-Discrimination Hypothesis," *Social Forces* 69 (March 1991):831–850.

Buss, Arnold H. "Instrumentality of Aggression, Feedback, and Frustration as Determinants of Physical Aggression," *Journal of Personality and Social Psychology* 3 (February 1966):153–162.

Bustamante, Jorge A. "Immigrants from Mexico: The Silent Invasion Issue," in Roy Simon Bryce-Laporte, ed. *Sourcebook on the New Immigration* (New Brunswick, N.J.: Transaction Books, 1980), 140–144.

Butler, John Sibley. "Institutional Racism: Viable Perspective or Intellectual Bogey," *Journal of the Black Sociologist* 7 (Spring-Summer 1978):5–25.

———. *Entrepreneurship and Self-Help Among Black Americans* (Albany: State University of New York Press, 1991).

Butler, John Sibley, and Wilson, Kenneth L. "The American Soldier Revisited: Race Relations in the Military," *Social Science Quarterly* 59 (December 1978):451–467.

———. "Entrepreneurial Enclaves: An Exposition into the Afro-American Experience," *National Journal of Sociology* 2 (Fall 1988):127–166.

Cafferty, Pastora San Juan; Chiswick, Barry R.; Greeley, Andrew M.; and Sullivan, Teresa A. *The Dilemma of American Immigration* (New Brunswick, N.J.: Transaction Books, 1983).

Camejo, Antonio. "Texas Chicanos Forge Own Political Power," in Livie Isauro Duran and H. Russell Bernard, eds. *Introduction to Chicano Studies* (New York: Macmillan, 1973), 552–558.

Caplan, Nathan; Choy, Marcella H.; and Whitmore, John K. *Children of the Boat People: A Study of Educational Success* (Ann Arbor: The University of Michigan Press, 1992).

Caplan, Nathan; Whitmore, John K.; and Choy, Marcella H. *The Boat People and Achievement in America* (Ann Arbor: The University of Michigan Press, 1989).

Cardenas, Gilberto. "United States Immigration Policy toward Mexico: An Historical Perspective," *Chicano Law Review* 2 (Summer 1975):66–89.

Carmichael, Stokely. "Black Power" (Chicago: Student Nonviolent Coordinating Committee, 1966); reprinted in Gilbert Osofsky, ed. *The Burden of Race* (New York: Harper & Row, 1968), 629–636.

Carmichael, Stokely, and Hamilton, Charles. *Black Power* (New York: Vintage Books, 1967).

Caudill, William, and DeVos, George. "Achievement, Culture, and Personality: The Case of the Japanese Americans," *American Anthropologist* 58 (December 1956):1102–1126.

Cazares, Ralph B.; Murguía, Edward; and Frisbie, W. Parker. "Mexican American Intermarriage in a Nonmetropolitan Context," in Rodolfo O. de la Garza, Frank D. Bean, Charles M. Bonjean, Ricardo Romo, and Rodolfo Alvarez, eds. *The Mexican American Experience*

(Austin: University of Texas Press, 1985), 393–401.

Chaudhuri, Joyotpaul. "American Indian Policy: An Overview," in Vine Deloria, Jr., ed. *American Indian Policy in the Twentieth Century* (Norman: University of Oklahoma Press, 1985), 15–33.

Chronicle of Higher Education 34 (July 6, 1988):A20.

Church, George J. "The Fire This Time," *Time* (May 11, 1992):18–25.

Clark, Kenneth B. *Prejudice and Your Child,* 2nd ed. (Boston: Beacon Press, 1963).

Clark, Kenneth B., and Clark, Mamie K. "The Development of Consciousness of Self and the Emergence of Racial Identification in Negro Preschool Children," *Journal of Social Psychology* 10 (November 1939):591–599.

———. "Racial Identification and Preference in Negro Children," in Eleanor E. Maccoby, Theodore M. Newcomb, and Eugene L. Hartley, eds. *Readings in Social Psychology* (New York: Henry Holt, 1958), 602–611.

Clark, W. A. V., and Mueller, Milan. "Hispanic Relocation and Spatial Assimilation: A Case Study," *Social Science Quarterly* 69 (June 1988):468–475.

Clines, Francis X. "With Casino Profits, Indian Tribes Thrive," *New York Times* (January 31, 1993):A1.

Cobas, Jose A. "A New Test and Extension of Propositions from the Bonacich Synthesis," *Social Forces* 64 (December 1985):432–441.

Cohen, Elizabeth G. "Design and Redesign of the Desegregated School," in Walter G. Stephan and Joe R. Feagin, eds. *School Desegregation* (New York: Plenum Press, 1980), 251–280.

Colburn, David R., and Pozzetta, George E., eds. *America and the New Ethnicity* (Port Washington, N.Y.: Kennikat Press, 1979).

Cole, Stewart G., and Cole, Mildred Wiese. *Minorities and the American Promise* (New York: Harper and Brothers, 1954).

Coleman, James S., et al. *Equality of Educational Opportunity* (Washington, D.C.: U. S. Department of Health, Education and Welfare, 1966).

Collison, Michele N-K. "A Seldom-Aired Issue: Do Black-Student Groups Hinder Campus Inte-

gration?" *Chronicle of Higher Education* 35 (October 5, 1988):A35.

Connell, Evan S. *Son of the Morning Star* (San Francisco: North Point Press, 1984).

Connor, John W. "Acculturation and Family Continuities in Three Generations of Japanese Americans," *Journal of Marriage and the Family* 36 (February 1974): 159–165.

———. "Changing Trends in Japanese American Academic Achievement," *The Journal of Ethnic Studies* 2 (1975):95–98.

Conroy, Hilary, and Miyakawa, T. Scott, eds. *East Across the Pacific* (Santa Barbara, Calif.: American Bibliographical Center-CLIO Press, 1972).

Conzen, Kathleen Neils. "Germans," in Stephan Thernstrom, Ann Orlov, and Oscar Handlin, eds. *Harvard Encyclopedia of American Ethnic Groups* (Cambridge, Mass.: The Belknap Press, 1980), 405–425.

Cook, James. "The American Indian Through Five Centuries," *Forbes* (November 1981).

Cotton, Jeremiah. "More on the 'Cost' of Being a Black or Mexican American Male Worker," *Social Science Quarterly* 66 (December 1985):867–885.

Coward, Barbara E.; Williams, J. Allen; and Feagin, Joe R. "The Culture of Poverty Debate: Some Additional Data," *Social Problems* 21 (June 1974):621–634.

Crevecoeur, J. Hector St. John, "Welcome to My Shores, Distressed European," in Moses Rischin, ed. *Immigration and the American Tradition* (Indianapolis: Bobbs-Merrill, [1782]/1976).

Cronon, Edmund David. *Black Moses* (Madison: The University of Wisconsin Press, 1968).

Crosby, Alfred W., Jr. *The Columbian Exchange* (Westport, Conn.: Greenwood Press, 1972).

Cué, Reynaldo A., and Bach, Robert L. "The Return of the Clandestine Worker and the End of the Golden Exile: Recent Mexican and Cuban Immigrants in the United States," in Roy Simon Bryce-Laporte, ed. *Sourcebook on the New Immigration* (New Brunswick, N.J.: Transaction Books, 1980), 257–269.

Cuéllar, Alfredo. "Perspective on Politics," in Joan W. Moore, ed. *Mexican Americans* (Englewood Cliffs, N.J.: Prentice-Hall, 1970), 137–156.

Curran, Thomas J. *Xenophobia and Immigration* (Boston: Twayne Publishers, 1975).

Daniels, Roger. *The Politics of Prejudice* (New York: Atheneum, 1969).

———. *The Decision to Relocate the Japanese Americans* (Philadelphia: J. B. Lippincott, 1975).

Darden, Joe T. "Black Inequality and Conservative Strategy," in Edgar A. Schuler, Thomas Ford Hoult, Duane L. Gibson, and Wilbur B. Brookover, eds. *Readings in Sociology,* 5th ed. (New York: Thomas Y. Crowell, 1974), 643–663.

Davie, Maurice R. *Negroes in American Society* (New York: McGraw-Hill, 1949).

Davis, Sally M.; Hunt, Ken; and Kitzes, Judith M. "Improving the Health of Indian Teenagers—A Demonstration Program in Rural New Mexico," *Public Health Reports* 104 (May-June 1989):271–278.

Day, Robert C. "The Emergence of Activism as a Social Movement," in Howard M. Bahr, Bruce A. Chadwick, and Robert C. Day, eds. *Native Americans Today* (New York: Harper & Row, 1972), 506–532.

DeFleur, Melvin L., and Westie, Frank B. "Verbal Attitudes and Overt Acts," *American Sociological Review* 23 (December 1958):667–673.

Degler, Carl N. "Slavery and the Genesis of American Race Prejudice," in Donald L. Noel, ed. *The Origins of American Slavery and Racism* (Columbus, Ohio: Charles E. Merrill, 1972), 61–80.

del Castillo, Richard Griswold. *The Treaty of Guadalupe Hidalgo: A Legacy of Conflict* (Norman: University of Oklahoma Press, 1990).

Delany, Martin R. "Destiny of the Colored Race: 1852," in Paul Jacobs and Saul Landau, eds. *To Serve the Devil,* vol. 1 (New York: Vintage Books, 1971), 148–157.

De Leon, Arnoldo. *They Called Them Greasers* (Austin: University of Texas Press, 1983).

Deloria, Vine, Jr. *Custer Died for Your Sins* (New York: Avon Books, 1969).

———. "This Country Was a Lot Better Off When the Indians Were Running It," in Howard M. Bahr, Bruce A. Chadwick, and Robert C. Day,

eds. *Native Americans Today* (New York: Harper & Row, 1972), 498–506.

———. "Native Americans: The Indian American Today," *The Annals: America as a Multicultural Society* 454 (March 1981):139–149.

———, ed. *American Indian Policy in the Twentieth Century* (Norman: University of Oklahoma Press, 1985a).

———. "The Evolution of Federal Indian Policy Making," in Vine Deloria, Jr., ed. *American Indian Policy in the Twentieth Century* (Norman: University of Oklahoma Press, 1985b), 239–256.

———. "Introduction," in Vine Deloria, Jr., ed. *American Indian Policy in the Twentieth Century* (Norman: University of Oklahoma Press, 1985c), 3–14.

Dennis, Henry C. *The American Indian 1492–1976* (Dobbs Ferry, N.Y.: Oceana Publications, 1977).

Dent, David J. "The New Black Suburbs," *The New York Times Magazine* (June 14, 1992):18–25.

Denton, Nancy A., and Massey, Douglas S. "Residential Segregation of Blacks, Hispanics, and Asians by Socioeconomic Status and Generation," *Social Science Quarterly* 69 (December 1988): 797–817.

Desbartes, Jacqueline. "Ethnic Differences in Adaptation: Sino-Vietnamese Refugees in the United States," *International Migration Review* 20 (Summer 1986):405–427.

Deutsch, Morton, and Collins, Mary Evans. "Interracial Housing," in William Petersen, ed. *American Social Patterns* (Garden City, N.Y.: Doubleday, 1956), 7–61.

Devine, Patricia G. "Stereotypes and Prejudice: Their Automatic and Controlled Components," *Journal of Personality and Social Psychology* 56 (January 1989):5–18.

De Witt, Karen. "Scores on SAT Edge UP," New York Times News Service, *Austin American-Statesman* (August 27, 1992):A1, A11.

Dinnerstein, Leonard, and Jaher, Frederic Cople, eds. *The Aliens* (New York: Appleton-Century-Crofts, 1970).

Dinnerstein, Leonard, and Reimers, David M., eds. *Ethnic Americans* (New York: Dodd, Mead, 1975).

Dobzhansky, Theodosius. *Mankind Evolving* (New Haven, Conn.: Yale University Press, 1962).

Dollard, John. *Caste and Class in a Southern Town,* 3rd ed. (Garden City, N.Y.: Doubleday, 1957).

Dollard, John; Doob, Leonard; Miller, Neal; Mowrer, O. H.; and Sears, R. R. *Frustration and Aggression* (New Haven, Conn.: Yale University Press, 1939).

Dovidio, J. F., and Gaertner, S. L. eds. *Prejudice, Discrimination, and Racism* (Orlando: Academic Press, 1986).

Dowdall, George W. "White Gains from Black Subordination in 1960 and 1970," *Social Problems* 22 (December 1974):162–183.

Doyle, Bertram W. *The Etiquette of Race Relations in the South* (Chicago: University of Chicago Press, 1937).

Drury, D. W. "Black Self-Esteem and Desegregated Schools," *Sociology of Education* 53 (April 1980):88–103.

Ducas, George, ed. (with Charles Van Doren). *Great Documents in Black American History* (New York: Praeger, 1970).

Dunn, L. C., and Dobzhansky, Theodosius. *Heredity, Race and Society* (New York: New American Library, 1964).

Dunne, John Gregory. *Delano* (New York: Farrar, Straus & Giroux, 1967).

Durant, Will. *The Life of Greece* (New York: Simon & Schuster, 1939).

———. *Ceasar and Christ* (New York: Simon & Schuster, 1944).

Dworkin, Anthony Gary. "A City Founded, A People Lost," in Livie Isauro Duran and H. Russell Bernard, eds. *Introduction to Chicano Studies* (New York: Macmillan, 1973), 406–420.

Easterlin, Richard A. "Immigration: Social Characteristics," in Stephan Thernstrom, Ann Orlov, and Oscar Handlin, eds. *Harvard Encyclopedia of American Ethnic Groups* (Cambridge, Mass.: The Belknap Press, 1980), 476–486.

Eckberg, Douglas Lee. *Intelligence and Race* (New York: Praeger, 1979).

Edwards, R. C.; Reich, Michael; and Gordon, David M., eds. *Labor Market Segmentation* (Lexington, Mass.: D. C. Heath, 1975).

Eggebeen, David J., and Lichter, Daniel T. "Race, Family Structure, and Changing Poverty Among American Children," *American Sociological Review* 56 (December 1991):801–817.

Ehrlich, Howard J. *The Social Psychology of Prejudice* (New York: Wiley, 1973).

Ehrlich, Howard J., and Rinehart, James W. "A Brief Report on the Methodology of Stereotype Research," *Social Forces* 44 (December 1965):171–176.

Ehrlich, Paul R., and Feldman, S. Shirley. *The Race Bomb* (New York: Ballantine Books, 1977).

Eisenbruch, Maurice. "The Mental Health of Refugee Children and Their Cultural Development," *International Migration Review* 22 (Summer 1988):282–300.

Eitzen, D. Stanley. "Two Minorities: The Jews of Poland and the Chinese of the Philippines," *The Jewish Journal of Sociology* 10 (December 1968):221–240.

———. *In Conflict and Order,* 4th ed. (Boston: Allyn and Bacon, 1988).

Elias, Thomas D. "Official English Gains Momentum as 17 States Amend Constitutions," Cox News Service, *Austin American-Statesman* (December 11, 1988):D8.

Elkins, Stanley M. *Slavery,* 2nd ed. (Chicago: University of Chicago Press, 1968).

Ellis, David. "L.A. Lawless," *Time* (May 11, 1992):26–29.

Ellison, Christopher G., and London, Bruce. "The Social and Political Participation of Black Americans: Compensatory and Ethnic Community Perspectives Revisited," *Social Forces* 70 (March 1992):681–701.

Ellison, Ralph. *Shadow and the Act* (New York: Random House, 1964).

Elson, R. M. *Guardians of Tradition* (Lincoln: University of Nebraska Press, 1964).

Embree, Edwin R. *Indians of the Americas* (New York: Collier Books, 1970).

Essed, Philomena. *Understanding Everyday Racism* (Newbury Park, Calif.: Sage Publications, Inc., 1991).

Farley, Reynolds. "Racial Integration in the Schools: Assessing the Effect of Governmental Policies," *Sociological Focus* 9 (January 1975):3–26.

———. "Trends in Racial Inequalities: Have the Gains of the 1960s Disappeared in the 1970s?"

American Sociological Review 42 (April 1977):189–208.

———. "School Integration in the United States," in Frank D. Bean and W. Parker Frisbie, eds. *The Demography of Racial and Ethnic Groups* (New York: Academic Press, 1978), 15–50.

———. "Three Steps Forward and Two Back? Recent Changes in the Social and Economic Status of Blacks," in Richard D. Alba, ed. *Ethnicity and Race in the U.S.A.* (New York: Routledge, 1988), 4–28.

Farley, Reynolds, and Allen, Walter R. *The Color Line and the Quality of Life in America* (New York: Russell Sage Foundation, 1987).

Farmer, James. *Freedom—When?* (New York: Random House, 1965), 60–62; reprinted in August Meier, Elliott Rudwick, and Francis L. Broderick, eds. *Black Protest Thought in the Twentieth Century,* 2nd ed. (Indianapolis and New York: Bobbs-Merrill, 1971), 183–202.

Faulkner, Harold Underwood. *American Political and Social History,* 5th ed. (New York: Appleton-Century-Crofts, 1948).

Feagin, Joe R. "Indirect Institutionalized Discrimination," *American Politics Quarterly* 5 (April 1977):177–200.

———. "The Continuing Significance of Race: Antiblack Discrimination in Public Places," *American Sociological Review* (February 1991):101–116.

Feagin, Joe R., and Fujitaki, Nancy. "On the Assimilation of the Japanese Americans," *Amerasia Journal* 1 (February 1972):13–30.

Feagin, Joe R., and Hahn, Harlan. *Ghetto Revolts* (New York: Macmillan, 1973).

Featherman, David L., and Hauser, Robert M. *Opportunity and Change* (New York: Academic Press, 1978).

Feldstein, Stanley, and Costello, Lawrence, eds. *The Ordeal of Assimilation* (Garden City, N.Y.: Anchor Press/Doubleday, 1974).

Festinger, Leon. *A Theory of Cognitive Dissonance* (New York: Harper & Row, 1957).

Firebaugh, Glenn, and Davis, Kenneth E. "Trends in Antiblack Prejudice, 1972–1984: Region and Cohort Effects," *American Journal of Sociology* 94 (September 1988):251–272.

Fligstein, Neil, and Fernandez, Roberto. "Educational Transitions of Whites and Mexican-Americans," in George J. Borjas and Marta Tienda, eds. *Hispanics in the U.S. Economy* (Orlando: Academic Press, 1985), 161–192.

Flynn, James R. "Massive IQ Gains in 14 Nations: What IQ Tests Really Measure," *Psychological Bulletin* 101 (March 1987):171–191.

Fogel, Robert William, and Engerman, Stanley L. *Time on the Cross: The Economics of American Negro Slavery* (Boston: Little, Brown, 1974).

Foner, Laura, and Genovese, Eugene D., eds. *Slavery in the New World* (Englewood Cliffs, N.J.: Prentice-Hall, 1969).

Footnotes "ABS Statement Assails Book by Wilson," 6 (December 1978):4.

Forbes, Jack D. *Aztecas Del Norte* (Greenwich, Conn.: Fawcett, 1973).

Ford, W. Scott. "Interracial Public Housing in a Border City: Another Look at the Contact Hypothesis," *American Journal of Sociology* 79 (May 1973):1426–1447.

Fossett, Mark A.; Galle, Omer R.; and Burr, Jeffrey A. "Racial Occupational Inequality, 1940–1980: A Research Note on the Impact of the Changing Regional Distribution of the Black Population," *Social Forces* 48 (December 1989):415–427.

Fossett, Mark A.; Galle, Omer R.; and Kelly, William R. "Racial Occupational Inequality, 1940–1980: National and Regional Trends," *American Sociological Review* 51 (June 1986):421–429.

Fox, David Joseph, and Jordan, Valerie Barnes. "Racial Preference and Identification of Black, American Chinese, and White Children," *Genetic Psychology Monographs* 88 (1973):229–286.

Francis, E. K. *Interethnic Relations* (New York: Elsevier, 1976).

Franklin, John Hope. *Reconstruction* (Chicago: University of Chicago Press, 1961).

Franklin, John Hope, and Moss, Alfred A., Jr. *From Slavery to Freedom,* 6th ed. (New York: Alfred A. Knopf, 1988).

Frazier, E. Franklin. *The Negro Family in the United States* (Chicago: University of Chicago Press, 1939).

————. *The Negro in the United States,* rev. ed. (New York: Macmillan, 1957).

Fredrickson, George M. "Toward a Social Interpretation of the Development of American Racism," in Nathan I. Huggins, Martin Kilson, and Daniel M. Fox, eds. *Key Issues in the Afro-American Experience* (New York: Harcourt Brace Jovanovich, 1971), 240–254.

————. *White Supremacy* (New York: Oxford University Press, 1981).

Frethorne, Richard. "The Experiences of an Indentured Servant, 1623," in Frederick M. Binder and David M. Reimers, eds. *The Way We Lived* (Lexington, Mass.: D. C. Heath, [1923] 1988), 35–37.

Friedman, Robert. "Institutional Racism: How to Discriminate without Really Trying," in Thomas F. Pettigrew, ed. *Racial Discrimination in the United States* (New York: Harper & Row, 1975).

Frisbie, Parker. "Illegal Migration from Mexico to the United States: A Longitudinal Analysis," *International Migration Review* 9 (Spring 1975):3–13.

Fugita, Stephen S., and O'Brien, David J., "Structural Assimilation, Ethnic Group Membership, and Political Participation Among Japanese Americans: A Research Note," *Social Forces* 63 (June 1985):986–995.

Fujimoto, Isao. "The Failure of Democracy in a Time of Crisis," in Amy Tachiki, Eddie Wong, Franklin Odo, and Buck Wong, eds. *Roots: An Asian American Reader* (Los Angeles: The Regents of the University of California, 1971), 207–214.

Furstenberg, Frank, J., Jr.; Hershberg T.; and Modell, John. "The Origins of the Female-Headed Black Family: The Impact of the Urban Experience." *Journal of Interdisciplinary History* 6 (Autumn 1985):211–233.

Galitzi, Christine A. *A Study of Assimilation Among the Rumanians in the United States* (New York: Columbia University Press, 1929).

Gans, Herbert J. "Symbolic Ethnicity: The Future of Ethnic Groups and Cultures in America," in Norman R. Yetman, ed. *Majority and Minority,* 4th ed. (Boston: Allyn and Bacon, 1985), 429–442.

————. "Deconstructing the Underclass: The Term's Danger as a Planning Concept," *Journal of the American Planning Association* 56 (Summer, 1990):271–277.

Garcia, John A. "Yo Soy Mexicano . . . : Self-Identity and Sociodemographic Correlates," *Social Science Quarterly* 62 (March 1981):88–98.

Garrett, Henry E. "Comparison of Negro and White Recruits on the Army Tests Given in 1917–1918," *American Journal of Psychology* 58 (October 1945):480–495.

Garvey, Amy Jacques. *Garvey & Garveyism* (London: Collier-Macmillan, 1970).

Garvey, Marcus. "An Appeal to the Conscience of the Black Race," in Gilbert Osofsky, ed. *The Burden of Race* (New York: Harper & Row, 1968a), 290–295.

————. "Declaration of Rights of the Negro Peoples of the World," in Gilbert Osofsky, ed. *The Burden of Race* (New York: Harper & Row, 1968b), 296–302.

Geen, Russell G., and Berkowitz, Leonard. "Some Conditions Facilitating the Occurrence of Aggression After the Observation of Violence," *Journal of Personality* 35 (December 1967):666–676; reprinted in Leonard Berkowitz, ed. *Roots of Aggression: A Reexamination of the Frustration-Aggression Hypothesis* (New York: Atherton Press, 1969), 106–118.

Genovese, Eugene D. *Roll, Jordan, Roll* (New York: Pantheon Books, 1974).

Gerard, Harold B.; Jackson, Terrence D.; and Conolley, Edward S. "Social Contact in the Desegregated Classroom," in Harold B. Gerard and Norman Miller, eds. *School Desegregation: A Long-Term Study* (New York: Plenum Press, 1975), 211–241.

Gerard, Harold B., and Miller, Norman. *School Desegregation: A Long-Term Study* (New York: Plenum Press, 1975).

Geschwender, James A. "Explorations in the Theory of Social Movements and Revolutions," *Social Forces* 47 (December 1968):127–135; reprinted in James A. Geschwender, ed. *The Black Revolt* (Englewood Cliffs, N.J.: Prentice-Hall, 1971).

Geschwender, James A.; Carroll-Seguin, Rita; and Brill, Howard. "The Portuguese and Haoles of

Hawaii: Implications for the Origin of Ethnicity," *American Sociological Review* 53 (August 1988):515–527.

Gibbs, Jack P. *Control: Sociology's Central Notion* (Urbana and Chicago: University of Illinois Press, 1989).

Gilbert, G. M. "Stereotype Persistence and Change among College Students," *Journal of Abnormal and Social Psychology* 46 (April 1951):245–254.

Glazer, Nathan. "Blacks and Ethnic Groups: The Difference, and the Political Difference It Makes," *Social Problems* 18 (Spring 1971): 444–461.

———. "America's Race Paradox," in Peter I. Rose, ed. *Nation of Nations* (New York: Random House, 1972), 165–180.

———, ed. *Clamor at the Gates* (San Francisco: Institute for Contemporary Studies, 1985).

———. *Affirmative Discrimination,* 1st and 2nd eds. (Cambridge, Mass.: Harvard University Press, 1975 and 1987).

Glazer, Nathan, and Moynihan, Daniel Patrick. *Beyond the Melting Pot,* 1st and 2nd eds. (Cambridge, Mass.: MIT Press, 1964 and 1970).

Glenn, Norval D. "Occupational Benefits to Whites from the Subordination of Negroes," *American Sociological Review* 28 (June 1963):443–448.

———. "White Gains from Negro Subordination," *Social Problems* 14 (Fall 1966):159–178.

Glick, Paul C. "Demographic Pictures of Black Families," in H. P. McAdoo, ed. *Black Families* (Newbury Park, Calif.: Sage Publications, 1988), 111–132.

Glickstein, Howard A. "Discrimination in Higher Education," in Barry R. Gross, ed. *Reverse Discrimination* (Buffalo, N.Y.: Prometheus Books, 1977), 14–18.

Goff, Regina. "Educating Black Americans," in Mabel M. Smythe, ed. *The Black American Reference Book* (Englewood Cliffs, N.J.: Prentice-Hall, 1976), 410–452.

Goldman, Peter. *Report from Black America* (New York: Simon & Schuster, 1970).

Gómez-Quiñones, Juan. "The First Steps: Chicano Labor Conflict and Organizing, 1900–20," in Manuel P. Servín, ed. *An Awakening Minority: The Mexican Americans,* 2nd ed. (Beverly Hills, Calif.: Glencoe Press, 1974), 79–113.

Goodchilds, Jacqueline D.; Green, James A.; and Bikson, Tora Kay. "The School Experience and Adjustment," in Harold B. Gerard and Norman Miller, eds., *School Desegregation: A Long-Term Study* (New York: Plenum Press, 1975), 151–166.

Gordon, Milton M. *Assimilation in American Life* (New York: Oxford University Press, 1964).

———. *Human Nature, Class, and Ethnicity* (New York: Oxford University Press, 1978).

———. "Models of Pluralism: The New American Dilemma," *The Annals* 454 (March 1981):178–188.

Gossett, Thomas F. *Race: The History of an Idea in America* (Dallas: Southern Methodist University Press, 1963).

Gould, C. W. *America, A Family Matter* (New York: Scribner's, 1922).

Graglia, Lino A. *Disaster By Decree* (Ithaca, N.Y.: Cornell University Press, 1976).

Graham, Hugh Davis, "The Origins of Affirmative Action: Civil Rights and the Regulatory State," in Harold Orlans and June O'Neill, eds. *The Annals: Affirmative Action Revisited,* (September 1992):50–62.

Graham, W. A. *The Story of the Little Big Horn* (Harrisburg, Penn.: Military Service Publishing, 1952).

———. *The Custer Myth* (Harrisburg, Penn.: The Stackpole Company, 1953).

Grebler, Leo; Moore, Joan W.; and Guzman, Ralph C. *The Mexican-American People* (New York: The Free Press, 1970).

Greeley, Andrew M. *Why Can't They Be Like Us?* (New York: E. P. Dutton, 1971).

———. "The Ethnic Miracle," in Norman R. Yetman, ed. *Majority and Minority,* 4th ed. (Boston: Allyn and Bacon, 1985), 268–277.

Green, James A. "Attitudinal and Situational Determinants of Intended Behavior Toward Blacks," *Journal of Personality and Social Psychology* 22 (April 1972):13–17.

Greenhouse, Linda. "Supreme Court Civil Rights Rulings Follow Reagan's Conservative Line," *Austin American-Statesman* (June 11, 1989): D6.

Grenier, Gilles. "Shifts to English as Usual Language by Americans of Spanish Mother Tongue," in Rodolfo O. de la Garza, Frank D. Bean, Charles M. Bonjean, Ricardo Romo, and Rodolfo Alvarez, eds. *The Mexican American Experience* (Austin: University of Texas Press, 1985), 346–358.

Grodzins, Morton. *The Loyal and the Disloyal* (Chicago: University of Chicago Press, 1956).

Gross, Andrew B., and Massey, Douglas S. "Spatial Assimilation Models: A Micro-Macro Comparison," *Social Science Quarterly* 72 (June 1991):347–360.

Gross, Barry R., ed. *Reverse Discrimination* (Buffalo, N.Y.: Prometheus Books, 1977).

Gruson, Lindsey. "Sensing Betrayal Again, Senecas Are Angry Again," *The New York Times* (July 18, 1992):12.

Gundlach, James H., and Busch, Ruth C. "Reservation Residence and the Survival of Native American Languages," *Current Anthropology* 22 (February 1981):96–97.

Gurak, Douglas T., and Kritz, Mary M. "Intermarriage Patterns in the U.S.: Maximizing Information from the U.S. Census Public Use Samples," *Public Data Use* 6 (March 1978):33–43.

Gutierrez, Armando, and Hirsch, Herbert. "The Militant Challenge to the American Ethos: 'Chicanos' and 'Mexican Americans,'" *Social Science Quarterly* 53 (March 1973):830–845.

Gutman, Herbert G. *Slavery and the Numbers Game: A Critique of Time on the Cross* (Urbana: University of Illinois Press, 1975).

———. *The Black Family in Slavery and Freedom, 1750–1925* (New York: Pantheon Books, 1976).

Hachen, David S. "Industrial Characteristics and Job Mobility Rates," *American Sociological Review* 57 (February 1992):39–55.

Hacker, Andrew. *Two Nations* (New York: Charles Scribner's Sons, 1992).

Hagan, William T. *American Indians* (Chicago: University of Chicago Press, 1971).

Haines, David W. "Kinship in Vietnamese Refugee Resettlement: A Review of the U.S. Experience," *Journal of Comparative Family Studies* 19 (Spring 1988):1–16.

Hallinan, Maureen T., and Williams, Richard A. "The Stability of Students' Interracial Friendships," *American Sociological Review* 52 (October 1987):653–664.

———. "Interracial Friendship Choices in Secondary Schools," *American Sociological Review* 54 (February 1989):67–78.

Hamilton, Alexander; Madison, James; and Jay, John. *The Federalist Papers* (New York: New American Library, [1787] 1961).

Hamilton, David L., and Bishop, George D. "Attitudinal and Behavioral Effects of Initial Integration of White Suburban Neighborhoods," *Journal of Social Issues* 32, no. 2 (1976):47–67.

Hamilton, David L., and Trolier, Tina K. "Stereotypes and Stereotyping: An Overview of the Cognitive Approach," in John F. Dovidio and Samuel L. Gaertner, eds. *Prejudice, Discrimination, and Racism* (Orlando: Academic Press, 1986).

Handlin, Oscar. *Race and Nationality in American Life* (Garden City, N.Y.: Doubleday, 1957).

Hansen, Marcus Lee. *The Problem of the Third Generation Immigrant* (Rock Island, Ill.: Augustana Historical Society, 1938).

———. *The Atlantic Migration 1607–1860* (Cambridge, Mass.: Harvard University Press, 1945).

Harrison, Roderick J., and Weinberg, Daniel H. "Changes in Racial and Ethnic Residential Segregation, 1980–1990," U.S. Bureau of the Census, Racial Statistics Branch, Population Division, 1992 (mimeographed).

Hartz, Louis. *The Founding of New Societies* (New York: Harcourt, Brace & World, 1964).

Hatchett, Shirley J.; Cochran, Donna L.; and Jackson, James S. "Family Life," in James S. Jackson, ed. *Life in Black America* (Newbury Park, Calif.: Sage Publications, 1991), 46–83.

Hazuda, Helen P.; Stern, Michael P.; and Haffner, Steven M. "Acculturation and Assimilation Among Mexican Americans: Scales and Population-Based Data," *Social Science Quarterly* 69 (September 1988):687–706.

Heer, David M. "Negro-White Marriage in the United States," *Journal of Marriage and the Family* 28 (August 1966):262–273.

———. "Intermarriage," in Stephan Thernstrom, Ann Orlov, and Oscar Handlin, eds. *Harvard Encyclopedia of American Ethnic Groups* (Cambridge, Mass.: The Belknap Press, 1980), 513–521.

Heiss, Jerold, and Owens, Susan. "Self-Evaluation of Blacks and Whites," *American Journal of Sociology* 78 (September 1972):360–370.

Herberg, Will. *Protestant-Catholic-Jew* (Garden City, N.Y.: Doubleday, 1960).

Hernandez, José; Estrada, Leo; and Alvírez, David. "Census Data and the Problem of Conceptually Defining the Mexican American Population," *Social Science Quarterly* 53 (March 1973):671–687.

Herskovits, Melville J. *The American Negro: A Study in Racial Crossing* (New York: Alfred A. Knopf, 1928).

———. *The Myth of the Negro Past* (Boston: Beacon Press, 1958).

Hertzberg, Hazel W. *The Search for an American Indian Identity* (Syracuse: Syracuse University Press, 1971).

Hewstone, Miles. "Contact is Not Enough: An Intergroup Perspective on the 'Contact Hypothesis,'" in Miles Hewstone and Rupert Brown, eds. *Contact and Conflict in Intergroup Encounters* (Oxford: Basil Blackwell, 1986), 1–44.

———. "Intergroup Attribution: Some Implications for the Study of Ethnic Prejudice," in Jan Pieter van Oudenhoven and Tineke M. Willemsen, eds. *Ethnic Minorities* (Amsterdam: Swets & Zeitlinger, 1989), 25–42.

Higham, John. *Strangers in the Land: Patterns of American Nativism 1860–1925* (New York: Atheneum, 1963).

Hill, Robert B. *The Strengths of Black Families* (New York: Emerson Hall Publishers, 1971).

Hirschman, Charles. "America's Melting Pot Reconsidered," in Ralph Turner and James F. Short, Jr., eds. *Annual Review of Sociology* (Palo Alto, Calif.: Annual Reviews, 1983), 397–423.

Hirschman, Charles, and Wong, Morrison G. "Socioeconomic Gains of Asian Americans, Blacks, and Hispanics: 1960–1976," *American Journal of Sociology* 90 (November 1984): 584–607.

———. "Trends in Socioeconomic Achievement among Immigrant and Native-Born Asian-Americans, 1960–1976," in Norman R. Yetman, ed. *Majority and Minority,* 4th ed. (Boston: Allyn and Bacon, 1985), 290–304.

———. "The Extraordinary Educational Attainment of Asian-Americans: A Search for Historical Evidence and Explanations," *Social Forces* 65 (September 1986):1–27.

Hoffman, Abraham. *Unwanted Mexican Americans in the Great Depression: Repatriation Pressures 1929–1939* (Tucson: University of Arizona Press, 1974).

Hofstetter, Richard R., ed. *U.S. Immigration Policy* (Durham, N.C.: Duke University Press, 1984).

Holle, Melvin G., and d'A. Jones, Peter, eds. *The Ethnic Frontier: Group Survival in Chicago and the Midwest* (Grand Rapids, Mich.: Eerdmans, 1977), 293–330.

Hollingshead, August B. "Cultural Factors in the Selection of Marriage Mates," *American Sociological Review* 15 (October 1950):619–627.

Holm, Tom. "The Crisis in Tribal Government," in Vine Deloria, Jr., ed. *American Indian Policy in the Twentieth Century* (Norman: University of Oklahoma Press, 1985), 135–154.

Hook, Sidney. "The Bias in Anti-Bias Regulations," in Barry R. Gross ed. *Reverse Discrimination* (Buffalo, N.Y.: Prometheus Books, 1977), 88–96.

Hoppe, Sue Keir, and Heller, Peter L. "Alienation, Familism, and the Utilization of Health Services by Mexican Americans," *Journal of Health and Social Behavior* 16 (September 1975):304–314.

Horn, Miriam, "The Return to Ellis Island," *U.S. News & World Report* (November 21, 1988):63.

Horowitz, E. L. "The Development of Attitude Toward the Negro," *Archives of Psychology* 29 (January 1936):5–47.

Horton, John. "Order and Conflict Theories of Social Problems as Competing Ideologies," *American Journal of Sociology* 71 (May 1966):701–713.

Hosokawa, Bill. *Nisei: The Quiet Americans* (New York: William Morrow, 1969).

Howery, Carla B. "Update on Human Rights Cases," *Footnotes* (Washington, D.C.: American Sociological Association 14 November 1986:9).

Hoxie, Frederick E. *A Final Promise: The Campaign to Assimilate the Indians, 1880–1920* (Lincoln: University of Nebraska Press, 1984).

Hughes, Michael, and Demo, David. "Self Perceptions of Black Americans: Self-Esteem and Personal Efficacy," *American Journal of Sociology* 95 (July 1989):132–159.

Huggins, Nathan I.; Kilson, Martin; and Fox, Daniel M.; eds. *Key Issues in the Afro American Experience* (New York: Harcourt Brace Jovanovich, 1971).

Hwang, Sean-Shong; Murdock, Steven H.; Parpia, Banoo; and Hamm, Rita R. "The Effects of Race and Socioeconomic Status on Residential Segregation in Texas, 1970–80," *Social Forces* 63 (March 1985):732–747.

Hyman, Herbert H., and Sheatsley, Paul B. "Attitudes Toward Desegregation," *Scientific American* (July 1964):16–23.

Ichihashi, Yamato. *Japanese in the United States* (Palo Alto, Calif.: Stanford University Press, 1932).

Ichioka, Yuji. "Nisei: The Quiet Americans," in Amy Tachiki, Eddie Wong, Franklin Odo, and Buck Wong, eds. *Roots: An Asian American Reader* (Los Angeles: The Regents of the University of California, 1971), 221–222.

Ikeda, Kiyoshi. "A Different 'Dilemma,'" *Social Forces* 51 (June 1973):497–499.

Indians of All Tribes. "We Must Hold on to the Old Ways," in Alvin M. Josephy, Jr., ed. *Red Power* (New York: American Heritage Press, 1971), 197–201.

Institute for Research on Poverty. "Nature-Nurture Nonsense," *Focus* 1 (Spring-Summer 1976): 1–4.

Institute for Social Research. "Cross-Racial Contact Increases in Seventies: Attitude Gap Narrows for Blacks and Whites," *ISR Newsletter* (Autumn 1975):4–7.

Isaac, Larry, and Kelly, William R. "Racial Insurgency, the State, and Welfare Expansion: Local and National Level Evidence from the Postwar United States," *American Journal of Sociology* 86 (May 1981):1348–1386.

Iwata, Masakazu. "The Japanese Immigrants in California Agriculture," *Agricultural History* 36 (January 1962):25–37.

Jackson, Curtis E., and Galli, Marcia J. *A History of the Bureau of Indian Affairs and Its Activities Among Indians* (San Francisco: R & E Research Associates, 1977).

Jackson, James S., ed. *Life in Black America* (Newbury Park, Calif.: Sage Publications, 1991).

Jacobs, Paul, and Landau, Saul, eds. *To Serve the Devil,* vol. 1. (New York: Vintage Books, 1971).

Jacobson, Cardell K. "Internal Colonialism and Native Americans: Indian Labor in the United States from 1871 to World War II," *Social Science Quarterly* 65 (March 1984):158–171.

James, Lenada. "Activism and Red Power" (comment), in Kenneth R. Philp, ed. *Indian Self-Rule* (Salt Lake City: Howe Brothers, 1986), 229–231.

Jaynes, Gerald David, and Williams, Robin M., Jr., eds. *A Common Destiny* (Washington, D.C.: National Academy Press, 1989).

Jensen, Arthur R. "How Much Can We Boost IQ and Scholastic Achievement?" *Harvard Educational Review* 39 (Winter 1969):1–123.

———. "Race and the Genetics of Intelligence: A Reply to Lewontin," in N. J. Block and Gerald Dworkin, eds. *The IQ Controversy* (New York: Pantheon Books, 1976), 93–106.

Jiobu, Robert M. *Ethnicity and Assimilation* (Albany: State University of New York Press, 1988a).

———. "Ethnic Hegemony and the Japanese of California," *American Sociological Review* 53 (June 1988b):353–367.

Johnson, Dirk. "Mob Violence Continues in Las Vegas," *The New York Times* (May 19, 1992):A10.

Johnson, James Weldon. "Description of a Race Riot in Chicago," in Gilbert Osofsky, ed. *The Burden of Race* (New York: Harper & Row, 1968), 304–309.

Jones, Maldwyn Allen. *American Immigration* (Chicago: University of Chicago Press, 1960).

———. *Destination America* (New York: Holt, Rinehart and Winston, 1976).

———. "Scotch-Irish," in Stephan Thernstrom, Ann Orlov, and Oscar Handlin, eds. *Harvard Encyclopedia of American Ethnic Groups* (Cambridge, Mass.: The Belknap Press, 1980), 895–908.

Jordan, Terry G. "The 1887 Census of Texas' Hispanic Population," *Aztlan* 12, no. 2 (1981): 271–277.

Jordan, Winthrop D. "Modern Tensions and the Origins of African Slavery," in Donald L. Noel, ed. *The Origins of American Slavery and Racisim* (Columbus, Ohio: Charles E. Merrill, 1972), 81–94.

Jordan, Winthrop D., and Litwack, Leon F. *The United States,* 6th ed., vol. 1 (Englewood Cliffs, N. J.: Prentice-Hall, 1987).

Josephy, Alvin M., Jr. *The Patriot Chiefs* (New York: Viking Press, 1961).

———. *The Indian Heritage of America* (New York: Alfred A. Knopf, 1968).

———, ed. *Red Power* (New York: American Heritage Press, 1971).

Kagiwada, George. "Assimilation of Nisei in Los Angeles," in Hilary Conroy and T. Scott Miyakawa, eds. *East Across the Pacific* (Santa Barbara, Calif.: American Bibliographical Center-CLIO Press, 1972), 268–278.

———. "Confessions of a Misguided Sociologist," *Amerasia Journal* 3 (Fall 1973):159–162.

Kallen, Horace M. *Culture and Democracy in the United States* (New York: Boni and Liveright, 1924).

Kantrowitz, Barbara. "The Ultimate Assimilation," *Newsweek* (November 24, 1986):80.

Karlins, Marvin; Coffman, Thomas L.; and Walters, Gary. "On the Fading of Social Stereotypes: Studies in Three Generations of College Students," *Journal of Personality and Social Psychology* 13 (September 1969):1–16.

Karno, Marvin, and Edgerton, Robert B. "Perceptions of Mental Illness in a Mexican-American Community," in John H. Burma, ed. *Mexican Americans in the United States* (Cambridge, Mass.: Schenkman Publishing, 1970), 343–351.

Katz, Daniel, and Braly, Kenneth W. "Racial Stereotypes of One Hundred College Students," *Journal of Abnormal and Social Psychology* 28 (October-December 1933):280–290.

Katz, P. A., ed. *Toward the Elimination of Racism* (New York: Pergamon Press, 1976).

Keefe, Susan E., and Padilla, Amado M. *Chicano Ethnicity* (Albuquerque: University of New Mexico Press, 1987).

Keely, Charles. "Immigration Policy and the New Immigrants, 1965–1975," in Roy Simon Bryce-Laporte, ed. *Sourcebook on the New Immigration* (New Brunswick, N.J.: Transaction Books, 1980), 15–25.

———. "Population and Immigration Policy: State and Federal Roles," in Frank D. Bean, Jurgen Schmandt, and Sidney Weintraub, eds. *Mexican and Central American Population and U.S. Immigration Policy* (Austin, Tex.: The Center for Mexican American Studies, 1989), 161–178.

Kelly, Gail Paradise. *From Vietnam to America* (Boulder, Colo.: Westview Press, 1977).

Kennedy, Ruby Jo Reeves. "Single or Triple Melting-Pot? Intermarriage Trends in New Haven, 1870–1940," *American Journal of Sociology* 49 (January 1944):331–339.

Kephart, William M., and Jedlicka, Davor. *The Family, Society, and the Individual,* 6th ed. (New York: Harper & Row, 1988).

Kerr, Louise Año Nuevo. "Mexican Chicago: Chicano Assimilation Aborted, 1939–1952," in Melvin G. Holle and Peter d'A. Jones, eds. *The Ethnic Frontier: Group Survival in Chicago and the Midwest* (Grand Rapids, Mich.: Eerdmans, 1977), 293–330.

Kibbe, Pauline R. *Latin Americans in Texas* (Albuquerque: University of New Mexico Press, 1946).

Kifner, John. "At Wounded Knee, Two Worlds Collide," in David R. Colburn and George E. Pozzetta, eds. *America and the New Ethnicity* (Port Washington, N.Y.: Kennikat Press, 1979), 79–90.

Kikimura, Akemi, and Kitano, Harry H. L. "Interracial Marriage: A Picture of the Japanese Americans," *Journal of Social Issues* 29, no. 2 (1973):67–81.

King, James C. *The Biology of Race* (New York: Harcourt Brace Jovanovich, 1971).

King, Martin Luther, Jr. "The Case Against 'Tokenism,'" *The New York Times Magazine,* August 5, 1962, p. 11ff.

———. *Why We Can't Wait?* (New York: New American Library, 1964).

———. "The Use of Nonviolence," in Gilbert Osofsky, ed. *The Burden of Race* (New York: Harper & Row, 1968), 522–526.

———. "Our Struggle for an Interracial Society Based on Freedom for All," in August Meier, Elliott Rudwick, and Francis L. Broderick, eds. *Black Protest Thought in the Twentieth Century,* 2nd ed. (Indianapolis and New York: Bobbs-Merrill, 1971a), 291–302.

———. "We Still Believe in Black and White Together," in August Meier, Elliott Rudwick, and Francis L. Broderick, eds. *Black Protest Thought in the Twentieth Century,* 2nd ed. (Indianapolis and New York: Bobbs-Merrill, 1971b), 584–595.

Kinzie, J. D. "Evaluation and Psychotherapy of Indochinese Refugee Patients," *American Journal of Psychotherapy* 35, no. 2 (1981):251–261.

Kitano, Harry H. L. *Japanese Americans* (Englewood Cliffs, N.J.: Prentice-Hall, 1969).

———. "Asian-Americans: The Chinese, Japanese, Koreans, Filipinos, and Southeast Asians," *The Annals* 454 (March 1981):125–138.

Kitano, Harry H. L., and Daniels, Roger. *Asian Americans* (Englewood Cliffs, N.J.: Prentice-Hall, 1988).

Klanwatch (Montgomery, Ala.: The Southern Poverty Law Center, March 1981).

Klineberg, Otto. *Negro Intelligence and Selective Migration* (New York: Columbia University Press, 1935).

———. "Mental Tests," *Encyclopedia of the Social Sciences,* vol. 10. (New York: Macmillan, 1937), 323–329.

———. "Pictures in Our Heads," in Edgar A. Schuler, Thomas Ford Hoult, Duane L. Gibson, and Wilbur B. Brookover, eds. *Readings in Sociology,* 5th ed. (New York: Thomas Y. Crowell, 1974), 631–637.

Kluckhohn, Florence. "Dominant and Variant Value Orientations," in Clyde Kluckhohn,

Henry A. Murray, and David M. Schneider, eds. *Personality in Nature, Society, and Culture,* 2nd ed. (New York: Alfred A. Knopf, 1956), 342–357.

Kluegel, James R. "Trends in Whites' Explanations of the Black-White Gap in Socioeconomic Status, 1977–1989," *American Sociological Review* 55 (August 1990):512–525.

Kluegel, James R., and Smith, Eliot R. "Whites' Belief About Blacks' Opportunity," *American Sociological Review* 47 (August 1982):518–519.

Kramer, Michael. "What Can Be Done?" *Time* (May 11, 1992):41.

Kraut, Alan M. *The Huddled Masses: The Immigrant in American Society, 1880–1921* (Arlington Heights, IL: Harlan Davidson, Inc., 1982).

Krebs, Dennis, and Miller, Dale T. "Altruism and Aggression," in Gardner Lindzey and Elliot Aronson, eds. *Handbook of Social Psychology,* 3rd ed. (New York: Random House, 1985), 1–71.

Krickus, Richard J. "White Ethnic Neighborhoods: Ripe for the Bulldozer?" in Stanley Feldstein and Lawrence Costello, eds. *The Ordeal of Assimilation* (Garden City, N.Y.: Anchor/Doubleday, 1974), 434–439.

Kriegel, Leonard. "Last Stop on the D Train: In the Land of the New Racists," in Stanley Feldstein and Lawrence Costello, eds. *The Ordeal of Assimilation* (Garden City, N.Y.: Anchor/Doubleday,1974), 418–434.

Kristol, Irving. "The Negro Today Is Like the Immigrant of Yesterday," in Peter I. Rose, ed. *Nation of Nations* (New York: Random House, 1972), 197–210.

Kritz, Mary M.; Keely, Charles B.; and Tomasi, Sylvano M., eds. *Global Trends in Migration* (Staten Island, N.Y.: CMS Press, 1981), 279–297.

Kunz, E. F. "The Refugees in Flight: Kinetic Models and Forms of Displacement," *International Migration Review* 7, no. 2 (1973)125–146.

Lacayo, Richard. *Time* (March 13, 1989):58–68.

———. "Anatomy of an Acquittal," *Time* (May 11, 1992):30–32.

Lai, H. M. "Chinese," in Stephan Thernstrom, Ann Orlov, and Oscar Handlin, eds. *Harvard Encyclopedia of American Ethnic Groups* (Cambridge, Mass.: The Belknap Press, 1980), 256–261.

Lake, Robert W. *The New Suburbanites: Race and Housing in the Suburbs* (New Brunswick, N.J.: Center for Urban Policy Research, Rutgers University, 1981).

Landry, Bart. *The New Black Middle Class* (Berkeley: University of California Press, 1987).

LaPiere, Richard T. "Attitudes vs. Actions," *Social Forces* 13 (December 1934):230–237.

LaViolette, Forrest E. *Americans of Japanese Ancestry* (Toronto: Canadian Institute of International Affairs, 1945).

Lawson, Stephen F. *Black Ballots: Voting Rights in the South, 1944–1969* (New York: Columbia University Press, 1976).

Lazarus, Emma. *Poems* (Boston: Houghton Mifflin, 1889).

Lea, Tom. *The King Ranch,* vol. 1. (Boston: Little, Brown, 1957).

Lee, Barrett A. "Racially Mixed Neighborhoods During the 1970s: Change or Stability?" *Social Science Quarterly* 66 (June 1985):346–364.

Lee, Everett S. "Negro Intelligence and Selective Migration: A Philadelphia Test of the Klineberg Hypothesis," *American Sociological Review* 16 (April 1951):227–233.

Leighton, Alexander. *The Governing of Men* (Princeton, N.J.: Princeton University Press, 1946).

Lenski, Gerhard E. *Power and Privilege* (New York: McGraw-Hill, 1966).

Lenski, Gerhard E., and Lenski, Jean. *Human Societies,* 5th ed. (New York: McGraw-Hill, 1987).

Leo, John. "An Apology to Japanese Americans," *Time* (May 2, 1988):70.

Lerner, Richard M., and Buehrig, Christie J. "The Development of Racial Attitudes in Young Black and White Children," *Journal of Genetic Psychology* 127 (September 1975):45–54.

Levine, Gene N., and Rhodes, Colbert. *The Japanese American Community* (New York: Praeger, 1981).

Levine, Lawrence W. *Black Culture and Black Consciousness* (New York: Oxford University Press, 1977).

Lewis, Oscar. *La Vida* (New York: Random House, 1965).

Leyburn, James G. "Frontier Society," in Leonard Dinnerstein and Frederick Cople Jaher, eds. *The Aliens* (New York: Appleton-Century-Crofts, 1970), 65–76.

Lieberson, Stanley. "A Societal Theory of Race and Ethnic Relations," *American Sociological Review* 26 (December 1961):902–910.

———. *A Piece of the Pie* (Berkeley: University of California Press, 1980).

———. "Stereotypes: Their Consequences for Race and Ethnic Interaction," in Robert M. Hauser, David Mechanic, Archibald Haller, and Taissa S. Hauser, eds. *Social Structure and Behavior: Essays in Honor of William Hamilton Sewell* (New York: Academic Press, 1982), 47–68.

———. "Unhyphenated Whites in the United States," in Richard D. Alba, ed. *Ethnicity and Race in the U.S.A.* (New York: Routledge, 1988), 159–180.

Lieberson, Stanley, and Fuguitt, Glenn V. "Negro-White Occupational Differences in the Absence of Discrimination," *American Journal of Sociology* 73 (September 1967): 188–200.

Lieberson, Stanley, and Waters, Mary C. *From Many Strands* (New York: Russell Sage Foundation, 1988).

Liebow, Edward R. "Category or Community? Measuring Urban Indian Social Cohesion with Network Sampling," *Journal of Ethnic Studies* 16 (Winter 1989):67–100.

Liebow, Elliot. *Tally's Corner* (Boston: Little, Brown, 1967).

Light, Ivan H. "Kenjin and Kinsmen," in Rudolph Gomez, Clement Cottingham, Jr., Russell Endo, and Kathleen Jackson, eds. *The Social Reality of Ethnic America.* (Lexington, Mass.: D. C. Heath, 1974), 282–297.

Lin, Keh-Ming; Tazuma, Laurie; and Masuda, Minoru. "Adaptational Problems of Vietnamese Refugees: Health and Mental Health Status," *Archives of General Psychiatry* 36 (August 1979):955–961.

Lincoln, C. Eric. *The Black Muslims in America* (Boston: Beacon Press, 1961).

Lindzey, Gardner, and Aronson, Elliot, eds. *Handbook of Social Psychology,* 3rd ed. (New York: Random House, 1985).

Linn, Lawrence S. "Verbal Attitudes and Overt Behavior: A Study of Racial Discrimination," *Social Forces* 43 (March 1965):353–364.

Linton, Ralph. *The Study of Man* (New York: Appleton-Century, 1936).

Lipset, Seymour Martin. *The First New Nation* (New York: W. W. Norton & Co., 1979).

Littlefield, Alice; Lieberman, Leonard; and Reynolds, Larry T. "Redefining Race: The Potential Demise of a Concept in Physical Anthropology," *Current Anthropology* 23 (December 1982):641–655.

Lobel, Sharon Alisa. "Effects of Personal Versus Impersonal Rater Instructions on Relative Favorability of Thirteen Ethnic Group Stereotypes," *Journal of Social Psychology* 128 (February 1988):29–39.

Loehlin, John C.; Lindzey, Gardner; and Spuhler, J. N. *Race Differences in Intelligence* (San Francisco: W. H. Freeman, 1975).

Logan, John R., and Schneider, Mark. "Racial Segregation and Racial Change in American Suburbs: 1970–1980," *American Journal of Sociology* 89 (January 1984):874–888.

Lohman, Joseph D., and Reitzes, Dietrich C. "Note on Race Relations in Mass Society," *American Journal of Sociology* 57 (November 1952):240–246.

Lopez, Manuel Mariano. "Patterns of Interethnic Residential Segregation in the Urban Southwest, 1960 and 1970," *Social Science Quarterly* 62 (March 1981):50–63.

Lopreato, Joseph. *Italian Americans* (New York: Random House, 1970).

———. *Human Nature and Biocultural Evolution* (Boston: Allen & Unwin, 1984).

Lurie, Nancy Oestreich. "The American Indian: Historical Background," in Norman R. Yetman, and C. Hoy Steele, eds. *Majority & Minority,* 3rd ed. (Boston: Allyn and Bacon, 1982):131–144.

Lutz, Donald S. "The Changing View of the Founding and a New Perspective on American Political Theory," *Social Science Quarterly* 68 (December 1987):669–686.

McAdam, Doug. *Political Process and the Development of Black Insurgency, 1930–1970* (Chicago: University of Chicago Press, 1982).

McCarthy, John, and Yancey, William. "Uncle Tom and Mr. Charlie: Metaphysical Pathos in the Study of Racism and Personal Disorganization," *American Journal of Sociology* 76 (January 1971):648–672.

McCone, John A. "The Watts Riot," in Gilbert Osofsky, ed. *The Burden of Race* (New York: Harper & Row, 1968), 608–621.

McCool, Daniel. "Indian Voting," in Vine Deloria, Jr., ed. *American Indian Policy in the Twentieth Century* (Norman: University of Oklahoma Press, 1985), 105–133.

McFee, Malcolm. "The 150% Man, A Product of Blackfeet Acculturation," in Howard M. Bahr, Bruce A. Chadwick, and Robert C. Day, eds. *Native Americans Today* (New York: Harper & Row, 1972), 303–312.

McKitrick, Eric L., ed. *Slavery Defended* (Englewood Cliffs, N.J.: Prentice-Hall, 1963).

MacLeish, Archibald. *A Time to Act* (Boston: Houghton Mifflin, 1943).

McLemore, S. Dale. "Ethnic Attitudes Toward Hospitalization: An Illustrative Comparison of Anglos and Mexican Americans," *Southwestern Social Science Quarterly* 43 (March 1963): 341–346.

———. "The Origins of Mexican American Subordination in Texas," *Social Science Quarterly* 53 (March 1973):656–670.

McLemore, S. Dale, and Romo, Ricardo. "The Origins and Development of the Mexican American People," in Rodolfo O. de la Garza, Frank D. Bean, Charles M. Bonjean, Ricardo Romo, and Rodolfo Alvarez, eds. *The Mexican American Experience* (Austin: University of Texas Press, 1985), 3–32.

McNeill, William H. *Plagues and Peoples* (Garden City, N.Y.: Anchor Books, 1976).

McNickle, D'Arcy. *Native American Tribalism* (London: Oxford University Press, 1973).

McWilliams, Carey. *California: The Great Exception* (New York: A. A. Wyn, 1949).

———. "Getting Rid of the Mexicans," in Wayne Moquín and Charles Van Doren, eds. *A Docu-*

mentary History of the Mexican Americans (New York: Bantam Books, 1972), 383–387.

———. *North from Mexico* (New York: Greenwood Press, 1973).

Malcolm X. "Malcolm X Founds the Organization of Afro-American Unity," in August Meier, Elliott Rudwick, and Francis L. Broderick, eds. *Black Protest Thought in the Twentieth Century,* 2nd ed. (Indianapolis and New York: Bobbs-Merrill, 1971), 412–420.

Malcolm X and Farmer, James. "Separation or Integration: A Debate," in August Meier, Elliott Rudwick, and Francis L. Broderick, eds. *Black Protest Thought in the Twentieth Century,* 2nd ed. (Indianapolis and New York: Bobbs-Merrill, 1971), 387–412.

Maldonado, Lionel, and Moore, Joan, eds. *Urban Ethnicity in the United States* (Newbury Park, Calif.: Sage Publications, 1985), 51–71.

Martin, W. Allen; Hammond, Clark; and Hardy, Hiroko. "Entrepreneurship among the Vietnamese of Port Arthur." Paper presented at the annual meeting of the American Sociological Association, Atlanta, August 1988 (mimeographed).

Martinez, Jose. "Michigan College on Edge After Racial Brawl," *Austin American-Statesman* (April 4, 1992):A5.

Marquez, Benjamin. "The Politics of Race and Class: The League of United Latin American Citizens in the Post-World War II Period," *Social Science Quarterly* 68 (March 1987): 84–101.

Marumoto, Masaji. "'First Year' Immigrants to Hawaii & Eugene Van Reed," in Hilary Conroy and T. Scott Miyakawa, eds. *East Across the Pacific* (Santa Barbara, Calif.: American Bibliographical Center-CLIO Press, 1972), 5–39.

Marx, Herbert L., ed. *The American Indian* (New York: H. W. Wilson, 1973).

Massey, Douglas S. "Effects of Socioeconomic Factors on the Residential Segregation of Blacks and Spanish Americans in U.S. Urbanized Areas," *American Sociological Review* 44 (December 1979):1015–1022.

———. "Dimensions of the New Immigration to the United States and the Prospects for Assimilation," in Ralph J. Turner and James F. Short, Jr., eds. *Annual Review of Sociology* 7 (1981):57–85.

Massey, Douglas S.; Condran, Gretchen A.; and Denton, Nancy A. "The Effect of Residential Segregation on Black Social and Economic Well-Being," *Social Forces* 66 (September 1987):29–56.

Massey, Douglas S., and Denton, Nancy A. "Trends in the Residential Segregation of Blacks, Hispanics, and Asians: 1970–1980," *American Sociological Review* 52 (December 1987): 802–825.

Massey, Douglas S., and Eggers, Mitchell L. "The Ecology of Inequality: Minorities and the Concentration of Poverty, 1970–1990" *American Journal of Sociology* 95 (March 1990):1153–1188).

Matarazzo, Joseph. "Psychological Testing and Assessment in the 21st Century," *American Psychologist* 47 (August 1992):1007–1018.

Matsumoto, Gary M.; Meredith, Gerald M.; and Masuda, Minoru. "Ethnic Identity: Honolulu and Seattle Japanese-Americans," in Stanley Sue and Nathaniel Wagner, eds. *Asian-Americans* (Ben Lomand, Calif.: Science and Behavior Books, 1973), 65–74.

Mazon, Mauricio. *The Zoot Suit Riots: The Psychology of Symbolic Annihilation* (Austin: University of Texas Press, 1988).

Meer, Bernard, and Freedman, Edward. "The Impact of Negro Neighbors on White Home Owners," *Social Forces* 45 (September 1966): 11–19.

Meier, August; Rudwick, Elliott; and Broderick, Francis L.; eds. *Black Protest Thought in the Twentieth Century,* 2nd ed. (Indianapolis and New York: Bobbs-Merrill, 1971).

Meister, Richard J., ed. *Race and Ethnicity in Modern America* (Lexington, Mass.: D. C. Heath, 1974).

Mercer, Jane R.; Iadicola, Peter; and Moore, Helen. "Building Effective Multiethnic Schools," in Walter G. Stephan and Joe R. Feagin, eds. *School Desegregation* (New York: Plenum Press, 1980), 281–307.

Meriam, Lewis, et al. *The Problem of Indian Administration* (Washington, D.C.: Brookings Institution, 1928).

Merton, Robert K. "Discrimination and the American Creed," in Robert M. MacIver, ed. *Discrimination and National Welfare* (New York: Harper & Row, 1949), 99–126.

Metzger, L. Paul. "American Sociology and Black Assimilation: Conflicting Perspectives," *American Journal of Sociology* 76 (January 1971):627–647.

Michner, Charles, and Brinkley-Rogers, Paul. "Success Story: Outwhiting the Whites," *Newsweek* (June 21, 1971):24–25.

Middlekauff, Robert. "The Assumptions of the Founders in 1787," *Social Science Quarterly* 68 (December 1987):656–668.

Middleton, Russell. "Ethnic Prejudice and Susceptibility to Persuasion," *American Sociological Review* 25 (October 1960):679–686.

———. "Regional Differences in Prejudice," *American Sociological Review* 41 (February 1976):94–117.

Mikulski, Barbara. "Who Speaks for Ethnic America?" in Stanley Feldstein and Lawrence Costello, eds. *The Ordeal of Assimilation* (Garden City, N.Y.: Anchor/Doubleday, 1974), 440–943.

Miller, Arthur G., ed. *In the Eye of the Beholder* (New York: Praeger, 1982).

Miller, Neal E. "The Frustration-Aggression Hypothesis," *Psychological Review* 48 (July 1941):337–342; reprinted in Leonard Berkowitz, ed. *Roots of Aggression: A Re-Examination of the Frustration-Aggression Hypothesis* (New York: Atherton Press, 1969), 29–34.

Miller, Norman. "Making School Desegregation Work," in Walter G. Stephan and Joe R. Feagin, eds. *School Desegregation* (New York: Plenum Press, 1980), 309–348.

Milner, Lucille B. "Letters from a Segregated Army," in Gilbert Osofsky, ed. *The Burden of Race* (New York: Harper & Row, 1968), 414–420.

Mindiola, Tatcho, Jr. "Age and Income Discrimination Against Mexican Americans and Blacks in Texas, 1960 and 1970," *Social Problems* 27 (December 1979):196–208.

Mintz, Sidney W. "Slavery and Emergent Capitalisms," in Laura Foner and Eugene D. Genovese, eds. *Slavery in the New World* (Englewood Cliffs, N.J.: Prentice-Hall, 1969), 27–37.

Mittlebach, Frank G., and Moore, Joan W. "Ethnic Endogamy—The Case of Mexican Americans," *American Journal of Sociology* 74 (July 1968): 50–62.

Miyamoto, S. Frank. *Social Solidarity Among the Japanese of Seattle* (Seattle: University of Washington Press, 1939).

———. "An Immigrant Community in America," in Hilary Conroy and T. Scott Miyakawa, eds. *East Across the Pacific* (Santa Barbara, Calif.: American Bibliographical Center-CLIO Press, 1972), 217–243.

Modell, John. *The Economics and Politics of Racial Accommodation: The Japanese of Los Angeles, 1900–1942* (Urbana: University of Illinois Press, 1977).

Monahan, Thomas P. "An Overview of Statistics on Interracial Marriage in the United States, with Data on Its Extent from 1963–1970," *Journal of Marriage and the Family* 38 (May 1976):223–231.

Monk, Maria. "Few Imaginations Can Conceive Deeds So Abominable as They Practiced," in Moses Rischin, ed. *Immigration and the American Tradition* (Indianapolis: Bobbs-Merrill, [1836] 1976).

Monsho, Kharen. "Kwanzaa Celebrates Community of Blacks," *Austin American-Statesman* (December 16, 1988):F2.

Montejano, David. *Anglos and Mexicans in the Making of Texas, 1836–1986* (Austin: University of Texas Press, 1987).

Montero, Darrel. *Vietnamese Americans: Patterns of Resettlement and Socioeconomic Adaptation in the United States* (Boulder, Colo.: Westview Press, 1979).

———. *Japanese Americans: Changing Patterns of Affiliation Over Three Generations* (Boulder, Colo.: Westview Press, 1980).

———. "The Japanese Americans: Changing Patterns of Assimilation over Three Generations," *American Sociological Review* 46 (December 1981):829–839.

Montero, Darrel, and Tsukashima, Ronald. "Assimilation and Educational Achievement: The Case of the Second-Generation Japanese

American," *Sociological Quarterly* 18 (1977): 490–503.

Moore, Joan W. *Mexican Americans,* 1st and 2nd eds. (Englewood Cliffs, N.J.: Prentice-Hall, 1970 and 1976).

————. "American Minorities and 'New Nation' Perspectives," *Pacific Sociological Review* 19 (1976):447–467.

————. "Is There a Hispanic Underclass?" *Social Science Quarterly* 70 (June 1989):265–284.

Moore, Joan W., and Pachon, Harry. *Hispanics in the United States* (Englewood Cliffs, N.J.: Prentice-Hall, 1985).

Moquín, Wayne, and Van Doren, Charles, eds. *A Documentary History of the Mexican Americans* (New York: Bantam Books, 1971).

Morganthau, Tom; Mabry, Marcus; Washington, Frank; Smith, Vern E.; Yoffe, Emily; and Beachy, Lucille. "Losing Ground," *Newsweek* (April 6, 1992):20–22.

Morland, J. Kenneth. "A Comparison of Race Awareness in Northern and Southern Children," *American Journal of Orthopsychiatry* 36 (January 1966):22–31.

Morris, Aldon. *The Origins of the Civil Rights Movement: Black Communities Organizing for Change* (New York: The Free Press, 1984).

Morison, Samuel Eliot. *The Oxford History of the American People,* vol. I (New York: New American Library, 1972).

Morse, Joseph Laffan, and Hendelson, William H., eds. "Indochina." *Funk & Wagnalls New Encyclopedia* 13(1972a):262–268.

————. "Vietnam." *Funk & Wagnalls New Encyclopedia* 24(1972b):317–326.

Morse, Samuel F. B. "Riot and Ignorance in Human Priest-Controlled Machines," in Moses Rischin, ed. *Immigration and the American Tradition* (Indianapolis: Bobbs-Merrill, [1835] 1976).

Moskos, Charles C., Jr. *Greek Americans* (Englewood Cliffs, N.J.: Prentice-Hall, 1980).

Moynihan, Daniel Patrick. *The Negro Family* (Washington, D.C.: U.S. Department of Labor, 1965).

Mura, David. "Japanese Americans: Strangers at Home," *New York Times* (April 29, 1992):A15.

Murguía, Edward. *Chicano Intermarriage* (San Antonio, Tex.: Trinity University Press, 1982).

————. *Assimilation, Colonialism, and the Mexican American People* (Lanham, Md.: University Press of America, 1989).

Murguía, Edward, and Frisbie, W. Parker. "Trends in Mexican American Intermarriage: Recent Findings in Perspective," *Social Science Quarterly* 58 (December 1977):374–389.

Mydans, Seth. "Japanese-Americans Face New Fears," *The New York Times* (March 4, 1992):A8.

Myrdal, Gunnar. *An American Dilemma* (New York: McGraw-Hill, [1944] 1964).

NARF Legal Review. Boulder, Colo.: Native American Rights Fund (Summer 1991).

————. Boulder, Colo.: Native American Rights Fund (Summer 1992).

Nash, Gary B. *Red, White, and Black* (Englewood Cliffs, N.J.: Prentice-Hall, 1974).

Nash, Philleo. "Termination" (comment), in Kenneth R. Philp, ed. *Indian Self-Rule* (Salt Lake City: Howe Brothers, 1986), 164–169.

National Advisory Commission. *Report of the National Advisory Commission on Civil Disorders* (New York: The New York Times Co., 1968).

National Center for Health Statistics. *Health, United States 1979* (Washington, D.C.: U.S. Department of Health, Education and Welfare, 1980).

Neidert, Lisa, and Farley, Reynolds. "Assimilation in the United States: An Analysis of Ethnic and Generation Differences in Status and Achievement," *American Sociological Review* 50 (December 1985):840–850.

Newby, Robert G., ed. *The Truly Disadvantaged: Challenges and Prospects,* Special Issue, *Journal of Sociology and Social Welfare* 16 (December 1989).

Newman, William M. *American Pluralism* (New York: Harper & Row, 1973).

The New York Times. "The AIDS 'Plot' Against Blacks," (May 12, 1992):A14.

————. "F.B.I. Agents Raid Casinos on 5 Indian Reservations," (May 13, 1992):A8.

————. "Of 58 Riot Deaths, 50 Have Been Ruled Homicides," (May 17, 1992):A17.

————. "Skinheads and Klansmen March Through Downtown Birmingham," (June 14, 1992):21.

————. "Tribe's Land Claim Voided in Vermont," (June 18, 1992):A12.

————. "Coroner Drops Toll in Los Angeles Riot to 51 After Review," (August 13, 1992):A11.

Newsweek. "For Indians, by Indians," in Herbert L. Marx, ed. *The American Indian* (New York: H. W. Wilson, 1973), 108–110.

Nhan, Chau Kim. "Foreword," in Darrel Montero, *Vietnamese Americans: Patterns of Resettlement and Socioeconomic Adaptation in the United States* (Boulder, Colo.: Westview Press, 1979).

Noel, Donald L. "A Theory of the Origin of Ethnic Stratification," *Social Problems* 16 (Fall 1968): 157–172.

————. *The Origins of American Slavery and Racism* (Columbus, Ohio: Charles E. Merrill, 1972).

Norton, Robert E. "The Myths of Foreign Investment," *U.S. News & World Report* (May 29, 1989):44–46.

Nostrand, Richard L. "'Mexican American' and 'Chicano': Emerging Terms for a People Coming of Age," *Pacific Historical Review* 62 (August 1973):389–406.

Novak, Michael. *The Rise of the Unmeltable Ethnics* (New York: Macmillan, 1971).

Novotny, Ann. *Strangers at the Door* (Toronto: Bantam Pathfinders, 1974).

O'Brien, David J., and Fugita, Stephen S. "Mobilization of a Traditionally Petit Bourgeois Ethnic Group," *Social Forces* 63 (December 1984):522–537.

O'Brien, Sharon. "Federal Indian Policies and the International Protection of Human Rights," in Vine Deloria, Jr., ed. *American Indian Policy in the Twentieth Century* (Norman: University of Oklahoma Press, 1985), 35–61.

Officer, James E. "Termination as Federal Policy: An Overview," in Kenneth R. Philp, ed. *Indian Self-Rule* (Salt Lake City: Howe Brothers, 1986), 114–128.

O'Hare, William. "Reaching for the Dream," 14 *American Demographics* (January 1992):32–36.

O'Hare, William P.; Pollard, Kelvin M.: Mann, Taynia L.; and Kent, Mary M. "African Americans in the 1990s," *Population Bulletin* 46, No. 1 (Washington, D.C.: Population Reference Bureau, Inc., July, 1991).

O'Hare, William P., and Usdansky, Margarett L. "What the 1990 Census Tells Us about Segregation in 25 Large Metros." *Population Today* 20: September 1992):6–7.

Okimoto, Daniel. "The Intolerance of Success," in Amy Tachiki, Eddie Wong, Franklin Odo, and Buck Wong, eds. *Roots: An Asian American Reader* (Los Angeles: Regents of the University of California, 1971), 14–19.

Old Person, Earl. "The IRA Record and John Collier" (comment), in Kenneth R. Philp, ed. *Indian Self-Rule* (Salt Lake City: Howe Brothers, 1986), 107–108.

Olson, James S., and Wilson, Raymond. *Native Americans in the Twentieth Century* (Urbana and Chicago: University of Illinois Press, 1984).

Olzak, Susan. "Labor Unrest, Immigration, and Ethnic Conflict in Urban America," *American Journal of Sociology* 94 (May 1989): 1303–1333.

One Feather, Gerald. "Relocation" (comment), in Kenneth R. Philp, ed. *Indian Self-Rule* (Salt Lake City: Howe Brothers, 1986), 171–172.

Orfield, Gary. *Must We Bus* (Washington, D.C.: Brookings Institution, 1978).

————. *Desegregation of Black and Hispanic Students from 1968 to 1980;* quoted in Mary Swerdlin, ed. *Education Daily* 15 (September 10, 1982):1–2.

Orlans, Harold, and O'Neill, June, eds. *The Annals: Affirmative Action Revisited* (September 1992).

Osofsky, Gilbert, ed. *The Burden of Race* (New York: Harper & Row, 1968).

Pachon, Harry P., and Moore, Joan W. "Mexican Americans," *The Annals* 454 (March 1981):111–124.

Padilla, Felix M. "On the Nature of Latino Ethnicity," in Rodolfo O. de la Garza, Frank D. Bean, Charles M. Bonjean, Ricardo Romo, and Rodolfo Alvarez, eds. *The Mexican American Experience* (Austin: University of Texas Press, 1985), 332–345.

Papademetriou, D. G. "The Immigration Reform and Control Act of 1986: America Amends Its Immigration Law," *International Migration* 25 (September 1987):325–334.

Paredes, Raymund. "The Origins of Anti-Mexican Sentiment in the United States," in Ricardo Romo and Raymund Paredes, eds. *New Directions in Chicano Scholarship* (La Jolla, Calif.: Chicano Studies Program, University of California, San Diego, 1978), 139–166.

Parenti, Michael. "Ethnic Politics and the Persistence of Ethnic Identification," *American Political Science Review* 61 (September 1967): 717–726.

Park, Robert E. "The Concept of Social Distance," *Journal of Applied Sociology* 8 (July-August 1924):339–344.

———. "Our Racial Frontier on the Pacific," *Survey Graphic* 56 (May 1926):192–196; reprinted in Robert E. Park, ed. *Race and Culture* (New York: The Free Press, 1964a), 138–151.

———. *Race and Culture* (New York: The Free Press, 1964b).

Park, Robert E., and Burgess, Ernest W. *Introduction to the Science of Sociology* (Chicago: University of Chicago Press, 1921).

Parkman, Margaret A., and Sawyer, Jack. "Dimensions of Ethnic Intermarriage in Hawaii," *American Sociological Review* 32 (August 1967):593–607.

Patchen, Martin; Davidson, James D.; Hoffmann, Gerhard; and Brown, William R. "Determinants of Students' Interracial Behavior and Opinion Change," *Sociology of Education* 50 (January 1977):55–75.

Patterson, Orlando. "Slavery," in Alex Inkeles, ed. *Annual Review of Sociology* (Palo Alto, Calif.: Annual Reviews, 1977), 407–449.

Peach, Ceri. "Ethnic Segregation and Ethnic Intermarriage: A Re-examination of Kennedy's Triple Melting Pot in New Haven, 1900–1950," in Ceri Peach, Vaughan Robinson, and Susan Smith, eds. *Ethnic Segregation in Cities* (London: Croom Helm, 1981).

Penalosa, Fernando. "The Changing Mexican-American in Southern California," in John H. Burma, ed. *Mexican Americans in the United States* (Cambridge, Mass.: Schenkman, 1970), 41–51.

Perez, Lisandro. "Cubans," in Stephan Thernstrom, Ann Orlov, and Oscar Handlin, eds. *Harvard Encyclopedia of American Ethnic Groups* (Cambridge, Mass.: The Belknap Press, 1980), 256–261.

Peroff, Nicholas G. "Termination Policy and the Menominees: Feedback of Unanticipated Impacts," in John G. Grumm and Stephen L. Wasby, eds. *The Analysis of Policy Impact* (Lexington, Mass.: Lexington Books, 1981), 123–131.

Petersen, William. *Japanese Americans* (New York: Random House, 1971).

———. "Concepts of Ethnicity," in Stephan Thernstrom, Ann Orlov, and Oscar Handlin, eds. *Harvard Encyclopedia of American Ethnic Groups* (Cambridge, Mass.: The Belknap Press, 1980), 234–242.

Pettigrew, Thomas F. *Racially Separate or Together?* (New York: McGraw-Hill, 1971).

———. "A Sociological View of the Post-Milliken Era," in U.S. Commission on Civil Rights, *Milliken v. Bradley: The Implications for Metropolitan Desegregation* (Washington, D.C.: U.S. Government Printing Office, 1974).

———. *Racial Discrimination in the United States* (New York: Harper & Row, 1975).

———, ed. *The Sociology of Race Relations* (New York: The Free Press, 1980).

Pettigrew, Thomas F., and Martin, Joanne. "Shaping the Organizational Context for Black American Inclusion," in George Levinger, ed. *Black Employment Opportunities: Macro and Micro Perspectives,* Special Issue, *Journal of Social Issues* 43, no. 1 (1987):41–78.

———. "Organizational Inclusion of Minority Groups: A Social Psychological Analysis," in Jan Pieter van Oudenhoven and Tineke M. Willemsen, eds. *Ethnic Minorities* (Amsterdam: Swets & Zeitlinger, 1989), 169–200.

Philp, Kenneth R., ed. "The Indian Reorganization Act Fifty Years Later," in Kenneth R. Philp, ed. *Indian Self-Rule* (Salt Lake City: Howe Brothers, 1986), 15–25.

Philpott, Thomas Lee. *The Slum and the Ghetto* (New York: Oxford University Press, 1978).

Piore, Michael J. *Birds of Passage: Migrant Labor and Industrial Societies* (New York: Cambridge University Press, 1979).

Porter, Judith R., and Robert E. Washington. "Black Identity and Self-Esteem: A Review of Studies of Black Self-Concept, 1968–1978," in Alex Inkeles, James Coleman, and Ralph Turner, eds. *Annual Review of Sociology,* vol. 5 (Palo Alto, Calif.: Annual Reviews, 1979), 53–74.

Portes, Alejandro. "Dilemmas of a Golden Exile: Integration of Cuban Refugee Families in Milwaukee," *American Sociological Review 34* (August 1969):505–518.

———. "Modes of Structural Incorporation and Present Theories of Immigration," in Mary M. Kritz, Charles B. Keely, and Sylvano M. Tomasi, eds. *Global Trends in Migration* (Staten Island, N.Y.: CMS Press, 1981), 279–297.

Portes, Alejandro, and Bach, Robert L. *Latin Journey* (Berkeley: University of California Press, 1985).

Portes, Alejandro, and Rumbaut, Ruben G. *Immigrant America: A Portrait* (Berkeley: University of California Press, 1990).

Poston, Dudley L., Jr., and Alvírez, David. "On the Cost of Being a Mexican American Worker," *Social Science Quarterly* 53 (March 1973):697–709.

Poston, Dudley L., Jr.; Alvírez, David; and Tienda, Marta. "Earnings Differences between Anglo and Mexican American Male Workers in 1960 and 1970: Changes in the 'Cost' of Being Mexican American," *Social Science Quarterly* 57 (December 1976):618–631.

Pottinger, J. Stanley. "The Drive Toward Equality," in Barry R. Gross, ed. *Reverse Discrimination* (Buffalo, N.Y.: Prometheus Books, 1977), 41–49.

Price, John A. "The Migration and Adaptation of American Indians to Los Angeles," in Howard M. Bahr, Bruce A. Chadwick, and Robert C. Day, eds. *Native Americans Today* (New York: Harper & Row, 1972), 428–439.

Proshansky, Harold. "The Development of Intergroup Attitudes," in Lois Wladis Hoffman and Martin L. Hoffman, eds. *Review of Child Development Research,* vol. 2 (New York: Russell Sage Foundation, 1966), 311–371.

Prucha, Francis Paul. *American Indian Policy in the Formative Years* (Cambridge, Mass.: Harvard University Press, 1962).

Quint, Howard H.; Cantor, Milton; and Albertson, Dean; eds. *Main Problems in American History,* 4th ed., vol. 1. (Homewood, Ill.: Dorsey, 1978).

Rainwater, Lee, and Yancey, William L. *The Moynihan Report and the Politics of Controversy* (Cambridge, Mass.: MIT Press, 1967).

Randolph, A. Philip. "The Call to the March on Washington," in Gilbert Osofsky, ed. *The Burden of Race* (New York: Harper Torchbooks, [1941] 1967a), 396–399.

———. "Let the Negro Masses Speak," in Gilbert Osofsky, ed. *The Burden of Race* (New York: Harper Torchbooks, [1941] 1967b), 392–396.

———. "Address to the Policy Conference," in August Meier, Elliott Rudwick, and Francis L. Broderick, eds. *Black Protest Thought in the Twentieth Century,* 2nd ed. (Indianapolis and New York: Bobbs-Merrill, 1971a), 224–233.

———. "A. Philip Randolph Urges Civil Disobedience Against a Jim Crow Army," in August Meier, Elliott Rudwick, and Francis L. Broderick, eds. *Black Protest Thought in the Twentieth Century,* 2nd ed. (Indianapolis and New York: Bobbs-Merrill, 1971b), 233–238.

Reich, Michael. "The Economics of Racism," in David M. Gordon, ed. *Problems in Political Economy* (Lexington, Mass.: D. C. Heath, 1971).

Reimers, David M. "Post-World War II Immigration to the United States: America's Latest Newcomers," in Milton M. Gordon, ed. *The Annals: America as a Multicultural Society 454* (March 1981):1–12.

———. *Still the Golden Door* (New York: Columbia University Press, 1985).

Reinhold, Robert. "Police Are Slow to React as the Violence Spreads," *The New York Times* (May 1, 1992):A1, A12.

Reisler, Mark. *By the Sweat of Their Brow: Mexican Immigrant Labor in the United States, 1900–1940* (Westport, Conn.: Greenwood, 1976).

Reynaldo, Rosaldo; Calvert, Robert A.; and Seligman, Gustav L., Jr.; eds. Chicano: *The Evolution of a People* (Malabar, Fla.: Krieger, 1982), 269–272.

Rhoades, Everett R.; Mason, Russell D.; Eddy, Phyllis; Smith, Eva M.; and Burns, Thomas R. "The Indian Health Service Approach to Alcoholism Among American Indians and Alaska Natives," *Public Health Reports* 103 (November-December 1988):621–627.

Richardson, Lynda. "A Suburb Seeks Clues After a Lawless Night," *The New York Times* (May 13, 1992):A13.

Riis, Jacob A. *How the Other Half Lives* (New York: Hill and Wang, [1890] 1957).

Rischin, Moses, ed. *Immigration and the American Tradition* (Indianapolis: Bobbs-Merrill, 1976).

Rist, Ray C., ed. *Desegregated Schools* (New York: Academic Press, 1979).

Rives, George Lockhart. *The United States and Mexico, 1821–1848* (New York: Scribner's, 1913).

Roberts, Sam. "Milestone in Queens: Black Households Reach Income Parity," *New York Times,* Monday, (June 8, 1992):A1.

Robinson, J. W., and Preston, J. D. "Equal-Status Contact and Modification of Racial Prejudice: A Re-examination of the Contact Hypothesis," *Social Forces* 54 (June 1976):911–924.

Robinson, William L., and Spitz, Stephen L. "Affirmative Action: Evolving Case Law and Shifting Philosophy," *The Urban League Review* 10 (Winter 1986–87):84–100.

Roche, John P., and Gordon, Milton M. "Can Morality Be Legislated?" in Kimball Young and Raymond W. Mack, eds. *Principles of Sociology,* 3rd ed. (New York: American Book, 1965), 332–336.

Rodman, Hyman. "Technical Note on Two Rates of Mixed Marriage," *American Sociological Review* 30 (October 1965):776–778.

Romano, Octavio Ignacio. "The Anthropology and Sociology of the Mexican Americans," *El Grito* 2 (Fall 1968):13–26.

Romo, Ricardo. *East Los Angeles: History of a Barrio* (Austin: University of Texas Press, 1983).

Romo, Ricardo, and Paredes, Raymund, eds. *New Directions in Chicano Scholarship* (La Jolla, Calif.: Chicano Studies Program, University of California, San Diego, 1978).

Romo, Ricardo, and Romo, Harriett. "Introduction: The Social and Cultural Context of the Mexican American Experience in the United States," in Rodolfo O. de la Garza, Frank D. Bean, Charles M. Bonjean, Ricardo Romo, and Rodolfo Alvarez, eds. *The Mexican American*

Experience (Austin: University of Texas Press, 1985), 317–331.

Roosevelt, Franklin D. "Executive Order 8802," in Gilbert Osofsky, ed. *The Burden of Race* (New York: Harper Torchbooks, [1941] 1967), 400–401.

Rose, Peter I., ed. *Nation of Nations* (New York: Random House, 1972).

Rosen, Bernard. "Race, Ethnicity, and the Achievement Syndrome," *American Sociological Review* 24 (1959):47–70.

Rosenbaum, Robert J. *Mexican Resistance in the Southwest: "The Sacred Right of Self-Preservation"* (Austin: University of Texas Press, 1981).

Rosenberg, Morris, and Simmons, Roberta. *Black and White Self-Esteem: The Urban School Child* (Washington, D.C.: American Sociological Association, 1972).

Rostow, Eugene V. "Our Worst Wartime Mistake," *Harper's Magazine* (September 1945):193–201.

Roy, Prodipto. "The Measurement of Assimilation: The Spokane Indians," in Howard M. Bahr, Bruce A. Chadwick, and Robert C. Day, eds. *Native Americans Today* (New York: Harper & Row, 1972), 225–239.

Rubenstein, Richard E. *Rebels in Eden* (Boston: Little, Brown, 1970).

Rustin, Bayard. ". . . A Workable and Christian Technique for the Righting of Injustice," in August Meier, Elliott Rudwick, and Francis L. Broderick, eds. *Black Protest Thought in the Twentieth Century,* 2nd ed. (Indianapolis and New York: Bobbs-Merrill, 1971), 233–238.

Ryan, William. *Blaming the Victim* (New York: Vintage Books, 1971).

St Cartmail, Keith. *Exodus Indochina* (Auckland, New Zealand: Heinemann, 1983).

St. John, Nancy H. *School Desegregation Outcomes for Children* (New York: Wiley, 1975).

Salholz, Eloise, and Miller, Mark. "Curbing the Hatemongers," *Newsweek* (September 19, 1988):29.

Samora, Julian, ed. *La Raza: Forgotten Americans* (South Bend, Ind.: University of Notre Dame Press, 1966).

Sanchez, George I. "Pachucos in the Making," in Wayne Moquin and Charles Van Doren, eds. *A Documentary History of the Mexican Amer-*

icans (New York: Bantam Books, 1972), 409–415.

Sandefur, Gary D., and McKinnell, Trudy. "American Indian Intermarriage," *Social Science Research* 15 (December 1986):347–371.

Sandefur, Gary D., and Scott, Wilbur J. "Minority Group Status and the Wages of Indian and Black Males," *Social Science Research* 12 (March 1983):44–68.

Sanders, Jimy M., and Nee, Victor. "Limits of Ethnic Solidarity in the Enclave Economy," *American Sociological Review* 52 (December 1987): 745–773.

Saunders, Lyle. *Cultural Difference in Medical Care* (New York: Russell Sage Foundation, 1954).

Sawhill, Isabel V. "What About America's Underclass?" in Kurt Finsterbusch, ed. *Sociology 91/92* (Guilford, Conn.: Dushkin Publishing Group, 1991), 175–184.

Schermerhorn, Richard A. *These Our People* (Boston: D. C. Heath, 1949).

———. *Comparative Ethnic Relations* (New York: Random House, 1970).

Schlesinger, Arthur M., Jr. *The Disuniting of America* (New York: W. W. Norton & Company, 1992).

Schoen, Robert, and Cohen, Lawrence E. "Ethnic Endogamy among Mexican American Grooms: A Reanalysis of Generational and Occupational Effects," *American Journal of Sociology* 86 (September 1980):359–366.

Schoen, Robert, and Kluegel, James R. "The Widening Gap in Black and White Marriage Rates: The Impact of Population Composition and Differential Marriage Propensities," *American Sociological Review* 53 (December 1988):895–907.

Schoen, Robert; Nelson, Verne E.; and Collins, Marion. "Intermarriage among Spanish Surnamed Californians, 1962–1974," *International Migration Review* 12 (1978):359–369.

Schofield, Janet Ward. "Black-White Contact in Desegregated Schools," in Miles Hewstone and Rupert Brown, eds. *Contact and Conflict in Intergroup Encounters* (Oxford: Basil Blackwell, 1986), 79–92.

Schofield, Janet Ward, and Sagar, H. Andrew. "The Social Context of Learning in an Interracial School," in Ray C. Rist, ed. *Desegregated Schools* (New York: Academic Press, 1979), 155–199.

Schuman, Howard, and Bobo, Lawrence. "Survey-Based Experiments on White Racial Attitudes toward Residential Integration," *American Journal of Sociology* 94 (September 1988): 273–299.

Schuman, Howard, and Hatchett, Shirley. *Black Racial Attitudes: Trends and Complexities* (Ann Arbor: The University of Michigan Institute for Social Research, 1974).

Schuman, Howard, and Johnson, Michael P. "Attitudes and Behavior," in Alex Inkeles, ed. *Annual Review of Sociology* (Palo Alto, Calif.: Annual Reviews, 1976), 161–207.

Schuman, Howard; Steeh, Charlotte; and Bobo, Lawrence. *Racial Attitudes in America* (Cambridge, Mass.: Harvard University Press, 1985).

Scott, Douglas D., and Connor, Melissa A. "Postmortem at the Little Bighorn," *Natural History* 95 (June 1986):46–55.

Scott, Robin Fitzgerald. "Wartime Labor Problems and Mexican-Americans in the War," in Manuel P. Servín, ed. *An Awakening Minority: The Mexican Americans,* 2nd ed. (Beverly Hills, Calif.: Glencoe Press, 1974), 134–142.

See, Katherine O'Sullivan, and Wilson, William J. "Race and Ethnicity," in Neil J. Smelser, ed. *Handbook of Sociology* (Newbury Park, Calif.: Sage Publications, 1988), 223–242.

Seller, Maxine S. "Historical Perspectives on American Immigration Policy: Case Studies and Current Implications," in Richard R. Hofstetter, ed. *U.S. Immigration Policy* (Durham, N.C.: Duke University Press, 1984), 137–162.

Semyonov, Moshe, and Cohen, Yinon. "Ethnic Discrimination and the Income of Majority-Group Workers," *American Sociological Review* 55 (February 1990):107–114.

Servín, Manuel P., ed. *An Awakening Minority: The Mexican Americans,* 2nd ed. (Beverly Hills, Calif.: Glencoe Press, 1974).

Sheldon, Paul M. "Community Participation and the Emerging Middle Class," in Julian Samora, ed. *La Raza: Forgotten Americans* (South Bend, Ind.: University of Notre Dame Press, 1966), 125–157.

Sherwood, Mary. "Striving Toward Assimilation," *Corpus Christi Times-Caller* (December 29, 1988):D14–16.

Shuey, Audrey M. *The Testing of Negro Intelligence,* 2nd ed. (New York: Social Science Press, 1966).

Siegel, Paul M. "On the Cost of Being a Negro," *Sociological Inquiry* 35 (Winter 1965):41–57.

Simmel, Georg. "The Stranger," in Kurt H. Wolf, translator, *The Sociology of Georg Simmel* (Glencoe, Ill.: Free Press, [1908] 1950), 402–406.

Simmons, Roberta G. "Blacks and High Self-Esteem: A Puzzle," *Social Psychology* 41 (March 1978):54–57.

Simon, Julian L. "Don't Close Our Borders," *Newsweek* (February 27, 1984):11; reprinted in Steven Anzovin, ed. *The Problem of Immigration* (New York: H.W. Wilson, 1985), 129–131.

Simpson, George Eaton, and Yinger, J. Milton. *Racial and Cultural Minorities,* 4th ed. (New York: Harper & Row, 1972).

Singer, Lester. "Ethnogenesis and Negro Americans Today," *Social Research* 29 (Winter 1962): 419–432.

Skinner, B. F. *About Behaviorism* (New York: Alfred A. Knopf, 1974).

Sklare, Marshall. "American Jewry: Social History and Group Identity," in Norman R. Yetman and C. Hoy Steele, eds. *Majority & Minority,* 2nd ed. (Boston: Allyn and Bacon, 1975), 261–273.

Skolnick, Jerome H. "Black Militancy," in Norman R. Yetman and C. Hoy Steele, eds. *Majority & Minority,* 2nd ed. (Boston: Allyn and Bacon, 1975), 557–577.

Sly, David F., and Pol, Louis G. "The Demographic Context of School Segregation and Desegregation," in Thomas F. Pettigrew, ed. *The Sociology of Race Relations* (New York: The Free Press, 1980), 397–407.

Smith, Abbot Emerson. *Colonists in Bondage* (Chapel Hill: University of North Carolina Press, 1947).

Smith, James P., and Welch, Finis. *Race Differences in Earnings: A Survey and New Evidence* (Santa Monica, Calif.: The Rand Corporation, 1978).

———. *Closing the Gap: Forty Years of Economic Progress for Blacks* (Santa Monica, Calif.: The Rand Corporation, 1986).

Smith, Lillian. *Killers of the Dream* (Garden City, N.Y.: Doubleday, 1963).

Smothers, Ronald. "Klan Vows to 'Have Our Say' After Mayor Cancels Permit," *New York Times* (May 9, 1992):5.

Snipp, C. Matthew. *American Indians: The First of This Land* (New York: Russell Sage Foundation, 1989).

Snipp, C. Matthew, and Sandefur, Gary D. "Earnings of American Indians and Alaskan Natives: The Effects of Residence and Migration," *Social Forces* 66 (June 1988):994–1008.

Sørensen, Annmette; Taeuber, Karl E.; and Hollingsworth, Leslie, Jr. "Indexes of Racial Residential Segregation for 109 Cities in the United States, 1940–1970," *Sociological Focus* 8 (April 1975):125–142.

Sowell, Thomas. "'Affirmative Action' Reconsidered," in Barry R. Gross, ed. *Reverse Discrimination* (Buffalo, N.Y.: Prometheus Books, 1977), 113–131.

Spector, Rachel E. *Cultural Diversity in Health and Illness,* 2nd ed. (Norwalk, Conn.: Appleton-Century-Crofts, 1985).

Spencer, Robert F. "Language-American Babel," in Robert F. Spencer, Jesse D. Jennings, et al., eds. *The Native Americans,* 2nd ed. (New York: Harper & Row, 1977), 37–55.

Spencer, Robert F., Jennings, Jesse D., et al., eds. *The Native Americans,* 2nd ed. (New York: Harper & Row, 1977).

Spicer, Edward H. "American Indians," in Stephan Thernstrom, Ann Orlov, and Oscar Handlin, eds. *Harvard Encyclopedia of American Ethnic Groups* (Cambridge, Mass.: The Belknap Press, 1980a), 58–114.

———. "American Indians, Federal Policy Toward," in Stephan Thernstrom, Ann Orlov, and Oscar Handlin, eds. *Harvard Encyclopedia of American Ethnic Groups* (Cambridge, Mass.: The Belknap Press, 1980b), 114–122.

Spickard, Paul R. *Mixed Blood: Intermarriage and Ethnic Identity in Twentieth-Century America* (Madison: The University of Wisconsin Press, 1989).

Stanfield, John H., II. "Absurd Assumptions and False Optimism Mark the Social Science of Race Relations," *Chronicle of Higher Education* (July 6, 1988):B2.

Steele, C. Hoy. "The Acculturation/Assimilation Model in Urban Indian Studies: A Critique," in Norman R. Yetman and C. Hoy Steele, eds. *Majority & Minority,* 3rd ed. (Boston: Allyn and Bacon, 1982), 282–289.

Steinberg, Stephen. *The Ethnic Myth* (New York: Atheneum, 1981).

Steiner, Stan. *The New Indians* (New York: Harper & Row, 1968).

Stephan, Walter G. "Intergroup Relations," in Gardner Lindzey and Elliot Aronson, eds. *Handbook of Social Psychology,* 3rd ed. (New York: Random House, 1985).

———. "The Effects of School Desegregation: An Evaluation 30 Years After Brown," in Michael J. Sax and Leonard Saxe, eds. *Advances in Applied Social Psychology* (Hillsdale, N.J.: Lawrence Erlbaum, 1986), 181–206.

———. "The Contact Hypothesis in Intergroup Relations," in Clyde Hendrick, ed. *Group Processes and Intergroup Relations* (Newbury Park, Calif.: Sage Publications, 1987), 13–40.

———. "School Desegregation: Short-Term and Long-Term Effects." Paper presented in Tuscaloosa, Alabama, June 10, 1988 (mimeographed).

Stephan, Walter G., and Feagin, Joe R., eds. *School Desegregation* (New York: Plenum Press, 1980).

Stevens, Gillian. "The Social and Demographic Context of Language Use in the United States," *American Sociological Review* 57 (April 1992):171–185.

Stevens, Gillian, and Swicegood, Gray. "The Linguistic Context of Ethnic Endogamy," *American Sociological Review* 52 (February 1987): 73–82.

Stewart, Kenneth M. "American Indian Heritage: Retrospect and Prospect," in Robert F. Spencer, Jesse D. Jennings, et al., eds. *The Native Americans* (New York: Harper & Row, 1977), 501–522.

———. "The Urban Native Americans," in Robert F. Spencer, Jesse D. Jennings, et al., eds. *The Native Americans* (New York: Harper & Row, 1977), 523–537.

Stonequist, Everett V. *The Marginal Man* (New York: Scribner's, 1937).

Strand, Paul J., and Jones, Woodrow, Jr. *Indochinese Refugees in America* (Durham, N.C.: Duke University Press, 1985).

"Success Story: Japanese American Style," *The New York Times Magazine* (January 9, 1966):20–43.

Sugimoto, Howard H. "The Vancouver Riots of 1907: A Canadian Episode," in Hilary Conroy and T. Scott Miyakawa, eds. *East Across the Pacific* (Santa Barbara, Calif.: American Bibliographical Center-CLIO Press, 1972), 92–126.

Sumner, William Graham. *Folkways* (Boston: Ginn and Co., 1906).

Swinton, David H. "Economic Status of Blacks 1987," in Janet Dewart, ed. *The State of Black America 1988* (New York: The National Urban League, 1988), 129–152.

Svensson, Frances. *The Ethnics in American Politics: American Indians* (Minneapolis: Burgess, 1973).

Sydnor, Charles S. *American Revolutionaries in the Making* (New York: The Free Press, 1965).

Szymanski, Albert. "Racial Discrimination and White Gain," *American Sociological Review* 41 (June 1976):403–414.

Tabb, William K. "What Happened to Black Economic Development?" *The Review of Black Political Economy* 9 (Summer 1979):392–415.

Tachiki, Amy. "Introduction," in Amy Tachiki, Eddie Wong, Franklin Odo, and Buck Wong, eds. *Roots: An Asian American Reader* (Los Angeles: The Regents of the University of California, 1971), 1–5.

Taeuber, Karl E., and Taeuber, Alma F. "The Negro as an Immigrant Group: Recent Trends in Racial and Ethnic Segregation in Chicago," *American Journal of Sociology* 69 (January 1964):374–394.

———. *Negroes in Cities* (New York: Atheneum, 1969).

Tajfel, Henry, and Turner, J. C. *An Integrative Theory of Intergroup Conflict* (Monterey, Calif.: Brooks/Cole, 1979).

Takagi, Paul. "The Myth of 'Assimilation in American Life,'" *Amerasia Journal* 3 (Fall 1973): 149–158.

Taylor, D. Garth; Sheatsley, Paul B.; and Greeley, Andrew M. "Attitudes Toward Racial Integration," *Scientific American* (June 1978): 42–49.

Taylor, Howard F. *The IQ Game* (New Brunswick, N.J.: Rutgers University Press, 1980).

Taylor, Patricia Ann. "Education, Ethnicity, and Cultural Assimilation in the United States," *Ethnicity* 8 (1981):31–49.

Taylor, Paul S. *An American-Mexican Frontier* (Chapel Hill: University of North Carolina Press, 1934).

Telles, Edward E. "Residential Segregation by Skin Color in Brazil," *American Sociological Review* 57 (April 1992):186–197.

Telles, Edward E., and Murguía, Edward. "Phenotypic Discrimination and Income Differences among Mexican Americans," *Social Science Quarterly* 71 (December 1990):682–696.

———. "The Continuing Significance of Phenotype among Mexican Americans," *Social Science Quarterly* 73 (March 1992):120–122.

tenBroek, Jacobus; Barnhart, Edward N.; and Matson, Floyd W. *Prejudice, War, and the Constitution* (Berkeley and Los Angeles: University of California Press, 1954).

Thernstrom, Abigail. "The Drive for Racially Inclusive Schools," in Harold Orlans and June O'Neill, eds. *The Annals: Affirmative Action Revisited* (September 1992):131–143.

Thernstrom, Stephan; Orlov, Ann; and Handlin, Oscar; eds. *Harvard Encyclopedia of American Ethnic Groups* (Cambridge, Mass.: The Belknap Press, 1980).

Thomas, Dorothy Swaine. *The Salvage* (Berkeley and Los Angeles: University of California Press, 1952).

Thomas, Dorothy Swaine, and Nishimoto, Richard S. *The Spoilage* (Berkeley and Los Angeles: University of California Press, 1946).

Thomas, Melvin E., and Hughes, Michael. "The Continuing Significance of Race: A Study of Race, Class, and Quality of Life in America, 1972–1985," *American Sociological Review* 51 (December 1986):830–841.

Thompson, Charles H. "The Conclusions of Scientists Relative to Racial Differences," *Journal of Negro Education* 19 (July 1934):494–512.

Thurow, Lester. *Poverty and Discrimination* (Washington, D.C.: The Brookings Institution, 1969).

Time. "Bad Landmark" (November 21, 1983).

———. Special Issue. (July 11, 1988):46–84.

———. "A National Apology" (October 22, 1990):35.

Tinker, John N. "Intermarriage and Ethnic Boundaries: The Japanese American Case," *Journal of Social Issues* 29, no. 2 (1973):49–66.

de Tocqueville, Alexis. *Democracy in America* ed. by J. P. Mayer (New York: Harper & Row, Perennial Library, [1835] 1988).

Todorovich, Miro M. "Discrimination in Higher Education," in Barry R. Gross, ed. *Reverse Discrimination* (Buffalo, N.Y.: Prometheus Books, 1977), 12–14.

Tolnay, Stewart, and Beck, E. M. "Racial Violence and Black Migration in the American South, 1910–1930," *American Sociological Review* 57 (February 1992):103–116.

Tolnay, Stewart E.; Beck, E. M.; and Massey, James L. "Black Lynchings: The Power Threat Hypothesis Revisited," *Social Forces* 67 (March 1989):605–623.

Ton, Mark. "America's Mixed Neighborhoods Need Support," *The New York Times* (July 10, 1992):A14.

Trotter, Monroe. Editorial, *Boston Guardian,* December 20, 1902; reprinted in August Meier, Elliott Rudwick, and Francis L. Broderick, eds. *Black Protest Thought in the Twentieth Century,* 2nd ed. (Indianapolis and New York: Bobbs-Merrill, 1971), 32–36.

Tuchman, Barbara W. *The First Salute* (New York: Alfred A. Knopf, 1988).

Turner, Frederick Jackson. *The Frontier in American History* (New York: Henry Holt, 1920).

Tussman, Joseph, ed. *The Supreme Court on Racial Discrimination* (New York: Oxford University Press, 1963).

Tyler, Leona. *The Psychology of Human Differences* (New York: Appleton-Century-Crofts, 1965).

Ueda, Reed. "Naturalization and Citizenship," in Stephan Thernstrom, Ann Orlov, and Oscar

Handlin, eds. *Harvard Encyclopedia of American Ethnic Groups* (Cambridge, Mass.: The Belknap Press, 1980), 734–748.

U.S. Bureau of the Census. *U.S. Census of Population: 1950,* vol. 2, "Characteristics of the Population," part 1, United States Summary (Washington, D.C.: U. S. Government Printing Office, 1953a).

———. *U.S. Census of Population: 1950,* vol. 4, part 3, chapter c, "Persons of Spanish Surname" (Washington, D.C.: U.S. Government Printing Office, 1953b).

———. *Historical Statistics of the United States, Colonial Times to 1957* (Washington, D.C.: U.S. Government Printing Office, 1960).

———. *U.S. Census of Population: 1960* vol. 1, "Characteristics of the Population," part 1, United States Summary (Washington, D.C.: U.S. Government Printing Office, 1964).

———. *U.S. Census of Population: 1970,* Subject Reports. Final Report PC(2)-1F, "American Indians" (Washington, D.C.: U.S. Government Printing Office, 1973a).

———. *U.S. Census of Population: 1970* vol. 1, "Characteristics of the Population," part 1, United States Summary—section 2 (Washington, D.C.: U.S. Government Printing Office, 1973b).

———. *U.S. Census of Population: 1970,* Subject Reports. Final Report PC(2)-1G, "Japanese, Chinese, and Filipinos in the United States" (Washington, D.C.: U.S. Government Printing Office, 1973c).

———. *U.S. Census of Population: 1960,* Subject Reports PC(2)-1B, "Persons of Spanish Surname" (Washington, D.C.: U.S. Government Printing Office, 1973d).

———. *U.S. Census of Population: 1970,* Subject Reports PC(2)-1D, "Persons of Spanish Surname" (Washington, D.C.: U.S. Government Printing Office, 1973e).

———. *Historical Statistics of the United States, Colonial Times to 1970* (Washington, D.C.: U.S. Government Printing Office, 1975).

———. Current Population Reports, Series P-23, No. 80, *The Social and Economic Status of the Black Population in the United States: An Historical View, 1790–1978* (Washington, D.C.: U.S. Government Printing Office, 1978).

———. *Statistical Abstract of the United States: 1979,* 100th ed. (Washington, D.C.: U. S. Government Printing Office, 1979).

———. Current Population Reports, Series P-20, No. 354, *Persons of Spanish Origin in the United States: March, 1979* (Washington, D.C.: U.S. Government Printing Office, 1980).

———. *Statistical Abstract of the United States: 1988,* 108th ed. (Washington, D.C.: U.S. Government Printing Office, 1987).

———. Current Population Reports, Series P-20, No. 438, *The Hispanic Population in the United States: March, 1988* (Washington, D.C.: U.S. Government Printing Office, 1989a).

———. *Statistical Abstract of the United States: 1989,* 109th ed. (Washington, D.C.: U.S. Government Printing Office, 1989b).

———. Current Population Reports, Series P-20, No. 455, *The Hispanic Population in the United States: March 1991* (Washington, D.C.: U.S. Government Printing Office, 1991a).

———. *Statistical Abstract of the United States: 1991,* 111th ed. (Washington, D.C.: 1991b).

U.S. Commission on Civil Rights. *Fulfilling the Letter and Spirit of the Law.* (Washington, D.C.: U.S. Government Printing Office, 1976).

———. *Milliken v. Bradley: The Implications for Metropolitan Desegregation* (Washington, D.C.: U.S. Government Printing Office, 1974).

———. *Civil Rights Update* (March 1979a).

———. *Civil Rights Update* (August 1979b).

———. *Affirmative Action in the 1980s: Dismantling the Process of Discrimination* (Washington, D.C.: U.S. Government Printing Office, 1981a).

———. *Civil Rights: A National, Not a Special Interest* (Washington, D.C.: U.S. Government Printing Office, 1981b).

———. *Civil Rights Update* (September/October 1988).

———. *Civil Rights Update* (November 1988).

———. *Civil Rights Update* (March 1989).

———. *Civil Rights Update* (June 1989).

———. *Civil Rights Update* (March/April 1992).

———. *Civil Rights Update* (May/June 1992).

U.S. Department of Commerce. *Commerce News* (September 16, 1982).

———. *Commerce News* (June 12, 1991).

U.S. Department of Labor. *Facts on U.S. Working Women,* Fact Sheet No. 86-2 (Washington, D.C.: U.S. Department of Labor, Women's Bureau, 1986).

U.S. Immigration and Naturalization Service. *1985 Statistical Yearbook of the Immigration and Naturalization Service* (Washington, D.C.: U.S. Department of Justice, 1986).

———. *1990 Statistical Yearbook of the Immigration and Naturalization Service* (Washington, D.C.: U.S. Government Printing Office), 1991.

U.S. News & World Report (May 15, 1989):45–46.

U.S. Senate Committee on the Judiciary. *Immigration Reform and Control,* Report No. 97-485 (Washington, D.C.: U.S. Government Printing Office, 1982).

Vaca, Nick C. "The Mexican-American in the Social Sciences," *El Grito* 4 (Fall 1970):17–51.

Valdez, Luis. "The Tale of the Raza," in Renato Rosaldo, Robert A. Calvert, and Gustav L. Seligman, eds., *Chicano: The Evolution of a People* (Malabar, FL: Krieger, 1982), 269–272.

Valdivieso, Rafael, and Davis, Cary. *U.S. Hispanics: Challenging Issues for the 1990s* (Washington, D.C.: Population Reference Bureau, 1988).

van den Berghe, Pierre L. *Race and Racism* (New York: Wiley, 1967).

———. *Man in Society,* 2nd ed. (New York: Elsevier, 1978).

Van Every, Dale. "Cherokee Removal," in Francis Paul Prucha, ed. *The Indian in American History* (Hinsdale, Ill.: Dryden, 1971), 29–38.

van Oudenhoven, Jan Pieter. "Improving Interethnic Relationships: How Effective Is Cooperation?" in Jan Pieter van Oudenhoven and Tineke M. Willemsen, eds. *Ethnic Minorities* (Amsterdam: Swets & Zeitlinger, 1989), 25–42.

Van Til, Sally Bould, and Van Til, Jon. "The Lower Class and the Future of Inequality," in Edgar A. Schuler, Thomas Ford Hoult, Duane L. Gibson, and Wilbur B. Brookover, eds. *Readings in Sociology,* 5th ed. (New York: Thomas Y. Crowell, 1974), 313–321.

Van Valey, Thomas L.; Roof, Wade Clark; and Wilcox, Jerome E. "Trends in Residential Segregation: 1960–1970," *American Journal of Sociology* 82 (January 1977):826–844.

Vigil, James Diego. *From Indians to Chicanos* (St. Louis: Mosby, 1980).

Wagar, Linda. "Reclaiming Tribal Lands," in John A. Kromkowski, ed. *Race and Ethnic Relations 92/93,* 2nd ed. (Guilford, Conn.: The Dushkin Publishing Group, 1992):92–93.

Wagley, Charles, and Harris, Marvin. *Minorities in the New World* (New York: Columbia University Press, 1958).

Waldinger, Roger. "The Occupational and Economic Integration of the New Immigrants," in Richard R. Hofstetter, ed. *U.S. Immigration Policy* (Durham, N.C.: Duke University Press, 1984), 197–222.

Walls, Thomas. *The Japanese Texans* (San Antonio: University of Texas, Institute of Texan Cultures, 1987).

War Relocation Authority. *WRA, A Story of Human Conservation* (Washington, D.C.: U.S. Government Printing Office, 1946).

Ware, Caroline F. "Immigration," *Encyclopedia of the Social Sciences,* vol. 7 (New York: Macmillan, 1937), 587–594.

Warner, Lyle G., and DeFleur, Melvin L. "Attitude as an Interactional Concept: Social Constraint and Social Distance as Intervening Variables Between Attitudes and Action," *American Sociological Review* 34 (April 1969):153–169.

Warner, W. Lloyd, and Srole, Leo. *The Social Systems of American Ethnic Groups,* 2nd ed. (New Haven, Conn.: Yale University Press, 1946).

Warren, Robert. "Volume and Composition of U.S. Immigration and Emigration," in Roy Simon Bryce-Laporte, ed. *Sourcebook on the New Immigration* (New Brunswick, N.J.: Transaction Books, 1980), 1–14.

Washburn, Wilcomb E. "The Status Today," in Herbert L. Marx, Jr., ed. *The American Indian* (New York: H. W. Wilson, 1973), 102–104.

Washington, Booker T. *Up from Slavery* (New York: Bantam Books, 1959).

Waters, Mary C. *Ethnic Options* (Berkeley: University of California Press, 1990).

Wax, Murray L. *Indian Americans* (Englewood Cliffs, N.J.: Prentice-Hall, 1971).

Wayne, Leslie. "New Hope in Inner Cities: Banks Offering Mortgages," *The New York Times* (August 14, 1992):1, 6.

Weaver, Jerry L. "Mexican American Health Care Behavior: A Critical Review of the Literature," *Social Science Quarterly* 54 (June 1973):85–102.

Webb, Walter Prescott. *The Texas Rangers* (Austin: University of Texas Press, [1935] 1987).

Webster, Murray, Jr., and Driskell, James E., Jr. "Status Generalization: A Review and Some New Data," *American Sociological Review* 43 (April 1978):220–236.

White, Lynn C., and Chadwick, Bruce A. "Urban Residence, Assimilation and the Identity of the Spokane Indians," in Howard M. Bahr, Bruce A. Chadwick, and Robert C. Day, eds. *Native Americans Today* (New York: Harper & Row, 1972), 239–249.

Wilhelm, Sidney M. *Black in a White America* (Cambridge, Mass.: Schenkman, 1983).

Wilkerson, Isabel, "Interracial Marriage Rises, Acceptance Lags," *The New York Times* (December 2, 1991:A1).

Wilkinson, Doris Y. "Toward a Positive Frame of Reference from Analysis of Black Families: A Selected Bibliography," *Journal of Marriage and the Family* 40 (November 1978):707–708.

Williams, J. Allen, Jr. "Reduction of Tension Through Intergroup Contact," *Pacific Sociological Review* 7 (Fall 1964):81–88.

Williams, J. Allen, Jr.; Beeson, Peter G.; and Johnson, David R. "Some Factors Associated with Income among Mexican Americans," *Social Science Quarterly* 53 (March 1973):710–715.

Williams, J. Allen, Jr.; Nunn, Clyde Z.; and St. Peter, Louis. "Origins of Tolerance: Findings from a Replication of Stouffer's Communism, Conformity, and Civil Liberties," *Social Forces* 55 (December 1976):394–418.

Williams, J. Allen, Jr., and Ortega, Suzanne T. "Dimensions of Ethnic Assimilation: An Empirical Appraisal of Gordon's Typology," *Social Science Quarterly* 71 (December 1990): 697–710.

Williams, John E., and Morland, J. Kenneth. *Race, Color, and the Young Child* (Chapel Hill: University of North Carolina Press, 1976).

Williams, Norma. *The Mexican American Family: Tradition and Change* (Dix Hills, N.Y.: General Hall, 1990).

Williams, Robin M., Jr. *The Reduction of Intergroup Tensions* (New York: Social Science Research Council, 1947).

———. *Strangers Next Door* (Englewood Cliffs, N.J.: Prentice-Hall, 1964).

Wilner, Daniel M.; Walkley, Rosabelle P.; and Cook, Stuart W. *Human Relations in Interracial Housing: A Study of the Contact Hypothesis* (Minneapolis: University of Minnesota Press, 1955).

Wilson, Kenneth L., and Martin, W. Allen. "Ethnic Enclaves: A Comparison of the Cuban and Black Economies in Miami," *American Journal of Sociology* 88 (July 1982):135–160.

Wilson, Kenneth L., and Portes, Alejandro. "Immigrant Enclaves: An Analysis of the Labor Market Experiences of Cubans in Miami," *American Journal of Sociology* 86 (September 1980):295–319.

Wilson, William J. "Race Relations Models and Explanations of Ghetto Behavior," in Peter I. Rose, ed. *Nation of Nations* (New York: Random House, 1972), 259–275.

———. *The Declining Significance of Race* (Chicago: University of Chicago Press, 1978).

———. *The Truly Disadvantaged* (Chicago: University of Chicago Press, 1987).

———. "A Response to Critics of *The Truly Disadvantaged,*" in Robert G. Newby, ed. *The Truly Disadvantaged: Challenges and Prospects,* Special Issue, *Journal of Sociology and Social Welfare* 16 (December 1989):133–148.

———. "Studying Inner-City Social Dislocations: The Challenge of Public Agenda Research," *American Sociological Review* 56 (February 1991):1–14.

Wirth, Louis. "The Problem of Minority Groups," in Ralph Linton, ed. *The Science of Man in the World Crisis* (New York: Columbia University Press, 1945), 347–372.

Wittke, Carl. *We Who Built America,* 3rd ed. (Englewood Cliffs, N.J.: Prentice-Hall, 1964).

Wong, Morrison G. "Post-1965 Immigrants: Demographic and Socioeconomic Profile," in Lionel Maldonado and Joan Moore, eds. *Urban Ethnicity in the United States* (Newbury Park, Calif.: Sage Publications, 1985), 51–71.

Wood, Ralph, ed. *The Pennsylvania Germans* (Princeton, N.J.: Princeton University Press, 1942).

Woodrum, Eric. "Japanese American Social Adaptation over Three Generations." Ph.D. dissertation, University of Texas at Austin, 1978.

Woodward, C. Vann. *The Strange Career of Jim Crow* (New York: Oxford University Press, 1957).

Woodworth, R. S. "Racial Differences in Mental Traits," *Science* (February 4, 1910):171–186.

Works, Ernest. "The Prejudice-Interaction Hypothesis from the Point of View of the Negro Minority Group," *American Journal of Sociology* 67 (July 1961):47–52.

Wright, Mary Bowen. "Indochinese," in Stephan Thernstrom, Ann Orlov, and Oscar Handlin, eds. *Harvard Encyclopedia of American Ethnic Groups* (Cambridge, Mass.: The Belknap Press, 1980), 508–513.

Wrong, Dennis H. "How Important Is Social Class?" in Dennis H. Wrong and Harry L. Gracey, eds. *Readings in Introductory Sociology,* 3rd ed. (New York: Macmillan, 1977), 480–488.

Yancey, William L.; Ericksen, Eugene P.; and Juliani, Richard N. "Emergent Ethnicity: A Review and Reformulation," *American Sociological Review* 41 (June 1976):391–403.

Yarbrough, Tinsley E., ed. *The Reagan Administration and Human Rights* (New York: Praeger, 1985).

Yerkes, Robert M., ed. *Psychological Examining in the United States Army,* vol. 15. (Washington, D.C.: National Academy of Sciences), 1921.

Yetman, Norman R., ed. *Majority and Minority,* 4th ed. (Boston: Allyn and Bacon, 1985).

Yetman, Norman R., and Steele, C. Hoy, eds. *Majority & Minority,* 2nd and 3rd eds. (Boston: Allyn and Bacon, 1975 and 1982).

Zangwill, Israel. *The Melting Pot* (New York: Macmillan, 1909); abridged in Richard J. Meister, ed. *Race and Ethnicity in Modern America* (Lexington, Mass.: D. C. Heath, 1974), 15–21.

Zhou, Min, and Logan, John R. "In and Out of Chinatown: Residential Mobility and Segregation of New York City's Chinese," *Social Forces* 70 (December 1991):387–407.

Author Index

Abernathy, Ralph, 317
Ablon, Joan, 394
Abrams, Franklin, 75, 88, 94, 107, 108
Acuña, Rodolfo, 234, 240–242, 279
Adam, Barry D., 137
Adamic, Louis, 53, 63, 65, 70, 116
Adams, John Quincy, 19, 237
Adams, Romanzo, 29
Adorno, T. W., 154
Alba, Richard D., 77–79, 80, 93, 216, 350, 407, 408, 439–444, 455
Albertson, Dean, 47
Allen, Walter R., 214, 280, 297, 298, 329–333, 335–338, 350
Allsup, Carl, 257
Alvarez, Rodolfo, 5, 234–247, 256
Alvírez, David, 268, 271, 279, 280
Amherst, Jeffrey, 41
Amir, Yehuda, 161, 162
Anderson, Charles H., 56
Anderson, Mad Bear, 402
Angel, Ronald, 280
Armor, David J., 182
Aurelius, Marcus, 156
Austin, Stephen F., 238
Ayres, E. D., 253, 254

Bach, Robert L., 77, 80, 83–85, 87, 93, 223, 224, 234, 251, 346, 426, 434
Bache, R. Meade, 104
Bachman, Jerald, 137
Bahr, Howard M., 375, 380, 385

Bailey, Thomas, 223, 224
Baker, Ross K., 302
Bakke, Allan, 176
Ball, Harry V., 166
Baltzell, E. Digby, 81, 82
Banfield, Edward C., 315
Banks, Dennis, 381
Banneker, Benjamin, 102
Bardolph, Richard, 102, 284
Barker, Eugene C., 239
Barnard, William A., 160, 161, 162
Barnhart, Edward N., 106, 187, 188, 189, 200, 203, 227, 228
Baron, Harold M., 152
Baron, Robert A., 129
Barrera, Mario, 275, 278, 279
Barringer, Felicity, 145, 332
Bean, Frank D., 87, 89, 90, 260, 261, 265–268, 271, 280
Beck, E. M., 145, 147, 301, 313
Beeson, Peter G., 280
Benedict, Ruth, 117
Benn, Mark S., 160–162
Bennett, Lerone, Jr., 63, 283
Benokraitis, Nijole V., 173–175
Benteen, William, 366, 401
Berelson, Bernard, 127, 157
Berg, Ruth, 267
Berger, Morroe, 165, 168
Berkowitz, Leonard, 129, 130, 154
Bernard, William S., 75, 88, 109
Bernhard, Virginia, 43, 44, 53, 54, 63, 83, 94, 240, 282–284
Berry, Brewton, 16
Biddle, Francis, 202
Bierce, Ambrose, 121
Big Foot, 372
Bikson, Tora Kay, 163

Billingsley, Andrew, 328
Binder, Frederick M., 312
Binet, Alfred, 104
Bishop, George D., 162
Black, Virginia, 178
Black Kettle, 366, 401
Blackmun, Harry A., 177
Blatchford, Herbert, 380
Blau, Zena Smith, 117
Blauner, Robert, 233, 234, 278, 288
Block, N. J., 117
Blumenbach, Johann Friedrich, 11
Blumer, Herbert, 17
Bobo, Lawrence, 150, 154, 170, 171, 340, 449
Bodnar, John, 63
Bogardus, Emory S., 128
Bohara, Alok K., 280
Bolino, August C., 75, 93
Bonacich, Edna, 84, 145, 146, 188, 221, 222, 224, 229
Bongartz, Roy, 402
Bonjean, Charles M., 153
Bonney, Rachel A., 381, 382
Bosomworth, Thomas, 395
Boston, Thomas D., 351
Boswell, Terry E., 106, 146
Bowman, Phillip J., 332
Boyd, Robert L., 347
Boyer, William H., 114
Bradford, William, 62
Bradshaw, Benjamin S., 271
Braly, Kenneth W., 124, 125, 126
Brasher, Philip, 393
Brigham, Carl C., 105, 110–112
Brill, Howard, 80
Brink, William, 433
Brinkley-Rogers, Paul, 185
Brisbane, Robert H., 323
Broderick, Francis L., 300, 301

Broman, Clifford L., 137
Broom, Leonard, 154, 206, 210, 228
Brown, Dee, 364–367, 372, 402
Brown, Roger, 124–126, 133, 136, 143, 153, 158, 164
Bruner, Frank G., 104
Bryan, Samuel, 244
Buffalohead, W. Roger, 383
Buffon, Georges L. L. de, 12, 102
Bullard, Sara, 318, 431, 432, 435
Bunche, Ralph J., 304
Burgess, Ernest W., 38
Burma, John H., 216, 229, 339, 350
Burner, David, 43, 44, 53, 54, 83, 94, 240, 282, 283, 284
Burner, Davie, 63
Burns, W. Haywood, 317
Burr, Jeffrey A., 16, 148, 331
Busch, Ruth C., 387
Bush, George, 323
Buss, Arnold H., 130
Bustamante, Jorge A., 431
Butler, John Sibley, 154, 182, 223, 224, 289, 300–302, 346–348, 351

Cafferty, Pastora San Juan, 75, 96, 108, 109
Calhoun, John, 368
Camejo, Antonio, 279
Cantor, Milton, 47
Caplan, Nathan, 422, 424–426, 429, 430, 434
Carmichael, Stokely, 151, 322
Caroli, Betty B., 78
Carroll-Seguin, Rita, 80, 426, 434
Castro, Fidel, 86, 87, 413
Caudill, William, 218, 219
Cazares, Ralph B., 271
Chadwick, Bruce A., 375, 380, 385, 396
Chaney, James, 318
Chapa, Jorge, 267
Chaudhuri, Joyotpaul, 359, 360
Chiswick, Barry R., 75, 96, 108, 109

Chivington, J. J., 366
Choy, Marcella H., 422, 424–426, 429, 430, 434
Church, George J., 325, 349
Clark, Kenneth B., 135, 137
Clark, Tom C., 202
Clark, W. A. V., 269
Clines, Francis X., 382
Cobas, Jose A., 222
Cochran, Donna L., 328
Cody, William ("Buffalo Bill"), 372
Coffman, Thomas L., 126
Cohen, Elizabeth G., 164
Cohen, Lawrence E., 272
Cohen, Yinon, 146, 147, 154
Collier, John, 374
Collins, Marion, 271
Collins, Mary Evans, 161, 167
Collison, Michele N-K., 339
Condran, Gretchen A., 337
Connell, Evan S., 366, 401
Connor, Eugene "Bull," 317
Connor, James, 366
Connor, John W., 211, 219
Conolley, Edward S., 163
Conzen, Kathleen Neils, 63
Cook, James, 62
Cook, Stuart W., 161
Coon, Carleton S., 12
Cortina, Juan N. ("Cheno"), 235, 241, 242
Costello, Lawrence, 98, 407, 411
Cotton, Jeremiah, 268
Coward, Barbara E., 350
Crazy Horse, 364–367, 401, 402
Crevecoeur, J. Hector St. John, 27
Cronon, Edmund David, 303
Crook, George, 365, 367, 401, 402
Crosby, Alfred W., Jr., 278
Crow King, 401
Cruse, Harold, 351
Cué, Reynaldo A., 85, 87
Cuéllar, Alfredo, 235, 256, 257
Curran, Thomas J., 106, 109
Custer, George Armstrong, 365, 366, 401

Daniels, Roger, 106, 116, 187–190, 196, 201, 212, 218, 221, 225, 228, 417, 419
Darden, Joe T., 334
Davie, Maurice R., 284, 285, 289, 292, 296, 298, 312
Davies, James C., 321
Davíla, Alberto, 280
Davis, Cary, 266
Davis, Kenneth E., 150
Davis, Sally M., 393
Day, Robert C., 375, 380, 381, 385
DeFleur, Melvin L., 142, 143
Degler, Carl N., 50
Delaney, Martin, 284, 288
Delaware Prophet, 356
del Castillo, Richard Griswold, 240, 279
De Leon, Arnoldo, 279
Deloria, Vine, Jr., 368, 376, 377, 398, 403
Demo, David, 137, 154
de Montaigne, M. E., 119
Denevan, William M., 354
Deniker, Joseph, 12
Dennis, Henry C., 62, 401
Dent, David J., 338
Denton, Nancy A., 213, 214, 269, 280, 351
Desbartes, Jacqueline, 434
Deutsch, Morton, 161, 167
Devine, Patricia G., 124
DeVos, George, 218, 219
DeWitt, John L., 200–202, 208, 253
De Witt, Karen, 114
Díaz, José, 253
Díaz, Porfírio, 242, 243
Diem, Ngo Dinh, 416
Dinnerstein, Leonard, 63, 65, 72, 80, 439
Dobzhansky, Theodosius, 12, 16
Dollard, John, 129, 130, 148
Douglas, Kirk, 130
Douglas, William O., 208
Douglass, Frederick, 284, 315
Dowdall, George W., 147
Doyle, Bertram W., 148

Driskell, James E., Jr., 164
Drury, D. W., 137
DuBois, W. E. B., 281, 300, 301, 303
Ducas, George, 284, 285
Dunn, L. C., 12
Dunne, John Gregory, 251
Dworkin, Anthony Gary, 252
Dworkin, Gerald, 117
Dymowski, Robert F., 90

Easterlin, Richard A., 58
Eastman, Charles (Ohiyesa), 378, 401
Eckberg, Douglas Lee, 103, 113
Edgerton, Robert B., 280
Edwards, R. C., 278
Eggebeen, David J., 329, 343, 346
Eggers, Mitchell L., 351
Ehrlich, Howard J., 124–127, 153
Ehrlich, Paul R., 113
Eisenbruch, Maurice, 428
Eisenhower, Dwight David, 87, 173, 310, 375
Eitzen, D. Stanley, 229
Elias, Thomas D., 432
Eliot, John, 20
Elkins, Thomas D., 285–287, 341
Ellis, David, 325
Ellison, Christopher G., 152
Ellison, Ralph, 287, 330
Elson, R. M., 127
Embree, Edwin R., 62
Endo, Mitsuye, 209
Engerman, Stanley L., 286, 287
Ericksen, Eugene P., 80
Espenshade, Thomas J., 90
Essed, Philomena, 35
Estrada, Leo, 279
Evans, John, 366

Fard, W. D., 304
Farley, Reynolds, 171, 172, 214, 280, 297–329, 330–338, 343, 345, 346, 350, 442, 448, 449
Farmer, James, 307, 319

Faulkner, Harold Underwood, 63, 98, 239, 240, 290, 360
Feagin, Joe R., 151, 173–175, 211, 229, 348–351
Featherman, David L., 344
Feldman, S. Shirley, 113
Feldstein, Stanley, 98, 407, 411
Fernandez, Roberto, 266, 267
Festinger, Leon, 131
Fetterman, William, 364
Fillmore, Millard, 99
Firebaugh, Glenn, 150
Fishman, Joshua, 279
Fligstein, Neil, 266, 267
Flynn, James R., 113
Fogel, Robert William, 286, 287
Forbes, Jack D., 455
Ford, Gerald R., 417
Ford, W. Scott, 161
Fossett, Mark A., 16, 148, 229, 331
Fox, David Joseph, 136
Fox-Genovese, Elizabeth, 43, 44, 53, 54, 63, 83, 94, 240, 282–284
Francis, E. K., 62, 71, 93, 445, 446, 454
Franklin, Benjamin, 56, 63
Franklin, John Hope, 49, 50, 284, 289, 290, 301, 312
Frazier, E. Franklin, 49, 51, 52, 63, 293, 294, 297, 326–328, 346
Fredrickson, George M., 45, 62
Freedman, Edward, 162
Frenkel-Brunswik, Else, 154
Frethorne, Richard, 50
Freud, Sigmund, 154
Friedman, Robert, 151
Frisbie, W. Parker, 259, 271
Fugita, Stephen S., 213, 215, 224
Fuguitt, Glenn V., 154
Fujimoto, Isao, 212
Fujitaki, Nancy, 211, 229
Furstenberg, Frank J., Jr, 329

Galitzi, Christine A., 38
Gall, 366
Galle, Omer R., 16, 148, 229, 331

Galli, Marcia J., 357, 367, 368, 370, 371, 374, 377, 401
Galton, Francis, 103, 104
Gans, Herbert J., 344, 405, 433, 437, 443, 444
Garcia, John A., 278
Garcia, Macario, 252
Garrett, Henry E., 112
Gartner, S. L., 150
Garvey, Amy Jacques, 303
Garvey, Marcus, 281, 302–305, 319
Geen, Russell G., 130
Genovese, Eugene D., 312
Gerard, Harold B., 162, 163
Geschwender, James A., 80, 321
Giago, Tim, 383
Gibbon, John, 365
Gibbs, Jack P., 16, 17
Gilbert, G. M., 126
Glazer, Nathan, 2, 4, 29, 82, 88, 170, 176, 178, 407–410, 438, 439, 444, 452
Glenn, Norval D., 144, 147, 148, 154
Glick, Paul C., 329
Glickstein, Howard A., 155, 176, 177
Godfrey, 401
Goff, Regina, 333
Golden, Reid M., 216, 350, 455
Goldman, Peter, 350
Gómez-Quiñnes, Juan, 244, 247, 248
Goodchilds, Jacqueline D., 163
Goodman, Andrew, 318
Gordon, David M., 278
Gordon, Milton M., 21, 23, 24, 30, 37–39, 49, 65, 134, 166, 168, 178, 179, 217, 218, 226, 232, 265, 272, 330, 350
Gossett, Thomas F., 44, 102, 103
Gould, C. W., 105
Graglia, Lino A., 169, 170, 182
Graham, Hugh Davis, 177
Graham, W. A., 401
Grant, Madison, 95
Grant, Ulysses Simpson, 99

Grebler, Leo, 243, 248, 250, 251, 262, 270, 271, 278, 279
Greeley, Andrew M., 10, 75, 80, 96, 108, 109, 157, 405, 412, 439, 443, 449, 455
Green, James A., 143, 163
Greenhouse, Linda, 175
Grenier, Gilles, 263
Grodzins, Morton, 228
Gross, Andrew B., 213
Gruson, Lindsey, 382
Gundlach, James H., 387
Gurak, Douglas T., 217, 339
Gutierrez, Armando, 279
Gutman, Herbert F., 286, 287, 327, 329, 350
Guzman, Ralph C., 243, 248, 250, 251, 262, 270, 271, 278, 279

Hacker, Andrew, 101, 121, 173, 229, 333, 350, 351
Haffner, Steven M., 279
Hagan, William T., 359, 362, 363, 364, 366
Hahn, Harlan, 348, 349
Haines, David W., 428
Hallinan, Maureen T., 164, 182, 339
Hamilton, Alexander, 58
Hamilton, Charles, 151
Hamilton, David L., 153, 154, 162
Hammond, Clark, 430
Handlin, Oscar, 49, 50, 443
Hanh, Phung thi, 428
Hanihara, Masanao, 197, 198
Hansen, Marcus Lee, 5, 38, 54, 71, 72, 212, 228
Hardy, Hiroko, 430
Harlan, John Marshall, 295
Harris, Louis, 433
Harris, Marvin, 62
Harrison, Roderick J., 269, 337
Harrison, William Henry, 358
Hartz, Louis, 63
Hatchett, Shirley J., 328, 350
Hauser, Robert M., 344
Hayakawa, S.I., 406
Hazuda, Helen P., 279

Heer, David M., 339, 396
Heiss, Jerold, 137
Heller, Peter L., 280
Hendelson, William H., 415, 416
Heraclitus, 16
Herberg, Will, 29, 408, 455
Hernandez, José, 279
Hershberg, T., 329
Herskovits, Melville J., 326, 327, 350
Hertzberg, Hazel W., 368, 371, 374, 378, 379, 388, 402
Hewstone, Miles, 125, 157, 158, 161
Higham, John, 103
Hill, Richard J., 153
Hill, Robert B., 328
Hirabayashi, Gordon, 208, 209
Hirsch, Herbert, 279
Hirschman, Charles, 29, 38, 39, 106, 185, 225, 227
Hitler, Adolph, 112
Ho Chi Minh, 415
Hoffman, Abraham, 249
Hollingsworth, Leslie, Jr., 336
Holm, Tom, 402
Hook, Sidney, 176
Hoover, Herbert, 94
Hoppe, Sue Keir, 280
Horn, Miriam, 75
Horowitz, E. L., 136
Horton, John, 39, 312
Hosokawa, Bill, 185, 199, 203, 209, 212, 228
Howery, Carla B., 209
Hoxie, Frederick E., 369, 371, 402
Hughes, Charles Evans, 197
Hughes, Michael, 137, 154, 351
Hump, 401
Humphrey, Hubert, 177
Hunt, Ken, 393
Hwang, Sean-Shong, 337
Hyman, Herbert H., 150

Iadicola, Peter, 163
Ichihashi, Yamato, 187, 190–192, 195, 199
Ichioka, Yuji, 212

Ikeda, Kiyoshi, 166, 221
Iron Thunder, 401
Isaac, Larry, 349
Iwata, Masakazu, 196

Jackson, Andrew, 360, 361
Jackson, Curtis E., 357, 367, 368, 370, 371, 374, 377, 401
Jackson, Helen Hunt, 378
Jackson, James S., 328
Jackson, Robert H., 208
Jackson, Terrence D., 163
Jacobs, Paul, 51, 284, 312
Jacobson, Cardell K., 383, 403
Jaher, Frederic Cople, 63
James, Lenada, 381
James I, King of England, 42
Jaynes, Gerald David, 114, 164, 171, 178, 182, 335, 349, 350, 448
Jedlicka, Davor, 134
Jefferson, Thomas, 102, 237, 239
Jennings, Jesse D., 45
Jensen, Arthur R., 113, 117
Jiobu, Robert M., 105, 214, 215, 223, 230, 422, 423, 424, 426, 427, 429, 434
Johnson, Andrew, 290
Johnson, David R., 280
Johnson, Dirk, 350, 382, 383
Johnson, James Weldon, 302
Johnson, Lyndon B., 93, 173, 174, 318, 376, 406
Johnson, Michael P., 154
Johnston, Harry, 63
Jones, Maldwyn Allen, 54, 57, 63, 68, 69, 70, 72, 74, 75, 78, 79, 81, 93, 94, 97–99, 100, 108
Jones, Woodrow, Jr., 415–420, 422–426, 430, 434
Jordan, Terry G., 279
Jordan, Valerie Barnes, 136
Jordan, Winthrop D., 44, 46, 62, 182, 240, 312
Joseph (Chief), 367
Josephy, Alvin M., Jr., 356, 358, 360, 361, 364, 365, 367, 390, 400
Juliani, Richard N., 80

Kagiwada, George, 215, 227, 229
Kallen, Horace, 19, 30
Kantrowitz, Barbara, 214, 229
Karenga, Mavlana Ron, 350
Karlins, Marvin, 126
Karno, Marvin, 280
Katz, Daniel, 124, 125, 126
Kearny, Stephen, 240
Keefe, Susan E., 263, 264, 265, 280
Keely, Charles B., 88, 89, 90
Kelly, Gail Paradise, 416, 417, 418, 421, 426, 427, 428, 429, 433, 434
Kelly, William R., 229, 331, 349
Kennedy, John Fitzgerald, 87, 174, 318, 413
Kennedy, Ruby Jo Reeves, 216, 271, 407, 408
Kephart, William M., 134
Kerr, Louise Año Nuevo, 247
Kessler, Ronald C., 408
Kibbe, Pauline R., 239
Kifner, John, 381
Kikimura, Akemi, 217
King, James C., 11
King, Martin Luther, Jr., 156, 167, 307, 315, 316, 318, 323, 348
King, Rodney, 324, 431
King Philip (Metacom), 48
Kinzie, J. D., 428
Kitano, Harry H. L., 85, 116, 185, 194, 198, 199, 210, 211, 212, 217–220, 225, 228, 417, 419, 431
Kitsuse, John L., 206, 210, 228
Kitzes, Judith M., 393
Klineberg, Otto, 104, 117, 124
Kluckhohn, Florence, 273, 274, 350
Kluegel, James R., 150, 154, 178, 184, 351
Knox, Henry, 357
Korematsu, Fred, 208, 209
Kramer, Michael, 325
Kraut, Alan M., 75, 77, 81, 83, 84, 93, 94
Krebs, Dennis, 130
Krickus, Richard J., 411
Kriegel, Leonard, 411

Kristol, Irving, 298, 444
Kritz, Mary M., 217, 339
Kunz, E. F., 434
Kuo, Wen H., 185

Lacayo, Richard, 325, 340
La Guardia, Fiorello, 94
Lai, H. M., 106, 108
Lake, Robert W., 337
Landau, Saul, 51, 284, 312
Landry, Bart, 345
LaPiere, Richard T., 141–143
LaViolette, Forrest E., 191, 193, 194
Lawson, Stephen F., 294
Lazarus, Emma, 1
Lea, Tom, 241
Lee, Barrett A., 337
Lee, Everett S., 117
Left Hand, 366
Leighton, Alexander, 202, 203, 228
Leo, John, 209
Lerner, Max, 65
Levine, Gene N., 213, 215, 225, 226, 228
Levine, Lawrence W., 327
Levinson, Daniel J., 154
Lewis, Oscar, 341
Leyburn, James G., 63
Lichter, Daniel T., 329, 343, 346
Lieberman, Leonard, 12
Lieberson, Stanley, 10, 16, 63, 78, 81, 83, 93, 144, 154, 214, 216, 221, 229, 278, 297, 339, 340, 346, 408, 438, 439, 440, 441–444, 449, 455
Liebow, Edward R., 395
Liebow, Elliot, 342
Light, Ivan H., 194
Lin, Keh-Ming, 428
Lincoln, Abraham, 95, 99, 240, 289, 290
Lincoln, C. Eric, 302, 304
Lindzey, Gardner, 12, 17, 113, 117
Linn, Lawrence S., 142
Linnaeus, Carolus, 12
Linton, Ralph, 29
Lippmann, Walter, 117, 124, 228

Lipset, Seymour Martin, 65
Littlefield, Alice, 12
Litwack, Leon F., 44, 46, 62, 182, 240, 312
Lobel, Sharon Alisa, 126, 127
Lodge, Henry Cabot, 197, 198
Loehlin, John C., 12, 17, 113, 117
Logan, John R., 213, 337
Lohman, Joseph D., 142
London, Bruce, 152
London, Jack, 189
Lopez, Manuel Mariano, 268
Lopreato, Joseph, 77–80, 134, 135
Louis XVI, King of France, 414
Lovidio, J. F., 150
Low Dog, 401
Lurie, Nancy Oestreich, 80, 360, 363
Lutz, Donald S., 63

McAdam, Doug, 317
McCarthy, John, 137
McCone, John A., 320, 321
McCool, Daniel, 402
McFee, Malcolm, 25
McKinnell, Trudy, 396, 397
MacLeish, Archibald, 2
McLemore, S. Dale, 153, 279, 280
McNeill, William H., 354
McNickle, D'Arcy, 279, 355, 357, 359, 360, 369, 373–376
McWilliams, Carey, 106, 185, 186, 242, 250, 252–255
Malcolm X, 305, 319, 320
Maldonado, Lionel, 89
Marquez, Benjamin, 256
Marshall, Humphrey, 106
Marshall, John, 359, 380
Marshall, Thurgood, 433
Martin, Joanne, 150, 158, 165, 167, 182
Martin, W. Allen, 62, 223, 346, 430
Martinez, Jose, 431
Martínez, José P., 255
Marumoto, Masaji, 227
Marx, Karl, 145

Masaoka, Mike, 183
Massasoit, 47
Massey, Douglas S., 85, 87, 89, 213, 214, 269, 280, 337, 351
Masuda, Minoru, 211, 428
Matarazzo, Joseph, 114
Matson, Floyd W., 106, 187–200, 203, 227, 228
Matsumoto, Gary M., 211
Mazon, Mauricio, 254
Mazzoli, Romano, 90
Means, Russell, 381
Meer, Bernard, 162
Meier, August, 300, 301
Meister, Richard J., 30
Mendel, Gregor, 16
Mercer, Jane R., 163
Meredith, Gerald M., 211
Meriam, Lewis, 402
Merton, Robert K., 143, 164
Metacom (King Philip), 48
Metzger, L. Paul, 115
Meyer, Dillon S., 385
Michner, Charles, 185
Middlekauff, Robert, 63
Middleton, Russell, 138, 159
Miele, Stefano, 78
Miksch, Amos, 366
Mikulski, Barbara, 410, 411
Miles, Nelson, 366
Miller, Arthur G., 154
Miller, Dale T., 130
Miller, Mark, 431, 432
Miller, Neal E., 129
Miller, Norman, 162, 163, 164
Milner, Lucille B., 308
Mindiola, Tatcho, Jr., 280
Mintz, Sidney W., 286
Mittlebach, Frank G., 271, 272
Miyamoto, S. Frank, 191, 193, 194, 219, 228
Modell, John, 221, 222, 224, 229, 329
Monahan, Thomas P., 339–350
Monk, Maria, 97
Monsho, Kharen, 350
Montero, Darrel, 85, 213, 215, 218, 224, 414, 417, 418, 421–423, 425, 426, 428, 430, 434, 435

Montezuma, Carlos (Wassaja), 378
Moore, Helen, 163
Moore, Joan W., 89, 235, 241, 243, 248–251, 260–262, 270–272, 275, 278, 279
Moquín, Wayne, 240, 241
Morganthau, Tom, 150, 323
Morison, Samuel Eliot, 43, 283, 284
Morland, J. Kenneth, 136
Morris, Aldon, 317
Morse, Jedidiah, 401
Morse, Joseph Laffan, 415, 416
Morse, Samuel F. B., 97
Moskos, Charles C., Jr., 229
Moss, Alfred A., Jr., 49, 50, 284, 289, 290, 301, 312
Moynihan, Daniel Patrick, 4, 29, 328, 329, 407–409, 410, 438, 439, 444, 452
Mueller, Milan, 269
Muhammad, Elijah (Elijah Poole), 304, 305, 319, 320
Mura, David, 431
Murguía, Edward, 39, 235, 271, 280
Murieta, Joaquin, 235
Murphy, Frank, 208, 209
Músquiz, Ramón, 238
Mydans, Seth, 431
Myrdal, Gunnar, 122, 140, 145, 156, 165, 306, 326, 327, 350

Nash, Gary B., 45, 46, 395, 400
Nash, Philleo, 355, 356, 403
Navarro, José Antonio, 238
Nee, Victor, 229
Neidert, Lisa, 442, 448, 449
Nelson, Verne E., 271
Newby, Robert G., 345
Newman, William M., 30
Nguyen-Anh, 414
Nhan, Chau Kim, 416
Nishimoto, Richard S., 206, 228
Nixon, E. D., 316
Nixon, Richard M., 173, 377, 412, 416

Noel, Donald L., 144, 241, 279
Norton, Robert E., 435
Nostrand, Richard L., 278
Novak, Michael, 407, 412, 437
Novotny, Ann, 77, 83
Nunn, Clyde Z., 154

O'Brien, David J., 213, 215, 224
O'Brien, Sharon, 402
Officer, James E., 385, 402
O'Hare, William, 224, 333, 338, 343, 346, 350
Okimoto, Daniel, 220, 225
Old Person, Earl, 402
Oliver, Symmes C., 401
Olson, James S., 354, 376, 377, 380, 381, 387, 402, 403
Olzak, Susan, 313
O'Malley, Patrick M., 137
One Feather, Gerald, 395
Orfield, Gary, 168, 172, 182
Ortega, Suzanne T., 229, 272
Osofsky, Gilbert, 137, 170, 174, 302, 308–310, 318
Owens, Susan, 137

Pachon, Harry P., 235, 249, 250, 260–262, 271, 275, 279
Padilla, Amado M., 263–265, 280
Papademetriou, D. G., 90
Paredes, Raymond, 279
Parenti, Michael, 455
Park, Robert E., 20, 21, 24, 37, 38, 49, 54, 55, 127, 128, 210, 217, 218, 232–439, 243, 265, 452
Parker, Arthur (Gawasowannah), 378
Parkman, Margaret A., 217
Parks, Rosa, 316
Pastorius, Franz Daniel, 63
Patchen, Martin, 164
Patterson, Orlando, 286, 312
Peach, Ceri, 408
Penalosa, Fernando, 231, 272
Penn, William, 54
Perez, Lisandro, 85
Peroff, Nicholas G., 376

Pershing, John J. ("Blackjack"), 242
Petersen, William, 3, 11, 12, 17, 185, 191, 194, 196, 209, 218, 219, 229
Pettigrew, Thomas F., 150, 158, 165, 167, 171, 182, 355
Phelan, J. D., 187, 228
Philp, Kenneth R., 374
Philpott, Thomas Lee, 94, 287, 335
Piore, Michael J., 78
Pocahontas, 395
Pol, Louis G., 182
Polk, James K., 240
Pontiac, 356, 399, 400
Poole, Elijah (Elijah Muhammad), 304, 305, 319, 320
Porter, Judith R., 136, 137
Portes, Alejandro, 6, 10, 77, 80, 83–85, 87, 89, 93, 94, 116, 223, 224, 230, 234, 251, 275, 279, 346, 434
Poston, Dudley L., Jr., 268, 280
Pot, Pol, 419
Pottinger, J. Stanley, 176, 177
Pratt, Richard A., 371, 402
Preston, J. D., 160
Price, John A., 385, 395
Proshansky, Harold, 154
Prosser, Gabriel, 284, 303
Prucha, Francis Paul, 357, 358, 367

Quatrefages de Breau, J. L. A., 12
Quint, Howard H., 47

Rainwater, Lee, 328
Randolph, A. Philip, 172, 173, 304, 306, 309, 318
Rawle, William, 65
Reagan, Ronald, 323
Red Cloud, 364, 365, 366, 372
Reich, Michael, 147, 278
Reimers, David M., 63, 65, 72, 80, 87, 88, 107, 250, 251, 312, 413, 432, 435, 439
Reinhold, Robert, 324

Reisler, Mark, 248
Reitzes, Dietrich C., 142
Rendon, Armando B., 231
Reno, Marcus, 366, 401
Reynolds, Larry T., 12
Rhoades, Everett R., 393
Rhodes, Colbert, 213, 215, 225, 226, 228
Rice, Thomas D., 182
Richardson, Lynda, 182
Riis, Jacob A., 80, 83
Rinehart, James W., 126
Rives, George Lockhart, 239
Roberts, Owen J., 208
Roberts, Sam, 350
Robinson, J. W., 160
Robinson, James R., 307
Robinson, William L., 174, 175, 178
Roche, John P., 166, 168
Rodino, Peter, 90
Rodman, Hyman, 229
Rolfe, John, 395
Romano, Octavio Ignacio, 274
Romo, Harriett, 278
Romo, Ricardo, 242–254, 278–280
Roof, Wade Clark, 336
Roosevelt, Franklin D., 172, 173, 200, 379, 411
Roosevelt, Theodore, 190
Root, Elihu, 190
Rosen, Bernard, 229
Rosenbaum, Robert J., 241, 432
Rosenberg, Morris, 137
Ross, E. A., 187, 188
Rostow, Eugene V., 201, 202, 209
Roy, Prodipto, 396
Rubenstein, Richard E., 59, 100
Rudwick, Elliott, 300, 301
Rumbaut, Ruben G., 6, 10, 87, 89, 93, 94, 116, 230, 275, 279, 434
Rustin, Bayard, 307, 308
Ryan, William, 94

Sagar, H. Andrew, 164
St Cartmail, Keith, 419, 434
St John, Nancy H., 162, 163
St Peter, Louis, 154

Salholz, Eloise, 431, 432
Salter, Patricia J., 127
Sanchez, George I., 278
Sandefur, Gary D., 394, 396, 397
Sanders, Jimy M., 229
Sanford, R. Nevitt, 154
Santa Anna, Antonio Lopez de, 239
Saunders, Lyle, 274
Sawhill, Isabel V., 351
Sawyer, Jack, 217
Saxton, Alexander, 106
Schermerhorn, Richard A., 16, 77–83, 94
Schlesinger, Arthur M., Jr., 437, 451
Schneider, Mark, 337
Schoen, Robert, 271, 272, 351
Schofield, Janet Ward, 164
Schuman, Howard, 150, 154, 170, 171, 340, 350, 449
Schwerner, Michael, 318
Scott, Robin Fitzgerald, 255, 256
Scott, Wilbur J., 394
Scott, Winfield, 240
See, Katherine O'Sullivan, 134, 160, 452
Seller, Maxine S., 54, 89
Semyonov, Moshe, 146, 147, 154
Sequoyah, 359
Sheatsley, P. B., 150, 157, 449
Sheldon, Paul M., 280
Sheridan, Phillip, 365
Sherman, William Tecumseh, 364, 365
Sherwood, Mary, 271
Shuey, Audrey M., 117
Simmel, Georg, 128
Simmons, Roberta G., 137
Simon, Julian L., 91
Simon, Theodore, 104
Simpson, Alan, 90
Simpson, George Eaton, 132, 145, 153, 166
Sitting Bull, 365, 367, 372, 401
Singer, Lester, 80
Sjoberg, Gideon, 351
Skinner, B. F., 154
Sklare, Marshall, 80, 81

Skolnick, Jerome H., 451
Sly, David F., 182
Smith, Abbott Emerson, 62
Smith, James P., 333
Smith, Lillian, 148
Smothers, Ronald, 432
Snipp, C. Matthew, 47, 62, 354, 370, 386, 387, 390–393, 400, 402, 403
Sowards, Kathryn, 267
Sowell, Thomas, 173, 177, 178, 182
Spector, Rachel E., 274
Spencer, Robert F., 45
Spicer, Edward H., 45, 62, 354, 359, 361, 363, 369, 375, 376, 384, 387–389
Spickard, Paul R., 15, 216, 217, 229, 340
Spitz, Stephen L., 174, 175, 178
Spotted Tail, 366
Spuhler, J. N., 12, 17, 113, 117
Squanto (Tisquantum), 62
Sørensen, Annmette, 336
Srole, Leo, 16
Stanfield, John H., II, 344
Stanford, Leland, 106
Steeh, Charlotte, 150, 154, 170, 171, 340, 449
Steele, C. Hoy, 389
Steinberg, Stephen, 35, 221, 225, 229, 410
Steiner, Gary A., 157
Steiner, Stan, 379, 380, 381, 402
Stephan, Walter G., 137, 154, 160, 161, 163, 171, 182
Stern, Michael P., 279
Stern, William, 104
Stevens, Gillian, 216, 261, 279
Stevenson, Coke, 252
Stewart, Kenneth M., 354, 384, 389, 403
Stonequist, Everett V., 16
Strand, Paul J., 415–420, 422–426, 430, 434
Sugimoto, Howard H., 227
Sullivan, Teresa A., 75, 96, 108, 109, 350
Sumner, William Graham, 62, 119, 133, 166–168

Svensson, Frances, 375, 402, 403
Swicegood, Gray, 216, 279
Sydnor, Charles S., 58
Szymanski, Albert, 147

Tabb, William K., 323
Tachiki, Amy, 183, 186, 220
Taeuber, Alma F., 214, 335, 336
Taeuber, Karl E., 214, 335, 336
Tajfel, Henry, 133
Takagi, Paul, 225, 227
Taylor, D. Garth, 157, 449
Taylor, Howard F., 113
Taylor, P. A., 63
Taylor, Paul S., 239, 279
Taylor, Zachary, 240
Tazuma, Laurie, 428
Tecumseh, 358, 399
Telles, Edward E., 280, 285
tenBroek, Jacobus, 106, 187–189, 200, 203, 227, 228
Tenskwatawa, 358
Terman, Lewis M., 117
Terry, Alfred, 365, 401
Thernstrom, Abigail, 114
Thom, Mel, 380, 381
Thomas, Dorothy Swaine, 206, 228
Thomas, Melvin E., 351
Thompson, Charles H., 111, 112
Tienda, Marta, 87, 89, 260, 261, 265–268, 280
Tinker, John N., 217
Tisquantum (Squanto), 62
Tocqueville, Alexis de, 452
Todorovich, Miro M., 177
Togo, Heihachiro, 190
Tolnay, Stewart, 301, 313
Ton, Mark, 182
Trolier, Tina K., 153, 154
Trotter, Monroe, 300
Truman, Harry S., 173, 309
Truth, Sojourner, 284
Tsukashima, Ronald, 218
Tubman, Harriet, 284
Tuchman, Barbara W., 22
Turner, Frederick Jackson, 28
Turner, J. C., 133
Turner, Nat, 285, 303

Tussman, Joseph, 204, 208, 294, 295, 310
Two Moon, 365, 366
Tyler, Leona, 102

Ueda, Reed, 96
Usdansky, Margarett L., 350

Vaca, Nick C., 275
Valdez, Luis, 257
Valdivieso, Rafael, 266
van den Berghe, Pierre L., 134, 335
Van Doren, Charles, 240, 241
Van Every, Dale, 361
van Oudenhoven, Jan Pieter, 101, 164
Van Til, Jon, 350
Van Til, Sally Bould, 350
Van Valey, Thomas L., 336
Vernez, George, 90
Vesey, Denmark, 284, 285, 303
Vigil, James Diego, 278
Villa, Francisco ("Pancho"), 242
Voltaire, 453

Wagar, Linda, 382
Wagley, Charles, 62
Waldinger, Roger, 91, 223, 224
Walker, David, 284
Walkley, Rosabelle P., 161
Wallace, George, 412
Walls, Thomas, 228
Walsh, Paul, 114
Walters, Gary, 126
Ware, Caroline F., 110
Warner, Lyle G., 143
Warner, W. Lloyd, 16
Warren, Earl, 228, 309
Warren, Robert, 88
Warrior, Clyde, 353, 380
Washburn, Wilcomb E., 391
Washington, Booker T., 281, 299–301, 303, 351
Washington, George, 357
Washington, Robert E., 136, 137
Waters, Mary C., 4, 10, 63, 78, 81, 83, 93, 144, 154, 214, 216, 339, 340, 408, 438–442, 444, 449, 455

Wax, Murray L., 362, 363, 374, 388, 389
Waymouth, George, 62
Wayne, Leslie, 433
Weaver, Jerry L., 280
Webb, Walter Prescott, 241
Webster, Murray, Jr., 164
Weinberg, Daniel H., 269, 337
Welch, Finis, 333
Westie, Frank B., 142, 143
White, Lynn C., 396
White, Michael J., 90
White Antelope, 366, 401
Whitmore, John K., 422, 424–426, 429, 430, 434
Wilcox, Jerome E., 336
Wilhelm, Sidney M., 351
Wilkerson, Isabel, 340
Wilkie, Bruce, 381
Wilkins, Roy, 281
Wilkinson, Doris Y., 328
Willemsen, Tineke M., 101

Williams, J. Allen, Jr., 154, 229, 272, 280, 350
Williams, John E., 136
Williams, Norma, 263, 264, 275, 280
Williams, Richard A., 164, 182, 339
Williams, Robin M., Jr., 16, 114, 135, 164, 171, 178, 182, 335, 349, 350, 448
Williams, Roger, 47
Wilner, Daniel M., 161
Wilson, Kenneth L., 182, 223, 300, 301, 302, 346
Wilson, Raymond, 354, 376, 377, 380, 381, 387, 402, 403
Wilson, William J., 134, 160, 312, 343–345, 347, 348, 351, 452
Wilson, Woodrow, 108, 242
Wirth, Louis, 16, 35

Wittke, Carl, 56, 70, 73, 77, 79, 81, 93
Wong, Morrison G., 106, 185, 225, 227
Woodrum, Eric, 211, 217
Woodward, C. Vann, 182, 293, 294
Woodworth, R. S., 104
Works, Ernest, 161
Wovoka, 372
Wright, Mary Bowen, 85, 416, 417
Wrong, Dennis H., 453

Yancey, William L., 80, 137, 328
Yarbrough, Tinsley E., 177
Yerkes, Robert M., 116
Yinger, J. Milton, 132, 145, 153

Zangwill, Israel, 19
Zhou, Min, 213

Subject Index

Abenaki Indians, 382
Accommodation, cycle of race relations and, 20
Acculturation, 4. *See also* Inclusion
Achievement, rewards on basis of, 14
Affirmative action, 172–179
  in education, 175, 176–179
  in employment, 172–179
African Americans, 282–312, 315–349, 448–449.
     See also Civil Rights Movement; Slavery
  assimilation of
    cultural, 325–330
    marital, 339–340
    structural, primary, 338–339
    structural, secondary, 330–338
  cultural assimilation of, 287–288
  emancipation and Reconstruction and, 289–291
  as immigrants versus colonized minority,
    287–288
  income of, 144–145
  intelligence of. *See* Intelligence
  IQ controversy and, 102–105
    before 1924, 104–105
  migration, urbanization, and employment of,
    297–299
  prejudice and discrimination against, 142–143,
    144–145, 147
    regional and educational differences in
      whites' attitudes and, 157–158
    shifts in attitudes and, 150–151
  residential segregation and, 150
  restoration of white supremacy and, 292–297
  school segregation and. *See* School
    desegregation; School segregation
  self-hate and, 135–137
  success of, 341–348
  three-generations process and, 5, 6
  voting rights and, 294
Aggressive cues, 130
Alien and Sedition Acts of 1798, 97
Alien Land Law of 1913, 195, 196
Alien Land Law of 1920, 197
Alpha test, 104, 111–112
American Colonization Society, 288

American Creed, 122, 165
American Federation of Labor (AFL), 305
American Indian(s). *See* Native American(s)
American Indian Chicago Conference, 380
American Indian Exposition, 389
American Indian Movement (AIM), 381–382
Americanization, 2–5
American Socialist Party, 189
Anglo-American ethnic model, 22–23
  as standard, 58–60
Anglo-American society
  colonial, 22
  rise of, 41–62
    colonial Germans and, 55–57
    colonial Irish and, 53–55
    English legacy and, 42–45
    Native American-English relations and, 45–49
    during Revolutionary period, 57–60
    servants and slaves and, 49–53
Anglo conformity ideology of assimilation,
    25–26, 450–451
  Native Americans and, 373–377
Antiassimilationist theories, 36. *See also*
    Immigrant model
Anticoolie clubs, 106
Anti-Defamation League of B'nai Brith, 431
Anti-Semitism, 431
Apache Indians, 383, 387, 388
Arapaho Indians, 363, 364, 366
Army testing program, 104–105, 110, 111–112
Aryans, 112
Ascription, rewards on basis of, 14
Ashkenazim, 80–82
Asian Americans. *See also specific groups*
  education and work skills of, 86
  hostility toward, 431–432
Asiatic Exclusion League, 189, 190
Assembly centers, 203, 204
Assimilation, 4. *See also* Cultural assimilation;
    Inclusion; Marital assimilation; Structural
    assimilation
  Anglo conformity ideology of, 25–26
  cultural pluralism ideology of, 30–37

501

Assimiliation, *(continued)*
  cycle of race relations and, 21
  melting pot ideology of, 27–30, 36
    Mexican Americans and, 237
  subprocesses of, 21–25
Atlanta Compromise, 299–300

Bay Area American Indian Council of San
    Francisco, 389
Beta test, 104, 111–112
Bilingualism
  among Mexican Americans, 263
  among Native Americans, 386
Binet-Simon scale, 104
Biographies, reducing prejudice and
    discrimination through, 158–159
Birmingham, Alabama, social protest in, 317–318
Black(s). *See* African Americans
Black Codes, 290, 293
Black Eagle Flying Corps, 303
Blackfoot Indians, 363
Black Hand, 79
Black Hills, 365–367
Blacklisting, 411
Black Muslims, 304–305, 319
Black Power, 319–325
Black price, 136
Black Renaissance, 302
Black Star Steamship Line, 303
Boat people, 419–420
Boycott
  of buses, 316
  economic, African Americans and, 306
Bracero program, 87, 250–252, 255
Braceros Act of 1943, 91
Brown v. Board of Education of Topeka
    decisions, 150, 169–170, 176, 309–310,
    319, 334
Bruder Schweigen Strike Force Two, 431
Brulace Indians, 363
Buffalo, 361–362
Bureau of Indian Affairs (BIA), 368, 370–371,
    376, 379, 384, 391
Bus boycott, 316

California, anti-Asian sentiment in, 186–192
  anti-Japanese protest and, 187–189
  employment and land ownership and, 195–196
  school segregation and, 189–191
California gold rush, Chinese immigration and,
    106
Cambodia, 418–419

Carlisle School, 371
Carpetbaggers, 290
Castle Garden, 75
Caucasians. *See headings beginning with term*
    Anglo-American
Cayuga Indians, 361
Census Bureau, identification of Mexican
    Americans by, 259–261
Chapter 1 education program, 114
Cherokee Indians, 357–358, 359–360, 360, 361,
    382, 386, 389
Cherokee Nation v. Georgia decision, 359–360
Cheyenne Indians, 363, 364, 365, 366, 367
Chicago American Indian Center, 389
Chicanismo, 235–236
Chicksaw Indians, 357–358, 60
Chinese, 87
  immigration restriction and, 105–108
Chinese Exclusion Act of 1882, 91, 107–108, 110,
    111, 187, 195
Chippewa Indians, 356, 357–358, 363
Choctaw Indians, 357–358, 360, 361
Christianity. *See also* Roman Catholicism
  among Native Americans, 388
Christianization, of Native Americans, 371–373
  Spanish, 236–237
Cities
  African Americans in, 297–298, 336–337
  ethnic neighborhoods in, 409–411, 451
  Irish in, 70
  Italians in, 77, 78, 79–80
  Native Americans in, 384–386
  Russian Jews in, 82
  second great wave of immigration and, 77
Citizenship
  eligibility of Japanese Americans for, 195–196
  eligibility of Native Americans for, 373
Citizen's leagues, Japanese American, 199
Civil Rights Act of 1866, 290
Civil Rights Act of 1964, 170, 174, 176–177, 318
Civil Rights Act of 1991, 323
Civil Rights Movement, 149–150, 299–311,
    316–325
  Booker T. Washington and, 299–300
  interracial violence and, 301–302
  legal victories and, 309–311
  NAACP and, 301, 302, 305–306
  Niagara Movement and, 300–301
  rise of direct action and, 316–325
    Black Power and, 319–325
  separatism and, 302–305
  strategy, tactics, and conflict and, 305–309

Civil War
  African American military service in, 289
  immigration patterns and, 74
  loyalty of immigrants and, 99
  slave resistance and, 285
Cognitive dissonance, prejudice and, 131–132
Coleman Report, 391
Colonialism, internal, theory of, 36
Colonial model, 444, 446–447
  African Americans and, 287–288
  Mexican Americans and. *See* Mexican
    American(s), colonial model and
  Native Americans and, 383–386
Colonies
  African, 233
  English, 21–22, 42–45
    Native Americans and, 45–49, 236, 355
    slavery in, 282–284
    Spanish colonies compared with, 236
  Germans in, 55–57
  Irish in, 53–55, 57
  servants and slavery in, 49–51
  Spanish, 236–238
    English colonies compared with, 236
Comanche Indians, 361–362, 363, 388
Community cohesion, Japanese-American
    success and, 219–220
Community Service Organization (CSO), 257
Competition, cycle of race relations and, 20
Confederate Hammer Skins, 432
Congress of Racial Equality (CORE), 307–308,
    309, 316, 317, 320, 449
Constitution of the United States, 58–59
  Fifteenth Amendment to, 294
  Fifth Amendment to, 309
  Fourteenth Amendment to, 290, 309
  Thirteenth Amendment to, 290
Contact, cycle of race relations and, 20
Contact hypothesis, 160
Cosa Nostra, 79
Cotton, 292
Crackers, 293
Creation Generation, 234, 240
Creed-deed discrepancy, discrimination and,
    140–144
Creek Indians, 360, 361
Crime
  among Italians, 79
  among Mexican Americans, 253–255
Crow Indians, 363, 364
Cubans, 86
  education and work skills of, 86–87

Cultural assimilation, 23, 24
  of African Americans, 287–288, 325–330
  of Japanese Americans, 210–212
  of Mexican Americans, 261–265
  of Native Americans, 49, 386–390
  of Vietnamese, 4220425
Cultural pluralism ideology of assimilation,
    30–37, 450–451, 452
  Native Americans and, 373–377
Cultural similarity, inclusion and, 9–10
Cultural transmission theories of prejudice,
    123–128
  social distance and, 127–128
  stereotypes and, 124–127
Culture of poverty thesis, 341–346
Cyclical migration, 77, 78

Dakota Indians, 362, 363
Dawes Act of 1887, 369–370, 371, 373, 374, 378,
    384, 397
Declaration of Rights of the Negro Peoples of
    the World, 303
Delaware Indians, 356, 357–358, 361
Department of Health, Education, and Welfare
    (HEW), 170, 171
Deportation, of Mexican aliens, 249–250
Desegregation. *See* School desegregation
Dillingham Commission, 108
Discrimination, 139–152. *See also* Prejudice and
    discrimination, reducing
  definition of, 120–121
  in education, affirmative action and, 175, 176–179
  in employment, affirmative action and, 172–179
  group gains theories of, 144–149
  institutional structure theories of, 149–152
  against Mexican Americans, in schools, 266
  situational pressures theories of, 140–144
Displaced people, 85–86, 87–89
Displaced Persons Act of 1948, 87–88, 91
Dissimilarity, indexes of, 213–214
Dissonance, prejudice and, 131–132
Dolls test, 135–136
Draft Riots, 99
Dual economy theory, 223. *See also* Split labor
    market
Dutch, cultural assimilation of, 24–25

Economic boycott, African Americans and, 306
Education. *See also* School desegregation; School
    segregation
  affirmative action and, 175, 176–179
  of African Americans, 333–335

Education, *(continued)*
Anglo conformity versus cultural pluralism and, 450–451
desegregation in, 176–179
employment and, 151
of Mexican Americans, 266–267
of Native Americans, 390–391
of native Americans, 370–371
second great stream of immigration and, 86–87
of Vietnamese, 425
Educational approach, to reducing prejudice and discrimination. *See* Prejudice and discrimination, reducing
Ellis Island, 75
Emancipation Proclamation, 289
Emergency Quota Act of 1921, 108–109, 197
Emergent ethnicity, 80
Employment
affirmative action and, 172–179
of African Americans, 297–298, 305, 330–332, 343–344
of Chinese, 106
educational requirements for, 151
institutional discrimination in, 151–152
of Italians, 77, 78
of Japanese Americans, 195, 196
of Jews, 84
German, 81
Russian, 82–83
of Mexican Americans, 247–248, 249, 265–266, 275
Bracero program and, 250–252
of Native Americans, 391–393
primary and secondary labor markets and, 222
second great stream of immigration and, 86–87
split labor market and, 146–148
Mexican Americans and, 275
of Vietnamese, 425–427
Endogamy, 216
Endo v. United States decision, 209
Entrepreneurial minorities, 84, 346–347
Environmentalists, 101
Equal Employment Opportunity Commission (EEOC), 174
Ethnic enclave theory, 84, 223
Ethnic hegemony, theory of, 223–224
Ethnicity
concept of, 10–13
emergent, 80

future of, 437–454
primary and secondary ethnic groups and, 445–447, 452
white ethnic assimilation and, 439–445
revival of, 406–412
Ethnic neighborhoods, 409–411, 451. *See also* Residential segregation
Ethnocentrism
biocultural view of, 134–135
colonial, 44–45
prejudice and, 133–135
Ethnogenesis, 80
Evacuation Claims Act of 1948, 209
Executive Order 8802, 173, 306–307
Executive Order 9066, 200
Executive Order 10308, 173
Executive Order 10557, 173
Executive Order 10925, 174
Executive Order 11246, 174–175, 177
Exogamy, 216

Factual information, reducing prejudice and discrimination through, 157–158
Fair Employment Practices Committee (FEPC), 173, 307
Families
African-American, 329–330
Japanese American, 192–195
Mexican-American, 263–265
Vietnamese, 428
Federal Acknowledgement Program, 377
Federal Housing Administration, 411
Federation for Immigration Reform (FAIR), 90
Fetterman Massacre, 364
Films, reducing prejudice and discrimination through, 158–159
First-generation Americans, 3
Fishing rights, Native Americans and, 381, 382
Five Civilized Tribes, 360, 369, 378, 395
Five Nations of the Iroquois. *See* Iroquois
Forty-Eighters, 73–74, 98
Fox Indians, 361, 386
Freedmen's Bureau, 289, 291
Freedom Ride, 317
French and Indian War, 356
French explorers, 355–356
Frontier thesis, 28
Frustration-aggression hypothesis, prejudice and, 129–133
Fugitive Slave Law of 1850, 284

Full-blood, 396
Fundamental attribution error, 143

Gaming, Native Americans and, 382–383
Garment industry, 83
General Allotment Act of 1887, 369–370, 371,
    373, 374, 378, 384, 397
Geneva Accords of 1954, 416
Geneva Agreements of 1954, 415–416
Gentleman's Agreement, 159
Gentlemen's Agreement, 190–191, 192, 197, 198
Georgia Colony, slavery in, 283
Germans
    antiforeign sentiment directed against, 98
    colonial, 55–57
    Jewish, 80–82
    nineteenth-century immigration of, 71–74
    stereotypes of, 126
Ghetto poor, 343344
Ghost Dance Religion, 372, 373
G.I. Forum, 257
Grandfather clause, voting and, 294
Great Depression, 110
    Mexican Americans and, 249–250
*Green v. County School Board of New Kent
    County* decision, 170
Greenville Treaty of 1795, 358
Griggs v. Duke Power Co. decision, 175
Group gains theories of discrimination, 144–149
Group identification theories of prejudice,
    133–137
    ethnocentrism and, 133–135
    self-hate and, 135–137
Group size, inclusion and, 9
Guadalupe Hidalgo, Treaty of, 241, 363
Haciendas, 237

Handsome Lake Religion, 388
Harlem, 298
Hart-Cellar Act of 1965, 88, 91
Haymarket Square bombing, 100
Head Start program, 114
Health and illness behavior, of Mexican
    Americans, 274
Health care, of Native Americans, 393
Hereditarians, 101
Hirabayashi v. United States decision, 208
Hispanics, education and work skills of, 86
Home sweatshops, 83
Homologous affiliation, prejudice and, 134–135
House Concurrent Resolution 108, 375, 377, 379

Hungarian Revolution of 1956, 413
Hunkpapa Indians, 363
Huron Indians, 356

"I Have a Dream" speech, 318
Illegal immigrants. *See* Undocumented workers
Immigrant model, 444–445, 446–447
    African Americans and, 287–288
    Mexican Americans and, 243–247
        colonial model compared with, 236–237,
        244–247
    Native Americans and, 383–386
Immigration, 66–93. *See also specific groups*
    changing patterns of, 74–76
    control of, 74–75, 84–85, 87–90, 91, 105–115
        Chinese and, 105–108
        Immigration Act of 1924 and, 108–111
        IQ controversy and, 111–115
        parole provision and, 87, 416
        preference system and, 89
        quotas and, 87, 88, 108–110, 197, 249
        undocumented workers and, 89–90
    first great stream of, 67–74, 441–442
        German, 71–74
        Irish, 68–71
    second great stream of, 76–85, 108, 441–442
        antiforeign sentiment and, 100
        Italian, 77–80
        Jewish, 80–85
    third great stream of, 85–92, 412–430
Immigration Act of 1875, 75, 111
Immigration Act of 1917, 108, 111
Immigration Act of 1921, 108–109, 111, 197
Immigration Act of 1924, 84–85, 105, 109–110,
    111, 406
    open door policy for Mexicans under, 248
Immigration Act of 1990, 89, 91
Immigration and Nationality Act (INA) of 1952,
    91, 413
    1965 Amendments to, 88, 89, 91, 110
    quota approach of, 88
Immigration and Nationality Act of 1965, 406
Immigration Quota Act of 1924, 197
Immigration Reform and Control Act (IRCA) of
    1986, 89, 91
Immigration Restriction League, 108
Inclusion, 6–13. *See also* Assimilation
    group size, cultural similarity, and time of
        entry and, 9–10
    race and ethnicity and, 10–13
    voluntary entry and race and, 6–9

Income
of African Americans, 332–333, 343, 345–346
discrimination and, 144–148
of Japanese Americans, 185
of Mexican Americans, 266, 267–268
of Native Americans, 393
of Vietnamese, 426–427
Indexes of dissimilarity, 213–214
Indian(s)
American. *See* Native American(s)
Mexican, relations with Spanish, 236–237
Spanish-Indians, 235
Indian Citizenship Act of 1924, 373
Indian Civil Rights Act of 1968, 376–377
Indian Removal Act of 1830, 360
Indian Reorganization Act (IRA) of 1934,
374–375, 384
Indian Rights Association, 378
Indian Self-Determination and Educational
Assistance Act of 1975, 377
Indian Territory, 360–363
Indian Trade and Intercourse Act of 1793, 367
Indian Trade and Intercourse Act of 1834, 368
Indochina Migration and Refugee Assistance Act
of 1975, 416
Indochinese War, 416
Informal training system theory, 224
Information, factual, reducing prejudice and
discrimination through, 157–158
Institutional structure theories of discrimination,
149–152
Integrated neighborhoods, Mexican Americans
and, 270
Integration, 4. *See also* Inclusion
Intelligence
heritability of, 113
IQ testing and, 110
before 1924, 104–105
since 1924, 111–115
racial differences in, 102–105
Interagency Task Force for Indochinese
Refugees (IATF), 417–418
Intergenerational conflict
Japanese Americans and, 207, 219
Mexican Americans and, 258–259
Intergroup contact, reducing prejudice and
discrimination through, 159–165
Intermarriage. *See* Marital assimilation
Internal colonialism, theory of, 36
Interracial housing, reducing prejudice and
discrimination through, 161–162

Interracial violence, 301–302, 308, 318, 320–322,
324–325, 431, 432
Irish
colonial, 53–55
Draft Riots and, 99
nineteenth-century immigration of, 68–71
opposition to Catholicism of, 97–98
Iroquois confederacy, 45
Iroquois Indians, 356, 357–358, 361, 386, 388
relations with English, 355
Iroquois League, 361
Isei. *See* Japanese Americans, first-generation
Italians, 77–80
assimilation of, 439–440
marital, 442
Russian Jews compared with, 82–83
Jamestown colony, 21–22, 42–43
Native Americans and, 46–47
slavery in, 282
Japanese, stereotypes of, 126
Japanese American(s), 184–227
anti-Asian sentiment and, 186–187
assimilation of, 210–218
cultural, 210–212
marital, 215–218
structural, primary, 215
structural, secondary, 213–215
citizenship eligibility of, 195–196
discrimination against, 185
employment of, 195, 196
evacuation and relocation of, 200–209
camp life and, 204–207
legal issues pertaining to, 207–209
relocation program and, 202–204
exclusion of, 197–198
family and community cohesion and, 192–195
first-generation, 192–195, 199, 201
cultural assimilation of, 210, 211
intergenerational conflict and, 207, 219, 258
fourth-generation, cultural assimilation of, 212
income of, 185
land ownership and, 195, 196
picture brides and, 191–192
protest against, 187–189
school segregation and, 189–191
second-generation, 192, 193, 198–200, 201
cultural assimilation of, 210, 211
intergenerational conflict and, 207, 219, 258
marital assimilation of, 217
structural assimilation of, 215
success of, 219–220

success of, 218–226, 346
  comparison of theories of, 224–226
  cultural view of, 218–221
  structural view of, 221–224
  third-generation, 192, 199
    cultural assimilation of, 210–211, 212
    marital assimilation of, 217
    structural assimilation of, 215
    success of, 219–220
Japanese American Citizen's League (JACL),
  199
Japanese and Korean Exclusion League,
  189
Japanese Association, 194
Japanese Language School, 194, 210
Jews, 80–85
  anti-Semitism and, 431
  assimilation of, 441
  German, 80–82
  Grant orders to leave Tennessee, 99
  Russian, 81–84
Jim Crow system, 174, 293, 296–297, 298, 301,
  335
  Plessy v. Ferguson decision and, 169
Johnson Act, 108–109, 111, 197
Johnson-Reid Act of 1924, 84–85, 105, 109–110,
  111, 406
  open door policy for Mexicans under, 248

Kenjin, 194
Kenjinkai, 194, 199
Keyes v. School District No. 1, Denver, Colorado
  decision, 170
Khmer Rouge, 418–419
Kickapoo Indians, 356, 361
Kiowa Indians, 388
Klamath Indians, 375–376
Know-Nothing Party, 98–99
Korematsu v. United States decision, 208–209
Ku Klux Klan, 291, 302, 310, 431, 432

Labor market. *See also* Employment
  primary and secondary, 222
Lakota Higher Education Center, 391
Lakota Indians, 362
Land ownership
  Japanese Americans and, 195, 196
  voting and, 294
Language
  Cherokee, 359
  German, 56

Japanese, transmission of, 194–195
  Native-American, 386–388, 389
  of Russian Jews, 81
  second great immigration stream and,
    76
  Spanish, Mexican Americans and, 246,
    261–263, 273
  Vietnamese, 4220425
Laos, 418
La Raza, 235, 256
  pride in, 276
League of the Iroquois, 356
League of United Latin American Citizens
  (LULAC), 256, 257
Legal approach, to reducing prejudice and
  discrimination. *See* Prejudice and
  discrimination, reducing
Legal issues, Japanese American evacuation and
  relocation and, 207–209
Legislation. *See also specific laws*
  controlling immigration. *See* Immigration,
    control of
  naturalization, 96–97
  reducing prejudice and discrimination
    through. *See* Prejudice and discrimination,
    reducing
  regarding slavery, 49–51
Liberia, 288
Literacy tests
  immigration restriction and, 108
  voting and, 294
Little Bighorn, battle at, 365–366
Little Italys, 79–80
Little Rock, Arkansas, school desegregation and,
  310
Longhouse Religion, 388
Lost Nation of Islam, 304–305, 319
Louisiana Purchase, 237
Louisville Platform of 1854, 98
Loyalty leagues, Japanese American, 199
Luiseno Indians, 386
Lynchings, 301

MCarran-Walter Act. *See* Immigration and
  Nationality Act of 1952
Mafia, 79
Makah Indians, 381
Mandan Indians, 363
Man-Stealing Law, 284
March on Washington Movement, 173, 306,
  307–308, 309, 318, 449

Marital assimilation, 23, 442
  of African Americans, 339–340
  ethnic revival and, 407–408
  of Italians, 442
  of Japanese Americans, 215–218
  of Mexican Americans, 271–272
  of Native Americans, 395–397
  of Vietnamese, 429
Massachusetts Bay Colony, 44
  Native Americans and, 47–48
Melting pot ideology of assimilation, 27–30, 36
  Mexican Americans and, 237
Mennonites, 55–56
Menominee Indians, 376
Meriam Report, 373, 374
Mestizos, 238
Mexican American(s), 231–278, 447–448
  assimilation of, 261–272
    cultural, 261–265
    marital, 271–272
    structural, primary, 269–271
    structural, secondary, 265–269
  census identifiers and, 259–262
  colonial model and, 232–243
    borderland conflicts and, 239–243
    immigrant model compared with, 236–237, 244–247
    Indian-Spanish relations and, 236–237
    Texas frontier and, 237–239
  immigrant model and, 243–247
    colonial model compared with, 236–237, 244–247
  income of, 144–145
  intergenerational overlap and, 258–259
  migration of, 245–246
  native reaction to immigration of, 247–257
    bracero program and, 250–252
    Chicano awakening and, 255–257
    during Great Depression, 249–250
    zoot suit riots and, 252–255
  success of, 272–276
  three-generations process and, 5–6
  transformation of population of, 244
Mexican American Political Association (MAPA), 257
Mexican Americans, 86
  braceros, 87
  undocumented, 89, 249, 251
Mexican American Youth Organization (MAYO), 257
Mexican Indians, relations with Spanish, 236–237

Miami Indians, 361
Middleman minority theory, 84, 221–222
Migration
  of African Americans, 297–299
  cyclical, 77, 78
  of Mexican Americans, 245–246
Migration and Refugee Assistance Act of 1962, 88, 414
Military service
  African Americans and, in Civil War, 289
  Japanese Americans and, 206, 207
  Mexican Americans and, 255, 256–257
Milliken v. Bradley decision, 172
Minneconjoux Indians, 363, 372
Missionary schools, 371
Mixed-blood, 396
Modernization, of social organization, 13–15
Mohawk Indians, 356
Montgomery, Alabama, bus boycott in, 316

Narragansett Indians, 386
National Association for the Advancement of Colored People (NAACP), 169, 301, 302, 304, 305–306, 309, 317, 449
National Congress of American Indians (NCAI), 379
National Farm Workers Association (NFWA), 257
National Indian Youth Council (NIYC), 380
Nationalist Movement, 431
National Liberation Front, 416, 418
National Negro Business League, 300
National Socialist White People's Party, 431
Native American(s), 353–400, 448
  alternations between Anglo conformity and cultural pluralism and, 373–377
    Indian Reorganization Act and, 374–375
    termination policy and, 375–377
  Anglo-American policies toward, 357–358
  assimilation of, 386–397
    cultural, 386–390
    marital, 395–397
    structural, primary, 394–395
    structural, secondary, 390–394
  cultural assimilation of, 49
  diversity of, 45
  English colonists' relations with, 45–49
  as immigrants versus colonized minority, 383–386
  move toward Anglo conformity and, 367–373
    Bureau of Indian Affairs and, 368
    Dawes Act and, 369–370

education and, 370–371
end of treaty making and, 368–369
Ghost Dance and Wounded Knee and, 371–373
pan-Indian responses and initiatives and, 377–383
new tribalism and, 380–383
protest organizations and, 377–380
Plains wars and reservations and, 362, 363–367
removal of, 359–362
legal issues pertaining to, 359–360
Trail of Tears and, 360–362
success of, 397–398
three-generations process and, 5, 6
Native American Church (NAC), 388
Native American Party, 98
Nativism, 96–100
resurgence of, 430–432
Naturalization, requirements for, 96–97
Navajo Community College, 391
Navajo Indians, 386–387, 395
Nazis, 112
New Deal, 379, 411
New immigration, 85–90, 412–430
New Negro Alliance, Inc., 306
Nez Perces Indians, 388
Niagara Movement, 300–301
Nisei. *See* Japanese Americans, second-generation
Nonresistance thesis, 51
Northwest Territory Ordinance, 357
Novels, reducing prejudice and discrimination through, 158–159

Office of Federal Contract Compliance (OFCC), 174–175
Oglala Indians, 363, 365
Olivet College, 431
Omaha Indians, 386
Oneida Indians, 361
Order of the Star-Spangled Banner, 98
Organization of Afro-American Unity, 320
Osage Indians, 361–362
Ottowa Indians, 357–358, 361
Outing system, 371
Ozawa v. United States decision, 196

Paiute Indians, 372
Pale of Settlement, 81
Parole provision, 87, 416

Pasamaquoddy Indians, 382
Pathet Lao, 418
Pauchucos, 252–255
Pawnee Indians, 361–362, 388
Pearl Harbor, Japanese attack on, 200
Pennsylvania
German immigration to, 55–56
Irish immigration to, 54
Pennsylvania Dutch, 56
Penobscot Indians, 382, 386
Peons, 237
Peoria Indians, 361
Personal control, 137
Personality theories of prejudice, 128–133
Personal worth, 137
Picture brides, 191–192
Plains wars, 362–367
Plantation system of agriculture, slavery and, 51
Plays, reducing prejudice and discrimination through, 158–159
Plessy v. Ferguson decision, 169, 294–295, 296, 299
Plymouth colony, 42, 43–44
Political activity
attempts to deny vote to African Americans and, 294
of German immigrants, 73–74
of Germans, 98
of Irish immigrants, 70, 97–98
of Native Americans, 373
Political Association of Spanish-Speaking Organizations (PASO), 257
Poll tax, 294
Ponca Indians, 378
Potato famine, Irish immigration and, 68, 69–70
Potawatomi Indians, 356, 361, 388
Poverty, culture of poverty thesis and, 341–346
Power, inclusion and, 7
Powhatan Indians, 46
Prairie Band, 388
Prejudice, 123–139
cultural transmission theories of, 123–128
social distance and, 127–128
stereotypes and, 124–127
definition of, 120–121
group identification theories of, 133–137
ethnocentrism and, 133–135
self-hate and, 135–137
personality theories of, 128–133
sources of, 122–123

Prejudice and discrimination, reducing, 156–181
  educational approach to, 157–165
    factual information and, 157–158
    intergroup contact and, 159–165
    vicarious experience and, 158–159
  legal approach to, 165–180
    affirmative action and, 172–179
    laws and mores and, 165–168
    organized social protest and, 179–180
    school busing and, 169–172
Preschool Racial Attitudes Measure (PRAM), 136
Prestige gain, 148
Primary ethnic groups, 445–447, 452
Proclamation of 1763, 357
Proclamation of Amnesty and Reconstruction, 289
Professionals
  Mexican-American, 265–266
  native-American, 378
Propinquity, 216
Protest. *See* Civil Rights Movement; Social protest
Psychological gains, 148
Public transportation, segregation of, 294–295

Quotas
  in educational institution admissions, 176
  immigration, 87, 88, 108–110, 197, 249

Race
  concept of, 10–13
  inclusion and, 6–9
Race relations, cycle of, 20–21, 232
Race riots, 320–322, 324–325
  zoot suit, 252–255
Racism, 100–105
  definition of, 101, 121
  environmentalists and, 101
  hereditarians and, 101
  IQ controversy and
    before 1924, 104–105
    since 1924, 111–115
  Mexican Americans and, 238
  racial differences and, 101–103
  resistance to, 432
  scientific, 100
Radical Republicans, Reconstruction and, 289–291
Recolonization, 302–303
Reconstruction, 289–291
Redlining, 411
Red Power, 380
Red Summer, 302, 308
Refugee(s), 85–86, 87–89, 413–414
  as involuntary immigrant minority, 420–421
  Vietnamese, 414–420

Refugee Act of 1980, 88–89, 416
Refugee Relief Act of 1953, 88, 91, 413
Refugee Resettlement Program, 416
Regents of the University of California v. Bakke
  decision, 176, 177
Relative deprivation hypothesis, 321
Religion. *See also specific religions*
  of Native Americans, 372, 373, 388
  second great immigration stream and, 76
Relocation, of Native Americans, 384–385
Relocation, of Japanese Americans, 203–207
Relocation centers, life in, 204–207
Reservations, Native Americans and, 362–367
Residential segregation. *See also* Ethnic
  neighborhoods; Interracial housing
  African Americans and, 150, 296, 335–338
  Japanese Americans and, 213–215
  of Mexican Americans, 268–269
  of Vietnamese, 427
Revolutionary War, rise of Anglo-American
  society during, 57–60
Riots, 320–322, 324–325
  zoot suit, 252–255
Rise and drop hypothesis, 321
Rising expectations hypothesis, 321
Roman Catholicism
  Irish, 70
  opposition to, 97–98
Rosebud, Battle of the, 365
Russians
  Jewish, 81–84
    Italians compared with, 82–83
  stereotypes of, 126

Sac Indians, 361, 386
Sand Creek Massacre, 366
Sandia Pueblo Indians, 382
San Francisco *Chronicle*, 189, 190
San Francisco *Morning Call*, 187
Sansei. *See* Japanese Americans, third-generation
Santee Sioux Indians, 363, 382
Scalawags, 290
Scapegoating, 131–132
Scholastic Aptitude Test (SAT), 114
School boys, 195
School busing, 169–172
  for school desegregation, objections to,
    170–171
School desegregation, 150, 309–311, 334–335
  reducing prejudice and discrimination
    through, 162–164
  school busing for, objections to, 170–171

School segregation
  African Americans and, 150
  Japanese Americans and, 189–191
  Mexican Americans and, 252, 256
Scientific racism, 100
Scotch-Irish, colonial, 53–55, 57
Secondary ethnic groups, 445–447, 452
Second-generation Americans, 3–4
Segregation
  legal, 296
  of public transportation, 294–295
  of schools. *See* School desegregation; School
    segregation
Self-hate, prejudice and, 135–137
Seminole Indians, 360, 361
Seneca Indians, 356, 361
Separate but equal case, 294–295
Separatism, 33–34, 35–36, 451
  African Americans and, 302–305
Sephardim, 80
Servants, rise of Anglo-American society and,
    49–50
Sexual gain, 148
Sharecropping, 292–293
Shawnee Indians, 356, 357–358, 361
Silas John Religion, 388
Simpson-Rodino Act, 89, 91
Sinte Gleska College, 391
Sioux Indians, 362, 363, 364, 365–367, 367, 372,
    382, 388, 395
Situational pressures theories of discrimination,
    140–144
Skinheads, 431
Slavery, 282–287
  colonial, 282–284
  Emancipation Proclamation and, 289
  Latin American and American, 285–286
  legislation regarding, 49–51
  racism and, 102–103
  rise of Anglo-American society and, 49–53
  slave resistance and, 51–52, 283–285
Sleepy Lagoon trial, 253–255
Social Darwinism, 103
Social desirability bias, 126
Social distance, prejudice and, 127–128
Social organization
  of Irish immigrants, 70
  transition from premodern to modern form of,
    13–15
Social protest. *See also* Civil Rights Movement
  against Japanese Americans, 187–189
  Native-American organizations for, 377–380

reducing prejudice and discrimination
    through, 179–180
Society for American Indians (SAI), 378–379
Southern Christian Leadership Conference
    (SCLC), 316, 449
Spanish, Mexican Indians' relations with, 236–237
Spanish-Indians, 235
Spatial assimilation, theory of, 213
Split labor market, 146–148
  Mexican Americans and, 275
Stereotypes, prejudice and, 124–127
Stratification system, 120
Structural assimilation, 23–24
  primary, 23–24
    of African Americans, 338–339
    of Japanese Americans, 215
    of Mexican Americans, 269–271
    of Native Americans, 394–395
    of Vietnamese, 428–429
  secondary, 23
    of African Americans, 330–338
    of Japanese Americans, 213–215
    of Mexican Americans, 265–269
    of Native Americans, 390–394
    of Vietnamese, 425–428
Student Nonviolent Coordinating Committee
    (SNCC), 316
Success
  African-American, 341–348
  Japanese-American, 218–226, 346
    comparison of theories of, 224–226
    cultural view of, 218–221
    structural view of, 221–224
  Mexican-American, 272–276
  Native-American, 397–398
*Swann v. Charlotte-Mecklenburg County Board
    of Education* decision, 170

Tanomoshi-ko, 194
Tejanos, 238–239
Television, reducing prejudice and
    discrimination through, 158–159
Tenancy, 292–293
Termination policy, Native Americans and,
    375–377
Teton Sioux Indians, 363
Texas, Mexican Americans in, 237–243
  borderland conflicts and, 239–243
  frontier and, 237–239
Texas Rangers, 242
Third-generation Americans, 4, 5
Thirty-eighth Street gang, 253

Three-generations process, 3–6
Timing, inclusion and, 10
Trade and Intercourse Acts, 357
Trail of Broken Treaties, 381
Trail of Tears, 360–362
Transcontinental railroad, Chinese immigration
    and, 106
Treaties, with Native Americans, end of, 368–369
Treaty of 1868, 365, 366, 381
Triple melting pot thesis, 408
Truncated middleman minority, 347
Turnvereine, 74, 81
Tuskegee Institute, 299
Twilight metaphor, 443–444
Two-way migration, 77, 78

Ulstermen, colonial, 53–55
Underclass, 324, 344
Underground Railroad, 283, 284
Undocumented aliens, 89–90
    Mexican, 89, 249
        Bracero program and, 251
Unemployment, among Native Americans,
    391–392
United Nations High Commission for Refugees
    (UNHCR), 416, 420
Universal African Legion, 303
Universal Black Cross Nurses, 303
Universal Negro Improvement Association
    (UNIA), 302–304, 305
Urban League, 449
Ute War, 367

Vacuum domicilium doctrine, 47
Value compatibility, Japanese-American success
    and, 218–219
Vaqueros, 241
Veterans Administration, 411
Vicarious experience, reducing prejudice and
    discrimination through, 158–159
Vicious circle, prejudice and discrimination and,
    131, 140
Vietcong, 416, 418
Vietminh, 415, 416, 418
Vietnamese, 86, 414–420
    assimilation of, 421–430
        cultural, 422–425
        marital, 429
        structural, primary, 428–429
        structural, secondary, 425–428
Voluntary Relocation Program, 385

Vote, attempts to deny to African Americans, 294
Voting Rights Act of 1965, 176, 318, 406

Ward's Cove Packing v. Antonio decision, 175
War of 1812, rise of Anglo-American society
    and, 59
War on Poverty, 376, 409
War Relocation Authority (WRA), 203–204, 206,
    209
War Relocation Work Corps, 204
Watts riot, 320–321
Western Hemisphere Act of 1976, 88, 91
Wheeler-Howard Act of 1934, 374–375, 384
White(s). *See headings beginning with term
    Anglo-American*
White Aryan Resistance, 431
White supremacy
    doctrine of, 45, 102
    restoration of, 292–297
Women's National Indian Association, 377–378
Worcester v. Georgia decision, 359–360
Work gangs, of Mexican Americans, 248
Workingmen's Party, 106
World War I
    African-American migration and, 297
    ethnic revival and, 407
World War II, 110
    African Americans and, 306–307, 308
        migration of, 298
    ethnic revival and, 407
    evacuation and relocation of Japanese
        Americans and. *See* Japanese Americans,
        evacuation and relocation of
    Japanese Americans and, military service and,
        206, 207
    Mexican Americans and, 256–257
        military service and, 255, 256–257
    refugees and, 85–86, 87–89, 413–414
    stereotypes and, 126
Wounded Knee Creek, South Dakota, 372–373
Wyandot Indians, 357–358, 361

Xenophobia, 96, 110
    resistance to, 432

Yankton Sioux Indians, 363, 382
Yiddish, 81
Yonsei, cultural assimilation of, 212
Yuwipi cult, 388

Zoot suit riots, 252–255